W9-CND-835

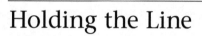

Holding the Line

*Edited by Heather N. Nicol
and Ian Townsend-Gault*

Holding the Line:
Borders in a Global World

UBC Press · Vancouver · Toronto

15   14   13   12   11   10   09   08   07   06   05   5   4   3   2   1

Printed in Canada on acid-free paper

Library and Archives Canada Cataloguing in Publication

Holding the line : borders in a global world / edited by Heather Nicol and Ian Townsend Gault.

   Includes bibliographical references and index.
   ISBN 0-7748-0931-0

   1. Boundaries. 2. Sovereignty. 3. Globalization. 4. International relations.
I. Nicol, Heather N. (Heather Nora), 1953- II. Townsend Gault, Ian, 1952-

   JC323.H64 2004   320.1'2   C2004-903247-X
   2005
Canada

UBC Press gratefully acknowledges the financial support for our publishing program of the Government of Canada through the Book Publishing Industry Development Program (BPIDP), and of the Canada Council for the Arts, and the British Columbia Arts Council.

This book has been published with the help of the K.D. Srivastava Fund.

Printed and bound in Canada by Friesens
Set in Stone by Brenda and Neil West, BN Typographics West
Copy editor: Joanne Richardson
Proofreader: Gail Copeland

UBC Press
The University of British Columbia
2029 West Mall
Vancouver, BC V6T 1Z2
604-822-5959 / Fax: 604-822-6083
www.ubcpress.ca

Contents

Introduction

Heather Nicol and Ian Townsend-Gault

The recurrent themes in this volume are those of the survival and redefinition of border arrangements under the processes of social, economic, cultural, and political globalization. Since 9/11, and following the very recent war in Iraq, the citizenry of Western states seem to agree concerning the degree to which national security can be compromised by "terrorists" and fanatics from the outside, yet they continue to look for, and find, a very great deal of what they want (in terms of information, culture, goods, and services) from outside the borders of the political unit of which they are a part. In this sense, they want national borders to be porous and permeable, at least in one direction – their own. Yet they also want to keep "threats" at a distance, seeing the border as a zone for risk management and the process of management an outcome of the new "risk politics" agenda[1] – risk being defined by the rising tide of terrorism and ethnic nationalism.

Both of these "threats" (terrorism and ethnic nationalism) have had a real impact upon the orientation of national and international relations, policy, and perception in the opening years of the twenty-first century. To some extent, this has reoriented debate about the nature of state governance, public welfare, and the role of public and private sectors – all themes that were of enormous concern as the twentieth century drew to a close and a new century began. While there is no doubt that, in some areas, citizens expect and want less from their governments than was the case fifty years ago, a new "risk agenda" demands from governments an unprecedented degree of protection and requires new rounds of border debate. Consider the tight state controls on the economy and the means of production that were required during the Second World War and its difficult aftermath. In some countries not involved in that conflict, government controls were seen as an essential aspect of the grip of the authorities on as many facets of life as possible. But the forces of deregulation have been pervasive, totalitarian regimes have fallen, democratic (or more-or-less accountable) administrations have been installed in countries that seemed to be mired in red tape, authoritarianism, and regimented political orthodoxy. At the same time, however, bombings and destruction by seemingly unpredictable and irrepressible groups raises the need for even tighter security. All of this has had an impact on boundaries too: indeed, how could they escape being affected by such seismic forces?

Given these realities, one strategic concern for decision makers, legislators, and scholars is how to conceptualize, explain, and at times restructure border and border issues to better accommodate the demands of globalization and the concerns of national sovereignty. This is not an easy task, the irony being that, although most governments and peoples are concerned with the potential threat of open borders, deterritorialized states, and loss of national sovereignty, as a general rule accessible borders are usually stress-free borders that are maintained by collaborative measures and cooperative management. Still, in the popular mind, problems such as illegal migrants, refugees, terrorist threats (real and perceived), smuggling, and drugs are often attributed to deterioration of border security and, therefore, are used to buttress claims for more stringent border controls. In the wake of the 2001 Trade Center and Pentagon attacks, the war in Iraq, and the seemingly failed new rounds of peace initiatives in Israel – all of which may prove to have a protracted aftermath in terms of their impact within the larger Southwestern Asia/Middle East region – virtually all governments are under pressure to control terrorist activities through more stringent border functions. Reactionary policies aimed at closing borders emerge from the perception of extreme threat lying on the other side. Yet realistic assessment and response to threat is an extremely important area for policy intervention because stress-free borders are essential to healthy cross-border functions as well as to the overall well-being of the state.

The chapters in this volume offer different perspectives on the nature of these new seismic forces. They are divided into eight parts, each part focusing on a specific issue, and each chapter adopting a distinctive approach. It is our intention to transport the reader on a journey that begins with speculation about the permeable nature of borders and their vulnerability to cross-border flows, and that finishes with the acknowledgment that borders are both open and closed – that they are both continua and fences – simultaneously. In doing this, *Holding the Line* acknowledges that borders and borderlands are as much metaphors as realities, that they are as much constitutive of border relations as they are walls that divide one nation from another (or one discourse concerning effective territorial control from another).

The World Stage – New Opportunities and Problems

In Chapter 1, "Boundary Permeability in Perspective," Gerald Blake discusses the complex nature of border interaction and the inadequacy of simplistic definitions of border functions. He suggests that the popular viewpoint – that state boundaries are containers or barriers permanently fixed by geopolitical and military objectives, and that governments must "hold the line" – is based upon ideas that are not only outmoded but that were probably never particularly accurate. In reality, borders vary from being totally "closed" to totally "open" and represent a broad continuum. It is at the border that legal, geographical, historical, and social forces respond to, as well as shape, borders and borderlands, and are sensitive to pressures on the boundary from people, goods, capital, and ideas. The barrier properties of borders change over time and are different from area to area. Because of this, any discussion that evokes notions of "borderlessness" misconstrues the active role that borders play in the construction of territorial interaction and definition.

Chapter 2, "Information Geopolitics: Blurring the Lines of Sovereignty," by Tom Edwards, shifts the emphasis away from strategic territorial concerns in order to demonstrate how policy formulations can garner greater control over transnationalism while still allowing cross-border flows of information and capital. Edwards's analysis of the structuring of information systems, corporate strategies, and conditions in which recontextualizing occurs raises the possibility of the development of "soft" means of territorial control. His comments concerning the market implications of localization are prescriptive, giving support to the concept that government must encourage interfacing services and that there needs to be an arena within which to promote cooperative interaction between transnational corporations (TNCs) and national governments. There are inherent opportunities to build bridges between the interests of these two groups of actors rather than to develop rigid positions based upon conflicting interests.

Building bridges is also the theme of Chapter 3, "Law, Sovereignty, and Transnationalism: Delivering Social Goods Using a Functional Approach to Borders," in which Robert Adamson brings a legal perspective to the question "whither border security in the twenty-first century?" and notes that, throughout the second half of the twentieth century, the trend towards internationalization and extraterritorialization has been increasingly marked in the development of law and policy. The recent desire to promote the setting of standards across borders reflects not just a desire for harmonization or uniformity for its own sake but, rather, the realization that the business of government increasingly involves dealing with an extraordinary number of issues that, by their nature, are international or transnational: law and policy response must come from the same perspective. While once seen as operating inside the watertight compartment of national territory, more or less immune from foreign influence, this is no longer true. The changing legal definition of internationalization and transnational activity, its norms and practices, is indeed part of the set of constitutive processes influencing border functions in an increasingly global world.

Regionalism and Subregionalism in Europe

The chapters in Part 2 recognize that, at a conceptual level, borders are convenient political constructions. They are not carved in stone but exist to enhance specific functional requirements of political territoriality. Chapters 4 and 5, by Eberhard Bort and James Scott, respectively, look more closely at the parallel functions of boundaries – both to contain and to innovate – suggesting that opening and coordinating internal borders within the European Union (EU) has encouraged regionalism, enhancing the political, administrative, and identity-making function of substate boundaries. Like Blake, Bort and Scott both suggest that, in the real world of the EU, the internal and external frontiers of Europe are not static but are in transition, and that they are less unilinear and more complex than slogans like "a Europe without frontiers" might suggest. Indeed, Bort argues that, while border disputes themselves are less common and less critical in the EU of the twenty-first century than they were in twentieth-century Europe, the frontier zones are constantly under debate and reconstruction.

Bort suggests that the major revolution in EU border making comes not from the death throes of nationalism but, rather, from the pragmatic devolution of federal power and the rising strategic importance of regions. Borders are not "erased" but redefined. As internal borders "soften," external borders "harden," making it possible for the EU to gain effective control over territories well outside the parameters of *Schengen* and other EU protocols and treaties. Scott agrees with Bort, arguing that the political construction of the EU has brought with it increasing sophistication of the formal institutions of integration and existing political, economic, and social networks. Transnational regional cooperation is essential to European integration and empowers local communities, regions, and cities, creating strategic alliances for the diffusion of social, political, and economic innovations. The result is not the end of the nation-state but "the emergence of subnational diplomatic activities on a large scale, and in very different geographical contexts."

In the final analysis, the chapters in Part 2 define the evolving EU borders as a set of spatial relationships that responds to a new territorial logic of activity. The experience of the EU highlights the process of creating structurally complex and multifaceted initiatives to cultivate community on a large geographical scale and under varied cultural, economic, and political conditions. While many nation-states have long regarded state, regional, and provincial demands for different treatment as unorthodox and unacceptable within the context of national unity, and have demanded a degree of conformity to a seamless set of "values" and "national" or "ethnic" identities, the experience of the EU has shown that flexibility is exactly what is required to build community. It is clear that there are lessons to be learned about the nature of multisectoral planning initiatives and the efficacy of structural policy agendas of state actors in fostering regional political communities.

Emerging Perspectives

The European model developed in Part 2 is clearly relevant to other regions, not all of them comprised of Western Hemisphere nation-states. In Part 3, emerging perspectives on borders in the twentieth century are explored, with particular emphasis on Africa and Southeast Asia. In Chapter 6, Anthony Asiwaju looks closely at the impact of European attitudes towards colonial terrestrial borders and argues for recognition of the theoretical compatibility between African and European border studies. This work is groundbreaking – at least from the perspective of Western scholarship.

Asiwaju's focus is upon the structural implications of African transborder frontiers, which function not only as conduits for effecting linkages along the edges of the states created by "erstwhile European colonizers" but also as a means of organizing transnational relations and devolving pressures within postcolonial Africa. He broaches the idea that the serious study of African borders arrangements is both necessary and legitimate, and that national borders in contemporary Africa are much more than relict borders from a previous era. Indeed, Asiwaju suggests that Africa's contemporary economic problems "have stemmed from the fact of territorial division into a large number of competitive rather than complementary national economies" as well as "the arbitrary nature of the colonial boundaries that were disruptive and artificial." But, unlike many other African scholars, Asiwaju suggests that such realities do not make Africa unique – "if anything, the comparative assessments ... have demonstrated a replication of the quintessence of the European experience in Africa."

Part 3 deals with more, however, than just the possibility of finding similarities in issues and approaches to terrestrial borders among European and emergent postcolonial nations within the developing world. It also deals with the issue of regional and subregional cooperative mechanisms in maritime border arrangements, which have often been overlooked in discussions about globalization, integration, and the borderless world. Chapter 7, Clive Schofield's "Trans-Maritime Boundary Cooperation in Southeast Asia: Enhancing or Eroding the Importance of International Boundaries," addresses this deficiency, observing that cooperative maritime initiatives, although based upon territorialization of marine regions, are no less state-centred than are terrestrial borders. As such, joint development zones in Southeast Asia are at the cutting edge of reterritorialization yet are similar to the transnational processes described by Bort, Scott, and Asiwaju. Indeed, as becomes clearer somewhat later in the volume (see Chapter 8), maritime cooperation has become a means by which many regions have been able to overcome territorial disputes by placing sovereign claims on the "back-burner," along with strategic control of resources.

Redefining Boundaries in the Americas
One of the key issues raised in Part 4 is the limited utility of the "global world" metaphor among countries that have never developed according to a Eurocentric model of the nation-state. This is made clear in Chapter 9, Roy Bradshaw's "Redefining the Nature and Functions of Boundaries: A South American Perspective." South American boundaries are different, says Bradshaw, because the relationship between national borders and national identity weighs differently and is differently constructed in South America than it is in other parts of the world. The world of "tensions, sentiments and social groupings," which now characterize South American countries, are a colonial product and have their roots in the power relations of fifteenth-century Spain. Indeed, "the very factor that attracted Bolivar to the possibility of creating a united South America, the uniformity in the origins and nature of society, was the very factor that facilitated territorial claims and boundary disputes throughout the region." Bradshaw suggests that cooperation of the kind seen elsewhere in the "borderless world" is highly improbable in South America.

Chapter 8, Heather Nicol's "Neoliberal Caribbean Integration: The Role of the ACS in Restructuring Borderlines," also looks at the state of boundary making in areas of Latin America, although in South America the focus is clearly upon those states that are linked to integration efforts emanating from the Caribbean. Nicol demonstrates that the new integration movement in the Caribbean relies upon economic-centred processes to create a potentially friction-free trade region capable of surmounting the divisive postcolonial geography among Caribbean countries searching for a common identity and common space in order to counteract the insular tendencies of the region and its complex geography and maritime borders. The solution for the region has been to develop neoliberal policy frameworks and development strategies that stress common linkages among all sectors. Globalization has indeed made inroads in redefining the edges of this region through a new integrated maritime territory movement, although whether unity or diversity will prevail is still an open question.

Ultimately, the chapters in Part 4 demonstrate the co-existence of very different border-making processes within the same geographical and geopolitical regions, highlighting the propensity for border issues to resist simple classification. If Bradshaw suggests that, in this region, boundaries remain a paradox, an area both of restraint and activity, Nicol demonstrates the relevance and impact of globalization in various areas of Latin America and the Caribbean. While Bradshaw suggests that there are boundary areas of South America that still remain outside the domain of global processes, it is equally clear that these border areas are increasingly under pressure.

A Borderless North America?

In Part 5, the spotlight turns from the "periphery" of North America to explore the ramifications of the North American Free Trade Agreement (NAFTA) and a new Western cross-border consciousness. The four chapters in this section measure the degree of cross-border cooperation that has occurred between North American nations and all are using a different yardstick. Moreover, the authors disagree as to the nature and extent of transnational regionalism in Western Canada and the United States. While in Chapter 11, "Conflicting Transborder Visions and Agendas: Economic and Environmental Cascadians," Donald Alper looks at environmental cooperation, in Chapter 10, "Cascadian Adventures: Shared Visions, Strategic Alliances, and Ingrained Barriers in a Trans-border Region," Ted Cohn examines the degree of transportation and competitiveness among North American cross-border regions. In Chapter 12, "Cascadian Adventures: Shared Visions, Strategic Alliances, and Ingrained Barriers in a Transborder Region," Alan Artibise suggests that, at the macro level – that is, in terms of the initiatives that engage national decision makers in Canada and the United States – there is reason to believe that Western Canada has achieved a considerable degree of regional integration. Interestingly, Alper disagrees with the arguments put forward by Daniel Turbeville and Susan Bradbury in Chapter 13, "NAFTA and Transportation Corridor Improvement in Western North America: Restructuring for the Twenty-First Century." Turberville and Bradbury highlight the existence of critical weaknesses at the infrastructure level, particularly in the area of transportation, focusing exclusively on the movement of goods and peoples through post-NAFTA transportation systems. "NAFTA moves by trucks," they conclude, identifying the fact that policy frameworks and outcomes are not all that well articulated in other areas. While some of these deficiencies can be resolved through instrumental policies that ease cross-border transit, others can only be addressed by sustained effort at the national and local levels.

In the final analysis, the larger question for North Americans introduced by the problem of Cascadia and highlighted by NAFTA is whether considerable cross-border integration is possible (1) without the erosion of national institutions or national sovereignty and (2) within the framework of limited and specifically targeted instruments and issue areas. The chapters in Part 6 suggest that the answer is "yes" since the Cascadia region has been historically and functionally connected for decades prior to NAFTA, and yet each side of the region – Canada and the United States – has undisputed and separate territorial and institutional dimensions. In this context, the history of cooperative ventures at the municipal, regional, and national levels represents an opportunity for cultivating the positive effects of transnational development rather than a threat to national security.

Borders as Metaphors

In Part 6 Steven Jackson and Mathew Coleman dwell on the conceptual divides that justify and orient "bordering activity." They support the critical analysis of conventional thinking about borders and the role of symbolic and textual metaphors in organizing borderlands. Clearly, all boundaries are not created equal – nor do they all serve the same function (i.e., to divide geographical territories by conventional political markers); rather, boundaries reflect spatial arrangements that reinforce rigid class, racial, national, and gendered hegemonies. As Jackson demonstrates in Chapter 15, "Technopoles and Development in a 'Borderless' World: Boundaries Erased, Boundaries Constructed," these may have the ultimate function of restricting power according to social and economic conditions. Or, as Coleman suggests in Chapter 14, "Permeable Borders and Boundaries in a Globalizing World: Feeling at Home amidst Global Poverty," they may serve instead as conceptual constructs justifying inequitable spatial arrangements beyond that of national boundaries, reflecting comprehensive ideological, social, and political agendas consistent with an evolving twenty-first-century discourse on environment, security, and race.

The dominant theme of Part 6 is that boundaries are metaphors: the way we construct our world is consistent with "the stories we tell about it." Focusing on information-led growth strategies in Malaysia, or the Multimedia Super-Corridor (MSC) projects, Jackson suggests that, "despite its connotations of liberty and claims to informational free-flow, the drive to create and promote the MSC has contributed significantly to a discursive closure that has undermined broader social discussion of the means and ends of technological development in Malaysia." In abandoning nationalist discourse and policy as a basis for organization of development strategies, proponents of the MSC promoted, instead, marginalization for those who fell on the wrong side of the "distribution of power between public and private actors embedded in [its and the information society's] long-term vision." The new border was as intractable as the old – "the latest field for the iteration of long-standing socio-economic divisions."

In his reading of Lefebvre and borders, Coleman suggests that there are further dimensions to be considered: boundaries are textual and scripted as well as artistically rendered; they are "naturalizations" encouraging us to demarcate or understand them as "conventional realist international maps" that "itemize supposedly distinct peoples, environments, and policies." Coleman brings us back to a theme raised by Blake in Chapter 1 – the myth of "firm borders." In the area of demarcation of "cultural visions and material interests," for example, Coleman suggests that realist interpretations of borders become increasingly problematic. Here in particular it becomes evident that borders are merely an expression of cultural appraisals (us versus them) reified as objective and stable spatial appraisals. Borders do more than mark the end of one territory and the beginning of another: they also devise spatial themes that reinforce power structures. Ultimately, borders are constitutive of spatial arrangements; but they are also a product of the very spatial arrangements they encode, "scripting human lives and experiences in spatial terms."

Rethinking Borders – Lines, Spaces, and Continua

Part 7 emphasizes the changing meaning of borderland in the international area. It is clear, in this section of the volume, that interaction across boundaries works to define new transnational relationships. Both cartographic conceptualizations and textual efforts to shape the processes of border making are critical to ensure that borders become zones of synthesis that both divide and unite.

For example, picking up the threads of Adamson's arguments concerning the increasingly transnational character of international law, in Chapter 16, "Complex Emergency Response Planning and Coordination: Potential GIS Applications," William Wood identifies a new theme in border studies: a growing international agenda has created the necessity for new cartographic conceptualizations and methodological approaches to humanitarian relief efforts. Cross-border initiatives involve strategic alliances that challenge old technologies and old internationalist formulas.

While focusing on cross-border, multilateral humanitarian relief efforts – specifically, those in Kosovo – Wood emphasizes the continuing importance of the state as an actor and its role in reassessing the geographical definition of borderlands in conflict via new and more complex cartographies. He urges us to think about the use of technology to resolve complex cross-border boundary problems such as massive humanitarian relief efforts under conditions of internal or civil war. "As diplomats, peacekeepers, human rights monitors, and relief agencies continue to wrestle with the challenge of implementing peace operations, relief deliveries, and even civil administrations in war-ravaged areas, they will need to rely more on new geographic information technologies and methodologies." Decision makers should be encouraged to explore the possibility of greater use of geographical information support and geographic information systems

(GIS) in boundary, immigration, and identity-building exercises. Closer attention should be paid to the interface between concept and technological solution, and a greater appreciation should be nurtured between the dynamic and complex nature of border issues and the need for new modes of cartographic representation.

Part 7 concludes by looking at the geopolitical discourses and processes that define border relations. In Chapter 17, "Good Neighbour Diplomacy Revisited," Alan Henrikson observes that, without mutually acceptable relations across borderlands, satisfactory relations between states are impossible to achieve. Good neighbours result from consociative border relations in which attention is give to "facing across borders" and to the vital process of allowing the effects of positive transborder relations to flow across borders and throughout respective national territories. The concept of "good neighbour" or "good neighbourhood," although diplomatically viable, differs dramatically from conventional approaches to borders. It is distinct from the "capital-to-capital" diplomacy focused on national centres, with little or no reference to national peripheries. It is a consociative process, within which "fences make good neighbours."

Conclusions

In the final analysis, *Holding the Line* is more than a challenge to the notion of a world without borders. Indeed, in Chapter 18, "Towards a Geopolitics of Life and Living: Where Boundaries Still Matter," Stanley Brunn et al. argue that we live as if borders still matter. Borderlands are places where diplomacy must often give way to the "politics of plants and animals." Brunn et al. do not deny the importance of cross-border flows (indeed, Brunn has been in the forefront of writing about informational technologies and the pressure they exert to refine borders and borderlands in ways that connect as much as divide). However, they appreciate the complexity of borders and of the problem raised by virtually every author in this book: "borders for whom?"

Similarly, in Chapter 19, "From the International to the Local in the Study and Representation of Boundaries: Theoretical and Methodological Comments," David Newman continues to focus on reconceptualization but at both the theoretical and methodological levels. He suggests that, with regard to border representation, we need not take consistency as a given. Indeed, consistency of representation undermines attempts to define borders fairly, effectively, and (ultimately) on the basis of clear and mutually agreed upon principals. While Newman does not claim that GIS and computer-aided cartography will resolve border conflict, he does argue that more attention should be given to marrying theory and methodology in order to arrive at clearly understood and mutually agreed upon border definitions – definitions that reflect the contingency of the border condition itself.

Holding the Line concludes on the same note that it begins – that traditional political maps give a false impression, an impression of uniformity or stability, or, as Blake argues, "of somehow being the finished product, a tidier version of older maps that were evolving towards the ideal." But stability is indeed deceptive, and border making is an ongoing process. As such, it is not particularly remarkable that new economic and political relationships among the world's nations require new modes of border making. The increasing importance of international security, economic power, and transnational regionalism has had tremendous consequences upon global and local scales of boundary making. 11 September 2001 and recent events of the "war on terror" notwithstanding, realist approaches to boundary making are increasingly challenged, and the problem has become one of understanding how new borders are formed at all levels and scales.

Notes
1 See Ulrich Beck, *World Risk Politics* (Cambridge: Polity Press, 1999).

Part 1
The World Stage –
New Opportunities and Problems

In Part 1 the issue of the changing nature of borders is discussed from a global perspective. The authors challenge the status quo, questioning the stability of borders in an increasingly international context. In Chapter 1, Gerald Blake claims that, overall, we fail to appreciate how dynamic borders can be and that they are indicators of broader geopolitical, economic, and cultural processes. Blake discusses border interaction and the inadequacy of simplistic definitions of border functions from a cartographic perspective, suggesting that state boundaries are not permanently fixed by geopolitical and military objectives. Similarly, in Chapter 2 Thomas Edwards focuses on cross-border flows of information and capital. He suggests that new geopolitical discourses will develop to accommodate the changing basis of borders – a basis focused upon informational flows and the accommodation of transnational economic forces. As such, the real challenge, as dictated by information geopolitics, is to proactively discern the proper "interfaces" between the global and local information contexts long before the "products" are released. Unlike Edwards, however, Blake questions the assumption that borders are by necessity "firm," and he looks to underlying perceptual and cartographic conventions that define the world simply as a stage divided among discrete nation-states. The problem is not so much with the map itself, but with the viewer.

This raises the question, of course, of how the viewer develops his or her viewpoint and of the role of geopolitics in influencing conventional viewpoints. To Edwards, a geopolitical revolution is under way, and it involves informational flows and transnational corporate politics challenging the geographical basis of the nation-state. It will result in the creation of informational geopolitics and redefine national-international power structures and conventional borders.

In Chapter 3 Robert Adamson focuses on a related but somewhat different theme – the role of law and its influence on globalization – or, more accurately, on internationalism. Adamson argues that domestic law and policy were once seen as operating inside the watertight compartment of national territory, more or less immune from foreign influence. Now law and policy makers must reinvent the concepts of sovereignty and jurisdiction in a way that best delivers social goods. Taking a fresh look at the concept of the internationalization of domestic legal processes, Adamson argues that the latter remain important and have increasing significance in a rapidly globalizing world. The prospect of unilateral responses to international events is growing proportionately, particularly in the United States, where internationalism and international law was having a diminishing influence even prior to the American invasion of Iraq in the spring of 2003.

Part 1 is concerned with redirecting our discussions towards an interrogation of the nature of "new" borders and the nature of border "retrenchment." The three chapters in this section of *Holding the Line* begin this project by recasting the question "what is the role of geopolitics within a global context?" to "has it changed in discursive substance or critical importance?" Two of the authors in this section would argue that geopolitical perceptions have indeed shifted, leading to new insights and new viewpoints. The third argues that strategic or international geopolitics is no longer a viable consideration as states and policy makers must reinvent the concepts of sovereignty and jurisdiction to reflect the growing importance of the local over the global.

1
Boundary Permeability in Perspective
Gerald Blake

World Political Maps Can Be Dangerous

The world political map has a powerful hold over most of us. World maps tend to be printed in bright colours, and the deep blue of the oceans provides an attractive setting for the mosaic of states that occupies the land. They also appeal to us because they are familiar, from our recollections of the map on the schoolroom wall to the tiny version of the same we can look at in our diaries when we are bored on the train or the bus. World maps are commonly part of the decor in offices and railway and airport waiting rooms all over the globe. Some of the finest world maps are triumphs of cartography and printing, and within the limits of scale and cost they convey an impression of reality that has genuine value.

Such maps are also misleading sources of information, quite apart from the distortions of various projections. They give an impression of stability, of somehow being the finished product, a tidier version of older maps that were evolving towards the ideal. Every part of the land is occupied by states usually outlined with thick red, green, or black lines, each state named and with its capital city shown. Few world maps show boundary disputes. Even fewer show maritime boundaries, although there are now some 160 maritime boundaries (or about one-third of the potential) formally agreed between states. No distinction is made between boundaries marked out on the ground and those that are delimited but not demarcated. Many maps carry dated or inaccurate information that should have been known at the time of printing. Part of the problem, of course, is not with the map itself, but with the viewer. Most maps are clearly dated, and it is our fault if we forget that the map is merely a snapshot of political arrangements at a point in time. In reality the pattern evolves constantly, sometimes dramatically (as in the past decade) and sometimes imperceptibly (as during the period of the Cold War). The world map of 100 years ago was very different to our map of today, and ours may be equally unrecognizable 100 years from now.

Another problem (for which we can hardly blame cartographers) is that international boundaries are three-dimensional, and our one-dimensional maps have conditioned us to overlook this vital fact. States control the airspace above their land territories and above their territorial seas to twelve nautical miles offshore horizontally but vertically to an undefined height. Coastal states have rights to resources in their exclusive economic zones (EEZs) and continental shelves. In the case of the EEZ, this means exclusive rights to the resources of the water column and the seabed to a distance of 200 nautical miles offshore. In the case of the continental shelf, it means exclusive rights to seabed resources to more than 200 nautical metres offshore. States jealously guard their rights to airspace over their offshore waters and over their land territories. To evaluate the permeability of the boundary system of a particular state, one must consider all these dimensions. There is much evidence to suggest that state control of offshore areas is being avidly asserted and reinforced all over the world, as witnessed by the growing volume of national legislation, the proliferation of island and maritime disputes, and state spending on patrol vessels and surveillance systems. Similarly, airspace intrusions are taken very seriously, as is shown by the aftermath of 11 September 2001. But even less dramatically, and outside of the continental United States, events such as the shooting down of a Pakistani aircraft in Indian airspace (which occurred in August 1999) had already raised a red flag. In an item on BBC TV news on 13 August 1999 concerning air traffic control chaos over central Europe, a BBC reporter speaking from an aircraft said that, while we may not see boundaries on the ground nowadays, "they are very much in evidence up here."

Perhaps the feature of our world political maps that is most misleading is their depiction of international boundaries as though they all have the same status, age, and function. Of course there is a limit to what can be shown at world scale, but it is surprising that, in this respect, cartography has hardly moved on since the beginning of the twentieth century. In the days when state boundaries were containers and barriers, and were fixed with military and geopolitical objectives in mind, thick lines indistinguishable from each other may have been appropriate. Now that the functions of state boundaries are changing, it is time for cartographers to take up the challenge. Indeed, the late Bradford Thomas called for us to consider new ways of showing international boundaries and, indeed, many of the contributors to this volume (see Bort, Nicol, Jackson, Scott) undertake analyses that reject a "linear" approach to borders. A good starting point may be to indicate, broadly, the permeability of international boundaries, all of which lie somewhere on a spectrum from totally closed to totally open. At least some distinction could be made between "hard" and "soft" boundaries, with an indication of those that remain in dispute. Greater cartographic sophistication may prove possible, and of course the opportunity to produce CD-ROM versions with impressive detail is now available.

Mapping Permeability: Desirable but Daunting

"Permeability" is a term borrowed from the physical sciences, where it has a precise meaning and the process is measurable. The permeability of a geological stratum is the result of the physical characteristics of the rock as a barrier and the frequency and volume of rainfall. Boundary permeability is the product of the barrier characteristics of the boundary (the outcome of legal, geographical, historical, and social factors) and the pressures on the boundary from people, goods, capital, ideas, and so on. Permeability is, however, most often used as convenient shorthand for transboundary collaboration, borderland initiatives, and openness.

The task of mapping boundary permeability at global scale is probably beyond the capacity of any research team or publishing group anywhere in the world. A proper analysis would involve data collection across 308 or more land boundaries separating approximately 190 independent states and some 70 dependencies, not to mention maritime and airspace boundaries. National statistics about the circulation of people and goods are often either unavailable or cannot be related to particular points of entry. The communications revolution and the growing volume of information and ideas crossing international boundaries are the inspiration for much of the debate about the fading of the state and the collapse of boundaries. At the beginning of the twenty-first century, in spite of breathtaking growth, access to the Internet remains uneven and is still massively concentrated among relatively few of the world's approximately 6,000 million people and in relatively few well-off states (dominated by the anglophone world). Even if detailed statistics about the Internet were available as an indicator of permeability, much thought would need to be given to weighting this phenomenon in relation to flows of people and goods.

Nevertheless, mapping permeability at world scale should be attempted. Membership of the world's most active political and economic blocks could be highlighted, distinguishing between internal boundaries (with a growing level of permeability) and the external boundaries (which tend to become less permeable). The greatest concentration of open borders in the world is in the European Union (EU), where, even by 1999, the EU member states shared twenty internal EU boundaries (see Bort, this volume). Although representing only 6.5 percent of the world's land boundaries, they ought to show up on a world map. When the new members of the EU are added (those that joined in May 2004), the proportion of internal EU boundaries becomes almost 10 percent of the world total. The outer margins of the EU, where borders are "hardening," also need to be depicted differently. The outer perimeter of the EU clearly has to be properly controlled if internal borders are to remain open.[1] NAFTA (North American Free Trade Agreement), ASEAN (Association of South-East Asian Nations), and other major associations of states could be similarly distinguished. The majority of states today belong to an economic or political grouping of some kind.

At the other end of the spectrum it is not too difficult to identify a number of closed (or effectively closed) boundaries, most of which are heavily militarized and in dispute. Turkey-Syria, North-South Korea, India-Pakistan, Iraq-Kuwait are examples. Such boundaries are clearly quite unlike those, for example, in the EU, which are peaceful and highly permeable. A large proportion of the world's land boundaries no doubt fall somewhere between these two extremes of open and closed. It would be highly instructive to break these down into levels of permeability. In the meantime, there are arguments for doing what we can to create a more realistic political map of the world, even if our categories are rather crude and incomplete. More detailed maps would have the great advantage of providing visual evidence to supplement the discourse about vanishing borders and the borderless world. Vanishing borders may (or may not) be a desirable outcome, but their advent may be more remote than is sometimes assumed.

The good news is that for a few individual boundaries, some illuminating data are being collected by a new generation of geography researchers. Much of this research throws light on boundary permeability, although that is not always the prime objective. Newman and Paasi have noted the need for such empirical studies.[2] If boundaries are becoming increasingly permeable, as is clearly the case in many parts of the world, then boundary and borderland management are becoming increasingly important. Terrorist activities leading to the tragedy of 11 September 2001, indicate that boundaries need to be open for legitimate crossings while acting as an effective filter to unwanted people (terrorists, bandits, criminals, smugglers, illegal migrants) and goods (drugs, weapons, biological threats, pornography). It is a difficult balancing act. Detailed knowledge of the rhythms, procedures, and processes at border crossings; profiles of the people who cross, their origins and destinations, purposes of travel or other similar reasons provide the basis for controlled and humane management. Recent events have created a new and pressing imperative for countries to get it right.

Certainly the need for enhanced border security vis-à-vis global terrorists is important; however, as Abdullatif Al Shaikh – who analyzed survey questionnaires in 1998-99 at a number of Saudi Arabia's border crossings with Kuwait, Bahrain, and the United Arab Emirates – demonstrates, borders also need to be fluid to be efficient. Abdullatif Al Shaikh observed that about one-third of all arrivals and departures in this area were for the purpose of visiting relatives. A large proportion of arriving travellers passed through the checkpoints in less than twenty minutes, whereas truck drivers with local destinations typically spent two or more hours getting through. All these states are members of the Gulf Co-operation Council, whose eventual aim has been open borders. This raises the question of how to interpret Al Shaikh's findings. On this evidence, are these borders open or not? What does permeability mean, and for whom? What more could be reasonably expected? Maybe open and closed borders are not as easily recognizable or as clear-cut as we would like to think.

Permeability Is Not Always Good
In general, the events of 9/11 notwithstanding, the most accessible borders are also the most stress-free borders. They are characterized by a fair measure of political goodwill on either side. The boundary itself is likely to have been formally agreed upon and demarcated, and will be routinely maintained and managed by both parties. In all probability there will be collaborative arrangements in place for transboundary resource exploitation and control of pollution. There may be a standing boundary commission to oversee boundary and borderland affairs. The classic models for boundary commission activities are the Canada-US and the Mexico-US international boundary commissions. Stress-free borders are usually easy to reach, have good road or rail links, and lack stringent military controls. Tourists as well as local people engaged in commuting, shopping, or visiting friends and relations account for much of the usage of open and stress-free borders. The dilemma is that, in today's world, borders are not necessarily limited to transnational flows; rather, they are more international than ever, often for economic purposes. In the Middle East the most common reasons given for border crossings are social rather than economic; within this kind of environment, permeability is clearly desirable and beneficial to the borderland communities.

There are, regrettably, many parts of the world where permeable borders bring negative results. In these areas governments may be well advised to impose strict border controls or to effectively close their borders. In the aftermath of September 11, the point hardly needs to be laboured. All the indications seem to point to more and more international boundaries coming under stress from a variety of potentially costly and threatening phenomena. Equally, citizens of the states affected expect their governments to prevent such threats, which most of them perceive to be a function of the state boundary (although in practice this may not be the case). Five examples are:

1 Illegal migrants and refuge-seekers. Caused by political upheavals and economic deprivation, the international movement of illegal migrants

is on a colossal scale and growing. For obvious reasons nobody knows the precise figure; however, worldwide, illegal migrants already number millions. Most rich states are vulnerable. Indeed, by the end of the twentieth century, the United Kingdom seemed to be particularly popular with asylum seekers.

2   Refugees. Civil wars and famine are major causes of large-scale refugee movements. Some large refugee groups are semi-permanent while others (like those in Central Africa) disperse after a short time. Refugees create enormous political, economic, and environmental strains and stresses on the host country. One of the most abnormal international boundaries is Burma-Thailand, where large numbers of Karen refugees settled in Thailand retain cross-border contacts.[3] There are some 20 million refugees in the world today, a significant proportion of whom remain permanently close to the borders of their homelands.

3   Smuggling. The greatest concern is with drug smuggling, with North America and Europe being the most favoured target areas. Much of the drug trade is overland, and a considerable number of states are involved in attempting to intercept supplies. In practice many drug seizures are made away from international boundaries.

4   War lords and bandits. Several borderlands in Africa and elsewhere are beyond the effective control of central governments. They have become the power domains of rebels whose objectives may be either political or criminal or both. The state boundaries bordering these regions may be extremely permeable, although hardly to the advantage of the local population or to the state.[4]

5   Terrorism. In the aftermath of the September 11 crisis, stricter enforcement of the security function has been directed towards preventing terrorism not just in the United States but also in much of the "developed" and "developing world."

Permeable Boundaries Do Not Negate Sovereignty

The modern state system can be said to have had its formal beginning with the Treaty of Westphalia in 1648, which ended thirty years of war in Europe. The treaty established the right of the state to exercise its functions within its own territory to the exclusion of all other states, thus confirming the link between sovereignty and territory. Only states (and not the church) were able to exercise political control, and no state could interfere in the domestic affairs of another state. Within state territory sovereignty was absolute, extending to limits defined by boundary lines of no thickness. The drawing of state boundaries had the effect of creating national consciousness through exclusion. With European imperial expansion, the Westphalian nation-state concept was exported to all the corners of the globe and became the cornerstone of international order. In the context of thousands of years of political history the state is a relatively new idea, and international boundaries are almost a novelty. Few expect the state system as we know it today to survive forever, and the character and purpose of international boundaries will evolve with new forms of political organization. It is, however, difficult to envisage a world without boundaries.

The processes, which we all agree are creating more permeable boundaries, are undoubtedly powerful. Similarly, it is undeniable that the modern state has a considerably reduced capacity to control its own economic affairs, deliver security to all its citizens, and ensure a clean and healthy environment. These facts have led to the assumption by some observers that borders are losing their meaning and, in time, will wither away. While it is true that boundaries have lost a number of their former functions as military and economic barriers, they retain the fundamentally important role of defining the limits of the territorial sovereignty of the state. Dittgen[5] regards this legal function as the most important of all, and this view seems to be held by many international lawyers, including Marcel Kohen:

> The exercise of power, whether "national" or "supranational," remains essentially a territorial one. Laws continue to be adopted in order to be applied over a given territory, the Executive continues to take decisions applicable within the limits of its territorial jurisdiction, judges are competent to deal with cases only if they have territorial jurisdiction. Even "supranational" decisions taken by organs of the European Union are applicable only to the extent of the territorial limits designated by its member States. Hence, territory continues to mark the sphere of jurisdiction of States and international institutions.[6]

Although states increasingly transfer power to international institutions for certain purposes, they have usually not abandoned these powers and, therefore, remain sovereign.[7] In the majority of cases they have transferred, but not relinquished, these powers (see, for example, Chapter 4, this volume). There are also a number of other kinds of territorial status, including neutral zones, condominiums, joint development zones, dependencies, and so on in which the state is not sovereign. These should not detain us here. The essential point is that high levels of permeability along state boundaries do not diminish the constitutional necessity for boundaries, nor do they remove the important function of defining different legal systems.

There is not much evidence to suggest that governments anywhere in the world recognize the phenomenon of withering boundaries and loss of territorial sovereignty. On the contrary, states are as eager as ever to define and protect their territories and offshore areas. Land boundary agreements continue to be made, while existing land boundaries are being more accurately mapped through the use of modern techniques such as global positioning system (GPS). Considerable sums are being spent on the demarcation and redemarcation of land boundaries. Offshore, there is great interest in delimiting the remaining 270 or so maritime boundaries that have not yet been agreed upon. The process is lengthy and often costly. Far from being a borderless world, about one-third of ocean space is currently being partitioned between coastal states. The territorial instinct is still very strong among states, and few matters can ignite nationalist fervour more readily than threats to territory.

Estimates as late as 1999 provide further evidence of the vitality of state sovereignty in the plethora of land and maritime boundary disputes, probably more than at any time since the Second World War. Recent estimates identified sixty unresolved land boundary disputes, twenty-six unresolved maritime boundary disputes, and thirty-two ongoing disputes over island sovereignty.[8] In pursuit of their claims states are increasingly resorting to arbitration or the International Court of Justice. Substantial costs are involved, and senior government officials may be preoccupied with cases for months (or even years). Although in recent decades maritime disputes have resulted in the temporary creation of some sixteen joint development zones, the preferred option is invariably the negotiation of a line delimiting sovereignty.

More States More Boundaries?

David Newman and Anssi Paasi undertook a comprehensive and timely review of the literature on boundary narratives in political geography.[9] Their work revealed a wide range of opinions among top scholars across a range of disciplines concerning the future of the state and state boundaries. Yet, in all this uncertainty, one feature of the future world political map seems highly probable: there will be more states and thus more borders. They will emerge in response to several processes, including:

• Secession. As a growing number of the "suppressed" nationalities of the Fourth World assert themselves, some will undoubtedly achieve statehood. E.W. Borntrager has argued that the time has come to unequivocally open up the right of self-determination as the only possible way to relieve rising tensions in the world political map. He detects an increasing tendency for international law to consider the claims of territorial self-determination.[10] While there may be some 4,000 "Fourth World" peoples in the world, not all would wish for statehood or be able to make a credible case for it. A more realistic indicator may be the fifty-plus members of the Unrepresented Nations and Peoples Organisation, comprising over 100 million people.[11] In mid-August 1999, all during the same week, there were press reports of bids for secession in Russia's Daghestan and Namibia's Caprivi Strip, in addition to the long-running struggles in Chechnya and elsewhere.

- Independence. Some of the seventy dependencies are likely to opt for independence from their possessors, which include (notably) the United Kingdom and France.
- Break-up of federal states. There are eighteen federal states in the world, with a total of something like 280 federal units. A number are undergoing serious strains and stresses, and seem destined to lose constituent members if not to disintegrate altogether, as did Yugoslavia.

Saul Cohen predicted the emergence, through a variety of processes, of forty new states in the twenty-first century.[12] Most of these would be "gateway states" at favourable geopolitical and economic locations, thriving on manufacturing, trade, tourism, and financial services. A number of his cases seem improbable today, but forty is a useful figure for speculation. Still, there is by no means universal agreement that greater economic cooperation will lead to more super states and fewer small states. A 1997 study, quoted in the *Financial Times,* showed that economic openness is likely to create more rather than fewer states. Politics will become more local as markets become more global because political separatism is less costly within a global economy.[13]

Conclusions: Back to the Future?

"If people are familiar with any map of the world at all, it is likely to be the map of so-called sovereign states."[14] That map, as we have seen, massively influences our conceptualization of global political space and has fostered the perception that all states share the same essential characteristics. This is just as absurd as is the assumption that all the world's 308 or so land boundaries have the same origins, the same physical characteristics, fulfil the same roles, and will evolve in the same way. In reality, the sovereign states, which comprise today's political map, were carved out of a rich diversity of geopolitical, cultural, and historic environments. Pre-state political space was organized in a considerable variety of ways, many of which did not recognize absolute sovereignty or conceive of precise boundary lines. The state system widely superimposed on these traditions, largely by Europeans, was alien and unpopular, and rarely coincided with the underlying human geographies.

Against this background, it seems inevitable that as a new world order emerges there will be marked regional contrasts in the types of political entity and the boundaries that enclose them. Instead of looking for global trends, political geographers in the coming decade should take up the challenge of tracking regional differences. There is plenty of evidence to suggest that boundary and state futures in Europe are likely to be, and indeed are, divergent from those of the former Soviet Union. Similarly, sub-Saharan Africa, the Indian subcontinent, and the Middle East may develop quite differently.

Of heightened interest, in view of recent terrorist activities and resulting political and military coalitions, is the relationship between border permeability and Islamic fundamentalist traditions. Pre-state territorial traditions in Islam provide a classic example, where, "In short, sovereignty in Islamic constitutional theory is concerned only with community and not with territory. It was only with the explicit introduction of the nation state that concepts of territorial sovereignty began to emerge."[15] Precise boundaries and territorial sovereignty were therefore unimportant in Islam, and there have been calls for a return to this tradition. Besides the major groupings of states based on common cultures, history, and political experience, the world's thirty island states must not be forgotten. They are invariably overlooked in the debate about the future of the state, but they are a fundamental part of the picture.

There is fear that, in the midst of rapid change, several competing cultural and ideological blocks might emerge, in which the "past," or nationalistically charged versions of the past, could reassert themselves. In devising such a global breakdown of geopolitical/territorial traditions as a tool to examine the boundary futures, there might be some hints of Huntington's "clash of civilizations." In his view the separating fault lines between civilizations will mark the most important future conflicts.[16] This may be far-fetched, but, as the contemporary world order disintegrates, there could be a rush to retrieve old political styles and identities, many of which lie dormant under today's political map.

Much data needs to be assembled, and regional experts need to be consulted before we can make any worthwhile predictions about where such "hot spots" might occur.

Notes

1 See M. Anderson, *Frontiers: Territory and State Formation in the Modern World* (Cambridge: Polity Press, 1996), 178-91.
2 D. Newman and A. Paasi, "Fences and Neighbours in the Postmodern World: Boundary Narratives in Political Geography," *Progress in Human Geography* 22, 2 (1998): 186-207.
3 C. Grundy-Warr, "The Karen: A Troubled Borderland People and a Destroyed State," *Boundary and Security Bulletin* 6, 3 (August 1998): 79-85.
4 Two recent examples in the media are:

   (1) 140 Ugandans were killed in Turutuko and Wolinyang villages near the borders with Sudan and Kenya. The attackers were alleged to be Turkana cattle thieves from Kenya (*London Times*, 13 August 1999).
   (2) Four Western aid workers were seized in Liberia by armed bandits operating from inside Guinea. The bandits had occupied part of northwest Liberia (*London Times*, 9 August 1999).

5 H. Dittgen, "World without Borders? Reflections on the Future of the Nation-State," *Government and Opposition* 34, 2 (1999): 161-79.
6 M. Kohen, "Is the Notion of Territorial Sovereignty Absolute?" (paper presented at the IBRU Conference, "Borderlands under Stress," Durham, England, 15-17 July 1998).
7 Ibid.
8 G.H. Blake, "Is the Time Ripe for a National Register of Boundary Status with the United Nations?" in *The Peaceful Resolution of Major Internal Disputes*, ed. J. Dahlitz (New York: United Nations, 1998), 145-67.
9 D. Newman and A. Paasi, "Fences and Neighbours," 186-207.
10 E.W. Borntrager, "Borders, Ethnicity and National Self-Determination," *Ethnos* 52 (1999): 72.
11 The Unrepresented Nations and Peoples Organisation Web site is at <http://www.unpo.org>.
12 S.B. Cohen, "The World Geopolitical System in Retrospect and Prospect," *Journal of Geography* 89, 1 (1990): 2-12.
13 A. Alesina, E. Spoloore, and R. Warziorg, "Economic Integration and Political Disintegration" (NBEI Working Paper 6163, Cambridge, MA, September 1997), quoted in the *Financial Times*, 22 December 1997, by Joachim Fells.
14 A.B. Murphy, "International Law and the Sovereign State: Challenges to the Status Quo," in *Reordering the World: Geopolitical Perspectives on the Twenty-First Century*, ed. G.J. Demko and W.B. Wood (Boulder, CO: Westview Press, 1994), 227-45.
15 G. Joffe, "Concepts of Sovereignty and Borders in North Africa," in *International Boundaries and Boundary Conflict Resolution: Proceedings of the 1989 IBRU Conference*, ed. C. Grundy-Warr (Durham, UK: International Boundaries Research Unit, 1990), 221-40.
16 See S.H. Rudolph, "Dehomogenizing Religious Formations," in *Transnational Religion and Fading States*, ed. S.H. Rudolph and J. Piscatori (Boulder, CO: Westview Press, 1997), 243-61.

2
Information Geopolitics: Blurring the Lines of Sovereignty
Thomas M. Edwards

The geographic landscape of the past several decades has seen upheaval and redirection that is unprecedented in preceding decades. This reassessment was under way before the events of 11 September 2001, and continues with the war on terrorism in its various forms. The new landscape consists of not only the basic territorial boundaries with which we are familiar but also the cultures, economies, security concerns, and controlling philosophies that contribute to geographic differentiation. For many decades, the discipline of "geopolitics" has guided the discussion on how these aspects of the geographic landscape interact on a political level, how real world geography is influenced by the presence of boundaries and their sovereign creators. Indeed, much of the recent past's geographic transitions has been focused on changes within and between sovereign national entities.

Despite the events that shook the faith of many in the potential of a new focus on transnationalism and globalization, and despite the recent emergence of power politics in relation to a "war on terror," there still remains an emerging trend that reveals a strong movement of the power base away from a focus on territorial sovereignty and towards one centred on economic control. Stated simply, this trend is "the receding power of the state relative to the global economy in mastering space." Much attention in this area has been given to transnational corporations (TNCs), which have been growing exponentially in response to robust international markets demanding their goods. While this has worked well for TNCs, it leaves open many questions as to how such corporate entities are affecting, altering, and shaping the territorial entities within which they thrive. Because they function on a global scale, within and between sovereign entities, TNCs have begun to operate on a plane similar to that of sovereign nations protecting their interests abroad.

When coupled with very rapid advances in information technology, global interpersonal connectivity, and a shifting paradigm of information usage (all developed and distributed by TNCs), these new interactions challenge the notion of territoriality and the presence of "real" and meaningful boundaries. The resultant effect of this interaction between a global information force and local traditional sovereignties is a "global versus local" clash of information contexts. Information geopolitics is an attempt to describe this clash and discern how it will affect real world social, political, and economic developments. This chapter explores the nature of this evolving relationship between sovereign nations and what could be emerging forms of sovereignty for new geopolitical entities founded more in virtual than in real space. It addresses the meaning and function of international boundaries in the coming century in relation to what has been called "information geopolitics," identifying possible geopolitical trends on the horizon as they are related to the global infusion of information technology.

Redefining Geopolitics

Geopolitics has been a guiding discipline for defining global political interactions, yet we need to be clear about the definition of the term "geopolitics" as it is used in the context of this discussion. Today, the term itself is often associated with concepts that do not always agree with those of one of the discipline's founders. Indeed, new times do require new definitions. Classical geopolitics dealt primarily with the notion of political spheres of influence, such as the Eastern Bloc, the West, and other supranational aggregations. Theories of such early geopoliticians as MacKinder concerning this relationship were revolutionary for their time, but today it is clear that the "command of a particular part of the earth's surface does not apparently give a special advantage in spite of arguments developed earlier in the century that control of East Europe and the interior of Asia would give control of the world island."[1] At its best, this version of geopolitics served as a proactive mechanism for discerning potential problems within various geographies by studying the socio-political factors influencing local geography. At its worst, it was contorted and manipulated to function as a propaganda device for purely nationalistic aims, such as those of Nazi Germany.

More recently, still other forms of geopolitics have evolved, such as "critical geopolitics." This newer concept envisions geopolitical theory as a critical filter for discerning the nature of the global power structure and its various influences on political and social systems. Here, geopolitics functions as a voice of conscience in the field, taking a step back to examine how perceptions of politics have been formed and moulded over time. While there is much that can be said about this recent revision of geopolitical thought, for now it is sufficient to point out that critical geopolitics is a useful aspect of broader geopolitics and that it helps to draw out the deus ex machina behind real world events. It also "deliberately attempts to avoid appearances of supporting or justifying the policies and arguments of any individual state."[2]

Another recent iteration in geopolitical thought is Dijkink's concept of "geopolitical visions." To Dijkink, a geopolitical vision is "any idea concerning the relation between one's own and other places, involving feelings of (in)security or (dis)advantage (and/or) invoking ideas about a collective mission or foreign policy strategy."[3] In line with postmodernist thinking, this definition of geopolitics incorporates a cognitive/perceptive dimension but still "requires at least a Them-and-Us distinction and emotional attachment to a place."[4] It deviates from the classic definitions in that it devolves itself of the strict inclusion of political structures and allows room for an individualistic perception of geography and place.

Since we are no longer in the era where "geopolitics rest[s] on the realist theory of international relations, and on the geography of states,"[5] modern geopolitics should not be viewed as a static study of social and political environments. It has become a dynamic tool, or a mechanism, a temporal snapshot of a particular state or region or people as well as a mechanism for predicting large-scale processes and changes in the short- and long-term futures. Still focused on the political mechanisms that exist between states, it realizes that the world today is a much more complex system than it used to be. In response to the dynamic social, economic, and political forces of our time, the scope of geopolitics continues to change to accommodate a world in flux.

Few of the preceding definitions of geopolitics, however, serve the purpose of this discussion, which is focused upon understanding how geopolitics could be used in combination with the concept of "information," as in "information geopolitics." Nor do conventional definitions address the nature of the recent and rapidly evolving information-based economy. Geopolitics must be redefined within the context of a world that is interacting more and more frequently via information exchange. Indeed, information technology is rapidly altering the way in which nation-states interact with one another, although we are still far from reaching the ultimate goal of implementing what software giant Microsoft calls a "*Digital Nervous System* (DNS)," DNS being a system for managing information within a homogeneous organization at both a small and large scale – whether in one's home, in a corporation, or even in a country.[6] Its purpose is to realize and establish the notion that, at all scales, "information" is the backbone of a modern organization.

This is of particular importance at the level of the nation-state as well as at the corporate level since most governments today are still wallowing in decades (or even centuries) of political dogma and administrative procedure that is quite difficult to overcome, and they are far from realizing the benefits of a DNS-like structure. It is inevitable that most organizations will adopt some form of DNS as we move further into the Information Age. However, it is important to bear in mind that all DNSs are not alike: we are not discussing a single approach or solution to the problem. As the notion of the DNS propagates (in whatever form), it, like any other by-product of a particular organization, political regime, or culture, is the feature of a specific *cultural* and *political* context. This is due to the fact that most information is highly context-dependent – both in its source and in its destination.

If one imagines the future existence of many DNSs distributed globally – the DNSs not only of large transnational corporations but also of nation-states and supranational aggregates (e.g., the UN, NATO, etc.) – then the interaction of information between context-dependent DNSs can produce many problems. While the networks may be physically connected in the correct manner, and while information formats may be compatible, there exist no effective means of resolving context differences in the content of the information moving through and between the DNSs. When opposing viewpoints on the same information are not compatible, we have a potential geopolitical crisis.

Already the DNS, and other advanced technologies both achieved and potential, have or will have an increasing impact on geopolitical theory. Instead of reinforcing a focus chiefly on territoriality and power bases, for example, they encourage consideration of the new global interaction taking place in this new environment, arriving at a definition that is better suited for an Information Age. A definition of "information geopolitics" would consider, therefore, the political effects of two or more interacting DNSs on different geographic contexts.

However, the world is *not* currently populated with digital nervous systems. The existence of true DNSs is mostly in the realm of the transnational corporations who create them (and even then in incomplete stages of development); the vision of a broad paperless society is far from having arrived. It is appropriate then, to revise the above definition of information geopolitics to incorporate a generic perspective that works for the interim. When viewed on a broader, less technology-dependent scale, information geopolitics could be defined as the political effects of global information interacting with local information.

The terms "global" and "local" are used here to define the context of scale – information used and/or accepted transnationally as compared to information that remains locally significant to a country, an organization, or particular group of people. The "global information standard" involves a level of understanding and availability of knowledge that is beyond the grasp of local government and cultural control: it is information considered generally acceptable on a global basis, or the "international" viewpoint, or the shared opinion among nation-states and citizens. Global information is a pluralizing force. The "local information standard" contains strong references to local "reality" that may conflict with the global viewpoint, which could include: geographic facts, historical facts, the naming of people or features, the appearance of a map, and so on. For example, that Canada is the country that contains the hydrologic feature Hudson Bay is an accepted, international fact that could pass from geographic context to geographic context without challenge. However, declaring a single country as the sole sovereign power over all of Jammu and Kashmir will undoubtedly face opposition from the local information contexts involved with the dispute. Local information, then, is a divisive force.

The process of globalization is to be taken seriously. Its long-term effects remain to be seen, but indications are already clear that, when a globalizing force intrudes upon a particular local context, there is a greater chance for conflict. Hall points out that "the return to the local is often a response to globalization,"[7] and this response has been observed frequently in the software industry, where local markets respond to incoming "Western" software with a vehemence that parallels the staging of troops along its border. It has often been the experience of Microsoft, for example, that "you just have to wait for the local to erupt and disrupt the global."[8]

Notice, however, that this new definition is purposefully less specific about boundaries or nationality than are previous geopolitical definitions. In an informational geopolitical regime, boundaries are the constructs of the political systems and histories in which they were designed and established: we look past the boundaries themselves and towards the underlying culture that created them. It is this "real world" cultural interaction on the basis of information exchange that defines the geographic ramifications of information geopolitics. Information, while contained and transmitted virtually, has real-world geopolitical effects that must be considered on the global and local scale. It is to this problem of context that we now turn.

What's in a Nation?

What does it mean to be a "state" or a "nation" – or a "nation-state"? What forces define the aggregation of people into a homogeneous political body that can then declare itself "sovereign," and perhaps even peace-loving? In the previous section, we redefined geopolitics in order to proceed with a more relevant meaning for information-based economies. Likewise, the concept of the nation-state needs to be considered in light of evidence telling us "the clarity of the state frontier is now fading because the exercise of sovereign authority in certain domains is becoming either very difficult or impossible."[9]

There is no one, clear, and acceptable definition for what defines a "nation." In fact, the terms "nation-state," "nation," "state," and "country" are often used interchangeably in various discussions. Defining what is meant by these terms is important in that it will enable us to draw out the basic factors that contribute to the identity of a nation-like group. If one were to examine the various available definitions of "nation" and aggregate them into a generic definition, then a "nation," in the classic sense, would be a geopolitical entity consisting of three major factors:

1 People: a homogeneous group
2 Territory: a geographically defined area
3 Government: an organizing, nationalistic body.

Various sources appear to make a distinction between the terms "nation" and "nation-state." The key issue separating the two concepts is *territorial control*. If we adhere only to the definition of "nation" given above, we are left open to accepting the presence of many possible nations in today's geopolitical landscape: "estimates of the number of stateless nations in the world run as high as 9,000."[10] So we distinguish between a "nation" and a "nation-state" as follows: in the former the conditions of nationhood have been met, while in the latter the conditions of statehood have been met and the nation actually controls the territory it has defined as belonging to it. It becomes clear that "the nation is the basis of political legitimacy ... all assume that the nation is bounded, that it has frontiers."[11] For example, the Kurdish people generally meet the conditions of nationhood but they have not satisfied the condition of statehood: they don't control the territory they view as being their exclusive realm. The idea of territorial control incorporates some degree of political, economic, and militaristic influence over geography. One question to ponder would be: is territory an absolute necessity in establishing the legitimacy of a nation as a geopolitical force?

From the previous discussion we conclude that a nation-state is a nation that wholly controls its geographic space and, by so doing, has obtained *sovereign* status: obtaining sovereign status (i.e., statehood) solidifies political control, and it is this sovereignty that secures nation-states the right to self-determination. In short, "the exercise of a state's authority over its territory implies that sovereignty is complete and exclusive."[12] So the generic definition of "nation" given above can be revised, as follows, to reflect the "nation-state":

1 People: a homogeneous group *that demonstrates national consciousness*
2 Territory: a geographically defined area *exclusively controlled by the governing body*
3 Government: an organizing, nationalistic body *that solely represents the national interests abroad.*

Why is the definition of the nation-state so relevant to our focus on the notion of information geopolitics? Because, "in the broad sweep of history, nation-states have provided a transnational form of organisation for managing economic affairs."[13] The nation-state serves as the fundamental geographic unit through which international political and economic systems interact, evolve, and conflict. By understanding the current perception of the nation-state we can move forward and examine how this perception is being altered by technological change.

The Position of Modern Sovereignty

How relevant are the conditions of sovereignty in today's evolving information-based economies and cultures? Does considering the basis of geopolitics as the flow and interaction of information within various contexts continue to hold much meaning? These are not easy questions and certainly cannot be fully explored here, but an attempt should be made to make a surface evaluation of their relative importance. We begin with assessing the basic building block – people.

People

The geopolitical process of individuals becoming a people, a people becoming a nation, and a nation becoming a nation-state begins with human beings; thus, people are its most critical element. While many studies and texts have been produced on the subject of nationalism and identity, it is sufficient to note that the phenomenon of people organizing themselves into nations and nation-states is a global one. Small nations (such as Chechnya, East Timor, and Tibet) are taking advantage of the current opportunity to continue the process towards statehood. Cultural identities continue to remain strong in many regions, yet, without a doubt, "the processes of economic modernization and social change throughout the world are separating people from longstanding local identities. They also weaken the nation state as a source of identity."[14]

Kenichi Ohmae's commentaries on the state of nations and the emerging global economy reveal a keen understanding of how profoundly information market forces are reshaping social identities:

This late twentieth-century wave of immigration [from the old economy to the new borderless economy] is being driven, on the surface, by the development of global brands and popular culture and, at a much deeper level, by the infectious spread of new information-related technologies. It is a new kind of social process, something we have never seen before, and it is leading to a new kind of social reality: a genuinely cross-border civilisation, nurtured by exposure to common technologies and sources of information, in which horizontal linkages within the same generation in different parts of the world are stronger than traditional, vertical linkages between generations in particular parts of it.[15]

This powerful trend could be a temporary one, a transitional process as technology is further introduced into many aspects of life on the small and large scale. But even if this represents a limited process, there are enormous implications for the concept of the nation-state. A person will give allegiance to the primary force that provides her/him with identity. In the future, as TNCs and their products increasingly influence younger generations, individuals may take their identity less from the nation-state in which they were born and more from the powers that establish the information and cultural context upon which they rely. Ohmae concludes by mentioning that, "as more and more individuals pass through the *brutal filter* separating old-fashioned geographies from the global economy, power over economic activity will inevitably migrate from the central governments of nation states to the borderless network of countless individual, market-based decisions."[16]

The new social phenomenon involves the rise of the individual and "small interests" as potential players in the global political and economic system. Commonality still draws individuals together, and their nature to aggregate will not be suppressed. But the nation-state, depending on its will and goals, will maintain some level of control over globalization by restricting information flow and/or technological implementation. Will nation-states be successful as "the masses" become empowered by technology? It is helpful to observe that "our lives have been transformed by the struggle of the margins to come into representation. Not just to be placed by the regime of some other, or imperializing eye but to reclaim some form of representation for themselves."[17]

Yet, as long as multimedia and computing technology are produced with a global emphasis, and based upon global information context (even if "global information" is produced with a clear cultural bias), the information standards of local regions will continue to be threatened. When propagated for a long enough duration, perhaps over a few generations, the end result is a people whose nationalistic connections are wholly diluted if not completely severed.

Territory

The implications of a people losing interest in the goals and raison d'être of their nation-state are serious. Could this extend to the "real" territory upon which their nation's sovereignty and, in fact, their own personal freedoms have been based? For most of human history the importance of land and territorial control has been absolute. In fact, it could be argued that the great majority of conflicts were contests over geographic control (spurred on by religious/ethnic prodding). If individuals are conditioned to disregard the importance of geographic space through exposure to global information, then the perceived need for territorial control diminishes, and sovereignty as we know it today will be endangered. Territorial importance may have less and less significance as people travel faster and farther from home, both literally and virtually, as "perceptions of frontiers are changing, from one frontier to several, from line to zone, from physical to cultural, from spatial to functional, from impermeable to permeable."[18]

People are the architects of the geopolitical system in which they live, and "as with all regions that pertain to human social organisation, a state's territory is a social construct."[19] Perhaps territory does exist in the real world; however, without human beings imposing value upon the land, the concept would be empty. We cannot overlook the role that cartography plays in reinforcing the concept of geographic control. In fact, "claims to an identity between people and territory can be asserted through maps and extended back through time."[20] For centuries, maps have served as surrogates for that concept of abstract space – the nation-state – that we cannot see in the real world. Information technology has revolutionized visual communication and the individual expression of self. "As a consequence of the explosion of those new forms of cultural communication and cultural representation there has opened up a new field of visual representation itself."[21] So we can perceive evidence of the existence of a nation-state, the homogeneity of the people, the flag flying overhead, the national anthem, and the different language – all *symptoms* of statehood. We can measure the area of the nation-state and prove its existence geographically. However, in the end, "territory is more than just a physical and measurable entity. It is also something of the mind because people impute meaning to and gain meaning from territory."[22]

The proliferation of global information across local contexts weakens nationalistic tendencies and a connection to territorial value, while increasing the various information conflicts. The problem for the nation-states is that "the Internet brings forth a personal mode of communication that national authorities cannot regulate easily."[23] Nationalistic groups now seeking statehood realize the importance of territorial control and thus continue their struggles for independence from existing colonial powers. Yet for those nations that have attained sovereignty, and whose populace is "wired" to the global networks and influenced by TNC marketing, territorial control is not a serious issue in their daily lives. One might imagine that a form of technological transition occurs as nations become states and as states become technologically enhanced. This relates directly to Ohmae's "brutal filter": for the citizen, finding a connection with the land/territory is not as important or as cognitively significant as is finding connection to the global scene, to other people of similar ages or interests.

In the end, the overall value of territory must decrease in the face of globalized information, when identity is established with multiple states and territories. Yet, as local information contexts slowly dissolve, often by the economic intrusion by TNCs, *some* information context must take its place. Consider that "even if a few states can still defend their territory against an invading army ... none can control the flow of images and ideas that shape human tastes and values. The globalized 'presence' of Madonna, McDonald's, and Mickey Mouse make a mockery of sovereignty as exclusive territorial control."[24] Some praise the kind of liberation that a global information context can bring to the people of an oppressed nation-state, while others condemn it as the worst form of cultural destruction. Whatever the case may be, this process is currently under way, and, as a result, "real" geographic space is being forfeited in favour of virtual space, space where information resides and ideas are created and disseminated, where perception is much more relevant than reality. When one realizes that "the political boundaries of nation-states are too narrow and constricted to define the scope and activities of modern business,"[25] then one begins to see the kind of powerful forces that nation-states face.

Government
Sovereignty is essentially the aggregation of people and their territorial characteristics. The control of territory by a homogeneous people requires an organizing body to administer the state's affairs. It is not difficult to imagine how state governments might react in the face of the broad, aforementioned technological changes. If a people's national identity is eroded and, with it, the importance of territorial control, then the last bastion for maintaining state sovereignty will lie in the government that was originally created to protect the state's interests.

Many national governments have had to change their administrative practices and perspectives on governance in the face of rapid economic and technological advances. Over the past few decades, in the interest of maintaining economic solidarity and military control, regional military and economic alliances have led governments to yield some degree of their sovereignty to supranational groups. However, "sovereign states have only reluctantly surrendered parts of their sovereignty to supranational groups since the 1950s."[26] Reluctantly yes, but, at an ever-increasing rate: the close of the twentieth century saw the advent of the European Union and economic alliances such as the General Agreement on Tariffs and Trade (GATT), the North American Free Trade Agreement (NAFTA), the Association of South-East Asian Nations (ASEAN), and so on. One can hardly blame the governments for taking such action. The isolationism of the pre-Second World War era is long gone. In the face of regional economic powers, the need for aggregation in order to remain viable in a global market is paramount. It is this strong emphasis on economy, on the flow of goods, services, and information, that is significant here. Sovereign governments are beginning to work towards a level of economic cooperation and competition that is unprecedented, yet they are discovering that the transnational corporations have already "arrived"; the TNCs are already operating at a level of sophistication and market penetration that is far beyond the scope and capabilities of most nation-states. TNCs developed and thrived on the principles of economic gain and market savvy that nation-states are only now beginning to realize. But, more important, the TNCs appeal to basic individual needs and desires that nation-states simply cannot address.

The TNCs appreciate the advantages they possess in this emerging arena. As the development of a global information infrastructure continues, they have been politically active in protecting their interests within the nation-states. This has led some analysts to conclude, "all over the world, national, provincial, and local governments have become pawns of global corporations and the Corporate Agenda."[27] This might be an extreme viewpoint, but it does point to the reality that TNCs operate on a unique geopolitical plane. Some may argue, for example, that even the Microsoft/US Department of Justice confrontation was not about monopolistic practices; rather, it was about the United States trying to preserve its sovereign economic control in the face of a formidable new economic force – the information economy that was essentially birthed in that country. TNCs enjoy an almost untouchable status in some regions as the perceived carriers of economic advancement and prosperity for more impoverished regions. Does this mean that the role of national governments is diminishing to the point where they only serve as unwitting tools for TNCs? Some staunchly disagree with this and believe that "the role of the nation-state in creating an innovation society is critical to the well-being of its citizens in the information age."[28] At the moment, the need for partnership is apparent. We are in a transitional mode, and any type of overly rapid upheaval to the sovereignty system would undoubtedly cause widespread social and political confusion. Besides, TNCs care less than does the state for the daily welfare of the consumers. In the eyes of TNCs, the individual exists to consume: what they do beyond that is not particularly relevant. The severity of TNC infiltration into the processes of statehood has yet to be objectively evaluated; however, we can see some rudimentary signs. When governments begin to legislate or take other formal actions against TNC's at an increasing rate, the perception is that the nation-states are beginning to understand the nature of the global information economy and are taking action to secure their role within it, if not as technological innovators then as technological regulators. Indeed, "the political result of this development will likely be a reordering of international relations in a manner that suggests that undemocratic or authoritarian nations may find the regulation necessary to their survival impossible."[29]

The initial focus of information geopolitics will be on the relationship between national governments and TNCs: this is where the "battle lines" will be drawn. Whether or not a peaceful settlement is attained will remain to be seen. At this point in time, we can discern the early signs of a contention between the remnants of the nation-state paradigm (the governments) and the new entities of an evolving information-state paradigm (the TNCs). Keep in mind that this is directly related to the more fundamental aspect of information geopolitics. It is a conflict between the global (TNCs) and the local (national governments). What is clear at the present is that "the greater the political power of corporations and those aligned with them, the less the political power of the people, and the less meaningful democracy becomes."[30] This is so because the global information economy is much less reliant upon nation-states as the primary unit of interaction. Due to advanced, progressive, and relatively inexpensive information technology, the primary unit of interaction is becoming the region, the small group, and even the single individual acting of her/his own accord, by a "personal sovereignty." The nation-state begins to seem much less effective in representing constituent interests. If and when national societies reach this most intrinsic, personal level, then people will begin to connect, interact, aggregate, and socialize according to common factors that transcend nationalism and sovereignty – at which point the significance of the nation-state as a geopolitical entity will diminish even further.

On Being Transnational

At the global scale, we realize the fierce competition of many powerful TNCs to position themselves not only as the primary conduits of information but also as the primary originators of information. The notion that "multinational corporations and nation-states are key actors in shaping the direction of the information economy"[31] is generally true, but the roles they play and for what duration remain to be seen. Having briefly examined the nation-state and its changing applicability, it would be prudent at this point to do the same for the transnational corporation and other such entities that are disseminating the information revolution.

How one views a TNC and information technology depends primarily upon where one stands in terms of gaining or losing from the imposition of the technology. The real "threat" exists in the fact that much of the advancement of local and global societies rests on the achievements of the various TNCs and their relatively unhindered dissemination. In short, the TNCs are creating the global information infrastructure while nation-states are acting as the top-level political system with which TNCs must negotiate: but, typically, they function as a minor filter. What advantage does a TNC really have over a nation-state and why will this make a difference? Information technology – including mainframe and personal computers, software, peripherals, multimedia, and, most important, networks – is the fundamental means through which TNCs operate. The more proficient any individual, TNC, or nation-state becomes at realizing the potential of the technology, the more successful they are likely to be in managing their information flows. There are three main advantages that can be gained from implementing information technology: "(1) to compress time, (2) to overcome geography, and (3) to alter the structure of relationships, such as bypassing intermediaries."[32] This is an underlying power of the technology: the removal of information boundaries between states and, more important, between individual citizens. Information, for better or worse, acts as a binding medium when shared across diverse geographic contexts. It has the potential to create a familiarity between cultures that hundreds of years of international relations failed to yield. In other words, information is "the raw material of the economic process, itself quite indifferent to space, because the technologies of information transmission are now supposedly approaching the point where the friction of distance is nil."[33] The elimination of distance and the diminution of geographic space are key factors in the global information system. It is in this realm of "virtual space" that information geopolitics can be found, along with its constituent parts – TNCs and a growing host of individuals and emergent "nations" that are finding a home on the global networks.

Although somewhat laughable, we have already seen emerging attempts of "nations" to stake a claim in cyberspace, from the Dominion of Melchizedek[34] to the Hutt River Province.[35] Realizing that they are not real world territorial claims are moot points; these and others like them establish virtual kingdoms via Web sites and other means. In and of itself, this is not wholly remarkable, but the overwhelming response such efforts have received from ordinary citizens worldwide is something to note.

The modus operandi of a TNC working to build the global infrastructure is not entirely noble. The focus is on the global information economy: therefore, the goal is producing revenues wherever possible. Globalization allows TNCs "to look for ways to sell their product in as many different places as possible."[36] While some corporations may operate on a more philanthropic basis, the fact is that most exist to expand markets and to increase their global revenue. If they happen to raise the standard of living in some regions, or create a new infrastructure, or bring international citizenry towards a more common understanding: well, that is a by-product. Conversely, if they disrupt local customs and practices, it is most likely not by intention but simply by virtue of their global presence interacting on a local level. Consider, for example, how McDonald's restaurants have altered some basic practices in Asia: "children's birthdays (previously uncelebrated in many places), queuing in Hong Kong (previously a scrum; now more likely to be in a line), the way that Japanese eat their food (previously always sitting down; now more likely to be standing up), and even smiling at strangers (previously close to an insult in China)."[37]

TNCs are responsible for examining their markets very carefully and for discerning how to ease into them so as to cause the least amount of disruption. Disruption of culture, language, mores, and (almost always) sovereignty will occur, so it becomes crucial to minimize the effects as much as possible. Thus, unless the TNC wants to invite a conflict, some form of "recontexting" must take place wherein the intruding entity must establish how its imported information context must be adapted to the local context. Many TNCs try to consider the locale when preparing information content or preparing to physically move in and establish a foothold. However, because TNCs primarily operate on a global information standard, they may reach a point where the conflicts between the global and local information contexts become obvious and must be resolved. Typically, the TNC ends up prevailing, either because the nation-state does not have strong enough legislation or the citizens value the benefits of the TNC's presence enough to be willing to relinquish some former aspects of their cultural identity.

Information Geopolitics and Microsoft: A Case in Point
For Microsoft Corporation (and, indeed, the software world in general), the term "localization" is used to describe the process through which products are prepared for local markets. Localization is a complex exercise wherein the language is translated from American English and, just as important, the content is altered to fit the local information contexts of the target market. The software's global context has to be tailored to fit a local expectation. This is a difficult and painstaking task, and is usually where problems arise for software companies. This is particularly true for Microsoft Corporation, which attempts to consider both market geography and the best way of entering the market. Still, even with the utmost attention, problems inevitably arise. Usually they relate to the breakdown of the appropriate "interface" between the global information contained in the products and the local information expected in the market. This breakdown can be caused by a number of things, not the least of which is the lack of local understanding consequent upon the information creator being located in the wrong geographic context. For example, an American in Redmond, Washington, is not likely to understand the local information expectations of a Turk in Ankara, Turkey. So the aim of localization involves "achieving a balance between being global, with the scale

advantages associated with size and global scope, and being local within each regional or national market and network of resources."[38]

The history of geopolitical errors at Microsoft Corporation reads like a gallery of localization events in which crucial global-local information interfaces were not diligently considered. Some mistakes can be traced to ignorance of world geography; others to a critical lack of local knowledge. The majority of problems Microsoft has encountered has involved cartography and its various products, from Windows to Office to Encarta World Atlas. It is true that "maps can serve as tools of debate, highlighting ... spatial implications and thus apparently providing graphic evidence of the nature of the practice of power and of what can be seen as a need to challenge it."[39] However, Microsoft has had many significant problems with art images, flags, national anthems, religious symbols, and a plethora of other content; maps are only a part of the total picture.

Maps are one of the first things that customs agents in some countries will examine in Microsoft's software products. These are loaded onto computer systems and checked for compatibility with the local information market. In some cases, such as Turkey, India, and China, the maps are unacceptable. Tunisia's government, for example, disliked the commentary about their country in Encarta Encyclopaedia. In some countries, it is true that "unofficial maps, such as those made by or for one of the parties to a legal dispute, are sometimes admitted in court."[40] In Latin American countries, this legal complication can include *any* cartography sold in the country, regardless of the source, which then makes Microsoft a contributor of evidence in a potential real-world boundary arbitration (for or against their host market). In these situations, Microsoft is forced to make a market decision whether to comply with the local information needs and to change the product or to bypass the local information market completely and sell only in those countries where the global context is palatable. This is something of a simplification, but it does show the type of decision that must be made.

The problem for Microsoft is that a mistake found in one product might affect the sales potential of other products. As an illustration, the problem in India with Windows 95 threatened not only the Windows 95 software but also the sale of all Microsoft products in that market. Like any other TNC, Microsoft would prefer to expand into new markets; however, if the potential risks outweigh the benefits, then Microsoft may forsake the market in favour of one that is less volatile. Some nation-states are more adamant about enforcing their sovereignty than are others, and they do so by reinforcing their local information standard. In the end, it may make a small difference to the TNC; there are many potential markets. The reasons for choosing not to enter a market are complex, but they are always based on the give and take of information geopolitics. Microsoft, as a primary producer of information management tools as well as content, is unwilling to become embroiled in a dispute over competing local information contexts. It would, of course, prefer to work around such a dispute and enter the market.

In many of the geopolitical issues at Microsoft, the nation-state is struggling to reassert its sovereignty via the information medium. Indeed, Microsoft exemplifies the fact that "our very concept of 'world,' an ideological construct that is usually more philosophical than geographical in content, can be framed and articulated by cartography."[41] Many governments are fully aware of the power of cartography as well as of the global information venue provided by TNCs and their related information technology. Therefore, local governments strive to utilize the TNC as a means of incorporating their local information context into the global context. Why? Because if a country is successful in promoting its local viewpoint, and convinces a TNC to incorporate it into the broader, global information stream, then that context becomes globally legitimized (quite possibly at the expense of other neighbouring contexts). This is pure information geopolitics at play.

Thus a TNC, or any information provider/producer, may unwittingly be used to disseminate misinformation on the global scale. However, the provider is not always unaware of what it is getting into; this is where another problem occurs. In order to secure a foothold in a local market, a TNC may, on the basis of market reviews, *consciously* favour one local information context over another. For example, if Argentina yields significantly more revenue than Chile for a certain company's product in Latin America, then the company may decide to favour the Argentinean viewpoint at the expense the Chilean viewpoint. The product may not sell in Chile and may actually yield some negative public reactions there; however, in the TNC's broader perspective within the global economy, the loss in Chile is a trifle. The TNC gets what it is really after – the larger revenues – and appeases at least one local information market in the process (one that may then remain loyal and show great long-term promise). In fact, clearly biasing itself towards one local context would likely improve the TNC's ability to thrive in that particular market much more than would have been the case had it compromised between competing viewpoints. Some opponents believe that this strategy is precisely that of Microsoft: "by putting it [the technology] in the (operating system), they anoint. You give it credibility. You give it distribution."[42] While this comment was made in reference to a specific technology's deployment in Windows software, it is true of content that is incorporated into software products generally.

Microsoft attempts to avoid situations where the content in its products is employed as a tool for local geopolitical agendas. It also attempts to compromise between differing local information contexts. Microsoft is not interested in starting or participating in a geopolitical information war. This company has not always been successful in avoiding these problems, however, mainly due to a lack of a local geographic understanding. However, Microsoft is taking steps company-wide to be more attentive to these issues; for example, it has created the Geopolitical Product Strategy (GPS) group. GPS's mission is to help protect Microsoft's global markets against closure and, in the process, to preserve local market trust in Microsoft's product integrity. But even with the existence of the GPS group, Microsoft will continue to face difficult decisions on a market-by-market basis. The real challenge, as dictated by information geopolitics, is to proactively discern the proper "interfaces" between the global and local information contexts long before the products are released. This is the challenge Microsoft and many other TNCs face when globalizing their products for worldwide consumption.

The nation-state, with its unique local information context, is then in the position of having to compete with other nation-states to gain access to, and place itself within, the global information context. Because TNCs are not only the creators of this global information venue but also the administrators of it, nation-states struggle to reaffirm their sovereignty in a world where real boundaries, territorial control, and the notion of sovereignty are challenged by virtual markets, globalized information, and technologically empowered citizens.

Information Geopolitics and New Sovereignties

Consider the major trends outlined so far in this discussion and how they relate to the role of nation-states and TNCs in information geopolitics:

1   the profusion of information technology on a global scale and a subsequent, unprecedented level of individual access to knowledge
2   people becoming more connected with individuals in other countries and less attached to their own nationalistic tendencies
3   geographic territory becoming less important than information access and the control of the *image* of territory (e.g., cartographic information)
4   national governments yielding control to intranational bodies to form economic alliances to control information flows and to protect local/regional information contexts
5   transnational corporations acting as conveyors of global information, choosing to accept/reject local contexts as part of the global information system based on market viability
6   nation-states jockeying for access to the global information stream, each trying to assert its own local context as being globally significant – or else forfeiting the local context in favour of the global one.

When these trends are examined en masse, it becomes clear that those nation-states, TNCs, and individuals all have a unique role to play. These trends solidify the supposition that "the past two decades have seen the most rapid and sweeping institutional transformation in human history. It is a conscious and intentional transformation in search of a new world economic order in which business has no nationality and knows no borders."[43] The turnabout has been so rapid, in fact, that all the players (individuals, groups, nation-states, and TNCs) are not fully aware of the extent of this revolution. If there is any truth-value to this suggestion, and growing evidence indicates that there is, then the world may be poised for another geopolitical shift – one that remains grounded in a real world but that diverges significantly into a virtual world of information representation and manipulation. If the geopolitical landscape changes in response to information technology, creating a new interaction called "information geopolitics," then who might the players be on this stage, and what will their actions dictate?

At the present time, both nation-states and corporations are acting out somewhat uncoordinated but similar roles in the global information economy. Up to the present time, nation-states have been carrying out their individual "manifest destinies" and exercising their right to self-determination as gained through their sovereign status. Likewise, TNCs have been operating mostly as big businesses not only because that's what they are but also because of their unrealized, hegemonic nature on the world scene. When positioned together in the present global system, the nation-states and TNCs carry out mainly a contentious interaction that is based on one entity trying to circumvent the other's regulations or practices. That is to say, it is not necessarily always a constructive relationship. Of course, this is a broad generalization. Certainly not all of the interactions between these two entities are negative. When nation-states take notice of the advantages of borderless TNCs, they come to realize that "technological capacity gives many states the possibility of operating beyond boundaries, including space."[44] Both nation-states and TNCs manoeuvre for strategic economic control over markets, both adopting similar tactics and both relying more heavily on information technology as the means to this end. TNCs are realizing, however, that technological infrastructure must have a real world, geographic basis: they have to install services in a territory (unless keen advantages of emerging satellite technologies are realized) and thus must be subject to national regulations. Meanwhile, nation-states, while controlling the territory, understand that, "unlike other advances in communication, the Internet brings forth a personal mode of communication that national authorities cannot regulate easily."[45]

On the information geopolitics field of play, we have one side where the nation-states are trying to maintain their sovereign control over the perception of national homogeneity and another side where the TNCs are trying to globalize geographic information and homogenize national citizens into being good transnational consumers. While TNCs have the option of catering to specific local contexts (and some do), it is more cost-effective and beneficial to future revenues to create a more homogenous consumer base. The goal of the two forces is the same, to maintain the national citizens as consumers of information. The realization here is the role of the individual and the small interest groups in dictating how the large, global players may interact, along with the recognition of a level of personal empowerment that had not previously existed. At this personal level boundaries and territory are much less significant. The only boundaries that matter are those of perceived personal space and the amount of freedom one has to gain access to information.

Possible Geopolitical Entities

As the global information economy grows and develops, we will see unique roles ascribed to the primary players of the former geopolitics model. We may see nation-states become more "corporation-like" and TNCs become more "state-like," but, realistically, the information economy of the future will allow for many new kinds of geopolitical interaction. New players will undoubtedly enter the information geopolitics scene, and new roles will be concomitant with the evolution of new forms of power. We will see many of these roles performed by diverse geopolitical entities, ranging widely in scale and power, and varying in technological adaptation and ability. While information, the primary fuel of the system, will be more clearly defined as a commodity, the acting players and their interactions will become *very* complex. The spectrum proposed here relies on the notion of scale, starting with a single individual and propagating the concept to the highest aggregation possible – the global state (Table 2.1).

The implications of such a system are prodigious, but this is only one possible model. There is no prescribed hierarchy with a simple transition from one state of existence to the next. Many of the new entities of information geopolitics may exist with no need to evolve, while others may aggregate and expand. Although the global state is not the positive, logical end to the process, it is at present the pinnacle of the hierarchy, a point at which information geopolitics is irrelevant on a global scale because all local contexts have been absorbed and aggregated. When viewing this system, "we need to ask again about the ways in which electronic information and mapping technologies are reconfiguring the contemporary world ... the techniques of data exchange and representation legitimize new

Table 2.1

New geopolitical entities arising out of an info-economy

	People	Space	Authority
Individual	A citizen empowered by information technology; an information user with a distinct identity.	The virtual networks; a virtual "home," local geography.	Adheres to the local information context as a convenience while accessing the global.
Community	A group of citizens united with a common identity; information users and distributors.	Shared virtual spaces, neighbourhoods, and small regions.	Builds its own local context, possibly combining with others, while accessing the global.
Nation	A homogeneous aggregation of individuals and clans, united by a common identity or purpose, connected via information technology; creates, distributes, and uses information.	Large, distributed virtual spaces, possible geographic space but not necessary.	Self-determining with its own local context, with its own global access.
Virtual nation	A virtual nation-state, comprised of a people, virtual territory, and a governing system; maintains a unique information domain.	A nation without geographic territory; possesses a well-established virtual presence. Sovereignty is based on control of information.	Self-determining, with its own local context on the basis of a non-geographic context, with its own form of global access via virtual means.
Transnational economic entity	A transnational business operation established for the purpose of creating, disseminating, and controlling information technology.	Exists both real and virtually, distributed across many geographic contexts. May be based in one nation-state.	Follows nation-state regulations as much as necessary to penetrate local markets. Thinks globally, acts locally.

▲

▲ *Table 2.1*

New geopolitical entities arising out of an info-economy

	People	Space	Authority
Nation-state	Classic definition: a defined people, geographic territory, and government body.	Exists geographically – sovereignty is based on control of territory.	Governments exists to regulate and legislate, to protect national citizenry (i.e., reinforce the local context).
Corporate nation	A unified corporate body of individuals, together for the purpose of succeeding in the global economy.	Exists virtually or geographically or both; geographic space is secondary to control of information space.	Self-governing, tolerates nation-state governments (local contexts) as a hindrance, interfaces with other corporate nations (other global contexts).
Supranation or regional alliance	An aggregation of nations, info-nations, nation-states, and/or corporate nations, based on common goals and regional information contexts.	Virtual or geographic, the space is an aggregation of individual national entities.	Control is relinquished to a higher body for decision making, local contexts are aggregated into regional contexts for better interface to the global context.
Global state	A fully aggregated political-economic system wherein the global information context has absorbed all local information contexts.	Exists virtually and geographically; de facto control over most territory – despite possible rogue nations.	Disaggregated sovereignty is gone; self-determination exists only at the highest level by a governing body.

social practices and institutions in ways we have only begun to recognise and regulate."[46] At this point in time, we can only begin to surmise what kinds of geopolitical entities may arise in response to the information paradigm shift that is under way.

In addition, we need to closely examine the role of the individual in this future scheme. The geopolitics of the past involved, primarily, a diplomatic plane among nation-states, but the information geopolitics that will arise in addition to or in replacement of traditional statecraft must account for the empowerment of individual citizens. Barlow, speaking on behalf of cyberspace-users, states in his "Declaration of Independence of Cyberspace to the Nation-States" that "we must declare our virtual selves immune to your sovereignty, even as we continue to consent to your rule over our bodies ... we will create a civilisation of the Mind in Cyberspace. May it be more humane and fair than the world your governments have made before."[47] Whether taken seriously or not, such statements begin to indicate the rise of a mentality that all national governments will need to address.

Conclusions

This chapter has not focused directly on boundaries and territoriality in relation to information geopolitics, seeing them, rather, as the by-products of a broader geopolitical sphere of action. However, the implication for boundaries and territoriality remain clear. There still exist many barriers that can prevent the global information economy from reaching fruition. Some of these barriers are painfully obvious, such as the fact that "more than 1.3 billion people live on less than a dollar a day, about 60 percent of them in South Asia and Sub-Saharan Africa."[48] And offering just as much a barrier is the fact that "the majority of the people in the world have never even seen a computer, much less thought about accessing the Internet and broadcasting local difficulties."[49] The serious economic and political disparity that exists between nation-states today cannot be overlooked. One may find Coca-Cola in the middle of a Third World country, but this by no means indicates that that country reaps the benefits of information technology.

We are, at present, in a time of transition: Individuals, nations, nation-states, cultural movements, and corporations must realize that "economic globalization is neither in the human interest nor inevitable. It is axiomatic that political power aligns with economic power. The larger the economic unit, the larger its dominant players, and the more political power becomes concentrated in the largest corporations."[50] If this trend remains strong into the next century, then the field of information geopolitics will be ripe for development, and the evolution of new forms of sovereignty will be likely. The current global system is still far removed from the world of information geopolitics outlined here, but potential exists: the necessary mentality is emerging, whether for purposes of economic compatibility or of global security. It is more frequently being realized, across distances, that "production of information is shaping politics and, by default, establishing new rules for post-industrial society."[51] As attention increasingly focuses on the state of geopolitics and the future viability of nation-states, we must consider what the new rules for information geopolitics might be, and who will be writing them.

Notes

1   J.P. Cole, *Geography of World Affairs*, 6th ed. (London: Butterworths, 1983).
2   John O'Loughlin, *Dictionary of Geopolitics* (Westport, CT: Greenwood Press, 1994).
3   Gertjan Dijkink, *National Identity and Geopolitical Visions: Maps of Pride and Pain* (London: Routledge, 1996), 11.
4   Ibid.
5   Jeremy Black, *Maps and Politics* (Chicago: University of Chicago Press, 1997), 110.
6   Bill Gates, "Speech to the National Governor's Association," Microsoft Corporate Information (Microsoft internal Web source), 30 July 1997.
7   Stuart Hall, "The Local and the Global," in *Culture, Globalization, and the World-System*, ed. Anthony D. King (University of Minnesota Press, 1997), 33.
8   Ibid., 39.
9   Malcolm Anderson, *Frontiers: Territory and State Formation in the Modern World* (Cambridge: Polity Press, 1996), 178.
10 James Minihan, *Nations without States* (Westport CT: Greenwood Press, 1996), xvi.
11 Anderson, *Frontiers*, 42.
12 David B. Knight, "People Together Yet Apart: Rethinking Territory, Sovereignty, and Identities," in *Reordering the World: Geopolitical Perspectives on the Twenty-First Century*, ed. G.J. Demko and W.B. Wood (Boulder, CO: Westview Press, 1994), 75.
13 Kenichi Ohmae, *The End of the Nation State: The Rise of Regional Economies* (New York: Free Press, 1995), 141.
14 Samuel P. Huntington, *The Clash of Civilizations* (New York: Simon and Schuster, 1996), 161.
15 Ohmae, *The End of the Nation State*, 138.
16 Ibid.
17 Hall, "The Local and the Global," 34.
18 Anderson, *Frontiers*, 190.
19 Knight, "People Together Yet Apart," 76.
20 Black, *Maps and Politics*, 143.
21 Hall, "The Local and the Global," 28.
22 Knight, "People Together Yet Apart," 77.
23 Johnathan Neilsen, "Cyberspace: Doom of the Undemocratic Nation State," *Harvard Political Review* (Spring 1999), online edition.
24 Joel Kreiger, "Sovereignty," in *Oxford Companion to Politics of the World*, ed. Joel Kreiger (Oxford: Oxford University Press, 1993), 853.
25 David C. Korten, *When Corporations Rule the World* (West Hartford, CT: Kumarian Press, 1995), 123.
26 Cole, *Geography of World Affairs*, 233.
27 Jeremy Brecher and Tim Costello, "Reversing the Race to the Bottom," in *The Geopolitics Reader*, ed. Gearóid Ó Tuathail, S. Dalby, and P. Routledge (London: Routledge, 1998), 301.
28 Martin Carnoy, "Multinationals in a Changing World Economy: Whither the Nation-State?" in *The New Global Economy in the Information Age: Reflections on Our Changing World*, ed. Stephen S. Cohen, Martin Carnoy, Manuel Castells, and Fernando Cardoso (University Park: Pennsylvania State University Press, 1993), 91.

29 Neilsen, "Cyberspace."
30 Korten, *When Corporations Rule the World,* 140.
31 Carnoy, "Multinationals in a Changing World Economy," 8.
32 Edward J. Malecki, *Technology and Economic Development* (Essex, UK: Addison Wesley Longman, 1997), 208.
33 Michael Storper, *The Regional World-Territorial Development in a Global Economy* (New York: Guilford Press, 1997), 237.
34 G. Bruce Knetch, "A Nation in Cyberspace Draws Fire from Authorities," *Wall Street Journal,* 9 February 1999, B1.
35 Leonard Casley ("Prince Leonard"), the Hutt River Province Web site, <http://www.huttriver.net>, 1999.
36 "The Science of Alliance," *The Economist,* 4 April 1998, 69-70.
37 "The Personal Touch," *The Economist,* 16 May 1998, 4-5.
38 Malecki, *Technology and Economic Development,* 202.
39 Black, *Maps and Politics,* 120.
40 Alec McEwen, "Temple of Dispute: The Fine Line of Border Negotiation," *Mercator's World* 3, 4 (July/August 1998): 19.
41 Alan K. Henrikson, "The Power and Politics of Maps," in *Reordering the World: Geopolitical Perspectives on the Twenty-First Century,* ed G.J. Demko and W.B. Wood (Boulder, CO: Westview Press, 1994), 50.
42 Jay Greene, "Software Giant Portrayed as Kingmaker," *Seattle Times,* 29 May 1999, section B.
43 Korten, *When Corporations Rule the World,* 121.
44 Kreiger, "Sovereignty," 853.
45 Neilsen, "Cyberspace: Doom of the Undemocratic Nation State."
46 John Pickles, ed., *Ground Truth: The Social Implications of Geographic Information Systems* (New York: Guilford Press, 1997), 231.
47 John Perry Barlow, "A Declaration of Independence from Cyberspace," Ariga: Cyberspace Nation Web site, <http://www.eff.org/~barlow/Declaration-Final.html>, 6 February 1996.
48 World Bank, *The World Bank Atlas* (World Bank, 1997), 4.
49 Neilsen, "Cyberspace."
50 Korten, *When Corporations Rule the World,* 140.
51 Richard J. Barnet and John Cavanagh, *Global Dreams: Imperial Corporations and the New World Order* (New York: Simon and Schuster, 1994), 334.

3
Law, Sovereignty, and Transnationalism: Delivering Social Goods Using a Functional Approach to Borders
Robert Adamson

Our twenty-first-century world accentuates trend-forecasting pitfalls. Trend-tellers are often foiled by the complex nature of people and events, which seemingly defy pattern and continuity, as well as by perceptual boundaries imposed by disciplinary focus and content: while we see the rise of European integration and the proliferation of multilateral trade zones, we also see the resurgence of ethnic and religious conflict and the emotional protests of those who question the benefit of current international trading regimes. While some seek internationalization, others seek decentralization. While some seek a unifying goal to transcend borders, others seek the comfort, predictability, and commonality of small community and locally defined purpose.

The tension between internationalization and localization is demonstrated by recent developments in insecurity and terrorism, which have rippled through the international community, as well as in the type of transnational corporate and communications developments described in the previous chapter. Similar tensions exist in the relationship between law and transnationalism. 9/11 and the Iraq crisis seem to demonstrate only too well that, while there has been a continuing proliferation of the instruments of international law (treaties, agreements, protocols, etc.), there has been a concomitant recognition of, and frustration with, the ineffectual nature of international legal obligation and enforcement. The skills and tenacity of international terrorists, drug and human traffickers, and other forms of organized crime far outmatch the vaguely worded, inadequately funded, and enforced international agreements created to thwart them. As a result, many states, particularly those to whom these illicit activities represent the greatest threat and who have other options, are working beyond international law. These states are choosing to pursue national objectives through the extension of the jurisdiction of their domestic laws. Although there is still a commitment to the development of international law and the consensus it attempts to build, domestic solutions are increasingly being preferred where international law has not pro-vided, and perhaps cannot provide, an immediate solution to an immediate problem.

The purpose of this chapter is not just to acknowledge that, in terms of the "big picture," borders are becoming more permeable but also to elaborate how lawmakers are responding to this increased permeability. There are various events that are exerting increased pressure on our current formulation of state sovereignty, jurisdiction, and the ability of any state, no matter how powerful or wealthy, to control what goes on within its borders. As a result of these events, it is argued that law and policy makers must reinvent the concepts of sovereignty and jurisdiction in a way that best delivers social goods. In order to achieve this end, it is also argued that borders must be defined and used functionally rather than geopolitically.

Where borders inhibit the realization of a social good, those borders and the sovereignty that they define must give way to international cooperation, multiple jurisdiction, and various other forms of legal multilateralism. As noted above, however, international cooperation is not always an effective way of delivering a social good. There are many institutional impediments to achieving consensus on the goal of cooperation, let alone the best way of achieving it. In these circumstances unilateralism, including the unilateral extension of domestic jurisdiction, may be the only option. As unilateral action by one or several states outside of the presently conceived sovereign jurisdiction of that state or states is understandably controversial, it will have to be used judiciously and strategically. Unilateralism will be reserved for those situations where the need for such action is so compelling that the state actor is able to withstand international political and moral scrutiny.

National Borders and Legal Regimes

States are sovereign entities with international rights and duties. Subject to the obligations assumed under international law, both through convention and customary law, states are free to create their own domestic legal regimes and to promulgate laws. Domestic laws are the instruments that theoretically articulate the rights and obligations of the state, its citizens, and the overall purposes and objectives of the state. Domestic laws are also the instruments through which states attempt to deliver social goods such as security and liberty of the person as well as the protection of one or several religious practices, infrastructure, and various other benefits. These benefits are meant to compel individuals to enter a social contract of statehood rather than to persist in the unpredictable world of what Locke and others have described as the state of nature.

In many cases, laws work well to promote and defend certain principles and to deliver social goods. Increasingly, however, numerous factors are intervening to thwart the ability of the state to provide these social goods.

Although there are a variety of reasons for these new challenges (lack of consensus on desirable social goods, increased pressure on the state to reduce its influence, limited financial resources, etc.), there is a particularly problematic obstacle for the modern state: the internationalization of problem solving. As the mobility of capital, people, ideas, and crime increases, the ability of the state to make good on the social contract correspondingly decreases. The less powerful, wealthy, and resourceful the state, the more likely its domestic laws will be ineffectual in addressing many of these increasingly transborder problems.

It is true that internationalization is not an entirely new phenomenon. Capital, people, ideas, and crime have long ignored borders. The fact is that these trends are accelerating at a pace, and with a level of sophistication, to which states have been able neither to predict nor respond. The rapidity of technological change has also contributed to internationalization and will continue to do so with increasing haste. The events of September 2001 prove that terrorists as well as people smugglers and other illicit activities seem to benefit from the difficulties of regulating the vastly increased numbers of people who arrive at various airports, ports, and land borders (let alone the thousands of kilometres of undefended borders, particularly between friendly nations). Moreover, new information technologies can also ensure that hate speech, fraudulent stock schemes, and recipes for home-made bombs all join the myriad of bits and bytes of information passing through and over the growing communications network of fibre-optic cables and radio-waves.

So although illicit activities have perforated borders for years, there are numerous other activities that challenge conventional ways of understanding and regulating transborder transactions. Technology has created new forms of transborder activity and new commodities that do not fit into existing legal regimes. Aided by technological advances, as our mobility increases, law and policy makers face new challenges and demands on their intellectual imagination. Issues of free speech (including hate speech), electronic commerce and fraud, privacy rights, environmental pollution, and reproductive technologies (including genetic manipulation and intellectual property rights) are all issues that demand more complete and nuanced legal responses.

Initial Response: Multilateral Legal Regimes

The intuitive response to these international dynamics is multilateral cooperation. Although states will prefer to resolve problems domestically, there are problems that, by definition, are not domestic. Depending on whether the state decides that multilateral cooperation is in its national interest or whether there are broader moral issues at stake, it will pursue some form of international cooperation and, if possible, some form of international legal regime to govern it.

This is not a new trend, and it is one that precedes the recent rapidity of transborder mobility. Even before the United Nations was created to represent the constructive face of international governance, states have been drawn together to pursue international purposes such as air travel, laws of war, settlement of international disputes: the list is long. In addition to these multilateral initiatives, there were even more bilateral arrangements to resolve problems between two states. With the United Nations in place to provide an institutionalized personality for the pursuit of international objectives, the number of areas for multilateral cooperation has proliferated. Human rights, environmental regulation, trade, finance, and police enforcement are but a few areas where states have joined to pursue social goods on an international scale.

It would not be difficult to anticipate that these international efforts would meet with limited success. States themselves are often unable to deliver social goods, even where there is little or no transborder obstacle. The problem of developing an effective international program of action is that much more formidable. All the problems of domestic politics multiply exponentially within an international system. Different political systems, historical animosities, vastly different financial and human resources, diplomatic posturing, national security interests all form an often insurmountable barrier to international action and, in particular, to the articulation of legal obligation enforceable in a court of law.

Despite these barriers, many efforts have been made and many successes can be noted. There is an undeniable presence of international laws (both conventional and customary) that regulate the conduct of state actors and qualify the nature of their sovereignty through obligations that states, either explicitly or implicitly, undertake. What is also undeniable is that many of these international laws have failed to mature to where they have become an effective (i.e., enforceable) means of encouraging certain activities and deterring others. States may choose not to participate in the international initiative. States may take initial steps to participate but little concrete action to implement the objectives and obligations. Governments may change. Resources may disappear. Years may pass without any action. Although international law has attempted to deal with many of these problems by agreeing on the rules of international obligation, the concept of state sovereignty ultimately remains most relevant in the realpolitik world of international law and relations. Although there are avenues for enforcing international obligations, they are few and largely ineffectual. It is often economic benefits or other political trade-offs that are used to deter rogue states and to bring the recalcitrant back in line.

The following factors have led states to search for other ways of achieving their objectives: inability to arrive at consensus for action, long delays in addressing urgent problems, internal dissent with respect to compromising national sovereignty through sharing jurisdiction, unwillingness to accept the lowest common denominator (often the outcome of international cooperation), requests for political or economic trade-offs, problems in enforcing international commitments, and the rapidity of technological change (necessitating immediate and resource-intensive responses). It is these factors, among others, that have led states, especially those with the political and financial resources and suasion to do so, to reconsider the benefits of unilateralism over multilateralism.

This increase in unilateralism may be a trend or a response to an international system in transition. As noted at the beginning of this chapter, trends are difficult to decipher and may often exist more vividly in the imagination of the commentator than in reality. Whether a trend or not, there are indications that certain states – the United States in particular – are willing to extend their national jurisdiction through domestic laws if international cooperation is neither feasible nor efficient. It is also important to note that domestic objectives may also be pursued through the guise of international cooperation, where certain state actors are able to persuade other states or, in some cases, impose upon them, a certain outcome.

Terrorism

Even before 11 September 2001, international terrorism had been a persistent national security threat to a great many states and their citizens. While recent initiatives may suggest a resurgence in multilateralism, the truth is that states have responded to these threats both through domestic measures to improve security and through international measures to collaborate on the prevention of terrorism and bringing international terrorists to justice. Prior to the United Nations' response and round on new resolutions to deal with terrorist actions targeting the United States, there existed a series of initiatives. The *Montreal Convention for the Suppression of Unlawful Acts against the Safety of Civil Aviation*, the *Tokyo Convention on Offences and Certain Other Acts Committed on Board Aircraft*, the *Hague Convention for the Suppression of Unlawful Seizure of Aircraft*, and the *International Convention against the Taking of Hostages* all illustrate these ongoing international efforts.

Despite these attempts, terrorism remains a potent force and is an obstacle to the ability of the state to ensure the security of its citizens both at home and abroad. As a result, some states are adopting more aggressive domestic approaches in combatting international terrorism. The United States has been most aggressive in asserting domestic jurisdiction over international terrorism. Although the United States also participates in multilateral efforts to respond to international terrorism, recent legislation and court cases have expanded the territorial jurisdiction of criminal law through the extension of the passive personality principle. The passive personality test expands the jurisdiction of US courts over penal law applicable to acts committed by non-nationals outside US territory, and it is one of the five traditional grounds in international law for asserting jurisdiction over an international crime: (1) territorial (including territorial effects), (2) universal, (3) protective, (4) nationality, and (5) nationality of the victim (passive personality). This extension of jurisdiction has been entrenched in such domestic legislation as the Omnibus Diplomatic Security and Antiterrorism Act, 1986 (Antiterrorism Act), and, more recently, in Congressional amendments to the Sabotage Act, 1996, where it is proclaimed that "the United States has a legitimate interest in punishing anyone who injures a U.S. national" (H.R. Conf. Rep. No. 104-518, at 122 [1996]). Other cases have reinforced this approach: *United States* v. *Yousef* (927 F. Supp. 673 [S.D. N.Y. 1996]), *United States* v. *Morin* (80 F. 3d 124 [4th Cir. 1996]), *United States* v. *Rezaq* (134 F. 3d 1121 [D.C. Cir. 1998]). Although before September 11 the United States was reluctant to use these new legislative provisions due, in part, to the precedent it sets for the passive personality principle and the possibility of its application to the United States itself, these provisions have become part of the legislative framework to combat terrorism and to assert unilateral jurisdiction where this was previously not possible.

International Trade

States are most reluctant to relinquish control of the levers of macroeconomic policy. As a result it has taken years of agonizingly slow negotiations to reach agreement on multilateral approaches to trade barriers, duties, anti-competitive practices, and the host of other components of the international trading regime. And, although notable advances have been made through the World Trade Organization (and the General Agreement on Tariffs and Trade, which governs it), the various bilateral or multilateral trade agreements such as the North American Free Trade Agreement, the EU and its expansion, and MERCOSUR, multilateralism has not satisfied the economic interests of many international actors. Many have argued that the world-trading regime is not reflective of multilateral consensus but, rather, of the imposition of trade practices to benefit those states that are best positioned to reap the rewards.

Even within those countries that tend to benefit disproportionately from existing trade regulation, there is often vociferous disagreement among trade unions, business, environmentalists, human rights activists, and other stakeholders concerning the benefits of trade liberalization. These disagreements become that much more heated when the dispute

settlement mechanisms set up to resolve trade disputes result in the imposition of restrictions on domestic macroeconomic policy. It is in these
cases that unilateralism begins to resurface. In the United States, legislation has been implemented to ensure that the domestic economic and
political interests prevail when the latter conflict with the conduct of
other states. The Sherman Act, 1994 (15 U.S.C. 1), asserts the extraterritorial prescriptive jurisdiction of US Congress. The act states: "every contract, combination ... or conspiracy, in restraint of trade or commerce ...
with foreign nations, is declared to be illegal." The United States thereby
maintains its jurisdiction to prosecute cases where the international trading
regime is unwilling or unable. Similarly, the Helms-Burton Act expresses
the preference for unilateral action when the international trading regime
does not incorporate domestic political policies. The Helms-Burton Act, in
its original formulation, asserted jurisdiction of US courts to prosecute
non-US companies doing business in Cuba who benefit from the expro-
priated land of US nationals.

Human Rights
Although human rights is arguably the most developed area of public
international law, and includes an extensive country reporting framework
administered through the United Nations, states are supplementing their
participation in international initiatives with unilateral action. The attempts to extend universal jurisdiction over certain international criminal
law matters through the creation of an International Criminal Court have
met with some important opposition from the United States (among others), whose concerns regarding the political manipulation of the court
reflect the inherent difficulties of international approaches to the enforcement of human rights. Instead, states are withdrawing from the international scrutiny and politicization of human rights in favour of domestic
and strategic choices regarding where and when to promote human rights
through unilateral action (such as trade policy and development assistance). The previous discussion of international trade illustrates that the
United States, for example, has used unilateral trade measures to (ostensibly) promote human rights in Cuba and China.

   In addition to these trade policy initiatives, states are using a variety of
different legal tools to assert influence, if not jurisdiction, over alleged
human rights abuses. Many states have provisions that allow citizens to
bring suit in domestic courts for human rights abuses suffered abroad. In
the United States, jurisdiction is provided under the Alien Tort Claims Act
(28 U.S.C. 1350 [1982]). Where the defendant is a foreign government or
leader, international law and the concept of foreign sovereign immunity
precludes legal remedy. The U.S. Foreign Sovereign Immunities Act (FSIA),
1976, articulates this element of international law. In the United States

there are, however, already nine general exceptions to the jurisdictional immunity of a foreign state as outlined in the FSIA, including provisions dealing with terrorism as outlined above. The Torture Victims Protection Act (28 U.S.C. 1350[2] [1994]) also provides avenues of redress against individuals acting under the authority of a foreign nation who commit acts of torture or extra-judicial killing. Case law represented by *Filartiga* v. *Pena-Irala* (630 F. 2d 876 [2d Cir. 1980]), *Chuidian* v. *Philippine National Bank* (912 F. 2d 1095, 1102 [9th Cir. 1990]), *Trajanos* v. *Marcos* (978 F. 2d 493 [9th Cir. 1992]), *Princz* v. *Federal Republic of Germany* (26 F. 3d 1166 [D.C. Cir. 1994]), and *Argentine Republic* v. *Amerada Hess* (488 U.S. 428 [1989]) illustrate further qualification on the concept of sovereign immunity in favour of the assertion of domestic jurisdiction.

The pressure on sovereign immunity in favour of domestic jurisdiction over human rights abuses has not been limited to the United States. A number of recent events prompted many states to challenge the nature and extent of the concept of sovereign immunity, particularly where human rights abuses are alleged. The recent attempt by Spain to extradite former Chilean president Pinochet for his role in the murder of Spaniards during the Pinochet regime reflects the pressure on this concept of state sovereignty. Although Pinochet's extradition was resolved largely through political accommodation, the legal decision of the House of Lords in the United Kingdom raised some important new issues and potential directions for domestic attempts to assert jurisdiction over extraterritorial abuses of international law by sovereign states and their leaders.

Intellectual Property
The law of intellectual property has also seen a significant degree of internationalization. There have been many initiatives undertaken through the World Intellectual Property Organization (WIPO) to promote common approaches to patent filing and the controversial issue of the patenting of genetic resources. Most recently, over 100 states convened to create a new international patent law, which will standardize the forms that all patent offices must accept and, most important, mandate the acceptance by signatories of any patent filed according to the international standard as outlined in the *Patent Co-operation Treaty*. Further negotiations in the fall of 2000 addressed the much more controversial issues of patent criteria such as novelty.

The development of the international law of intellectual property illustrates how even internationalization can, in fact, be interpreted as a unilateral action. Many states, particularly lesser-developed countries, argue that attempts to internationalize intellectual property protection through WIPO agreements and the Trade Related Aspects of Intellectual Property Rights (TRIPS) provisions of GATT merely reflect the desire and ability of powerful states, particularly the United States, to impose its domestic legislation on the international community. There is ample evidence to support arguments that the international law of intellectual property is increasingly mirroring US patent law. How closely international law will follow US law will be decided in the next several years of negotiations between the main players: the United States, the EU, and large developing countries such as China and India.

Environmental Law

The growing threat of environmental degradation has been the catalyst for a proliferation of international and regional legal responses. The Stockholm Declaration of the early 1970s and the 1992 Rio Declaration have become important landmarks on the international environmental legal landscape. Although there have been many successes in creating a legal and policy framework to address issues such as the protection of biodiversity, the protection of regional seas (such as the Mediterranean and the Baltic), global warming, and ship-source pollution, international environmental regulation continues to suffer from inadequate or ambiguous legal obligations, inadequate or non-existent enforcement, and inadequate human and financial resource allocation (even with regard to pursuing commitments already undertaken).

These flaws of the international environmental regime are not surprising, as many of these same criticisms can also be levelled against domestic environmental regulation. Yet, despite the similar limitations of domestic approaches to environmental problems, it is these that remain the focus of environmental policy. Where the environmental threat is urgent, and where the domestic political will exists, policy makers are embracing unilateral legislative responses. Even where the specific environmental problem is transboundary and not amenable to unilateral action, states with the resources and the directing political climate will promulgate national or subnational legislation that is intended to have an impact not only on the environmental problem but also on the adjacent state (which also needs to develop a regulatory response). In some cases, this attempt to extend domestic regulatory goals occurs through the vehicle of multilateral initiatives such as trade regimes. The North American Free Trade Agreement also includes environmental provisions and the implicit objective that regulatory responses in Mexico will eventually improve to approximate the more stringent environmental standards in Canada and the United States.

Towards Functionality

What have these examples illustrated? They have illustrated that there is some merit to the prognostications of both those who champion and those who bemoan the internationalization of the modern world. The examples also illustrate that borders are becoming more permeable and that this trend will continue to be aided by technological innovation that, even if not intentionally, makes borders less relevant. Beyond these general trends, the pundit's ability to accurately describe, let alone predict, the nature of the modern state and the maturation of the concept of state sovereignty is limited.

Although there is an inherent logic to the cooperative action of multilateralism, international cooperation may not be the most expedient way of achieving a certain result. It has not been so in the past and will not be so in the future. All the flaws of the international system may continue to exert pressure on states, particularly those with adequate resources, to pursue unilateral options in order to achieve their collective will. The main point is that the permeability of borders will continue to demand increasingly creative and hybrid legislative responses, both multilateral and unilateral, in order to be able to embrace and regulate internationalization. This does not mean that the modern state will or should become an anachronism in a new world order where universal collective purpose has triumphed over ethnic, linguistic, religious, and other differences. Although many have imagined such a utopia, the human need for community identity as defined more parochially than humankind will likely ensure that borders exist for a long time.

Despite this fact, the pressure that the permeability of borders will continue to exert on state sovereignty will, it is hoped, compel states to reassess the purpose of borders. Borders must be evaluated for their functionality and not only for their geopolitics. When borders inhibit or even prevent effective environmental management, when borders interfere with the free exchange of goods and ideas, when borders allow those who abuse fundamental human rights to go unpunished and undeterred, when borders provide refuge for those attempting to escape justice, then those borders prevent us all from realizing our collective aspirations. States should be willing to redefine sovereignty in a way that acknowledges borders as a tool for achieving certain social goods. If international cooperation is effective, efficient, and non-coercive, then this option should be pursued. If these criteria cannot be met, then unilateral action may provide the only path to a desired outcome. Although the issue of what constitutes an objectively defined desirable outcome has been long debated and would be the subject of a chapter much longer and more complex than this one, it is these issues that should be explored. Rather than persisting in intellectual servitude to outdated and counterproductive lines on a map and the international legal discourse that protects them, we should aspire to a more creative and productive way of embracing a larger world that is getting smaller.

Part 2
Regionalism and Subregionalism in Europe

The idea of a European Union (EU) is often misunderstood by those who stand outside of the geopolitical territory established by this large transnational association. To many it represents a collaboration of states that have given up sovereignty and have erased internal borders in an effort to gain economic security. The authors in this section of *Holding the Line* take a different tack in their explanation of this remarkable geographical territory, suggesting that new and more spatial models of borderlands associated with the EU (e.g., *Schengenland*) have increased the potential for transnational cooperation not only in the area of security but also in the area of environmental initiatives. Both of the chapters in this section deal with new regional approaches to border making within the EU and their role in reshaping security and environmental concerns. Indeed, in Chapter 4 Bort suggests that regionalism is clearly a process complementing and balancing centralizing tendencies and needs within the European Union, and that it relies, implicitly, upon the reorganization of borderlines by "frontiers," or spatial zones of contact with shared jurisdictions. Like Blake in Part 1, Bort presents the case for a Europe divided by territories that cannot be distinguished using traditional linear conventions with regard to borders. His concern is that the structure of the contemporary European community, as defined by Schengen, has created yet a new and broader geographical territory that now reaches into the heart of Eastern Europe, well beyond the original geographical edges of the EU.

In Chapter 5 Scott focuses upon new policy instruments for bridging nation-states through the creation of specific cross-border communities and cross-border initiatives. His concern is the process of devolution, from the perspective of transnational regional cooperation. According to Scott, transnational regional cooperation is an element of European integration that cuts across member-state jurisdictions and EU policy areas. It is a large-scale project designed, among other things, to empower local communities, create new strategic alliances between cities and regions, and to facilitate the diffusion of social, political, and economic innovation.

Scott's focus is the empowerment of communities and the restructuring of political arrangements at the regional level, while Bort's focus is the other end of the scale. However, both authors realize that the scalar differences they identify, and the differing nature of the initiatives discussed – one rooted in concerns about security and immigration, the other in concerns about the environment – are different sides of the same coin, or polar opposites with respect to a "continuum of bordering processes" (see Chapter 19, this volume). Moreover, while there is a vast literature on security, environmental cooperation, and transnationalism at the borders, these contributions are unique in the sense that they identify the redefinition of borders in Europe as spatial processes inculcated by a new geopolitical discursive. Indeed, Scott argues that "seeing itself as an example of prosperity and stability, the EU is actively promoting its principles and values both within and without its present borders." He suggests that European integration is "both an explicit political project and an unintentional, unguided process of societal interaction" – one "not without its contradictions. It must promote formal and informal means of integration, respect local and regional sensibilities, and secure the broad and long-term support of the EU citizenry." Thus, the chapters in this section define the challenges of sharing elements of national sovereignty within a much larger political community as well as the problems involved in not only reconciling different national and subnational perspectives on social and economic development but also in maintaining legitimacy through franchising and incorporating local communities.

4
European Borders in Transition: The Internal and External Frontiers of the European Union
Eberhard Bort

The Final Act of Helsinki, 1975, guaranteed the existing borders of Europe. To some this suggested that the discourse on European frontiers would now be relegated to specialist academic circles. Two major developments have since changed that situation. The first is that, within the European Union (EU), the "Euro-sclerotic" phase was overcome through the Single European Act, 1986, and the drive to abolish frontier controls at the European Union's internal borders, expressed in the Schengen agreements of 1985 and 1990. The second is that, outside the EU, the pivotal events that occurred between 1989 and 1992 (the fall of the Berlin Wall, the fall of the Eastern communist regimes, and the crumbling of the Soviet empire and the dissolution of the Soviet Union itself) opened the opportunity to heal the rift that had divided the Continent during the Cold War. Since then, over 20,000 kilometres of new international frontiers have been created in Europe, and the debate on the functioning and the perception of frontiers has gained new salience in political discourse.[1]

The Single European Market ("Europe '92") abolished border controls for the movement of goods, services, and capital. Regionalization has enhanced the political, administrative, and identity-marking function of substate boundaries. Since the mid-1990s the Schengen Agreement of 1985 and the Convention of 1990 have progressively been implemented, guaranteeing the free movement of people within "Schengenland." But both at its internal and its external frontiers, the opening of borders has not been seen solely as a positive step. Anxieties and even fears have accompanied the process, as decision makers wonder if open borders will be an invitation for criminals and illegal immigrants to cross freely and move easily between one European country and another. The Schengen Agreement insists that the abolition of border controls at the internal frontiers be matched by a standardized strengthening of controls at the external frontiers of Schengenland. Does that mean that the eastern frontier of the EU, opened in 1989/90, and most recently expanded in May 2004, is subsequently experiencing a degree of closure from the West? How does that match with attempts at developing institutionalized cross-border cooperation along that frontier? Part of the accession process of Central and Eastern European states is the demand by EU member states, and by the EU itself, that the applicant states police their eastern frontiers efficiently. Schengen standards are being exported eastward in order to secure the future eastern frontier of the EU, and Schengen now casts its shadow far into Central and Eastern Europe.

The result of this intricate, sometimes unclear or contradictory, picture of the functions of frontiers torn between enhanced cooperation and integration (requiring open frontiers) and the perceived need for strict controls (requiring limits to this openness) is a political discourse. This process highlights the issue of migration and the "security threat," promoting the need for harmonized and strict identity controls, at the borders and beyond, in what has been called a return to spatial approaches to security and control. The replacement of borderlines with border zones and police cooperation far beyond national frontiers reinforces the spatial approach. In 1986 the Chernobyl accident made it abundantly clear that international frontiers are no barriers to environmental pollution. Other global developments also challenge the role of frontiers as barriers and protective or regulatory instruments.

Consequently, the internal and external frontiers of the EU are in transition, presenting a less unilinear and more complex picture than slogans like "a Europe without frontiers" may suggest. This will be the case for the foreseeable future for at least seven reasons:

- The further political, economic, and social integration of the EU (tax and legal harmonization as well as the possible strengthening of the regional tier of European governance) may further blur the boundaries between member states and substate units of the EU.
- EU enlargement will transform external into internal EU frontiers and create new external EU frontiers.
- On the margins of the EU (in the Balkans and, further east, in the former Soviet Union) existing borders are being challenged and are far from stable.
- Wealth disparities in Europe, but also in a global context, will keep a focus on the topic of legal and illegal migration.
- Aspects of globalization – e-commerce, new communications technologies, and so on – will further challenge the role of frontiers as efficient regulatory instruments.
- Organized transfrontier crime seems to have replaced the military threat, and the fight against it is increasingly based on the linking of the internal and external in a new security discourse.
- EU applicant status for Turkey puts a new spin on the questions of the frontiers of Europe: where are the geographical limits of the Continent? Is there a defined *finalité politique* of the EU?

Internal EU Boundaries

Border Conflicts

There are no longer any significant border-related conflicts between EU member states, with the following exceptions:

- The most serious conflict, hindering implementation of European Union Justice and Home Affairs legislation, is between Spain and the UK over the territory of Gibraltar. Spain has used Schengen (and the fact that the UK has not signed) as a lever to impose rigid and time-consuming controls at its border with Gibraltar.
- Euzkadi Ta Askatasuna (ETA, translated as Basque Homeland and Freedom) in the Basque Country campaigns for an independent Euzkadi, which would encompass Basques on both sides of the international frontier between Spain and France. Yet there is little support from the Basques on the French side, and none from the French and Spanish governments, for any change of the international frontier.
- A plethora of more or less militant Corsican independence groups strive to break away from France.
- With the Belfast Agreement of Good Friday, 1998, and the subsequent change of the Irish Constitution, the conflict over the Northern Irish border has been defused – although the nationalist parties in the North (Sinn Féin and the Social Democratic and Labour Party), as well as the parties in the South, still aspire to a united Ireland (to be achieved by peaceful and democratic means).
- A minority movement in the north of Italy, led by Umberto Bossi and his Northern League, demands its separate state – Padania.
- The Scottish National Party (SNP) campaigns for Scotland's "independence in Europe" and would hold a referendum on parting from the UK in case of an election victory in Scotland.

Most of these cases do not have any influence on EU legislation and are seen as internal matters of the member states.

The Role of Schengen

Since the mid-1980s, as the European Economic Community transformed itself into the enlarged European Union, the Treaty of Rome goal of an "ever closer union of peoples," encompassing the four freedoms of movement of goods, services, capital, and people, has progressed in leaps and bounds. Customs formalities at internal frontiers had all but vanished by the late 1980s, a result widely welcomed although not without difficulties.[2] More controversial, however, have been the negotiation and implementation of both the Schengen Agreement of 1985 and the Schengen

Convention of 1990, which, together with hundreds of pages of rules and regulations, make up the *Schengen acquis*.

With the exception of Ireland and the UK, all present EU member states have signed. Germany, France, the Benelux states, and Spain implemented Schengen in March 1995; Austria and Italy followed on 1 April 1997. The Scandinavian EU countries of Denmark, Sweden, and Finland had "observer status" from 1996, in view of the difficulty of sharing a passport union and common travel zone with non-EU member state Norway. Meanwhile, the entire Scandinavian "Nordic Union" (including Norway and Iceland) has become party to the *Schengen acquis*, despite Norway's determination to remain outside the EU. Greece, whose airport controls at Athens have come under the Schengen regime, is still not deemed efficient enough in its external border controls. With its difficult external sea and islands frontier, Greece is the only EU country without a common land frontier with another EU member state.

Through the Amsterdam Treaty, ratified in 1999, Schengen has come under the institutionalized umbrella of the EU, managed by the Justice and Home Affairs Council of Ministers. In practice, Schengen has created border zones along the internal frontiers of Schengenland – usually twenty kilometres in depth, where police now have the right of "hot pursuit" across the frontier. In some cases, larger areas have been made into border zones, where random controls are legally allowed.[3] The Austrian Ministry of the Interior, for example, announced a thirty-kilometre-wide "security veil" along the German border, with a significantly increased police presence; German police could pursue criminals unlimited by space and time in Austria.[4] Dr. Horst Eisel, assistant director for frontiers at the German Ministry of Internal Affairs, covering internal as well as external frontiers, argued: "The spatial approach clearly ought to take precedence over the purely linear approach to geographic boundaries. The latter is no longer a match for today's challenges, because individual and collective security begins beyond our borders and continues well on this side of them."[5]

While border posts have vanished at the internal frontiers, this must not be confused with a Europe where borders no longer exist. Schengen has only been incompletely implemented and occasionally suspended. France, for example, decided to retain border checks on its Benelux frontier because the French government perceived liberal Dutch drugs policies as potentially dangerous.[6] Likewise, France suspended Schengen during "Vigipirate," after terrorist bombs had exploded in the Paris Metro in 1995.[7]

Perception of Frontiers

Internal frontiers within the EU vary widely in terms of geography and demography, from low-intensity frontiers, with very few crossings (or crossings concentrated at very few passages) in mountainous regions (Pyrenees, Alps) or in sparsely populated areas like Scandinavia, to high-intensity frontiers like, for example, those in the upper and lower Rhine valley. These historical, geographical, and demographic features have an impact on the function of frontiers and on the need for (and possibility of) cooperation across them. All frontiers are human constructs, yet it helps if natural and geographical features can be employed to support frontier claims. Indeed, some of the internal frontiers of the EU have long since acquired the status of "natural" frontiers. France, for example, came to regard the Pyrenees, the Alps, the Rhine, the Channel, and the Atlantic as its "natural" limits centuries after Caesar had described Gaul in the same terms. Despite the diverse history that followed, as Fernand Braudel observed, a relic boundary like the Roman *limes* between the Rhine and the Danube re-emerged as a new dividing line: "When the Reformation occurred, it was along virtually the same frontier that the split in Christianity became established: Protestants on one side and Catholics on the other."[8] Of course, there is no such thing as a "natural" frontier. "Frontiers tend to entrench frontiers and make them seem natural phenomena."[9]

Borders thus engraved in collective memory and public consciousness will not vanish with abolition of border controls. They mark different cultures and lifestyles, different languages, different legal and political systems.[10] In fact, the more the physical trappings of the frontier are erased, the more the frontier demands to be permanently imagined, created as a frontier of the mind in defence of culture and lifestyle but also in order to experience and cherish difference. The border, no longer viewed as an obstacle or a hindrance, becomes an attractive line to be criss-crossed in pursuit of difference, enhancing the quality of life in the "borders" and, thus, sometimes reverting the historical experience of having been sealed off, having been a backwater, peripheral, and underdeveloped.

Police Cooperation

Police cooperation at the EU's internal frontiers preceded Schengen, often in an informal way based on personal contacts, sometimes operating from a legal perspective in what might be considered as a grey zone. Schengen has generated a wealth of accords, agreements, and cooperative arrangements between law enforcement agencies, not all of them coordinated. Bilateral and multilateral arrangements, for example, often overlap. A good example is the Channel tunnel, covered by the Anglo-French Protocol of 1991.[11] In addition to the bilateral agreement, there are letters of understanding between Kent Constabulary and police authorities in France, Belgium, and the Netherlands. This, in turn, needs to be seen within the wider framework of the Cross-Channel Intelligence Conference, and, of course, this particular frontier also comes under the remit of Europol and, at least partly, of Schengen. Overarching all this is the global network of Interpol.[12]

On the one hand, this is a confusing complexity and is widely criticized for its lack of transparency and accountability. On the other, in practical terms of police activity, this situation offers alternative channels of communication should one network not function properly. In addition, cooperation, based on personal acquaintance and trust, has increasingly supplemented the institutional arrangements. Since 1996 the EU Commission has sponsored seminars and placements for border police to enhance the exchange of notes, with a view towards harmonizing border management.[13]

Substate Frontiers

"Europe of the Regions" and the discourse on the imminent death of the nation-state, which flourished in the 1980s, seem to have diminished in importance since the establishment of the Committee of the Regions provided by Maastricht. The big topics – engineering the introduction of the European single currency and tentatively opening the European Union towards the South and, particularly, the East – have put the member states and their (heads of) governments firmly at the helm of European politics.

The importance of the nation-state in future European governance has become the new emphasis,[14] echoing the turn taken by former chancellor Kohl and President Chirac in their letter to the 1997 Cardiff Summit, where they seemed to reduce the principle of subsidiarity to a two-polar exercise between Brussels and the member states rather than "the devolution of powers from Brussels and Strasbourg not to a national but to a sub-national or regional level."[15] This is clearly seen as a worrying turn of rhetoric in cross-border regions, particularly on the German side, where the emphasis had been on balancing national with European and regional identities.

Yet the twists of rhetoric on the one hand, and the actual development of cross-border regionalism on the other, may diverge. The EU clearly shows signs of multilevel governance. The Tübingen political scientist and integration theorist Rudolf Hrbek has defined four levels within the EU: the national level (formed by the member states), the supranational level (the EU institutions), the transnational level (transnational communication and cooperation of non-governmental actors), and the subnational level (encompassing the territorial units existing below the member states). Hrbek points out that these levels are not hierarchically related to each other but have their own impact.[16]

Identification with the region has undergone a dramatic change. While twenty or thirty years ago, region and "Heimat" were seen as parochial, backward, stifling, and narrow, if not outright reactionary, the emergence or re-emergence of local history, vernacular writing, grassroots movements, and citizens' initiatives has led to a nearly complete revaluation of regions as models of democracy, where one finds not only the parameters for one's identity but also, in Louis MacNeice's words, minted for Ireland, "the end of one's actions."

This is important if the discourse on the role of the regions in governance will not be restricted to constitutional questions, without reference to issues closer to the minds of the people. Accountability, transparency of political decision making, control over the affairs in one's environment are all of import, as are "bread-and-butter" questions such as: "How does regional government relate to economic performance?" Can it "raise the innovative capacity of the indigenous regional economy"?[17] Is a strong local culture conducive to inward investment and structural development? What are the synergy effects in regional cooperation? If a convincing case is to be construed, then constitutional questions have to be seen in conjunction with questions of political culture and economic policies.

Undoubtedly, there has been a European process of regionalization, transforming such centralist states as Italy, France, Spain, or Belgium; adding a touch of decentralization if not turning them into federal or at least semi-federal units. In 1970 Italy created twenty administrative regions, from the pre-industrial areas of the far south to the ancient city-states of the north and the special status regions of Val d'Aosta or South Tyrol. Under Mitterand, in the early 1980s, France decentralized (in what has been called "a silent revolution") administrative and planning power to twenty-two regions. Belgium's answer to its ethnic/linguistic divisions has been the federalization of the country, which has created the three regions of Wallonia, Flanders, and Brussels.[18] Spain embarked on a program of regionalization after Franco, with Euzkadi (the Basque Country), Catalonia, and Galicia paving the way for other regions. German unification meant the restitution of five federal states on the territory of the former centralist German Democratic Republic. And, endorsed by the overwhelming referendum result in Scotland on 11 September 1997 (and the cliff-hanger in Wales a week later along with the "Yes" vote in the Irish referenda of 1998), the UK and Ireland belatedly joined the European regionalization train, creating assemblies in Belfast and Cardiff and a Scottish Parliament in Edinburgh. Furthermore, in 2000, London got its elected mayor, with other cities set to follow that example. And English regions can be expected to demand their own devolved structures, particularly if, as in the Spanish case of rolling devolution, the Scottish, Welsh, and Northern Irish assemblies will be seen as producing the goods.[19]

Additional pressure comes from the need to restructure regional and cohesion funds in view of EU enlargement. Cornwall has been recognized as a target region of its own (its indicators showing 69 percent of the EU average when detached from the more affluent counties of Devon and Somerset), as has Western Wales, South Yorkshire and Merseyside, the Highlands and Islands of Scotland – all looking for priority status for regional funding.[20] Similar moves can be seen in Ireland and other European countries.

Regionalism is clearly a process complementing and balancing centralizing tendencies and needs within the EU. This is most obvious in the realm of environmental policies. Regional protest against nuclear power stations, polluted rivers, and poisonous industrial emissions informed regionalism in the 1970s as a grassroots movement. At the same time, this environmental consciousness helped to promote the idea that standards and frameworks of environmental protection must not stop at national borders. Acid rain, ozone depletion, and threats to wildlife all require international and cross-border cooperation. Many of these grassroots regional movements themselves have transcended national frontiers (e.g., the anti-nuclear movement in the Upper Rhine region).[21]

Transport policies, macroeconomic planning, and redistribution through regional and cohesion funds are other areas where power has been increasingly concentrated on the European level. In light of this, the preservation of cultural, linguistic, and historical identities, or "unity in diversity," requires strong regional structures. As a tier within the governmental structures of the EU, the regions can safeguard democratic participation of the citizens in the decision-making processes concerning their own affairs, applying in practice the principle of subsidiarity. Regionalism, in other words, brings government closer to the people. Regions seem, potentially, more competent in handling economic affairs. They seem better suited to the modern demands of "flexible specialization" in manufacturing.[22] States seem, on the one hand, too large, their political centres often too far away from the regions, to arrive at economic decisions that are properly informed about interconnections on the ground. On the other hand, they seem too small to provide the markets for industries and services.

Bernd Groß and Peter Schmitt-Egner distinguish between three phases of regionalism in Western Europe:

- "old" regionalism, which was conservative, tied-up with ethnic nationalistic ideals
- "new" regionalism, which involves a rebellion of the province against centralist policies of modernization, following autonomous, separatist, and autarkist goals (of decreasing impact but still to be observed in the Basque Country or in Corsica)
- "postmodern" regionalism, encompassing regional elites (rather than

marginal groups), integrated into the different levels of governance, aiming at cooperation in structural and industrial policies; neither making front against modernization nor passively suffering it.[23]

The last category – "postmodern regionalism" – strives at actively supporting regional culture by developing both internal instruments of governance and external cooperation. It plays an important role in the balance between integration and autonomy, unity, and diversity. Groß and Schmitt-Egner analyze what they call its vertical and horizontal dimensions. Why, Groß and Schmitt-Egner ask, is decentralization a necessity in Europe? Following Jens-Joachim Heese, they come to the conclusion that regions offer specific development potentials because they are close to the problems that have to be solved and can muster reserves, resources, and active participation.[24] Kenichi Ohmae has argued that the nation-state has become "an unnatural, even dysfunctional, unit for organizing human activity and managing economic endeavour in a borderless world."[25] This might be slightly exaggerated, but the role of the nation-state is certainly changing. Nation-states are, in the phrase of Michael Mann, "diversifying, developing, not dying."[26] Regions have, as Scott, Sweedler, Ganster, and Eberwein highlight, grown in importance because of "their greater flexibility and capacity to react rapidly to new economic circumstances."[27]

Groß and Schmitt-Egner summarize the regionalist agenda as follows:

- historically developed identities and cultural diversity can be preserved and developed;
- political action becomes more comprehensible, transparent, and democratic;
- acceptance of the overarching European level of governance is made easier; a stronger regional consciousness supports the identification with Europe;
- regional economic fine engineering as a regulative to economic centres can contribute to a more equal economic development in Europe;
- the so-called "third level," i.e. the regions besides the member states and the EU institutions, guarantees a vertical division of power, thus contributing to a harmonization of the distribution of power in Europe.[28]

It seems clear, therefore, that four major trends may be discerned in regional developments that correspond to the new regional agenda.

(1) Regionalism within the EU States
First, there is the trend towards regionalization within European states, as already alluded to in the cases of France, Italy, Spain, or, latterly, the UK. "The tide is still running strongly towards regional governance structures

across Europe."[29] In this sense, regionalism is a process. Rolling devolution, or uneven federalism, continues to develop in Spain, where Catalonia, the Basque Country, and Galicia have demanded recognition as
nations rather than, as at present, "nationalities." In their *Declaration of
Barcelona*, they have appealed to the EU to accept the transformation
of Spain into a confederation of states.[30] Similarly, Italy is encountering
problems with its federalization program. And in Germany the debate
about a reorganization of the Länder structure gathers pace, particularly
on the centre-right, as the discrepancies in viability and affluence are
accentuated by the new Länder, highlighting at the same time the structural weaknesses of small units like Bremen or the Saarland.[31]

(2) Interregional Partnerships
The second trend in regional development consists of interregional partnerships, like the Welsh tie-in with the Four Motors (Baden-Württemberg,
Lombardy, Rhone-Alpes, Catalonia), which have partly been made possible by the regionalization process and have progressed regardless of their
fashion-value in the media.[32] Other examples would include Scotland,
which is linked with Catalonia, Tuscany, and North-Rhine Westphalia, or
the West-German Länder twinning with the New Länder of East Germany
after 1990.

(3) Subregions
A relatively new phenomenon, particularly evident in Germany, is the
emergence of subregions. A good example is the Greater Stuttgart Region,
an area covering about 2.5 million people, which got its own directly
elected parliament in 1994. This created a new tier of governance between
the Land level and local government, with its remit concentrated on spatial and infrastructure planning. This regional assembly still has its
teething problems, as intense debates over competencies have shown,[33]
but it has already been copied in other subregions with similar congestion
problems, like Frankfurt or the Ruhrgebiet. A fourth phenomenon is cross-
border regionalism (which will be discussed below).

(4) Cross-Border Cooperation: Euroregions
Cross-border regionalism has flourished over the past two decades, beginning from the heartlands along the western border of Germany, and taking a new step in the 1990s, when – in response to the opening of the Iron
Curtain – Euroregions were set up from the Finno-Russian border down to
Austria, Slovakia, Hungary, and Slovenia.[34] This has the potential to question the basis of a "Europe of the Regions" as understood by Brussels
(where regions are defined as the substate level of governance within member states). Not only does cross-border regionalism challenge traditional

views of state sovereignty,[35] but it also transcends the external frontiers of the Union – certainly in the East (where nearly all the neighbouring states are to or have become members of the EU) but also in Switzerland, particularly on the Upper Rhine and in the Lake Constance region. In April 1998 the Upper Rhine Council was established – not quite a parliament but a political body made up of elected members (MPs, mayors, prefects) from Baden-Württemberg, Alsace, and the Swiss cantons of Basle-City and Basle-Land.[36]

Peripheral borderlands are one of the legacies of the nation-state. It is because of the memory of that fact that the returning rhetoric of the lasting importance of the nation-state is viewed with scepticism in the borderlands of Europe. Regionalism, and in particular cross-border regionalism, has been a tool to place formerly peripheral regions at the heart of developments.[37]

Wherever possible, cross-border Euroregions have been based on common cultural and historical experience; however, primarily they are a pragmatic enterprise for economic development funded by the EU's INTERREG and, at the external frontier, PHARE programs. The EU's introduction of the INTERREG programs[38] at the beginning of the 1990s gave transboundary planning of infrastructure investment a solid basis. Their objectives are to support border regions in their adaptation to the single market, to alleviate their economic and social peripherality, and to support cross-border cooperation.[39] The Euregio Meuse-Rhin, formally established in 1976, may serve as an example. With almost 3.7 million inhabitants at the meeting point between Germany, the Netherlands, and Belgium, and with three working languages, it is "a true laboratory for the European experiment,"[40] based on "a common artistic and cultural heritage."[41] Its "Euroregional council," established in 1995 and made up of representatives from elected political bodies (60 percent) and from societal organizations (40 percent) – trade unions, chambers of commerce, universities, employers' organizations – keeps it at the cutting edge of cross-border regionalism.[42]

Another example, straddling internal as well as external frontiers of the EU, is the International Lake Constance Conference (ILCC), a body born out of environmental concern, particularly focusing on the water quality of this important freshwater and fish reservoir. The ILCC was established in 1972 between the German *Länder* Baden-Württemberg and Bayern; the three Swiss cantons of St. Gallen, Schaffhausen, and Thurgau; and the Austrian *Land* Vorarlberg, "to solve cross-border problems through common policies, to work on cooperative projects and to contribute regionally to the transcending, of borders."[43] Since 1990 the Regio Bodensee has been formed, including the cantons of Appenzell-Ausserrhoden and Appenzell-Innerrhoden as well as Liechtenstein, which has observer status.

Schengen has created the possibility of cross-border regionalism without barriers, something felt particularly where international frontiers separated regions with common roots, as between Italy and Austria, in the case of North and South Tyrol.[44] Cross-border regionalism has helped to overcome deeply ingrained enmities and sources of conflict, as demonstrated in the Eastern and Western German borderlands. Maybe the Belfast Agreement of Good Friday, 1998, will play its part in finding a regional solution for the bitter conflict that has left its mark on Northern Ireland over the past decades. In its provision of safeguards for both majorities and minorities, and its complex three-stranded structure, it may yet be seen as a model for a postnationalist Europe.

Some of these regional developments seem to have found entry into the system of European governance through the Maastricht process. The Committee of the Regions, created through Article 198 of the Maastricht Treaty, and meeting for its inauguration on 1 March 1994, was "a significant step in institutionalizing the presence of regions in the Community but ... a long way short of the ideals of the more ardent regionalists who looked to a regionally based second chamber of the European Parliament."[45]

Despite its mere consultative role, and despite the wide and uneven diversity of its constituent members (from Northrhine Westphalia's eighteen million to British or Greek local councils), it must not be forgotten that, in negotiating the creation of this body, regions were integrated into the Maastricht process: the Committee of the Regions is an integral part of the decision-making structures of the EU. Many in the Committee of the Regions see it only as a beginning. "Rather than complaining what we have not [yet] achieved, we should make full use of the opportunities open to us," seems to have been the motto since its creation.[46] In view of the Convention on the Future of Europe and the Intergovernmental Conference of 2004, the seventy-five self-governing ("constitutional") regions within the EU – majorized by the local councils in the Committee of the Regions – have joined their efforts to gain direct access to the European institutions.

Regionalism, though, is not a panacea. It has to be seen as part of the process of European integration, fully tied into the way European affairs are being governed, from international relations to local matters. It would be fatal were people to discover that regionalism has left them with a meaningless playground where they can build their little castles in the sand, while the big decisions on the big issues are being made elsewhere, without the reach of their control and influence. Regionalism must also not serve as an excuse for nation-states to abandon policies of solidarity by devolving standards of social security to an uneven system of regions, most of them incapable of sustaining levels a redistributive state could manage. "The new European regional agenda presupposes devolution,"

Kevin Morgan has argued, "not least because regions need to be able to design and deliver policies attuned to their own circumstances, to act on their own knowledge and, yes, to make their own mistakes. But this should not be seen as an opportunity for central governments to relinquish responsibility for the fate of their poorer regions."[47]

It would be further detrimental if regionalism were to develop into regio-centrism. Competition between regions can be a motor for development, but if it deteriorated into a Darwinist wooing of investors, snatching them from other regions unable to offer large-scale tax incentives or other subsidies, distortion of European integration to the disadvantage of the taxpayer would be the flipside of a free-for-all for multi- and transnational concerns. Kevin Morgan speaks of "a regulatory regime that safeguards against their [the regions'] precipitating a race to the bottom by outbidding each other in debilitating subsidy wars to attract inward investment."[48]

For all these reasons, competence and tie-in are the keys for a regional European polity. Real competencies in the governance of their own affairs (i.e., effective subsidiarity) empowers the regions within a European framework, in the construction of which regions must have their constitutionally guaranteed part to play.

Is regionalism prone to be more open to corruption than are larger units of governance? Parochial politics certainly could be fostering nepotism and clientilism. Yet it also offers the chance of greater accountability and transparency, which will have to be emphasized in the institutions of local and regional democracy. The danger cannot be completely ruled out, but why it should be greater than in larger, more anonymous, units of governance, is difficult to conceive. Again, a system of checks and balances in an integrated system of interlinking levels of governance, from the local to the European, seems to be the best guarantee of the best possible democratic control of decision-making processes at all levels.

If there is any truth in the contrast between European "culture" and American "civilization," it rests to a great degree with the regions. Strong regional cultures have long been accepted as an important "soft factor" for industrial and economic development. Sustainable, "cultural" tourism is one of the most obvious areas where regional initiatives may both support local culture, traditions, and identities, and create infrastructure and jobs. Thus, the debate about regionalism is not simply an abstract constitutional game, perhaps enriched by some discourse on identity and belonging. These must not be underestimated, but what counts in the end is that real issues – poverty, unemployment, environmental hazards, and alienation – are being addressed. To do this efficiently, regions need to be empowered with competencies, both in their own area of responsibility and on a European level.

If, for example, the UK government wants to safeguard its union, it might be best advised to push for a strong regional tier in European governance. This would alleviate the pressure on stateless nations (not only in the UK) to press for full independence. If stateless nations were to find that nation-state rhetoric and practice does deny them the input and access to governance on the European level that small nations like Denmark or Finland enjoy (let alone newcomers to the EU like Estonia, Slovenia, or Malta), then that would be grist to the mills of separatist "big N" Nationalism – not necessarily atavistic or ethnic in itself, but separatist along the lines of the Scottish Nationalists' "Independence in Europe" program. If, on the other hand, there was sufficient provision for participation in the governance of the EU for stateless regions/nations, then these might yet settle for "small n" nationalism in the form of autonomous, devolved regimes, perhaps aspiring towards federal solutions at home and at the European level, avoiding the disruption of existing EU member states and the setting up of new international frontiers. Yet, for that to be achieved, "a new regional vision of Europe is demanding attention, one that challenges the current Europe of the nation states and is likely to do so more strongly in the coming century. If it is to be democratic, this new Europe must have strong local and regional governments."[49]

The mosaic of regions as it presents itself in Europe at the moment is untidy, fuzzy, best illustrated by the unevenness of composition and inadequacy in power of the Committee of the Regions. It is a process, not least a learning process. "The Europe of the Regions," to quote John Osmond, remains fluid and unfocused, "a direction of the will" more than a blueprint. "No one map can capture its sense. Yet it is on the map in the 1990s in a concrete economic way that was only dimly perceived in the 1970s, certainly so far as England is concerned. And at least one aspect of the direction now seems unmistakable: a transcendence of the rigidities of big, upper case Nation-State nationalism by the flexibilities of small, lower-case regionalism."[50]

External EU Boundaries

Schengen has created a common external frontier for those EU states that have implemented it. This frontier is policed and controlled according to rules and regulations laid down in the confidential Schengen manual and through a common visa policy. A central computer system, the Schengen Information System (SIS) based at Strasbourg and linked to national databases, has been installed to facilitate quick exchange of data on wanted persons, illegal immigrants, and stolen vehicles. Data protection is provided by an independent control board, yet its efficiency is being questioned by civil rights groups and from within the European Parliament. So-called SIRENE offices *(Supplément d'Information Requis à l'Entrée*

Nationale) have been established in all Schengen states as support structures, while Schengen also emphasizes closer police and law enforcement co-operation between the participating states – particularly in the border regions. It also calls for a common visa, asylum, and immigration policy.

There are two broad categories of EU external frontiers: first, those with the rich non-EU countries like Norway and Switzerland or with microstates like Andorra or Monaco, and those with relatively poor Central and Eastern European and Mediterranean countries. External borderlands of the EU "range from the most advanced regions in the core (EU borders with Switzerland) and northern periphery (outer borders with Norway) to the most poorly developed regions in the east."[51] A more refined typology distinguishes four different categories of external frontiers

- with highly developed EFTA/EEA[52] countries and rich microstates
- with Central and Eastern European countries on the threshold of becoming or having just become members of the EU, including the Baltic States, Cyprus, and Malta
- with African and Middle Eastern countries around the Mediterranean
- with other Central and Eastern European countries like Albania, Macedonia, Croatia, Yugoslavia,[53] Turkey,[54] Moldova, and Russia, which have no immediate perspective of membership.

The first category of frontiers can be considered "as if" frontiers. The EU and European countries themselves tend to treat these common borders "as if" they were internal frontiers. Bilateral agreements attempt to bring cooperation and control mechanisms in line with standards of the Schengen countries.[55] The Nordic Union, for example, based on conventions agreed upon in 1954 and 1957,[56] has straddled the EU external land frontier since the accession of Sweden and Finland in 1995. It has agreed with the EU on the granting of Schengen observer status to Norway and Iceland in May 1996. Similar practical arrangements are in place at the Swiss frontiers. EU INTERREG funding for frontier region cooperation on the EU side of the frontier is matched by national funding on the other side because INTERREG funds can only be used in EU territory. Financing of joint programs at the external frontier is undertaken in cooperation with other EU programs (such as TACIS, PHARE, and ECOS/OUVERTURE).[57]

This category also includes microstates and overseas territories, illustrating the ragged and fragmented character of the external frontier and its varied and anomalous relationships with member states, the EU, and, in the case of overseas territories, their close neighbours: the status of Europe's microstates, overseas territories, and autonomous regions, and their relation to the framework of the European treaties, is complex.

Special relationships fall into four categories:

- independent countries (microstates) within the European Community's boundaries
- French overseas *départements*
- European or nearby regions of member states that enjoy autonomous or semi-autonomous status
- overseas countries and territories, referred to in Part 4 of the Treaty of Rome and listed in Annex 1 to the Council Decision of 25 July 1991, that retain ties of varying intensity with a member state.

Notions of political sovereignty are scarcely relevant for microstates. Their very existence, throughout history, has depended on the goodwill of, and negotiated arrangements with, their larger neighbours.[58]

Another important consideration is the existence of what has been called the "blue frontier." All EU member states, except land-locked Luxembourg and Austria, have sea frontiers (enlargement will add Slovakia and the Czech Republic as land-locked states). Sea frontiers are very diverse but, except for fisheries (where there is a common regime for the territorial waters of the EU states), both seas and seaports form part of the external frontier. Some areas of the seas are polluted. Coastal protection problems can only be solved by cross-border cooperation, and regimes have been put in place to deal with them. Other areas for cooperation include improvements of sea infrastructure (transport, tourism and safety/emergency measures). Still perceived as natural barriers, "maritime borders are often characterized by common historic and cultural links and trading traditions."[59] Under the INTERREG programs, maritime borders were included as "exceptional," and programs for external maritime frontiers supported initiatives for the Baltic, the North Sea, Greece and Cyprus, and Spain and Morocco.

The Baltic

The disintegration of the USSR in 1991 created a new security situation in the Baltic. While the immediate military threat of the USSR disappeared, social and economic conditions in Russia were potentially destabilizing for the region. The environmental threat of the decaying Russian nuclear northern fleet was serious. New and vulnerable Baltic states re-emerged. The different forms of neutrality of Sweden and Finland seemed to lose some relevance. Poland unequivocally "joined" the West and aspired to membership of both the North Atlantic Treaty Organization (NATO) and the European Communities (EC).

During the Finnish presidency of the EU in the second part of 1999, Finland tried to promote its concept of a "Northern Dimension,"[60] focusing on trade with Russia and forging a regional cooperative for the Baltic Sea, both complementing and counterbalancing the Euro-Med Partnership. Russia's north harbours one-third of the world's gas resources, is oil-rich, and is the location of one-fifth of the world's forests. The Finns use these arguments to promote what they call the "Baltic chance" – a field of gigantic opportunity for investment and trade, with Finland as "Europe's gateway to the East."

The Mediterranean Frontier

The Mediterranean "blue frontier" is the most problematic of EU external maritime frontiers. Intractable political conflicts,[61] resulting in both wars and terrorist action, complicate political relationships between the EU and its neighbours. Trafficking and landing illegal goods and persons occurs on all EU sea frontiers, but the Mediterranean presents the most difficult problems.[62] Greece, Italy, and Spain have long coastal and island frontiers, in close proximity to unstable and relatively poor neighbouring countries. Migratory pressure and cross-border crime present serious policing problems. The gulf between the northern and southern shores of the Mediterranean, often dubbed "Europe's Rio Grande,"[63] is wide and getting wider.[64] The disparities are sometimes referred to as the three Ds – demography, development, and democracy – which present formidable barriers to close cooperation between the EU and the southern shore countries.

The Eastern Frontier

As the eastern neighbours joined the EU in May 2004, the erstwhile Iron Curtain has been transformed into an internal EU boundary. But it will not immediately become a control-free internal Schengen frontier.

When Austria and Italy implemented Schengen (between 1 October 1997 and 1 April 1998) the former Iron Curtain, opened from the east in 1989, became the external Schengen frontier of the EU. This was feared as a threat to cross-border relations in the neighbouring states to the east. And when there was a trial run of Schengen external frontier controls at the Italian-Sloven border in October 1997, this caused considerable disruption.[65] Yet by April 1998 the expected barrier did not materialize – at least not to the extent expected.[66] The Slovenian border authorities had taken the Schengen threat seriously and persuaded their own government to adopt the Schengen criteria (of identity and customs checks) at their Croatian frontier. And they convinced the Italian, Austrian, and EU authorities that Slovenia has – practically – implemented Schengen (without being part of it) at its external non-EU frontiers. This, obviously, made it possible for border controls with Italy and Austria to remain relatively flexible, even after Schengen had become fully operational on 1 April 1998.

Yet this does not obscure the unease about the Schengen process that was felt beyond the external frontier of the EU. From Poland to Slovenia there was concern at being obliged to implement Schengen norms, the negotiations of which were conducted to the exclusion of these countries.[67] Slovenia may have been successful in saving its partially open frontiers with Italy and Austria. Slovakia was not as successful, or at least did not try as hard to implement Schengen-type frontier controls at its eastern frontier. Cooperation between the border authorities in Germany, Poland, and the Czech Republic seemed better developed – with regular meetings, comparing notes, frequent communications, common training, and exchanges – than was the case further south (e.g., at the Austrian-Slovak crossing of Berg/Bratislava, where communication between both sides was rare and often had to be conducted indirectly via Vienna and Bratislava). Improvements have been achieved since the end of the Meciar regime. From the Austro-Hungarian border (historically, certainly one of the most symbolic frontiers of Europe) long queues have been reported since Schengen was fully implemented by Austria on 1 April 1998. These queues are caused by Austrian border police, a new special police force with a "martial outlook."[68]

The Future Frontier
From the start of accession negotiations in March 1998, the candidate states came under increasing pressure to efficiently police their eastern frontiers. This has resulted in far-reaching changes of border controls, particularly in Poland but also in the Czech Republic and Hungary. A closure of the Hungarian-Romanian frontier, for example, has implications for the large Hungarian minority in Romania.

The Schengen Agreements thus cast a shadow beyond the present EU. The EU commissioner in charge of the Single Market, Mario Monti, told the Polish government that Poland's chances of joining the EU depended to a great deal on how well it could police its borders. The strengthening of Poland's eastern frontier is seen, particularly in Germany, as the attempt to erect a first serious obstacle to illegal migration and illegal trade from east to west.

Marek Bienkowski, in charge of the Polish border guards, announced fifteen new border crossings on the eastern frontier by 2001, along with an increase in the number of border guards and the installation funded by EU PHARE of electronic passport-reading equipment at border checkpoints. In 1998 Poland also introduced a new "alien" law, which led to protests from Russia. Several border crossings were blocked by Russians. Belarus withdrew its ambassador from Warsaw. But there was also protest from Polish traders who depend on cross-border traffic. Ukrainians and Lithuanians must now prove that they have sufficient means to sustain themselves in Poland.

Russians and Belarussians must have Polish invitations or pre-paid hotel vouchers if they want to cross into Poland.[69]

The economic price for these measures is heavy. In east Poland more than 1,000 local traders rallied against the "economic catastrophe" caused by tighter border controls. Incomes in eastern border towns dropped dramatically and unemployment rose. There was a sharp fall in trading not only in the border areas but also at Warsaw's economically important "Russian bazaar." Here, trading fell by about 30 percent after the introduction of a new aliens law and visa regime. In 1997 the turnover of the Warsaw bazaar had been, according to Poland's Market Economy Research Institute, in the region of £350 million.

But there are also problems of policing because Poland's eastern neighbours cannot, or will not, cooperate. "Chaos and corruption"[70] was the verdict of the respectable *Süddeutsche Zeitung,* summing up the situation at the frontiers between Poland and Kaliningrad in the north as well as Lithuania, Belarus, and the Ukraine – the extensive "green border": 407 kilometres with Belarus, 526 kilometres with the Ukraine. While in Belarus, as at the time of the Soviet Union, the army still exercises a measure of control from the east, the Ukrainian side is totally deficient in its policing of the border. When Ukrainian frontier guards ceased to receive their salaries in 1997, they were wont to recoup the money by assisting illegal migrants to cross the frontier. But corruption is supposed to be widespread on both sides of the Polish-Ukrainian border.[71] Frontiers are only controllable if there is cooperation with the other side: Poland attempts a delicate balancing act, stabilizing and effectively controlling the borders but avoiding total closure towards the East. "Poland, too, does not want barriers at its eastern frontiers," Poland's foreign secretary, Bronislaw Geremek, stressed on a visit to Bonn in November 1997.[72] And the minister for Europe, Ryszard Carnecki, spoke of a tightly controlled border that could, at the same time, function as a bridge to the large markets of Russia, Belarus, and the Ukraine. Stabilizing the states that have emerged from the rubble of the Soviet Union, he stated, must be in both Poland's and the West's interest.[73]

Cross-Border Crime

Cross-border crime, although often exaggerated, must also not be underestimated. Leslie Holmes has argued that, "at their most extreme, substantial rises in the proportion of illegality in international economic activity can destabilize national economies."[74] The rise in internal and cross-border crime in Eastern Europe, particularly in the countries of the former Soviet Union, can be pinned down to the difficult transitional situation in these countries: postcommunist states attempting, in Claus Offe's term, a "triple transition" – the rapid and simultaneous transformation of their political systems, their economic systems, and their boundaries and identities.[75]

This "triple transition" is grafted onto the pre-1989 experience under communism, where corruption and dodging the state were part of the political culture, "creating an environment of institutionalized illegality."[76] Economic decline had long laid the foundations of a flourishing shadow economy, and then the fraught transformation into market economies provided new opportunities for criminals to exploit deficiencies in inadequately regulated markets, which could not match demand and supply. Yet this is not just an internal problem of the postcommunist countries. There seems to be widespread interaction between organized criminals in postcommunist states and established criminal structures in the West, as "all sorts of crime can cross borders"[77] or operate in the border zones, from street prostitution to money laundering and drug trafficking, and from arms smuggling to human trafficking.

It is estimated that human trafficking earns well organized, internationally operating criminal cartels up to $5 billion per year.[78] The most popular routes for human trafficking are, according to the *Bundesgrenzschutz*, the "eastern channel" (Almaty, Moscow, St. Petersburg, Minsk, Vilnius) and the "Balkan channel" (Romania, Hungary, Moldova, Russia, Ukraine, Poland).[79] The *Süddeutsche Zeitung* noted the connection between the drastic tightening of the German asylum laws in 1993 and the increase of illegal migration. As the door was closed in the face of asylum, refugees were driven into the arms of unscrupulous human smuggling organizations, paying up to £5,000 per head for their services.[80] A particularly sad chapter involves the casualties at the border, particularly refugees who drowned in the Oder and Neisse Rivers, led by their smugglers to remote river banks and dangerous currents because these are the least policed spots of the border. Nearly a hundred corpses have been fished out of the rivers in the past few years, a watery grave putting an end to journeys that had often covered thousands of kilometres.[81]

The discourse of migration control has become intricately linked with the discourses on crime and security in what Huysmans and Bigo have both called a process of "securization."[82] Security has become a much broader concept, compared with the focus on military concerns that dominated the discourse until the changes of 1989/90, encompassing new risks and threats to society, the economy, and the polity itself.[83] This constitution of a security continuum, including the control of frontiers and immigration among police activities in the fight against crime, is, Bigo argues, "not a natural response to the changes in criminality" but, rather, a proactive mixing of crime and immigration issues.[84] Barry Buzan has coined the term "societal security" to describe the shift of security concerns from protection of the state to protection against threats, or perceived threats, against society and identity (or the identity and security of groups within a society).[85]

Refining border controls as a means of exclusion can be seen as a response to the threat to societal security. Yet, even after the terrorist attacks of 11 September 2001 reinforced borders in many regions, a fortress mentality (often invoked when Schengen is criticized) is no longer really conceivable as a practical solution to internal security needs. It is undeniable that the security of individuals has become deterritorialized.[86] As highlighted by the "war on terrorism," internal security now implies collaboration with foreign countries and is thus linked to foreign policy; and the 1980s and 1990s marked the beginning of a public debate on policing, coinciding with the emergence of a discourse on urban insecurity and the city on the one hand, and discourses on stopping immigration of unskilled workers on the other.[87] There have been two predominant modes of reaction to the challenges of cross-border crime: increased security protection at borders (not necessarily restricted to the actual borderline) and increased international cross-border cooperation.

Cross-Border Cooperation

In an attempt to combat the rise in cross-border criminality, police forces are intensifying their cooperation across frontiers. Cooperation between border police at the German-Polish and the German-Czech borders was already highly developed prior to Poland's joining the EU, with a permanent exchange of notes, common training, daily communication, and joint patrols.[88] As mentioned earlier, in 1996 the European Commission started to sponsor seminars and a placement scheme for EU border police, with the intention of creating an institutionalized network of exchange and cooperation.[89] Seminars on detection of fraudulent documents are being held, and the collaboration between, for instance, car rental firms and police organizations in the East and Central European states are being intensified, which has already led to arrests and the disruption of smuggling routes.[90] This is not only happening within an internal European context. The US State Department has invested more than $8 million in police training in Hungary. In 1995 the International Law Enforcement Academy (ILEA) was founded in Budapest, offering eight-week courses for law enforcement agents from Hungary and other East-Central European states, concentrating on combating terrorism, drug-related crime, and economic criminality. This seems to go hand in hand with a much needed improvement that the Hungarian government is providing for its underpaid, and allegedly corrupt, police force and efforts to establish closer cooperation between the secret services in the East and in the West.[91] The EU summit at Seville in 2002 put improved cooperation at the EU's external frontiers at the top of the agenda, even envisaging a joint European Border Guard.

Following the example of cross-border Euroregions (particularly on Germany's western frontier), informal contacts developed into formalized cross-border institutions along the Eastern Frontier. In the north we find the regional cooperation model of Kuhmo-Kostamuksha (1992) on the Finnish-Russian border; in the German-Polish border regions the Euroregions of Neisse-Nysa (1992), Spree-Neisse-Bober (1993), Pro Europa Viadrina (1993), and Pomerania (1995) were created. Further south there are the Euroregions on the German-Czech border: Elbe-Labe, Erzgebirge, Egrensis, the Euregio Bayerischer Wald/Böhmerwald (including the Austrian *Mühlviertel*), and the Region Triagonale between Austria, Hungary, and Slovakia. Further east there are cross-border Euroregions like the Carpathian Region (1993) and the quadrilateral Niemen cooperation (1996), involving Poland, Lithuania, Belarus, and Russia (Kaliningrad).

The establishment of institutionalized cross-border cooperation seems to show that a translation of practical concerns from West to East is well under way. The frequently expressed need for cross-border cooperation (environment, infrastructure, tourism, and security) matches certain regional reform concepts, devolving planning authority and decision-making processes to the regions. The regional context may also be more conducive to solving problems of national minorities, and it may even provide regional solutions to international problems. Regionalization and "integrated borderlands,"[92] rather than a nineteenth-century model of the nation-state, could offer a more tranquil future for non-homogenous states with large ethnic minorities within their borders.

The implementation of Schengen and the accession of Central European states to the EU, highlighted by the establishment of these Euroregions, which, in order to function effectively, require a high permeability of borders – border as bridge, as communicative channel, rather than as barrier – add up to a confusing (sometimes even contradictory) and ambiguous picture of a frontier with elements of both openness and closure.[93]

Conclusions

The internal and external frontiers of the EU are in transition. How border management develops at the internal frontiers will depend to a great extent on the enlargement process and its impact on the integration project. Will the boundaries between strong regions and small member states be further blurred? If not, then established regions – or nations within multinational states – like the German *Länder* or the Spanish regions, or Scotland and Wales, might have to gain greater European competence within their states (if not strive for independence) in order to fully participate in a European system of governance that would be predominantly intergovernmental rather than multilevel and integrated.

Michel Foucher noted that borders are "time inscribed into space or, more appropriately, time written in territories."[94] That is to say, they are temporary, functional arrangements. He contends that borders in a Europe that embarked on fundamental changes in 1989/90 will – for the foreseeable future – be marked by "a 'fuzzy logic,' less rational, less rigid, but allowing historical transition to take place."[95]

Notes

1 See for example, M. Foucher, *Fronts et frontières, un tour du monde géopolitique* (Paris: Fayard, 1990); H. Donnan and T. Wilson, eds., *Border Approaches* (Lanham, MD: University Press of America, 1994); S. Raich, "Grenzüberschreitende und interregionale Zusammenarbeit," in *Europa der Regionen* (Baden-Baden: Nomos, 1995); Malcolm Anderson, *Frontiers: Territory and State Formation in the Modern World* (Cambridge: Polity Press, 1996); L. O'Dowd and M. Wilson, eds., *Borders, Nations, and States: Frontiers of Sovereignty in the New Europe* (Aldershot: Avevery Press, 1996); Paul Ganster, A. Sweedler, J. Scott, and W.D. Eberwein, eds., *Borders and Border Regions in Europe and North America* (San Diego: San Diego State University Press, 1997); R. Krämer, *Grenzen der Europäischen Union* (Potsdam: Brandenburgische Landeszentrale für Politische Bildung, 1997); G. Brunn and P. Schmitt-Egner, eds., *Grenzüberschreitende Zusammenarbeit in Europa – Theorie – Empirie – Praxis* (Baden-Baden: Nomos, 1998); Beate Neuss, Peter Jurczek, and Wolfram Hilz, eds., *Grenzübergreifende Kooperation im östlichen Mitteleuropa* (Tübingen: Europäisches Zentrum für Föderalismus-Forschung, 1998); Malcolm Anderson and E. Bort, eds., *The Frontiers of Europe* (London: Pinter, 1998); Monica den Boer, ed., *Schengen Still Going Strong: Evaluation and Update* (Maastricht: European Institute for Public Administration, 2000); Malcolm Anderson with Eberhard Bort, *The Frontiers of the European Union* (Basingstoke: Palgrave, 2001); Jan Zielonka, ed., *Europe Unbound: Enlarging and Reshaping the Boundaries of the European Union* (London: Routlege, 2002).

2 Abolition of customs affected border communities that had depended on checkpoints (and their personnel) as well as on trade generated by customs differences.

3 The constitutional legality of this was challenged in some German *Länder* (like Baden-Württemberg), following a controversial decision of the Mecklenburg-Vorpommern High Court in November 1999.

4 See Claus Pándi, "Bayerische Polizei bekommt in Österreich mehr Kompetenzen," in *Neue Kronen Zeitung*, 17 April 1997.

5 Quoted in Patrice Molle, *External Borders Pilot Project: Placement Report* (Strasbourg: Centre des Etudes Européennes, 1996), 6.

6 The doping scandal subsequently overshadowing the 1998 *Tour de France* was detected at the Belgian-French border.

7 Reinforced during the football World Cup '98, this time targeted against cross-border football hooliganism.

8 F. Braudel, *The Perspective of the World* (*Civilization and Capitalism*, vol. iii) (London: Collins, 1985), 66.

9 Ibid.

10 Even at the local level, ancient divides can still exercise their influence on present-day culture and politics. The northern-English neighbouring cities of Gateshead and Newcastle are jointly bidding to become European city of culture. But there are still difficulties to be overcome in bridging the Tyne, which separates the "sister cities." Gateshead's director of arts, Bill Macnaught, was quoted in the *Guardian* (24 August 1999): "It's a narrow river, but it has been a big divide."

11 This Protocol provides for a French police presence at Folkestone and a British police presence at Fréthun.

12 See Jim Sheptycki, "Police Co-operation in the English Channel Region, 1968-1996," *European Journal of Crime, Criminal Law and Criminal Justice* 6, 3: 216-35.
13 See Molle, *External Borders Pilot Project*, 6.
14 See Peter Schenk, "Die Nation ist noch nicht überholt," *Badische Zeitung*, 6 July 1998.
15 Christopher Harvie, *The Rise of Regional Europe* (London: Routledge, 1994), 1.
16 Ibid., 17-18.
17 Kevin Morgan, "Let's Get Regionalism Right This Time," *New Statesman*, 26 June 1998.
18 See Benedikt Jonas, "A Disintegrating Belgium at the Heart of an Integrating Europe?" in *Borders and Borderlands in Europe*, ed. E. Bort (Edinburgh: ISSI, 1998), 53-71.
19 In *London's Mayor and the Prospects for English Regional Government Renewal, 1998.* Mike Craven predicts that London's mayor will pave the way for regionalism in England, bringing in its wake directly elected assemblies for the North, the North-West, Yorkshire, and the South-West within the next decade. See also the "Regions" supplement in the *New Statesman*, 26 June 1998. At the time of writing (April 2000), the Northern Irish institutions were suspended due to the impasse over the issue of decommissioning paramilitary weapons.
20 European Parliament, *EP News*, July 1998.
21 See Thomas Lehner, "Einige Sätze über das Elsaß," in *Thema: Regionalismus*, Lars Gustafsson, ed., *Tintenfisch 10* (Berlin: Wagenbach, 1976), 121-23.
22 See E. Bort and Neil Evans, "Networking Europe: Understanding the European Union from Below," in *Networking Europe: Essays on Regionalism and Social Democracy*, ed. E. Bort and N. Evans (Liverpool: Liverpool University Press, 2000), 5-24; 17.
23 Bernd Groß and Peter Schmitt-Egner, *Europas kooperierende Regionen: Rahmenbedingungen und Praxis transnationaler Zusammenarbeit deutscher Grenzregionen in Europa* (Baden-Baden: Nomos, 1994), 16.
24 Ibid.
25 Kenichi Ohmae, "The Rise of the Region State," *Foreign Affairs* 72, 2 (1993): 78-87; 78.
26 Michael Mann, "Nation-States in Europe and other Continents: Diversifying, Developing, not Dying," *Daedalus* 122, 3 (1993): 115-40.
27 James Scott, Alan Sweedler, Paul Ganster, and Wolf-Dieter Eberwein, "Dynamics of Transboundary Interaction in Comparative Perspective," in Ganster et al., *Borders and Border Regions*, 3-23; 5.
28 Ibid.
29 Patrick Dunleavy and Stuart Weir, "Home Rule for Yorkshire?" *New Statesman*, 26 June 1998.
30 See Friedrich Kassebeer, "Wie Spanien in Stücke zerfällt," *Süddeutsche Zeitung*, 3 August 1998.
31 See Bernt Conrad, "Die Kraft des Föderalen," *Die Welt*, 23 December 1997; Ralf Neubauer, "Föderaler Reformbedarf," *Die Welt*, 22 January 1998; and Philip Kunig, "Vielfalt ist gut, weniger Vielfalt wäre besser," *Die Welt*, 22 August 1998.
32 Phil Cooke and Kevin Morgan, "The Wales–Baden-Württemberg Accord," in Bort and Evans, *Networking Europe*, 45-55.
33 See Helmut Doka, "A Region Is a Region Is a Region: Is It? Planning in the Stuttgart Region," in Bort and Evans, *Networking Europe*, 463-71.
34 See E. Bort, "*Mitteleuropa:* The Difficult Frontier," in Anderson and Bort, *The Frontiers of Europe*, 91-108; E. Bort, "Crossing the EU Frontier: Eastern Enlargement of the EU, Cross-Border Regionalism and State Sovereignty," *Interregiones* 6 (1997): 20-31.
35 The German *Grundgesetz* in Art. 24, 1 (introduced in 1992) already allows the transfer of sovereignty rights across frontiers. See Ulrich Beyerlin, "Neue rechtliche Entwicklungen der regionalen und lokalen grenzüberschreitenden Zusammenarbeit," in Brunn and Schmitt-Egner, *Grenzüberschreitende Zusammenarbeit in Europa*, 118-34, esp. 129-33.
36 It cannot really be called a parliament, as only half the Baden-Württemberg members are MPs (the other half are mayors and elected *Landräte*, with no specific mandate to represent the region). The Swiss representatives come closest to the parliamentary tag, as they are delegates from the canton parliaments.
37 See the late Hans Briner (d. 1996), "Das Europa der Regionen – die Perspektive des 21.

Jahrhunderts," in *Boundaries and Identities: The Eastern Frontier of the European Union,* ed. M. Anderson and E. Bort (Edinburgh: ISSI, 1996), 39-46.

38 INTERREG I (1990-94), INTERREG II (1995-99), INTERREG III (2000-4).

39 See James Scott, "Dutch-German Euroregions: A Model for Transboundary Cooperation?" in Ganster et al., *Borders and Border Regions,* 107-40, esp. 118-19 and 136-39.

40 INTERREG, ed., *Euregio Meuse-Rhin,* n.d.

41 Ibid., 6.

42 Bas Denters, Rob Schobben, and Anne van der Veen, "Governance of European Border Regions: A Legal, Economic and Political Science approach with an Application to the Dutch-German and the Dutch-Belgian Border," in Brunn and Schmidt-Egner, *Grenzüberschreitende Zusammenarbeit in Europa,* 135-61; 144.

43 Regio Bodensee, ed., *Bodenseeleitbild* (Constance: Regio-Büro Bodensee, 1995), 9.

44 See Michael Frank, "Vereinigung nach Art der Tiroler," *Süddeutsche Zeitung,* 8 April 1998.

45 B. Jones and M. Keating, *The European Union and the Regions* (Oxford: Oxford University Press, 1995), 15.

46 Dietrich Pause, the former secretary general of the committee, quoted in N. Schöbel, *The Committee of the Regions: A Preliminary Review of the Committee's Work during its first two Years in Operation* (Tübingen: European Centre for Research on Federalism, 1997), 6.

47 Morgan, "Let's Get Regionalism Right This Time."

48 Ibid.

49 John Osmond, "The Welsh Assembly 1979 and 1997," in Bort and Evans, *Networking Europe,* 375-88; 382.

50 John Osmond, "Unitary Britain," in Bort and Evans, *Networking Europe,* 81-99; 97.

51 Association of European Border Regions/European Commission, eds., *Practical Guide to Cross-border Cooperation,* 2nd ed. (Gronau: AEBR, 1997), A2/10.

52 European Free Trade Area; European Economic Area.

53 Following the Kosovo war, the European Union announced its Balkans initiative, creating an inclusive perspective for all Balkan countries to eventually become members of the EU.

54 Turkey was accepted in 1999 as a candidate country; negotiations for accession started on 28 March 2000.

55 Bilateral police cooperation is often easier between Switzerland and Germany than it is between France and Germany because both of the former have decentralized police organizations.

56 There are three main differences between its modus operandi and the Schengen system: random controls at the internal Scandinavian frontiers are allowed; external frontier checks are regulated by a five-paragraph guideline rather than by the 250 pages of the Schengen manual; and exchange of information between frontier police is decentralized, contrasting with the centralized Schengen Information System in Strasbourg.

57 TACIS: Technical Assistance for the Commonwealth of Independent States (i.e., the countries of the former USSR). PHARE: Poland and Hungary Assistance for Economic Recovery (subsequently extended to the Czech Republic, Bosnia-Herzegovina, Albania, and Macedonia). ECOS/OUVERTURE is a European Commission Programme for external interregional cooperation, promoting cooperation between regions and cities in the EU and their counterparts in Central and Eastern Europe, the New Independent States, and the Mediterranean non-member countries.

58 See Tom Nairn, "After Brobdingnag: Micro-States and Their Future," in Anderson and Bort, *The Frontiers of Europe,* 135-47.

59 AEBR, *Practical Guide to Cross-border Cooperation,* A2/12.

60 While the Finno-Russian border zone is very thinly populated, the population of the St. Petersburg area is larger than that of the whole of Finland and is "one of the reasons why this frontier is the European Union's window on Russia." R Veijalainen, "Security Arrangements at the External Borders of Schengen: A View from Finland," in *Schengen's Final Days? The Incorporation of Schengen into the New TEU, External Borders and Information Systems,* ed. Monica den Boer (Maastricht: EIPA, 1998), 101-11; 102.

61 Greeks and Turks dispute the Aegean frontier, which led to the brink of armed conflict (between two NATO states) in 1996; both countries are also in conflict over divided

Cyprus. In order to qualify for EU membership, proximity talks started in December 1999 at the UN in an attempt to solve the Cypriot question. There are also signs that the Spanish and the British governments will attempt to find an agreement over the status of Gibraltar (see Cornelia Bolesch, "Das felsige Hindernis soll aus dem Weg," *Süddeutsche Zeitung*, 27 March 2000). Other disputes, from the Western Sahara to the Palestinian-Israeli conflict, are beyond the immediate remit of the EU.

62   Crossing the fourteen-kilometre Strait of Gibraltar illegally costs, according to unofficial estimates, over a thousand lives every year. See Beat Leuthardt, *An den Rändern Europas* (Zürich: Rotpunktverlag, 1999).

63   See Russell King, "The Mediterranean: Europe's Rio Grande," in Anderson and Bort, *The Frontiers of Europe*, 109-34.

64   See E. Bort, "Frontiers or Intermediaries: Mitteleuropa, the Mediterranean and the Middle East," in *The Mediterranean: Cultural Identity and Intercultural Dialogue*, ed. Biserka Cvjeti-canin (Zagreb: Institute for International Relations, 1999), 233-46.

65   Melita Richter-Malabotta, "Some Aspects of Regional and Transfrontier Co-operation in a Changing Europe," in *Schengen and the Southern Frontier of the European Union*, ed. M. Anderson and E. Bort (Edinburgh: ISSI, 1998), 41-72, esp. 65-67.

66   See Marko Gasperlin, "Schengen needs Modification: A Slovenian Perspective," in *Schengen and EU Enlargement: Security and Co-operation at the Eastern Frontier of the European Union*, ed. M. Anderson and E. Bort (Edinburgh: ISSI, 1997), 102-3.

67   A point emphasized by Jazek Sayusz-Wolski in a lecture for the Europa Institute in Edinburgh on 30 April 1998.

68   Michael Frank, "Da gerät Europa an seine Grenzen," *Süddeutsche Zeitung*, 5 January 1999.

69   Ian Traynor, "Fortress Europe Shuts Window to the East," *The Guardian*, 9 February 1998.

70   "Deutsch-polnische Hausaufgaben," *Süddeutsche Zeitung*, 20 August 1998.

71   See Thomas Urban, "Nach Westen isoliert," *Süddeutsche Zeitung*, 18 September 1998.

72   Quoted in "Kohl sagt Polen Unterstützung zu," *Süddeutsche Zeitung*, 20 November 1997.

73   "Deutsche profitieren von Polens Beitritt," *Süddeutsche Zeitung*, 9 April 1998.

74   Leslie Holmes, "Crime, Corruption and Politics: International and Transnational Factors," in *Democratic Consolidation in Eastern Europe: International and Transnational Factors*, ed. Jan Zielonka and Alex Pravda (Oxford: Oxford University Press, 2001), 192-230.

75   Claus Offe, "Capitalism by Design? Democratic Theory Facing the Triple Transition in Eastern Europe," *Social Research* 58, 2 (1996): 3-13.

76   Mark Galeotti, "Cross-Border Crime and the Former Soviet Union," *Boundary and Territory Briefing* 1, 5 (1995): 1.

77   Ibid., 1, 6.

78   Peter Scherer, "Zustrom von Illegalen wächst," *Die Welt*, 16 June 1998.

79   Peter Scherer, "Schleuser gehen jetzt Weg über Tschechien," *Die Welt*, 13 October 1998.

80   Christoph Schwennicke, "Abwehrmauer an den Ostgrenzen," *Süddeutsche Zeitung*, 3 January 1997. For reports on human trafficking, see also Jens Schneider, "Spezialisten für Grenzfälle," *Süddeutsche Zeitung*, 3 September 1998; and Hans-Werner Loose, "Schmuggelware Mensch," *Die Welt*, 8 September 1998.

81   See Olaf Kaltenborn, "Die neue Todesgrenze an der Neiße," *Süddeutsche Zeitung*, 12 June 1997; and Markus Lesch, "Die Eltern ließen ihr totes Kind zurück," *Die Welt*, 14 January 1998.

82   Didier Bigo, "The Landscape of Police Co-operation," in *The Boundaries of Understanding*, ed. E. Bort and Russell Keat (Edinburgh: ISSI, 1998), 59-74; 69. See also Jef Huysmans, "Migrants as a Security Problem: Dangers of Securitizing Societal Issues," in *Migration and European Integration: The Dynamics of Inclusion and Exclusion*, ed. Robert Miles and Dietrich Thränhardt (London: Pinter, 1995), 52-73.

83   See Jan Zielonka, "Europe's Security: A Great Confusion," *International Affairs* 67, 1 (1991): 127-37.

84   Bigo, "The Landscape of Police Co-operation," 67-68.

85   Barry Buzan, *People, States and Fear: An Agenda for International Security Studies in the Post-Cold War Era* (London: Harvester Wheatsheaf, 1991), 18-19.

86   Bigo, "The Landscape of Police Co-operation," 73.

87 See, for example, Malcolm Anderson, Monica den Boer, Peter Cullen, William Gilmore, Charles Raab, and Neil Walker, *Policing the European Union: Theory, Law and Practice* (Oxford: Clarendon Press, 1995); see also James Sheptycki, "Transnational Policing and the Makings of a Postmodern State," *British Journal of Criminology* 35, 4 (Autumn 1995): 613-35; and J. Sheptycki, "Law Enforcement, Justice and Democracy in the Transnational Arena: Reflections on the War on Drugs," *International Journal of the Sociology of Law* 24 (1996): 61-75.

88 Sheptycki, "Transnational Policing and the Makings of a Postmodern State," 61-75.

89 Molle, *External Borders Pilot Project.*

90 Stefan Simon, "Wenn der Mietwagen nie mehr auftaucht," *Süddeutsche Zeitung,* 3 November 1998.

91 Thomas Becker, "Wo Polizisten pauken müssen," *Süddeutsche Zeitung,* 7 January 1999. See also E. Bort, "EU Enlargement: Policing the new Borders," *International Spectator* 1 (2003): 51-68.

92 O.J. Martinez, "The Dynamics of Border Integration: New Approaches to Border Analysis," in *Global Boundaries,* ed. C.H. Schofield (London: Routledge, 1994), 1-15.

93 Malcolm Anderson, "Transfrontier Co-operation: History and Theory," in Brunn and Schmitt-Egner, *Grenzüberschreitende Zusammenarbeit in Europa,* 78-97.

94 Michel Foucher, "The Geopolitics of European Frontiers," in Anderson and Bort, *The Frontiers of Europe,* 235-50; 249.

95 M. Foucher, "Europe and its Long-Lasting Variable Geography," in *The Boundaries of Understanding,* ed. E. Bort and R. Keat (Edinburgh: ISSI, 1999), 163-69; 169.

5

Transnational Regionalism, Strategic Geopolitics, and European Integration: The Case of the Baltic Sea Region

James Wesley Scott

By design or default, the European Union (EU) has become a geopolitical actor of more than economic significance. Evolving out of a core community of West European states with the purpose of organizing economic integration and promoting postwar reconciliation, the EU encompassed twenty-five members by May 2004. Despite some recent scepticism regarding the EU's Common Security and Foreign Policy, it is clear that, in the long run, interstate integration and the process of EU enlargement will enhance its role with respect to pan-European development issues and security. Democracy, cohesion, a market economy, peaceful relations with neighbouring states, minority rights, and international solidarity are, for example, all powerful normative elements in defining a European "zone of peace."[1] Seeing itself as an example of prosperity and stability, the EU is, furthermore, actively promoting its principles and values both within and without its present borders.

As the political construction of Europe has progressed, so have the complexity and sophistication of its formal institutions and the scope of its political, economic, and social networks. Consequently, European policy is channelled both through formal and informal avenues in an attempt to maintain conditions for economic strength and political stability. Furthermore, the creation of new and flexible subnational and transnational contexts for governance within the EU has emerged as an important policy innovation since the mid-1980s. "Integrative" European geographies are being defined, among other means, through symbolic planning concepts, the transnationalization of space through networks and flexible regionalization, and network-like forms of governance.[2]

Transnational regional cooperation is an element of European integration that cuts across member-state jurisdictions and EU policy areas. It is a large-scale project designed, among other things, to empower local communities, create new strategic alliances between cities and regions, and facilitate the diffusion of social, political, and economic innovation.[3]

Transnational regionalism, the subject of this chapter, implies the emergence of subnational diplomatic activities on a large scale and in very different geographical contexts.[4] It can be seen both as a response to the new territorial (network) logic of economic activity and as a product of global interdependence and the limited capabilities of nation-states to address global concerns.[5] Transnational regionalism is thus driven by a desire to develop new, more responsive and effective forms of collective action – or governance – in protecting the environment, safeguarding peaceful coexistence, and promoting economic development. Furthermore, demand for governance and governability in these areas appears to be steadily increasing.[6]

Geopolitics, as a way of looking at international relations, has generally been more concerned with power relationships between nation-states or military blocs, ignoring more complex processes of supranational community building. With the increasing importance of regional organizations in the international order it would appear necessary to relate community-building processes with the strategic interests of the involved states and regions. Hence, within the EU, the idea of greater economic and political interdependence is closely tied to political stability, competitiveness, empowerment, and other values.[7] In the case of the EU, and in contradistinction to other regional arrangements, this provides a powerful rationale for supporting more intense local and regional transboundary cooperation. In fact, an explicit regionalization policy with respect to border regions and transboundary cooperation has emerged in the EU since the mid-1980s. This policy is informed by theoretical and political debate that imbues the issue of transboundary and transnational cooperation with programmatic, even normative, qualities. This is manifested in (1) material incentives and other formal opportunity structures provided by the EU and member states, and (2) a political discourse that accords transnational regionalization legitimacy and meaning.

This chapter deals with project-oriented transnational networks developing in the Baltic Sea Region (BSR) in terms of a "geopolitics" of community building. Through the EU's INTERREG initiatives targeted for regional cooperation in spatial planning issues, a large number of new interorganizational alliances have emerged that serve as broad regional development fora. These networks are remarkable in their ability to bring together actors from very different levels of government – often with the participation of non-state actors – and to define regional development agendas. Their main objective is to introduce alternative regional perspectives into the strategic orientations of the EU and nation-states. However, while they are informed by EU policy they also bear the stamp of senior government involvement. Assuming then that transboundary regionalism is a highly regulated experiment in region building and governance, what can realistically be expected from it? Are new forms of regional policy emerging that cut across local, regional, and national jurisdictions? And, if so, what ramifications might this have for European integration and cohesion? These questions cannot be answered here in full; institutional change is a gradual, long-term process and forecasting the trajectories of that change is a highly speculative business. In attempting nevertheless to shed some light on these issues, I argue that substantive change is occurring at the ideational level. Viewed in the long term, transnational regionalism, such as that developing in the BSR, could become a central activity of local and regional governments, irrespective of changes in the cooperation incentives provided by the EU.

Transnational Regionalism as Strategic Geopolitics: Some Theoretical Issues

Markets are perhaps the most conspicuous arenas for European integration. Since the introduction of the Euro as a currency unit in 1999, cross-border mergers and acquisitions have increased dramatically, facilitating the formation of pan-European industrial and business groups. In 1999 over $US1,200 billion were spent on mergers and acquisitions in Europe, of which 40 percent were cross-border. National capital markets have merged into a much larger European pool, transforming the strategic perspectives of firms, investors, and banks.[8] As impressive as these numbers are, however, community building at the scale of the EU is a complex process that cannot be reduced to economic interaction alone. Structural policies involving large interregional financial transfers, environmental security fora, new European research networks, student mobility schemes, as well as a vast array of market and non-market forces, are all contributing to the construction of the EU. Along with the European Parliament and other supranational bodies, the European Commission is itself an institution of integration, creating a new transnational civil service and new elite networks that transcend the traditional national-oriented career trajectories. These developments seem in fact to imply the emergence of a new European identity.

European integration is hence both an explicit political project and an unintentional, unguided process of societal interaction. However, it is not without its contradictions. It must promote formal and informal means of integration, respect local and regional sensibilities, and, ultimately, secure the broad and long-term support of the EU citizenry. The challenge of sharing elements of national sovereignty within a much larger political community therefore involves not only reconciling different national and subnational perspectives on social and economic development but also maintaining legitimacy through franchising and incorporating local communities. Similarly, new regional forms of political integration must strike

a balance between perceived imperatives of globalization and more immediate local concerns.

The idea of European citizenship as manifested by "membership to a
polity" has been identified as a crucial element of interstate integration.[9]
Similarly, Anthony Smith has argued that a sense of common cultural
identity is a general prerequisite for the constitution of political community, regardless of the spatial level involved. Europe's linguistic and cultural heterogeneity and the lack of a truly common language can be seen,
however, as important barriers to the development of a common identity
and, thus, of a European public sphere.[10] It is self-evident that the construction of the EU is a continuous process and that a truly European
demos and public sphere as represented, for example, by transnational
political party structures, media, interest groups, and NGOs, must eventually emerge. A notable element of the Maastricht Treaty, 1992, was the
introduction (in Articles 8-8e) of legal and conceptual elements of formal
European citizenship into an integration process hitherto characterized
primarily by economic issues. Going a step further, one of the implicit
goals of the Treaty of Amsterdam, 1998, is the promotion of a European
public sphere through the establishment of common (i.e., unifying) constitutional principles and intergovernmental processes. These arrangements could very well support the emergence of common values in the
area of human rights, women's rights and democracy, and so on.[11]

Traditionally, the study of geopolitics has concerned itself with power
relations and conflict between nation-states as basic elements of international order. More recently, the field of geopolitics has widened, introducing a more inclusive definition of security and challenging the monopoly
of normative state-centred perspectives.[12] An "enlightened" geopolitical
perspective, focusing on social-spatial elements of region building, would,
in my view, provide insights into how cooperation and conflict are being
managed through the construction of transnational political communities.
European macroregionalization is a complex geopolitical phenomenon
that can only be comprehended as a multilevel and multifaceted exercise.
Furthermore, material constraints and discursive elements are inseparable
and mutually interdependent aspects of regionalization processes. Consequently, macroregionalization patterns vary with the ideas promoted by the
respective communities of private- and public-sector actors.[13] The paradigm of "open" economic regionalism has held sway in the Latin American,
North American, and Asia-Pacific context but has provided few institutional mechanisms to promote cross-border cooperation or deal with wider
political issues.[14] In the case of the EU, integration requires adherence to a
comprehensive set of political and ethical values as well as membership
within a plethora of supranational institutions.

Here, a notion of geopolitics is introduced that reflects a concern for both the "immaterial" realm of integration discourse and the actual patterns of political integration. Carlsnaes relates doctrines, as socializing ideas, to dispositional political behaviour and the resulting pursuit of political goals.[15] Thus, the intentionality of political action is supported by ideologies, belief systems, and normative ideas. In a similar vein, Richard Higgott[16] has argued that there are distinct links between structures and processes of regional (and hence interstate) cooperation on the one hand and mutually accepted leitmotifs guiding action on the other. As such, the paradigmatic interlinking of transnational regionalism with value-laden concepts such as "cohesion," "sustainability," "empowerment," and "partnership" has, at least in the European case, greatly increased the significance of the former within domestic and community politics. Oftentimes, spatial metaphors provide a cognitive link between ideas and political action. Spatial metaphors such as "networks" and "glocalism" enhance our conceptions of material spaces, and, conversely, our conceptions of material (physical) spaces contribute to the creation of spatial metaphors.[17] As is illustrated below, visionary spatial development perspectives and maps of new European zones of cooperation visualize and thus make more tangible the notion of transnational regionalism.

Integration and the encouragement of European affinities are also seen as contingent upon regional empowerment and the strengthening of regional identity. EU policies must therefore bridge gaps between European unification at the political and cultural levels and the realities of divergent national identities, perceptions, and identities within Europe. Accordingly, the promotion of local cross-border and wider transnational cooperation has, since 1988, become firmly anchored within European politics: they are seen as vital elements within the construction of a multinational political community and in stabilizing political relationships with neighbouring states. The elaboration of cross-border cooperation policies within the broader political context of the EU is thus both an institutional response to global policy challenges and a manifestation of values, ideology, and received common elite knowledge.[18]

The EU Integration Policy Environment:
Symbolic and Material Aspects
The construction of the EU is very much a process of integrating ideas, values, and identities in order to assure political cohesion and popular legitimacy. This integration process can also be defined in terms of region building at different spatial scales. The evolution of postwar European cooperation from the limited economic communities of the 1950s to a fully fledged union in the 1990s, with its powerful supranational institutions, is a clear expression of interstate regional cooperation, of defining an international community of states. The consolidation of a European

political and economic space is implied by the objectives of the Treaty of Maastricht, which include "harmonious and balanced development of economic life with the European Union, sustainable, non-inflationary and environmentally sensitive growth, a high (great) degree of convergence in economic development, high levels of employment, and social protection, the improvement of the quality of life, economic and social cohesion and solidarity between the member states" (Article 2).

Within the nation-states of the EU, however, parallel processes of regionalization have taken place in which subunits of the state have been accorded a larger role in defining their futures and influencing European policy. While often based upon historical and cultural traditions, this more local form of regionalism has also been promoted by state policy as a means of rationalizing administration and managing internal conflict. Finally, and more recently, transnational regionalism has emerged as partly directed, partly spontaneous, processes of cooperation between communities and regions across national boundaries but not necessarily in a spatially contiguous manner.[19]

What is the specificity of the European situation with regard to multi-level regionalization processes? Michael Keating[20] has described a basic tension that has evolved between an induced (or "top-down") regionalism, aimed primarily at the rationalization of territorial control and maintenance of socioeconomic balance, and locally based ("indigenous") regionalisms that have sought to claim larger economic, cultural, and/or political autonomy within the European system of nation-states. The EU has also tried to reconcile economic with social equity concerns: according to Liesbet Hooghe,[21] "the social counterpart (of economic liberalization) is centred on a specific understanding of cohesion: growth needs to be stimulated and organized in the less advantaged areas and groups, 'les forces vives' in these areas need to be encouraged, and collaboration between the widest coalition of forces for growth actively assisted."

At yet another level, the regionalization question is also related to European identity. Reacting to a lack of awareness of Europe's history and cultural heritage, the Treaty of Maastricht was designed to increase local and citizen involvement in EU affairs and to reinforce a sense of community.[22] Romano Prodi, now president of the EU Commission, has argued that Europe needs an overall "vision" of its future, shape, and strategic role: "Europe must not simply become a sort of inter-governmental marketplace in which Member States simply haggle over national interests. The European Union I want to see ... is a Community of shared values, underpinned by a shared vision of what we want to achieve together."[23] In fact, according to Brigid Laffan,[24] there exist three basic policy elements designed to provide this vision: (1) a shift of political focus in treating member populations as European citizens rather than as mere economic subjects, (2) a politics of identity and symbols, and (3) the creation of non-economic cross-national networks.

Contemporary policies of the EU, focused as they are on issues of cohesion, identity, and competitiveness, involve both symbolic campaigning for a borderless Europe and generous regional development incentives to encourage local initiative and cross-border networking. European planning and structural policy documents emphasize a need for spatially integrated forms of political cooperation and problem solving.[25] Transboundary regionalism is thus seen to address a need to transcend the limits of nationally based administrative practice and to attempt to create (or recreate, as the case might be) a sense of community across national boundaries. Transcending boundaries is still a leitmotif of European politics, even after forty years of gradual progress in integrating nation-states, and is supported by the INTERREG structural initiative, which provides incentives for both local/regional cross-border and transnational cooperation.[26] This is evidenced by visionary cartography depicting new cooperative regions such as the Baltic Sea, the Atlantic Arc, or Mediterranean region.[27]

Furthermore, the symbolic importance of "regional anchoring" is also evident in political documents and statements that support the idea of transboundary cooperation. Former EU commissioner Monika Wulf-Matthies has suggested that a more direct experience with European integration and greater understanding of the importance of promoting integration can only develop out of a sense of "regional-local empowerment."[28] It has also been argued that transnational regionalism contributes to community building through promoting processes of Deutschian "social learning" and that political support of cooperative projects addressing specific regional problems will help create a "citizen's Europe."[29]

The Policy Framework
Within the EU the creation of regional transboundary cooperation institutions has been advanced as a vital element in the process of interstate integration and as a means of improving the implementation of regional policy. Since 1990 a formalized EU policy has emerged that promotes transboundary regionalism and provides support for development initiatives within border regions.[30] This policy comprises a bundle of regional development instruments and procedural guidelines. Material incentives for cooperative projects are conditional upon the establishment of joint planning and management structures, which directly impose an institutionalization "requirement." Institutionalization has indeed proceeded apace and has been greatly influenced by German, Dutch, and French experiences in transboundary multilevel governance. In concrete terms this has meant the establishment of bilateral (and multilateral) agencies at national,

subnational, and local levels dealing with various aspects of public policy. Ideally, these three levels should interact in a form of partnership guaranteeing a local voice while maintaining the comprehensive perspectives of state policies. This partnership is reinforced by distributive measures of the EU; many aspects of programming and employing EU resources for regional development involve central-local reciprocity.

The most conspicuous manifestation of transboundary regionalism is situated at the local level and is known by the generic term "Euroregions." These municipal associations were pioneered and developed as locally based cooperation initiatives in Dutch-German border regions as early as the 1960s.[31] Since then, Euroregions have become part of complex policy networks at the European and national levels. The main goal of these organizations is to promote mutual learning and cooperative initiatives across borders in order to address specific regional economic, environmental, social, and institutional problems.[32] These associations, many with transboundary local parliaments (or councils), represent an additional, albeit strictly advisory, regional governance structure and play a vital role in channelling European regional development aid into the border regions.

Euroregions represent a spatial metaphor in that they evoke a sense of region, developed in free association, which contributes to wider European integration. As such, the Euroregion concept has proved a powerful tool with which to transport European (and, to an extent, national) values and objectives. The popularity of the concept is evident in its proliferation within the EU, particularly along Germany's borders.[33] More striking, however, is the fact that, since 1993, Euroregions have rapidly materialized in Central and Eastern Europe in areas characterized by decades of conflict, closure, and non-cooperation. Indeed, it appears that the model of multilevel institutionalization, perfected in West European border regions, has been transferred to the EU's borders with Central and Eastern Europe as part of a pre-integration policy to combat regional marginalization and to facilitate a long-term basis for cooperation.[34] Together with generous project incentives financed out of European structural and economic cooperation funds, this "model" theoretically constitutes a powerful framework (regime) for the development of new policy-making capacities across national boundaries.

The rapid spatial diffusion of Euroregions is largely due to the perception that they represent "laboratories" of European integration[35] – a perception that has prompted direct political encouragement. It has also been a conscious political project: the EU, the German Federal Ministry of Planning, and local level activists, for example, have been instrumental in providing expertise, funds, and moral support. Furthermore, national, subnational, and local governments have been systematically persuaded to facilitate the development of Euroregions (along Dutch-German lines) in the German-Polish and German-Czech border regions.[36]

At another level, structural policy has decisively influenced the development of cross-border cooperation in Europe. As of the present programming phase (2000-6) the most prominent policy instruments available for promoting transboundary regionalism are: (1) the INTERREG IIIA initiative earmarked for local projects, including physical development and investments; (2) INTERREG IIIB, aimed at facilitating transnational networking in spatial planning issues; and (3) PHARE/TACIS/MEDA, programs aimed at developing cooperation with neighbouring non-EU states (Central and Eastern Europe, the Community of Independent States, and Mediterranean countries, respectively).[37] Almost $ECU4 billion from structural fund budgets were dedicated to INTERREG II for the 1994-99 programming period, making it the largest community structural development initiative. This amount was increased for the present programming period of 2000-6. With co-financing from national and local sources, the total amount available within the present INTERREG III framework could well exceed $ECU6 billion.[38] In addition, programs targeted for Eastern and Central Europe, most prominently PHARE and TACIS, provide supplemental funds for cross-border projects on the EU's external boundaries. These programs were strategically important as they served to prepare neighbouring states (e.g., Poland, Hungary, the Czech Republic, Slovenia, and Estonia) for EU membership and to expedite the transfer of EU norms, policies, and regulations.

In addition to these formal instruments of regional policy, more informal attempts to develop a set of shared European values with respect to spatial development and the environment have served to promote transnational regionalism. The process of elaborating a European Spatial Development Perspective (ESDP) was inaugurated in 1994 at a pan-European meeting of regional planning agencies in Leipzig, Germany. After five years of debate and numerous regional meetings, the European ministers of spatial planning agreed upon a framework document that enshrines sustainable economic development, socioeconomic cohesion, regional equity, and polynucleated (and thus balanced) urban development as common objectives. Although not a community-level policy in the sense of agriculture or regional development, ESDP could play an important role as a policy guideline and as a means of conflict avoidance in industrial, environmental, transportation, and other spatial development policy areas. More important perhaps, ESDP is a framework for structural transnational cooperation within the EU (and with neighbouring countries) based on macro- and mesoregionalization processes, multilevel governance partnerships, and agenda setting in spatial development issues.

Case Study: An Emerging Baltic Sea Regionalism?

The BSR is a complex zone of interstate cooperation within Europe. Characterized by great disparities in economic development and living standards, it comprises member states of the EU, future EU members, and Russia (and, arguably, parts of Belarus). Manifold environmental problems originating from agricultural, urban, industrial, and military sources have imperiled the Baltic Sea and large stretches of coastline. Meaningful multilateral cooperation within the entire region has only really been possible since 1990 and the abrupt end of confrontational Cold War politics. Before that, cooperation platforms were limited either in terms of the number of partners involved or in terms of their forcefulness. The rapid development of multilateral cooperation in the BSR in the last decade, on the other hand, has been remarkable. Presently dozens of initiatives involving cities, regions, chambers of commerce, universities, national governments, NGOs, and other actors are either under way or in preparation.

The emergence of a renewed sense of "region" in the Baltic context has as much to do with historical relationships as with an acute sense of mutual interdependence. The "revival" of old trading networks (the famed Hanse) as well as the surmounting of historical animosities are highly symbolic (and emotionally rooted) elements of Baltic Sea regionalism. Pragmatism (i.e., the knowledge that national well-being can only be guaranteed through macroregional stability) provides the political rationale for cooperation. A major step in creating institutions of Baltic Region cooperation in spatial planning and environmental protection was taken in March 1992 at a summit of foreign ministers of the so-called Baltic Rim states. On this occasion, a Baltic Sea Region Council of States was formally established. The council's agenda includes the promotion of new democratic institutions as well as interregional cooperation in economic, technological, humanitarian, scientific, cultural, and spatial development matters. As Joeniemmi[39] has pointed out, security issues were deliberately excluded from the council's activities in order to emphasize *functional* international cooperation and the strengthening of institutions of a democratic civil society. In addition to the Baltic Rim states, the European Union also maintains a seat in the council.

Multilateral cooperation in the BSR potentially represents a new dimension in the promotion of economic development, environmental protection, and security regimes. It is not surprising that the Nordic Council, having met with only partial success in the past with its own Baltic cooperation initiatives, has actively supported this process. The Nordic countries, sensitive to the complex political and ecological situation of the region, have seized the opportunity to encourage multilateral political fora in the BSR. Here, they have received support from Germany (and especially the state of Schleswig-Holstein) and, with the accession of Finland

and Sweden to the EU, from Brussels. As a result, the multilateral exercise that defines Baltic Sea regionalism is evolving out of subregional "cores" of cooperation, particularly those long established between the Nordic countries; those developing between Sweden, Finland, and the newly independent Baltic States; and the local transboundary cooperation initiatives emerging between Germany and Poland, Finland and Russia, and other countries. A decidedly European dimension has been added thanks to the aforementioned community initiatives facilitating multilateral cooperation in spatial planning and regional development; in fact, the EU is attempting to promote economic and other forms of "positive" interdependence in the BSR as a basic strategic objective.[40] This latter objective goes hand in hand with the adoption of the *acquis communautaire* (i.e., the norms, legal frameworks, and standards of the EU) by Estonia, Latvia, Lithuania, and Poland as a prerequisite for membership in the EU.[41]

The development of multilateral collaborative relationships in the BSR is being promoted by a wide variety of project-oriented initiatives and networks. Heterogeneous in nature, these are establishing subregional working agendas at various administrative levels as well as bringing NGOs and other organizations together. Since 1990 an impressive variety of single- and multipurpose consortia of pubic agencies, universities, advocacy groups, and business organizations have developed. Examples of these are the Baltic Sea States' Subregional Co-operation (BSSSC), coordinated by the German state of Schleswig-Holstein, and Ballad (Independent Forum for Networking in the Baltic Sea Region), a forum for NGOs.[42] BSSSC maintains three working groups dealing with (1) institution building, (2) economic development, and (3) environmental protection, and it is developing a number of collaborative projects in these areas. These large multilateral cooperation platforms are only one facet of new "geo-governance" structures developing in the Baltic Sea Region. In addition, a plethora of local and regional initiatives have blossomed that involve bilateral partnerships and/or regional subgroups. As such, for example, Scandinavian authorities at the national, regional, and local levels have all been active establishing their own forums for dialogue and information exchange on various administrative problems. Baltic Sea regionalism is therefore manifested by at least four different levels of organization. These are:

1   intergovernmental institutions that provide a state-centred cooperation forum
2   global development concepts and strategies
3   interregional fora involving state, non-state, and private-sector actors (often organized around specific issues)
4   local projects and initiatives.

A certain degree of integration between these levels of cooperation has been achieved through a spatial development forum supported by the EU. Baltic perspectives for sustainable economic growth and balanced regional development predate ESDP but have now been integrated into this pan-European strategy. Reciprocally, the Visions and Strategies around the Baltic 2010 (VASAB), discussed in more detail below, form the basis of an EU initiative for the BSR. The INTERREG IIIB program provides, as did its predecessor INTERREG IIC, co-financing for interregional/transnational projects that pursue basic substantive planning and organizational goals. INTERREG IIIB-BSR, as it is officially referred to, is coordinated by Germany and Sweden. It provides a broad platform for projects, conferences and exchanges of information and experience between various projects under way in the BSR.

In the following, the global development concept VASAB 2010 and two transnational cooperation initiatives that received support during the INTERREG IIC programming phase are discussed in terms of their goals and strategic rationales as well as their symbolic and ideational content.[43] This forms the basis for a critical appraisal of the contribution of transboundary regionalism to the development of Baltic and European political communities.

The VASAB 2010 Initiative: Environmental Regionalism as Vision
The need for new organizational patterns of cooperation within the region to meet the challenges of globalization and the opportunities for enhanced European cooperation are now widely acknowledged by nation-states and regions on or near the Baltic Sea. After the creation of the Council of Baltic Sea States in 1990, further attempts to promote interregional cooperation in this part of Europe followed. An advisory body, the so-called Helsinki Commission (HELCOM), was, for example, established with the express purpose of protecting maritime and coastal biotopes. Recognizing that the future of the Baltic Sea – and indeed of the greater macroregion – would hinge upon the reconciliation of competing and conflicting activities as well as the various interests of Baltic Sea states, national and regional representatives of ministries for spatial planning and development resolved in August 1992 to prepare a common and comprehensive strategy for environmentally sustainable spatial development. The initiative "Visions and Strategies around the Baltic 2010 (VASAB 2010)" was developed with the assistance of the Baltic Institute in Karlskrona, Sweden, and unveiled in December 1994. Since then it has been periodically updated, most recently in 2000 with the preparation of the VASAB 2010 PLUS report.[44]

VASAB 2010 represents a potentially vital nexus between European integration objectives and those of regional transnational cooperation. VASAB

has been promoted as an innovative approach to transnational cooperation in dealing with a complex array of problems, ranging from water
resources management and urban development to the restructuring of
postsocialist economies in crisis. Unavoidably, all these issues are either
directly or indirectly related to the maintenance of economically and
politically viable forms of regionalism in the BSR. Although underwritten
by the ministers for spatial planning and development of the eleven Baltic
Rim states, VASAB is a process that explicitly includes local and regional
actors, representatives of the private sector, and civil society.[45] The EU

Map 5.1   The "self-defined" Baltic Sea region

plays an essential role, both in promoting its values and strategic objectives through representatives of involved member states and in providing funds for transnational projects via INTERREG and other initiatives. For their part, Scandinavian planning authorities and the German federal government provided political pressure to maintain the momentum of the process.

Four main principles, intentionally idealistic in tone, form the basis of VASAB 2010: development, environmental sustainability, freedom, and solidarity. Briefly expressed, these principles outline a form of interregional cooperation that emphasizes flexibility, pragmatism, and the open participation of local, regional, and state actors in a planning process that strikes a balance between specific regional development goals and ambitions and the pressing need to halt environmental deterioration. In its own – perhaps limited – fashion, VASAB 2010 also envisages interregional cooperation as a means of diminishing socioeconomic disparities between East and West and, thereby, eliminating sources of possible future conflict. The broad scope of VASAB 2010 is evidenced by four strategic focal points that are intended to guide common action: (1) the urban network; (2) communications and transportation; (3) regions, natural areas, and border areas; and (4) the spatial planning system.

In helping establish a new multilateral and multilevel framework for planning action – in effect, precedents for subregional implementation of VASAB and ESDP – a variety of national and international planning documents have been considered, including national and regional planning concepts (i.e., guidelines, physical and structural plans, recommendations concerning the spatial development of coastal zones, and the like). Beyond that, planning dialogue and consensus building, supported by well-defined national and supranational policies, are seen as the means by which a multilevel planning regime can be gradually pieced together and institutionalized. The structure of this envisaged planning regime is seen to involve the horizontal integration of ministerial policies at the national level and the vertical integration of local and regional authorities in the decision-making process. It is to be based on a partnership between various levels of government and allow for the open participation of interested citizens.

As well as being pragmatic, VASAB 2010 is also a highly "philosophical" document in that it promulgates paradigms of global governance that challenge traditional state-centred approaches to regional development. VASAB is also portrayed as a regional mechanism for implementing the Rio Declaration and post-Rio initiatives such as Agenda 21. Sustainability and the paradigm of global environmentalism, understood as a reaction to ecologically destructive urban growth and economic globalization, represent one of VASAB's primary ideational foundations. At the same time, the internationalization of domestic politics – and the need to develop forms of global environmental governance[46] – provides arguments for advancing VASAB. VASAB supports the principle of "partnership" as defined in the Rio and Habitat II contexts, underscoring the necessity of multilevel fora that include state and non-state actors and greater citizen participation in planning processes.

The basic premise of VASAB, very much in tune with contemporary environmental and governance paradigms, makes it an attractive platform with which states can depict themselves as supportive of "sustainability" and "partnership" and, thus, as cooperative. Indeed, refusal to participate in the VASAB process could appear rather awkward. However, this major strength of VASAB's is also its central weakness: its general character facilitates participation but reserves the hard work of implementation and conflict resolution for other intergovernmental arrangements. Realizing that a non-committal approach could quickly reduce VASAB to pure symbolism, the EU and national sources with a vested interest in VASAB's success (the German Federal Ministries of Planning and of the Environment being a prominent example) have provided a financial and political fillip to the process.

Hence, VASAB provides a political umbrella for a wide variety of regional development initiatives and facilitates cooperation experiments that, at some time, should translate into affective institutional action. In fact, in order to flesh out the general objectives of VASAB, a plethora of planning networks have developed since 1995 that are, by and large, unbureaucratic, inclusive, and (perhaps) somewhat contrived exercises in regional cooperation. In a rather remarkable case of policy coordination, EU programs, along with the ESDP and national and region policy initiatives, have combined to support VASAB. Most crucially, INTERREG has provided a financial guarantee and political forum for project-oriented cooperation.

Baltic Bridge

This project refers to a regional and urban planning forum that involves German, Polish, and Swedish regions and that was supported by the INTERREG IIC-BSR initiative between 1999 and 2001. The Baltic subregion defined by the Baltic Bridge (BB) is situated in a transitional area between advanced Western European economies (Denmark, Germany, and Sweden to the west and to the north) and Central European countries in transition (Poland to the east and eastern German regions in a process of rapid structural change). It is also characterized by large areas of protected natural landscapes. Furthermore, this subregion will be increasingly exposed to spatial effects generated by the growth potentials of two major urban agglomerations: the Berlin metropolitan region and the Øresund region, with Copenhagen and the Malmö-Lund conurbation. Major trans-European transportation axes that connect these nodes of international transaction traverse the BB area. Hence, this trinational space will, in future, likely require solutions to the very problems identified by the VASAB 2010 document in 1994: the need for the development of a sustainable settlement structure and for the improvement of communications and transportation in an environmentally sensitive border area. Participants in the project, which was formally initiated in 1999, are representatives of planning authorities in northeastern Germany, northwestern Poland, and southern Sweden. The "lead partner" is the Joint Planning Office of Berlin-Brandenburg (Gemeinsame Landesplanung). As with many other INTERREG projects for the BSR, the BB was able to provide an informal and unbureaucratic platform for organizing cooperation between German-Polish Euroregions, existing urban networks, and state agencies.

The principal rationales motivating involvement in the project were both political and geographical. While state agencies saw for themselves an enhanced role as mediators between national and European institutions, cities sought to avoid marginalization within an intensifying interregional competition. Szczecin, a major Polish city and an important Baltic port, has been frustrated by Warsaw's refusal to support the improvement of its road and rail links to Germany and other Polish cities. Despite its strategic location and a population of over 500,000, Szczecin does not enjoy high priority in Poland's national development schemes, perhaps due to perceptions that proximity to Berlin will, in any case, guarantee the city's prosperity. Sweden's port cities on the Scania coast risk losing importance as transportation centres with the opening of the Øresund Bridge between Sweden and Denmark. Furthermore, the German cities between Berlin and the Polish border area are in every sense of the word peripheral centres. Here, the traumatic impacts of rapid job losses in agriculture and industry since unification have not been overcome.

The BB project concept developed out of local networking initiatives between Brandenburg-Berlin and Poland. It involved, among others, the cities of Schwedt, Prenzlau, Szczecin, and Eberswalde; representatives of the Polish Voivodship of Szczecin; and Berlin-Brandenburg's Joint Planning Office. Focusing on the construction of urban networks, the BB project set out to open up a new cooperative space in the BSR and to promote open dialogue on spatial planning and regional development among experts and politicians from Germany, Poland, and Sweden, concentrating on specific project elements, with the ultimate aim being to form a transnational planning regime that is flexible and responsive to changing planning exigencies. If functional interconnection through communication and project-oriented cooperation was the nucleus of this project, then transportation infrastructures, tourism development, and strategic planning were its practical elements. This project prioritized the development of functional networks connecting important centres and clusters of urban centres located between Berlin, Szczecin, and southern Sweden, connecting them to regional development initiatives of similar orientation in other parts of the BSR. As such, this project represented an exercise in the subregional implementation of VASAB.

In addition, the BB was conceived as a framework for sectoral cooperation initiatives in the South Baltic Sea Region. Together with a joint spatial planning platform, it aims to assist planning agencies and actors to promote cooperative processes for carrying out further measures in the countries involved. The project comprises four focal points around which activities are organized:

1   the creation of a strategic regional management for cross-border cooperation on sustainable spatial development
2   the development of urban networks as a means for a sustainable settlement structure
3   the reinforcement and the improvement of communication and transport systems
4   the development of rural areas and areas with structural weaknesses in accordance with the principle of sustainability.

The four corresponding working groups met four times a year individually and twice a year as a group. Each of the working groups was responsible for developing projects in its respective areas and locating funding sources. Overall coordination of the project was entrusted to external organizations, the World Trade Centre in Frankfurt (Oder), and private consulting firms.

Despite the commitment of the project's lead partners, the BB encountered considerable problems. To begin with, recruiting the participation of most German municipalities was difficult and required considerable pressure from the Joint Planning Office. The EU initially provided only about $ECU1 million, and several larger towns were obliged to contribute to the overall budget. Financially speaking, this did not make for a very attractive project from the standpoint of struggling East German municipalities. Interestingly, Swedish and Polish communities, who from the beginning were attracted more by the project's European orientation than by additional local revenues, did not share these reservations. Problems facing the BB came from other, rather unexpected, quarters; namely, from procedural requirements demanded by the European Commission. Here, the EU has tended to apply rigorous conditions for the release of project funds and has (at least in the past) demanded more or less strict adherence to project goals defined in initial proposals submitted for consideration. Should, in the course of practical cooperation, substantive changes in focus take place, the EU can threaten or cancel financial support. These organizational aspects proved unexpectedly cumbersome and were the source of much frustration for the lead partners. Furthermore, these administrative burdens generated high transaction costs for the understaffed Joint Planning Office, prompting some officials to call into question the overall utility of the project.

Via Baltica

This network developed directly out of deliberations over the implementation of VASAB in 1994 and 1995. It began as a concept for a development corridor between Tampere, Helsinki, Tallinn, and Riga, thus connecting Finland more directly with the Baltic states of Estonia and Latvia. The THTR Development Zone, as it was known, was inaugurated by the Ministries of the Environment of the three participating countries, but with Finnish regional administrations playing a central role. The goal of the pilot project was to establish working relationships between various administrative levels and to specifically train Estonian and Latvian planners in modern management techniques. The THTR focused on settlement structures and economic cooperation, mobility, and infrastructure issues as well as the environmental and cultural heritage. The THTR also pursued the political objective of increasing awareness of the spatial consequences of European integration on the Eastern Baltic and thus promoting strategic, long-term planning.[47] Problems were encountered in financing the project out of EU funds, as INTERREG and PHARE are destined to different groups of states (i.e., EU member and non-member countries). Funds taken from these two initiatives cannot be combined to jointly fund cooperative projects. The local PHARE offices in the Baltic state, responsible for coordinating EU development aid, have also tended to be nationally oriented and much less open to assisting transnational cooperation.[48]

These financing difficulties were eventually overcome through national funding and thus proved only a temporary setback. The THTR eventually evolved into a much larger network during discussions over future "Trans-European Networks," in which a Helsinki-Warsaw route along the Baltic coast (feeding in to the major East-West axis between Paris and Moscow) was identified as a priority infrastructure project. The decision was made by the THTR partners to adopt the so-called Via Baltica (VB) as a unifying concept for a long-term project involving Finland, Estonia, Latvia, Lithuania, Poland, and Germany. VB was submitted to the INTERREG IIC selection committee for consideration and was approved. Work on the project began in 1998.

In keeping with the principles of VASAB, VB dealt with the development of new contexts for cooperation in spatial planning and regional policy that bring "centre" (Finland, Germany) and "periphery" (Poland and the

Baltic States) together and that promote a more open political dialogue in the BSR. Perhaps not unsurprisingly, the major focal points of the project evolved around issues dealing with transportation corridors. Indeed, the larger European situations of Baltic Sea cities and regions, as well as that of Berlin and Brandenburg, clearly demonstrate the importance of diagonal connections not necessarily located on the main communications axes between major European centres.[49]

The strategic rationale for VB was both straightforward and compelling. National transportation strategies, particularly in the case of Poland, are focused on investments in high-speed links to major European capitals. Fiscal pressures and the push for EU membership in May 2004 drove the Polish government to prioritize the East-West axis (Paris-Berlin-Poznan-Warsaw-Moscow) above all other capital investment projects. The other transportation axis that is favoured is a north-south link between the Baltic port of Gdansk (Danzig) and Warsaw. Hence, as is the case with Szczecin, many Polish regions lying off these main corridors continue to face the prospect of being cut off from future economic development. Indeed, Poland could be split between an easily accessible metropolitan core (Warsaw, Poznan, and Gdansk) integrated into the larger European economy and a nationally oriented periphery. This scenario could have drastic consequences for northeastern Polish regions centred around Bialystok, especially if transportation links to Lithuania, Latvia, and Estonia, presently in a miserable state, are not greatly improved. Logically, the Baltic States are greatly interested in developing a Baltic corridor that connects their capitals (Vilnius, Riga, and Tallinn, respectively) with Warsaw and Berlin. Presently, the most important international links of the Baltic States are maritime connections to the Nordic countries. While the Baltic States are vitally interested in a high-speed VB (i.e., a diagonal connection between them and the Berlin region), their limited resources and weak political voice do not provide them with much leverage. Finland, perhaps the most influential partner, also welcomes the prospect of improved terrestrial connections through Estonia to the rest of Europe. However, Finland is more interested in rapidly integrating the Baltic States politically and economically within a "Western" context, particularly given the unstable situation in Russia and Belarus.

In this way, VB united states, regions, and cities that sensed a need for action in order to avoid being marginalized within an enlarging EU. VB, taking advantage of the EU's INTERREG initiatives, was a proactive measure intended less as a challenge to national policies than as an attempt to elaborate alternative regional perspectives. The project partners also seemed to agree that the need to develop informal networking and cooperation in broad political, economic, and cultural areas was, in the long run, more important than was the immediate objective of modernizing transportation corridors. Similarly, the project partners attached considerable importance to emphasizing the greater European dimension of VB and the shared values that might stem from a common cultural heritage.[50]

Given that particularistic national perspectives are driven by short-term considerations and frugality, the project partners were quite cognizant of the need to apply political pressure in order to achieve their aims. The EU and its respective national governments will play an essential role in supporting large-scale transportation projects in the BSR. However, the competition between different project proposals (both in the BSR and on a European scale) is intense and will certainly increase. As such, lobbying was understood to be absolutely vital to the promotion of VB's goals, and the importance of the corridor for regional and, thus, national development was emphasized. The VB steering committee warned, however, that, in order to lobby effectively, the regions would have to set priorities and concentrate on a few key areas, thus avoiding putting forth fragmented regional initiatives or promoting too many objectives simultaneously.[51]

INTERREG IIC and Problems of "Regional Fragmentation"

Above and beyond the experiences of individual cooperation projects, general evaluations of the INTERREG IIC program for the BSR illustrate several contradictions inherent in the EU's attempts to promote transnational regionalism. The most critical drawback of the program, and one addressed by the INTERREG IIIB-BSR Secretariats (2000), has been a countervailing element of regional fragmentation, evident both in a low level of coherence between individual projects and in the incompatibility of funding mechanisms between "East" and "West."

INTERREG IIC-BSR was heavily criticized for failing to take advantage of the possible synergy effects available by interlinking projects and/or systematizing the cooperation objectives in order to ensure that projects would complement each other. Instead, a "mixed-bag" of projects resulted, and these pursued a wide variety of objectives. This lack of linkages between the projects could not be counterbalanced by the twin secretariats in Rostock and Karlskrona, who attempted to put the most favourable "regional" gloss on the program. Furthermore, the experiences of the two INTERREG networks discussed above are illustrative of the contradictory role of European opportunity structures for regional cooperation. Ironically, European involvement has resulted in dividing the region according to degrees of affiliation with the EU. Financial restrictions as well as complex procedural requirements tend to highlight and perhaps exacerbate asymmetries between unequal partners in the BSR (i.e., between EU member states, associated states, and the long-term "non-EU"). In certain cases involving cooperation with Poland and the Baltic States, partnership was complicated by "diplomatic" protocol and a lack of continuity in the persons representing the respective partner institutions.

INTERREG IIIB: Continued Support for Transnational Networking in the BSR

As were the majority of planning initiatives for the BSR, the Baltic Bridge and Via Baltica represented ambitious attempts to develop "social capital" with very limited resources. Project activities were focused on the constitution of a cohesive network and on identifying all partners in order to close "gaps" within the Berlin-Baltic trajectory. However, while regional development agendas were established, the two-year duration of the project did not allow time for the development of cohesive strategies with which to further these agendas. Within the scope of the present INTER-REG IIIB structural initiative (which ends in 2006), resources have been targeted for the continuation of transnational cooperation in the BSR and other focal areas of transnational activity. Among the forty-three projects now receiving support, "second generation" initiatives have assured the continuity of the networks established within the BB and VB frameworks.[52]

Nordregio,[53] in its ex-ante evaluation of the INTERREG IIIB program for the BSR, has voiced the expectation that this third phase of the initiative will result in more concrete benefits to the BSR program area. The Nordregio document also stresses the need for more aggressive marketing of project activities as well as for orienting work towards decision making and producing political agreements with concrete results. Indeed, INTERREG IIIB-BSR has been conceived along more strategic lines than had the preceding initiative. VASAB, for example, serves in the INTERREG IIIB-BSR programming context as an overall vision of Nordic/Baltic development and, hence, as an integrating concept from which the initiative's main parameters have been derived. Furthermore, attempts are under way to maximize the potential of transnational planning activities supported by INTERREG IIIB-BSR through clearer management structures, more context-sensitive indicators, and a stronger political focus.

There is a final point that should be mentioned here and that affects all cooperation projects involving non-EU member states. The program secretariats, located in Germany and Denmark, are also attempting to facilitate cooperation with non-EU member states by proving information on the co-financing of joint projects through different EU funding sources.

Conclusions

The rapid development of transboundary cooperation in the BSR appears to suggest the emergence of "networked" transnational spaces within the context of an enlarging EU. The significance of transnational networking lies in its potential for creating new problem-solving capacities and governance mechanisms in, among other policy areas, regional development and spatial planning. An optimistic reading of the events unfolding in the BSR is that cross-border regionalism and transnational networking are resulting in complementary spatial scales of governance within the complex European mosaic of nation-states and regions. However, such claims are, as yet, highly speculative. What, for example, do the short case studies presented here tell us about the possible political and geopolitical significance of transnational regionalism?

We can identify certain patterns that, while rather recent, may indicate some of the prospects and limitations of transnational regionalism. First, programmatic and pragmatic elements appear to be facilitating formal institutionalization and informal networking. These help to establish cooperative relationships and routines by de-emphasizing potentially controversial issues and focusing on areas where common interests can be identified. By using powerful spatial metaphors, such as development and transportation corridors, as unifying concepts, several BSR initiatives have succeeded in bringing together representatives of several different countries and a wide range of actors. In addition, the combination of global environmentalist values with objectives of European integration has provided a convenient ideational platform for securing overall political support. Finally, the available opportunity structures for actual projects have helped to translate ideas into action. Based on the VASAB process and a series of initiatives that explicitly aim to engender a sense of Baltic regionalism, we can identify the following elements of structural cooperation that appear to be contributing to the regionalization process in the BSR (see Table 5.1).

This process of agenda formulation and strategy building, while certainly a logical means of promoting cooperation, is only one element in the transnational regionalist equation. In fact, structural cooperation centred on general planning forums and EU initiatives might be providing a springboard for new political communities and transnational public spheres, but it suffers clear limitations. Indeed, few concrete cooperation results have as yet materialized.

Two basic problems deserve special mention here: (1) a relative lack of political influence and (2) an often one-sided dependence upon EU and national support. Influenced by intense competitive pressures between regions, lobbying for national and EU support appears to be one of the main raisons d'être of these regionalist exercises. This fact raises questions as to whether the regionalist initiatives are actually contributing anything original to the construction of European union or whether a one-way (i.e., "top-down") communication of European values to the regional and local level is taking place. Furthermore, the strong EU orientation of the regionalist initiatives brings with it administrative drawbacks, with emphasis on procedure rather than process and, ironically, many bureaucratic restrictions.

Typical of European political traditions is the important state role in guiding (or trying to guide) regionalization processes. While valuable as a vehicle for communication and cultural understanding, transnational regionalism does appear subservient to the policies and interests of the European suprastate and member nations. It is enmeshed within the structural policy agendas of state actors and, of necessity, dependent upon formal politics. Geopolitical considerations of EU nation-states are very prominent in this regard.

Despite these considerations, it must be said that the EU's regionalization experience goes much further, and is more profound, than similar attempts in other parts of the world. Unlike the cases of NAFTA or APEC, where national sovereignty, cultural identities, and ideology are so intertwined as to preclude true political integration, the EU is characterized by a complex project of supranational institution building. In contrast to the EU, for example, Asian regional organizations are geared towards sovereignty enhancement rather than to the sharing of national sovereignty, which, in the Asian case, is highly territorially contingent. The popular

Table 5.1

Programmatic elements of transnational region building in the EU

	Contents	Methods
Agenda	Visions, strategies, scenarios	Documents, political declarations, events
Program formulation	Incentives for cooperation, recommendations, formulation of regional visions	Institutionalization, structural policies
Implementation	Experiences of existing cooperation	Cooperative activities on specific topics, project activities
Evaluation	Accomplishment of aims, stabilization of cooperation	Critical reflection on cross-border activities and and action
Reformulation of the agenda	Proposals, innovations, modification of the program	Transformation of the actor's criticism and self-reflection into political action

image of hegemonic neoliberalism, which, in the opinion of Agnew, Brenner,[54] and others, characterizes developments within the European integration project as yet another accumulation strategy within global capitalism, glosses over deep cultural and ideological differences underlying microregionalization in different continental contexts.

This chapter has raised the possibility that substantive change at the ideational level might, with time, translate into institutional change and shifts in spatial scales of European governance. If we interpret the enrichment of social capital as a primary goal of local and regional development, then, despite their limitations, interorganizational networks indeed seem to be playing an essential role in linking actors and agencies. Social capital is an essential counterpart of structural regionalism built around general development concepts. As there appears to be a need for broader local and regional participation in order to compensate for the cooptation of transnational regionalism by states and the EU, these two elements, working together and incorporating European symbolism and "universal" values (such as sustainability and solidarity), might signal a change in governance. In closing, the slow institutional change that might be induced in this manner need not involve a new, complicated institutionalization process. Transnational regional governance in Europe could emerge as flexible systems of policy coordination juxtaposed with formal national and European structures. Should the momentum of such initiatives increase and tangible results become evident, then perhaps a new dimension in political, economic, and social integration in Europe might be achieved.

Notes

1 See Max Singer and Aaron Wildavsky, *The Real World Order: Zones of Peace, Zones of Turmoil* (Chatham, NJ: Chatham House, 1996). See also Björn H. Inotai and András and Osvaldo Sunkel, eds., *National Perspectives on the New Regionalism in the North*, vol. 2 (Basingstoke: Macmillan, 2000).

2 Spatial planning and regional development cooperation attempts are conspicuous elements of this wider European strategy. See, for example, the European Spatial Development Perspective, EU Commission, 1999.

3 Bjarne Lindström, Lars Hedegaard, and Noralv Veggeland, *Regional Policy and Territorial Supremacy: Nordic Region Building and Institutional Change in the Wake of European Integration* (Copenhagen: NordRefo, 1996).

4 Panayotis Soldatos defines transnational regionalism in governance terms as: "direct international activity by subnational actors (federated units, regions, urban communities, cities) supporting, complementing, correcting, duplicating, or challenging the nation-state's diplomacy; the prefix 'para' indicates the use of diplomacy outside of the traditional nation-state framework." The primary reason for its emergence in the last forty years has been dissatisfaction with the means and priorities of foreign policy as practised by the nation-state. See Panayotis Soldatos, "Cascading Subnational Paradiplomacy in an Interdependent and Transnational World," in *States and Provinces in the International Economy*, ed. David Brown and Earl Fry (Berkeley: University of California, Institute of Governmental Studies Press, 1993), 45-64. As Soldatos has stated (48), it is a phenomenon

symptomatic of "dysfunction" and, at the same time, an attempt to rationalize policy making in order to make foreign diplomacy more responsive to subnational needs and, thus, more effective. See also Ivo Duchacek, "International Competence of Subnational Governments: Borderlands and Beyond," in *Across Boundaries: Transborder Interaction in Comparative Perspective,* ed. Oscar J. Martinez (El Paso: Texas Western Press, 1986), 11-28.

5 Liam O'Dowd, "The Changing Significance of European Borders," *Regional and Federal Studies* 12, 4 (2002): 13-36.

6 Oran Young, "Global Governance: Towards a Theory of Decentralized World Order," in *Global Governance: Drawing Insights from the Environmental Experience,* ed. Oran Young (Cambridge, MA, and London: MIT Press, 1997), 273-99.

7 Alexander Sergounin, "Russia and Transborder Security Interests in Northern Europe: Defining a Co-operative Agenda," in *Regional Dimensions of Security in Border Areas of Northern and Eastern Europe,* ed. Pertti Joenniemi and Jevgenia Viktorova (Tartu, Estonia: Pepsi Centre for Transboundary Cooperation, 2001), 133-71.

8 Lex Column, "The Construction of Europe," *Financial Times,* 1 February 2000, 26.

9 Massimo De la Torre, "European Identity and Citizenship: Between Law and Philosophy," in *European Citizenship, Multiculturalism and the State,* ed. Ulrich Preuss and Fusan Requejo (Baden-Baden: Nomos, 1998), 87-104.

10 Richard Münch, *Das Projekt Europa: Zwischen Nationalstaat, regionaler Autonomie und Weltgesellschaft* (Frankfurt am Main, Germany: Suhrkamp, 1993).

11 Victor Pérez Diaz, "The Challenge of the European Public Sphere." ASP Research Paper, 4/1994, Madrid.

12 Gearóid Ó Tuathail, "Thinking Critically about Geopolitics," in *The Geopolitics Reader,* ed. Gearóid Ó Tuathail, Simon Dalby, and P. Routledge (London and New York: Routledge, 1998), 1-12.

13 Richard Higgott, "The International Political Economy of Regionalism: The Asia-Pacific and Europe Compared," in *Regionalism and Global Economic Integration,* ed. William D. Coleman and R.D. Underhill (London and New York: Routledge, 1998), 42-67.

14 It is important, of course, not to lump the regional cooperation organizations of North America (North American Free Trade Areas, Latin America [MERCOSUR], and the Asia-Pacific Economic Co-operation Forum [APEC]) together, as they are characterized by different institutional arrangements, treaties, and openness to interaction with other regions (Ramino Pizarro, "Comparative Analysis of Regionalism in Latin America and Asia-Pacific," *Comercio Internacional* 6 [1999]). See also Clark Reynolds, "Regionalismo abierto y acceso social: nuevos enfoques hacia la integracion en las Americas," in *El Ecuador en el Mercado Comun,* ed. German Creamer Guillen, S. Kim Kwan, and Clark Reynolds (Quito, Ecuador: Corporacion Editora Nacional, 1997), 13-70.

15 Walter Carlsnaes, *Ideology and Foreign Policy: Problems of Comparative Conceptualization* (Oxford and New York: Basil Blackwell, 1986), 175.

16 Higgott, "The International Political Economy of Regionalism," 42-67.

17 Neil Smith, "Homeless/Global: Scaling Places," in *Mapping the Futures: Local Cultures, Global Change,* ed. Jon Bird, Barry Curtis, Tim Putnam, and George Robertson (London and New York: Routledge, 1993), 87-119.

18 James W. Scott, "European and North American Contexts for Cross-Border Regionalism," *Regional Studies* 33, 7 (1999): 605-17.

19 Ibid.

20 Michael Keating, *The Politics of Modern Europe: The State and Political Authority in the Major Democracies* (Aldershot: Edward Elgar, 1993), 17.

21 Liesbet Hooghe, ed., *Cohesion Policy and European Integration: Building Multi-Level Governance* (Oxford: Oxford University Press, 1996).

22 Anthony Smith argues, for example that "relatively little attention had been devoted to the cultural and psychological issues associated with European unification – to questions of meaning, value, and symbolism." See Anthony D. Smith, "National Identities and the Idea of European Unity," *International Affairs* 68, 6 (1992): 55-76.

23 Romano Prodi, "Solidarity: The Foundation on which Europe Stands." Speech delivered at the opening session of the European Forum on Economic and Social Cohesion, Brussels, 21 May 2001 (Document: SPEECH/01/236), 3.

24 B. Laffan, "The Politics of Identity and Political Order in Europe," *Journal of Common Market Studies* 34, 1 (1996): 96.

25 European Commission, "Interregional and Crossborder Co-operation in Europe," *Proceedings of the Conference on Interregional Co-operation-Regions in Partnership*, Brussels, 14 and 15 December 1992, EC Regional Development Studies No. 10 Brussels/Luxemburg: ESCS-EC-EAEC. See also the European Parliament, *Report on Transboundary and Inter-Regional Co-operation* (prepared by the Committee on Regional Policy, Rapporteur: Ritta Myller), 1997, DOC EN\RR\325\325616.

26 For information on INTERREG, see the European Commission's Web site at <http://www.inforegio.cec.eu.int>.

27 See European Commission TERRA, *An Experimental Laboratory in Spatial Planning* (Luxembourg: Office for Official Publications of the European Communities, 2000); and Nordregio (Nordic Centre for Spatial Development), *Ex-Ante Evaluation of Baltic Sea INTERREG IIIB Programme*, Final Report (Stockholm: Nordregio/Eurofutures, November 2000).

28 Comments made at the Conference of Transboundary Co-operation in Breisach (Germany) on 18 September 1998.

29 Sabine Weynand, "Inter-Regional Associations and the European Integration Process," in *The Regional Dimension of the European Union: Towards a Third Level in Europe*, ed. J. Charlie Jeffery (London and Portland, OR: Frank Cass, 1997), 166-82.

30 Markus Perkmann, "Euroregions: Institutional Entrepreneurship in the European Union," in *Globalization, Regionalization and Cross-Border Regions*, ed. Markus Perkmann and Ngai-Ling Sum (Basingstoke: Palgrave Macmillan, 2000), 103-24.

31 Jens Gabbe, "Institutionelle Aspekte dergrenzüberschreitenden Zusammenarbeit," in *Grenzübergreifende Raumplanung: Erfahrungen und Perspektiven der Zusammenarbeit mit den Nachbarstaaten Deutschlands*, ed. Akademie für Raumforschung und Landesplanung (Hanover: Verlag der ARL, 1992), 174-86.

32 Jonathan Grix and Vanda Knowles, "The Euroregion and the Maximization of Regional Capital: Pro Europa Viadrina," *Regional and Federal Studies* 12, 4 (2002): 154-76.

33 James W. Scott, "Transboundary Co-operation on Germany's Borders: Strategic Regionalism through Multilevel Governance," *Journal of Borderlands Studies* 15, 1 (2000): 143-67.

34 György Eger, "Az eurégió mint az europai integráció sajátos térbéli területe," *Külpolitika Foreign Policy* 4, 4 (1998): 76-87; Gabor Novotny, "The Institution of Euroregions: Prerequisite for Success?" paper presented at the Regional Studies Association Conference, Bilbao, Spain, September, 1999; Tadeusz Stryjakiewicz, "The Changing Role of Border Zones in the Transforming Economies of East-Central Europe: The Case of Poland," *GeoJournal* 44, 3 (1998): 203-13.

35 M. Kessler, "Laboratory for European Integration: The Euroregions," *Inter Nationes, Basis-Info*, 14-1999/European Integration, 1999, 14.

36 Institute for Regional Development and Structural Policy, Zusammenfassender Projektbericht, Project Report no. 1.18.

37 *Grenzübergreifende Regionalentwicklung* (Project Report on Transboundary Regional Development) (Erkner by Berlin: IRS, 1999).

38 See the October 2000 issue of *Inforegio Panorama*, the European Commission's magazine on regional development, for a detailed discussion of INTERREG III (available at <http://www.inforegio.cec.eu.int>).

39 Pertti Joenniemi, "Interregional Cooperation and a New Regionalist Paradigm," in *Borders and Border Regions in Functional Transition: European and North American Perspectives*, ed. James Scott, Alan Sweedler, Paul Ganster, and Eberwein Wolf-Dieter (Berlin: Institut für Regionalentwicklung und Strukturplanung, 1996), 53-61.

40 Hiski Haukkala, *Two Reluctant Regionalizers? The European Union and Russia in Europe's North*, UPI Working Papers, No. 32, UPI (Helsinki: Finnish Institute of Foreign Affairs, 2001).

41 See the EU Web site regarding the enlargement process and the EU's AGENDA 2000: <europa.eu.int/comm/agenda2000/index-en.htm>.

42 This has also resulted in a dense virtual environment: the Internet now provides extensive information about projects, conferences, organizations, general cooperation, and other matters.

43 Based on research carried out by the author between 1997 and 2000 at the behest of the Berlin-Brandenburg Joint Office of Spatial Planning.
44 Nordregio (Nordic Centre for Spatial Development), *Ex-Ante Evaluation of Baltic Sea INTERREG IIIB Programme,* Final report of November 2000 (Stockholm: Nordregio/Eurofutures, 2002).
45 See the EU *Committee on Spatial Development* 1997, 9-10.
46 Ingemar Elander and Rolf Lidskog, "The Rio Declaration and Subsequent Global Initiatives," in *Consuming Cities: The Urban Environment in the Global Economy After the Rio Declaration,* ed. Nicholas Low, Brendan Gleeson, Ingemar Elander, and Rolf Lidskog (London and New York: Routledge, 2000), 30-53.
47 Juri Lass, "Transport Infrastructure Networks in the Countries of Northern Europe and Links with the European Network," in *The Challenges Facing European Society with the Approach of the Year 2000: Strategies for the Sustainable Development of Northern States in Europe,* European Regional Planning Series, No. 61 (Strasbourg, France: Council of Europe Publishing, 1998), 69-76.
48 Ibid.
49 The trajectory Berlin-Riga is presently 1,303 rail-kilometres in length and requires a net travel time of 21.5 hours. By way of comparison, the route between Avignon-Berlin, which are 1,585 kilometres apart, can be travelled in 13.5 hours (including transfer time).
50 Documentation of the "Via Baltic" Workshop, 9 December 1999, Berlin (prepared for the Joint Planning Office of Berlin-Brandenburg by the Institute of Regional Development and Structural Planning, in Erkner, Germany).
51 Ibid.
52 See the INTERREG IIIB Web site at <http://www.spatial.baltic.net>.
53 Nordegio (Nordic Centre for Spatial Development) Background Study for VASAB 2010 PLUS, *The Baltic Sea Region Yesterday, Today and Tomorrow: Main Spanish Trends* (Stockholm: Nordregio, 2000).
54 John Agnew, "How Many Europes? The European Union, Eastward Enlargement and Uneven Development," *European Urban and Regional Studies* 8, 1 (2001): 29-38; Neil Brenner, "Building 'Euro-Regions': Locational Politics and the Political Geography of Neoliberalism in Post-Unification Germany," *European Urban and Regional Studies* 7, 4 (2000): 319-45.

Part 3
Emerging Perspectives

The chapters in this section of *Holding the Line* highlight an important but overlooked geographical process – the emergence of new regions in the non-Western world. These regions are key actors who, as Anthony Asiwaju argues in Chapter 6, are "compelled to interact because they have common interests in human and natural resources (straddling a shared international boundary) and also because of common concerns about the cross-border environmental impacts of human and natural processes." Yet, by definition, emergent non-Western regions (unlike Europe or North America – see Parts 3 and 6, this volume) are located on the margins of the core of the global economy and find themselves subject to political, institutional, environmental, and economic pressures to cooperate.

The necessary response in parts of postcolonial Africa has been to interrogate borders from the perspective of their potential for building "Afrio-regions" along the lines of the EU – something that traditional African and European scholars have often thought incompatible with the African experience. For example, Asiwaju suggests, from the perspective of African scholarship, that "contrary to popular belief, state territories and boundaries in postcolonial Africa are structurally and functionally not so different from those found elsewhere in the wider world of the nation-state. They were created in consequence of preceding centuries of imperialist expansion and colonial domination by metropolitan powers, which are now core member states of the Council of Europe and the EU." While he does not deny important differences in the details of history and geography between Europe and Africa, his argument that "significant similarities have been identified between Africa and Europe, especially with regard to local perceptions of the arbitrariness of the processes and overall artificiality of the partition effects," is breathtaking in its critique of traditional understandings of Africa's nation-state structure outside the continent.

Asiwaju's discussion of the issue of the potential of regional and sub-regional cooperative mechanisms for building a true transnationalism among African nation-states is a good foundation for Chapter 7, by Clive Schofield, where the theme of the compatibility of international instruments and cross-border regimes outside of "core" countries is repeated. While recognizing that, in many respects, maritime transnational pressures and instruments for cooperation are geographically and historically specific to Thailand, Schofield suggests that they are also nested in common broad institutional, economic, and instrumental mechanisms as well as in global protocols that place them at the heart of the international community and at the cutting edge of transnational cooperation. Moreover, geographical context, particularly the physical character of the transborder community (i.e., its maritime geography) is, to a large extent, constitutive of the degree of cooperative transnationalism that follows as well as its potential success or efficacy.

While Schofield's discussion deals with a subject similar in some respects to Scott's (Chapter 5, this volume) in that it focuses on regional cooperation issues which have a maritime environment in common, there is a world of difference between these two approaches. In Europe, the development of transborder community as a way of aiding devolutionary processes is designed to rebuild a broad-based EU from the bottom up. In Southeast Asia, the structure is legalistic and the initiative comes from the top down. This puts one in mind of the point made by Adamson in Chapter 3: "desire to promote the setting of standards across borders reflects not just a desire for harmonization or uniformity for its own sake but, rather, the realization that the business of government increasingly involves dealing with an extraordinary number of issues that, by their nature, are international or transnational: law and policy response must come from the same perspective."

6

Transfrontier Regionalism: The European Union Perspective on Postcolonial Africa, with Special Reference to Borgu

Anthony I. Asiwaju

Transfrontier regionalism is a novel category of internationalism focused on adjacent sovereign states. These states are compelled to interact because they have common interests in human and natural resources (straddling a shared international boundary) and also because of common concerns about the cross-border environmental impacts of human and natural processes. Although transfrontier regionalism, as described in this chapter, is concerned with artificially partitioned ethnic groups giving rise to the global phenomenon of peoples of identical languages and cultures found across international boundaries, it is essential to bear in mind the other closely interrelated manifestations of transfrontier regions; namely, the wide spectrum of transboundary natural resources ranging from land, water (surface and underground), and air to liquid and solid minerals as well as to flora, fauna, and inherently indivisible environments and eco-systems. Depending on the policy put in place by one or the other state vis-à-vis its geographically contiguous neighbours, the international interactions generated by such transboundary human and natural resources may be one of conflict and war or of cooperation and peace. While conflict has been the dominant perspective, cooperation has always remained conceptually open and adoptable.

In Europe, since the end of the Second World War policy emphasis has shifted from a disposition towards war to an ever-increasing commitment to the exploration and systematic utilization of peace. This has involved developing cooperative potentials of international boundaries and shared borderlands. Uncoordinated, informal local initiatives have developed based on the spontaneous reactions of transborder peoples or vivisected ethnic groups across several of the international boundaries in Western Europe. The organization of "European Regions," or "Euregios,"[1] has evolved into a well-coordinated powerhouse of European integration.[2] "Euregios" now operate everywhere in the region as formal institutions and are recognized by both domestic and international laws. They have also become effectively coordinated at both regional and subregional levels.

So successful has been the practice of transborder cooperation, and so manifest its contributions to the spectacular achievement of European integration, that it has attracted policy makers outside the primary diffusion centre in Western Europe. Not only has it become standard practice in Northern Europe (notably the Scandinavian countries) and in Central and Eastern Europe but, since the fall of the Berlin Wall, it is also being actively canvassed and replicated outside Europe.[3] The 1998 centenary of the Anglo-French partition of Borgu, one of the several prospective African Regions, or "Afregios," created in consequence of the European partition and the subsequent emergence of independent African states, has provided the opportunity for a renewed reflection on a whole range of African potentials begging for policy exploration and application.[4]

This chapter is divided into four sections. The first explores European historical experience and the current practice of transfrontier regionalism; the second indicates the relevance of European history and its applicability to Africa; the third illustrates Africa's, "transfrontier regions," with special reference to Borgu and the crucial roles of vivisected culture areas; and the fourth attempts to identify the conditions required if African potential for transfrontier regionalism is to be realized. It explores Nigeria and Benin, with special reference to the active participation of the Borgawa on both sides of the shared boundary. Special emphasis is placed (1) on the role of policy making at the level of the Organisation of African Unity (now African Union) and (2) on the imperative of appropriate research support. I conclude with pointers for policy initiatives and developments, the latter aimed at refounding African regional integration endeavours on the cornerstones of transborder cooperation between geographically adjacent states and, therefore, on the cornerstones of grassroots historical, socioeconomic, and environmental cross-border linkages.

The European Model

As we have seen in earlier chapters, European transfrontier regionalism developed as a companion movement to the evolution of European integration. Indeed, the aim of transfrontier regionalism was the achievement of transfrontier microintegration, which would dovetail with European macrointegration. Originally a product of the Council of Europe (founded in 1949), and still a prime mover, transfrontier regionalism was boosted in the 1980s by the adoption of a regional approach to planning and development by the better-resourced European Economic Community (EEC), now the European Union (EU), and by the systematic promotion of a new "Europe of the Regions" in contradistinction to the old Europe of nation-states.

Giuseppe Vedovato observes that "the starting point for the development of transfrontier regions is found after the Second World War, when 'insurmountable political and ideological barriers' descended on Europe and problems of reconstruction made it necessary to look to new openings and new territorial cooperation 'models.' It was a time that saw the almost spontaneous establishment of contacts between local communities that were to render frontiers more 'permeable' and give rise to a variety of different organizational forms."[5]

By 1986, when the European Single Act was initiated in anticipation of regions as choice units for planning and development in the European Community, "Euregios" and associated transfrontier cooperative initiatives had become permanent features of European life, with special reference to member states of the Council of Europe and the EEC. The European Charter on Frontiers and Transfrontier Regions, adopted by the Association of European Border Regions (headquarters in Bonn), contains a list of forty-six regions and associations located throughout Western and Northern Europe but concentrated on the Rhine (the Waal, in the Netherlands), which serves as the international boundary between Germany and France and between Germany and the Netherlands.[6]

The organizations of the individual transfrontier regions draw considerable strength from their multisectoral nature, each combining social, economic, environmental, and other interests and thus involving a large number of stakeholders. Also adding to the strength of the organizations is their disposition to being consolidated into larger and stronger regional formats,[7] although there are other successful transfrontier cooperation models emphasizing specialized functions.[8] Over the years, especially since the late 1970s, transfrontier regionalism in Europe has gained tremendously in lobbying power and political influence. This growth has been achieved by a growing capacity for self-empowerment, evidenced by European borderlanders who exploit to the fullest the advantages of the wider political environment (characterized by the post-1945 embrace of democracy). This capacity was exhibited in the building of certain strategic institutions, which won recognition and support for transfrontier regionalism at both national and international levels in Europe. First was the establishment, in the early 1980s, of the Association of European Border Regions (AEBR), based in Bonn, which has since functioned as a common front at the continental level. Next was the creation of the Liaison Office of the European Regional Organizations, with the AEBR as its core, and strategically located in Strasbourg, which is also the seat of Council of Europe and the European Parliament.

The adoption not only of the European Outline Convention on Transfrontier Co-operation between Territorial Authorities and Communities but also of the Additional Protocols to the Outline Convention by the Council of Europe (in 1980 and 1993, respectively), as well as the creation within the council's secretariat of the specialized Office for Local and Regional Authorities (in 1984) and the institutionalization of the Conference of Ministers Responsible for Regional Planning, provide part of a wide array of evidence of the tremendous influence that transfrontier regionalism came to wield on the European institutions in Strasbourg.

For the EEC and the European Economic Commission in Brussels, proof of an equally effective penetration by transfrontier regionalism is provided by the coming into effect of the Single European Act and the enthronement therein of regions as the primary planning and development units in Community Europe. Border regions, which constitute the heart and the bulk of the so-called "transregional" category (i.e., regions in different states, especially those on both sides of borders between members states) recognized in the act, have been the main beneficiaries of the European Region Development Fund created by the European Commission and disbursed under the INTERREG programs.

With the widespread collapse of communist regimes in the early 1990s and the subsequent establishment of democratic, political, and economic pluralism in Central and Eastern Europe – events that have raised the prospects for the ultimate admission of former Communist Europe into the EU – transfrontier regionalism has spread its influence into Central and Eastern Europe.[9] There are two main categories of transborder cooperative institutional frameworks. First are institutions such as the Pomeranian Euroregion, astride the Oder-Neisse border between Poland and Germany, which link the former communist states with Western Europe or the EU. Second are actively organized transfrontier regions in Central and Eastern Europe, which link the former communist states directly with themselves. This may be illustrated by the Carpathian Euregio project initiated in 1992. According to Vedovato,[10] the project covers approximately 118,000 square kilometres of land and about 12.5 million people. It is made up of the adjacent borderlands of Poland, Hungary, Slovakia, and Ukraine, with Romania participating as an observer because of its two proximate provinces in northern Transylvania. It is assisted by the institute for East-West Studies of Atlanta, Georgia, in the United States and the Sasakawa Peace Foundation of Japan. The contributions from outside are made to a specially created Foundation for the Development of the Carpathian Euro-region. As with the older transfrontier regional development projects in the West, the new transborder regional development initiatives in Eastern and Central Europe are also supported by the European Region Development Fund of the EU, especially under its so-called PHARE program.

African Comparability

Overview

Contrary to popular belief, state territories and boundaries in postcolonial Africa are structurally and functionally not so different from those found elsewhere in the wider world of the nation-state.[11] They were created in consequence of preceding centuries of imperialist expansion and colonial domination by metropolitan powers, which are now core member states of the Council of Europe and the EU. While not denying important differences in the details of history and geography, significant similarities have been identified between Africa and Europe, especially with regard to local perceptions of the arbitrariness of the processes and overall artificiality of the partition effects. Comparative studies of the localized impacts of the boundaries in Africa and Europe point more to similarities than to differences. Traditional lamentations about Africa often ignore these crucial similarities and block a clearer vision of the vital lessons that Africa can learn from the European historical experience.

It is generally lamented, for example, that Africa was badly partitioned; that African boundaries are artificial and arbitrarily drawn with little or no regard for pre-existing socioeconomic patterns and networks on the ground; that the boundaries have erratically split unified culture areas and mindlessly fragmented coherent natural planning regions and ecosystems; that a great deal of Africa's contemporary economic problems have stemmed from the fact of territorial division into such a large number of competitive, rather than complementary, national economies; and, finally, that much of the continent's current political problems have originated from the arbitrary nature of the inherited colonial boundaries that (among other things) resulted in artificially juxtaposing incompatible groups.

However, none of the claims that point to Africa as unique have been sustained by focused comparisons with Europe. If anything, the comparative assessments, based on detailed case studies, have demonstrated a replication of the European experience in Africa. In Europe, as in Africa, neighbouring border regions represent areas of opposing official languages, national cultures, and histories as well as differing economic systems, disharmonious legal regimes, and parallel administrative traditions, all superimposed upon invariably distinct local indigenous cultures that straddle the intersovereignty boundaries.

Hence the extremely close similarities that have been found between the Catalans (an ethnic group neither French nor Spanish)[12] in the Cerdanya Valley of the Eastern Pyrenees and the Western Yoruba, and the Hausa (ethnic groups neither French nor British, each of which came to be split into the officially different worlds of the French and the British by the present-day Nigeria-Benin and Nigeria-Niger borders, respectively).[13] Needless to say, these are but a few of the numerous vivisected ethnic groups, or transborder peoples, found across virtually all state frontiers in the two continents.

Partitioning Europe and partitioned Africa are, through the same processes, continents consisting of a multiplicity of state territories and state frontiers – in Europe even more so than Africa. Quite apart from the obviously larger number of states in Europe, considering its size relative to Africa, is the greater instability of the European territorial framework of the nation-state. This contrast is clearest in the fact that Africa's widespread and ever deepening political crises have produced little or no changes in state territories and boundaries while Europe's crises have led to widespread and fundamental cartographic revisions. It has been estimated, for example, that "more than 60 percent of [Europe's] present borders [were] drawn during the twentieth century" and that no fewer than "8,000 miles [12,800 kilometres] of new political lines" have been drawn to frame present-day Central and Eastern European countries (including the dissolution of old states and the creation of new ones) as a sequel to the collapse of communist regimes in the late 1980s and early 1990s.[14]

In Europe, as in colonial and postcolonial Africa, state territories and boundaries share an essential arbitrariness in their creation and their locally felt artificiality. These have resulted in similar forms of territorial absurdities, evident in the ludicrous shapes and sizes of state territories and the comparable incidents of such inherently dependent entities as land-locked states and enclaves. There have also been similar experiences with the artificial partition of natural regions (seas, lakes, rivers, mountains, valleys, forests, deserts, and so on) and coherent ethnic groups and culture areas. The latter subcategory has proved to be important to the production of ethnic or national minorities and the associated questions of irredentism and the frightful practice of "ethnic cleansing." Both in Europe and postcolonial Africa state frontiers are notorious for their roles as precipitants of disputes and conflicts within and, more especially, between states.

These and other problems of state territories and boundaries in Europe and Africa ought not to surprise us since the boundaries of the one continent have remained more or less as created by imperialists from the other. These people drew boundaries and managed them as though they were existing in their own respective metropolitan countries. Indeed, it has been well established that in Europe, as in Africa, the boundary-making processes, as well as the structures and functions of the resultant state frontiers, are more similar than dissimilar.[15] The same observation goes for the legal instruments and political engineering that have been designed for their management: the same kind of "treaties," "protocols," and "exchange of notes" – the same pattern of diplomacy. The point, then, is that, given these essential similarities, lessons learned from the experiences in the one continent cannot and must not be lost on the other.

Transfrontier Regionalist Pressure in Africa

Africa experiences local historical and geopolitical pressures for transborder cooperation and wider regional integration that are similar to those that operated, and still operate, in postwar Europe. With respect to transborder cooperation, it is pertinent to draw attention to widespread replications of vibrant transfrontier regions that await policy adjustments that will stimulate them into becoming formidable transfrontier regional organizations. These could be capable of galvanizing the various fledging subcontinental organizations and transforming them into an African regional organization envisioned in the African Economic Community Treaty and initiated in 1991 on the model of the European Economic Community Treaty, 1957.

Much like Europe, the prospects for transfrontier regionalism in Africa appear to be irresistibly driven by four interlocking forces: (1) local populations; (2) border economies; (3) natural resources and the environment; and (4) the widely recognized necessity to ground African regional/subregional integration projects on the realities of local African history and culture. In fact, the continuous operation of these factors has led to various microintegration formations across Africa's international boundaries, each begging to be formalized and thereafter used as cornerstones for the wider regional integration projects being pursued by states in the various subregions of the continent.

The first and the most fundamental of the four forces compelling transfrontier regionalism in Africa is the commanding presence, everywhere, of vivisected or partitioned ethnic groups and culture areas. This has ensured a systematic and sustained contradiction and, with it, the obliteration of the normal barrier effects of the intersovereignty boundaries.

This effacing impact of Africa's "transborder peoples" is produced by the cross-border operation of strong networks of cultural, socioeconomic, and even political interactions between borderlanders. These peoples are located astride specific segments of every border where people speak identical indigenous languages and share related cultural identities (such as traditional religions, memories of common ancestral origin, identical socioeconomic and political institutions, and close kinship ties). In cases such as that of the Shona across the Monica sector of the Zimbabwe-Mozambique border, the Ketu-Yoruba astride the Nigeria-Benin border, or, as we will shortly see, the Baatonu of the Nikki kingdom of Borgu (who also straddle the Nigeria-Benin border), memories of common allegiance to the same precolonial state are often retained in order to strengthen the feeling of solidarity that binds territorial communities on both sides of the boundaries. The significance of this ethnic dimension of transfrontier solidarity in Africa is underscored by its solidly documented ubiquity.[16]

The second interrelated factor forging transfrontier regionalism is cross-border trade. A measure of the significance of this often ignored factor is that it has now become a focus of attention by researchers and consultants working for such high-profile international development and donor agencies as the World Bank, the United States Agency for International Development (USAID), and the Paris-based Club du Sahel of the Organisation for Economic Co-operation and Development (OECD). The widely circulated studies, reports, and publications that have resulted from these endeavours leave no further doubt about the dominance of the mostly unofficial forms of inter-African business transaction vis-à-vis the recorded forms. The continent-wide spread of this phenomenon is indicated by such publications as those by MacGaffee (which focus on former Zaire as being a typical Central African case); by Ackello-Ogutu and Echessah with regard to Eastern Africa (funded by USAID); and by Egg and Igue with regard to the West African subregion (funded separately and severally by the French Ministry of Co-operation and the Club du Sahel of the OECD in Paris).[17]

The realization of the magnitude of cross-border trade flows and the truly regional character of its operational dynamics has led the experts of the West African studies to suggest the need for a radical reorientation of current approaches to integration in favour of a new strategy, which they refer to as "market-driven integration."[18] The essence of this suggestion is that, instead of continuing to be pursued along the lines of the model of traditional international organizations, regional integration in Africa should be rooted in the alternative realities of transnational interactions as manifested in cross-border trade. The Economic Community of West African States (ECOWAS) has, therefore, been conceptually reorganized into three separate subgroupings based upon the degree of cross-border business transactions among the states so grouped. The suggested restructuring of the West African subcontinent has thus resulted in the identification of three overlapping units:[19]

1   the West, embracing the wider Senegambia region that comprises Gambia, Senegal, Mauritania, Mali, Guinea (Conakry), Guinea (Bissau), and Cape Verde
2   the Centre West, made up of Côte d'Ivoire, Ghana, Burkina Faso, Liberia, and Sierra Leone
3   the East-West, consisting of Nigeria and the neighbouring states of Benin, with Togo, Niger, Chad, Cameroon, and Equatorial Guinea.

A similar suggestion is possible for the identification of Tanzania and its neighbours; the Republic of South Africa and its territorially adjacent countries; and the Democratic Republic of the Congo (former Zaire) and its immediate neighbours.

The third factor in cross-border pull in Africa is the irresistible force imposed by the wide array of transborder natural resources, natural habitats, and ecosystemic entities. The importance of this crucial factor is emphasized not only by the high incidence in the use of rivers (such as the Zambezi, the Limpopo, and the Mano), lakes (such as Chad, Victoria, and Malawi), and mountains (Cameroon, Adamawa, and Kilimanjaro) as boundaries but also by the commonplace characteristics of transnational rivers such as the Nile, the Niger, the Senegal, and the Orange – Africa's rivers of unity.

The potentially strong stimulus provided for transborder cooperation in planning, development, and joint management is also demonstrated, paradoxically, by conflicts over transboundary strategic resources – local conflicts that have often precipitated international conflicts. For example, the offshore hydro-carbon deposits in the Gulf of Guinea have provoked a prolonged border dispute and recently triggered armed conflicts and aggressive litigation between Nigeria and Cameroon; and the Libya-Chad and Mali-Burkina Faso border conflicts led to international litigation over stretches of shared boundaries suspected to be rich in solid minerals (the Aouzur strip and the Agacher corridor, respectively). Similarly, cross-border flora and fauna, critical to the important tourist industries of most Eastern and Southern African countries, can produce either conflict or solidarity.

The fourth and final indication of prospects for transfrontier regionalism in Africa is the evidence of an increasing number of advocacies. Arguments about a reorientation of regional integration projects on the more solid foundations of local African cultures, inspired by known affinities of history and cultural traditions, have been supplemented by advocacy for a "market-driven" perspective based upon scientific data collection and analysis regarding transborder business transactions and their wider regional dynamics and networks.

There are reliable indicators as to the existence, in most African border locations, of potential regional groups made up of local political figures, experts in economic and social affairs, and scientists able and willing to devise appropriate scenarios of the type that has played critical roles in European transfrontier regionalist organizations. If the current tempo for democratization in Africa is maintained, then there are chances for the African regional groups to transform into transborder cooperation pressure groups. Indeed, in the Great Lakes Region, the Horn, West Africa (notably Sierra Leone and Liberia), and Angola the deepening African crises have produced spectacular refugee movement as well as the cross-border spillover of armed rebellions. All this is stimulating an ever-increasing awareness of the imperative for transborder cooperation.

The Borgu Case Study

Borgu, characterized by a vibrant indigenous transborder population consisting of identical ethnic and linguistic compositions and alignments, is distinguished by the extraordinary feeling of allegiance on the part of its diverse constituent communities. Throughout their history, the latter have been known to jealously guard and collectively defend Borgu's territorial integrity. Situated on the right bank of the Niger River, Borgu has been estimated to cover a territory of approximately 70,000 square kilometres and has about two million inhabitants,[20] yet the hallmark of its history is the unity within this diversity of ethnicity, culture, and polities.

Since the late-nineteenth-century Anglo-French partition and subsequent colonial governance, which lasted until August and October 1960 (in the French and British territories, respectively), Borgu has consisted of two distinct parts. The communities to the west of the border were incorporated into the former French colony of Dahomey (present-day Republic of Benin) and include principal settlements such as Nikki, Parakou, Djougou, Kouande, Kandi, and Bembereke. In the east is Nigerian Borgu, formerly administered as part of the British Protectorate of Northern Nigeria. It includes settlements and chiefdoms such as Bussa, Illo, Kaoje, Koenji, Agwara, Rofia, Aliyara (Babana), and Wawa in the north, and, in the south, Kaima, Kenu, Okuta, Ilesha, Gwanara, and Yashikera.

Today, not only has Borgu remained divided into two main official blocs – Francophone Benin and Anglophone Nigeria – but each of the different parts of this historic land has been further "scattered" by reason of the vicissitudes of the territorial arrangements made for each during both the colonial and postcolonial eras. On the Nigerian side of the border[21] precolonial sensitivity about the overall integrity of Borgu was completely ignored, first by restructuring it into two aggressively competing emirates (Kaima in the south and Bussa in the north) and then by instituting a series of territorial excisions and restorations in the north. In 1905, for example, Illo, Kaoje, Lefaru, and Gendernni in the northeast were merged with Gwandu Emirate to compensate the Sokoto Caliphate for parts of its territory that the British had conceded to the French. Although Agwara and Rofia were eventually restored to Borgu, Illo, Kaoje, and Koenji remained in the Gwandu Emirate, now part of the recently created Kebbi State. Moreover, in the colonial period Borgu identity was further disturbed by attachments to other larger provinces like Yauri, Kontagora, and, finally, Ilorin. Nigerian Borgu ended up being organized into four or so distinct local government areas scattered across the boundaries of the three adjacent states of Kwara, Niger, and Kebbi.

Similar internal territorial dismemberment occurred in the French portion of Borgu. Apart from being divided into smaller territorial units explicitly for administrative convenience (rather than due to any historical antecedents), there was the mindless merging of the Barba people of Borgou with non-Barba people in new administrative units like Gourma and Middle Niger, two of the four cercles into which the French initially organized their portion of Borgu. The other two, predominantly Barba in population, were the Cercles of Borgou and Djougou-Kouande. Eventually, French Borgou was organized into two main cercles – Parakou, comprising the subdivisions of Parakou, Bembereke, and Nikki; and Kandi, made up of the subdivisions of Kandi, Malanville (predominantly Dendi in population), and Kouande. The location of the headquarters of Kandi Cercle in Natitingou in Somba country, outside historic Borgu, was as culturally irritating to the Barba in the French sphere as the merger of Illo with Gwandu has been to their kinsmen in the Nigerian Borgu. Today, the Beninese portion of historic Borgu is embraced in the departments (the equivalent of states in Nigeria) of Borgou and Attacora and their constituent sous-prefectures (the equivalent of local governments in Nigeria).

However, these colonial and postcolonial territorial arrangements and their accompanying administrative practices were viewed as unacceptable by the vast majority of the Borgawa (the term used by the Hausa [their neigbours] to collectively refer to the peoples of Borgu), who came to see the developments as an affront to their perception that the larger culture area and the specific state territories within it were sacred and inviolable. This point is extremely vital to a proper understanding of the systematic and sustained reactions against European imperialist partition and differential colonial rule – reactions that continued, if subtly, into the postcolonial era. Since the details of history are so well known, it will suffice simply to emphasize that the most central theme in the history and culture of Borgu is unity within diversity. This unique quality has not only permitted the peoples to perceive themselves as Barba but it has also justified the objective identification of Borgu as a definable culture area.

It is remarkable that, in spite of the internal differentiation into several distinct ethnic and linguistic groups and subgroups (of which the most dominant are the Baatonu and the Boko), the majority and ruling elite, the Borgawa, collectively view themselves, as "one people" and relate to Borgu as "our country." This country is seen as an indivisible common patrimony, despite its traditional organization into numerous, and even competing, kingdoms – of which there were three main power blocs centred in Bussa, Nikki, and Illo, respectively. And, in spite of the overall emphasis that Anene's study placed on fission rather than fusion with regard to the culture areas through which the boundaries of Nigeria were drawn, Borgu was, from its "ancient" beginning, a distinct political area the integrity of which the Borgawa (Baatonu or Boko; Bussa, Nikki, or Illo) were determined to defend with their blood.[22]

This extraordinary sense of collective allegiance to Borgu as the "patrie" of all Borgawa has been demonstrated throughout history. Patriotic responses by all and sundry to the call to defend the entire land resulted whenever the territorial integrity of Borgu was threatened. This threat could come from within, as, for example, when any of the constituent states or a combination thereof engaged in actions capable of disturbing the delicate balance between all the states; or, more often, from without, as when outsiders threatened the safety and security of the corporate culture area. As Anene is known to have acknowledged, the Borgawa proudly claim that, "until the partition of their country by the Europeans, they had never yielded to alien domination."[23] The Borgawa were known to have collectively fought and successfully warded off the invasions of Songhai under the Askias in the sixteenth and seventeenth centuries, the Habe (or Hausa) states in the eighteenth century, and the Fulani jihadist in the first half of the nineteenth century. It was probably these collective defence actions that led Kenneth Lupton to categorize the political system of the Borgawa as a "standing alliance."[24]

Apart from the collective claim of the Borgawa on Borgu as a common patrimony, there are other pieces of historical evidence that buttress the argument for identifying the area as a coherent region. Flowing from the issue of collective allegiance and the history of the culture area as a defended area is the unmistakable evidence regarding the clarity of the peoples' notions about territory and boundary. However, as occurs elsewhere in precolonial Africa, and as is still manifest in most indigenous African societies, the sense in which the concept of boundaries is understood among the Borgawa is not one of the inflexible lines of demarcation that Europeans established to separate respective areas of territorial jurisdiction. Whether between states within Borgu or between Borgu and adjacent lands such as those of the Yoruba to the south and southeast, the Nupe to the east, the Hausa to the north, or the Somba to the west, the notion of boundary entertained by the Borgawa was one of mutual inclusion.

Indeed, as Obare Bagodo has explained, boundaries as expressed in Baatonu, the language of the largest single ethnic group in Borgu, are references to zones of contact and convergence of interests – points of meeting and interaction rather than points of separation.[25] Politically, for example, Borgu has often been described as a confederation or a standing alliance. While each of the constituent states maintained its own autonomy, states such as Bussa, Nikki, Wawa, or Kaima (the actual number varied) were interconnected by several factors, including common Aboriginal foundations; the derivation of the ruling dynasties from the same culture-hero, Kisra; exchange of gifts among the rulers; participation in one another's traditional festivals; and the use of identical ritual and ceremonial instruments such, as the *kakaki*, or royal trumpets.

The emphasis on boundaries as points of contact and mutual interaction is found to have been even more widely applied to the overall benefit of the evolution of Borgu as a significantly integrated region, one with a disposition for alliance formation with tested states and societies outside Borgu. The notion of boundary entertained by the Borgawa is also known to have consolidated the tradition of a symbiotic relationship between the distinct ethnic and linguistic groups and subgroups (e.g., those of the Baatonu and the Boko), and advanced the process of a continuous fusion of the otherwise distinct cultures and subcultures. While the preservation of the integrity of Borgu remained the constant concern of all Borgawa, military alliances (such as the one that the kingdoms of Borgu were known to have forged with the ancient Yoruba state of Oyo) point to the extent to which the Borgawa were prepared to permit the permeability of the external boundary of their collective homeland if this would enhance safety and security. Although the Eleduwe War of 1835, fought collectively by the Borgawa and the Yoruba against the Fulani, brought defeat rather than victory (and was particularly disastrous for the Borgawa states of Nikki and Wawa), the corporate existence of Borgu was preserved.

This flurry of activities across the border, especially the mass movement of supporters of contesting princes from the Nigerian side (Yashikera and Aliyara) to Nikki, took place as a result of a number of succession struggles during the colonial era.[26] These were constant reminders that the local people have not quite accepted the fact of the Anglo-French partition, including the separate roles and functions of the interstate frontier negotiated by the European authorities. Other factors blurring the separation functions and effects of the boundary included a series of protest migrations that took place when there were political-administrative problems on either side of the border; cross-border trade with special reference to smuggling; and the indeterminate character of the border, arising from its controversial delimitation and the totally unsatisfactory demarcation of the segment of the Nigeria-Benin border through Borgu.[27] The last factor has led to farmers from either side clearing the lands with little or no regard for the position of the boundary.

Consequently, Borgu has remained a distinct region in spite of the international (formerly intercolonial) boundary running through it. There is, of course, no doubt that differential colonial over-rule of the French and the British has made an indelible impact. There have been parallel socialization processes by which the obviously different languages and cultures of the two colonizing powers have been adopted as the official languages and cultures of the succeeding independent states. But the effects have been more deeply felt by Western-educated elites on either side than by the non-literate majority of the local populations, who remain more attached to the indigenous culture and its traditions – including the view of Borgu as an indivisible entity. The persistence of the tradition of Borgu as one land, and the diverse peoples as one cultural community, is evident in the continuity of relations and interactions of kinship groups, including those of the Wassangari (or traditional ruling elites) across the border. All of this points to Borgu as being one of Africa's most prospective transfrontier regions.

Policy Reflections and Recommendations

If there are in postcolonial Africa as many potentials and even pressures for transfrontier regionalism as there are in postwar Europe, then why has the actualization in Africa lagged so far behind the events and developments in Europe? What are the obstacles in Africa, and what are the hopes for the future?

These questions, like the preceding argument itself, are not new. However, the recent centenary of the Anglo-French partition of Borgu, an act that completed the admittedly problematic delimitation of the present-day Nigeria-Benin border, provides a golden opportunity for a renewed discussion and a necessary update on transborder cooperation and policy promotion as a cornerstone of regional integration endeavours in Africa. In the twenty-first century, finding satisfactory answers to these essential policy questions must engage attention in view of the obvious relevance to the realization of a future that is widely viewed to lie not in an Africa of the nation-state but, rather, in an Africa of regions and peoples modelled on the European Union.

With regard to the question of obstacles, it bears repeating that the entrenchment of the nation-state structure and its non-embrace of the principles and practice of democratic governance must be targeted. First is the extolling of nation-state structure and its interrelated negative features, such as the unbridled assertions of territorial sovereignty and what has been called state nationalism. The absorption of these features by the Western-educated elites, who provided the leadership at all levels for the new sovereign states in postcolonial Africa, are the hardest nuts to be cracked. This is as much the case in the core as in the border areas of the new states, but it is particularly so with regard to the new elites in the border areas, who must now be converted into active membership of regional groups. Here assimilation into contrastive European cultures has given rise to a mindset that has produced the familiar type back-to-back, rather than the more desirable face-to-face, relationships across the borders. The effects have been especially dramatic in the several cases in Africa where the elites on the different sides of the borders are also products of the same indigenous cultures.[28] While their non-literate parents and relations cross the borders (in keeping with cherished kinship and other sociocultural ties or in order to exploit the business advantages of the border locations), educated elites among partitioned Africans are rarely known to develop cross-border relationships. They prefer to cultivate relationships with their peers inside the states, even when these people belong to other indigenous cultures.

There is a very interesting irony that emerges when comparing the history of postcolonial Africa to the history of contemporary Europe: it was precisely when Europeans, in the immediate aftermath of the last world wars (which had been fostered on them by three centuries of state nationalism), embarked upon systematically converting from a nationalist to a regionalist ideology that, in Africa, nation-state aspirations reared their ugly heads. Thus, while in Europe, since 1945 the upward swing has been towards the achievement of a trans- and supranational integration and the defunctionalizing, devaluating, and overcoming of national boundaries, in Africa and the wider world of former European colonies the boundaries "traced by (erstwhile) European colonial powers became utterly sacred and one of the main political concerns is to demarcate, sharpen, strengthen, and harden them."[29]

In Europe, finally, while one frequently hears and reads about popular criticisms of the nation-state as an "obsolete" mode of societal organization, of the need to "efface, toward higher levels (EU) and lower levels (local and regional communities) ... and of borderlands communities as miniature exemplars of the new United Europe,"[30] in Africa, the contemporary states remain firmly grounded in the doctrine and practice of territorial sovereignty, and regional integration projects are pursued on the model of classical international organizations. In Africa, international boundaries and borderlands are officially held and are treated more as points of discontinuities than as continuities – as barriers rather than as bridges between them. In Community Europe, the emphasis is on decentralization of territorial, administrative, and decision-making processes; in postcolonial Africa, the trend is to the ever-increasing centralization of control.

The ruling elites of postcolonial Africa are prepared to continue to draw their inspirations from a prewar Europe – a time that contemporary Europeans themselves are determined to forget. Lamentably, African elites seem set to turn their back on their own ancestral pasts, characterized – as Basil Davidson has aptly pointed out and as we have amply demonstrated by the Borgu case study – by "a genius ... for integration ... by conquest ... [and] also by an ever fruitful mingling and migration and an inherent impatience with exclusive boundaries."[31]

The sharp contrast between the histories of Africa and Europe since 1945 goes beyond the question of the ideologies of nationalism and regionalism. While postwar Europe represents a conversion not only from nationalist to regionalist political ideology but also from militarism and totalitarianism to full-fledged democracy and commitment to the defence and preservation of human rights and fundamental freedoms, contemporary Africa has progressively degenerated into an era of undemocratic governance, the popularization of repressive authoritarian regimes, unbridled human rights abuses, massive official corruption, a total lack of transparency and accountability of the leadership, and ever-increasing and worsening political crises that have resulted in the continent having the most civil and interstate wars since the end of the Second World War.

The sum total of the difference between Africa and Europe must be viewed as the gauge for measuring the gap that has to be bridged if developments of the state in today's Africa is to be redirected so as to achieve a future Africa of the regions and of the peoples on the model of the EU, firmly grounded in the active and systematic practice of transfrontier regionalism and nourished by a regionwide acceptance of the principles and practice of democratic governance, administrative decentralization, and accountability, plus a total commitment to the defence of fundamental freedoms. It was the commitment to the respect for human rights and, no doubt, the deep resentments that postwar Europeans came to have towards state nationalism, militarism, and authoritarianism (and their concomitant embrace of democracy, transparency, fundamental human rights, and freedoms) that gave border communities, hitherto thoroughly suppressed and downtrodden, the chance to organize themselves into the ever-thriving transfrontier territorial communities and authorities that have become the cornerstone for the realization of Community Europe. Similar sociopolitical conditions must be created and nourished if Africa is to become like this Europe, which has long replaced the one that created its colonial and neocolonial states, territories, and frontiers.

While not doubting that the European experience in the field of overcoming state nationalism and alleviating the problems of border peoples can be of some inspiration, elsewhere (most notably in Africa), Strassoldo has expressed the hope that "transnational unions in other continents will be grounded" on bases other than the immense heaps of rubble and corpses in Europe.[32] He deeply hopes "that European horrors [will] not be replicated elsewhere."[33]

The facts in Africa have not matched Strassoldo's hopes and wishes. The details have not been and cannot be the same in Africa as in Europe, but the "horrors" generated by malfunctions of Africa's postcolonial states have not been less terrifying than were those of pre-1945 Europe. Records of Africa's ever-worsening sociopolitical crises point to African equivalents of the "heaps of rubble and corpses" of European history. Witness, for example, the genocides, mass killings, and mass graves as well as the wanton destruction of property and infrastructure that have accompanied the several cases of armed conflicts in Congo/Kinshasa, Nigeria, Angola, Mozambique, Zimbabwe, South Africa, Namibia, Uganda, Rwanda, Burundi,

Congo/Braziville, Somalia, Sudan, Liberia, Sierra Leone, and Algeria; and between each of Morocco and Somalia and its neighbours, Libya and Chad, Mali and Burkina Faso, Senegal and Mauritania, Nigeria and Cameroon, Ethiopia and Eritrea. To the human-made crises must be added the several instances of natural disaster, notably the droughts and famines in the entire Sahelian zone from Senegal in the west to Djibouti in the east in the mid-1970s and mid-1980s.

Yet, in all their variety, what the African crises demonstrate is the inherent ineffectiveness of the individual states acting in isolation from one another and the imperative of transborder cooperation and regional integration. Consider such manifestations as the massive movements of refugees across the boundaries of many a troubled nation and the high incidence of the cross-border spillover of armed revolt, including the many instances of secessionist wars. It is quite instructive, for example, that one of the great thoughts that the crises in the Great Lakes Region has provoked is the innovative suggestion to turn the area into a platform for a new subregional organization. If and when this happens, the initiative can draw its main inspiration from such existing establishments as the Ouagadougou-based Inter-State Commission for the Campaign against Drought in the Sahel and the Inter-Governmental Authority for Development, based in Djibouti, both created in response to the environmental disaster consequent upon the Sahelian droughts and famines of the 1970s and 1980s.

There is no doubt, judging from the gaps to be bridged in order to attain the levels of developments in Europe, that Africans still have a long way to go. But the future is predictably one of a steady gravitation towards an ever-increasing appreciation of institutionalized transfrontier cooperation as an indispensable cornerstone for the realization of durable regional integration projects. The evidence for this is twofold: (1) the significant renewal of efforts at the creation of new subregional organizations, along with the radical reconceptualization and reorientation of existing institutions, and (2) the promotion of border-specific cooperation policy initiatives, especially in the Maghreb, West Africa, and Eastern and Southern Africa.[34]

In the first category of new developments are such renaissances as have led to the upgrading of ECOWAS into a supranational organization for the region, based on the adoption of a revised ECOWAS treaty in 1993; the reorientation of the Southern Africa Development and Co-ordination Council (SADCC) of the apartheid era into a new post-apartheid Southern African Development Community (SADC); and the creation of the Arab Maghrebian Union (AMU), rooted in the practice of transfrontier cooperation, especially the co-development of border regions between the member states of Morocco, Mauritania, Libya, Algeria, and Tunisia.

With regard to the second category of developments, mention must be made of the series of initiatives among member states of the AMU. Other pertinent illustrations include the highly dramatized but no so well sustained initiative that Nigeria proposed to its immediate neighbours. This featured a series of bilateral workshops, the first being the resoundingly successful session with the Republic of Benin at Topo, Badagry, in May 1988. This session had the active participation of the territorial authorities and local communities from both the Nigerian and Beninese sides of Borgu. The Nigeria-Benin transborder cooperation policy initiative has since been followed by similar efforts with regard to Niger, Cameroon, and Equatorial Guinea.[35] A more systematic policy innovation in West Africa is the concept of *"pays frontières,"* recently launched by the Republic of Mali, aimed at promoting shared borderlands as areas of common concern for peace and sustainable development.[36]

Finally, there is the ongoing Research Project on the Development of Border Regions in Eastern and Southern Africa, initiated in 1992 by the United Nations Centre for Regional Development Africa Office in Nairobi, Kenya. This laudable project has featured two highly successful international workshops, one in Kariba, Zimbabwe, on the border with Zambia, in August 1995;[37] and the other in Mutare, also in Zimbabwe, on the border with Mozambique. Among the credits that this project can claim is a range of concrete developments in cross-border cooperative initiatives, including the launching in 1996 of a progressive local periodical entitled *Bridging the Borders: Kariba-Siavonga Newsletter* and published twice yearly. It is being very well received on both sides of the Zimbabwe-Zambia border. Also on the Kariba-Siavonga border sector, a bilateral steering committee has been established to accelerate the process for a general reorientation from a prevailing back-to-back to a more desirable face-to-face relationship between the local elites and the local authorities on both sides of the border.

Policy Recommendations

To sustain these admittedly modest developments, and to ensure their acceleration and spread, there is an obvious need for a radical reorientation of the mindset of postcolonial Africa's so-called inheritance elite. This calls for three interrelated recommendations:

1   an urgent action plan on the part of policy makers in Africa
2   a rededication of support on the part of African and Africanist research communities inside and outside the continent
3   appropriate assistance by donor communities, especially Friends of Africa in the EU and the North American Free Trade Area.

With regard to relevant policy decisions, the African Union as successor to the Organization of African Unity (OAU) must be specially targeted. Having maintained in its Consultative Act the provisions of the Charter of 1963 and the Cairo Declaration of 1964 to legitimize the inherited colonial boundaries in the interest of continental peace and stability, the AU must not permit itself to advance into the twenty-first century without taking the long overdue next logical step: that of ensuring the conversion of the inherited borders from their prevailing official postures as barriers into new dispositions as bridges between the member states. In so doing, the union stands to profit from the experience of Europe, erstwhile colonizer of Africa, where border problems similar to those in postcolonial Africa are being tackled with noticeable success. Especially recommended is the adoption of instruments of a continent-wide application, on the model of the European Outline Convention on Transfrontier Co-operation between Territorial Authorities and Communities, which took effect in 1984 and has since been ratified and adopted by an ever-increasing number of European states (notably Hungary and Poland) in the recently decolonized subregions of Central and Eastern Europe. The AU, possibly through the African Development Bank, should create an African Regional Development Fund on the analogy of the European Regional Development Fund (ERDF) and for purposes similar to the INTERREG program in Community Europe.

Second, African and Africanist researchers must shift emphasis from the traditional statist, and a predominantly conflictual, perspective and refocus on projects that emphasize peace and the cooperative and regional integration potentials of African boundaries. African research institutions outside the continent, such as the imaginative border-focused Program on International Co-operation in Africa (PICA) inaugurated at Northwestern University, Evanston, Illinois, in 1989, must collaborate actively with parallel institutions within Africa, such as the Centre for African Regional Integration and Border Studies recently established at the University of Lagos, in order to focus specially on the factor of boundaries with regard to regional integration both in Africa and in wider comparative contexts.

The final policy recommendation relates to the role expected of the wider international community, especially the EU, which embraces the erstwhile imperial and colonial powers who partitioned Africa, including Borgu, at the turn of the nineteenth century. Borgu offers a rare opportunity for postwar Europe to be specially sensitized not only to the wrongs done and the debts owed to formerly colonized Africa but also to the compelling moral duty to make necessary amends through establishing appropriate programs of assistance. It is in this regard that I make the following specific recommendations:

1   It is crucial to radically adjust the current practice of the International Monetary Fund and the World Bank, both of which support only

nationally based projects. This lending policy has tended to accord attention to the nation-state territorial structure and must be blended with increased support for regional and transborder development initiatives.

2   It is crucial that developed countries, especially those of the EU and NAFTA, actively support the repatriation of "ill-gotten wealth" invested by corrupt African leaders and government officials in their economies, especially the money markets and real estate sectors. This will boost transparency, a major component of democratic governance and a requirement for the realization of transfrontier regionalism in Africa.

3   It is crucial that the EU, especially the European Economic Commission, extend to Africa the same kind of funding support that it has extended to Eastern and Central Europe with regard to transfrontier regional development programs.

4   It is crucial to twin exemplar "Euregios" (e.g., Regio Basiliensi) with prospective African transfrontier regions such as Borgu.

I conclude this chapter by calling on the governments and peoples of Britain, France, and Germany,[38] and those European nation-states whose nationals were responsible wholly or in part for the arbitrary partition of Borgu and other fragmented peoples and cultures of Africa, to make such contributions that would accelerate their evolution as exemplar "Afregio's" on the model of the "Euregios" that, since the 1950s, have been nurtured across the borders of the European Metropolitan States – especially those of France and Germany, the emerging "Framany" of the EU.

Acknowledgment

An earlier version of this chapter was published in 1999, as Occasional Publication 12, by IFRA-Ibadan Institut Français de Recherche AFRIQUE-French Institute for Research in Africa, University of Ibadan. This institute partly funded my research. I gratefully acknowledge the support of IFRA and its encouragement for the present publication.

Notes

1   G. Vedovato, *Transfrontier Co-operation and the Europe of Tomorrow* (Strasbourg: Council of Europe, 1995), 2.

2   Ibid.

3   For sample essays on North and Latin America, see L. Lambi, "The Venezuela-Colombia Borderlands: A Regional and Historical Perspective," *Journal of Borderland Studies* 4, 1 (1989) 1-38; P. Ganster, "The Andean Border Integration: Report on a Seminar in Lima, Peru," *Journal of Borderland Studies* 5, 1 (1990): 95-110; and Niles Hansen, "European Transboundary Cooperation and Its Relevance to the United States-Mexico Border," *Journal of the American Institute of Planners* 49, 3 (1983): 336-43. For a reference to transfrontier regionalism in Asia, see W. Gooneratne and E. Mosselman, "Planning across the Borders: Border Regions in Eastern and Southern Africa," *Regional Development Dialogue* 7, 2 (1996): 136-55, esp. 148-49.

4 For the writer's antecedent writings on the subject of African potentials for transfrontier regionalism, see A.I. Asiwaju, *Artificial Boundaries* (Lagos: University of Lagos Press, 1984); A.I. Asiwaju, ed., *Partitioned Africans: Ethnic Relations Across Africa's International Boundaries, 1884-1984* (London: C. Hurst and Co., 1984); A.I. Asiwaju, "Borders and Borderlands as Linchpins for Regional Integration in Africa: Lessons of the European Experience," in *Africa Development* (Dakar: CODESRIA, 1992), xvii, 2, 345-63; and A.I Asiwaju, "Borderlands in Africa: A Comparative Research Perspective with Special Reference to Western Europe," in *African Boundaries: Barriers, Conduits and Opportunities*, ed. Paul Nugent and A.I. Asiwaju (London: Frances Pinter, 1996).

5 Vedovato, *Transfrontier Co-operation*, 3.

6 See Association of European Border Regions (AERB), European Charter on Frontier and Transborder Regions: Aims and Tasks of the Association of European Border Regions (AERB offices, Bonn). Among typical examples of organized Euroregions are the Regio Basiliensi, created in 1963, around the Swiss-French-German trinational conurbation of Basel. This is the nucleus of a larger transfrontier region that embraces the Swiss Jura, the German Black Forest, and the French Vosges. It covers a region of about two million inhabitants who commonly speak a local German dialect. For discussion, see H.J. Briner, "Regional Planning and Transfrontier Cooperation: The Regio Basiliensi," in *Across Boundaries: Transborder Interaction in Comparative Perspective*, ed. O.J. Martinez (El Paso: Western Texas Press, 1986). Then there is the Rhine-Waal Euregio, launched in 1970 to promote German-Dutch cooperation in the area along and across the binational boundary. The regional organization of the Central, the Eastern, and the Western Alpine regions connected Italy with particular Alpine neighbouring countries, including former communist Yugoslavia (in the case of the Alps Adria in the heyday of the Iron Curtain). In Northern Europe, where the Scandinavian countries (Denmark, Finland, Norway, and Sweden) have developed a series of bilateral and multilateral agreements to curb activities that could lead to the pollution of the air, soil, fresh water, and the sea, regions most advanced in transfrontier cooperation promotion include the North Calotte Area, the West Nordic Region, Archipelago Arko, Osfield-Bohus, the Orsund Canal and the Bornholm Southeastern Skane. See R. Strassoldo, "Perspective on Frontiers: The Case of Alpe Adria," in *The Frontiers of Europe*, ed. M. Anderson and E. Bort (London: Frances Pinter, 1998).

7 Examples include the Committee for the Promotion of the Alpine Region (headquarters in Turin, Italy) and the Conference of the Upper Rhine Valley Planners.

8 Examples include the Euroregions of the cities and municipalities; the Euroregion of the Chambers of Commerce, the Co-operation Agreement between Vice-Chancellors or Rectors of the Universities of Liege (France), Maastricht (Netherlands) and Aix-la-Chapelle (Germany), and the more imaginative International Scheldt Faculty linking higher education and applied research in Zeeland and Flanders.

9 Vedovato, *Transfrontier Co-operation*, 9-13.

10 Ibid.

11 See, in particular, Asiwaju, "Borderlands in Africa."

12 P. Sahlin, *Boundaries: The Making of France and Spain in the Pyrenees* (Berkeley: University of California Press, 1989).

13 A.I Asiwaju, *Western Yoruba and Under European Rule, 1889-1945: A Comparative Analysis of French and British Colonialism* (London: Longman, 1976); and W.R.S. Miles, *Hausaland Divided: Colonialism and Independence in Nigeria and Niger* (Ithaca, NY: Cornell University Press, 1994).

14 M. Foucher, "The Geopolitics of European Frontiers," in *The Frontiers of Europe*, ed. M. Anderson and E. Bort (London: Frances Pinter, 1998), 235.

15 Asiwaju, "Borders and Borderlands," 345-63.

16 See Asiwaju, *Partitioned Africans*.

17 For the detailed references, see Janet MacGaffee, ed., *The Real Economy of Zaire: The Contributions of Smuggling and Other Unofficial Activities to National Wealth* (Philadelphia: University of Philadelphia Press, 1991); C. Ackello-Ogutu and P.N. Echessah, *Unrecorderd Cross-Border Trade Between Tanzania and Her Neighbours: Implications for Food Security* (Nairobi, USAID Regional Economic Development Support Office, Draft Report, 1997).

18 Ibid.

19 Ibid.

20 This estimate is owed, at least partly, to Obare Bagodo, "Liens Ethniques et Systèmes de Chefferie Traditionelle Comme Element de Cooperation Transfrontalière des 'Bariba,'" in *The Nigerian-Benin Transborder Cooperation, Proceedings of a Bilateral Workshop,* ed. A.I. Asiwaju and J. Igue (Lagos: University of Lagos Press, 1994), 63.

21 See O.D. Akinwunmi, "The Nigerian Borgu, 1898-1989: A History of Inter-Group Relations" (PhD diss., University of Ilorin, 1995). Older relevant studies include M. Crowder, *Revolt in Bussa: A Study of British Native Administration in Nigerian Borgu, 1902-1934* (London: Faber and Faber, 1973); M.H. Stewart, "The Borgu People of Nigeria and Benin: The Disruptive Effects of Partition on Traditional Political and Economic Relations," *Journal of the Historical Society of Nigeria* 12, 4 (1984-85): 95-119; and K. Lupton, "The Partitioning of Borgu in 1989 and the French Enclaves in Nigeria," *Journal of the Historical Society of Nigeria* 12, 4 (1984-85): 77-94.

22 See J.C. Anene, *The International Boundaries of Nigeria: The Framework of an Emergent African Nation* (London: Longman, 1970), 194.

23 Ibid.

24 Lupton, "The Partitioning of Borgu."

25 Obare Bagodo, "Liens Ethniques et Systèmes de Chefferie Traditionelle Comme Element de Cooperation Transfrontalière des 'Bariba,'" in Egg and Igue, *Market Integration,* 63.

26 This kind of protest migration took place in 1907 when Woru Yaru, the dethroned Sarkin Yashikira, migrated with virtually the entire population of Yashikira to Nikki, where he eventually succeeded to the throne as the Sina Boko in 1917. Similar migrations took place from Kenu, Ilesha, and Aliyara in protest against British colonial arrangement, which forced chiefdoms formerly under Nikki to be subjected to new territorial authorities, especially that of the British-created Emirate of Kaiama.

27 To date, there are two conflicting definitions for this sector of the boundary: the Anglo-French Agreement of 1906, generally adjudged impossible to translate as a viable tool for the actual demarcation; and the modification reached by 1960 as a result of two preceding years of meetings between the surveyors-general of Nigeria and Dahomey, authorized by the two central governments. The demarcation of this sector of the boundary, based on the 1960 description, was initially contested by Dahomey and has remained controversial.

28 For a detailed case study see A.I. Asiwaju, "Formal Education in Western Yorubaland, 1889-1960: A Comparison of the French and British Colonial Systems," *Comparative Education Review* 19, 3 (1975): 434-50. See also "Educating the Hausa," in *Hausaland Divided: Colonialism and Independence in Nigeria and Niger,* W.F.S. Miles (Ithaca: Cornell University Press, 1995), 227-47.

29 R. Strassoldo, "Border Studies: The State of the Arts In Europe," in *Borderlands in Africa: A Multidisciplinary and Comparative Focus on Nigeria and West Africa,* ed. A.I. Asiwaju and P.O. Adeniyi (Lagos: University of Lagos Press, 1989). For a more systematic comparison of Africa, see A.I. Asiwaju, "Public Policy for Overcoming Marginalization: Borderlands in Africa, North America and Western Europe," in *Margins of Insecurity: Minorities and International Security,* ed. Sam Nolutshungu (New York: Rochester University Press, 1996).

30 See Strassoldo, *Border Studies,* 393.

31 See Anene, *International Boundaries of Nigeria,* 2.

32 See Strassoldo, *Border Studies,* 392.

33 Ibid.

34 See A.I. Asiwaju, "Fragmentation or Integration: What Future for African Boundaries?" in *Borderlands under Stress,* ed. M.A. Pratt and J.A. Brown (London: Kluwer Law International, 2000).

35 See A.I. Asiwaju and O.J. Igue, eds., *The Nigeria-Benin Transborder Cooperation: Proceedings of a Bilateral Workshop* (Lagos: University of Lagos Press, 1994); A.I. Asiwaju and B.M. Barkindo, eds., *The Nigeria-Niger Transborder Cooperation: Proceedings of a Bilateral Workshop* (Lagos: Malthouse Press, 1993); and A.I. Asiwaju, B.M. Bakindo, and R. Mabale, eds., *The Niger-Equatorial Guinea Transborder Cooperation: Proceedings of a Bilateral Workshop* (Lagos: National Boundary Commission, 1996).

36 See the *Rappport Général: Séminaire Sous-Regional sur le Concept de Pays Frontières* (Bamako: Ministère de l'Administration Territoriale et des Collectivités Légales-Direction Nationale des frontières, 2002).

37 The proceedings of the two workshops are contained in A.I. Asiwaju and Marlies de Leeuw, eds., *Border Region Development in Africa: Focus on Eastern and Southern Sub-Regions* (Nairobi: UN Center for Regional Development, 1998).

38 The three colonial powers showed interest in Borgu: Germany conceded the area to France as a result of the bilateral convention of 23 July 1897, whereby France, in return, conceded Kirikiri, Bafilo, and the so-called "Mono triangle" to German Togo. The Anglo-French Convention of 14 July 1898 settled the conflicting interest through a bilateral partition.

7
Trans-Maritime Boundary Cooperation in Southeast Asia: Eroding or Enhancing the Importance of International Boundaries?
Clive Schofield

The Rationale for Cooperation

It is undeniable that many marine resources are transnational both by nature and in their distribution. Many maritime activities are also inherently transboundary in character. Moreover, the ocean environment, as a continuous, fluid system, transmits pollutants and the consequences of states' actions without regard for national jurisdictional limits.[1] The practical importance and desirability of cooperation is therefore clear-cut. This chapter examines the rise of such regional and subregional cooperative mechanisms in Southeast Asia, which is host to several noteworthy examples of bi- and multilateral cooperation in the maritime sphere, especially maritime joint development zones. Additionally, fisheries cooperation and conflict in the Gulf of Thailand serves as a case study of the challenges involved in realizing transboundary maritime cooperation in the region. The chapter is set within the context of the opportunities and challenges afforded by globalization and worldwide trends in environmental and resource security, and it points towards the impact of these processes on the significance and functions of international maritime boundaries in the region.

Opportunities and Obligations

The legal rationale for transboundary cooperation can be drawn from the UN Convention on the Law of the Sea (UNCLOS). Cues can also be taken from Chapter 17 of Agenda 21, arising from the UN Conference on Environment and Development (UNCED). These documents call for cooperation, coordination, and the harmonization of approaches with respect to a wide variety of ocean management issues.

The list of areas where cooperation is required under UNCLOS is, however, daunting, covering such phenomena as marine scientific research and management of living resources. This includes fishing, marine environmental protection, environmental monitoring and response, search and rescue efforts, and safety of navigation.

Furthermore, Article 123, dealing with cooperation of states bordering enclosed and semi-enclosed seas, provides even more stringent requirements relevant to much of Southeast Asia. It requires that:

States bordering an enclosed or semi-enclosed sea should cooperate with each other in the exercise of their rights and in the performance of their duties under this Convention. To this end they shall endeavour, directly or through an appropriate regional organization:

a to coordinate the management, conservation, exploration and exploitation of the living resources of the sea;

b to coordinate the implementation of their rights and duties with respect to the protection and preservation of the marine environment;

c to coordinate their scientific research polices and undertake where appropriate joint programmes of scientific research in the area;

d to invite, as appropriate, other interested States or international organizations to cooperate with them in the furtherance of the provisions of this article.

This requirement represents recognition that the biophysical and natural resource characteristics of semi-enclosed seas are more sensibly regarded as "shared" entities, or as "a subregional commons," than as partitioned entities.[2]

As a number of commentators have observed, there is a tension between these requirements and traditional concepts of state sovereignty.[3] It should, however, be remembered that, in ocean affairs, obligations and opportunities are two sides of the same coin. At the conclusion of the Third Conference on the Law of the Sea, the president observed that, while the fundamental aim of the conference was to produce a comprehensive and lasting *"constitution for the oceans,"* he went on to make it explicit that

the provisions of the Convention are closely interrelated and form an integral package. Thus it is not possible for a State to pick what it likes and to disregard what it does not like ... rights and obligations go hand in hand and it is not permissible to claim rights under the Convention without being willing to shoulder the corresponding obligations.[4]

In essence there is a distinction between approaches that tend to emphasize *responsibilities* in the public interest for environmental and resource management purposes, and approaches that tend to give priority to *statist entitlements*. Central to any discussion concerning subregional and transborder cooperation is the question of whether the states concerned are willing to accept a compromise that involves a balance between *sovereign* entitlement and environmental responsibility.[5] In the Southeast Asian context it is generally fair to say that states have exhibited a preference for acquiring rights rather than responsibilities.

It is also worth observing that, while the obligation for states to cooperate on ocean resource management issues, particularly in the context of enclosed and semi-enclosed seas, is quite clear, it is unclear what is actually meant by the term "cooperation."

Joint Development Zones

Perhaps the most obvious instances of transboundary cooperation in Southeast Asia are the maritime joint development zones hosted by the region. These arrangements represent the most significant innovative form of functionalist-oriented dispute resolution, or at least deferral, that has developed over recent years. Joint development arrangements are encouraged under UNCLOS. Both Articles 74(3) and 83(3), dealing with the delimitation of the exclusive economic zone and continental shelf, respectively, state:

> Pending agreement as provided for in paragraph 1, the States concerned, in a spirit of understanding and cooperation, shall make every effort to enter into provisional arrangements of a practical nature and, during this transitional period, not to jeopardize or hamper the reaching of the final agreement. Such arrangements shall be without prejudice to the final delimitation.

Joint development zones have been heralded as a means of overcoming seemingly intractable maritime boundary disputes, where the parties concerned inflexibly cling to overlapping claims. In this situation, where there appears to be no prospect of agreement on a boundary line in the foreseeable future, it has been argued that joint development agreements seem to offer an ideal way forward. As Richardson noted in his influential article, if the parties agree to such an arrangement, "the focus would be placed where it belonged: on a fair division of the resources at stake, rather than on the determination of an artificial line, thus ... eliminating competition over the ownership of resources ... especially where the resources are unknown."[6]

The rationale behind this contention is that such cooperative arrangements are entirely logical – allowing states to retain their claims unaltered in principle and to proceed with desired offshore development (e.g., of oil and gas resources) or fisheries management. Joint development zones have also been welcomed as evidence of the emergence of a more broad-based, functionalist, and comprehensive approach to ocean management as opposed to more traditional legalistic and, thus, confrontational approaches focusing on the definition of a particular dividing line.[7] Additionally, the drawing of a definitive boundary line can be regarded as a "once and for all" process and can represent something of a lottery with regard to undiscovered resources. With a joint zone, lack of knowledge as to the precise location of resources assumes less importance and no longer acts as a deterrent to resolution; instead, both sides can be confident that a fair and equitable sharing has been achieved – no "winners" and "losers" should therefore emerge from such arrangements.

Conversely, it seems inappropriate to promote joint development arrangements simply because the parties to a dispute have proved unable to resolve their differences over overlapping maritime claims. Furthermore, the practical task of establishing and maintaining such potentially dauntingly complex arrangements should not be underestimated as this requires considerable political commitment from all parties. Joint development zones cannot, therefore, be divorced from the overall political context between the states involved. As Stormont and Townsend-Gault maintain, joint development should not be suggested lightly: "The conclusion of any joint development arrangement, in the absence of the appropriate level of consent between the parties, is merely redrafting the problem and possibly complicating it further."[8]

Similarly, Jagota has noted that "sensitive security conditions in the area, incompatible political relations between the disputants, vertical or dependent economic relations, reluctance to transfer technology or to co develop [sic] technology, and other similar inconsistencies may generate resistance to joint development zones, with or without a maritime boundary."[9] Nevertheless, it is clear that emerging state practice appears to favour joint development arrangements and that this accords with the evolving general duty of states to facilitate optimum ocean management. As such, joint development arrangements do offer a functional, flexible, and equitable way forward for states with seemingly intractable disputes over overlapping maritime claims with their neighbours. Such a practical, problem-solving approach, with the emphasis firmly placed on promoting interstate cooperation and effective ocean resource development and management, must be considered welcome and is likely to prove of increasing significance in the future. At least twenty-two such zones have come into being around the world to date and are not confined to a particular geographical region, although Southeast Asia is well represented.[10]

Southeast Asia is host to five fully fledged joint development agreements:

- Japan-South Korea Agreement of 30 January 1974
- Australia-Papua New Guinea: Torres Strait, 1978
- Malaysia-Thailand Memorandum of Understanding of 21 February 1979 (see Map 7.1)

- Australia-East Timor Timor Sea Treaty of May 2002 (largely based on the now defunct Australia-Indonesia Treaty of 11 December 1989)
- Malaysia-Vietnam Memorandum of Understanding of 5 June 1992 (see Map 7.1).

Additionally, a further joint arrangement exists in respect of the Cambodia-Vietnam Historic Waters Agreement. Further to this, in June 2001 Cambodia and Thailand signed a Memorandum of Understanding committing them to delimitation coupled with the establishment of a joint development zone in their large area of overlapping claims in the central Gulf of Thailand, although no formal agreement to date has been forthcoming (see Map 7.1).

The latter development is potentially highly significant because Thailand had, in the course of negotiations spanning years, previously been extremely reluctant to consider joint development with Cambodia. Indeed, Thailand resisted joint zone proposals in its maritime boundary negotiations with Vietnam, successfully holding out for a delimitation solution instead. This negative attitude towards joint development probably stems from the difficulties experienced in implementing the Thai-Malaysian joint development area. In the end, however, the potential benefits of joint development seem to have overcome Thai reluctance, as has been demonstrated by successful exploration activities in both the Thai-Malaysian JDA and Malaysia-Vietnam "Defined Area." Indeed, the estimated eleven trillion cubic feet of gas reserves in the Thai-Malaysian JDA have been touted by both governments concerned as providing the foundation for their economic recovery.

Together these agreements make Southeast Asia a place where it is possible to find one of the leading concentrations of state practice in joint development worldwide. However, as cooperative transboundary measures these arrangements are subject to significant restrictions. With the notable exception of the Torres Strait Treaty, the joint zones established in Southeast Asia are unifunctional in nature. They are concentrated on seabed resource exploration and exploitation – essentially a drive for oil and gas resources – to the benefit of participating states. National rights rather than responsibilities are therefore the motivation for these cooperative efforts.

The establishment of joint zones does not indicate that the states involved have, in principle, compromised over their sovereignty claims. The agreements on joint development are generally without prejudice to such claims (in legal parlance they are "sovereignty neutral"); they are often strictly temporary in nature, being bound by a time limit, and frequently include a commitment to continue to seek a delimitation through the area of overlapping claims forming the joint zone.

Fishing

The Gulf of Thailand is an example of joint development initiatives in Southeast Asia. The gulf has traditionally been an important source of fish for all the littoral states.[11] However, rising demand for fish from increasing coastal populations for food, as well as for export, has resulted in rapid increases in marine fishery production.[12] In the 1970s Thailand emerged as a major commercial fishing nation, ranked among the top ten in the world, with a significant distant-water fishing fleet (the largest in Southeast Asia) accustomed to fishing throughout the Andaman Sea and South

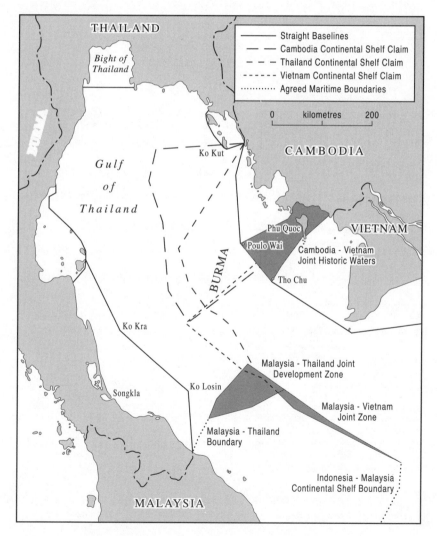

Map 7.1   Maritime boundary delimitation in the Gulf of Thailand.

China Sea as well as the Gulf of Thailand.[13] Fish products therefore became an important facet of the Thai economy.[14] Fisheries development in Malaysia also gathered pace from the 1960s onward (albeit largely outside the Gulf of Thailand), while that of Cambodia and Vietnam has lagged behind, gaining momentum only since the 1980s.[15] As a result of these developments, the total fishery catch of the four littoral states was estimated at 5.95 million tonnes for 1996, having achieved an average annual increase of a startling 4.9 percent per annum in the period from 1988 to 1994.[16]

Mohamed describes the threat of overfishing in the Gulf of Thailand as "real and ominous."[17] This assessment is backed up with analysis showing dramatic declines in catch per unit effort (CPUE) in the gulf, indicating that overfishing is evident.[18] If the trends outlined continue unchecked, then the possibility of the eventual collapse of fisheries in the Gulf of Thailand must be addressed. The need for strict ecosystem-wide, and therefore transboundary, management of these threatened resources is incontrovertible.[19]

Illegal fishing has proved a particularly poisonous issue in relations between the Gulf of Thailand coastal states and has generated a considerable body of literature devoted to the problem.[20] The main problem appears to stem from activities by Thai fishers, but incidents have also occurred between the other Gulf of Thailand states, particularly involving

Table 7.1

Fish catch and per capita consumption of the Gulf of Thailand coastal states

Country	Total catch (tonnes)	Catch in Gulf of Thailand	Percentage of catch in the gulf	Consumption (kg/capita)
Cambodia	103,200	30,960[1]	1.2[1]	21.6
Malaysia	1,181,763	–	–	36.6
Thailand	3,522,233	2,297,575	89.8	34.6
Vietnam	1,150,000	230,000[2]	8.99	12.5
Total/Average	5,957,196	2,558,535		26.3[3]

Source: Mohd. Ibrahim Hj. Mohamed, "Overfishing in the Gulf of Thailand: Issues and Resolution," in *Integrated Studies of the Gulf of Thailand*, vol. 2, ed. D.M. Johnston (Bangkok: Southeast Asian Programme on Ocean Law, Policy and Management [SEAPOL], 1998), 4.

1 Based on 30 percent of Cambodia's catch being composed of marine fish according to Sour and Vuthy (1997), as referred to in Mohamed, "Overfishing," 24.

2 Based on a 20 percent contribution to Vietnam's total catch from its southwestern region, according to Pham Thouc and Huy Son (1997), as referred to in Mohamed, "Overfishing," 24.

3 This compares with average global consumption per capita of 14.5 kg. See D. Menavesta, Fisheries Management Needs and Prospects for the Countries Bordering the Gulf of Thailand," in *Integrated Studies of the Gulf of Thailand*, vol. 1, ed. D.M. Johnston (Bangkok: SEAPOL, 1998), 53.

Malaysia and Vietnam. The key causes of fisheries conflicts between Thailand (and, to a lesser extent, Malaysia) and its maritime neighbours have been identified as being:

- *The development and implementation of the EEZ concept* – This must be viewed as the crucial factor in generating fisheries conflict in the Gulf of Thailand. The declaration of exclusive economic zones (EEZs) by Thailand's neighbours placed large maritime areas traditionally fished by Thai fleets out of bounds. It has been estimated that this development has entailed a loss to Thailand of around 300,000 square kilometres of fishing grounds formerly used by Thai fishers.[21]
- *Fishing capacity* – Thailand's large fishing fleet, 85 percent of which is based on Thailand's Gulf of Thailand coast, was faced with the fact that Thai waters had been subject to overfishing and had been effectively "fished out," while those of its neighbours, where Thai fishers had in any case traditionally fished, were relatively plentiful.[22] In McDorman's words, the temptation for Thai fishers to stray into Cambodian, Malaysian, or Vietnamese waters in these circumstances was "very great."[23] As a result it has been estimated that as much as 30 percent to 40 percent of Thailand's marine catch has come from outside Thai waters.[24] As time has progressed it is also clear that Thailand's neighbours have enhanced their own fishing capacities, resulting in increased friction with "poaching" Thai vessels.
- *Maritime boundary disputes* – Uncertainties over the limits of jurisdiction of the Gulf of Thailand states because of overlapping continental shelf claims and reticence concerning the limits of EEZ claims have clearly contributed to disputes over access to fisheries.
- *Politics* – As McDorman has noted, "fishery conflicts between Thailand and its Indochinese neighbours were intensified by the broader bilateral animosity" between the communist regimes of Cambodia and Vietnam and Thailand.[25]
- *Fisheries regulation and enforcement* – In the wake of making EEZ declarations, the Gulf of Thailand states have sought to enact legislation designed to protect and conserve the resources therein. Of particular note here is Malaysia's Fisheries Act of May 1985.[26] This legislation appears to have been framed with Thai fishing activities in mind, and its strict enforcement resulted in countless seizures of Thai fishing vessels and arrests of Thai fishers.[27] The Malaysian act requires fishing vessels in transit through Malaysian waters to give prior notification to the Malaysian authorities to stow their gear and to proceed without lingering. Failure to do so automatically gives rise to a presumption that illegal fishing has been undertaken or attempted.

Thailand has protested against these provisions, arguing that they seriously undermine freedom of navigation and that they are inconsistent with the relevant provisions of UNCLOS.[28] These incidents have also repeatedly led to violent clashes between Thai fishers and Malaysian coastguards.[29] In the mid-1980s and 1990s, therefore, the fisheries issue proved the most significant strain on relations between Malaysia and Thailand. Over time all the Gulf of Thailand states have sought to increase their surveillance and enforcement capabilities, resulting in an enhanced likelihood of confrontation between suspected illegal fishers and the coastal state authorities.[30]

With the notable exception of improved political relations between Cambodia and Vietnam and the other gulf states, none of the factors contributing to conflict over fisheries in the Gulf of Thailand has been removed or even very significantly reduced. EEZs are now clearly established in international maritime law, and Thailand has reluctantly been forced to acknowledge that reality. Thailand has complained bitterly that its acceptance of the EEZ concept was "conditional upon the equitable sharing of the living resources in the zone between the coastal States and developing countries which had traditionally or habitually exercised in the EEZ areas that had previously been the high seas the right of exploitation of the living resources."[31]

However, the key provisions of UNCLOS dealing with this issue, contained in Articles 61 and 62 (whereby once a state has determined the total allowable catch [TAC] within its waters and its own harvesting capacity, "where the coastal State does not have the capacity to harvest the entire allowable catch, it shall ... give other States access to the surplus of the allowable catch"),[32] have failed to address Thai concerns and requirements. This is because "even under the strict wording of the LOS Convention, the coastal state has discretion in determining domestic harvesting capacity, resource surpluses, and to whom and upon what terms the surpluses would be distributed to other states."[33] In any case, none of the Gulf of Thailand littoral states (including Thailand) has adopted TAC in their fisheries management practices.[34]

Additionally, Thailand in particular has failed to address the problem of fishing capacity, which is described as the "key to the reduction and elimination of future fishery conflicts in the Gulf of Thailand,"[35] and to regulate the Thai fishing industry effectively – a problem that the Thai government has itself recognized.[36] In McDorman's words: "A reduced Thai fishing effort, ... containment within Thai waters, or access agreements rely upon the Government of Thailand obtaining and exercising a degree of control over the Thai fishing industry that is currently unimaginable."[37]

Fundamentally, the profitability of illegal fishing activities, despite the escalating risks posed both by Thai efforts at regulation and the increasing efforts of the other Gulf of Thailand states to enforce their rights, argues against swift resolution of the problem. Furthermore, extensive areas of overlapping claims to jurisdiction in the Gulf of Thailand persist, the littoral states have remained guarded concerning the precise extent of their EEZ claims, and tension continues to be generated over Malaysia's enforcement of its controversial fisheries regulations.

Some encouragement can, however, be gleaned from private joint ventures into which Thai companies have entered with their counterparts in other Gulf of Thailand coastal states, giving Thai fishers legal access to fishery resources in other states' EEZs.[38] Furthermore, progress has recently been made on joint management of fish stocks, including joint survey work, and on joint patrolling operations. For instance, Thailand and Vietnam agreed in principle on joint patrols in the overlapping claims area in April 1996.[39] The two states have also established a Thai-Vietnamese Joint Commission on Fisheries and Law and Order at Sea and, in the wake of their August 1997 maritime boundary agreement, have agreed to conduct a joint survey of fisheries resources in their formerly disputed area.[40] In addition, the Thai and Vietnamese navies reached agreement in May 1998 on procedures for joint maritime boundary patrols.[41] Similarly, Malaysia and Thailand have in the past established join patrols under the auspices of their Joint General Border Committees,[42] and Thailand and Cambodia agreed to undertake joint maritime patrols in July 1998.[43]

Prospects for, and Limitations on, Trans-Maritime Boundary Cooperation in Southeast Asia

There is general agreement among marine policy experts and practitioners that trans-maritime boundary cooperation and management is essential and even inevitable – a stance fully supported by UNCLOS. Undoubtedly, the political and legal frameworks for significant transborder cooperation are very often based on and shaped by international agreements, and are often the culmination of lengthy processes of bi-, tri-, or multilateral negotiations at the level of states and the appropriate official bodies thereof. This has certainly been the case for transboundary cooperative endeavours in Southeast Asia.

Nevertheless, central governments are not always or necessarily the major players in the formation and development of transborder cooperation. In Europe, North America, and other parts of the world, there are a variety of localized mechanisms of cooperation on substantive economic, social, environmental, and resource issues that have arisen as a result of what can best be described as processes of "subnational paradiplomacy." These are cases where transborder cooperation is largely the result of interaction between actors and agencies at the level of local provinces, districts, or municipalities rather than formal international or interstate relations.

In other cases, ingenious forms of local-level transboundary cooperation have been created and developed within a broad framework established by agreement between two or more states. The fact that there are often several mechanisms and institutions within one specific borderland and subregion suggests that there are many shapes, forms, and functions to subregional institutionalization, and that a whole variety of appropriate players can be involved. Indeed, the notion of transboundary regionalism necessitates the creation of multiple forms of cross-border linkage and multiple levels of transboundary institutionalization.

Such subnational efforts to promote transboundary cooperation are, however, in their infancy in Southeast Asia. State elites are still aloof from these processes. Furthermore, there are all too often close vested interests between government officials and big business in the resource sectors, which undermine efforts aimed, for example, at achieving long-term environmental management.

State sensitivities over issues of boundaries, sovereignty, and compromises to their national jurisdiction have been highlighted by SEAPOL's painstaking progress in encouraging the Gulf of Thailand states to adopt some form of cooperative management framework, such as a Gulf of Thailand Commission. Despite the apparently compelling arguments that can be made in favour of such a body, there remains considerable suspicion among the governments concerned with regard to the need for another international body in the region. Particular worries include costs in terms of finance and personnel and reluctance to contemplate compromises in national sovereignty.

However, does this abiding fixation on the part of governments with boundaries and the limits of sovereignty necessarily forestall maritime cooperation? As mentioned, the marine environment and its resources clearly transcend national maritime claims and tend to frustrate exclusively national attempts to address them. Uncertainty over jurisdictional limits inevitably exacerbates these problems, leading to uncoordinated policies that, in turn, can result in destructive competition for resources and ultimately to political tension. The severe overfishing that afflicts the Gulf of Thailand can be viewed as symptomatic of this trend: it has led to numerous armed clashes, including fatalities, and has soured diplomatic relations. The short- and long-term economic, environmental, and political impacts of these conflicts may be extremely serious.

Rather than attempting to remove boundaries and sovereignty issues from the equation, an alternative way to look at fostering maritime cooperation is to view maritime boundary delimitation as an opportunity to remove a potentially explosive issue from bilateral agendas, facilitating subsequent transboundary management of resources. In Southeast Asia and elsewhere around the world these problems, particularly relating to fisheries and pollution, are likely to multiply in the future as a function of increasing coastal populations, economic development, escalating resource requirements, and the associated pressures that this places on the marine environment. The littoral states' desire to gain access to ocean resources is likewise set to increase. This situation *demands* the delimitation of maritime boundaries as a prelude to collaborative and peaceful management of the littoral states' shared resources, environment, and heritage.

Maritime boundary delimitation can therefore be viewed as an essential precursor to the full realization of the resource potential of ocean space and its peaceful management. With regard to seabed resources that could prove crucial to the well-being and political stability of the economically disadvantaged countries surrounding the gulf, extensive overlapping claims areas forestall development while maritime boundaries remain unsettled. The rational exploitation and preservation of the important living resources of the Gulf of Thailand is similarly undermined by failure to address jurisdictional issues in a comprehensive and cooperative manner. According to this admittedly optimistic perspective, the delimitation of maritime boundaries could, in fact, act as a catalyst to transboundary cooperation with the boundaries themselves acting more as tools for environmental and resource management than as barriers to cooperation.

Notes

1 George Kent and Mark J. Valencia, eds., *Marine Policy in Southeast Asia* (Berkeley: University of California Press, 1985), 369.
2 Indeed, the precautionary principle, when applied to semi-enclosed seas and to coastal zones divided by political boundaries, necessitates that contiguous states make appropriate efforts to collect and share enormous amounts of scientific, socioeconomic, and other relevant data. In order to prevent long-term environmental harm and to manage resources more sustainably it may also be necessary to create new mechanisms for managing the gulf as a subregional unit. Evidence from other parts of the world, including the Gulf of Maine, the Baltic Sea, and the Mediterranean Sea, all point to the desirability of subregional institutional mechanisms for improving resource management.
3 For example, Ian Townsend-Gault, "Regional Maritime Cooperation Post-UNCLOS/UNCED: Do Boundaries Matter Any More?" in *International Boundaries and Environmental Security*, ed. G.H. Blake (London: Kluwer Law International, 1997), 3.
4 Tommy T.B. Koh, "A Constitution for the Oceans," introduction to UN Convention on the Law of the Sea, <http://www.un.org/Depts/los/convention_agreements/texts/koh_english.pdf>, p. xxxiv.
5 This delicate balance has already been faced by states in several other areas of the world. Indeed, transboundary agencies are often grappling with similar dilemmas, but their very existence shows that states are at least willing to compromise a little of their sovereign entitlements in order to reap the benefits of shared responsibilities.
6 E.L. Richardson, "Jan Mayen in Perspective," *American Journal of International Law* 82 (1988): 443-58.
7 D. Ong, "Southeast Asian State practice on the Joint Development of Offshore Oil and Gas Deposits," in *The Peaceful Management of Transboundary Resources*, ed. G. Blake, W. Hildesley, M.A. Pratt, R. Ridley, and C.H. Schofield (London: Graham and Trotman,

1995), 91; and S.P. Jagota, "Maritime Boundary and Joint Development Zones: Emerging Trends," *Ocean Yearbook* vol. 10 (Chicago: University of Chicago Press, 1993), 114.

8   W.G. Stormont and Ian Townsend-Gault, "Offshore Petroleum Joint Development Arrangements: Functional Instrument? Compromise? Obligation?" in Blake, *Peaceful Management*, 52.

9   Jagota, "Maritime Boundary," 117.

10 C.H. Schofield and Martin Pratt, "Cooperation in the Absence of Maritime Boundary Agreements: The Purpose and Value of Joint Development," in *The Aegean Sea 2000: Proceedings of the International Symposium on the Aegean Sea* (Bodrum, Turkey: 2000), 152-64.

11 J.R.V. Prescott, *The Gulf of Thailand* (Kuala Lumpur: MIMA, 1998), 11; and D.J. Dzurek, "Boundary and Resource Disputes in the South China Sea," *Ocean Yearbook* vol. 5 (Chicago: University of Chicago Press, 1985), 264-65, describe the countries bordering the South China Sea as a whole as being "extraordinarily dependent" upon the fisheries of the region, obtaining 13 percent of their protein from marine products in comparison to 3 percent for the United States. For a review of fisheries throughout Southeast Asia, see E.D. Samson, "Fisheries," in Valencia and Kent, *Marine Policy in Southeast Asia*, 101-54.

12 Mohd. Ibrahim Hj. Mohamed, "Overfishing in the Gulf of Thailand: Issues and Resolution," in *Integrated Studies of the Gulf of Thailand*, vol, 2, ed. D.M. Johnston (Bangkok: Southeast Asian Programme on Ocean Law, Policy and Management [SEAPOL], 1998), 4.

13 See T.L. McDorman, "Thailand and the 1982 Law of the Sea Convention," *Marine Policy* (October 1985): 298; "International Fishery Relations in the Gulf of Thailand," *Contemporary Southeast Asia* 12, 1 (1990): 41; and "Thai Fisheries and Fishing Industry: Its Development and Prospects with Regard to the 1982 UN Convention on the Law of the Sea," in *The United Nations Convention on the Law of the Sea in Southeast Asia: Problems of Implementation* (Bangkok: SEAPOL, 1991), 37-93. See also M. Torell, "Thailand's Fishing Industry: Future Prospects," in *Ocean Yearbook* vol. 7 (Chicago: University of Chicago Press, 1988), 144.

14 By 1984 the export of fishery products from Thailand accounted for almost 9 percent of Thailand's total exports. See also M. Torell, "Thailand's Fishing Industry," 132.

15 D. Menavesta, "Fisheries Management Needs and Prospects for the Countries Bordering the Gulf of Thailand," in *Integrated Studies of the Gulf of Thailand*, vol. 1, ed. D.M. Johnston (Bangkok: SEAPOL, 1998), 209. Nevertheless, it has been estimated that the fisheries sector accounts for up to 5 percent of Cambodia's gross domestic product. See Cambodia/UNEP, *Cambodia: First State of the Environment Report* (Phnom Penh: Ministry of the Environment of the Royal Government of Cambodia and the United Nations Environment Programme, 1994), 105. See M.J. Valencia, *Malaysia and the Law of the Sea* (Kuala Lumpur: Institute of Strategic and International Studies, 1991), 5-8, in relation to Malaysian fishing activities.

16 Mohd. Ibrahim Hj. Mohamed, "Overfishing in the Gulf of Thailand," 6.

17 Ibid., 3. It should be stressed that this problem is by no means exclusive to the Gulf of Thailand. Indeed, most marine fisheries around the world are in danger of severe depletion, with the UN's Food and Agriculture Organization (FAO) estimating that eleven of the world's fifteen major fishing areas and 69 percent of the world's main fish species are in decline. See A.P. McGinn, "Promoting Sustainable Fisheries," in *State of the World 1998* (London: Worldwatch Institute, Earthscan, 1998), 60. See also P. Weber, "Net Loss: Fish, Jobs and the Marine Environment," in *Worldwatch Paper 120* (Washington, DC, 1994). See also K.I. Matics, "Development of the Mekong River and Law: Some Environmental Problems," in Blake, *International Boundaries and Environmental Security;* E.D. Samson, "Fisheries," in *Marine Policy in Southeast Asia*, ed. G. Kent and M.J. Valencia (Berkeley: University of California Press, 1985), 101-54; and P. Tangsubkul, *ASEAN and the Law of the Sea* (Singapore: Institute of Southeast Asian Studies, Tangsubkul, 1982) for assessments of the prospect for Southeast Asia as a whole.

18 According to Mohd. Ibrahim Hj. Mohamed, "Overfishing in the Gulf of Thailand," 3, long-term systematic surveys by the Thai Department of Fisheries indicates that the daytime CPUE has declined from 290 kg/hr in 1963 to approximately 50 kg/hr in 1993, while the nighttime CPUE has declined from 57 kg/hr in 1976 to 21 kg/hr in 1995 – less than half its previous value. The same author states that these findings are also supported by surveys conducted in Vietnamese waters.

19 For an overview of transboundary fishery management needs in Southeast Asia, see G.R. Munro, "Fishery Diplomacy in the 1990s: The Challenges and Constraints," in *SEAPOL International Workshop on Challenges to Fishery Policy and Diplomacy in Southeast Asia: Selected Papers,* ed. K.I. Matics and T.L McDorman (Bangkok: SEAPOL, 1993), 3-10; and A. Soegiarto, "Sustainable Development of Fisheries in Southeast Asia," in *SEAPOL International Workshop,* 11-18.

20 See, for example, C. Ake-uru, "Thailand and the Law of the Sea," in *The Law of the Sea: Problems from the East Asian Perspective,* ed. C. Park and J.K. Park (Honolulu: The Law of the Sea Institute, University of Hawaii, 1987), 414-25; B.A. Hamzah, "Malaysia and the Law of the Sea: Post-UNCLOS III Issues," in Park, *The Law of the Sea,* 356-71; Hamzah, *Malaysia's Exclusive Economic Zone: A Study in Legal Aspects* (Selangor: Pelanduk Publications, 1988); Hamzah, "Malaysia," in *Regional Maritime Management and Security,* ed. S. Bateman and S. Bates (Canberra: Strategic and Defence Studies Centre, Australian National University, 1998), 51-60; K. Kittichaisaree, *The Law of the Sea and Maritime Boundary Delimitation in South-East Asia* (Oxford: Oxford University Press, 1987); Kittichaisaree, "Development of Ocean Law, Policy and Management in Thailand," *Marine Policy* (July 1990): 315-33; and T.L. McDorman, "Thailand's Fisheries: A Victim of 200-Mile Zones," *Ocean Development and International Law* 16, 2 (1986): 183-209.

21 McDorman, "Thailand's Fisheries," 183. In contrast, C. Ake-uru, "Thailand and the Law of the Sea," 418, puts the figure at "300,000 square miles."

22 See McDorman, "International Fishery Relations," 42. McDorman has also commented that the Thai fishers' retreat to Thai waters in the Gulf of Thailand "led immediately to serious overfishing and the grave potential of severely damaging the stocks that were already in a poor state."

23 Ibid., 42.

24 Ake-uru, "Thailand and the Law of the Sea," 418; Kittichaisaree, *The Law of the Sea;* Kittichaisaree, "Development of Ocean Law, Policy and Management in Thailand," 315-23; Asian Development Bank, *Thailand Fisheries Sector Study* (Manila: Asian Development Bank, 1985), 72, qtd. in Torell, "Thai Fisheries and Fishing Industry," 134-36.

25 McDorman, "International Fishery Relations," 46. An appreciation of the scale of the problem is provided by the fact that, during the period between 1983 and 1986 alone, Vietnam arrested and detained 1,000 Thai fishers. See M.J. Valencia and J.M. Van Dyke, "Vietnam's National Interests and the Law of the Sea," *Ocean Development and International Law* 25 (1984): 231.

26 For a copy, see B.A. Hamzah, *Malaysia's Exclusive Economic Zone: A Study in Legal Aspects* (Selangor: Pelanduk Publications, 1988), 53-95.

27 For example, in the three-year period following the enactment of the Malaysian fishery legislation (1985-87), Malaysia arrested 178 Thai vessels (see McDorman, "International Fishery Relations," 46).

28 For example, Thailand formally protested the Malaysian Fisheries Act, 1985, in a memorandum dated 15 December 1987 (see Kittichaisaree, "Development of Ocean Law," 321). It is also highly likely that Thailand had Malaysia in mind when it issued its Statement of the Ministry of Foreign Affairs to the UN Secretary-General, 3 May 1993 (copy on file with the author). Kittichaisaree, "Development of Ocean Law, Policy and Management in Thailand," 321, described the Malaysian act's provisions as "not well-found in international law and ... impractical"; he also found the requirement of prior notice to be unreasonable and excessive. In contrast, B. Hamzah, *Malaysia's Exclusive Economic Zone,* 1988, has offered a robust defence of Malaysia's fisheries legislation, concluding that the core issue is the sovereign right of a nation to explore and exploit, conserve and manage its natural resources: "Malaysia, as a sovereign nation, cannot be coerced or intimidated to give up its rights to others no matter what the pretext may be" (2). See also Valencia, "National Marine Interests in Southeast Asia," in Kent and Valencia, *Marine Policy,* 33-57; and R. Haller-Trost, "Some Comments on the Territorial Sea," *Ocean Yearbook* vol. 12 (Chicago: University of Chicago Press, 1996), 328-32.

29 For example, in one of the worst incidents in recent years, in early November 1995 a clash between a Malaysian patrol boat and a Thai trawler led to two Thai fishers being shot dead. This provoked a furious response from the Thai fishing community, who variously

threatened to go on strike and blockade key ports in order to pressure the Thai government to resolve the problem. The incident even led the director-general of the Thai Fisheries Department, Plodprasob Surassawadee, to threaten to lead a Thai fishing fleet into Malaysian waters in protest (*Bangkok Post,* 29-30 November 1995, 27 December 1995; *The Nation,* 10 November 1995, 28-29 November 1995, 1 December 1995, 5 December 1995, 20 December 1995). Such incidents are also not unique to Thai-Malaysian fisheries relations. For instance, it was reported in early June 1995 that a Thai naval vessel had exchanged fire with three armed Vietnamese boats (believed to belong to the Vietnamese navy) that had allegedly attacked several Thai trawlers, leaving one Thai and two Vietnamese sailors dead (*Bangkok Post,* 4 June 1995; *The Nation,* 2-4 June 1995).

30 For example, in July 1999 Vietnam issued a decree on the management of fishing activities by foreigners and, in the following month, established a marine police force to enforce the decree's provisions. VNA news agency, Hanoi, 16 July 1999, 31 August 1999 (SWB FE/3282 and 3321).
31 Kittichaisaree, "Development of Ocean Law," 316.
32 UNCLOS, Article 62.
33 McDorman, "International Fishery Relations," 42.
34 Menasveta, "Fisheries Management Needs," 209.
35 McDorman, "International Fishery Relations," 50.
36 McDorman, "Thailand's Fisheries: A Victim of 200-Mile Zones," 51.
37 Ibid.
38 Ibid., 47. It should be noted, however, that there has been significant resistance, for example from the Malaysian fishing community, to granting Thailand formal access agreements as a result of "perceived destructive Thai fishing practices and alleged intimidation of Malaysian fishermen" (ibid., 50).
39 *Bangkok Post,* 29 April 1996.
40 Ibid., 5 November 1997, 22 November 1997.
41 Ibid., 29 May 1998.
42 Hamzah, "Malaysia and the Law of the Sea," 366.
43 *Bangkok Post,* 15 July 1998.

Part 4
Redefining Boundaries
in the Americas

The following chapters describe general trends in boundary redefinition among South and Latin American countries, including the Caribbean. Here traditional approaches focusing upon state-oriented practices have underestimated the strength of integration efforts in some areas, while overestimating them in others. Indeed, one of the key issues raised in Part 4 is whether there is any utility to the "global world" concept among countries that have never developed according to the classic Eurocentric model of the nation-state.

In Chapter 8 Heather Nicol argues that, among Caribbean decision makers, neoliberalism is an indigenous policy response to the demands of economic globalization and free trade. In recent years, neoliberalism has become the mantra of decision makers within this region, resulting in significant rethinking about domestic and economic policy within Caribbean countries and, in some cases, promoting structural adjustment policies and similar instruments of change. Interestingly, however, because it stresses self-sufficiency, the legitimacy of Caribbean neoliberalism has often been suspect among scholars outside the region. Much like Schofield in Chapter 7, Nicol suggests that the Caribbean is an emergent region in which internationalization of domestic economic, political, cultural, legal, and environmental policies has been promoted from the top down in order to reconcile local developmental gaps with the demands of globalization. The latter demands increased cooperation and resource sharing among small developing nations, particularly coastal and maritime states. Like Asiwaju in Chapter 6 (with regard to Africa), Nicol reassesses the innate reservations many development scholars have towards applying Eurocentric models to emergent regions. In this sense, her chapter has much in common with those in Part 3.

In contrast, Chapter 9, by Roy Bradshaw, suggests that the flexibility seen in Caribbean political borders is unlike that seen in South America. Bradshaw argues that the boundaries of South America are highly distinctive.

"Whether in origin, historical development, or present-day role and function, the boundaries of South America are seen to be quite unlike those found anywhere else in the world." Unlike Europe, where national identity and the related concept of territoriality have helped to determine the location and function of national boundaries, in South America, "most of these elements are missing." Indeed, over most of South America, "people have the same ethnic origins, they speak the same language, have the same religion, the same colonial history, the same basis for their legal and administrative systems, and so on." According to Bradshaw, this is further evidence that "national identity and, with it, national territory and national boundaries, are based on factors quite distinct from those found elsewhere on the globe." He suggests that the precedent in South America is not in favour of the types of cooperation between states that globalization requires. "Historical experience and geopolitical thinking has left behind a legacy of mutual suspicion. The dismantling of border controls and the opening of economies to outside influences goes against almost every instinct of current geopolitical and nationalistic thinking."

The chapters in this section return us to an important element in our understanding of borders not only within the Americas but also in all world regions: the constitutive role of geopolitics and geopolitical discourse in setting the terms of transborder dialogue. As we observed in the introduction to *Holding the Line*, the co-existence of very different border-making processes within the same geographical and geopolitical regions highlight the propensity for border issues to remain resilient and to stay at the very core of "reterritorialization."

8
Neoliberal Caribbean Integration: The Role of the ACS in Restructuring Borderlines
Heather Nicol

This chapter explores regional integration and globalization within the greater Caribbean area. It argues, much like Serbin[1] and Scott (Chapter 5, this volume), that many of the traditional political theories of international relations, such as the recently revived "realist tradition," are inadequate to understanding new regional integration movements. The reason for this is that traditional approaches focus upon state-oriented practices and fail to appreciate the importance of linkages among forces of globalization, neoliberalism, and the regional restructuring that took place throughout the late twentieth and early twenty-first centuries. They also fail to appreciate, or even to address, the fact that, through a restructuring of scalar relationships, globalization has produced new regional geographies. One of the most critical outcomes of this scalar restructuring is, according to Roberts, that, in various ways, the global becomes interfluent with the local and vice versa.[2]

This chapter builds upon the assumption that there is a critical link between globalization and regional restructuring, examining how newly popular neoliberal development approaches now gaining currency within the Caribbean foster local restructuring of political, economic, and spatial processes. Using the greater Caribbean area as a case study (including the islands of the Caribbean, the coastal states of South and Central America that border the Caribbean Sea, and Mexico), I argue that globalization and neoliberal economic policies are important building blocks in the new scalar relationships of globalization, resulting in the "(re)territorialization" of the Caribbean region, particularly in terms of efforts to have the Caribbean Sea declared a "Special Area" under joint control of members of the new regional institution, the Association of Caribbean States.

I suggest that the supranational regional agendas, discourses, and relationships emerging within the Caribbean result from specific political, economic, and environmental "spillover effects" that are themselves the direct result of the application of new neoliberal ideologies and development agendas that have infused the region at the institutional level. In recent years, neoliberalism has become the mantra of decision makers within this region, resulting in significant rethinking about domestic and economic policy within Caribbean countries, in some cases promoting structural adjustment policies and similar instruments of change.

These changes in policy orientation and the revision of the decision-making community has resulted in the reimagining of regional boundaries and a new functional cooperation among Caribbean nations. However, it is a cooperation based as much upon conventional and ecological consideration regarding maritime resources as upon a desire for heightened levels of trade. Much like Scott's Chapter 5 (this volume), which argues that the European Union (EU) is the result of efforts to build a new community "driven by a desire to develop new, more responsive and effective forms of collective action – or governance – in protecting the environment, safeguarding peaceful co-existence, and promoting economic development," this chapter suggests that, within the Caribbean, too, new regionalism is "distinguished by a range of [new] possibilities for institutionalized co-operation."[3] This is an institutionalized cooperation in which new environmental and economic agendas comprise the foundations for the new policy frameworks.[4]

In order to demonstrate this point, I investigate the emergent structure and spatial arrangements of one of the newest of Caribbean integration initiatives – the Association of Caribbean States (ACS). I look at the contribution of its working agenda to the reformulation of regional cooperation, territorial definition, and economic interdependence. Although it is not the first time that governments within the Caribbean have attempted to make common policies for regional economic development, the ACS is the most recent and comprehensive initiative. Other integration attempts include that of the West Indies Federation (1958-62) as well as a number of less ambitious and longer-lived subregional associations, including the Caribbean Community (CARICOM), the Organization of Eastern Caribbean States (OECS), and the Caribbean Basin Initiative (CBI). Unlike all of these earlier initiatives, however, the ACS has attempted to widen and deepen the Caribbean community in unprecedented ways, transforming the region's lead subregional economic institution, CARICOM (which has traditionally been focused on the Eastern Caribbean area), into a larger, independent, regionwide free trade association. This would include all of the thirty or so countries and contemporary colonial dependencies that border on the Caribbean Sea, and a population of over 200 million people. To date, the ACS counts over twenty-five countries among its members, along with most of the region's major powers and largest economies.

Why, specifically, have Caribbean countries adopted trade liberalization policies as the basis for their new regional integration effort? Is this attempt to build community on the basis of economic development realistic?

Clearly, part of the impetus for regional integration came from the recommendations of the West Indian Commission, struck in the early 1990s, to promote a single market within the Caribbean. Indeed, the idea of a liberal trade association has been on the books for decades. It has been part of the Caribbean agenda since 1958, continuing and growing in importance as an integral component of present-day ACS and CARICOM agendas for trade relations among regional states with the context of a global framework of economic interrelationships. In the new millennium, this constitutes a "global survival plan," the importance of which goes well beyond banana wars and the circulation of traditional regional exports.

While it is not difficult to identify the nature of policy frameworks upon which the new Caribbean integration movement is based, the more difficult question remains: how will the new integration agenda influence the interactions of member states along existing political and conceptual boundaries? There are some guideposts within geographical, political, and economic scholarship that describe the growing phenomenon of supranational and transnational integration and the ensuing restructuring of boundaries that result. But before beginning my analysis of the Caribbean situation, it is worth reviewing some of the ways in which regional integration and "(re)bordering" in general – or, as Newman, calls it, the process of "(re)territorialization" – has been linked to global events. In other words, I review the ways in which global and local scalar relations, both processes in integration and fragmentation, have been conceptualized as interfluent systems.

Globalization and Integration

Globalization has evoked changes to world political systems, and, as Rosati, Sampson, and Hagan note, in order to understand international developments, one must attempt to comprehend change in policies.[5] How will governments respond to these global changes? What is foreign policy change? When and why does it occur? How would it affect world politics? To this list of questions we might just as easily add "What new spatial patterns will emerge from new policy?" as it is clear that policies under liberalized trade regimes produce very different outcomes for international relations than do policies based on realist perspectives. Painter[6] and Serbin[7] both observe that policy points and foci differ tremendously between the two perspectives, each placing different emphasis upon interdependence, domestic concerns, and internationalism. The hallmarks of neoliberalism include free trade, new productive regimes, fiscal austerity, deregulation, and other policies that "shakedown" previous modes of international order and lead to new and different modes of interaction between states. The most notable example in contemporary terms is "Europe of the Regions" as defined by both Scott and Bort (Chapters 5 and

4, respectively, this volume) and by Harvie.[8] These new modes of interaction may produce new territorial affiliations or, indeed, new territories as countries attempt to revise policy frameworks (in aid of regional cooperation) or to meet the needs of domestic policies and new domestic political regimes.

Serbin argues that nowhere is the ongoing process of economic, political, and, consequently, spatial restructuring clearer than in the contemporary Caribbean, where liberalized trade policies, economic integration initiatives, and new rounds of regionally based strengthening of identity are being constructed by policy makers from the "top down."[9] In this area, not only does the implementation of new trade policies require the formulation of a supranational regional institution to coordinate and oversee trade liberalization but it also requires the establishment of new territorial boundaries or new ways to physically and structurally demarcate trade regulation with respect to regional and global imperatives.[10] These boundaries are both real and perceptual precisely because neoliberalism, as a policy framework, is concerned with the construction of a world empowered by new technologies and communications networks that, simultaneously, encourages common-minded political and economic goals. Moreover, it is a world in which intensification and diversity of interconnection has brought about a remarkable integration of geographical regions.

Or has it? Barber suggested that this world of homogenized economies is actually sustained by ethnic, political, and religious cleavages resulting from transnational corporate and consumer cultures.[11] This is evident in the global map – particularly maps of global information flows or flows of goods and peoples. Geographers have documented only too well that, even within the global economy, economic and cultural inequities promote development within carefully prescribed core and periphery regions: divisions that remain remarkably resilient despite the "new world order."[12]

Consequently, it may be more realistic to depict the new world order not as one of homogenized trade networks but, rather, with the tacit recognition that neoliberalism creates and works through a series of trade blocs formed in response to the prevailing economic, cultural, and political realities of a global economy – a sort of regionalism nested within multilateralism, making globalization and fragmentation interdependent, both sides of the same coin and constitutive of a local-global dialect.[13]

While numerous studies on fragmentation and integration have been undertaken, there still appears to be limited appreciation of the relationship between the experience of fragmentation and integration within the geographical literature. Some scholars, for example, suggest that stability within the new world order has created impetus for the creation of newly independent states at the same time that many political and military alliances are reinforcing the status quo. But this avoids the issue of the unprecedented extent to which new regional alliances have formed. Indeed, the recent trend towards supranational regionalism, and a usurping of the traditional role of the state by regional alliances, is a fact of international relations in the twenty-first century. Mattli observes, for example, that, although the EU is a focal point for scholarship on political processes of integration, more than half a dozen new integration projects haved formed in Latin America in recent years, the most notable being the Mercado Común del Sur (MERCOSUR). In North America, a Free Trade Agreement grew into the North American Free Trade Agreement (NAFTA). In Asia the most notable regional grouping is the Association of South-East Asian Nations (ASEAN).[14]

To this list we may now add the ACS, a regional trade group with linkages to broader global markets. Serbin argues that the Caribbean has experienced significant political restructuring over the past few decades as a direct consequence of globalization. Serbin argues that:

> World trade and production underwent rapid restructuring in the 1980s, as increasing globalization of the world economy led to the elimination of national boundaries in the process of capital accumulation at the world level ... While the European Community advance[d] towards integration in 1992, North America has tended to become a free trade zone, forming a block that is gradually integrating the U.S. economy with those of Canada and Mexico, and that anticipates the future incorporation of the Caribbean Basin.[15]

Rethinking the Caribbean: Theoretical Issues
The recognition of the emergence of a new international agenda and a global economy based upon free trade and multilateralism is still very recent in the Caribbean. In the past, "realist" and "neorealist" theories have most often been used to explain political arrangements among powers within this area of the world.[16] Realism, as a theoretical framework, presumes that power relations between states determine the structure of international relations and that states are discrete players, responding strategically to issues on the basis of their own self-interest (although not directly as a result of domestic policy formulations). Hegemonic relations are necessary in order to promote stability in the world system, and the balance of power is clearly maintained by the most powerful states because "the absence of centralized international authority precludes attainment of common goals."[17] Regionalism and supranational institutions are viewed, within realist frameworks, as weak, short-term coalitions. Cooperation is not precluded but emerges as an alternative to hegemonic relations only under specific conditions, where, in the long term, it promotes strategic gain.[18]

This "winner-take-all" attitude towards international events has been revised in recent years. But neoliberalism has also proven inadequate as a theory. Recognizing the limitations of traditional realist theories (i.e., they preclude the analysis of domestic economies as strategic in nature), neorealists have attempted to incorporate economic relations into their theoretical models of internationalism. Kahler argues, for example, that, at the end of the Cold War, greater attention has been given to the consequences of domestic change for foreign policies and that there has been increasing recognition of the role of domestic priorities in international relations.[19] He observes that this has also "accelerated the erosion of neo-realist theoretical pretensions in international relations. Neo-realist hostility towards reductionist arguments based upon the domestic determinants of foreign policy has been an important barrier to serious, systematic investigation of such relationships."[20]

The dilemma for Caribbean nations is, therefore, that most analyses of Caribbean international relations have, until quite recently, evoked realist theories to explain regional structure and interests. While issues of power, and the source of power, are inimical to any understanding of regionalism within the Caribbean, traditional realist interpretations of Caribbean international relations have placed near exclusive emphasis upon the strategic importance of the region to North American political, economic, and security interests. These strategic concerns have tended to reflect those of North American countries, in particular the United States, rather than those countries within the region. Until the end of the Cold War, the Caribbean was seen quite literally as a part of the "American backyard" or the "American lake" rather than as a world region in its own terms. Today, pretensions of American hegemony within the region are more muted. Realist interpretations of North American regional destiny are generally avoided, except in connection with discussion of the new concept of a Free Trade Area of the Americas (FTAA) and of the North American Free Trade Agreement (NAFTA). Yet they still haunt the region in several important ways. The ACS, the regional economic bloc, has rejected the US veto on strategic and trade alliances with Cuba, allowing Cuba to become a member state and thus ruling out the participation of Puerto Rico and those American states that border on the Caribbean Sea. Given the importance of Miami to regional flows of people, goods, and capital within the Caribbean, this is an assertion of political confidence that would give pause to even the most stolid of international decision makers.

The significance of this break with realist interpretations for Caribbean countries cannot be overemphasized. It is consistent with the contemporary tendency for nation-states to define international interests, "including their commercial interests, more narrowly and regionally."[21] Serbin suggests that, in stepping away from a realist perspective, a breathing space emerges for the countries of the Caribbean, allowing the possibility of cultivating a regional identity. Although Serbin is ultimately pessimistic about the outcome of regional community building, he recognizes a number of venues for imagining identity within the new development paradigm – regional identity being a point to which I will return when discussing new maritime border initiatives.

What are the elements of the new development paradigm? As we have seen, new policy frameworks that are embraced by most Caribbean countries are those that could loosely be defined or grouped into the category of "neoliberalism" or "liberalized trade policies." Their hallmarks involve deficit reduction, trade liberalization, development of market mechanisms, deregulation, privatization, the creation of trade blocs, and the implementation of common borders and currencies.[22] These represent top-down strategies for economic development that have been initiated at the national government level and may, indeed, be characterized as a movement that supports neoliberalism less as a set of theoretical or methodological tools and more as an ideology. These project "an image of transnational liberalism as an unstoppable revolution that will inaugurate a borderless world of frictionless, superconductive capitalism."[23]

According to Serbin, Caribbean neoliberal policy reforms have created pressures for the transformation of the international system as well as

> concerns about marginalization from the international economic system [which] have stimulated the process of economic adjustment, trade liberalization and opening, and subregional integration. These pressures have also led to a series of political reforms that affect the role of the state and political society, with significant social and political costs, generally under the banner of the neo-liberal logic of the predominance of the market.[24]

It is clear, however, that while the late 1990s saw a new movement that identified Caribbean regional interests in economic terms, what began as a concern with economic issues has developed into a more comprehensive plan for the economic recovery of the Caribbean Basin and its insertion into the global economy. Serbin suggests that regional integration is a halting process lurching forward between the "conservative pragmatism of the CARICOM governments" and a "pressing onwards to regional integration."[25] "The latter alternative, despite its limited economic scope, is perceived as a viable response to the consolidation of the increasingly centripetal world economic blocs."[26]

In general terms, the new integration policies have had tremendous implications for the changing spatial configuration of the Caribbean Basin. They encourage the weakening of interregional borders while strengthening intraregional linkages. They encourage increasing interconnectivity among Caribbean states, while redefining the linkages among individual states and those outside the trade bloc. Finally, they provide a means by which Caribbean countries can respond to developments outside of the region, particularly in terms of the nature and number of linkages within the global economy. In the case of the Caribbean, it is clear that events in the new global marketplace have already begun to define the parameters of the new regionalism. Key to the concept of supranationalism in the Caribbean, therefore, is the central role played by policies promoting market deregulation, privatization, and fiscal austerity.

Caribbean Regionalism: More than Neoliberalism Writ Large?

It is important, at this juncture in the discussion, to move a step beyond the fairly simple assertion that the emergent regionalism in the Caribbean is merely an expression of neoliberalism writ large. As Barry and Keith argue with regard to the rise of new regional trade blocs in general, "although globalization has served as a catalyst for regionalism, internal factors have coincided with the form that this collaboration has taken."[27] Consequently, the fact that the ACS has adopted liberal trade policies does not, in and of itself, fully explain the nature of Caribbean integration and the spatial restructuring that is inimical to this event. While it is true that market-oriented policies and the desire to be a contender in the global marketplace has promoted the development of a regional association designed to deliver these goals, some consideration must be given to the way in which common rules and policies have developed to structure or implement regionalism, the identification of the common good that ensues from regionalism, and the role of external events on regional formation.[28] Naim, in his re-evaluation of the new liberalized trade policy agenda for developing countries known as the "Washington consensus," argues that the ideas derived from neoliberalism had a huge impact on the economic reforms of many countries.

> Yet, the way these countries interpreted such ideas varied substantially, and how they chose to implement them did even more so. Additionally, the original ... policy prescriptions ... reigned unchallenged only for a short time. Changes in the international economic and political environment, as well as new domestic conditions in reforming countries, created problems that the original proponents of the consensus did not envision, thus forcing the search for new answers ... Reforming governments everywhere saw how policy goals that just a few years ago, or even months, earlier had been identified as the final frontier of the reform process became mere preconditions for success.[29]

Inequity, lack of investment, economic instability, and other variables often create diversity in developing regions and change the nature and results of neoliberal prescriptions. Indeed, Naim suggests that in the wake of known failures have come regional innovations such as "the search for the free-market oriented model that recognizes a role for the state to play and pays more attention to social policies." This is particularly true within the Caribbean, where the specific institutional context and goals of neoliberal integration have played an important role in broadening the discourse of the integration process to include a discussion of civil society and social equity.[30]

One of the most remarkable features of the Caribbean integration process is the fact that, unlike many of their South and Central American counterparts, Caribbean countries have created a broad institutional context for integration under the umbrella of the ACS. No such institution existed before it. It would not be an exaggeration to say that efforts to broaden regional identity and economic integration have been strengthened by a compatible institutional structure in this region. At the most fundamental level, the response of the ACS to its goal of achieving sustainable development, social equity, and a strong civil society within the Caribbean area has been the formation of a permanent secretariat and decision-making body that coordinates the participation of member states. Although there was CARICOM, a powerful force in the Eastern Caribbean, as well as the OECS and the Caribbean Free Trade Area (CARIFTA), all were influential only at the subregional level. Faced with the prospect of "widening and deepening" CARICOM (which was a subregional trade group) in order to achieve the goals of regional integration and a single market, it was decided instead to sponsor a new regional institution, the ACS, which would promote the goal of regional integration in a much more inclusive format. CARICOM has already established itself as an economic trade bloc whose interest lies principally with the Eastern Caribbean, a group of primarily English-speaking countries whose agenda was sometimes seen as being at odds with that of its Spanish neighbours.

Like CARICOM, the organizational structure of the ACS is relatively formal.[31] Although its formality makes it potentially elitist, it also gives the ACS a degree of autonomy and permanency, which is important to its ongoing task of regional policy coordination. The United Nations' Economic Commission for Latin America and the Caribbean (ECLAC) has argued that formal structure is necessary for regional organizations whose goal is to promote changes to economic productivity. If the initiative involves policy coordination, then "it eventually must provide for some centralization of decision-making power, if [common] policies are to be implemented or the coordinated management of indicators if a joint macroeconomic policy is envisaged."[32]

While the ACS provided the much-needed regionwide institutional structure for integration, as well as a centralizing framework for policy formulation, it was also apparent that the association was concerned as much with providing an ideological basis as with providing an institutional basis for the new liberalized trade agenda. It has successfully articulated regionwide economic goals that have proven to be sufficiently inclusive to attract a broad regional membership and that have set the course for the new Caribbean regional integration movement. There is a deeply felt consensus among Caribbean countries that a liberal trade agenda will encourage cooperation, new investment, and further deregulation in transportation, and that these, when coupled with a new emphasis on tourism, will stimulate productive capacity within the region. The underlying rationale is that a regional effort will allow the Caribbean Basin to reinsert itself into the global economy and allow the area to carry some weight in trade negotiations with NAFTA, the EU, and other regional trade blocs. The fear within the region is that efforts to enhance interregional trade will be weakened without access to larger non-Caribbean marketplaces.

Although the ACS Secretariat has created a formal decision-making body to meet the challenge of regional decision making, it has, nonetheless, signalled that its role will be facilitating rather than deterministic. Consequently, the ACS has called for a "partnership of existing regional actors, as well as the private sector," and, indeed, it sees itself as "an arm of coordination rather than an originator of activity," or even an elite organization.[33] Yet the process is driven from the top down and is inherently slow because of the nature of institutional change. As Scott suggests (Chapter 5, this volume), similar multisectoral approaches to regional integration have been utilized within the EU as a means of adjusting community building at the supranational level to local regional subunits. Consequently, while the high-level status of decision making within the ACS leads some to claim that it is elitist, it may well be that there is little alternative when attempting to create policies for broad geographical regions.

Moreover, the scale of the integration effort generates other problems, making the exercise a delicate political balancing act. Not the least important issue is that the ACS member states are often members of more than one regional organization. Subregional trade blocs co-exist within a region, which itself sees tremendous asymmetries in the flow of goods and services. In this sense, for many member states the ACS is one of several simultaneous membership options within the Caribbean.

These divided loyalties mean that there are inherent frictions within the ACS. Moreover, the potential for the contribution of member states is limited by historical and political circumstances as well as by linguistic and cultural divisions. The motivation for the new emphasis upon economic productivity and the market-centred policies of the ACS stems from the fact that most Caribbean economies are driven by trade and tourism agendas over which they have little control. Since most of them are small island states with small economies, few broker significant economic power within the broader world economy. Consequently, their economies tend to be competitive rather than complementary: this competitiveness is then carried over into the policy-making arena.

Despite these obstacles, the ACS has constructed a common ground and a common set of institutional infrastructures primarily to coordinate policies of member states with respect to economic development. The agenda of issues discussed by the ACS Special Committees reflects these priorities and concerns. But it also indicates that what began as an economic agenda has developed into a broader regional development initiative. It has developed into a comprehensive integration agenda and ideology that seeks to promote social equity, to strengthen civil society, to preserve cultural distinctiveness, and to promote general welfare in areas such as education and employment.

In this sense, the activities of the ACS at the committee level are very instructive with regard to understanding its plans for meeting the potential of integration. At the most fundamental level, policy formulations to encourage regional trade and restructure perceptual boundaries in order to build a more inclusive region include:

- the removal of obstacles to the restructuring of the regions' productive capacities
- identification and coordination of cooperative activities to remove regional barriers to trade and investment
- research into the nature of tariff boundaries between countries
- identification of issues in investment and transportation sectors that might influence integration
- inventory of public and private sector trade funding and payment mechanisms within the area and advocacy for the establishment of a single-visa system for the ACS area.

It is probably too early to identify the efficacy of the ACS with regard to improving trade. But some regional experts have claimed that the ACS is likely to play only a small role in regional economic development, if only because the development of a Free Trade Area of the Americas (FTAA) "has rendered the broader free trade aspects of the ACS ineffectual."[34] Gibbings argues that "there is nothing to support the claim that such a process would eventually lead to the kind of ACS-centric cohesions required to justify the eventual financial and political cost of the exercise" but that "there are far more realistic possibilities for action and change."[35] These possibilities include collaboration and cooperation in science and technology, health, education, disaster mitigation, and the strengthening of civil society. According to Gibbings,

> Only in these areas, will there exist real scope for engaging the challenge of converting the WIC metaphor of Latin American/Caribbean commonality into working reality. Greater emphasis on these areas may suggest tacit concessions in matters of trade and political cohesion, but may also serve as catalysts for the promotion of a new way of harnessing the tremendous economic and political potential of the region.[36]

This is consistent with general observations that neoliberalism as a policy framework is often the point of departure for new policy formulations rather than the end-point of economic development in developing regions.[37] In the course of achieving economic goals other relationships become reorganized, and other institutional arrangements for cooperation are altered. The end result is that, although trade represents a central point in the whole network of international economic interaction envisioned by the ACS,[38] whether or not the trade agenda takes root is not the only measure of integration or success.

The possibility of spillover from trade issues to other institutional sectors within the ACS is tremendous and becomes increasingly clear over time. As Mattli notes, "spillover" is based upon the assumption that "the different sectors of a modern society are highly interdependent and that any integrative action in one sector creates a situation in which the original goal can be assured [only] by taking further actions in related sectors."[39] Moreover, this can result in "political spillover," "the process of adaptive behaviours ... the incremental shifting of expectations, the changing of values, and coalescing at the supranational level of interest groups and political parties in response to sectoral integration."[40] The result can best be understood as a process whereby "political actors in several distinct national settings are persuaded to shift their loyalties, expectations and political activities towards a new and larger centre whose institutions possess or demand jurisdiction over pre-existing states."[41] It is this process that has occurred within the Caribbean as a result of ACS initiatives, and it is this process that holds the greatest potential for influencing the contours of a new regionalism and establishing its borders.

Broadening Out the ACS Agenda: From Tourism to New Maritime Boundaries

To appreciate how these spillovers might influence Caribbean boundaries requires that we first examine the ACS integration agenda as a whole. Despite the ambivalent record of the ACS in initiating new levels of trade within the region, trade-related economic-policy frameworks have been instrumental in reorganizing the structural basis of the region's transportation agenda, drawing together public- and, most recently, private-sector participants to confront the obstacles to sustainability within the transport and tourism sector.

Since transportation and tourism are considered, along with trade, to be the most important economic activities (and the ones possessing the greatest growth potential) within the region, the problem of enhancing mobility and increasing the circulatory system of peoples and goods is considered to be crucial to the ongoing development of the region. Since the founding of the ACS in the mid-1990s, these have included considerations of the restructuring of port authorities and port ownership, and the investigation of the viability of a non-vessel-owner carrying capacity company (NVOCC) system. Through policy research, the ACS has attempted to identify the potential for NVOCCs to serve a coordinating and load-brokering function, and to enhance the efficiency of private-sector shipping interests. The ACS has also initiated a new roster of marine transportation policies for the development of new systems, to promote cooperation between Port Authorities and marine operators; provision of port services, as well as reduction of costs of improvement to the efficiency of shipping operators, and the encouragement of the use of computerized systems for the exchange of electronic data, training, and safety.[42]

In the area of air transportation policies, the ACS also expressed interest in changing the regulatory framework of aviation in order to encourage open skies. These changes were to encourage considerable deregulation of national carriers, abandonment of government subsidization, and harmonization of bilateral agreements. In the late 1990s, ACS policy makers have supplemented their governmental meetings with consultations with "real actors" – meeting with the executive officers of regional airlines and developing a consensus to work together on the issues of enhancing cooperation and harmonization of air transportation policies and practices.

Indeed, moving beyond the level of building consensus and identifying areas for policy formulation, one finds a number of specific ACS projects. These include studies of hub and gateway facilities in marine transport, the Colombian initiative on air transportation routes and schedules, the Cuban effort to define the regulatory framework of bilateral agreements in air transport, and ACS initiatives to coordinate airline policies and public agendas.[43]

In its push for trade and enhanced productive capacity, the ACS has also identified tourism as an important arena for policy formulation. In 1995, in the Declaration of Principles and Plan of Action on Tourism, Trade and Transportation, adopted at the ACS Summit of Heads of States and Government, trade, tourism, and transportation were identified as the three "critical sectors" that "should be accorded priority in our concerted efforts to promote coordination."[44] In June 1998, the Caribbean Tourism

Organization (CTO), one of the region's most important NGOs, prepared a diagnostic document that outlined issues and challenges to tourism sectors in the Caribbean in response to the new mandate of the Special Committee on Tourism, as specified by the Ministerial Council request in December 1996. The new goal was to establish what was to become a "sustainable tourism zone" within the Caribbean and to produce a draft proposal on how this zone might be established and regulated. Consequently, the ACS agreed upon an initiative to establish policies among member states to encourage cooperation between government and private sectors. Inimical to this agenda, however, is the desire to control the impact of all sectors of the economies on environment and culture, as well as to share the benefits generated by tourism with the communities.[45]

The sustainable tourism zone has been accepted in principle as well as actively promoted by the ACS, emerging as a policy framework and as a set of definable interventions. This represents a significant spillover effect from the general economic agenda originally conceived by the ACS – one that was confined to establishing a free trade area. A number of more specific initiatives, derived from a sustainable tourism agenda, are also being considered in order to safeguard cultural values while consolodating Caribbean identity. Suggested areas of intervention include protection of cultural diversity, coordination with private-sector initiatives, education, training, and tourism awareness.

Moreover, while the ACS has given the CTO ample opportunity to make policy recommendations – many of which have been incorporated into the ACS proposal for a sustainable tourism zone – it has also attempted to bring the issue of sustainable tourism to the attention of other committees, particularly those that deal with transportation and environmental issues, and may have real concerns in this area. For example, an important component of the thrust towards a sustainable tourism zone is a new round of considerations regarding the impact of increasing numbers of cruise liner visits and passenger stopovers within the ACS member states. Although this is clearly consistent with the ACS desire to enhance tourism, a rising tourist agenda within the Caribbean region cannot be uncoupled from environmental policy. Currently, the ACS Secretariat is considering means to deal with the new levels of environmental risk posed by tourism, while devising ways to increase the capacity and human resources of the region to accommodate and, indeed, to promote gains in this industry.

Another intervention linked to tourism occurred when the Special Committee on the Protection of the Environment and the Caribbean Sea and the Special Committee on Natural Resources met jointly on several occasions. Their aim is to develop and to evaluate broad strategies for the coordination of issues in the area of environmental conservation, protection of natural resources, and mitigation of natural disasters within the region. In its draft strategy of 1997 the Special Committee on Protection and Conservation of the Environment and of the Caribbean Sea prioritized many issues that it considered of importance within the region.[46] Its objectives, which included preservation of the environment, rational and controlled use of natural resources, preven tion and mitigation of natural and environmental disasters, intraregional cooperation, and cooperation with specialized regional and international agencies, were incorporated into an environmental strategy in June of 2000.[47] This amounted to a document that stressed the need for cooperation between ACS member states with regard to integrated management and the identification of a short- and medium-term work program to heighten environmental agendas and cooperative networks of expertise.

Among the long-term initiatives encouraged by ACS environmental committees have been the identification of vulnerable sectors of member states; the potential consequences of marine erosion; the potential problems of pollution, oil, and hydrocarbon spills; the protection of fisheries and marine resources from overexploitation; and the development of energy resources. ACS committees have worked to explore the active protection and conservation of natural resources and environments by developing political strategies and partnerships with existing regional authorities, and by promoting cooperative agreements among them. In this sense the ACS has signalled its intention to tap into the existing body of "soft law" – official and unofficial protocols, including those of the United Nations Environmental Programme (UNEP) and the Land-Based Sources of Pollution Protocol (LBS) as well as the global conventions that provide benchmarks and consensus for environmental policy and economic development. The draft environmental strategy developed in June 2001, for example, was undertaken in anticipation of the need for a coherent environmental strategy to be finalized and prioritized prior to the 2002 meeting.[48]

Although the strategic plans of ACS committees still reflect an overwhelming concern with the importance of economic resources and their renewal, it is clear that much more is at stake. The ACS is now considering the importance of economic protection as a goal in and of itself. This is increasingly clear in the progression of policy frameworks established by this supranational organization since its founding.[49] With its proposal for a Regional Cooperative Agreement on Natural Disasters, its consideration of the LBS Protocol, its engagement with UNEP, and its heightened awareness of the need to strategize and prioritize environmental issues, the ACS has achieved a degree of institutional maturity. It has signalled its intent to seriously consider environmental policies as core strategies of regional integration. The impetus for the remarkable degree of political consensus and resolve may well lie in the wake of several recent and severe natural disasters as well as in the recognition of the physical vulnerability of the region.[50] These circumstances make environmental agendas equal to economic development agendas – both are critical for survival.

The environmental strategy, as well as the nature of other ACS work programs and agendas, clearly demonstrate that, within the Caribbean, the desire for regional integration has moved beyond the simple desire for a customs union, free trade zone, or common currency area. The desire for regional integration has become nothing short of a desire for harmonization between production functions and social goals – for welfare maximization (delivered through supranational institutions that stress utilitarian goals) and broadening the range of market-led policy tools in order to achieve integration. Consequently, institutional and political factors are highly relevant, along with regional security and the protection of human rights. Strengthening democracy and social partnerships has also become important, along with the coordinatinating external policies, preserving the cultural identity of the Caribbean, protecting the environment, expanding the telecommunications network, human resource development, joint management of the exclusive economic zones (EEZs), and disaster preparedness and emergency response. These are all important new areas in which functional cooperation is beginning to be exercised.

Bordering the New Regionalism

We have seen that if free trade constitutes the nexus of the ACS initiative, then there are many significant spillover effects from liberalized trade policies that have a tremendous impact upon common goals (other than market performance). Perhaps the best example of how spillovers from the economic agenda have resulted in new functional cooperation and a redefinition of the political space for regional activity is an attempt to broker new maritime border relations by ACS member states. The ACS has attempted to build resolve for new regional borders embedded within an environmental paradigm and promote a cooperative approach to maritime zones as "frontiers" for integrated management and disaster prevention. Although they have not yet been successful in this area, efforts are ongoing.

For example, in June 1999 the ACS met to discuss the concept of a Special Area in Context of Sustainable Development in Guyana. This concept was developed into a formal resolution and presented to the UN General Assembly in the fall of the same year. An important part of the resolution, apart from its emphasis upon functional cooperation in maritime zones within the Caribbean region, was the definition of a new functional boundary for the area of the ACS – one that relied upon a common acceptance of new functional cooperation in environmental issues within maritime zones. Obviously, this resolution involved a clear understanding of regional boundaries and interfaces. In fact, the boundary for the special region was originally defined by the Convention for the Protection and Development of a Marine Environment of the Wider Caribbean Region by the Cartagena Convention of 1983, and it included the Gulf of the Mexico and the Caribbean Sea proper, the bays and seas within the region, and a portion of the Atlantic Ocean (within a boundary lying southeast of Florida and northeast of French Guiana).

In reality, however, the boundary represented less of a scientific concern with the edges of distinctive ecological zones and more of a general understanding of what constitutes a Caribbean region and Caribbean identity. Where the high seas begin, the Caribbean ends, and the new territorial boundary represents an attempt to insert a modicum of precision into a somewhat imprecise process.

While the June 1999 meetings in Guyana provoked discussion concerning the most effective borders for the new special area as well as work on the resolution to be presented to the United Nations, there was really no dissent concerning the actual concept of a special zone – except in so far as the United Nations environmental representatives were concerned. They felt, and continue to feel, that the structuring and monitoring of a special zone was the responsibility of UNEP – the United Nations Environment Programme – and that adequate protocols existed outside of a regional integration movement. The resolution for a special area was defeated at the United Nations General Assembly in the fall of 1999, and UNEP continues to press for integrated management and adherence to established programs and protocols in the region.[51]

This has not deterred the ACS, however. It has resolved to continue its efforts to have the Caribbean Sea declared a special area rather than an integrated management zone. It noted that Resolution 54/225, which replaced the special area concept with the integrated management concept, "however tentative, watered-down and mutilated, has fulfilled a key mandate of the ACS Heads of Government for the proposal to be introduced into the UN system."[52] The ACS has requested that all ACS member states take ownership of the resolution and explore the reasons for the failure of their attempt to redefine the borders of the region.

In doing this, and in defining the Caribbean Sea as a special area, or common source of identity for all member states, the ACS has signalled its intention to create a functional space and common identity that crisscrosses linguistic, cultural, and political divisions. It has organized efforts to develop regionwide policies and mechanisms for environmental protection, conservation, and disaster coordination along these lines, and it encourages member states to cultivate a common set of political instruments in relation to Caribbean Sea issues. Although yet untested, the unifying concept of a sea that sustains the economy of the member states has been a powerful perceptual metaphor, and it has been useful in enabling member states to arrive at a consensus on environmental and maritime transportation agendas. It builds upon the conventional wisdom that semi-enclosed seas such as the Caribbean are unique spaces that offer unique opportunities for cooperation among coastal states. It also builds upon several decades of strengthening exercises in which the United Nations and other international bodies have promoted the need for more holistic and environmentally sound approaches to the use of this maritime region.[53]

Consequently, the special area is a powerful metaphor in that it constitutes an important rallying point for regional cooperation and legislative frameworks that support an environmental agenda. But the attempt by the ACS to create a common space using a maritime context also amounts to much more than a tentative common bond based upon regional identity and a shared history (although common identity is important). It is the recognition of a common geopolitical space in which environmental hazards and resource exploitation are common threats and opportunities, and in which all member states have a stake. Much of the success of the ACS integration initiative rests upon its ability to reinforce holistic environmental and political thinking with respect to the Caribbean Sea and its resources.

Moreover, although the rationale for the development of this new special area is ostensibly rooted in the consideration of environmental factors and the sustainability of maritime resources (what Schofield calls a "responsibilities approach" in Chapter 7) – particularly the concern that a newly revitalized tourism industry within the region could serve as a threat to fragile ecosystems – upon inspection, economic integration goals are well served. If the special area represents a new territorial definition of the changing economic and strategic interests of the Caribbean states, and the development of a new venue for functional cooperation, then, at the end of the day, it is expressed in a joint resolution to declare the Caribbean Sea a common territory and supranational region. This initiative is consistent with a push towards policy frameworks that identify a broader, less structured, and more complex institutional and international agenda – one that "incorporat[es] a much more diffuse range of interests and much more extensive team of actors than [has been the case] in the past [and that is] no longer reduced to exclusively nation states."[54]

Conclusions

Liberalized trade policies, or, more specifically, neoliberalism, within the Caribbean can best be understood in terms of the spillover effects that have created the potential for new border relationships within the region.

As such, Caribbean integration has been given a substantial boost. The new neoliberal agenda has politicized environmental issues and has led to a new goal – the redefinition of regional responsibility for resource protection. This new mode of political integration simultaneously challenges the traditional power relations within the region and promotes new modes of functional cooperation at the supranational level. However, there is more at stake than "defusing" the problem of political borders and the expression of traditional sovereignty in the maritime environment. The extension of political control in the form of cooperative agreements between states into areas such as maritime environments, which were previously out of reach of individual states, means that the power of the traditional state has been successfully transformed. The state has become simultaneously more diffuse and more powerful – extending its control, albeit based upon tacit consensus, into regions that were previously out of reach. This constitutes an extension of power and a blurring of borders, and this entails a process that is not simply a "secondary effect" or outcome of the process of regional integration but, rather, an integral component of that integration process. One cannot exist without the other.

It is clear that neoliberalism in the Caribbean cannot be simplistically understood merely as a function of global marketplaces; rather, it must be seen in relationship to broader processes of political, social, and economic development. The institutional context and independent nature of policy formulations inherent in neoliberal integration is a significant force in reworking the boundaries of national interest and in creating distinctive regional agendas.

Notes

1 Andres Serbin, *Sunset over the Islands: The Caribbean in an Age of Global and Regional Challenges* (New York: St. Martin's Press, 1998).
2 Susan M. Roberts, "Geo-Governance in Trade and Finance and Political Geographies of Dissent," in *Unruly World? Globalization, Governance and Geography,* ed. Andrew Herod, Gearóid Ó Tuathail, and Susan M. Roberts (London: Routledge, 1998), 116.
3 Donald Barry and Ronald C. Keith use this terminology in the introduction to their study "Introduction: Changing Perspectives on Regionalism and Multilateralism," in *Regionalism, Multilateralism, and the Politics of Global Trade* (Vancouver: UBC Press, 1999), 4. Although it refers to developments under global trade regimes in general, it is particularly pertinent to the Caribbean situation.
4 See Heather N. Nicol, "The ACS and Sustainable Development," in *Social and Economic Studies,* December 2000.
5 Jerel A. Rosati, Joe D. Hagan, and Martin W. Sampson III, *Foreign Policy Restructuring: When and Why Governments Alter Their Foreign Policy* (Columbia, SC: University of South Carolina Press, 1994).
6 Joe Painter, *Politics, Geography and Political Geography: A Critical Perspective* (London: Arnold, 1995).
7 Serbin, *Sunset over the Islands.*
8 See Christopher Harvie, *The Rise of Regional Europe* (London: Routeledge, 1994), 2-5.

9   See Serbin, *Sunset over the Islands.*

10 See, for example, Andrew Axline, "Free Trade in the Americas and Sub-Regional Integration in Central America and the Caribbean," *Canadian Journal of Development Studies* 21, 1 (2000): 31-53. United Nations, Economic Commission of Latin America and the Caribbean, *Strengthening Development: The Interplay of Macro and Microeconomics* (Santiago: ECLAC, 1996).

11 Benjamin Barber, *Jihad versus McWorld* (New York: Times Books, 1995).

12 See, for example, R.J. Johnson, P.J. Taylor, and M.J. Watts, *Geographies of Global Change* (Oxford: Blackwell, 1995), 8-9; and John Agnew, Paul Knox, and Linda McCarthy, *The Geography of the World Economy,* 4th ed. (London: Arnold, 2003).

13 Johnson, Taylor, and Watts, *Geographies of Global Change.*

14 Walter Mattli, *The Logic of Regional Integration: Europe and beyond Cambridge* (Cambridge: Cambridge University Press, 1999), 2-3.

15 Andres Serbin, *Caribbean Geopolitics: Towards Security through Peace* (London: Lynne Reinner Publications, 1990), 111.

16 For a discussion of realists' viewpoints see Painter, *Politics, Geography and Political Geography.* For a discussion of its application to the Caribbean area, see Serbin, *Caribbean Geopolitics* and *Sunset over the Islands.*

17 Kenneth A. Oye, "The Conditions for Co-operation in World Politics," in *International Politics: Enduring Concepts and Contemporary Issues,* ed. R.J. Art and Robert Jervis (New York: Harper Collins, 1996), 81-94.

18 See Robert O. Keohane, "Hegemony in the World Political Economy," in Art and Jervis, *International Politics,* 286-98.

19 Miles Kahler, "Introduction: Liberalization and Foreign Policy" in *Liberalization and Foreign Policy* (New York: Columbia University Press, 1997), 1.

20 Ibid., 2.

21 Michael Hart, "A Matter of Synergy: The Role of Regional Trade Agreements in the Multilateral Trading Order," in *Regionalism, Multilateralism, and the Politics of Global Trade,* ed. Donald Barry and Robert C. Keith (Vancouver: UBC Press, 1999), 29.

22 See Moises Naim, "Washington Consensus or Washington Confusion," *Foreign Policy* 118 (Spring 2000): 86-103.

23 See Timothy W. Luke and Gearóid Ó Tuathail, "Global Flowmations, Local Fundamentalisms and Fast Geopolitics," in Herod, Tuathail, and Roberts, *Unruly World?,* 74.

24 Serbin, *Sunset over the Caribbean,* 54.

25 Ibid., 54, 113.

26 See Donald Barry and Ronald C. Keith, "Introduction: Changing Perspectives on Regionalism and Multilateralism," in Barry and Keith, *Regionalism, Multilateralism, and the Politics of Global Trade,* 3-22.

27 Ibid., 4.

28 Mattli, *The Logic of Regional Integration,* 10-11.

29 Naim, "Washington Consensus," 88.

30 See Heather N. Nicol, *The ACS: Is It Working?* Draft Report (Ottawa: FOCAL, 1999).

31 Ibid.

32 United Nations, Economic Commission for Latin America and the Caribbean, *Open Regionalism in Latin America and the Caribbean: Economic Integration as a Contribution to Changing Production Patterns with Social Equity* (Santiago: ECLAC, 1994), 95.

33 The Latin American and Caribbean Center, Florida International University, *Annual Report on Trade, 1996/1997: Caribbean Integration Report* (Miami: Florida International University, 1996), 7-8.

34 Wesley Gibbings, "Future Directions of the ACS," in *Integrating the Caribbean* (Port of Spain: ACS, 1999), 71.

35 Ibid., 71-72.

36 Ibid., 74.

37 Naim, "Washington Consensus," 86-103.

38 Tom Nierop, *Systems and Regions in Global Politics: An Empirical Study of Diplomacy International Organization and Trade, 1950-1991* (New York: John Wiley, 1994), 22.

39 Mattli, *The Logic of Regional Integration,* 25.
40 Ibid., 26.
41 Ibid., 24.
42 The Association of Caribbean States, *Work Program: Follow-Up Mandate of the Mandates of the ACS in the Area of Transportation – First Meeting of the Special Working Group on Air and Maritime Transportation of the ACS Special Committee on Transportation* (Port of Spain: ACS, 1998).
43 Ibid.
44 *Cooperation Agreement between the Secretariat of the Association of Caribbean States and the Secretariat of the Caribbean Tourism Organization* (Port of Spain: ACS, 1996).
45 ACS, *Agreement for the Establishment of the Sustainable Tourism Zone in the Caribbean* (Port of Spain: ACS, 1998).
46 Association of Caribbean States. Special Committee on the Environment and Natural Resources. *Draft Proposal of Environmental Strategy and Work Programme* (Port of Spain: ACS, 1977).
47 Association of Caribbean States, *Fourth Meeting of the Special Committee for the Protection and Conservation of the Environment and the Caribbean Sea and Natural Resources* (Port of Spain: ACS, 2000).
48 Ibid.
49 Nicol, "The ACS and Sustainable Development."
50 See ACS, *Integrating the Caribbean* (Port of Spain: ACS, 1999).
51 ACS, *Fourth Meeting of the Special Committee for the Protection and Conservation of the Environment and the Caribbean Sea and Natural Resources* (Port of Spain: ACS, 2000).
52 Ibid.
53 See Winston Anderson, *The Law of Caribbean Marine Pollution* (London: Kluwer Law International, 1997) for a discussion of UN efforts.
54 Serbin, *Sunset over the Islands,* 4.

9
Redefining the Nature and Functions of Boundaries: A South American Perspective
Roy Bradshaw

The boundaries of South America are highly distinctive. Whether in origin, historical development, or present-day role and function, the boundaries of South America are quite unlike those found anywhere else in the rest of the world. In Europe national identity and the related concept of territoriality have helped determine the location and function of national boundaries. Asia appears similar in that, for most Asians, questions of identity and territorial location are reasonably clearly defined. In Africa (see Asiwaju, Chapter 6, this volume) the system of nation-states and national boundaries is largely nonsensical, defying all logic except that of the former colonial powers; yet it has been accepted as a fully working system that few have yet challenged or successfully been able to alter.

South America is different. Unlike Europe, where strong linguistic, ethnic, religious, and cultural differences have all combined to form the elements that we know as national identity, in South America most of these elements are missing. Over the region many of the peoples have the same ethnic origins, speak the same language, practise the same religion, and have the same colonial history, the same basis for their legal and administrative systems, and so on. In other words, national identity and, with it, national territory and national boundaries are based on factors quite distinct from those found elsewhere on the globe. South American boundaries are different, and the reasons for this difference are to be found in the circumstances surrounding their origin and formation and, above all, in the historical development of the modern South American state.

The Origins of Boundaries in South America
Shortly before his death in 1830, Simón Bolívar declared "[South] America is ungovernable. Those who have served the revolution have ploughed the sea." However, he did not mean that it was impossible to govern *in* South America but, rather, that it was impossible to govern *as* South America. Bolívar's great dream of a pan-American union had come to nothing. His

more limited plan for an Andean confederation consisting of Gran Colombia, Peru, and Bolivia was never given any serious consideration, and even his own state of Gran Colombia was shortly to split into the constituent elements of Colombia, Ecuador, and Venezuela. However, the Spanish Empire had successfully governed much of South America as a single unit, or collection of units, for over 300 years. The Spanish Crown, together with the Roman Catholic Church, had provided very effective unifying forces within the region throughout this time. Colonial America had not been ungovernable: it was postcolonial unity that had proved so impossible to achieve.

The formations of the boundaries, national territories, and national states in South America all have their origins in the earliest days of colonial rule. The tensions, sentiments, and social groupings that were vital to the origin and maintenance of the various independence movements can all be traced back to the earliest days of colonization and colonial administration (or even before). For the 700 years prior to 1492, any Spaniard wishing for personal advancement had been able to join in the *Reconquista*, the struggle against the Moors, in the search for fame and fortune. The fall of Grenada and the discovery of the Americas in 1492 had closed off one set of possibilities and, at the same time, opened up another. Many tough, self-reliant, and adventurous Spaniards had been able to switch from participating in the reconquest of the Iberian Peninsula to participating in the creation of an empire. As a result, the typical early Spanish settlers in America have been described as "rough, uneducated peasants from Extremadura and Western Andalucia who were quick to mutiny or to disregard authority, for they had come out to the Caribbean islands to make a quick fortune and then to go back home again."[1]

The seeds of dissension and rebellion were present right from the start. The problems of administration and government in South America began with Columbus's governorship of the earliest Spanish settlements. As early as 1494 a faction of Catalans rebelled against the rule of Columbus's brother, Diego, who had been left in charge during Christopher's absence. Not only was there rivalry amongst the new settlers but there was also tension between the settlers and the Spanish authorities, particularly over the treatment of the Native peoples. Although Queen Isabella and all subsequent Spanish monarchs expressly forbade any slavery or maltreatment of the Native peoples, a system of indented labour, *encomienda*, was introduced in which the employer was forced to pay reasonable wages but the labourer was still forced to work. It was little more than slavery and open to a great deal of abuse.

It was a constant concern of the Spanish authorities throughout the 1500s to ensure that the Americas were governed in an ethical and Christian manner. Some of the early governors were enlightened, but others were unashamedly exploitative and used their positions to seek personal gain and to mistreat the indigenous peoples. There was constant tension between the local administration and the colonial authority back in Spain, which was determined to carry out efficient but fair government. This tension soon resolved itself into a conflict between the local-born people of Spanish origin (the *criollos*, who were denied access to the highest posts in the administration) and the officials sent out from Spain (the *peninsulares*, who were charged with carrying out the policy of the Spanish Crown).

What happened in Columbus's reign was repeated in Pizarro's takeover of the Inca Empire in Peru. Constant squabbles between the Pizarro brothers led to conflicts and, eventually, to civil war amongst the Spaniards. At the same time the behaviour of the Spanish settlers towards the Native peoples ensured their deep censure by the Spanish authorities. As early as 1546 the surviving Pizarro brothers sought to make themselves independent from Spain, with Gonzalo Pizarro being declared king of Peru. In 1547 a royal army entered Peru, and in the following year defeated the Pizarristas. Gonzalo Pizarro was executed and royal authority reasserted.

Thus, the potential problems of governance in South America can be identified from the very earliest days of colonial rule. The tensions, which gave rise to these problems, can be summarized as follows:

- the desire to get rich and to exercise political power by the earliest Spanish settlers, soon to be succeeded by their equally ambitious offspring, the American-born *criollos*
- resentment at control exerted by the Spanish colonial (i.e., non-local) authority
- resentment at restrictions over the production and trade of agricultural and manufactured goods, which were all strictly controlled by metropolitan Spain
- the desire by the *criollo* elites to replace metropolitan Spain as rulers in south America
- the resentment of the indigenous Indian peoples against their *criollo* masters and the desire to be treated as free individuals and not subject to the conditions of semi-slavery.

The indigenous Indians were largely unsuccessful in this latter aim, and even today they have rarely gained equality within the state. During the various wars of independence, they were often used as cannon fodder, fighting for one or other of the groups formed by members of the *criollo* elite. Of the present-day South American peoples, many of those who are of Indian origin remain largely on the edge of society, while those of European origin still hold most of the highest offices.

What the Spanish Empire, and in particular the Roman Catholic monarchy, was able to offer its American colonies was legitimacy and stability. The monarchy ruled under a system of benign paternalism, which accepted the ethnic and cultural pluralism of its subject peoples. The only requirements were loyalty to the Crown and adherence to the Roman Catholic faith.

> The culture of the Catholic monarchy possessed enduring strengths: it pervaded all strata of society, linking high culture and low; it could accommodate *mestizaje* (cross-breeding) in all spheres, from sexual relations to architecture; and finally it was capable of reconciling great ethnic and regional diversity with a sense of underlying unity.[2]

The resentments harboured amongst the *criollos* were directed against the arrogance of incoming peninsular immigrants and officials rather than against the Roman Catholic monarchy, which, the *criollos* fully understood, was vital to the survival of their society. By the seventeenth century the *criollos* represented a frustrated ruling class who were often seething with resentment against Spain but not against the authority of the monarchy. In part this was because the Crown provided legitimacy to the rather privileged lifestyle of the *criollos*; in part it was because of enlightened self-interest. The *criollos* knew that, in the event of an uprising by the indigenous peoples, the Spanish Empire would send in forces to reestablish authority.

Although this belief in the monarchy was somewhat shaken by the rule of the Bourbon monarchs, especially Charles III, who tried to implement reforms according to the best principles of the Enlightenment,[3] the authority of the Crown was never seriously challenged. It was the intervention of Napoleon in Spain in 1808 that led to the collapse of the system. Napoleon forced Charles IV and his son Ferdinand to renounce the throne and delivered the Crown to his own brother, Joseph. This act broke the compact between the absolute ruler, the Spanish monarch, and the subject peoples. Within Spanish America this act produced a constitutional crisis. The abrupt removal of the constitutional monarch now posed the question as to where legitimate authority lay – with the new monarch, with the former monarch, or with the *criollos* themselves? This situation provided a number of radicals, most of them from the *criollo* elite, with the opportunity to seize power. After 1810 South America broke up into a series of fratricidal struggles and occasionally full-blown civil wars as the various *criollo* groups lurched towards gaining full-blown independence for their respective regions.

The reason for the former empire splintering into many smaller nation-states is explained quite simply by the fact that these latter represented the major groupings of colonial society. The Spanish Empire was very far from occupying all the lands of South America. Most of the settlements were clustered around the major administrative centres and in the coastal regions. It was around these largely isolated groups that the new nation-states were formed.

With independence from Spain came the practical problem of delimiting the extent of national territory. In 1810 the doctrine of *uti possidetis de jure* was formed as a guideline towards the establishment of the boundaries of the newly independent states. The doctrine of *uti possidetis de jure* was generally understood to mean that each new state was entitled to the territory formerly under the jurisdiction of the former colonial authority, which it replaced. This doctrine was of questionable legal validity and of even greater practical difficulty with regard to implementation. There had been frequent administrative changes within the Spanish Empire, particularly in the preceding century, so that it was not always clear to which legitimate former colonial authority the doctrine should be applied. For example, Caracas and Venezuela had variously been administered from Santo Domingo in the Caribbean, from Bogotá in neighbouring Colombia, and from Caracas itself. Added to this confusion was the fact that there were often few if any accurate maps of the boundary areas. Many of the borders were located in uninhabited areas and, in some cases, had never been properly explored at all. Indeed, this situation is still true for many border areas today, and it is only to be expected that South American governments should, even now, view such areas as frontiers of opportunity waiting to be exploited.

In these circumstances it is not surprising that, for most countries of South America, the postcolonial period is dominated by border disputes and the struggle to gain territory and resources. The problem was exacerbated by the lack of distinction between the peoples of the region. The very factor that caused Bolívar to believe in the possibility of creating a united South America – the uniformity in the origins and nature of its society – was the very factor that facilitated territorial claims and boundary disputes throughout the region. In other parts of the world any attempt to take over neighbouring territory soon had to take into account the local people, who were of a different ethnic type, who spoke a different language, and who had a different culture. It should be noted that questions of postcolonial nationality and territoriality were almost entirely restricted to the influential *criollo/mestizo* sector of the population. The indigenous peoples were either indifferent to these matters or simply followed the lead of the local *criollo* elite. In much of South America this has not been a problem. For example, to the people of the northern Atacama it mattered very little whether they were ruled from Santiago, Lima, or La Paz. Such uniformity has made it very easy to pursue irredentist policies, and the lack of a clearly defined "other" has made it much easier to lay claim to vast tracts of territory.

As a result of these particular circumstances it is not surprising that, for many of the newly independent states, much of the nineteenth century and large parts of the twentieth century were spent in territorial disputes. Details of these disputes have been chronicled elsewhere,[4] and little more need be said of them here, except to point out that most have been intricate and that few have been resolved to the satisfaction of both sides. In some cases they have led to quite bloody conflicts, most notably the War of the Triple Alliance (1870), during which over a million Paraguayans died in the conflict with Brazil, Argentina, and Uruguay, leaving fewer than 300,000 survivors.[5] In the twentieth century such disputes have, fortunately, become rarer and generally much less bloody. Nevertheless, disputes still occur, and the recent flare-up in the Ecuador-Peru conflict over the boundary area in the Cordillera del Condor shows that they have not lost their capacity for viciousness. However, to place these events in context, it is salutary to compare a map of South America in 1900 with a map of Europe in 1900. Within the twentieth century, far greater territorial changes and much greater associated loss of life have occurred in the Old World than in the New World. Although in South America many boundary disputes remain, and the rhetoric is frequently bellicose, in reality it is quite rare for these disputes to lead to major conflicts.

Geopolitics in South America

There is a surprisingly large literature on geopolitics in most countries of South America, little of which finds its way into the outside world. It forms a major subject of study in many academic institutions and most military academies, particularly those within Chile, Argentina, and Brazil. At a time when conventional geopolitics has been almost entirely discredited in Europe and North America, in South America geopolitical discourse has been a topic of rapidly growing interest, particularly within the last twenty years. The strength of this interest has meant that geopolitical thinking underlies much of the current policy towards boundaries throughout South America.

For South American authorities, especially governments and military planners, geopolitical issues are an obvious subject of concern. In a region where most issues are still in a very fluid state and where there remain considerable potential resources still to be tapped, each national government is concerned to be in the most advantageous position possible to take full advantage of any future resources that may be uncovered. At the same time, governments watch their neighbours very closely to make sure that they do not gain some advantage at their own expense. In South American politics it is normal to regard every potential situation as a zero-sum game, where one country's advantage is thought to be gained entirely at another country's expense.

There are plenty of precedents to support such views. Chile's territorial advance north up the Pacific coast during the nineteenth century was largely based on the desire to gain control over the valuable guano (phosphate) and nitrate deposits in the disputed areas. It was Chilean policy to use these resources to pay for the costs of the war.[6] The current dispute (which may or may not have been satisfactorily resolved) between Ecuador and Peru in the Cordillera del Condor area is based partly on the possible presence of oil in the area, which is of vital importance to Peru (which, unlike Ecuador, is a net importer of oil), and on the old Ecuadorean dream of gaining a navigable outlet on the Amazon River – or at least its subsidiary the Marañon River. The dispute between Chile and Argentina over the islands in the Beagle Channel was intensified by the discovery that the waters of the South Atlantic may contain rich deposits of hydrocarbons.

In a major study of geopolitics in South America, Child[7] lists at least twenty actual or potential major conflicts in all Latin America and the Caribbean, of which at least fourteen involve South American states. Furthermore, many of these conflicts are interlinked. Movement on any one of these issues is likely to have a knock-on effect elsewhere. Thus the defeat of the Argentinean armed forces in the Falklands/Malvinas War, together with the destruction of Argentinean war *matériel,* eased the pressure on Chile in terms of the dispute over the Beagle Channel and other border issues.

To these many actual and potential conflicts should be added a rich vein of geopolitical writings that provide, or at least purport to provide, a coherent account of national development, national destiny, territorial claims, and international relations with neighbouring states. These writings usually portray a harsh and cruel Darwinian world full of competitive states that are engaged in a vicious game of survival of the fittest. In this vision it is the most aggressive nations that not only survive but also manage to increase their power and influence and finally gain control over territory and resources.

Geopolitical thinking in South America has been developed out of a close study of the early pioneers, including Ratzel, Kjellen, Mahan, Mackinder, and Haushofer. However, whereas in Europe and North America their association with Nazism discredited these ideas, in South America the study of geopolitics was to continue unabated throughout the postwar period and to flourish particularly in the period following the 1960s. Many of the earliest writings were based on an organic theory of the state, an idea first developed by Ratzel and his followers in the nineteenth century. This metaphor was based on the idea that a state was like a living organism that had to be healthy and strong in order to prosper and grow. This concept was expanded to include many aspects of national life. For example, in 1968 Franco's Spain had adopted a new constitution based on an "Organic Law" that was intended to provide the framework for the entire political and social development of Spain in the post-Franco era.[8] Following Franco's death and the establishment of Western-style democracy, the concept of the organic state was discredited and abandoned in Spain. However, in South America, the concept was to continue in use as a guide to both the internal and external policies of nation-states. For example, in July 1983 the government of Venezuela passed the *Ley Orgánica para la Ordenación del Territorio* (Organic Law for Territorial Management), which was designed to coordinate and integrate the "internal geopolitics of the nation."[9] The aim of this law was to guide and promote the occupation and full use of national territory, including the establishment of new settlements and the promotion of new economic and social activities in interior areas, thereby ensuring the constant and sustained growth of Venezuela's economy and to help Venezuela become a great nation.

However, more typically, the organic theory of the state has been used as a basis for guiding a nation's external policy. Thus, organic concepts have often been used to promote highly nationalistic policies based on the creation of a strong domestic economy but with the ultimate aim of using this domestic economy to help advance the expansion of the state to its "natural frontiers." Such policies, adapted from the ideas of Karl Haushofer, have been summarized by the leading Chilean geopolitician, General Augusto Pinochet, as follows:

- that every state needs *lebensraum*, the vital space that a state needs in order to grow and expand
- that a state's boundaries should be based on natural features that should mark out the limits to this *lebensraum*
- that a state should develop a strong domestic economy and not be dependent on any other state – a policy of political and economic *autarchy*
- that a state should expand out into its sphere of influence in order to exercise its maximum power in the world.[10]

Such a policy takes no account of neighbouring states, which are either ignored or are assumed to be destined to lose out to the "fittest" states in the constant struggle for survival. A state becomes "fit" by pursuing the correct geopolitical policies. It is easy to see how this form of thinking can lead to bellicose policies and military confrontation, and why it is so attractive to military leaders as a means of justifying their position in society.

In South America geopolitics has, in extreme cases, been used to promote and justify a crude and often very confused form of *realpolitik*. The

American analyst Jack Child,[11] who was born and lived his early life in Buenos Aires, quotes the case of a senior Argentinean general who had been in charge of his country's border commission and who had been advocating a doctrine based on the "law of the orange." Behind this "law" was the idea that an orange, thrown anywhere into the River Plate Basin, would eventually float past Buenos Aires and therefore come under Argentinean influence. By implication this would be true of many other human activities as well. At its worst, this mode of thinking has given rise to a rhetoric that appears to be full of bombast and self-delusion. For example, the following is a section from the writings of one of Argentina's leading geopolitical writers, Jorge T. Briano:

> The exceptional historico-political formation of the Argentine nation has been made possible thanks to the marvellous conjunction of the most favourable geographic environment and the optimum ethnic conditions of the Argentine People, which probably cannot be found in any other country on earth. The spiritual currents of the human masses which make up the country – essentially and principally Graeco-Latin – have produced a philosophical and political conception that distinguishes it with unique characteristics, which are humanitarian, with a universal transcendence, which have made of Argentina the recipient of the friendship and consideration of all the people of the Earth.[12]

In keeping with this observation, Child goes on to note that the sense of Argentinean geopolitical greatness can "become wrapped up in the excessive pride and even arrogance and racism, that is the occasional dark side of the Argentine character."[13]

However, to put this into perspective, the first country to propound and execute geopolitical policies within the hemisphere was the United States, with the promulgation of the Monroe Doctrine and the long-held view that the Caribbean is an "American lake" and that the rest of Latin America forms "Uncle Sam's backyard." Indeed, the United States has been far more active in promoting its national policy overseas than have any of its southern neighbours, and it has directly interfered in the internal affairs of practically every state south of the Rio Grande.

In his study of South American geopolitical discourse and military thinking, Hepple[14] discusses the extraordinary power of the underlying organic metaphor for fuelling much of this geopolitical thinking. As he points out, the organic metaphor is one of the "big" metaphors in social and political theory. It provides a powerful and intuitively accessible explanation of the role and function of states. However, a metaphor is merely a way of making sense of some aspect of the world; it is not necessarily the "correct" way and is certainly not the only way of viewing the world, although hopefully it is a useful way. As Demeritt points out, "No metaphor can provide total, unmediated vision. Rather metaphors are enforcing devices that make the world knowable while always already precluding still other ways of ordering the world."[15] It should also be remembered that a metaphor is the application of a name or description to an object to which it is not literally connected.[16] Thus, the organic concept is a metaphor taken from the plant kingdom and applied to political and military situations. Demerritt goes on to warn of the dangers of "appropriative holism," of claiming unwarranted exclusivity for a metaphor. No matter how useful a metaphor has been at one stage in its existence it can easily become inappropriate and out of date.

Hepple[17] has discussed the possible death of the organic metaphor in geopolitical thinking and practice in South America, suggesting that the demise of many of the former right-wing military regimes would be accompanied by the demise of their policies as well. This judgment would seem to be somewhat premature. The tradition of the *cuadillo*, the populist nationalist leader, is still very strongly embedded in the South American psyche and is probably far too strong to have disappeared for good. Indeed, the continued survival of Fidel Castro and the more recent election of the ex-paratroop commander Hugo Chaves in Venezuela suggests that, in South America, the appeal of charismatic military leaders is as powerful as ever.

Hepple goes on to suggest that new metaphors are needed to replace the "state-as-organism" metaphor, which he regards as no longer acceptable. He pleads for a number of smaller, more focused metaphors that will clarify the legitimate needs and objectives of the state without attempting to link them together within this overarching organic framework that has done "such a disservice to political debate."[18] (This is further addressed below.)

The Globalization Thesis and the "End of the Nation-State"?

Throughout much of the 1990s it has been argued that, with the rise of transnational corporations (TNCs) and the extraordinary increase in the size and influence of the international financial system, there has been a concomitant reduction in the economic autonomy of the state. Indeed, there can be no doubt that we now live in a New World Order in which the globalization of trade and capital has undermined the economic sovereignty of nation-states.[19] Various authors have taken this further and argued that a loss of economic sovereignty will lead inevitably to the destruction of the basis for the nation-state as the focal point of political activity and authority, and that with globalization we are seeing the end of the nation-state.[20]

There has been much debate as to what constitutes globalization, but all of the following have been put forward as key factors in the globalization process:

- the rise of the international financial system. That the coming of modern electronic communication systems has made it possible to develop twenty-four-hours-a-day banking systems, which now account for enormous quantities of financial transactions (far greater than the volumes of money that a single nation-state can deploy, even one as powerful as the US).
- the rise in importance of TNCs. That global companies are now able to deploy their resources around the globe so that they can maximize their economic power and minimize any control that might be exerted by a national government.
- the rise of the global market. That the postwar years have seen the rise of global products such as Coca-Cola, Persil washing powder, and so on, and that, increasingly, companies are thinking in terms of products for global rather than national markets.
- the rise of global cultures. That increasingly companies such as Coca-Cola do not sell a product so much as a way of life, a feel-good factor, a part of the "American dream."
- the retreat of the state and the rise of the market in determining the prosperity of citizens. That as a result of the previous items the prosperity of citizens depends increasingly on factors such as interest rates and stock market performance, factors that are largely global and not national in behaviour.

Although there has been considerable debate as to whether globalization is a new phenomenon or, as some authors suggest, merely the recent and rapid extension of existing trends,[21] the more intriguing issue has been to try to identify the impact that this process of globalization is likely to have around the world. Ohmae[22] presents a convincing case that the countries of the "Triad" – Japan, North America, and Europe – are all well positioned to take full advantage of globalization. What is far less clear is how this will affect the economies located in the less favourable parts of the world. For example, South America hardly figures at all in Ohmae's analysis. In fact, there are a number of factors that indicate that South America is not well placed to take advantage of the new opportunities of the global economy.

One of these factors is history. As we have seen, the historical precedent in South America is not in favour of the types of cooperation between states that globalization requires. Historical experience and geopolitical thinking has left behind a legacy of mutual suspicion. The dismantling of border controls and the opening up of economies to outside influences goes against almost every instinct of current geopolitical and nationalistic thinking. Modern successful economies, as Fukiyama has noted, depend on high levels of trust; however, as noted above, in South American geopolitics the typical response tends to be one of paranoia rather than mutual cooperation.

Geography has also played an important role. As has been noted, most of the states of South America are based around core areas, and the border zones are frequently located in inhospitable territory with very few inhabitants. In such circumstances it is not possible to think in terms of the same levels of cross-border activities that are being promoted with such success in Europe. In fact, in many parts of South America there is no shortage of plans and projects to promote increased cross-border activity and cooperation. See, for example, any issue of the Venezuelan journal *Aldea Mundo*, which maintains a full record of such proposals for the Venezuelan-Colombian border. Notwithstanding the laudable intentions contained in these projects, the total level of activity remains low compared with the national economy as a whole. For most South American states the border areas are very much on the periphery of national territory, and the scope for cooperative ventures continues to remain very low.

Transportation has also been a key factor in inhibiting interaction and cooperation. Again, due to physical factors, much of South America is quite difficult of access. Most communication networks are centred on the core areas of the state, and cross-border crossings are often quite rare. For example, along the 1,600 kilometres of border between Venezuela and Colombia there are really only two or three worthwhile crossing points, and only one is presently suitable for carrying a large volume of international trade.

The modern economy also plays a key role in the development of borderlands and boundaries. The Venezuelan writer Kaldone Nweihed[23] has attempted to catalogue the winners and losers in the globalization process, using as his starting point Paul Streeten's analysis (see Table 9.1). Nweihed argues that, for every one of Streeten's categories, South America appears on the "losers" rather than the "winners" side of the ledger. He goes on to cite the work of Owen Lippert of the Fraser Foundation in support of his argument that the process of globalization is bound to increase the gap between rich and poor societies.[24] The states of South America, with poor communications, low levels of computer ownership, underdeveloped financial and service sectors, among other factors, are at a distinct disadvantage in the new globalized society. As far as globalization is concerned, much of South America falls into the "poor" category.

Few South American states enter into trade with the dominant Triad. The one major international trading partner is the US. Trade with Europe and Asia is, with very few exceptions, quite low. Even for the three largest economies in the region – Venezuela, Argentina, and Brazil – most trade is destined to remain in the hemisphere. For example, Venezuela sends 56.7 percent of its exports to, and receives 45.0 percent of its imports from, the US, while a further 38.4 percent of its imports and 21.5 percent of its exports remain within Latin America (all figures refer to exports by value for the year 1997). Very little of Venezuela's trade is with the rest of the world. The figures are rather better for Argentina and Brazil, where no more than about 50 percent of trade remains within the Americas, indicating a more diverse trading pattern. The situation worsens for many of the smaller countries, such as Ecuador and Uruguay, where 60 percent or more of the trade is conducted within the hemisphere. The pattern of trade by commodities can also indicate a very heavy reliance on the export of raw materials. Outstanding is the case of Venezuela, where 46.3 percent

Table 9.1

Winners and losers in the globalization process

Identity of sector affected	Winners	Losers
Level of the individual (biological)	Men	Women
Economic level	Those who can afford to pay for private services Savers	Those who cannot afford to pay for private services Borrowers
Labour	Qualified workers Flexible workforce Techno-specialists	Unqualified workers Inflexible workforce Basic producers
Level of the individual (social)	People with interests	People without interests
Cultural	The global	The local
Socio-economic functions	Production, utility	Employment, salary
Company level	International market Large enterprises Flexible firms	Local communities Small enterprises Inflexible firms
Geographical or macro-cultural region	East and South-East Asia	Africa and South America

Source: After K.G. Nweihed, *Globalización: Dos rostros y una máscara* (Caracas: Instituto de Altos Estudios de America Latina, Universidad Simón Bolívar, 1999).

of exports are made up of extractive industries (mainly oil). Ecuador, Bolivia, and Colombia are also very heavily reliant on the export of extractive products (again oil).

From the above, it can be seen that South America is extremely poorly placed to gain full advantage from the new, globalizing world economy. The impact of globalization on levels of cross-border activity within South America is likely to remain relatively small until a number of fundamental changes are brought about, ranging from basic improvements to communications and transportation structures through to new forms of political dialogue and ideology.

Conclusions

Hepple has argued for a new set of metaphors to explain the workings and function of the modern nation-state. He asserts that the old metaphor of the "state as organism" is both misleading and dangerous and that it needs to be replaced by less ambitious but more highly focused metaphors. These new metaphors would explain smaller but more clearly defined areas of social and political activity. In line with this recommendation, I offer a number of observations concerning the metaphors and theoretical concepts currently being used to explain borderland activities and developments concerning South American boundaries.

The dominant metaphor of boundaries at the present time is derived from Giddens's concept of the boundary as "container"[25] – the idea that boundaries represents the edge of the vessel that "contains" all the power relations of a modern state. However, this view is very centrist, conceptualizing boundaries from within the container and seeing them as the lines that indicate the locus where authority ends. It says nothing about cross-border activity. Taylor's more recent modification of this dominant metaphor has introduced the "leaky container" concept,[26] which emphasizes that the container is not entirely watertight and that some activities manage to seep through its gaps. This metaphor is an improvement in that it does permit cross-border activity. Unfortunately, it tolerates all activities seeping through, whereas in the real world restrictions are often placed on certain cross-border relations.

A further refinement might involve considering boundaries as the analogues of those chemical membranes that allow the passage of certain chemicals but restrain the movements of others. This would have the advantage of allowing both the restraining and the permissive aspects of a boundary to be included in the explanation. However, even these modifications do not throw light on the rich pattern of activities that can often be discerned in borderland areas. In South America borderlands are important for a whole range of activities, apart from the more traditional ones of trade and transport. Borderlands may be attractive to guerrilla movements seeking refuge across the border. They are frequently used by smugglers and for other criminal activities, including drug trafficking and kidnapping. Indeed, South America is no exception to the rule that all boundaries are leaky, no matter how well they are fenced and patrolled by police or military forces. Just as the boundary between North and South Korea, or the boundary formed by the Berlin Wall, was never completely sealed, so boundaries in South America remain permeable. In general it is possible to restrict the flows that cross a boundary, but it is never possible to stop them.

When conceptualizing the nature and functions of boundaries we may, in the past, have been all too ready to regard borderlands as limits, as places where activities and influences are terminated or at least "contained," rather than as phenomena in their own right, with their own range of possibilities and distinctive activities. Perhaps it is time to move on from Giddens's concept of the boundary as container, or even Taylor's concept of the leaky container. Perhaps our new conceptualization of boundaries and boundary areas, our new metaphors, should give more emphasis to the enabling and distinctive features of borderlands and borderland activities.

Notes

1 E. Williamson, *The Penguin History of Latin America* (London: Penguin, 1992), 13.
2 Ibid., 164.
3 J. Lynch, "The Origins of Spanish American Independence," in *The Cambridge History of Latin America*, vol. 3, ed. L. Bethell (Cambridge: Cambridge University Press, 1985), 15.
4 See, for example, J. Child, *Geopolitics and Conflict in South America* (New York: Praeger, 1985); G. Ireland, *Boundaries, Possessions and Conflicts in South America* (Cambridge: Harvard University Press, 1938); R. Bruce St. John, "The Boundary between Ecuador and Peru," *Boundary and Territory Briefing* 1, 4 (1994); International Boundaries Research Unit, University of Durham (or R. Bruce St. John), "The Bolivia-Chile-Peru Dispute in the Atacama Desert," *Boundary and Territory Briefing* 1, 6 (1994): 207.
5 M. Niedergang, *The Twenty-Nine Latin Americas* (London: Penguin, 1971).
6 Bruce St. John, "The Bolivia-Chile-Peru Dispute," 13.
7 Child, *Geopolitics and Conflict.*
8 See K. Medhurst, *The Government of Spain* (Oxford: Pergamon, 1972), 26.
9 See M. del Pilar Lliso, "La Ley Orgánica de Ordenamiento Territorial como fundamento para la solución de los problemas territoriales internos del país," in *Compendio de la Geopolítica en Venezuela*, ed. O. Quintana Castro, C.E. Celis Noguera, E. Siblez Vera, C. de Castro, J. Montesano, G. Gonzalez Eraso, A. Coello, F. Maduro, C. Lepervanche, S. Sanchez de Pacheco, M. Garcia Villasmil, and L. Diaz Gonzalez (Caracas: Ediciones Fundaiaeden, 1997), 370.
10 A. Pinochet Ugarte, *Geopolítica de Chile* (México: El Cid Editor, 1978).
11 See Child, *Geopolitics and Conflict.*
12 Ibid., 46. See also J.T. Briano, *Geopolítica y Geoestratégia Americana* (Caracas: Pleamar, 1966).
13 Child, *Geopolitics and Conflict.*
14 L.W. Hepple, "Metaphor, Geopolitical Discourse and the Military in South America," in *Writing Worlds,* ed. T.J. Barnes and J.S Duncan (London: Routledge, 1992).
15 D. Demeritt, "The Nature of Metaphors in Cultural Geography and Environmental History," *Progress in Human Geography* 18, 2 (1994): 81.

16 See M. Hesse, *Models and Analogies in Science* (London: Sheed and Ward, 1963); and "The Explanatory Function of Metaphors," in *Revolutions and Reconstructions in the Philosophy of Science* (Brighton: Harvestor, 1984).
17 Hepple, "Metaphor, Geopolitical Discourse," 152-54.
18 Ibid., 154.
19 H. Dittgen, "World without Borders? Reflections on the Future of the Nation State," paper presented at the Fifth International Conference of the International Boundaries Research Unit, University of Durham, Borderlands under Stress.
20 See Kenichi Ohmae, *The End of the Nation State* (London: Harper Collins, 1995); and S. Strange, *The Retreat of the State: The Diffusion of Power in the World Economy* (Cambridge: Cambridge University Press, 1996).
21 P. Hirst and G. Thompson, *Globalization in Question* (Cambridge: Policy Press, 1996).
22 Ohmae, *The End of the Nation State.*
23 K.G. Nweihed, *Globalización: Dos rostros y una máscara* (Caracas: Instituto de Altos Estudios de America Latina, Universidad Simón Bolívar, 1999).
24 Ibid., 104.
25 A. Giddens, *The Nation-State and Violence* (Cambridge: Polity Press, 1985).
26 P.J. Taylor, "The State as Container: Territoriality in the Modern World-System," in *Progress in Human Geography* 18, 2 (1994): 151-62; and "Beyond Containers: Internationality, Interstateness, Interterritoriality," *Progress in Human Geography* 19, 1 (1995): 1-15.

Part 5
A Borderless North America?

The chapters in this section address the issue of transborder regionalism in North America from the perspective of specific transnational experiences. Western Canada's border with the United States and the US-Mexican borderlands are explored from the perspective of ongoing regional efforts to diminish political, economic, cultural, and social divisions among border communities. The perspective of Part 5 is thus somewhat at odds with current thinking about North American borders promulgated by post-9/11 and/or the American invasion of Iraq and its "war on terrorism." Rather than regarding borders in North America as "weak zones" that must be strengthened by building walls, the chapters in this section focus on integration. While the changing geopolitics of American borders in the twenty-first century has resulted in a growing adherence to "risk politics" (where security issues dominate international agendas and popular journalism), the four chapters in this section take a different perspective. Rather than focusing upon American national security issues as played out along the Canadian and Mexican borders, they look at the continued validity of building cross-border regions and at the geographical potential and institutional initiatives that link communities that, for all intents and purposes, provide strategic bridges for regional development. Security becomes but one variable to be weighed in the building of transfrontier policy, transportation, and environmental agendas.

One of the important points made by the chapters in Part 5 is that, although NAFTA remains a viable transnational initiative, transnationalism within North America has not progressed to the same degree that it has, for example, in Europe. As all these chapters observe, the growing volume of trade between the three North American states has posed major new challenges for their cross-border transportation systems. Continental structures to promote continental integration, particularly in the area of transportation, have proven less effective than have regional responses to specific transborder issues. Yet, conceptually, regionalism has not been a mainstream concept in the study of international relations in North America, where, as Ted Cohen observes in Chapter 10, it has "aroused connotations of something small in scale, something provincial, practical, innocent, and weak."

Given this reality, the chapters in Part 5 indicate that, in the face of large deficits in infrastructural and institutional linkages among the national and international continental community, regionalism in North America may indeed be the only viable solution to problems of transborder communication. For example, Cohen compares Canadian and Mexican border interfaces, arguing that the latter are more successful because of the nature of regional linkages that have evolved, while Donald Alper, in Chapter 11, focuses upon Cascadian, or Washington State/British Columbia, regional efforts. Alper argues that, while the Canada-US border in western North America was always an area of cross-border interaction, "increased interdependencies within Cascadia have focused considerable attention on this north-south transboundary region. Particular attention has been given to regional economic development, environmental protection, transportation, border crossings, and other issues related to the notion of sustainability."

Virtually all of the essays in Part 5 touch upon the critical role of regional structures in building a new, if still limited, cross-border transnationalism that is regionally specific to Cascadia. In Chapter 12, Alan Artibise suggests that, at the macrolevel (i.e., in terms of the initiatives that engage national decision makers in Canada and the US), there is reason to believe that Western Canada has achieved a considerable degree of regional integration. At the same time, regional cooperation has forged a transborder community of cooperation in ways that broader initiatives have not; Cascadia now involves a wide variety of activities and frameworks for gathering and sharing information.

Most of the chapters in Part 5 would conclude that, although regional arrangements specific to Cascadia have spawned new patterns of functional interaction, new forms of cross-border governance and policy coordination are noticeably lacking. As Daniel Turbeville and Susan Bradbury indicate in Chapter 13 in their discussion of NAFTA, this is as true at the continental scale (where the grain of transportation infrastructure remains strongly east-west in orientation) as it is at the regional scale (where institutional initiatives are most affected in the limited policy areas of environment and transportation). NAFTA "moves by trucks" as a result – making border crossings at major vehicular checkpoints the primary transborder interface.

In comparison to earlier chapters in *Holding the Line*, which discuss the potential for regionalism in building transnational communities in Europe, the Caribbean, and Africa, the chapters in Part 5 suggest that the North

American transnational experience has been limited. In North America there remain, as some have described them, "good old-fashioned states" with strong borders, much like those Bradshaw discusses in South American nations (although perhaps for different reasons). Nonetheless, it is clear that the Old World and the New World remain differentiated by the degree to which territorial integration has advanced beyond traditional state-centred models of cooperation and transnationalism.

10
Transportation and Competitiveness in North America: The Cascadian and San Diego-Tijuana Border Regions
Theodore H. Cohn

The United States' trade and foreign investment linkages with Canada and Mexico were already extremely close before the North American Free Trade Agreement (NAFTA) came into effect in January 1994, and this agreement has further solidified these ties. The growing volume of trade between the three North American states has posed major new challenges for their cross-border transportation systems; this is because trucks carry almost 70 percent of the goods traded between the United States and Canada, over 80 percent of US-Mexico trade, and about 60 percent of Canada-Mexico trade.[1] The importance of rapid transport to trade liberalization objectives was in fact evident to the negotiators of NAFTA, who included in the agreement detailed provisions on liberalizing land transportation services.[2] Rapid transportation throughout North America depends on upgrading transport infrastructure and on modernizing and easing the regulations regarding cross-border transit. However, because of the different requirements and priorities of the various regional ports-of-entry, it is difficult to generalize about the effects of transportation on trade efficiency and competitiveness along the entire length of the Canada-US and Mexico-US borders.[3]

This chapter focuses on the efforts to facilitate rapid transport as a means of promoting competitiveness in two NAFTA cross-border regions: Cascadia and San Diego-Tijuana. Although regional and national competitiveness are complementary, the various regions (including cross-border regions) in large, diverse states such as the United States, Canada, and Mexico often compete with each other for trade and foreign investment. Thus, any given region must face "the possibility of being underbid or outbid by a competitor region."[4] After discussing the role of transportation in promoting regional competitiveness in general, I focus upon two aspects of cross-border transport: (1) the development of transport infrastructure for border areas and (2) the development of innovative regulations and procedures to facilitate cross-border travel. I also examine the major obstacles to promoting a more "seamless" border, ranging from funding shortages to disputes regarding the cross-border movement of trucks and people.

The two regions of special concern in this chapter are Cascadia and San Diego-Tijuana. I use the most common definition of "Cascadia," which includes the Canadian province of British Columbia (BC) and the American states of Washington and Oregon. While governmental and non-governmental actors at the provincial/state level have formed many of the Cascadia cross-border institutions discussed below, municipal governments have also established some cross-border institutions (such as the Cascadia Metropolitan Forum and the Cascadia Mayors Council).[5] Thus, with regard to the key actors, the Cascadia region is defined in rather diffuse terms. The San Diego-Tijuana region, by contrast, is defined primarily in terms of the two main cities in the area. A major reason for this difference relates to the location of the largest cities in relation to the two border areas. San Diego is only about thirty-two kilometres from the border with Mexico, while Tijuana extends up to and along the international border. Transborder regional concerns therefore tend to focus on these two cities, and a *Who's Who Directory* of institutions and individuals involved in cross-border activities states that "the important and growing ties between San Diego and Tijuana represent the emergence of a binational region with shared interests and challenges."[6] In the Cascadia case, by contrast, Vancouver, BC, is about fifty-three kilometres north of the Canada-US border, while Seattle and Portland are 178 and 453 kilometres south of the border. These cities are simply too far apart to establish a highly interdependent relationship. Vancouver, in fact, has a far greater impact on Bellingham and Blaine, Washington, which are much closer to the border than is Seattle. However, Bellingham and Blaine are too small to be significant focal points of the Cascadia region. (Some institutions in Bellingham, such as the Whatcom County Council of Governments, do play an important role in promoting transborder regionalism.)

Cascadia and San Diego-Tijuana were selected for this study because of their importance as NAFTA transborder regions and because of the possibilities of drawing comparisons between them. Tijuana has become a major site for foreign-based *maquiladora* plants, largely because of its proximity to San Diego; and the service industries of San Diego often utilize Mexican labour. There has also been an exponential growth of travel across the common border, and today the San Ysidro border crossing between the two cities is the busiest international land crossing in the world, with over ninety million persons crossing in 1998.[7] The San Diego metropolitan area is also the largest urban area in the entire US-Mexico border region, encompassing almost one-half of the population on the southern US border.[8] In Cascadia the cross-border ties have resulted from a strong feeling "that the natural and built environments, the economy of the region, and the socio-cultural characteristics of the residents ... [have] more in common than any part of the region ... [has] with other areas in either Canada or the United States."[9] Cross-border trade and tourism are important contributors to prosperity in the Cascadia region, and the Peace Arch Crossing between BC and Washington State is the third busiest along the Canada-US border, with nearly four million crossings in 1995-96. The BC-Washington State border ports, as a group, registered about seventeen million crossings in 1995-96.[10]

Mexico-US and Canada-US border relationships have some starkly different characteristics, largely because of Mexico's lower level of economic development. Despite these major differences, there are some important similarities between the Cascadia and San Diego-Tijuana experiences. Both regions have a Pacific coast orientation and place considerable emphasis on economic linkages along the Western coast of North America and the Asia Pacific. These two regions are also located a long distance from their national capitals in Ottawa, Mexico City, and Washington, DC. In Cascadia, this distance has contributed to feelings of "western alienation." BC governments, whether led by the Social Credit, Liberal, or New Democratic Party, have often pitted themselves against the federal government; and in Washington State, Seattle often seems to have "more in common with Vancouver, B.C., than Washington, D.C."[11] In the Tijuana-San Diego region, Governor Ernest Ruffo Appel (1989-95) from the opposition National Action Party (PAN) in Baja, California, strongly pressured the Mexican government (led by the dominant Institutional Revolutionary Party [PRI]) to transfer more fiscal capacity to the state and local levels. Thus, the geographic location of Cascadia and San Diego-Tijuana has contributed to a unique brand of activist politics in both regions.[12]

Before focusing on Cascadia and San Diego-Tijuana, it is necessary to examine what insights we can gain from the general literature on regionalism, competitiveness, and transportation.

Studies of Regionalism and Competitiveness

A striking characteristic of the literature on competitiveness is its almost exclusive focus on the competitiveness of nation-states and international firms, even though "regions are one of the essential bases of industrial organization in the emerging global economy."[13] Part of the reason for this oversight stems from the fact that regionalism has not been a mainstream concept in the study of international relations. Traditionally, regionalism has aroused "connotations of something small in scale, something provincial, practical, innocent, and weak. It has been depicted as one of the principles organizing political space within states, but as void of relevance in a broader context."[14] The tendency to overlook regional competitiveness also stems from the preoccupations of economists. For example, David

Ricardo's influential theory of comparative advantage explains the benefits of trade on the basis of the relative advantages of nation-states. Concentration on the national level has limited the number of relevant actors and made theories such as comparative advantage more manageable.[15]

In this age of globalization, the view of regionalism as a low-profile issue of little political significance – or as a negative influence – must be reconsidered. During the Cold War years state borders were quite rigid, and there was little room for cross-border regionalism. With the decline of the Cold War, however, the "high politics" of state security issues has had to share the stage with "low political" preoccupations such as economic growth, integration, and interdependence. Along with this shift towards socioeconomic issues has gone a heightened interest in regional relationships, including cross-border regionalism. Some writers have become more attuned to the importance of regional competitiveness. In her groundbreaking study entitled *Cities and the Wealth of Nations*, Jane Jacobs has focused on the limitations of examining competitiveness only at the national level. According to Jacobs, most states "are composed of collections or grab bags of very different economies, rich regions and poor ones within the same nation."[16] Explicitly adopting a regional view of competitiveness, Jacobs asserts that "a nation in which city economies have been enfeebled is necessarily a nation in process of becoming poor and backward."[17]

In *The Competitive Advantage of Nations*, Michael Porter argues that competitive advantage develops from geographic concentration, or from "clusters" of related industries within a nation-state. These "internationally successful ... industry clusters frequently concentrate in a city or region, and the bases for advantage are often intensely local ... While the national government has a role in upgrading industry, the role of state and local governments is potentially as great or greater."[18] In *The Work of Nations*, Robert Reich similarly refers to the development of competitive "symbolic-analytic zones" within nation-states, which have each developed a unique combination of institutions and skills over time. For example, the Los Angeles area is known for film and music; greater Boston and the San Francisco Bay area are known for science and engineering; and New York is known for law, advertising, publishing, and global finance.[19]

Kenichi Ohmae argues that "region states" are the important boundaries to consider in terms of global economic relationships today. The United States is, in fact, a collection of region states, some of which cross the border with Canada and Mexico; for example, Ohmae identifies Cascadia and the San Diego-Tijuana corridor as region states that overlap existing national boundaries. While a region state must be small enough for its citizens to share certain common interests, it must also be large enough to support the infrastructure needed to participate effectively in the global economy. Thus, a region state must have at least one international airport and one good harbour with international class freight-handling facilities.[20] Paul Krugman discusses the important historical role of the US manufacturing belt, a cross-border region that extended from the US Northeast and Midwest into Ontario. The manufacturing belt retained its dominance for so long because of the advantage to individual firms in clustering together, even after the US production of most raw materials had moved to other regions.[21] Since the manufacturing belt industries benefited from economies of scale, this region "had a better transport network than any other part of the country."[22] It is to the role of transportation in promoting competitiveness that we now turn.

Studies of Transportation and Competitiveness

Historically, advances in transportation have contributed to major breakthroughs in economic development. The world's first great commercial centres developed around seaports, and a second wave of economic development took place in river- and canal-based cities that were central to the Industrial Revolution. Railroads were critical to a third wave of industrial development, and a fourth wave resulted from the shift to trucks and cars for moving goods and people. A fifth wave of development is associated with a greater emphasis on high-speed jet airplanes and advanced telecommunications technologies.[23] Rapid transport has become even more important in promoting development and competitiveness in recent years, with the shift to global sourcing and exporting. The emphasis on speedy production processes became particularly evident in the early 1980s when auto manufacturers began implementing just-in-time (JIT) production techniques to reduce their stockpiles of raw materials and parts.[24] The JIT concept is straightforward – to deliver material to production points at the precise time and in the exact amount required. By synchronizing all stages of the value chain from raw material acquisition to finished products, JIT production shortens sourcing, production, and delivery times, and gives firms a competitive advantage in pricing. Closely associated with the JIT concept in production are the concepts of quick response (QR) in the retailing and apparel industries, and efficient consumer response (ECR) in the food and grocery industries. Increasingly, competitiveness will be determined by rapid response time, which, in turn, will depend on the timely movement of goods through railways, highways, seaports, and airports.[25]

Rapid transport has been essential to the economic vitality of cities and regions. While regions with high degrees of traffic congestion and pollution can lose important industries, regions in the forefront of transport infrastructure and technology reap significant economic benefits.[26] For example, a 1990 report listed London and Paris as being among the most desired locations for European business because of their good transportation facilities. Fifty-seven percent of the firms surveyed considered transportation to be an "absolutely essential" factor in their decision to locate in a particular city.[27] The sections that follow examine the special challenges in developing multimodel transport systems for cross-border regions such as Cascadia and San Diego-Tijuana. In comparing these two cases, it is useful to focus on two types of cross-border transport issues: (1) the development of transport infrastructure and (2) the development of innovative regulations and procedures to facilitate border crossings.

Cascadia

In the 1990s a number of government agencies, private business groups, and informal transborder institutions became committed to facilitating cross-border transport in Cascadia. The establishment of the Canada-US Free Trade Agreement in 1988 and NAFTA in 1994 increased these groups' awareness that an efficient and seamless transportation system was essential if Cascadia were to attain its competitive potential. Vancouver, Seattle, and Portland have a natural advantage as sea and air transport points because of their greater proximity to Japan and other areas in the Asia Pacific. Nevertheless, Cascadia faces serious competition from the ports and railroads in the Los Angeles-Long Beach area of California, which put aside their differences in developing the Alameda Corridor. Without similar cooperation in linking ports, airports, and cities with high-speed rail and roadways in Cascadia, its natural advantage in terms of distance to Asia will be eroded.[28] Due to political, bureaucratic, and economic obstacles, progress in developing a rapid and seamless transportation system in Cascadia has been slow. However, some initiatives that have shown considerable promise are discussed below: the PACE/CANPASS dedicated commuter lanes, the Cascadia Project, and the International Mobility and Trade Corridor Project (IMTC).

PACE/CANPASS

A number of transborder groupings in Cascadia, such as the Discovery Institute, the Cascadia Institute, the Pacific Northwest Economic Region (PNWER), and the Pacific Corridor Enterprise Council (PACE), have sought to facilitate the cross-border movement of goods, services, and people.[29] One result of these groups' efforts was the introduction of a Peace Arch Crossing Entry (PACE) dedicated commuter lane at the main border crossing between BC and Washington State in 1991, which permits frequent and low-risk travellers who have undergone a police background check to by-pass regular inspection lanes. The actual decision to introduce the PACE lane resulted from a 1990 regional agreement signed by two Canadian and two US officials, which required final approval by the US Department of State, Canada's Department of External Affairs, and customs and immigration in both countries.[30] One potential obstacle to gaining approval was the concern about cross-border shopping. Cross-border shopping by BC residents in Washington State was at its height in 1990-91, and some BC business groups feared that a PACE lane would facilitate this shopping and detract from their own sales revenue. These business groups were assured, however, that the PACE lane was in fact designed for people such as commuting workers and vacationers with summer cottages. In 1991 the PACE lane was finally approved at the Peace Arch crossing as a pilot project. PACE automobiles, marked by a window decal, travel through the lane without regular inspections. This was the first dedicated commuter lane in North America, and it proved to be so successful that the concept was extended to other regions on the Canada-US and also the Mexico-US borders. Although the term "PACE" was originally used on both sides of the Peace Arch border crossing, when the concept became more national in scope the name was officially changed in Canada to "CANPASS."

Currently, Canadian and American residents must apply separately for the US PACE and Canadian CANPASS programs, and undergo separate security checks to qualify for each country's program. A goal of many groups in Cascadia is to have joint US-Canadian administration of PACE and CANPASS so that the application processing and data management can be shared rather than duplicated. However, the differing policies of the two countries make such coordination difficult. Although Canada has already expanded CANPASS service to other border-crossing points for northbound traffic into BC, the United States has not yet extended PACE service beyond the Peace Arch crossing into Washington State (US federal funds have been allocated for expanding the PACE program, but they have not yet been utilized). In May 1999 Canada's minister of national revenue announced that users of the CANPASS program in BC would no longer be required to pay the twenty-five-dollar annual administrative fee; but the PACE program in Washington State still requires a twenty-five-dollar fee, and the US Immigration and Naturalization Service (INS) has no plans to emulate Canada in eliminating the fee. The procedures for the CANPASS and PACE programs in terms of number of lanes available, cost to commuters, and so forth will have to become standardized before US-Canada joint administration of the commuter lane program can be contemplated. The experience gained by current efforts to develop joint US-Canadian facilities at several smaller border crossings will help to determine whether a joint program can be developed for the commuter lanes. For example, the two countries have or are building new joint customs buildings that will be partly on the Canadian side of the border (for example, in Coutts, Alberta) and partly on the US side (in Sweetwater, Montana). Similar joint operations are also planned or already installed in the border areas adjoining Osoyoos, BC; Emerson, Manitoba; and Little Gold Creek, Yukon. Certain adjustments will have to be made in these joint facilities (e.g., US customs officials will have to disarm when they enter the Canadian side of the building because US officials carry guns and Canadian officials do not).[31] The results of this cross-border experiment should be useful in assessing the possibilities for developing binational procedures for commuter lanes.

The Cascadia Project
Created in 1993, the Cascadia Project supports binational cooperative planning to achieve common objectives in areas such as trade, tourism, and technology; but it identifies a rapid, seamless transportation system as being the most important objective. The Seattle-based Discovery Institute, a public policy think tank, manages the Cascadia Project in cooperation with the Vancouver-based Cascadia Institute. The project seeks to involve not only business groups and transportation providers and users but also provincial/state and local governments. In May 1997 the Cascadia Project launched a "Connecting the Gateways and Trade Corridors Initiative," which is designed to develop a twenty-year multimodal transportation plan for the Interstate 5 corridor connecting BC, Washington, and Oregon. Boeing Company and the Port of Seattle provided the initial funding for this initiative. Boeing is a prime example of a company that depends on subassemblies getting to its factories on time, and it is therefore "committed to the development of an intermodal transportation system for the enhanced movement of people and goods" in Cascadia.[32] By stimulating dialogue and providing a forum for cooperative work, the Connecting the Gateways and Trade Corridors Initiative is designed to achieve this objective.

The International Mobility and Trade Corridor Project
While the Connecting the Gateways and Trade Corridors Initiative is concerned with developing longer-term plans for transportation from BC to Oregon, the International Mobility and Trade Corridor project (IMTC) focuses on shorter-term transportation objectives in western Washington and BC, along the I-5/Highway 99 corridor. The original idea for the IMTC resulted from a "brainstorming meeting" of three individuals: James Miller of the Whatcom Council of Governments (WCCOG) in Bellingham, Washington; Bruce Agnew of the Discovery Institute; and David Sherwood of the Pacific Northwest Economic Region. The IMTC was formally launched in April 1997, and the WCCOG was selected as the lead agency in the project. To improve cross-border mobility, participants in the IMTC process have pressed for the expansion of PACE/CANPASS; the enhancement of infrastructure and approach roads to border areas; the development of intelligent transportation systems, shared border facilities, and bilateral financing; and the conclusion of international border-zone agreements.

Among the concrete achievements of the IMTC has been its ability to develop proposals (under the leadership of the WCCOG) for funding from US federal sources to improve corridor and border infrastructure. In response to IMTC information and pressure, the US Immigration and Naturalization Service earmarked $1.6 million in appropriations in October 1998 for expanding the PACE program in Cascadia. The WCCOG and the Washington State Department of Transport have also jointly submitted proposals for funding under the US Transportation Equity Act for the 21st Century (TEA-21), which authorizes US federal funds for highway safety and transit programs. Of particular relevance are Section 1119 of TEA-21, which deals with funding for border infrastructure, and (to a lesser extent) Section 1118, which deals with national corridor planning and development.[33] Under TEA-21 the US Department of Transportation has the authority to allocate up to $140 million each year over four fiscal years (1999-2003), for a total of $700 million. In the first year of TEA-21 three border projects submitted by the WCCOG and the Washington State Department of Transport received federal funding, and the State of Washington provided some matching grants. The first project grant will enable the IMTC to continue coordinating binational border planning; the second will be used to gather origin-destination and commodity flow data with the aim of adding new border facilities, upgrading existing facilities, and implementing new technologies; and the third will be used to expand and improve the PACE program.[34]

Continuing Obstacles in Cascadia

Despite the efforts to facilitate cross-border transportation in Cascadia, major problems remain and there are continuing obstacles to progress. A 1989 study by the Texas Transportation Institute referred to greater Seattle as the fifth most congested area in the US, and a more recent article by Seattle's Discovery Institute describes the inadequacy of the present transportation system on the I-5 corridor and in the US-Canadian border area.[35] Obstacles to cross-border cooperation in improving rapid transport result from differences in political systems; differences in priorities at the federal, provincial/state, and local levels; and competition and conflict among governments.

The ability of Cascadian state and provincial governments to establish formal relationships are of course limited by the control that the US and Canadian federal governments exert over international relations. Even in areas where provincial and state governments are able to establish their own linkages, the differences in political systems pose some serious obstacles. For example, in 1977 the Washington State Legislature established the Joint Legislative Committee on Washington/British Columbia Cooperation in hopes that a formalized relationship could be established between the Washington and BC legislatures. However, BC did not establish a comparable legislative committee, largely because of the difference in political systems. While the joint committee in Washington State could speak alone on behalf of the legislative branch, in BC, because of the fusion of the executive and legislative branches in a parliamentary system, this would be impossible. Thus, a formal relationship between the BC and Washington State legislatures has never been established. For similar reasons, BC premiers have been more reluctant than have Washington State governors to establish formal ties at the executive level. Unlike American states, where governors can develop structured relationships with each other, the government in Victoria "is in and of the legislative assembly, and must stand and answer to it."[36] Thus, the differences in political systems can impede efforts to develop provincial-state institutions in Cascadia on transportation and other issues.

Another factor interfering with cooperation on cross-border transport in Cascadia is the differences in priorities at the federal, state/provincial, and local levels. In this chapter, it is only possible to give a few examples of this problem. At the federal level, recent US actions to deal with illegal immigration – primarily from Mexico – threaten to interfere with cross-border transport throughout North America. In 1996 the US Congress passed Section 110 of the US Illegal Immigration Reform and Immigrant Responsibility Act. Although Section 110 was aimed at illegal immigration in the US, it would have resulted in massive delays and backups at the borders with Canada and Mexico for commuters, shoppers, tourists, and truckers who carry goods traded among the three NAFTA countries.[37] Partly because of strong protests, Section 110 was not implemented. However, increased US vigilance since the 11 September 2001 terrorist attacks on New York's World Trade Center has contributed to delays in transporting goods as well as people from Canada and Mexico across the US border.

At the provincial/state level, the political leanings of some recent BC governments have not been conducive to cooperative agreements with Washington and Oregon on transportation. BC has traditionally been less concerned about American domination than have some other provinces (such as Ontario). However, the former governing party in BC – the New Democratic Party (NDP) – was associated with economic and cultural nationalism, and opposition to NAFTA. The NDP-led government was therefore slow to push for cooperation in promoting cross-border transport. At the local level, priorities regarding community lifestyle also sometimes conflict with plans to upgrade the transport system. For example, a major goal of the Cascadia Project has been to develop a high-speed rail corridor extending from Vancouver, BC, to Eugene, Oregon. Plans are now under way to increase the one-round-trip-per-day Amtrak service between these cities to three, but a range of obstacles may interfere with these plans. The current Amtrak service travels through White Rock, BC, and there is considerable local pressure to have trains travel through that area at slower speeds. Local pressures may also interfere with US plans to expand its border facilities at the Peace Arch crossing. A number of local groups strongly oppose the expansion plans, which may encroach on the Peace Arch Park, the Peace Portal Golf Club, and residential areas.[38]

Finally, competition and conflict *within* Cascadia interfere with the region's efforts to form a unified front in competition with other regions. BC, for example, is concerned that competitive pressures from Washington and Oregon may detract from Vancouver's importance as a gateway city for transportation. In 1998 the Greater Vancouver Gateway Council, composed of senior executives from industry and government, identified some of these concerns:

1. Competing US gateways have public subsidies, and lower taxes and capital costs, which put Vancouver at a cost disadvantage. Canadian shippers are therefore using more US routes for their goods, and one major Canadian potash shipper has built a terminal in Portland, Oregon.
2. Although the weak Canadian dollar temporarily masks the cost disadvantages of Vancouver as a gateway, the lower valued Canadian dollar threatens Canadian ownership of transportation companies because of the aggressive acquisition efforts of US firms.
3. While the US TEA-21 program will provide benefits for cross-border transport in Cascadia, competitors in Washington State will be major beneficiaries of these funds. The Canadian government has no federal highways program for borders and corridors that compares with the US government's TEA-21.[39]

Efforts to develop cross-border transportation linkages are sometimes adversely affected not only by competition among governments within Cascadia but also by open conflict. BC, Washington, and Oregon all have important resource sectors that are competitive with each other, and there have been serious clashes in recent years over softwood lumber, salmon, and apples. At the height of conflict in the region over salmon fishing regulations, the BC government stopped participating with its two Cascadia partners in talks on a range of unrelated issues. Since the urban economies in Cascadia have more service- and technology-oriented industries, these disputes tend to centre on the rural areas of BC, Washington, and Oregon. Thus, much of the support for cross-border linkages is found in the large urban areas.[40] Within these cities, private business has often taken the lead in promoting cross-border transport, and the provincial and state governments have generally been followers. However, if Cascadia transportation initiatives are to achieve their objectives, it will be necessary to have political leaders emerge who "effectively champion the Cascadian cause."[41] One encouraging sign was the decision of the BC premier and Washington State governor in June 1999 to form a new joint corridor task force to improve cross-border transportation.[42]

San Diego-Tijuana

The San Diego-Tijuana region's estimated spending on port, rail, and airport development to expand Pacific Rim trade for the years 1996 to 2000 amounts to less than $400 million; this figure is far below those for other city regions such as Los Angeles ($4.3 billion), the San Francisco Bay area ($3.2 billion), and Seattle-Tacoma ($1.5 billion). As a result, San Diego-Tijuana is highly dependent on Los Angeles-Long Beach for its port, rail, and airport transportation. San Diego International Airport is unable to meet about one-quarter of the region's air passenger demand and from one-half to two-thirds of its air cargo needs; airports in the Los Angeles area meet most of this demand. About 90 percent of the vessel cargo shipped to and from San Diego-Tijuana goes through the ports of San Pedro Bay in Los Angeles-Long Beach. Thus, component parts for the *maquiladora* industry are shipped from East Asia through the San Pedro Bay ports, and then transported by truck to border plants. The cross-border region also lacks a direct rail connection to the east with the rest of North America, and its rail shipments are routed through Los Angeles.[43]

Some argue that San Diego-Tijuana's dependence upon Los Angeles is efficient because Los Angeles has world-class facilities that the border area could not match, and using these facilities has decreased the need for large local transport investments. However, others argue that the drawbacks of over-dependence outweigh the advantages. Although the border region will continue to depend on Los Angeles facilities, the extremely high degree of reliance interferes with San Diego/Tijuana's control over economic development in the border region. Reliance on Los Angeles area airports is also problematic because delays and controversies over environmental issues pose a threat to their expansion plans. Furthermore, traffic congestion will continue to increase travel times between the cross-border region and Los Angeles-area airports.[44]

In the cross-border region itself, the most immediate transport problem is the need to improve the highway system. Efficient highways and land ports of entry are essential because the San Diego/Tijuana trade flow is mainly north-south. San Diego's exports are largely NAFTA-oriented, with 44 percent going to Mexico, 9 percent to Canada, and only 23 percent to East Asia. For Tijuana, the main export market is the US, with a majority of exports being shipped to the western US states. San Diego serves as a major transhipment point for these goods as well as for goods shipped from East Asia for Tijuana's *maquiladora* industries. Component parts from Asia for the *maquiladoras* are trucked from Los Angeles-Long Beach to Mexico, and finished products are then trucked back across the border. NAFTA has resulted in a marked increase in the amount of goods being shipped, and congestion has become a major problem on local streets because of the lack of direct connections between border crossings and the interstate highway system. On a recent trip to Mexico, a California senator therefore indicated that a common problem on both sides of the border was the need for funds to construct and improve highway networks.[45]

Efforts to Improve the Cross-Border Transport System

In the early 1990s the US and Mexican governments created the Binational Liaison Mechanism (BLM) program, under which communities along the US-Mexico border would establish BLMs to deal formally with border-related matters of local concern. The San Diego-Tijuana/Tecate BLM has been actively involved in transport issues and has formed a working group – the Port of Entry Council for Tijuana-San Diego-Tecate – to advise it on developments related to the region's ports of entry. The council provides a forum for regional and federal agencies as well as community stakeholders to examine ways of improving the management of border crossings. It also considers the long-term expansion needs of the ports of entry and their integration with the highway systems on both sides of the border.[46] Another local institution involved in cross-border transport issues is the San Diego Association of Governments (SANDAG). As early as 1975 SANDAG designated a representative of the Tijuana and Baja California governments as an honorary member on its Board of Directors. In 1996 SANDAG signed an agreement with Baja California to establish the Bi-State Transportation Technical Advisory Committee (BTTAC). BTTAC, which brings together the agencies for transportation planning along the border of the two states, has supported a number of border-related transportation programs. At the state level, the California Department of Transportation (CALTRANS) has agreements with state and federal transportation agencies in Mexico to cooperate in transportation planning.[47] As is the case in Cascadia, SANDAG (along with CALTRANS) has successfully applied for US federal funding under the TEA-21 program for border improvement projects and planning.

Cross-border arrangements are of course not limited to governments; and business, civic, and academic groups have been cooperating to promote their transportation and development interests. The Border Trade Alliance (BTA), which deals with issues along the entire US-Mexico border, has had a significant effect on cross-border transport in the San Diego-Tijuana region. Formed in 1986, the BTA includes economic development corporations, chambers of commerce, banks, industrial parks, service providers, trade associations, manufacturers, and state and local government agencies from every state along the US-Mexico border. The BTA has been working with US customs to deal with such issues as the high turnover of US customs personnel at southern border ports; the need to expedite the shipment of high-volume, low-risk goods; the possibility of using high-technology equipment as an alternative to manual inspection at the border; and the possibilities for increasing communication between US and Mexican Customs.[48]

Another important group is the San Diego Dialogue, which was established in 1991 and is a partnership between the greater San Diego/Tijuana community and the University of California, San Diego. The membership includes university scholars and leaders from both sides of the border in business, the media, the arts, education, and government. In April 1994 the San Diego Dialogue published a study pointing to the high volume of border crossings by commuters, shoppers, and tourists in the San Diego-Tijuana region.[49] This report led the US Congress to authorize a dedicated commuter lane pilot project in 1995 – called the SENTRI (Secure Electronic Network for Traveller Rapid Inspection) lane – for businesspeople at the Otay Mesa port of entry. Patterned after the PACE/CANPASS lane in Cascadia, the Otay Mesa lane has been quite successful. Thus, two SENTRI lanes are ready to begin operating at the San Ysidro crossing (also between San Diego and Tijuana), and there are plans to develop other commuter lanes along the entire length of the Mexico-US border.[50]

Although the SENTRI lane was patterned after PACE/CANPASS, there are some significant differences that result partly from concerns about illegal immigration on the Mexico-US border. While the cost to commuters travelling to the United States at the Tijuana/San Diego crossing is $129, the cost to commuters going to the United States at the Cascadia crossing is only $25. The Mexico-US SENTRI system is also more automated than is the PACE/CANPASS system, and those applying for SENTRI permits in Tijuana-Cascadia must provide fingerprint samples. Those using the new SENTRI lane at San Ysidro will have a crossing card that they must "swipe" when crossing the border, and a radio transmitter placed in the owner's vehicle will aid in identification. When SENTRI lane users slide their cards through the optic reader, a computer will read their fingerprints. The SENTRI lane at the US-Mexico crossing is only on the US side of the border and is administered solely by the US. In Cascadia, by contrast, Canada has a CANPASS lane comparable to the US PACE lane, and there is discussion about developing joint administration of the commuter lanes.[51]

Continuing Obstacles in San Diego-Tijuana

As is the case with Cascadia, the political systems on the two sides of the border between San Diego and Tijuana limit progress in facilitating cross-border transport. For example, a highly fragmented governance system in San Diego interferes with binational cooperation in infrastructure planning and management. In some California cities, such as Los Angeles, Long Beach, San Francisco, and Oakland, city agencies have comprehensive authority over port, rail, and airport decision making. In San Diego, by contrast, the agencies responsible for infrastructure decision making, such as the Port District and the Metropolitan Transportation Development Board, are limited-purpose special authorities. This fragmented governance system compounds San Diego's difficulties in promoting bilateral cooperation with Tijuana on infrastructure issues.[52]

Tijuana has its own set of governance problems. The Mexican political system has had many of the characteristics of an authoritarian, unitary government. Although Mexico has been evolving in the direction of democratization and some regional devolution of authority, uncertainties and constraints regarding the decentralization process make it difficult for Tijuana to engage in binational cooperation. Mexican president Zedillo's willingness to accept increased democratization resulted in the election of the first opposition-dominated Chamber of Deputies in 1997, and the legislature has supported changes to the Mexican Constitution that would give municipalities greater control and responsibilities. "Baja California has been at the forefront of Mexican decentralization," and it has assumed greater responsibility from the federal government in transportation as well as education, health care, and sewage and water facilities.[53] Nevertheless, in the view of many US officials, this decentalization is proceeding at too slow a pace. Cross-border transportation planning is also difficult because Baja California does not have a metropolitan council of governments similar to SANDAG in the San Diego area. Furthermore, Mexico's rail, port, and airport services are being privatized, and the privatization process is creating considerable uncertainty with regard to planning and cross-border cooperation. For example, Mexico's attempt to privatize the seventy-kilometre Baja California spur of the San Diego and Arizona Eastern Railway has been an "on-again, off-again" affair, with a series of setbacks.[54]

As has been the case with BC's NDP government, another obstacle to cross-border cooperation on transportation issues in Tijuana-San Diego has been Mexico's concerns about sovereignty vis-à-vis its much larger neighbour to the north. Concerns about sovereignty are based on Mexico's lower level of economic development and its high degree of dependence on the US. Indeed, the most important constraint to cross-border transportation planning stems from the socioeconomic disparities between San Diego and Tijuana.[55] Tijuana's dependence on San Diego is most evident in the *maquiladora* operations. If Mexican labour costs become too high, then US investors can simply relocate their assembly operations to countries with lower wages. Another result of the economic disparities across the border is the problem with illegal immigration. The US Border Patrol has referred to the San Diego-Tijuana region as a "war zone" because so many people attempt to cross every night illegally,[56] and tensions resulting from the pressures for illegal immigration have impeded efforts to facilitate cross-border transport.

The economic disparity between Tijuana and San Diego is especially evident with regard to cross-border transport issues. While San Diego is concerned about its congested freeways, Tijuana is more preoccupied with the lack of paved roads in some of its newest neighbourhoods. Only about 40 percent of the Tijuana area's public roadway system is paved, and 60 percent of that system is in disrepair. The disparate abilities of San Diego and Tijuana to share costs pose a serious problem for joint infrastructure development. CALTRANS is actively involved in building new roads on the US side of the border to cope with expected increases in traffic; but these improvements will not produce the desired results if SAHOPE, the Baja California transportation agency, does not improve the highways on the Mexican side of the border. The disparities are also evident in light rapid transit. In the early 1980s San Diego built a light rail mass transit system that connected its downtown business district with the border at San Ysidro. Lack of finance, however, has interfered with Tijuana's ability to build a similar system connecting its downtown with the US system at San Ysidro.[57] Socioeconomic disparities also interfere with the development of the SENTRI lanes, one of the success stories in cross-border transport. The United States is the creator, promoter, and administrator of the SENTRI program, and Mexican authorities are not involved in the selection or inspection of SENTRI lane users. The Mexican government has argued against the $US129 fee for use of the SENTRI system, but the United States has been the sole decision maker on this issue.[58]

Socioeconomic disparities sometimes contribute to outright conflict. A primary example today is the US-Mexico trucking dispute. Canada and the United States agreed to expanded trucking operations with each other in the early 1980s, but significant barriers to cross-border trucking on both the Mexican and US sides of the southern US border remained.[59] NAFTA contains a timetable for the phased removal of barriers for transporting cargo between the United States and Mexico. On 18 December 1995 the US-Mexico border was to be opened for increased commercial truck traffic within the four US border states (Arizona, California, New Mexico, and Texas) and the six Mexican border states; and on 1 January 2000 all limits on access for international traffic were to be phased out.[60] In December 1995, however, the US Department of Transportation indicated that it would not remove the transport barriers until the safety of Mexican trucks improved. A US Department of Transportation official has stated that "what we would like to see is a comprehensive safety regime established in Mexico that would meet many of the kinds of safety demands that we require of our motor carriers here in the United States."[61] The US refusal to implement NAFTA provisions on transborder truck travel is highly contentious among some groups in both the United States and Mexico, and a detailed examination of the competing views on this issue are beyond the scope of this chapter.[62] At the point of this writing, the United States has still not agreed to implement the NAFTA provision on trucking, and Mexico (although it has mixed feelings about increased competition that cross-border trucking would bring) has launched a dispute settlement case on this issue under NAFTA Chapter 20.

Conclusion

David Ricardo viewed comparative advantage in national terms, but competitive advantage today is in fact a regional as well as a national phenomenon. This chapter points to the importance of a rapid, efficient transportation system for promoting competitiveness in two cross-border regions: Cascadia and Tijuana-San Diego.[63] In both of these regions nongovernmental and governmental institutions have identified transport problems and proposed solutions, and some significant breakthroughs have occurred. For example, Cascadia pioneered in developing the PACE dedicated commuter lane, and San Diego-Tijuana followed with a similar SENTRI lane; both regions have received funding for corridor and border transport from the US TEA-21 legislation; and both regions have highly innovative groups and projects that are looking to future as well as to present transport requirements. Nevertheless both regions continue to have transportation problems that seriously interfere with their competitiveness. San Diego-Tijuana continues to be too dependent on the Los Angeles-Long Beach area for its transport needs; congestion in both regions interferes with the smooth flow of traffic in the corridor and border areas; border-crossing procedures have not been updated sufficiently to take account of just-in-time production and other competitive requirements: and neither region has developed an adequate multimodal transportation system that coordinates the need for rapid air, sea, and land travel. Cross-border cooperation on transport is hindered by political governance and sovereignty issues; by competition and conflict among actors within both regions; and by major socioeconomic disparities between Tijuana and San Diego.

Steven Erie has referred to three necessary conditions for binational cooperation on transportation issues that are highly relevant for both Cascadia and San Diego-Tijuana: belief in a common destiny, leadership, and patience.[64] In some respects the destinies of Mexico, the US, and Canada may seem to be anything but common. Both Mexico and Canada have concerns about maintaining a degree of sovereignty vis-à-vis the US, and Mexico's status as a developing country clearly differentiates it from industrial states such as the United States and Canada. In an age of NAFTA and competing trade blocs, however, the three North American states have much to gain by cooperation. At the regional level, there are additional reasons for cooperation. Seattle, Vancouver, San Diego, and Tijuana are all middle-range cities that, individually, cannot compete with larger North American cities such as Los Angeles and New York in developing transport infrastructure, a large consumer market, and economies of scale in production. The subnational governments in the Cascadia and San Diego-Tijuana regions can only achieve the size critical for becoming more competitive by joining forces and cooperating. For example, Seattle and Vancouver have a natural advantage in sea and air transport over Los Angeles because they are closer to Japan and other parts of the Asia Pacific. Without cooperating in developing a multimodal transport system where trains and trucks can move rapidly between seaports and airports, this advantage will be of little benefit to the region.

Effective leadership is a second requirement for improving cross-border transport. In Cascadia, "no Governor or Premier has stepped forward to provide the political leadership involved ... in developing the institutional mechanisms necessary to further the concept"; and, similarly, "the heart of the problem" in San Diego-Tijuana "is that *somebody* has to lead."[65] Existing governmental agencies tend to have clearly delimited authority and are reluctant to engage in decision making in areas such as cross-border planning, which are outside their mandates. On the other hand, they are often resistant to the establishment of new transborder agencies that might infringe on their territory. As for elected officials, voters generally are not aware of the potential benefits of cross-border cooperation, and there is little political reward for politicians to pursue a cross-border agenda. Although non-governmental groups in both regions have developed innovative proposals for improving transport policies and infrastructure, effective leadership by major governmental actors in each region is essential if such proposals are to be implemented. Despite the problems with effective leadership, there are indications that political leaders are emerging who are willing to take effective action and to propose innovative ideas. In Cascadia, for example, BC and Washington State (which have often lagged behind private actors) recently agreed to set up a new joint task to improve cross-border transportation; and in San Diego-Tijuana, a California State senator has proposed that a multimodal transit centre be established that would preserve "the sense of neighbourhood" in San Diego and, at the same time, contribute to economic competitiveness in the region.[66]

Finally, patience is required because cross-border relationships and institutions develop only gradually. State/provincial and municipal governments also have only limited financial resources for cross-border ventures, and sometimes they are involved in disputes (such as the fisheries dispute in Cascadia) that seriously interfere with progress on cross-border transport issues. Patience has become much more important since the 11 September 2001 terrorist attacks on the World Trade Center in New York City and the Pentagon in Washington, DC (which occurred after this chapter was written). Understandable US concerns about further terrorist attacks have resulted in delays at the border and major new obstacles to improving cross-border transport. However, patience in developing a rapid, efficient transportation system is a "virtue" because the rewards in terms of competitiveness of cross-border regions such as Cascadia and San Diego-Tijuana can be great.

Acknowledgments
This chapter is part of a trinational (Canada-US-Mexico) project funded by the Technical Committee of the Inter-Institutional Studies Program for North America, based at El Colegio de México. Thanks are also due to Lawrence Taylor, Michael Pfau, James Miller, Blake Delgaty, Steven Erie, and others who provided information on cross-border transport issues.

Notes
1 Statement of the American Trucking Associations, Inc., "NAFTA, Border Infrastructure, and Motor Carrier Safety," in *Hearings before the Subcommittee on Surface Transportation of the Committee on Transportation and Infrastructure,* US House of Representatives, "Reauthorization of ISTEA: North American Free Trade Agreement, Border Infrastructure and Motor Carrier Safety, Laredo and Pharr, Texas," 104th Congress, 2nd session, 8-9 August 1996 (Washington, DC: US Government Printing Office, 1997), 74.
2 NAFTA provisions on land transportation services are contained in an annex to Chapter 12 on Services (Annex 1212) and in NAFTA Annex I. See *NAFTA Text: Including Supplemental Agreements,* final version (Chicago: CCH, 1994).
3 See statement of Dr. Demetrios G. Papademetriou and Deborah Waller Meyers before the Subcommittee on Immigration and Claims of the Committee on the Judiciary, US House of Representatives, 14 April 1999.
4 Michael Storper and Allen J. Scott, "The Wealth of Regions: Market Forces and Policy Imperatives in Local and Global Context," *Futures* 27, 5 (1995): 18.
5 A total of twenty-six cities in Washington, Oregon, and British Columbia were initially invited to participate in the Cascadia Mayors Council. The members of the Cascadia Metropolitan Forum are the Greater Vancouver Regional District, Portland Metro, and the Puget Sound Regional Council – which includes Seattle. ("Cascadia Metropolitan Forum: Conference Proceedings," various years; "Cascadia Mayors Council, 14 July 1998, Meeting Agenda.")
6 *Who's Who in San Diego-Tijuana Cross-Border Affairs* (San Diego: Center for US-Mexican Studies, University of California, San Diego, n.d.).
7 Caltrans District 11, "U.S./Mexico Border Activities," March 1999, 7.
8 Robert W. Duemling, "San Diego and Tijuana: Conflict and Cooperation between Two Border Communities," executive seminar in National and International Affairs, 23rd session, 1980-81, US Department of State, Foreign Service Institute, 1981, p. 1; John R. Weeks, "The Changing Demographic Structure of the San Diego Region," in *San Diego-Tijuana in Transition: A Regional Analysis,* ed. Norris C. Clement and Eduardo Zepeda Miramontes (San Diego: Institute for Regional Studies of the California, San Diego State University, 1993), 17-21.

9 Alan F.J. Artibise, "Cascadian Adventures: Shared Visions, Strategic Alliances, and Ingrained Barriers in a Transborder Region," unpublished paper, April 1997, 6. See also Chapter 12, this volume.

10 Ibid., 14-15.

11 Elaine Porterfield, "'Emerging Cascadia': Geography, Economy Bring Northwest Cities Ever Closer," *Christian Science Monitor*, 26 July 1999, 3.

12 David A. Shirk, "New Federalism in Mexico: Implications for Baja California and the Cross-Border Region," briefing paper for *San Diego Dialogue*, July 1999, 23; Joachim Blatter, "Explaining Crossborder Cooperation: A Border-Focused and Border External Approach," *Journal of Borderlands Studies* 12, 1 and 2 (1997): 163.

13 Storper and Scott, "The Wealth of Regions," 509.

14 Pertti Joenniemi and Ole Waever, "By Way of Introduction: Why Regionalization?" in *Cooperation in the Baltic Region*, ed. Pertti Joenniemi (Washington, DC: Taylor and Francis, 1993), 1.

15 Peter Karl Kresl, *The Urban Economy and Regional Trade Liberalization* (New York: Praeger, 1992), 14-15. This section of the paper draws upon some of the ideas discussed in the Kresl book.

16 Jane Jacobs, *Cities and the Wealth of Nations: Principles of Economic Life* (New York: Random House, 1984), 32.

17 Jacobs, *Cities and the Wealth of Nations*, 211.

18 Michael E. Porter, *The Competitive Advantage of Nations* (New York: The Free Press, 1990), 622.

19 Robert B. Reich, *The Work of Nations: Preparing Ourselves for 21st-Century Capitalism* (New York: Vintage Books, 1991), 117 and 234-40.

20 Kenichi Ohmae, "The Rise of the Region State," *Foreign Affairs* 72, 2 (Spring 1993): 79-85; *The End of the Nation State: The Rise of Regional Economies* (New York: The Free Press, 1995), 88-89.

21 Paul Krugman, *Geography and Trade* (Leuven, Belg, and Cambridge, MA: Leuven University Press and MIT Press, 1991), 11-14. For an earlier study that devotes considerable space to the importance of the US manufacturing belt, see Harvey S. Perloff, Edgar S. Dunn, Jr., Eric E. Lampard, and Richard F. Muth, *Regions, Resources, and Economic Growth* (Baltimore: Johns Hopkins Press, 1960).

22 Krugman, *Geography and Trade*, 25.

23 John D. Kasarda, "Transportation Infrastructure for Competitive Success," *Transportation Quarterly* 50-1 (Winter 1996): 37.

24 James Aaron Cooke, "Beyond Quality ... Speed," *Traffic Management* 33-6 (June 1994): 32. The emphasis on frequent and timely deliveries by suppliers is now widely referred to as *kanban*, after its Japanese innovators. See Porter, *The Competitive Advantage of Nations*, 43.

25 Douglas Gantenbein, "The Competitive Edge: The Role of Transportation in a Regional Economy," paper prepared for the Regional Transit Project and Trade Development Alliance of Greater Seattle, 30 July 1993, 4; "James Aaron Cooke, Beyond Quality ... Speed," 33; John D. Kasarda, "Transportation Infrastructure for Competitive Success," 38.

26 On problems of traffic congestion and alternate modes of regional development, see Gantenbein, "The Competitive Edge," 2-4; and Timothy Egan, "The Freeway, Its Cost, and Two Cities' Destinies," *New York Times*, 14 July 1999, A1 and A18.

27 Gantenbein, "The Competitive Edge," 3; Kasarda, "Transportation Infrastructure," 43-47.

28 Ross Anderson, "A Seamless Network Urged for Northwest," *Seattle Times*, 19 December 1997, B2.

29 For a discussion of these groupings, see Theodore H. Cohn and Patrick J. Smith, "Sub-national Governments as International Actors: Constituent Diplomacy in British Columbia and the Pacific Northwest," *BC Studies* 110 (1996): 25-59; and Artibise, "Cascadian Adventures."

30 The four officials were Blake Delgaty, John Watson, Richard Smith, and Thomas Eberhart. Interviews with Blake Delgaty, Director for Canada Customs Border Services, Pacific Region, in Vancouver, BC, 1 May 1998 and 9 August 1999.

31 Mike Trickey, "Guns Create Toilet Trouble at Border Post," *Vancouver Sun*, 11 August 1999, 3.

32　Letter from P.M. Condit, Boeing, to Paige Miller, Chair of Seattle Port Commission, 25 March 1997; International Mobility and Trade Corridor Project, "Status Report on the IMTC Scope of Work," paper prepared by Whatcom County Council of Governments for the Port of Bellingham, 12 January 1998; Whatcom Country Council of Governments, "The Cascade Gateway and the International Mobility and Trade Corridor Project," n.d.; Pacific Northwest Economic Region and Discovery Institute, "Connecting the Gateways and Trade Corridors," n.d.; Arthur C. Gorlick, "Joint Port Authority with BC on Agenda," *Seattle Post-Intelligencer,* 20 November 1997, D4.

33　US Public Law 105-178, 105th Congress, 9 June 1998.

34　Interview with James Miller, Executive Director, Whatcom County Council of Governments in Bellingham, Washington, 3 August 1999; International Mobility and Trade Corridor Project (IMTC), "Summary of Awarded FY 99 Project Applications to the Coordinated Border Infrastructure Program," n.d.

35　Gantenbein, "The Competitive Edge," 2; Bruce Chapman, Glenn Pascall, and Bruce Agnew, "Looking Ahead 50 Years to Solve Washington's Transit Problems," Special to the *Seattle Times,* 25 July 1999.

36　Gerard F. Rutan, "British Columbia-Washington State Governmental Interrelations: Some Findings upon the Failure of Structure," *American Review of Canadian Studies* 15, 1 (1985): 105; Gerard F. Rutan, "Legislative Interaction of a Canadian Province and an American State: Thoughts upon Sub-National Cross-Border Relations," *American Review of Canadian Studies* 11, 2 (Autumn 1981): 67-79. Blatter points out that such political differences need not be absolute barriers to cross-border cooperation. See Blatter, "Explaining Cross-Border Cooperation," 166-67.

37　For a detailed discussion of Section 110, see Theodore H. Cohn, "Cross-Border Travel in North America: The Case of US Section 110 Legislation," *Canadian-American Public Policy* 40 (October 1999).

38　Discovery Institute, "Cascadia Transportation/Trade Task Force," n.d.; Artibise, "Cascadian Adventures," 19-21; Gerry Bellett and Chad Skelton, "Border Project Draws Ire," *Vancouver Sun,* 7 September 1999, A1 and A2.

39　"Vision for the Future of the Greater Vancouver Gateway," Greater Vancouver Gateway Council, Summer 1999, 8.

40　On the differences between the urban economies and the hinterland in BC, see H. Craig Davis and Thomas A. Hutton, "The Two Economies of British Columbia," *BC Studies* 82 (1989): 3-15.

41　Artibise, "Cascadian Adventures," 25.

42　"Task Force to Improve Cross-border Transportation," *British Columbia News Release,* Employment and Investment 061, 18 June 1999.

43　Steven P. Erie, "Toward a Trade Infrastructure Strategy for the San Diego/Tijuana Region," San Diego Dialogue Briefing Paper, February 1999, 13; Steven P. Erie, "Trade Laggard: While Other West Coast Centers Prosper, the San Diego Region is Missing Out," *San Diego Union-Tribune,* 21 February 1999, G-1 and G-6.

44　Erie, "Toward a Trade Infrastructure Strategy," 14; Anthony Millican, "Port Director Prepares to Launch Strategy to Solve Air-travel Woes," *San Diego Union-Tribune,* 25 July 1999, B-1 and B-3; "Filling the Void: Airport Capacity Is Vital to San Diego's Economy," *San Diego Union-Tribune,* 25 July 1999, G-2.

45　Karla Gómez, "Deben Mejorar Infraestructura Carretera," *La Crónica de Baja California,* 11 July 1999, 1; Erie, "Toward a Trade Infrastructure Strategy," 9-12; Diane Lindquist and Valerie Alvord, "Trucking through Tecate," *San Diego Union Tribune,* 29 July 1999, C-1.

46　SANDAG, "Border Area Transportation: The Local, State, National, and International Connection," November 1996.

47　SANDAG, "Border Area Transportation," 16-17.

48　Theresa M. Sires, "The Border Trade Alliance: Improving US-Mexico Trade through Action and Education," *Twin Plant News* 6, 1 (1990): 74-80.

49　"Who Crosses the Border: A View of the San Diego/Tijuana Metropolitan Region," *A Report of San Diego Dialogue* (La Jolla: University of California, San Diego, April 1994).

50　Daniel Salinas, "Retrasa Cruce Rápido: México," *Frontera* (Tijuana), 5 September 1999,

4-5; Interview with Nancy Le Roy, Public Affairs Officer, and Adriana Mendiolea, Cultural Programs Coordinator, US Consulate in Tijuana, Mexico, 29 April 1998; Franciso J. Ortiz Franco, "Ingreso Rápido a San Ysidro con Revisión Electrónica," *Zeta* (Tijuana), 23-29 April, 1999, A37.

51 Salinas, "Retrasa Cruce Rápido," 4-5.
52 Erie, "Toward a Trade Infrastructure Strategy," 23.
53 Shirk, "New Federalism in Mexico," 1.
54 See Dean Calbreath, "Plans to Privatize Tijuana-Tecate Rail Are Rolling Again," *San Diego Union Tribune*, 18 June 1999, C-7; "Propuestas Para la Vía Corta Tijuana-Tecate: Concluirá Privatización del Sistema Ferroviario," *El Mexicano*, 3 July 1999, C-1; Diane Lindquist, "Mexico Spurns Bidder for Segment of Rail Line," *San Diego Union Tribune*, 14 July 1999, C-1.
55 For comparisons of Mexican and Canadian relations with the US, see Theodore Cohn, "Canadian and Mexican Trade Policies towards the United States: A Perspective from Canada," in *Canada and International Trade*, vol. 1, ed. John Curtis and David Haglund (Montreal: The Institute for Research on Public Policy, 1985), 7-61.
56 Milton H. Jamail and Margo Gutiérrez, *The Border Guide: Institutions and Organizations of the United States-Mexico Borderlands*, rev. ed. (Austin, TX: CMAS Books, University of Texas at Austin, 1992), 24-25.
57 "Planning for Prosperity in the San Diego/Baja California Region," Report of the Binational Task Force on Economic Development and Transportation Infrastructure, sponsored by the Greater San Diego Chamber of Commerce and managed by San Diego Dialogue, 30 September 1993, 42; James Gerber, ed., *Economic Profile of the San Diego-Tijuana Region: Characteristics for Investment and Governance Decisions* (San Diego, CA: Institute for Regional Studies of the Californias, San Diego State University, 1995), ch. 5; Lawrence A. Herzog, "International Boundary Cities: The Debate on Transfrontier Planning in Two Border Regions," *Natural Resources Journal* 31, 3 (1991): 604.
58 Salinas, "Retrasa Cruce Rápido," 4-5.
59 For a discussion of remaining restrictions on Canada-US trucking, see Darren Prokop, "In 1988 We Freed Trade. Now Let's Free Transport," *Policy Options* 20, 5 (1999): 37-40.
60 *NAFTA Text*, Annex 1 for the US on "land transportation." See also Michael P. Rhoades, "NAFTA's Implications for the Transportation Industry," *Transportation Quarterly* 48, 2 (1994), 135-48.
61 Testimony of Slater, in *Hearings before the Subcommittee on Surface Transportation*, 15 and 21. In the US view, its refusal to implement the agreement for safety reasons is permitted under NAFTA Article 904, which deals with the "right to establish protection."
62 Competing views on this issue in the US Congress are evident from US House of Representative letters to President Clinton on the NAFTA trucking issue dated 4 April 1997 and 2 July 1999.
63 See Thomas J. Courchene with Colin R. Telmer, *From Heartland to North American Region State: The Social, Fiscal and Federal Evolution of Ontario* (Toronto: University of Toronto Faculty of Management, Monograph Series on Public Policy, 1998), 268-74.
64 Erie, "Toward a Trade Infrastructure Strategy," 29-30.
65 Artibise, "Cascadian Adventures," 25; Erie, "Toward a Trade Infrastructure Strategy," 25.
66 Interview with California State Senator Steve Peace in *San Diego Dialogue Report* 2-10 September 1999, 9.

11
Conflicting Transborder Visions and Agendas: Economic and Environmental Cascadians
Donald K. Alper

In North America considerable attention is being paid to north-south border regions as they serve as sites for new forms of transnational economic, environmental, social, and political interaction. These regional processes are heavily influenced by business groups, environmental non-governmental organization (NGOs), and a wide array of civic officials. One area of North America where regional processes are well advanced is the Pacific Northwest/Western Canada transborder region that has come to be known as "Cascadia." Rapid population growth and economic expansion, fuelled by the high-tech economies of the West Coast and driven by Pacific Rim and other international trade, has stimulated new thinking about partnerships that transcend the border. While always an area with considerable cross-border interaction, increased interdependencies within Cascadia have focused considerable attention on this north-south transboundary region. Particular attention has been given to regional economic development, environmental protection, transportation, border crossings, and other issues related to the notion of sustainability. A number of cross-border alliances and partnerships have been formed, and notions of a "Cascadia economy" and a "Cascadia bioregion" have increasingly caught the attention of journalists and policy makers across North America and in Europe.

This chapter examines various notions of Cascadia and the ways in which transboundary cooperation and activity in this region is manifesting itself. It discusses many of the transboundary linkages that have formed and how they relate to one another. Of note in the case of Cascadia is the relative lack of development of operational models for the organization and management of transboundary cooperation. Although there are many governmental and private cross-border linkages, the scope and depth of institutionalization is minimal. In part this is due to the relatively late (compared to Europe and the Great Lakes and Atlantic regions of North America) onset of cross-border activity by subnational entities in the Pacific Northwest. Until the late 1980s, for ideological reasons as well as for reasons of economic self-interest, the BC government rejected formalized ties with its American neighbours.[1] Further, region building in Cascadia, unlike in European cross-border regions, has not been defined and nurtured within a broader national or continental context. Research findings indicate that transboundary environmental cooperation efforts are more likely to be effective when national and regional authorities work collaboratively.[2] For mostly political reasons, neither Ottawa nor Washington, DC, have expressed support for, or even a great deal of interest in, Cascadia initiatives. In turn, Cascadians have approached cross-border relations with a "go-it-alone" attitude. Indeed, with some exceptions (border security and transportation), officials and activists in the region tend to be suspicious of federal authority and generally regard federal institutions as distant, meddlesome, and unhelpful.[3]

Research has shown that there are at least three sets of factors that are influential in transboundary "region building." First, cross-border regions are viewed as vehicles for promoting socioeconomic cohesion in areas plagued by historical conflicts or disparities in incomes and living standards.[4] Second, transboundary economic regions are part of the logic of globalization where business and trade interests are not coincident with historical borders.[5] Third, increasing awareness of ecological interdependencies have given rise to ecosystem, as opposed to traditional jurisdictional, approaches to managing resource and environmental issues.[6] The Cascadia regional movement, which involves two nations with a history of harmonious relations and relative equality in standard of living, is best understood in the context of economic and environmental factors. In Cascadia the main drivers of regionalization are economic and environmental interests. These interests are functional in nature and generally not in alignment in terms of vision and goals. Although the normative goal of sustainability has the potential for integrating these visions and agendas, business-oriented and environmental-oriented Cascadians have found little common ground and, for the most part, have operated within their own domains. As Blatter points out,[7] most cross-border institutional connections in Cascadia thus far have been sectoral. Cross-border integration within sectors (environmental or economic) is much easier to achieve than is cross-sectoral integration. Further, the Cascadia movement, centred in these functional areas, has not connected with other important groups such as labour, cultural entities, and tribes/First Nations, nor has it penetrated the general public. In short, a Cascadia transboundary mindset has not developed.

The Idea of Cascadia

The idea of a Cascadia region derives from both geography and history. Geographically, Cascadia is made coherent by rainforests and mountain ranges that follow a north-south grid and a system of major rivers that flow east to west into the Pacific Ocean. Prior to European settlement, a common Native American culture pervaded the area. In the nineteenth century, the area known today as BC, Washington, and Oregon was controlled by the Hudson's Bay Company, and, later, the Oregon Country extended across today's national boundaries. The isolation of BC in the western corner of North America, and its links with the Pacific states, helped shape an identity remote from that of central Canada. Permeability of the Canada-US border, whether reflected by American miners going north in the nineteenth century or Canadians today travelling south to Washington State and Oregon in search of recreation land and more favourably priced goods, has reinforced perceptions of region. More recently, the upsurge of environmentalism and free trade have highlighted a new raison d'être for permeability. Finally, the idea of Cascadia has been advanced by the centrifugal tendencies in both federal systems, where both federal capitals (in Washington, DC, and Ottawa) are seen as remote from, and uninterested in, the affairs of the Pacific Northwest.

The name "Cascadia" comes from waterfalls and rivers that flow from the Cascade Mountain Range to the sea. It implies a major element in the region's identity – spectacular natural beauty, strong environmental consciousness, and distinctive northwest landscape and lifestyle. Geographically, the core of the region is the binational coastal corridor that extends north-south from Vancouver Island, to Portland, Oregon, and west-east from the Pacific to the Cascade and Coast Range Mountains. This growing area of approximately 7 million, anchored by three major cities – Vancouver, Seattle, and Portland – is the economic and cultural centre of the region. Within the corridor lie the shared transboundary marine waters of Georgia Basin and Puget Sound as well as rivers, freshwater aquifers, and wilderness areas that bisect the border.

As an economic region, Cascadia's vitality and global potential is linked to the new information economy and the region's cultural and trade ties to the Pacific Rim. From an ecological perspective, the Cascadia identity is rooted in the unifying nature of the natural environment, where boundaries are defined in bioregional as opposed to political terms. The Cascadia bioregion is an ecological unit that encompasses the Georgia Basin/Puget Sound inland sea (Salish Sea), the rainforests of Vancouver Island and the Olympic Peninsula, and the wilderness perimeter that includes the Coast Range Mountains to the east and north of Vancouver and the Cascade Range to the south in Washington and Oregon. Integral to the bioregion are the major watersheds that drain into the Pacific Ocean.

A more profound view of Cascadia rejects the traditional notion of spatial jurisdiction and, instead, emphasizes patterns of functional interactions, connections, and networks that are said to be reconstituting cultural and political life in the Pacific Northwest of North America and else-where.[8] According to this view, connections and networks are more impor-tant in creating commonalities than are traditional political jurisdictions. In effect, this view defines Cascadia not as territory but as a web of socio-cultural interdependencies that guide and structure community life.

Definitions of Cascadia vary according to academic and media perspec-tives and the interests of different groups pursuing regional goals. For the most part, these groups can be divided into business-oriented alliances and environmental activists. Although both have transborder agendas, their interests and goals are quite different.

Business-Oriented Cascadians: A Brief Summary

Although the idea of Cascadia implies commonalities related to culture, geography, environment, and economy, business and economic impera-tives have been the main drivers of transnational regionalism. The idea of economically integrated cross-border regions as necessary elements in the global economy is well established in Europe. In North America, scholars and policy makers are studying and promoting cross-border relationships as inevitable components of a new trilateral continentalism as well as globalism.[9] As free trade agreements have increased transnational interac-tions and interdependencies, greater attention has been focused on the advantages to be realized from economic cooperation by regional actors on both sides of the border. Research indicates that economic develop-ment interests are the principal stimuli to transborder cooperation.[10] Eco-nomic development actors in Cascadia include business councils, firms, public-private alliances, and government officials.

The Cascadia Project

Of all the business-oriented Cascadia initiatives, the Cascadia Project is the most visible and active. The Cascadia Project was begun in the early 1990s as a "strategic plan for environmentally sound economic development and urban management in the Cascadia transborder corridor."[11] The goal was to demonstrate the possibilities for sustainable development in a still unspoiled urban area experiencing rapid growth. The Cascadia Task Force, led by a former US congressman from Washington State, was formed as the instrument to bring together a coalition of regional leaders to pro-mote cooperative economic, transportation, and growth management initiatives. The original plan was to create a binational Cascadia corri-dor commission to manage binational issues and to serve as a kind of early warning system for regional conflicts. The commission idea went nowhere, largely because of fears in the BC government that the scheme was "politically dangerous" and "too American."[12]

Despite its somewhat rocky start, the Cascadia Project has taken the lead on numerous cross-border initiatives, especially ones related to transportation and border infrastructure. Numerous public-private alliances among business groups and state, provincial, federal, and municipal agencies have been created. These include a Cascadian Mayor's Council involving nine mayors from Oregon, Washington, and BC; the Cascadia Metropolitan Forum, linking Portland, Seattle, and Vancouver; the Cascadia Border Working Group, an alliance of officials from counties adjacent to the border; and the International Mobility and Trade Corridor (IMTC) project, a coalition of county, state, and federal agencies focused on upgrading transportation infrastructure that co-joins Canada and the US. The Cascadia Project operates under the auspices of the Discovery Institute, a conservative think tank based in Seattle. Its Canadian partner, the Cascadia Institute, is located in Vancouver, BC.

In recent years, the top priority of the Cascadia Project has been improved transportation throughout the corridor. The project's leading initiative, called "Connecting the Gateways and Trade Corridors," is an attempt to mobilize support for an ambitious regional transportation system – to link ports, freeways, and railways – from Portland to Vancouver. Part of this is a proposed fast train that would speed freight and passengers up and down the I-5 Corridor. To fund this ambitious regional project, Discovery Institute officials have proposed a Cascadia Corridor Development Bank that would oversee a $100 billion, twenty-year rebuild of the roads and bridges in the Interstate 5 corridor – Cascadia's 750-kilometre "Main Street."[13] The binational corporation would be a cooperative alliance of the numerous levels of government throughout the corridor. To date, regional heavyweights such as Boeing, Weyerhauser, and McCaw as well as area ports have endorsed the project, and federal transportation funding has been secured. However, the specifics of a regional transportation plan are mired in state and provincial politics and, as a result, little progress has been made.

Another priority of the Cascadia Project is finding ways to speed up border crossings – especially for commercial traffic. Since 11 September 2001, this has been complicated by new security concerns. As a result, border infrastructure planning has focused on enhancing security while facilitating trade. The north-south I-5/Highway 99 corridor is the second busiest Canada-US crossing. Growth in commercial crossings is about 10 percent per year. Pilot projects involving pre-clearance and the utilization of technology to speed truck inspections at the land border and freight handling at ports are examples of changes instituted due to effective politicking by the Cascadia Project. In addition, the Cascadia Project, working through the Cascadia Border Working Group, has engaged in an active lobbying effort opposing US congressional attempts to impose a border fee and has led the effort to institute dedicated commuter lanes.[14]

Promotion of regional tourism is also a major goal of the Cascadia Project. Glossy maps, brochures, and Web sites promote Cascadia as the "Gateway to the Pacific Northwest" and the "Two Nation Vacation." Recently, the Cascadia Project was a strong backer of the effort to bring the Olympic Games to Seattle, with events to be sited from BC to Oregon. Although not a major player, Cascadia Project leaders strongly backed the Whistler bid for the Olympic Games in 2010. Tourism is a rapidly growing industry in the region and a very competitive one. Because of this competition, close cooperation between BC and Washington State tourist officials is problematic.

Pacific Northwest Economic Region (PNWER)
Another version of Cascadia extends the territorial boundaries so that they encompass much of the Pacific Northwest and Western Canada. Known as the Pacific Northwest Economic Region (PNWER), this regional entity is an organization of legislators and businesspersons from five states (Oregon, Washington, Idaho, Montana, and Alaska), two provinces (British Columbia and Alberta), and one territory (Yukon). The organization is unique in that it has institutionalized representation and dues-based funding from provincial and state governments. PNWER grew out of a 1989 conference of BC, Alberta, and Pacific Northwest legislators following the signing of the Canada-US Free Trade Agreement in 1988. Its goal was to promote economic development and trade abroad and within the cross-border region.[15] The main work of the organization, in addition to trade promotion, has been fostering cooperation within industry sectors through nine working groups: agriculture, environment, export, forest products, government procurement, recycling, telecommunications, tourism, and transportation.

In concept and organization, PNWER resembles what Kenichi Ohmae calls a "natural global economic zone."[16] According to Ohmae, such zones are characterized by the presence of a geographically coherent internal market, usually involving parts of more than one country, where there exist common economic and environmental interests, and large ports that provide links with the global economy. The idea underlying PNWER is that, by rationalizing linkages among the region's economies, the regional entity as a whole could be situated to compete as a major world economic force in the twenty-first century. There is a strong feeling within PNWER that the respective federal governments have not done enough for regional exports and, thus, the region needs to take action on its own behalf.[17] As one PNWER booster said, "we want to sell the Northwest as the best place to get environmental technology; through working together, we can more effectively market our products to Asia, the EC and the rest of the world."

Although well funded and successful in such areas as helping exporters develop new markets, PNWER's effectiveness as a regional institution has been hampered by its unwieldy size and internal conflict about its focus and mission. Some question whether it makes any sense to think of PNWER as a region at all, given its size and internal heterogeneity. Another constraint is the absence of the economic integration within the PNWER states that Ohmae's region states are meant to have.[18]

In 1999 PNWER commissioned a group of regionalist thinkers from outside the organization to set out a vision for PNWER in the twenty-first century.[19] A key recommendation of the report was that PNWER could be most effective as an inclusive arena – a "neural network" – for fostering dialogue on concerns common to Pacific Northwest states and Western Canada. The report suggested that PNWER should model itself as more than an economic development group. The report highlighted the need for a regional organization equipped to bring together diverse constituencies and to consider environmental, economic, and social issues as mutually reinforcing rather than as oppositional categories.

PNWER's self-evaluation is significant for the debate about the future of the region. Clearly, with a funding base and representation from eight governments, PNWER can and often does have a strong voice on regional issues. So, too, it has been an effective lobbying voice on issues of common interest to the businesses in the extended region. Whether an organization made up primarily of businesspersons and politicians can be seen as a legitimate forum for developing alternative initiatives in areas such as environment, education, immigration, and labour remains to be seen.

Pacific Corridor Enterprise Council (PACE)

Another example of regional economic cooperation is the Pacific Corridor Enterprise Council (PACE), a private-sector business group involving more than 200 managers, owners, and entrepreneurs in the two-nation region. The Canada-US Free Trade Agreement and NAFTA inspired PACE. Its goal is to foster free trade throughout the region, including California and Mexico. PACE works closely with boards of trade and chambers of commerce throughout Cascadia.

The business-oriented Cascadians have been successful in creating alliances of local, state, and federal officials who, with support from business groups, have focused attention on the logic of enhanced cross-border linkages and cooperation, especially in the transportation area. Yet political boundaries remain entrenched, and funding for joint projects has been all but non-existent. Clearly, the weight of binational political relations in Cascadia has served as a drag on the forces of integration. From the Canadian side, with a historical sensitivity to the binational power imbalance, expanded linkages almost always heighten fears of "American influence."

In recent years, regional and national politics have intruded to confound cross-border relationships in the Cascadia region. Disagreements over salmon have prompted nasty incidents, such as Canada's imposition of a "licensing fee" on Alaska-bound US fishers in 1995, and a provincial government-supported blockade by BC fishers of an Alaskan ferry in Prince Rupert in 1997. At about the same time, cross-border harmony was not helped by Congress's passage of immigration legislation that, if implemented, would have severely tightened border controls. The impact of 9/11 has slowed momentum for de-bordering the region. Although functional linkages have proliferated, the border continues to serve as a barrier to closer regional economic cooperation.

A Framework for State-Province Coordination: The BC-Washington Corridor Task Force

, The efforts to improve cross-border mobility and to develop an efficient north-south transportation corridor have provided a unifying theme to the Cascadia movement. North-south integration, accelerated by NAFTA, has focused increasing attention on the movement of freight between the corridor states of Oregon and Washington and British Columbia, and even Alberta, Idaho, and further south to Mexico. While the Cascadia Project has focused on the Interstate-5 coastal corridor, the idea of an inland north-south freight corridor has become popular with politicians who represent interior constituencies and with those concerned about greater congestion in the Cascadia main street area. The inland corridor idea was the catalyst that led to the formation of the BC-Washington Corridor Task Force in 1998.[20] The task force, co-chaired by high-ranking provincial and state political officials, established terms of reference focused on improving border infrastructure, developing transportation corridors, coordinating state-provincial tourism, and promising binational cooperation to foster sustainability in the marine environment of the Georgia Basin/Puget Sound and the built environment surrounding it.

Although it is too early to assess the impact of the task force, it represents an effort to provide some level of institutional framework, involving provincial and state policy leaders, for dealing with regional issues. In this regard, the task force, backed by the top political leadership in the province and state, has the potential to raise the profile of "region-building" projects and to establish sustained leadership on binational issues.

Environmental Cascadians

In recent years, a great deal of attention has focused on environmental protection and restoration in the rapidly growing Cascadia corridor. Growth rates in the Seattle-Tacoma and Vancouver urban areas have been among the highest for metropolitan areas in Canada and the US. The resulting ecological impacts, such as habitat loss, declining air and water quality, traffic congestion, and loss of farmland, have prompted calls for new forms of cooperation, management, and planning processes.

Within the Cascadia region, environmental management agreements and institutions have evolved since the 1980s. The current transboundary governance framework includes the geographically focused BC-Washington Environmental Cooperation Council, regional institutions focused on specific issues such as the Pacific Salmon Commission and the State/BC Oil Spill Task Force, non-governmental alliances, and bilateral partnerships linking provincial, state, and federal ecosystem initiatives on either side of the border.

In terms of fostering cross-border environmental cooperation, the most important agreement to date is the BC-Washington Environmental Cooperation Agreement, signed between BC and Washington State in 1992. The agreement formed a unique binational coordinating body, the BC-WA Environmental Cooperation Council.

BC-Washington State Environmental Cooperation Council

In the late 1980s, a major oil spill off the Washington coast, which polluted beaches in both Washington and BC, focused attention on the need for further and deeper cross-border collaboration on environmental issues. In 1992 Washington governor Booth Gardner and BC premier Mike Harcourt signed the Environmental Cooperation Agreement pledging both governments to cooperate to preserve the shared environment.

The agreement created a BC-WA Environmental Cooperation Council (ECC) chaired by high-level provincial and state officials. The council is composed of the director of the Washington Department of Ecology and the deputy minister of the BC Ministry of Water, Land and Air Protection as well as officials from federal agencies in both countries. The council reports to the governor and premier, and meetings are held twice each year. The council's mandate includes marine and freshwater issues, air shed management, and Columbia River water quality. To carry out its mandate, the council has created five task forces to coordinate work in five priority areas: air quality, aquifer contamination, river flooding that spills over the border, contamination of the Columbia River, and protection and restoration of the Georgia Basin/Puget Sound (Salish Sea).

The council's purposes are twofold: to coordinate action on common environmental issues and to provide an institutionalized forum for communication among the parties.[21] Task forces and their work groups deal with specific issues, and scientific research has been fostered through commissioned research and conferences.

In 1997 ECC activities were disrupted by the US-Canada salmon dispute. When BC fishers blockaded a US ferry in July 1997, Premier Glen Clark suspended BC participation in ECC meetings. Resumption of council meetings did not occur until October 1998.

The ECC has worked well to improve cross-border communication among environmental actors, including government officials, NGOs, and academics. It has sponsored the most comprehensive scientific study of the quality of the shared waters. It has provided a framework for the signing of specific agreements and memoranda of understandings (MOUs) covering air quality issues, marine spill prevention in the shared marine waters, pollution issues involving the Columbia River, and contamination of an aquifer that spans the border. Another ECC success is a joint monitoring project to assess fish contamination in the Georgia Basin/Puget Sound waters.

The ECC was designed to be a "coordinating" and "information-sharing" body. In this regard, it has provided a badly needed framework for highlighting problems and developing common strategies for dealing with environmental issues. However, as a regional organization, the ECC has lacked the authority to engage in planning or management of the transboundary environment. It is essentially a coordinating body without legally or policy-based instruments for implementing environmental management. The question that has been raised by the critics of the ECC is whether the ECC process is the equivalent of "talk and log." NGO groups have become especially impatient with the lack of real progress in building a process where truly binational environmental problem solving can occur.

The ECC is limited by a lack of authority to make and enforce rules. Neither Washington State nor BC has given up decision-making power to this regional organization. Even if there existed the political will to do so, this would be difficult, if not impossible, given the mix of federal, provincial, and state jurisdictional authorities involved. The council has also been hampered by the unwillingness of political officials, especially those in Canada, to commit designated funding to support it.[22]

Transboundary NGOs

Increasingly, environmental NGOs have become major players in cross-border regions. In Cascadia, the major groups are the People for Puget Sound, Georgia Strait Alliance, and the Northwest Ecosystem Alliance. In 1995 the People for Puget Sound and the Georgia Strait Alliance joined together to form the Sounds and Straits Coalition. The coalition links numerous groups from around the Georgia Basin/Puget Sound bioregion. The work of the coalition and other environmental NGOs emphasizes research, education, information sharing, advocacy, and issue analysis. There are also numerous unaffiliated, locally based organizations scattered throughout the region.

Despite a strong and active network of NGOs throughout the Cascadia region, NGO transboundary activity is not well developed. Most environmental interest groups are focused on their own province, state, or country. Trade agreements like NAFTA have encouraged a good deal of cross-border NGO mobilization, but the arena in which this activity occurs is more often national and continental than regional.[23] Transnational cooperation among environmental NGOs tends to be protective and defensive. NGO groups are most effective when responding to highly focused issues and crises. In short, most environmental activists are not regionalists; instead, they coalesce to exert pressure on governments, businesses, and public opinion in the pursuit of objectives tied to national governments and multilateral trade organizations.

The different political and legal institutions in the two countries also serve as a constraint on cross-border NGO cooperation. The cross-border region is an abstraction as far as conventional politics is concerned. There is little incentive for NGOs to expend energy and resources where they cannot affect votes or legislative decisions. For NGOs, perhaps more than for economic organizations, the border is a formidable obstacle to building coherent regional organizations.

Further, environmental NGOs in Cascadia have lacked the citizen base and financial resources needed to focus and enhance public interest in the region as a whole. Hodge and West point out that the Cascadia bioregion lacks an organization equivalent to Great Lakes United (GLU),[24] a formal binational citizens' coalition that includes member groups of environmentalists, sportspersons, labour, and civic organizations from the Great Lakes states, Ontario, and Quebec.

Bioregional Initiatives

Basin-wide approaches to environmental management and sustainability have been a mainstay in Canada since the 1980s. A series of initiatives directed at the Georgia Basin/Puget Sound bioregion have been launched by provincial and federal governments to facilitate cooperation among levels of government and stakeholders. These include the Georgia Basin Initiative, the Fraser River Management Program, the Fraser River Action Plan, the Fraser River Estuary Management Plan, the Burrard Inlet Environmental Action Plan, the Georgia Basin Ecosystem Initiative, and the Fraser Basin Council. Although none of these initiatives has been explicitly transboundary in design, recognition that ecosystems do not respect borders has invited transboundary participation and perspectives. This was the central theme of a 1999 conference in Vancouver, BC, Basin Forum: A Workshop Focusing on the Georgia Basin and Puget Sound, which urged closer transboundary collaboration in order to achieve a more liveable Georgia Basin/Puget Sound bioregion. While governments, burdened by constituency and funding pressures, will continue to find it difficult to make transboundary work a priority, they are also finding it increasingly difficult to ignore.

Georgia Basin Ecosystem Initiative

This initiative, prompted by the Canadian federal government, explicitly recognizes the transboundary nature of the Lower Fraser/Georgia Basin area. The area has been designated as a top priority within the whole of Western Canada because of its projected growth, current levels of habitat loss, and worsening air quality in the Lower Mainland region.[25] Still in the planning stage, once implemented this initiative is intended to coordinate the work of federal agencies with the BC government in promoting sustainability in the shared Fraser Basin/Georgia Basin/Puget Sound ecosystem.

Puget Sound Action Team: Fraser Basin Council Memorandum of Understanding

In 1999 the Puget Sound Action Team, which has responsibility for overseeing the protection of Puget Sound water quality in Washington State, signed an MOU with the Fraser Basin Council, charged with responsibility for promoting sustainability in the Fraser Basin. The agreement explicitly made reference to the similar goals of the two organizations with respect to water quality and the biological well-being of the Fraser Basin and the Puget Sound. Most important, the agreement committed the two organizations to cooperate to develop strategies to improve the quality of the shared ecosystem. The agreement also provided for annual binational meetings of the two organizations.

Canada-United States Joint Statement of Cooperation on the Georgia Basin/Puget Sound Ecosystem

Transboundary governance was further supported in 2000 with the signing of the Canada-United States Joint Statement of Cooperation on the shared ecosystem. The joint statement affirms the commitment of the two governments to common action to achieve greater sustainability in the region and, significantly, recognizes the special interests of Coast Salish First Nations and tribes. It also commits the respective federal agencies to specific action plans and regular progress reports.[26]

Transboundary Marine Protected Areas

A coalition of Canadian and US environmental groups, including the People for Puget Sound and the Georgia Strait Alliance, have proposed a series of transboundary marine protected areas in the US San Juan and Canadian Gulf Islands. Ecologically stressed marine areas and islands on both sides of the border would be designated protected areas. The strategy has been to develop the scientific grounding and then work with constituent groups (island residents, fishers, Aboriginal groups) to build a consensus before engaging the respective governments. As a grassroots, bottom-up process, the Marine Protected Area campaign has the advantage of being well focused and less entangled in the complex jurisdictional politics at the state, provincial, and federal levels. This initiative, if successful, could serve as a model to inform the public and to help legitimate cross-border cooperation. Efforts to organize collaboration focused on the whole of the Georgia Basin/Puget Sound bioregion have proven to be extremely difficult, given that no single problem is the focus of attention and that end results are both vague and (most often) long-term in their realization. Although gaining protected area status for waters adjacent to the San Juan and Gulf Islands is quite a different political challenge than is saving an ecosystem, the transboundary marine protected areas initiative could be an interesting model for environmental regionalism.

Conclusion

This chapter has surveyed transboundary interactions and the factors shaping the dynamics of cross-border cooperation in Cascadia. Of interest is the extent to which Cascadia regional processes are structuring and organizing transboundary cooperation on behalf of a coherent regional agenda. The normative goal of sustainability is a central point of reference in the debates about direction and objectives in Cascadia. Although numerous sustainability projects have emerged – many with cross-border implications – there is little evidence that these initiatives have become the basis for a "regionwide" agenda or for cooperative actions. Different political and legal systems, historical sensitivities, and competing domestic political considerations related to resource and other cross-border issues have hampered efforts to articulate a common regional vision and to develop the structure and processes needed for cooperation. The Cascadia experience suggests that political jurisdictions are highly resistant to the "border-eroding" effects of global and regional exchanges. In fact, it appears that increased cross-border interactions often serve to strengthen, not weaken, the binary qualities of the border. Intensification of the flow of cross-border interactions, especially those perceived to be undesirable (economic competition, potential terrorists, drugs, certain immigrants) increases the pressure on political jurisdictions to reinforce barriers rather than to tear them down. In short, despite the increased interdependencies generated by the activities of Cascadia groups, the barrier effect of provincial and state jurisdictions remains relatively intact.

Perhaps most important, Cascadia represents a struggle between visions that are incompatible, if not contradictory. The economic visions advanced by the Cascadia project and PNWER are pro-growth, although moderated by the espousal of sustainable development, and are in favour of freer trade. The bioregional visions are generally anti-growth and either neutral or opposed to strategies aimed at enhancing the region's trade potential. Business actors are hoping to achieve the critical mass for competing in continental and global markets. This requires building and streamlining infrastructure (especially transportation and border crossings) and lobbying on behalf of private-sector interests. For them, a major goal is to promote the region in the global economy, especially across the Pacific and in Europe. Environmental actors have different agendas, most of which are aimed at managing growth, preserving biodiversity, and protecting and restoring the region's natural environment.

What the Cascadia visions have in common are transboundary perspectives that emphasize interdependencies and favour cooperative regional actions. These perspectives, however, contain values that are in opposition. On the one hand, economic Cascadians wish to shape the region in accordance with the borderless global economy. In contrast, the bioregional Cascadians call for a primary focus on conserving place and community. As the bioregionalist Patrick Mazza put it, "The issue comes down to focus and values. How do we envision our region, as a marketing district or a watershed; a marketplace or life place."[27]

These conflicting visions have ensured, at least so far, that most cross-border connections (both informal and institutional) are sectoral. In a very real sense, the economic and environmental groups that work across the border operate in separate ideological arenas, having little if any contact with their Cascadian counterparts. This lack of convergence across sectoral boundaries discourages broader cross-border cooperation and constrains the regional conversation.

Essentially, Cascadia involves a wide variety of activities and frameworks for gathering and sharing information. Although Cascadia has spawned new patterns of functional interaction, new forms of cross-border governance and policy coordination are noticeably lacking. Nor have fora or other processes for democratic conversations about the future of the region managed to evolve. Cross-border activity tends to be sectoral-based, bottom-up, problem-oriented, and, for the most part, exclusive (the voices of labour, Aboriginal groups, and human rights organizations are conspicuously absent in the Cascadia dialogue). Whether this web of interactions can be translated into a coherent approach to fostering a more sustainable border region remains to be seen.

Notes

1 P. Roff Johannson, "British Columbia's Relation with the United States," *Canadian Public Administration* 21 (Summer 1978): 213-33. See also James P. Groen, "British Columbia's

International Relations: Consolidating a Coalition Building Strategy," *BC Studies* 102 (1994): 54-82.

2 Anthony R. Hodge and Paul West, "Achieving Progress in the Great Lakes Basin Ecosystem and the Georgia Basin-Puget Sound Bioregion," in *Environmental Management on North America's Border,* ed. Richard Kiy and John D. Wirth (College Station, TX: Texas A&M Press, 1998).

3 Donald K. Alper, "Transboundary Environmental Relations in British Columbia and the Pacific Northwest," *American Review of Canadian Studies* 27, 3 (1997): 359-83.

4 R. Cappaellin, *Regional Networks, Border Regions and European Integration* (London: Pion, 1994). See also James W. Scott, "Planning Cooperation and Transboundary Regionalism: Implementing European Border Regions Policies in the German-Polish Context," *Environment and Planning: Government and Policy* 16, 5 (1998): 605-24.

5 K. Ohmae, "The Rise of the Region State," *Foreign Affairs* 72, 2 (1993): 78-88. See also Bruce Agnew and Glenn Pascall, "Cooperate Regionally, Compete Globally is a Strategy for 21st Century," *News Tribune,* 26 August 1997.

6 Anne Drost and Richard Brooks, "Civil Society Regimes and Ecosystem Management: Selected Problems in Lake Champlain," *Arizona Journal of International and Comparative Law* 15, 1 (Winter 1998): 289-317. See also Oran P. Young, "North American Resource Regimes: Institutional Cooperation in Canadian-American Relations," *Arizona Journal of International and Comparative Law* 15, 1 (Winter 1998): 47-68; and Joachim Blatter, "Cross-Border Cooperation and Sustainable Development in Europe and North America," paper prepared for Rodney Dobell, for manuscript entitled *North American Environmental Cooperation: Transition to Sustainable Development,* 1996.

7 Blatter, "Cross-Border Cooperation." See also Joachim Blatter, "Cross-Border Regions: A Step Toward Sustainable Development? Experiences and Considerations from Examples in Europe and North America," in *Cooperation, Environment and Sustainability in Border Regions,* ed. Paul Ganster (San Diego: San Diego State University Press, 2001).

8 R.J.B. Walker, "Does It Make Sense to Envisage a Regional Politics in Pacific Northwest?" in *PNWER in the 21st Century,* ed. Sukumar Periwal (Victoria, BC: Pacific Northwest Economic Region, 1999).

9 Robert L. Earle and John D. Wirth, eds., *Identities in North America: The Search for Community* (Stanford: Stanford University Press, 1995).

10 J. Rogers Hollingsworth and Robert Boyers, *Contemporary Capitalism: The Indebtedness of Institutions* (Cambridge: Cambridge University Press, 1997).

11 Bruce Agnew, "Overview of Washington State," paper presented to the BC Roundtable on the Environment and the Economy, 1992.

12 Alan F.J. Artibise, "Cascadian Adventures: Shared Vision, Strategic Alliances and Ingrained Barriers in a Transborder Region," paper presented to On Brotherly Terms: Canadian-American Relations West of the Rockies, symposium, University of Washington, Seattle, 12-14 September 1996.

13 Steven Goldsmith, "Planners Ponder the Future of Cascadia," *Seattle Post Intelligencer,* 26 April 1999.

14 Artibise, "Cascadian Adventures." See also Chapter 12, this volume.

15 Blatter, "Cross-Border Cooperation."

16 K. Ohmae, "The Rise of the Region State," *Foreign Affairs* 72, 2 (Spring 1993): 78-88. See also Bruce Agnew and Glenn Pascall, "Cooperate Regionally, Compete Globally is a Strategy for 21st Century," *News Tribune,* 26 August 1997.

17 Artibise, "Cascadian Adventures."

18 Matthew Sparke, "Excavating the Future in Cascadia: Geoeconomics and the Imagined Geographies of a Cross-Border Region," *BC Studies* 127 (2000): 26.

19 Sukimar Periwal, ed., *PNWER in the 21st Century* (Victoria, BC: Pacific Northwest Economic Region, 1999).

20 Anita Burke, "Freight Mobility Gets Attention," *Journal of Business, Spokane,* 29 July 1999, B-1.

21 Jamie Alley, "The British Columbia-Washington Environmental Cooperation Council: An Evolving Model of Canada-US Interjurisdictional Cooperation," in *Environmental*

Management on North America's Borders, ed. Richard Kiy and John D. Wirth (College Station, TX: Texas A&M Press, 1998).

22 Ibid.

23 Mildred Schwartz, "Political Parties and NGOs in the NAFTA Debates: Creating Cross Border Ties," paper presented to the International Sociological Association 14th World Congress of Sociology, Montreal, Canada.

24 Hodge and West, "Achieving Progress in the Great Lakes Basin Ecosystem."

25 Larry Hildebrand, Victoria Pebbles, and Holly Schneider Ross, "Cooperative Ecosystem Management, Canada and the US: Approaches and Experiences of Programs in the Gulf of Maine, Great Lakes and Puget Sound/Georgia Basin," paper presented to the Coastal Zone 97 conference.

26 See the US EPA website at <http://yosemite.epa.gov/r10/extaff.nsf/webpage/international+statement+of+Cooperation+-+English>.

27 Patrick Mazza, "The Curse against the Global Economy and for a Turn Toward the Local" (unpublished paper, 1997).

12
Cascadian Adventures: Shared Visions, Strategic Alliances, and Ingrained Barriers in a Transborder Region

Alan F.J. Artibise

At a recent conference entitled "On Brotherly Terms: Canadian-American Relations West of the Rockies," the keynote speaker observed that it is time for historians to overcome the "self-evident imperatives of the nation-state" and to address "the historically evident importance of regional connections and cross-border developments."[1] My exploration of Cascadia endeavours to take up this challenge by examining three key elements in the evolution of this transborder region. First, I explore the notion of a Cascadian culture, environment, geography, and economy, even while recognizing that distinctions between the American and Canadian portions of the region continue to exist; second, under the heading "Strategic Alliances," I argue that – despite scepticism on the part of some observers – there is a tangible, measurable, and functioning region called Cascadia; and third, I explore the barriers that continue to pose challenges to pursuing the goals of a Cascadian "movement."

The Foundations of Cascadia: Regional Definitions and Organizations

In recent years the notion of closer cooperation within the Cascadia Region has become increasingly popular. The region, which includes the US Pacific Northwest and part of Western Canada, is divided politically but united geographically and is rooted in the old Oregon Territory, which was severed by the fixing of the 49th parallel as the international boundary by the Treaty of Washington in 1846. As is often the case with political frontiers,[2] the settlement on a boundary did not define allegiance: British Columbia – the Canadian remnant of the Oregon Territory – remained tied economically and culturally to the rest of what was then a San Francisco-focused region. Establishing "Canadianness" in BC became one of the great challenges of Confederation after 1871.[3]

This continuing conflict between geographical and political forces has shaped the history, landscape, and attitudes of what until the 1960s was very much an isolated region.[4] The Canadian and American components of the region grew increasingly apart over the first half of the century as a result of the centralizing and standardizing tendencies of separate nation building. Yet, significant economic and cultural connections remained. Since the 1980s there has been increasing awareness of the potential for – and in some instances the necessity of – reviving the historic regional alliance.

Cascadia is best envisioned as three concentric semi-circles spreading eastward from the Pacific Coast (see Map 12.1). The largest unit is comprised of BC, Alberta, Yukon, Washington, Oregon, Idaho, Montana, and Alaska. This area is loosely, but formally, organized as the Pacific Northwest Economic Region (PNWER), a public-private partnership governed by a bipartisan delegate council and administered by a secretariat located in Seattle.[5] A more historically based and more common definition is limited to the Province of British Columbia and the States of Washington and Oregon. This definition is utilized by the Cascadia Project (sometimes referred to as the Cascadia Trade and Transportation Task Force) and is based in the Discovery Institute in Seattle and the Cascadia Education and Research Society in Vancouver.[6] The Cascadia Project represents a coalition of government, business, and non-governmental organizations (NGOs) in the three jurisdictions dedicated to developing transborder strategies that focus on sustainable communities, cross-border mobility, and improved regional transportation, trade, and tourism linkages. There is also a more thematically focused group, the Pacific Corridor Enterprise Council (PACE), a private-sector networking organization formed to encourage closer business, trade, and tourism links throughout the region. It has chapters in Oregon, Washington, BC, and Alaska.[7]

Other initiatives and organizations recognize elements of the more urbanized parts of the region. The Georgia Basin Initiative – a program of the Province of British Columbia – includes those portions of BC and Washington surrounding Puget Sound and the Georgia Basin. This inland sea stretches from Olympia, Washington, in the south to Campbell River and Powell River, BC, in the north.[8] A fifth configuration has recently emerged called "Cascadia's Main Street," encompassing the major cities, towns, and villages located on or near Interstate 5 from Eugene, Oregon, to those along Highway 99 in BC to Whistler, and the Island Highway on Vancouver Island from Victoria to Campbell River.[9] (See Map 12.2.)

Regardless of the definition of Cascadia, the region offers a spectacular array of natural and built environments, with wilderness and ocean coexisting in relative harmony with sophisticated urban centres. The defining physical characteristic of the area is its mountainous nature.[10] While geography and politics has created many boundaries, and the international border divides two national identities, the residents of the region have much in common.

Shared Visions

The notion of Cascadia can be approached from a variety of perspectives. At one level, it has strong roots in a wide variety of sources: historical, the natural and built environments, the economic characteristics of the region, and sociocultural traits. At another level, the Cascadia concept is being strongly influenced by a variety of external forces, ranging from globalization, the free trade agreement (FTA), and the North American Free Trade Agreement (NAFTA) to the changing nature of the nation-state, the politics of contemporary federalism, and the rise of citizen diplomacy.

Map 12.1   Three views of Cascadia; map by Eric Leinberger

Map 12.2   Main Street Cascadia; map by Eric Leinberger

In addition, the Cascadia region has increasingly moved from "symbol to reality"[11] as it receives attention from journalists and policy makers across North America and in Western Europe. Finally, the integrated region concept is one that an increasing number of theorists and policy experts are promoting as a requirement for meeting the economic and environmental challenges of the twenty-first century.

Historical Ties

Gaining a perspective on Cascadia's present and future can best start by examining the region's past. In the pre-European settlement period the area was tied together by a common, distinctive Native American culture.[12] Then, following the voyages of Captain George Cook in the late eighteenth century, the early European settlement of the region on both sides of the border was similar. The Washington State of today was for many years ruled by the British Hudson's Bay Company as part of BC, and the region had dual American and British sovereignty for several decades of the nineteenth century. "Though separate nations today, Canada and the United States are 'children with a common mother,' as the Peace Arch at the US-Canada border proclaims. The name "British Columbia" was, in fact, necessary to distinguish one part of Columbia from the other."[13]

One historian of the region described this common history by stating that, "from early on, people recognized that the area constituted a region unto itself. The natural resources were similar, as were the Maritime industries, the reality of mineral deposits in the mountains, and the possibility of agriculture in the interior. The natural boundaries that form the region don't divide it the way the political boundaries do."[14]

Until the 1960s the principal characteristic of Cascadia was its isolation from the rest of the continent. The economy was driven by boom-and-bust resource exploitation, as was the political life of the region. By the 1950s the major cities of Cascadia – Portland, Seattle, and Vancouver – were beginning to attain metropolitan status, but the marks of their more utilitarian origins remained and they "retained a frontier roughness."[15] All three cities were important ports that, until recently, were geared to the export of raw materials. The waterfront districts in all three were the original centres of lumbering operations, serving as rough and tumble recreation areas for transient maritime, hinterland, and local resource industry workers.[16]

Since the 1960s modernization in regional transportation and communications rapidly served to link the Cascadia region together, beginning with the completion of a freeway connection (Interstate 5 – Highway 99) in 1962.[17] Integration was also fuelled by a strong sense throughout Cascadia that the natural and built environments, the economy of the region, and the sociocultural characteristics of the residents had more in common than any part of the region had with other areas in either Canada or the US. As one observer wrote as early as 1963, in a volume on *The Pacific Northwest* (Oregon, Washington, and BC):

> The picture that emerges is that of a "last frontier" that ignores international boundaries and may be taken generally as a social, economic, and geographic entity. People attracted there seem to share the same penchant for natural beauty, for responding to challenge, for being resourcefully independent yet conservative in the sense that Thoreau was conservative. They also share related problems.[18]

The Natural and Built Environments

The most obvious shared characteristic of the Cascadia region is the natural environment. Many commentators have made note of this fact, but the most poetic description of the region was penned by David McCloskey, a Seattle University professor of sociology and human ecology and a proponent of an "ecocultural" movement that, for over a decade, has contended that the political lines dividing the region do not reflect its ecological and cultural realities. While McCloskey's "Cascadia" is somewhat larger than the States of Oregon and Washington and the Province of British Columbia, it is nonetheless based on a belief in the commonality that reaches across the region's political boundaries. McCloskey's description of Cascadia – "a great green land on the Northeast Pacific Rim," is as follows:

> Cascadia is a land rooted in the very bones of the earth, and animated by the turnings of sea and sky, the mid-latitude wash of wind and waters. As a distinct region, Cascadia arises from both a natural integrity (landforms and earth-plates, weather patterns and ocean currents, flora, fauna, watersheds) and a socio-cultural unity (native cultures, a shared history and destiny). One of the newest and most diverse places on earth, Cascadia is flowing land poured from the north Pacific Rim ... Cascadia is a land of falling waters.[19]

Another detailed description of the natural endowment of the Cascadia region was produced by the Northwest Environment Watch (NEW), a private, non-profit research centre based in Seattle. Its profile of Cascadia states:

> [Cascadia] is a region bound by climate, geology, and living things into an eclectic yet coherent whole ... Spanning deserts and rain forests, glaciers and kelp beds, fjords and prairies, the Northwest is nonetheless one region in a biological sense ... The rain forests of its coastal strip and the mountain ranges throughout recognize no political boundaries.

> [Cascadia's] defining features include four of the continent's largest rivers – the Columbia, Fraser, Skeena, Stikine – as well as countless smaller streams and rivers racing to the coast ... On land, the rugged, folded topography is dominated by three great, young mountain ranges, the Cascade, Coast, and Rocky Mountains.
>
> [The] region is biologically rich. The world's most massive conifer forests grow here, containing the biggest and longest-lived spruces, firs, and hemlocks found anywhere ... Just offshore lie some of the world's most productive waters ... [The region] is home to ... the greatest salmon runs in the world.[20]

In addition to these two versions, there are, literally, dozens of other writers, scientists, politicians, academics and journalists who have addressed the unique and unifying nature of Cascadia's natural environment.[21]

The shared characteristics of the region also extend to the built environment, whether in the burgeoning urban communities along Cascadia's Main Street or in the inland communities and farms of BC, Washington, and Oregon. Most notable, perhaps, are the numerous commentaries on the major cities, which range from statements by politicians, journalists, and policy planners to academic analysis. Councillor Gordon Price of the City of Vancouver, in an article in *The New Pacific* on Vancouver, Seattle, and Portland, wrote that the visions the residents had of their future were "almost indistinguishable."

> Is it so surprising that their desires are similar? Vancouver, Portland and Seattle are about the same age and size. They have been shaped by similar economic forces. Each is uncommonly blessed with a natural environment of stunning beauty for which its citizens care deeply. All share the same problems – how to maintain a highly desired quality of life while coping with the impacts of growth. And all are confronted with the same paradox: maintaining quality may mean changing the way of life that people came for in the first place.[22]

In a similar vein, the Greater Vancouver Regional District's manager of strategic planning, Ken Cameron, has analyzed three metropolitan regions in terms of their "common context" and "common policy issues." The results are remarkable in that it is virtually possible to speak of the transborder urban corridor as one region.[23] Other analysts have come to the same conclusion in numerous articles, editorials, and commentaries.[24]

The Cascadian Economy

Given these similarities in terms of history, environment, and community building, it comes as no surprise that the Cascadian economy can be described with few references to dissimilarities. With a significant part of Cascadia comprised of the great coastal rainforest, the economic (and cultural) base of the region has been centred on the harvesting and processing of forest resources. The forms of industrial relations and settlement patterns, as well as the character of everyday life, have been tied historically to the economic fluctuations of this export-driven industry.[25] As a result of the frontier nature of the region and an industrial base that produced the social isolation of workers in camps and company towns, Cascadia has been a highly unionized and strike-prone region.[26] In the postwar period, while there had been notable progress away from the traditional staples economy, the region remained primarily focused on resource exploitation into the 1960s. While Boeing of Seattle can be considered an exception to this generalization, the company's technological linkages outside the region have reduced its impact on the economic base in comparison with the historic sources of economic growth.[27] In more recent times, as a result both of the maturing of the regional economy and environmental pressures that forced major changes in resource exploitation, there has been an increasing emphasis on diversification. The evolving economic base is characterized by such firms as Microsoft in Seattle; LSI Logic in Portland; cultural industries related to music, television, and films in Vancouver; and tourism throughout the region.[28]

The new economy of Cascadia is highly export oriented, with a focus on the Pacific Rim, and it includes the traditional resource-based industries, value-added industries, aerospace, manufacturing, defence, transportation, energy, tourism, computer software, entertainment, environmental industries, and biotechnology. Throughout the region there is a complex network of trade relationships and associations; some, in sectors such as forestry and energy, are of long-standing; others, in such sectors as technology and services, are more recent.[29]

Intraregional and international trade is significant and growing, with high levels of cross-border commuting, shopping, and movement of goods and services. Trade within Cascadia is a very important contributor to the economic prosperity of the region. In addition, through a wide variety of government-industry associations, Cascadia is being promoted internationally. The regional thrust has attracted the attention of analysts outside of the region and has given Cascadia growing advantages in targeting investment from major financial centres. And, although the traditional large employers in the resource, defence, and aerospace sectors have remained dominant within the regional economy, value-added manufacturing, tourism, and knowledge-based, high-technology companies are providing much of the recent growth.

It is important to note, however, that, unlike the highly integrated regional economies of the Great Lakes Region, the Pacific Northwest and

BC have traditionally been competitors. The ports, airports, and railways serving the region compete fiercely as gateways for traffic to and from the continent. With parallel resource bases, many of the region's products are similar and competitive in sectors such as forest products, food, and wine. But this traditional perspective is rapidly being challenged and slowly but surely being overcome due to the influence of both the FTA and NAFTA, and the growing belief that "the advantages of regional economic cooperation are clear."[30]

Cascadian Culture

All the influences and factors cited – history, environment, and economy – have also combined to produce what to outsiders at least is a Cascadian culture. While too much can be made of this aspect of shared vision, there are many elements that do indicate both common views within the region and distinctions between the region and other parts of the continent. Most notable is Cascadia's commitment to the environment. For Cascadians, environmentalism has become a sort of secular religion. Residents might not always do the right thing, but they do know when they or someone else has sinned. As one analyst noted: "The notion of Cascadia has a reasonably solid grounding in the region's past and style. Residents share a common cultural heritage and a keen sense of their ecology's fragility: a fear sometimes expressed in virulent antigrowth politics."[31] For most Cascadians, the so-called "global village" is perceived as a "global garden."

Other common elements of the Cascadian culture, or style, include a powerful commitment to maintaining what is perceived to be a distinct quality of life. The "lotus land" stereotype associated with Cascadia is, in fact, quite accurate. This commitment is pursued by a strong sense of local autonomy in the communities of the region. At the same time, Cascadians – because of their historic and continuing role as exporters – understand the new global economy. They recognize that the future will not be a "borderless world" but, rather, a world of complex and multiple borders. They also know that powerful forces are at work that, simultaneously, are pushing power up to international and transborder regions, and down to local communities. In this context, Cascadians share "a certain bemused antipathy toward the two national capitals. Many Americans ... regard their place in the cosmos as ... 'so close to God, and so far from Washington, DC.' [Roger] Bull [a former Canadian diplomat and current executive-director of PNWER] contends that in British Columbia 'the real enemy is Ottawa' and that whatever the effects of Yankee dominance in other regions, the good people of Vancouver feel quite comfortable dealing with the people of Seattle as equals."[32]

Another shared trait is a strong belief in "citizen diplomacy." Cascadia residents are not overly deferential to authority or institutional elites; rather, they regularly take matters into their own hands with a confident view that governments and elites will follow. This is especially true in environmental areas but is becoming increasingly prevalent elsewhere. Many issues are handled via means short of government action, a tradition that has generated a bewildering array of informal organizations.[33] It may be true that the effort to maintain an economically, socially, and environmentally sustainable set of communities in Cascadia through consultation with and action by the public often consists of one step forward and two steps back, but in the end Cascadians believe it is worth the effort.

These shared characteristics should not be overstated. The Canadian and American residents of Cascadia have, and undoubtedly will retain, unique characteristics. While Canada and the United States are each affluent, pluralistic nations dedicated to the twin democratic ideals of freedom and equality, Canada has chosen to emphasize equality, the United States freedom. "There is no point kidding ourselves ... Canadians ... are not about to become Americans. Old Glory will not fly over the Vancouver Town Tennis Club. Nor are Americans about to relinquish individual liberty to construct a welfare state."[34] Notwithstanding this view, there is no question in the minds of many residents of Cascadia that similarities are more powerful than distinctions.

> The citizens of Cascadia share more than just a common geography of mountains and water, and a temperate climate. We have a love of the outdoors and a relatively high level of concern for the environment. The Native American regard for nature is a clearer influence than in the east. We share an openness to Asia as well as European influences, perhaps as a result of lying equidistant between the two continents and having had a long history of international trade.[35]

The Forces of Convergence

The internal forces that combine to form a shared vision in Cascadia are being assisted by a number of external forces that promote the creation of an integrated transborder region. Notably, Lewis Mumford recognized these forces as early as 1938 when he asserted that, in the interests of nationalism, states have often masked the true nature of human interaction and expression – the region: "Real communities and real regions do not fit into the frontiers and the ideological pattern of the nation state"; rather, people's daily lives are bounded regionally, and "thus regions should become the basic units of political and economic life."[36]

Mumford's theme has been rediscovered in the past fifteen years and to his notion of the importance of region has been added the concept of transnational regions. In North America the concept was perhaps best publicized in Neil Peirce's work on "citistates," but numerous journalists and scholars have explored the notion of city-centred regions that may (and sometimes must) cross natural borders.[37] In Europe the notion of integrated cross-border regions as necessary elements in the new global economy is well established.[38] In North America this dimension has already resulted in serious study by scholars and policy makers, and the notion of cross-border regions across the continent is growing rapidly, both in theoretical and practical terms.[39] There are even formal organizations dedicated to studying and promoting cross-border relationships, such as the Canadian/American Border Trade Alliance, the North American Institute (NAMI), the North American Institute for Comparative Urban Research (NAMICUR), and the Association of Borderland Scholars.

The logic behind this new interest in regions in general, and cross-border regions in particular, is quite straightforward. In the new, global economy, national borders are less and less important.[40] Regions are on their own and cannot count on much assistance from the nation-state. The message is, think globally but act locally (or, in this case, regionally). In short, the modern world – especially its technology – has transformed notions of territory, space, and nation.[41] In this new world, border disputes and intercity rivalry within regions are anathema. Prosperity will come only to regions that can plan strategically and cooperatively and that can show a stable, innovative, efficient face to the world.

These "economic imperatives" are understood by many in Cascadia and serve to fuel regional cooperation and to overcome competition. "We are only going to be stronger for the cooperation," says one policy maker. "The world is too big a place for us to try to go it alone. We can help one another out quite a lot."[42] Similarly, *The New Pacific* noted:

> The outside world cannot be wished away. If the future is not to be jeopardized by xenophobia, parochialism or just plain apathy, the New Pacific's leaders must seize and maintain the initiative. They must get to know one another, warts and all. They must see beyond lines that divide and invest time and human capital in turning a vision into a reality. For the Pacific Northwest the power of one will be more than the sum of the parts.[43]

The powerful forces of convergence can also be found in the changing nature of the federal systems of both Canada and the US. In both countries, national governments are overcome by deficits and, as a result, are increasingly devolving power to the states and provinces; some, not surprisingly, call the phenomenon "downloading." Nonetheless, the result is newly powerful states, provinces, and cities with a new-found interest in international and cross-border relations.[44] At the same time, the new context provided by both the FTA and NAFTA encourage a new north-south corridor relationship, whether in Cascadia or elsewhere.[45]

Strategic Alliances

The attitudes, perspectives, and shared visions explored here set the context for the Cascadia concept. But sharing attitudes and experiences and facing common opportunities and challenges does not necessarily lead to concerted or cooperative action. And there is no doubt that in Cascadia the rhetoric is often far ahead of the reality. Nonetheless, in the past decade a wide variety of informal and formal alliances have been forged in the region, and these alliances are fuelled and fostered by growing information and communication links and by Cascadian organizations and institutional arrangements. Indeed, there are so many initiatives and proposals that it is difficult to even list all of them, let alone analyze their origins, activities, and prospects. In an effort to do so, however, in this section I explore the topic under six headings: information, communications, organizations, and institutional arrangements; economic initiatives; border arrangements; transportation plans; the natural and built environments; and tourism.

Information, Communication, Organizations, and Institutional Arrangements

For any regional concept – and especially for a transnational region – to have meaning, it is critical that the people and the institutions of the region know each other and communicate with each other on a regular basis. In Cascadia, regional knowledge and understanding begins on a personal level, through travelling throughout the region. The Peace Arch Border Crossing is the third busiest along the Canada-US border, with almost four million crossings in 1995-96. As a group, the BC-Washington border "ports" registered seventeen million crossings in 1995-96. In terms of commerce, the Douglas Crossing is the largest "commercial port" in the region. And crossings – both personal and commercial – are increasing at rapid, even exponential, rates.[46] These figures provide solid evidence that citizens and companies are undertaking informal "diplomacy" on a regular basis, whatever the ebbs and flows of government-to-government relationships.

This first-hand knowledge is bolstered by an array of books, journals, and articles, and by television stations and programs that have growing Cascadian audiences. In addition to Callenbach's *Ecotopia* – which has sold over 650,000 copies,[47] Joel Garreau's *The Nine Nations of North America*, published in 1981, also helped popularize Cascadia.[48] Two specialized magazines – *The New Pacific* and *Cascadia Forum* – were also published for several years, although neither survived.[49] But any void created has been amply filled by the regular newsletters of organizations such as PNWER and the Cascadia Project, academic and business publications such as the *Northwest Journal of Business and Economics* and the annual *Regional Economic Review and Outlook,* and publications by such organizations as the Cascadia Education and Research Society and the International Centre for Sustainable Cities.[50] Articles in newspapers and magazines appear regularly,[51] and there is even planning under way to create a "Cascadia Communications Service" that would have bureaus in Seattle, Portland, Vancouver, and Victoria and that would distribute information by cable television and the Internet.[52] In 1996 the *Cascadia Times: An Independent Voice for the Northwest and Its Environment,* published monthly in Portland, went on the Internet. Another Oregon-based Internet service is "Cascadia Planet" (<http://www.tnews.com/>). It is also notable that Seattle's PBS channel is extremely popular with the BC market and that, when the removal of CBC TV from the Seattle market was threatened, there was a loud protest in that city. Another intriguing indicator is that several TV stations in the region provide weather reports that actually cross the border. Finally, one Washington television station, KVOS of Bellingham, produces its shows in the state but has an advertising office in Vancouver, and its audience is primarily located in the Lower Mainland.[53]

In sports, there have been ongoing discussions of the "Cascadia Mariners," and active planning is under way for a Cascadia Olympics.[54] In more formal cultural areas, there have been exchange performances by Portland, Seattle, and Vancouver symphonies, ballets, and operas.[55] And in 1990 the Seattle Chamber of Commerce broke with tradition and held its annual conference outside the state, in Vancouver.[56] Cascadia has even developed two regional flags and a marketing logo; the US Bank has proclaimed it is Cascadia's bank; the Vancouver Stock Exchange president has talked about a Cascadia Stock Exchange; lawyers are exploring a Cascadia Bar Association; and citizen environmentalists hold regular meetings on Cascadia's sustainability.[57]

Other forms of regular information and communication include conferences, seminars, and working groups. PNWER, the Cascadia Project, and PACE all hold regular conferences and seminars, while exchange tours by groups as diverse as planners, developers, university classes, and yacht clubs are frequent.[58] Finally, there have been a host of cross-border studies and research initiatives on such topics as the environment, tourism, the economy, the border, transportation, and governance.

In terms of Cascadia organizations, the list is long and diverse. In addition to organizations already mentioned, an incomplete listing of others include:

- the Pacific Northwest Economic Partnership
- the Cascadia Metropolitan Forum
- the Alliance of Border Communities
- the Cascadia Sustainable Communities Network
- the Cascadia Economic Roundtable
- the Cascadia Border Task Force
- the BC-Washington-Oregon Rail Working Group
- the nine working groups established by PNWER
- the BC-Washington Corridor Task Force.

In addition to these organizations, there are a number of formal institutional arrangements in place throughout the region to deal with common issues and opportunities. Most are between BC and Washington; there are, however, also a few trilateral or multilateral arrangements.[59]

These examples indicate that, while Cascadia has a long way to go in terms of integration, it has already achieved a good deal and further steps in the direction of cooperation are certain. It is also important to understand that the leaders of the Cascadia movement have deliberately chosen to move towards integration in a cautious, practical manner. Since some Cascadia residents have difficulty in coming to terms with the shared challenges and opportunities, the various groups and organizations – and, indeed, the Cascadia state and provincial governments and the governments of Canada and the United States – have set a limited but achievable agenda. The focus is on practical projects and cooperative efforts in a limited number of areas.

Economic Initiatives
At an early stage in the evolution of the Cascadia concept, business and government recognized that its key challenge was to find specific ways for businesses to collaborate and to develop the network and alliances necessary to enhance their competitive strengths, and better exploit trade opportunities in the Pacific Rim, while at the same time preventing the erosion of current market shares. An early but highly successful regional initiative was the Pacific Northwest Economic Partnership (PNEP). PNEP was established by Washington and BC in 1988 and was designed to encourage communication between businesses, with a goal of facilitating an exchange of information and ideas in such sections as biotechnology, environment, and software. A number of success stories can be told, including a joint marketing effort at the 1991 COMDEX in Las Vegas, joint biotechnology industry meetings, increased university-to-university communication on technology transfer, and increased cross-border cooperation in a number of sectors.[60]

Another regional initiative, PNWER, has also been very energetic in the economic sphere. PNWER undertakes the agenda for the two provinces and five state organizations through a series of working groups. By 1996 nine groups had been established: agriculture, environment, export, forest products, government procurement, recycling, telecommunications, tourism, and transportation.[61]

Other examples of regional economic cooperation include the Pacific Corridor Enterprise Council (PACE), a private-sector organization of 200 American and Canadian owners, managers, and entrepreneurs. It endeavours to make doing cross-border business easier and has established committees on such topics as venture capital. PACE also works closely with boards of trade and chambers of commerce throughout Cascadia.

Border Arrangements

One of the other major Cascadia organizations, the Cascadia Project, has also been active in the economic sphere, but it has chosen to pursue cross-border relationships in a less direct, more critical, fashion. One of its key areas of activity involves dealing with the border itself, attempting to overcome the "significant problems and barriers that exist."[62] This focus on the border as a barrier is based on the fact that the border has a significant impact on the region's ability to respond to the growing opportunities that have resulted from NAFTA and the dramatic rises in intraregional and international tourism. At the Cascadia Transportation and Trade Task Force Conference held in Vancouver in March 1994, Canada's then national revenue minister, David Anderson, pledged in his keynote address to work towards a "hassle-free border."[63]

Following this conference, the Cascadia Project formed a Cascadia Border Working Group, co-chaired by the mayors of Blaine and Surrey.[64] In May 1994 the US Federal Task Force on Border Infrastructure and Facilitation, representing all agencies involved in border crossings, held a hearing in Bellingham. Diverse organizations from Canada and the United States gave testimony about the impact of border issues and called for more action to address the problems.[65] Subsequently, in February 1995 Canada and the United States signed the Accord on Our Shared Border and developed an "Action Plan." The accord committed the two governments to an ambitious and innovative plan of action designed to achieve four objectives: the promotion of international trade; the facilitation of the movement of people; the reduction in costs for both governments and users; and enhanced protection against illegal movements.[66]

At the same time, the Cascadia Border Working Group has lobbied successfully to oppose the US Congressional attempt to impose a border fee, and it is working hard to permanently authorize the PACE dedicated-commuter lane. Other initiatives include efforts to have funds allocated to improve approaches to the border crossings, new commercial facilities, and improved technology for commercial clearances. The Canadian equivalent of PACE – CANPASS/PACE – has been added to the Pacific Highway and Sumas crossings for Canadian-bound traffic. CANPASS Airport has been put in place at the Vancouver International Airport with the use of "smart" cards for faster clearances, and a CANNPASS Marine clearance program is operational. As well, both BC and Washington State have enhanced the border delay warning systems to ease congestion.[67]

Together, these continuing efforts represent significant steps towards the achievement of a functioning Cascadia region. While only a few are keen on "bulldozing the checkpoints,"[68] most residents of the region share the sentiments expressed in the Shared Border Accord: "Canada and the United States are more than neighbours. Sharing a common past, many interests and objectives, we have become friends, allies and economic partners ... We already have the longest undefended border in the world. We now need to create the most efficiently managed border in the world."[69]

The Cascadia Transportation Corridor

The improvement of cross-border mobility in Cascadia involves more than creating an efficient border; it also focuses on trade corridor infrastructure. Again, significant progress is being made. Certainly the region has moved far beyond the 1960s sentiment of then Oregon governor Tom McCall, who was rumoured to have joked that "he would permit the freeway [Interstate 5] to go through Oregon only if there were no off-ramps." By 1994 Oregon senator Mark Hatfield stated bluntly: "We cannot afford to think that way any more. Our new problems and new opportunities do not respect jurisdictional boundaries."[70]

The focus of the trade corridor issue is on a binational, high-speed rail corridor. This is based on the belief that improved mobility will give Cascadia's major ports – Vancouver, Seattle, Tacoma, and Portland – a competitive advantage in the global economy. Moreover, in terms of NAFTA, Cascadia must compete with a growing number of other trade corridors being actively developed across the continent.[71]

Cascadia's ports sit halfway across the great circle route between Asia and Europe. If it is easy to move freight intraregionally, then business will improve; if there are bottlenecks at the border, congestion at the ports, and inadequate infrastructure, then cargo and jobs will go elsewhere. Improvements to passenger rail line services – with a focus on multimodal linkages – is also high on the agenda. High-speed rail development is seen as a necessary catalyst to future joint air capacity planning, especially in an era of "Open Skies."

A significant milestone was reached in spring 1995, with the renewal of regular train service between Vancouver and Eugene. With ridership levels at over 90 percent, plans are under way to increase the one-round-trip-per-day service to three in the coming years. This train – the *Mount Baker International* – is seen as a critical building block for future high-speed rail. Advocates say the high-speed rail corridor would form the "main street" of Cascadia, providing a transportation link that will make other forms of cooperation and integration possible.[72] The Cascadia Project is working with the Oregon High-Speed Rail Task Force, the Washington State Department of Transportation, BC's Employment and Investment Ministry, and regional transit agencies to forge the development of "seamless" connections and multimodal stations. Over the next several years, ongoing system upgrading on "Cascadia's Main Street" is planned in order to increase speeds and to reduce travel times.

In addition to pledging significant funds to upgrading, Oregon, Washington, Amtrak, and the Cascadia Project are working on public education programs to promote inter-city rail, including the "Main Street Tour," regional fora, and a citizen network.[73] The Cascadia Project is also currently developing a comprehensive Cascadia Trade Corridor Infrastructure/Finance Plan. The key will involve examining funding options that may include a cross-border infrastructure development bank similar to North American Development Bank, which was established through NAFTA to fund environmental projects on the Mexico-US border.

The Natural and Built Environments

Efforts within Cascadia to improve communication, to foster economic growth and global competitiveness, and to develop an efficient north-south transportation corridor are balanced by equally energetic efforts to preserve, protect, and enhance the natural and built environments. Cascadian traditions of environmental activism ("environmentalists are as thick on the ground as moss")[74] and stewardship, and the desire to maintain the liveability of the region, have been coupled with citizen diplomacy and "green" state, provincial, regional, and local governments to develop and sustain a strong environmental agenda.

There are a wide variety of initiatives in Cascadia that are directed at innovative ways of moving towards environmental sustainability. Underlying these efforts is a belief that "progress toward a sustainable environment will require changes to current management institutions and practices ... There is an urgent need to develop long-term strategies which cut-across traditional political, institutional, and community boundaries to create integrated environmental management."[75]

In 1992, the premier of BC and the governor of Washington signed an Environmental Cooperation Agreement, which states "environmental concerns and impacts respect neither physical nor political boundaries." It obliged the province and state to "promote and coordinate mutual efforts to ensure the protection, preservation and enhancement of our shared environment for the benefit of current and future generations." The premier and governor also created the Environmental Cooperation Council (ECC) to address numerous issues transcending the boundary between BC and Washington. The ECC meets biannually and has established five working groups to address the following priorities: marine water, quality, Nooksack River flood management, Columbia River/Lake Roosevelt water quality, the Abbotsford/Sumas aquifer, and Georgia Basin/Puget Sound air quality.[76]

In 1993 the ECC appointed the Marine Science Panel, consisting of six university and government marine scientists, to examine the state of the marine environment. After hearing the views of a wide spectrum of researchers, managers, and interest groups at a groundbreaking international public symposium and in small group meetings, the panel members presented their results to the council on August 1994 in a report entitled *Shared Waters: The Vulnerable Inland Sea of British Columbia and Washington.* Notably, this document involved cooperation not only between Washington and BC but also between federal departments in Canada and the US. The ECC has continued to meet on a regular basis, and there have been statements that the governor of Oregon will be involved in future discussions, just as BC officials have initiated meetings with their Oregon counterparts.

The other important initiative is the Cascadia Metropolitan Forum (CMF). Begun in an informal way at the Vancouver Cascadia Conference in March 1994, the CMF has since held formal meetings in Portland and Seattle, and another meeting was held in Vancouver in 1997. The forum brings together regional and local politicians, officials, experts, and academics from the Greater Vancouver Regional District, the Puget Sound Regional Council, and Portland Metro to discuss common problems and to share information on the development of effective regional urban management strategies.

Tourism: The Two-Nation Vacation

Another example of the practical value of Cascadia alliances is found in the tourism sector, an especially important segment of the economies of BC, Washington, and Oregon. As well, in terms of the larger PNWER, it is expected that tourism will soon be the largest employer and generator of foreign currency, accounting for regional revenues of over $20 billion annually; in BC, tourism is already the second most important sector of the economy. It is not surprising, therefore, that tourism alliances have an important place in the Cascadian Adventure, with the goal of putting the region "on the tips of tourists' tongues – especially the tongues of foreign tourists, a group that's the fastest growing segment of the tourism industry."[77]

Formal alliances in a Cascadia context became the focus of discussions following the completion of a major report in January 1994. Vancouver's Cascadia Institute received a grant from Tourism Canada to explore international tourism opportunities in Cascadia. In March 1994 a Cascadia Tourism Leaders' Forum was held in Vancouver, where the report was discussed in some detail. In particular, discussion focused on opportunities to expand tourism in such areas as the BC-Washington "Golden Triangle" of Whistler, Vancouver-Victoria, Seattle; rail touring; Aboriginal tourism; pre- and post-Alaska Cruise touring; an intermodal transportation pass; and partnerships with Alaska and Yukon for northern touring.[78]

Since then, a Cascadia Tourism Survey was undertaken, asking respondents to rank three international markets and to indicate their level of interest in a joint marketing program. Responses were received from over forty companies, and, in subsequent months, the Cascadia Tourism Working Group was established to guide the joint marketing project. Achievements to date include the development by the Port of Seattle of a colourful Cascadia poster illustrating the beauty and diversity of the region, the publication of *Two Nation Vacation: A Touring Guide to Cascadia* by Key Pacific Publishers of Victoria, and the development of a Cascadia logo, marketing concept, and rules for promoting the region. In September 1995 a "familiarization tour" of tour operators from the United Kingdom, Germany, and California visited Seattle, Vancouver, the San Juan Islands, and Victoria.

This review of an impressive array of Cascadia alliances suggests that the region is moving towards effective intraregional integration in a deliberate and coordinated fashion. The fact is, however, as one analyst put it, "Cascadia continues its stumbling march into the public imagination – part fantasy, part reality."[79] It is possible to portray Cascadia as an effective, functioning region with many elements of a shared vision of the past and future, and with many functioning and effective alliances in place. Certainly, the level of interest shown in the Cascadia concept by other transnational regions in North America and Europe strongly suggests that, on an international scale, Cascadia is indeed at the leading edge of transborder regional cooperation. Notwithstanding these facts, it is necessary to examine the ingrained barriers that work against the "Cascadia Adventure"; barriers that slow – and sometimes stop – plans for integration.

Ingrained Barriers

The barriers that stand in the way of the Cascadia Adventure can be analyzed under at least four headings: lack of coordination and political leadership; continuing points of friction over issues relating to trade and resources; cultural and economic nationalism; and internal divisions among Cascadia supporters.

Lack of Coordination and Leadership

As early as 1990, in a very perceptive analysis of the prospects for regional cooperation, the Northwest Policy Center of the University of Washington noted:

> In many respects there are an impressive array of cooperative efforts in the region ... Yet, in many ways, the Northwest has made progress where progress came easy, not where it was most needed ... Intergovernmental efforts have limited their potential by limiting size and scope. They fail to seek out lessons from others' experiences and apply the best of them across borders and departmental lines. They don't harness existing organizations to help foster new initiatives ... There is no shortage of groups interested in economic policy in our states, provinces, cities, countries, reservations, towns, and neighbourhoods ... But few regional organizations attempt to coordinate the activities of the diverse groups.[80]

It has already been noted that, in geographic terms, there are several competing versions of Cascadia. For each version there has been considerable effort made to forge new institutions and to coordinate a wide array of initiatives. But while this lack of agreement regarding Cascadia's geography is important, it is probably not as significant as is the fact that for none of the versions have political leaders emerged to effectively and consistently champion the Cascadian cause. Notwithstanding the laudable efforts of US senator Hatfield of Oregon, Seattle mayor Norm Rice, and Surrey mayor Bob Bose, no governor or premier has stepped forward to provide the political leadership involved in crystallizing a Cascadian definition or in developing the institutional mechanisms necessary to further the concept. Without this leadership, the sheer number and complexity of initiatives results in a loss of focus and – for some in the region – a loss of interest. Many residents become confused about what Cascadia really is, and no respected or important politicians are there to provide guidance or direction. One observer described the situation as "crossborder chaos."[81] In addition, the realities of politics are such that no leader gets elected to represent a region; there is, it seems, little direct political payoff in promoting Cascadia. As David Harrison of the Northwest Policy Centre noted, "few lofty regional aspirations have the desirable short-term positive impact on one's own constituency."[82]

The search for new institutional mechanisms is thus still under way. A growing number of Cascadians are recognizing that the traditional structures of government are no longer effective in responding to the challenges of an increasingly interdependent region. As a result, examples abound of new approaches to planning and organization that cut across jurisdictional boundaries and that have multiparty stakeholders and a broad regional mandate. But these processes typically fall back for decisions and delivery on traditional levels of government. And since governments are hierarchical and compartmentalized, they fail to respond effectively. The challenge is to make the Cascadia agenda the agenda of traditional governments. But despite a good deal of rhetoric, there has been little progress beyond the establishing of thematic, bilateral mechanisms.

One dimension of this reality is the lack of symmetry in Cascadia state-province relations. From a BC perspective, there has been the political will to work closely with Washington State and to enter into formal cooperative agreements. This familiar, bilateral pattern is firmly established and is certain to continue. The trilateral relationship that adds Oregon is, however, far more difficult to realize. On the BC side there is a growing but still fuzzy understanding of this larger, three-party relationship; certainly there is little enthusiasm in official circles for formalizing this version of Cascadia. Similarly, the Oregon-Washington relationship presents difficulties. Oregonians have always viewed their northern and southern neighbours with suspicion.[83] The prospect of placing Washington State in a central, "hinge" position between themselves and BC is not appealing. At another level – the five-state, two-province coalition of PNWER – there are also symmetry problems. In Canada there is little official affection between BC and Alberta. The mountains separating the two provinces are more than a physical barrier. On the American side, it is felt by some that the five-state coalition must stay together if it is to influence Washington, DC, and any smaller version of Cascadia (such as Washington, Oregon, and BC) may result in precipitating a defensive or even negative response by congressional leaders in Idaho, Montana, and Alaska. To date, these political realities have not been tackled and are rarely even discussed publicly; however, unless they are so discussed, and unless some new, innovative approach can be developed, the Cascadia concept will continue to suffer.

Trade and Resource Disputes

The difficulties in developing new mechanisms, institutional coordination, and political leadership is exacerbated in a period when, despite the FTA and NAFTA, trade and resource disputes continue to flare up between Canada and the US. In these situations, the familiar nationalistic responses tend to overwhelm the Cascadia concept. Even though the vast majority of trade within the region is free from bickering, the last several years have seen clashes over salmon, apples, lumber, wheat, and water-power. Each issue attracts intense interest since all are important aspects of the Cascadian economy.[84] In addition, because trade with the US states is more important to BC than is trade with BC to the American states, BC politicians are even more sensitive than are their American counterparts. BC simply has more to lose.[85]

Within the larger context of Cascadia, these specific disputes should not be exaggerated, but they do colour the nature of the cross-border relationship and can – and do – chill what may otherwise be increasingly warm relationships. Dispute problems are also exacerbated by the different political systems of the two countries, especially the different roles played by states and provinces in their respective federal systems. Efforts to harmonize issues, better manage state/provincial/national government relations, and facilitate adjustment as a result of NAFTA are being pursued. In the meantime, these ongoing points of friction slow down the integration of Cascadia.

Cultural and Economic Nationalism

Perhaps the most deeply ingrained barrier to closer cooperation and joint action is the fact that, in Canada, national debate has often been dominated by the assumption that closer economic and cultural association with the United States would lead to assimilation and annexation.[86] As one study indicated:

[The fear of domination] was dramatized by the reciprocal free trade agreement between the two countries prior to the American Civil War, the Canadian National Policy of the late 1870s, and the 1911 Canadian election, the key issue of which was reciprocity (the Conservative campaign slogan being "No truck nor trade with the Yankees"). Thus the loud, free trade debate of 1988 is part of a historical and ongoing dialogue about the connection between economic integration and political union. The discussion about the absorption of Canada into the US is historic; it has been carried out for more than a century; and it will continue ... The multiplication and cumulation of transactions does not add up to the integration of the two societies.[87]

In the cultural sphere, Canadian concerns about sovereignty are also strong. "For almost a century, Canadian governments have attempted to assert ... cultural sovereignty, and to control the allegedly deleterious effects of US newspapers, popular friction, magazines, comic books, motion picture (and now video tapes), radio, and eventually television and the associated recording industry."[88]

These general statements about Canadian economic and cultural nationalism do not apply equally across all of country's regions, and, in the case of BC and Alberta, the fear of American domination is relatively weak, while the strength of the international and continental outlook is strong. Nonetheless, at least two elements in this deeply ingrained barrier do work to slow the Cascadian Adventure. Until 2001 BC was governed by the NDP, a party with a tradition of economic and cultural nationalism, and a party that officially opposed both the FTA and NAFTA. There was, as well, a latent anti-Americanism evident in the views of some NDP Members of the Legislature, based – at least in part – on their memories of the Vietnam era.[89] A second element is the fact that, compared to their counterparts in the US, British Columbians are "highly sceptical of business"[90] and are distrustful – even fearful – of the entrepreneurial energies of their American neighbours; these views are evident in the relative lack of entrepreneurial spirit in the province. In 1993, for example, *Canadian Business* analyzed BC's situation and concluded by stating:

> It seemed that Vancouver would become a major international centre of business and finance. The combination of safety, liveability and a strategic location ... was supposed to do the trick. It's just not happening ... [The] people in BC are deluding themselves if they think they can succeed on attractiveness and lifestyle alone ...
>
> [There is] the dawning realization that natural advantages alone won't be enough to secure a glorious future. It's time to stop boasting about the scenery and get to work.[91]

These ingrained elements are not unique to Cascadia. The region "faces a generic problem of the nation-state: how to preserve sovereignty against a rising cross-border tide."[92] Indeed, as NAFTA continues to evolve, as American culture continues to influence, and as US and Canadian understandings of culture converge, it is virtually certain that cultural and economic nationalism will decrease in importance. And in terms of entrepreneurship, there are signs that BC and Alberta are becoming more "Americanized." As well, the shared visions in Cascadia appear to be stronger – and growing – while the ingrained barriers are declining in importance. Thus, while it is certainly more difficult to bridge deeply ingrained value systems than it is to cross political boundaries, Cascadia does represent an example of both.

Competing Cascadia Visions

A central characteristic of evolving transborder regions around the world is the differing visions groups within the region hold regarding the purpose and future of cooperation.[93] In Cascadia, the debate takes place between those who promote Cascadia as a fundamental imperative in the new global and continental economy, and those who envision Cascadia as a bioregion. For some – especially the environmental theologists and bioregionalists – the two groups represent diametrically opposed visions. The bioregionalists tend to be inward-looking and, in their view, place –

"Cascadia as a great green land" – is the essential bond – a bond that "may even prefigure a form of biologically rooted, ecological self-governance that transcends and essentially replaces the reign of nation states."[94] Alternatively, the bioregionalists portray other Cascadians, such as those involved in PNWER, PACE, or the Cascadia Project, as "free traders" who have "hijacked" and "imperilled" the Cascadia notion and who represent "big money interests."[95]

These divisions are exaggerated versions of reality. While there is no doubt some antipathy between the bioregionalists and the so-called "free traders," it is a one-way antipathy. Indeed, the free traders have developed a strong environmental agenda, and both formal agreements and working alliances in PNWER and the Cascadia Project, and between governments, regularly focus on sustainability. The distinction is that the free traders have a balanced view of sustainability, encompassing environmental, economic, and social challenges, while the bioregonalists tend to be focused almost exclusively on the environment.

Will these two visions converge? Undoubtedly they will. The power of the environmental imperative in Cascadia is simply too deep-rooted to be ignored or even submerged in any agenda for transborder cooperation. It may be that neither the so-called free trade nor the bioregionalist view of Cascadia will prevail in any supposedly pure form, but certainly the basis for a vision that encompasses the views of a vast majority of Cascadia's residents is firmly in place.

The Future of the Cascadian Adventure
In the space of a dozen years, the Cascadian Adventure has unfolded in a remarkable manner. When *The New Pacific* was launched in the fall of 1989, the lead editorial noted that, despite the shared visions held in Cascadia, there were "relatively few resources or regional institutions ... Although Washington, Oregon and British Columbia have shared similar economies, geography, climate, and development patterns for several hundred years, no entity has crossed the increasingly artificial state and national boundaries to examine or build regional awareness."[96] By fall 2001 this situation had changed dramatically. In a similar vein, the economic relationship between Canada and the US, and within Cascadia, was transformed. In 1989, at the dawn of the free trade era, most trade patterns ran east-west; in Canada inter-provincial trade amounted to 105 percent of trade with the US. By 1996 the overwhelming majority of trade patterns were flowing north-south. Trade across provincial boundaries amounted to only 60 percent of trade across the US-Canada border.[97]

These two examples suggest that the Cascadian Adventure will continue and, although many challenges remain, the story will unfold at an increasing pace. And while the tendency towards convergence "must be viewed through the lens of past divergence and ambiguity,"[98] the energy and drive of Cascadia proponents will certainly prevail. It is not a question of choosing between history and geography; rather, the strengthening of the Cascadia alliance can take place while each member state and province, and each country, maintains its distinctiveness. This approach to Cascadia – an approach that remains at the heart of the adventure – was best stated by Paul Schell and John Hamer in 1993:

> The [Cascadia] vision is not designed to alter the fundamental nature of our mutual region, or make it what it is not. Instead, the regional movement is intended to make the most of the people, the culture, the natural gifts and the geographic good fortune the region has been blessed with. In that sense the innovations in cooperation ... are meant to *conserve* the most prized feature of our lives, including some that distinguish us one from the other...
>
> [Cascadia] is a shared notion, and one in active evolution. We're still inventing ourselves as a regional culture. Cascadia is recognition of emerging realities, a way to celebrate commonality with diversity, a way to make the whole more than the sum of its parts. Cascadia is not a State, but a state of mind. But a state of mind can have important practical consequences.[99]

Notes

1 Ken Coates, "Border Crossings: Pattern and Process in the History of the Pacific Northwest," paper presented at On Brotherly Terms symposium, University of Washington, 12 September 1996, 28.

2 See, for example, W.G. East and I.R.V. Prescott, *Our Fragmented World* (London: Macmillan, 1975).

3 F.W. Howay, W.N. Sage, and H.F. Angus, *British Columbia and the United States* (Toronto: Ryerson, 1942).

4 See, for example, M.A. Ormsby, *British Columbia: A History* (Toronto: Macmillan, 1958); E.M. Gibson, "Lotus Eaters, Loggers and the Vancouver Landscape," in *Cultural Discord in the Modern World: Shared Visions, Strategic Alliances, and Ingrained Barriers in a Transborder Region,* ed. L.J. Evenden and F.F. Cunningham (Vancouver: Tantalus, 1974), 57-74; and Barry Sandford, *McCulloch's Wonder: The Story of the Kettle Valley Railway* (Vancouver: Whitecap Books, 1978).

5 PNWER can be contacted at First Interstate Center, 999 Third Avenue, Suite 1080, Seattle, WA, 98104. The organization holds regular meetings, publishes a newsletter, and has a variety of active projects designed to increase the global competitiveness of the region.

6 The Cascadia Project can be contacted at Discovery Institute, 1402 Third Avenue, Suite 400, Seattle, WA, 98101, or at the Cascadia Institute, 885 Dunsmuir Street, Suite 920, Hamilton Street, Vancouver, BC, V6C 1N5.

7 PACE can be contacted at 720 Olive Way, Suite 1300, Seattle, WA, 98101.

8 The GBI has published a major study and regularly releases a newsletter. GBI can be contacted at the Ministry of Municipal Affairs, Government of BC, Victoria, BC, V8V 1X4.

9 See, for example, Gary Piro, *Toward Sustainable Development on Cascadia's Main Street* (Vancouver: International Center for Sustainable Cities, Publication 3, 1995). Still another definition of Cascadia is the one pioneered by David McCloskey of the Seattle-based Cascadia Institute. His bioregional definition of Cascadia has been pursued by Doug Aberley and his students in the School of Community and Regional Planning at the University of

BC and has resulted in the publication in 1995 of *Envisioning Cascadia: A Bioregional Atlas* (Vancouver: SCARP, UBC, 1995), Map 7.

10 See McClosky, *Envisioning Cascadia;* and J. Lewis Robinson, *Concepts and Themes in the Regional Geography of Canada* (Vancouver: Talonbooks, 1989).

11 Philip Gold, "A Brave New World in the Old Frontier," *Insight,* 9 May 1994, 16.

12 See Map 12A, in McClosky, *Envisioning Cascadia.*

13 Eileen V. Quigley, "Coming of Age in the New Pacific Era," *The New Pacific* 1 (Fall 1989): 5.

14 Robert Soltvig of Seattle University, quoted in *The Christian Science Monitor,* 20 July 1992, 15.

15 See Martin Robin, *The Pillars of Profit: The Company Province, 1934-1972* (Toronto: McClelland and Stewart, 1973); Carlos A. Schwantes, *The Pacific Northwest: An Interpretative History* (Lincoln: University of Nebraska Press, 1989); A.P. Andrus, W.B. Beyers, et al., *Seattle* (Cambridge, MA.: Ballinger, 1976); W.G. Hardwick, *Vancouver* (Don Mills, ON: Collier-Macmillan, 1974); Carl Abbott, *Portland: Planning, Politics and Growth in a Twentieth-Century City* (Lincoln: University of Nebraska Press, 1983); Alan F.J. Artibise, Anne Vernez-Moudon, and Ethan Seltzer, "Cascadia," in *Cities in Our Future,* ed. R. Geddes (Washington, DC: Island Press, 1996); and P. Roy, *Vancouver: An Illustrated History* (Toronto: Lorimer, 1980).

16 Warren Gill, "Client Variations and Urban Nightclub Locations: A Case Study of Vancouver" (MA thesis, University of British Columbia, 1972). See also Alan F.J. Artibise, Bradley Condon, and Warren Gill, "Cascadia: Shared Visions and Strategic Alliances in a Transborder Region," in *Integrating Cities and Regions: North America Faces Globalization,* ed. J. Wilkie and C.E. Smith (Guadalajara and Los Angeles: UCLA Program in Mexico and Universidad de Guadalajara, Centro Internacional "Lucas Alamán" para el Crecimiento Economico [CILACE], 1996), 77-104.

17 L.J. Evenden, "Shaping the Vancouver Suburbs," in *Vancouver: Western Metropolis* (Victoria: University of Victoria, 1978), 179-99.

18 Anthony Netboy, ed., *The Pacific Northwest* (Garden City, NY: Doubleday, 1963), 7.

19 Cited in Eileen V. Quigley, "Cascadia," *The New Pacific* 2 (1990): 3. For detailed maps of all of the region's natural environment, see McClosky, *Envisioning Cascadia.* McCloskey's description can also be found on the Internet. See McCloskey, "Cascadia: A Great Green Land on the Northeast Pacific Rim," <http://tnews.com:80/text/mccloskey.html.Cascadia Planet>.

20 John C. Ryan, *State of the Northwest* (Seattle: NEW, 1994), 10-11.

21 See, for example, BC/Washington Marine Science Panel, *Shared Waters: The Vulnerable Inland Sea of British Columbia and Washington* (Seattle: State of Washington, 1994); Paul Schell and John Hamer, "What Is the Future of Cascadia? On the New Binationalism of Western Canada and the US Pacific Northwest," *Discovery Institute Inquiry* (Seattle: Discovery Institute, 1993); BC Round Table on the Environment and the Economy, *Georgia Basin Initiative: Creating a Sustainable Future* (Victoria: Province of British Columbia, 1993); Alan F.J. Artibise, *Opportunities for Achieving Sustainability in Cascadia* (Vancouver: International Center for Sustainable Cities, Publication 1, 1994); Timothy Egan, *The Good Rain: Across Time and Terrain in the Pacific Northwest* (New York: Vintage, 1991); and J.M.J. Brownson, *In Cold Margins: Sustainable Development in Northern Bioregions* (Missoula: Northern Rim Press, 1995).

22 G. Price, "Tale of Three Cities," *The New Pacific* 6 (1992): 30. See also US Senator Mark O. Hatfield, "Fulfilling the Promise of the Cascadia Region," *Seattle Times,* 22 February 1994; and former US Representative John Miller, "Pacific Northwest Can Meet the Cascadia Challenge," *Seattle Post-Intelligencer,* 3 August 1994. Notably, in BC, the Cascadia idea was pursued by the late M.P. Robert Wenman and resulted in the creation of the International Center for Sustainable Cities, which had, as one of its major projects, the urban corridor stretching from Eugene to Whistler. See Alan F.J. Artibise, *International Georgia Basin-Puget Sound Sustainable Urbanization Project, Rationale and Operational Plans: Final Report* (Vancouver: Cascadia Planning Group, 1992).

23 Cameron's analysis was presented at a meeting of the Cascadia Metropolitan Forum in Seattle in February 1996 and was unanimously endorsed by the audience. Under common

context was listed: population size/growth rate; economic base and opportunities; dominance of provincial/state life; remoteness from imperial capitals; physical constraints/assets-water, air, land; traditions of stewardship; traditions of local authority. Under common policy issues was listed: making two-tier government work; urban containment; promoting multicentred urban structure; promoting alternatives to the private automobile; building and financing light rail; regional air quality management; and Cascadia's future under NAFTA.

24 See, for example, Artibise, Vernez-Moudon, and Seltzer, "Cascadia"; Gary Pivo, *Cascadia's Main Street;* Alan F.J. Artibise, "Achieving Sustainability in Cascadia: An Emerging Model of Urban Growth Management in the Vancouver-Seattle-Portland Corridor," and T.H. Cohn and P.J. Smith, "Developing Global Cities in the Pacific Northwest: The Cases of Vancouver and Seattle," in *North American Cities and the Global Economy: Challenges and Opportunities,* ed. P.K. Kresl and G. Gappert (Thousand Oaks, CA: Sage, 1995). Notably, the Association of American Geographers Comparative Metropolitan Analysis Project stated that the three cities were "the most similar to each other in terms of size, economic function and social conditions." See Artibise, Condon, and Gill, "Cascadia: Shared Visions and Strategic Alliances."

25 See, for example, B. Wharf, "Regional Transformation, Everyday Life, and Pacific Northwest Lumber Production," *Annals of the American Association of Geographers* 78 (1988): 326-46; K.G. Denike and Roger Leigh, "Economic Geography," in *Studies in Canadian Geography: British Columbia,* ed. J.L. Robinson (Toronto: University of Toronto Press, 1972), 69-86; John Bradbury, "British Columbia: Metropolis and Hinterland in Microcosm," in *Heartland and Hinterland: A Geography of Canada,* ed. L.D. McCann (Scarborough, ON: Prentice Hall, 1982), 338-71; and Earl Pomeroy, *The Pacific Slope: A History of California, Oregon, Washington, Idaho, Utah and Nevada* (New York: Knopf, 1996).

26 Stuart Jamieson, "Regional Factors in Industrial Conflict," in *Historical Essays on British Columbia,* ed. J. Friesen and H.K. Rolston (Toronto: Carleton Library, 1980), 228-42.

27 R.A. Erickson, "The Regional Impact of Growth Firms: The Case of Boeing," in *Systems of Cities: Readings on Structure, Growth and Policy,* ed. L.S. Bourne and J.W. Simmons (New York: Oxford, 1978) 402-11.

28 For detailed discussions of the economies of the states and provinces, see Artibise, Condon, and Gill, "Cascadia." See also Earl H. Foy, M.G. Binks, and Leslie K. Smith, "The Economic Development and Tourism Profiles of the Western US States and the Canadian Provinces," paper prepared for "Strengthening the Economic Linkages between Canada and the US: Trade, Investment and Tourism," Salt Lake City, 25-26 June 1992.

29 For a good overview, see Alan Bluechel, "The Pacific Northwest Economic Region: A Multi-State, Multi-Province, Regional Approach to Economic Development," *Economic Development Review* (Winter 1993): 27-29. See also D. Bramham, "BC's Service Sector Growth Lauded," *Vancouver Sun,* 14 August 1996, C6 and C8; and Terry B. Chadwick, "Hands across the Border: The Pacific Northwest Economic Partnership," *The New Pacific* 1 (Fall 1989): 9-20.

30 See the statements cited in Chadwick, "Hands across the Border." Also, for a discussion of the "high-tech regional network," see D.J. Yang, "Magic Mountains," *The New Pacific* 6 (Autumn 1992): 18-23.

31 Gold, "A Brave New World," 15. See also Brownson, *In Cold Margins,* 169-70.

32 Ibid.

33 For a general discussion of this phenomenon, see D.K. McAllen, "Shifting from the Traditional to the New Political Agenda," *American Review of Canadian Studies* 25 (1995): 323-45; and North American Institute (NAMI) *News* 14 (May). On the topic of organizations, see *Sounding Board,* May 1995, the newsletter of the Vancouver Board of Trade. In an article entitled "Too Many Cooks in the Kitchen," the author notes that PACE has identified more than thirty associations with aspirations to assist businesses in free trade. The phenomenon of the past several years of government following rather than leading the public on Cascadia issues has also been noted by senior BC government officials. Based on a discussion with Peter Heap, International Relation Division, Office of the Premier, 27 August 1996.

34 Gerald Prosalendis, "The Power of One," *The New Pacific* 5 (Summer): 7.

35 Schell and Hamer, "Cascadia," 3. I have also explored this theme in "'Our Similarities Are Different': Perspectives on Canada's Development in a North American Context," address to the American Association of University Presidents, annual meeting, Whistler, BC, July 1992.

36 Lewis Mumford, *The Culture of Cities* (New York: Harcourt, Brace and Co., 1938), 351, 363. Notably, Mumford also wrote about the Cascadia region. See Mumford, "Regional Planning in the Pacific Northwest: A Memorandum," Portland, Northwest Regional Council, 1939.

37 Neil Peirce, *Citistates: How Urban America Can Prosper in a Competitive World* (Washington, DC: Seven Locks Press, 1993). See also Peirce's bibliography, which lists important works on this topic.

38 See, for example, P. Soldatos, "Strategic Cities Networking in the European Community," paper presented at conference, "New International Cities Era," Provo, Utah, 15-16 October 1993; and Leo van den Berg et al., "The Need for Organizing Capacity in Managing European Metropolitan Regions," paper presented at North American Institute for Comparative Urban Research (NAMICUR) Conference, "Metropolitan Regions in the Global Economy," Vancouver, BC, 11-13 April 1996. The European researchers are organized as the European Institute for Comparative Urban Research (EURICUR). It is based at Erasmus University in Rotterdam and was founded in 1988. NAMICUR was established in 1993 at the University of Missouri, St. Louis. See also three papers by Joachim Blatter: "Cross-Border Co-operation on Environmental Issues: Analytical Model, Western European Findings and Organizational Recommendations," paper presented at the Annual Meeting of the Association of Borderland Scholars, Reno, Nevada, 17-20 April 1996; "Political Co-operation in Cross-Border Regions: Two Explanatory Approaches," paper presented at European Regional Science Association, 36th European Congress, Zurich, Switzerland, 26-30 August 1996; and "Cross-Border Cooperation and Sustainable Development in Europe and North America," unpublished manuscript, 1996.

39 See, for example, Kresl and Gappert, *North American Cities;* L. McKinsey and V. Konrad, *Borderlands Reflections: The United States and Canada* (Orono, ME: Borderlands Monograph Series 1, Orono, University of Maine, 1989); and *Trade Flows: The Newsletter of the Red River Corridor* (Crookston, MN: University of Minnesota, 1989).

40 A view most strongly expressed by Kenichi Ohmae. Interestingly, Ohmae has a home in Cascadia at Whistler.

41 L.H. Herzog, "Cross National Urban Structure in the Era of Global Cities," *Urban Studies* 28 (1991): 519-33.

42 Quoted in Chadwick, "Hands across the Border," 20.

43 Gerald Prosalendis, "The Power of One," *The New Pacific* 5 (1992): 7.

44 For a case study, see T.H. Cohn and P.J. Smith, "Developing Global Cities in the Pacific Northwest: The Cases of Vancouver and Seattle," in Kresl and Gappert, *North American Cities,* 251-85. See also John Hamer and Bruce Chapman, *International Seattle: Creating a Globally Competitive Community* (Seattle: Discovery Institute, 1993).

45 See, for example, J.E. Garten, "The Changing Face of North America in the Global Economy," remarks by Under Secretary of Commerce for International Trade to Americas Society and the Council of the Americas, New York, 17 May 1994.

46 Statistics were obtained from Customs Border Services of Revenue Canada. The numbers for 1995/96 are as follows: Pacific Highway: 3,671,467; Douglas: 4,606,292; Huntington: 2,520,191; Aldergrove: 1,632,973; Boundary Bay: 2,023,356; and VIA 2,454,679. In 1994 the *Bellingham Herald* reported over twenty million crossings (20 September 1994). There has been a general decline in growth since then, largely as a result of the declining Canadian dollar.

47 For a discussion of *Ecotopia,* see E. Godley, "View from the Edge," *The New Pacific* 9 (Autumn 1993): 12-15.

48 Joel Garreau, *The Nine Nations of North America* (Boston: Houghton Mifflin, 1981).

49 *The New Pacific* was published between 1989 and 1994; the *Cascadia Forum* produced two issues in 1994.

50 The *Northwest Journal* is published by the College of Business and Economics at Western Washington University. WWU journalism students also published a *Borderlands* newspaper

in September 1995. An annual "portrait" of Cascadia is published by the Northwest Policy Center at the University of Washington and the US Bank. It has been published since 1990. The Vancouver Cascadia Institute published a major report, entitled *Opportunities for Expanding International Tourism in Cascadia*, in 1994, while the ICSC has two monographs on Cascadia (cited above) and has highlighted Cascadia in its newsletter.

51 Examples – in addition to those already cited above – include *The Economist* (May 1994); *Globe and Mail*, 25 January 1992; *Christian Science Monitor*, 20 July 1992; *Boston Globe*, 31 May 1992; *The Statesman Journal*, 3 October 1994; *Puget Sound Business Journal*, 10-16 November 1995; *Vancouver Courier*, 27 March 1994; *Business in Vancouver*, 5-11 April 1994; *Seattle Times*, 9 December 1994; *Eugene Register-Guard*, 7 October 1994; *Transporter: The Magazine of the Oregon and Washington Trucking Associations* (October 1994); *Bellingham Herald*, 20 September 1994; and *Business in Vancouver*, 20-26 August 1996.

52 A plan is being prepared by John Myrick, director of international communications, Third Avenue Productions, in Seattle.

53 Craig Stephens, "US Television Sold across the Border," *Borderlands*, 25 September 1995. See also *Vancouver Sun*, 4 September 1996.

54 See Charles Kelly, "Cascadia Mariners: A Winning Opportunity," *The New Pacific* 5 (1992): 9; "The Cascadia Olympics," *Seattle Times*, 9 December 1994; and "Momentum Building for Games Bid," *Seattle Times*, 14 June 1995.

55 Schell and Hamer, "What Is the Future of Cascadia?" 10.

56 Quigley, "Cascadia," 4-5.

57 *The New Pacific* held a flag competition in 1993. See "Cascadia Flag Competition," *The New Pacific* 8 (1993): 12-15. The Cascadia logo was developed by a Cascadia group of tourism officials in cooperation with the Cascadia Project. The Cascadia Institute in Seattle has also promoted a distinctive Cascadia flag. See also *Seattle Post-Intelligencer*, 3 August 1994.

58 To cite but one example, UBC and UW planning students undertake an annual exchange field trip. Also, Portland State University, UBC, and UW offer regular courses on Cascadia.

59 As of 2000, there were at least a dozen formal agreements in place.

60 See Don White and Tim Gallagher, "British Columbia and International Trade: Opportunities, Challenges and Prospects," paper presented at the Pacific Northwest Regional Economic Conference, Portland, Oregon, 3 May 1996. It is notable that BC and Washington cooperated at COMDEX, one of the largest computer expositions in the world, as early as 1988 when the name "Pacific Northwest Economic Partnership" was first used. See Chadwick, "Hands across the Border."

61 See PNWER *Newsletter*, January 1996.

62 Cascadia Institute, "BC-Washington Bi-National Trade Corridor Proposal," 11 October 1994.

63 Ibid.

64 See the report on the group in Discovery Institute, *Cascadia* 1, 2 (1994): 1. The Cascadia Project has also issued regular reports on the Border Working Group.

65 Cascadia Institute, "Trade Corridor Proposal."

66 In addition to the accord, see reports in the *Vancouver Sun*, 25 February 1995; and the *Globe and Mail*, 29 June 1995.

67 Based on Cascadia Project reports.

68 Schell and Hamer, "What Is the Future of Cascadia?" 7.

69 Shared Border Accord (published by the Government of Canada).

70 Hatfield, "Fulfilling the Promise of the Cascadia Region," *Seattle Times*, 22 February 1994. Hatfield's opinions were also published in *The Oregonian*.

71 See, for example, *Assessment of Border Crossings and Transportation Corridors for North American Trade: Report to Congress* (Washington, DC: US Department of Transportation, 1994).

72 John Henrikson, "Blurring Borders for the Future," *Salem Statesman Journal*, 3 October 1994. See also R. Eng, "Runaway Success of Cross-Border Rail Route," *Business in Vancouver*, 12-18 September 1995.

73 *Cascadia Project Report*, September 1995.

74 "Cascadia," *The Economist*, 21 May 1994.

75 *The Lower Fraser River Basin: A State of the Environment Synopsis* (Vancouver: Environment Canada, 1992), 9.

76 See Alan F.J. Artibise, "Opportunities for Sustainability in Cascadia," 7; and BC-Washington Marine Science Panel, *Shared Waters*.

77 C. Solomon, "Tourism Industry to Promote Cascadia Concept," *Seattle Times*, 7 June 1996.

78 M. Robson, *Opportunities for Expanding International Tourism in Cascadia* (Vancouver: Cascadia Institute, 1994).

79 *Business in Vancouver*, 20-26 August 1996.

80 *Northwest Resources for Regional Cooperation* (Seattle: Northwest Policy Center, 1990), 21-22.

81 Charles Kelly, "Crossborder Chaos," *The New Pacific* 9 (1993/94): 6.

82 David Harrison, "O, Cascadia!" *The Weekly*, 14 June 1995.

83 See, for example, Carl Abbott, Sy Adler, and Deborah Howe, eds., *Planning the Oregon Way* (Corvallis: Oregon State University Press, 1994).

84 For one synopsis of disputes, see the *Seattle Times*, 26 June 1994. Since that date disputes – especially over fishing and softwood lumber – have continued to colour the relationship. For one analysis of the disputes, see Groen, "British Columbia's International Relations."

85 See Artibise, Condon, Gill, "Cascadia."

86 See, for example, McKinsey and Konrad, *Borderlands Reflections*, 23-26; several of the articles in S.J. Randall and H.W. Konrad, *NAFTA in Transition* (Calgary: University of Calgary Press, 1995); and M. Sandler, "The Free Trade Agreement: A Betrothal of Two Economies?" *The New Pacific* 2 (1990): 9-20. For a current view of the relationship, see the special issue of the *American Review of Canadian Studies* 24, 4 (Winter 1994), entitled "Weathering the Calm: The State of the Canada-U.S. Relationship."

87 McKinsey and Konrad, *The United States and Canada*, 26.

88 J.H. Thompson, "Canada's Quest for Cultural Sovereignty: Protection, Promotion, and Popular Culture," in Randall and Konrad, *NAFTA in Transition*, 394.

89 This view is based on my discussions with several MLAs. Also, at least one NDP MLA migrated to Canada from the US during the early 1970s.

90 See BC *Premier's Summit* report, Province of British Columbia, January 1995, esp. 83-88.

91 D. Stoffman, "A Great Place to Visit," *Canadian Business* 66, 10 (October 1993): 107. This attitude problem was also identified as an important factor at the 1992 Premier's Summit on Trade and Economic Opportunity. See *Summary of Proceedings*, 17-19 June 1992.

92 McKinsey and Konrad, *The United States and Canada*, 25.

93 See, for example, Blatter, "Cross-Border Co-operation on Environmental Issues," 35.

94 The bioregionalist view is best represented by David McCloskey. See also Terry Morgan, "Cascadia," *Victoria Times Colonist*, 1 April 1995. See also Patrick Mazza, "Cascadia Emerging: The End and the Beginning of the World," and "Lifeplace or Marketplace? Bioregions, Region States and the Contested Turf of Regionalism." Both are located on the Internet: <http//www.tnews.com:80/text/emerge.html.Cascadia Planet> and <http.//www.tnews.com/text/lifeplace_marketplace.html.Cascadia Planet>, respectively.

95 Morgan, "Cascadia." See also *Puget Sound Business Journal*, 10-16 November 1995.

96 Quigley, "Cascadia," 5.

97 *Canadian Business* (January 1996): 38.

98 J.H. Thompson and S.J. Randall, *Canada and the United States: Ambivalent Allies* (Montreal and Kingston: McGill-Queen's University Press, 1994), 305.

99 Schell and Hamer, "What Is the Future of Cascadia?" 4 and 12.

13

NAFTA and Transportation Corridor Improvement in Western North America: Restructuring for the Twenty-First Century

Daniel E. Turbeville III and Susan L. Bradbury

The economical, political, and social character of North America has been profoundly shaped during the past decade by the globalization process and increased economic integration. While significant improvements in transportation and communication technology have made this possible, it has also involved deliberate – and often controversial – policy choices.[1] The policy choices involve two major trade agreements – the 1989 Canada-US Free Trade Agreement (FTA) and the 1994 North American Free Trade Agreement (NAFTA) – which have redefined the economic relationship between Canada, the US, and Mexico. As a result, economic restructuring is no longer just taking place on a national level but is now also occurring on a continental scale as traditional patterns of economic activity (such as trade, investment, and migration) are rapidly changing. Some of the literature suggests that globalization and regional restructuring has resulted in an increasingly borderless world – one where the consequence of international borders is vanishing and the importance of geography and distance is declining.[2] However, it is our contention that geography and borderlands, rather than declining, are actually taking on greater significance. Thus, while borderlines have blurred, borderlands require greater attention.

The term "borderlands" was developed by political geographers to refer to the distinctive regions that form along the boundaries of nation-states. While, by definition, borders divide nations, they also link them through trade and interaction, creating areas of common characteristics in the landscape and people.[3] It is in the borderlands where much of the interaction between countries takes place, for they provide the conduit and infrastructure that supports interaction between nations. As free trade and increased economic integration reconceptualize North America into a continental amalgam, it is in the borderlands where the greatest changes are taking place and where the success or failure of such economic policies will ultimately be determined.

The impact of these economic changes is largely uneven, affecting some regions of the continent and sectors of the economy more profoundly than others. While the assessment of impacts continues, sceptics lament the negative effects of NAFTA on job creation, economic expansion, and the natural environment.[4] The amount of trade – whether measured in terms of volume or value – has increased significantly among Canada, the US, and Mexico.[5] However, one aspect of NAFTA that has been largely unrecognized by politicians, economists, and planners is the overwhelming impact of the agreements on the continental transportation system.

The primary purpose of these agreements was to foster trade and investment among the three countries through the elimination of both tariff and non-tariff barriers. While the two treaties have been a success and trade has increased dramatically among the three participants, it is the very success of this economic/trade policy that is causing havoc with the existing continental transportation system. Since 1991 Canada/US/Mexico trade has increased by 9 percent per year, and estimates suggest that continental trade was expected to grow by at least 15 percent per year through the year 2003.[6]

Not surprisingly, this enhanced trade has resulted in increased traffic on North American highways and railroads, demonstrating weaknesses in the existing transportation infrastructure and policies as massive delays and congestion are becoming a normal occurrence in transborder corridors.[7] The very success of NAFTA and the resulting transportation problems clearly illustrate the failure to consider and create an integrated North American transportation system. NAFTA was simply written as a trade policy with no adjustment provisions for the resulting impacts on other related policy areas, such as transportation, security, and immigration. Until an efficient continental transportation system is developed and operating, the economic benefits associated with NAFTA cannot be fully realized. Despite acknowledgment of this fact, all three countries have been slow to respond to making the infrastructure improvements necessary to make NAFTA work.

This chapter focuses on the impact of NAFTA on the transportation patterns in the western border region of Canada and the United States. The western border region refers to the area from the western end of Lake Superior to the Pacific Coast. The decision to limit the focus to the western region was determined by a number of factors. First, transportation patterns and trends differ between the east and west. In the west distances are greater, travel times are longer, and transportation costs and competitiveness take on greater importance. Second, there is a difference in the type of commodities that are transported: the east mainly consists of higher-value, manufactured products, whereas the west involves large quantities of low-value, resource-based commodities.[8] Transportation networks in the east have long been better integrated between Canada and the United States, partly due to the close geographic proximity of the manufacturing heartlands of the two countries but also due to the Auto Pact of 1965.[9] Third, and perhaps most important, it is in the west where the greatest changes have occurred. Western border traffic has increased at a faster rate than has that in the east, and this trend is expected to continue.[10] Western transportation patterns are undergoing profound changes since the introduction of free trade, and these changes will affect not only the west but also the continent's global competitive position.

First, we briefly outline the comparative history of transportation development on the western border and demonstrate the role that geography and politics have played in creating the transportation networks that have emerged. Second, we describe the current transportation patterns that NAFTA has helped to shape and assess the ability of the current continental system to deal with this situation. Third, we explore the planning efforts that have been taking place in order to accommodate NAFTA. Despite efforts that have been under way for several years, very little has actually been accomplished. Transportation planning in the western borderland has failed largely because most of the decision making has occurred centrally rather than locally, and with a notable lack of coordination and cooperation. The lack of reliable comparative data has further hampered the ability of national governments to comprehend the changes that have been occurring in the border region, resulting in an overall lack of understanding of the issues at stake for each of the countries. Consequently, many of the transportation issues remain a mystery. Unlike the case of the European Union, NAFTA did not create a strong institutional structure to implement the agreement.[11] While planning at the federal level has largely failed, planning at the local and regional levels is showing more promise. We conclude with policy recommendations regarding what will be necessary to better implement NAFTA.

Historical Perspectives on National Transportation Infrastructure

The present continental transportation system was constructed incrementally and independently as Canada, the United States, and Mexico each pursued its own national transportation policy based on individual economic and political requirements. Obviously, much of the continental system was designed and built to respond to very different economic realities, and thus it fails to reflect the needs of today. Examination of the history of national transportation policies for both Canada and the United States illustrates that they were planned and structured according to conditions that existed over a century ago and that network expansion, whether rail or highway, has tended to merely reinforce, rather than to reorient, the existing structure.

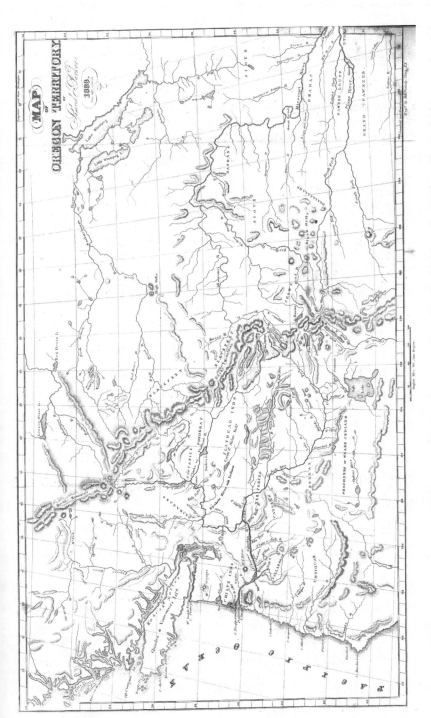

Map 13.1 Western North America in 1838, eight years before the Oregon Boundary Treaty. Note the north-south trend of topography and drainage, especially the Fraser, Columbia, and Okanagan Rivers; and the Cascade, Coast, and Rocky Mountain Ranges. *Source:* Oregon Historical Society.

Perhaps the most obvious way to begin is by noting that the 49th Parallel was drawn across the natural geographic "grain" of western North America. The most prominent physical features of the region all run in a north-south direction: the Great Plains and Prairies, the Rocky Mountains, the Cascade Range, and, most significantly, the Columbia and Fraser Rivers and their tributaries (see Map 13.1). In prehistory, First Nations peoples used this north-south system of waterways and trails for trade, communication, and warfare. This axis was later reinforced during the fur trade era of the late eighteenth and early nineteenth centuries when the Hudson's Bay Company organized its internal administrative departments in a north-south pattern. The Oregon Treaty of 1846 truncated this geographically logical arrangement, but it was not until the arrival of the first transcontinental railroads that the political and economic power of the two nation-states was able to overcome these natural barriers.[12]

The first national transportation policy for Canada was shaped by Prime Minister Sir John A. Macdonald, who recognized that trade and economic policies needed to be linked to the nation's transportation policy in order to succeed.[13] In 1879 Macdonald implemented what became known as the "National Policy," with Canada choosing "Canadianism" over "Continentalism." The National Policy linked a highly protectionist trade policy with building the first Canadian transcontinental rail line, the Canadian Pacific Railway (CPR). This economic policy had strong political overtones – it created a British-controlled "All-Red Route" across the continent, linking the mother country to its Pacific colonies as well as securing British Columbia to the bosom of Mother Canada in order to thwart the threat of Yankee imperialism and "Manifest Destiny," – and it obviously entrenched the national transportation network into a primarily east-west pattern (Map 13.2). The pattern was further enhanced by the 1915 completion of the more northerly transcontinental route of the Canadian Northern Railway (CNR), now Canadian National (CN).[14]

This predominantly east-west transportation pattern has continued to evolve through the construction of the national highway system. Of special note is the Trans-Canada Highway (TCH), whose construction began in 1949. The TCH was designed to reinforce the CPR/CNR linkage and, at the same time, bind the country together with an efficient all-weather highway. Although officially opened to traffic in 1962, it was not actually completed until 1970. Like the rails that preceded it, the TCH links the manufacturing heartland of the country with the resource hinterlands and the markets of the east and west. This transportation system supported the trade patterns of an era that was dominated by the tariff barriers that had remained between Canada and the United States since the 1880s. Although the Canadian economy has always been heavily dependent on trade, it was not until the mid-1980s that more trade occurred north-south between Canada and its largest trading partner, the United States, than occurred east-west among the provinces of Canada.[15]

The national transportation system of the United States has also followed an east-west axis. The railroad network of a century ago clearly reflects the east-west orientation inspired by "Manifest Destiny" and the need to bind the Atlantic and Pacific seaboards. Every major western railroad of the nineteenth century reflected this with an east-west trunk line: the Union Pacific-Central Pacific, the Northern Pacific, the Great Northern, and many smaller lines as well. Again, this east-west pattern was repeated and enhanced by virtually every piece of US highway legislation and construction from the 1916 Federal Highway Act (Maps 13.3 and 13.4) to the Defence Interstate Highway Act of 1956. This latter piece of legislation represents the last major transportation policy initiative in the United

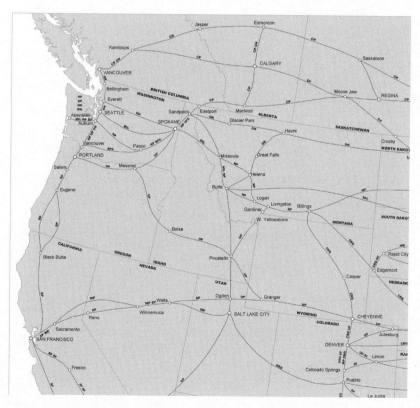

Map 13.2 Western railroad network, 1928. Trunk lines display the east-west pattern dictated by the international boundary, with limited border crossing points between networks.
Source: Rand McNally, *Auto Road Atlas of the United States* (Chicago: Rand McNally, 1928)

States until the 1990s. With over 69,000 kilometres completed, it was also the largest public works project in human history.

Today the interstate highway system is as much a relic of the Cold War as are empty missile silos and rusting nuclear submarines. The east-west mentality is clearly reflected in maps of the system (Map 13.5). The interstate highway system was designed to link the two coasts together, thus there are far fewer north-south than east-west links. In addition, where north-south linkages occur (with the exception of the two coastal and Mississippi Valley corridors), the remaining corridors seem to wander about connecting major western cities but not providing adequate direct links between western Canada and Mexico. Thus the design of the transportation network reflects a past era, when each country pursued independent

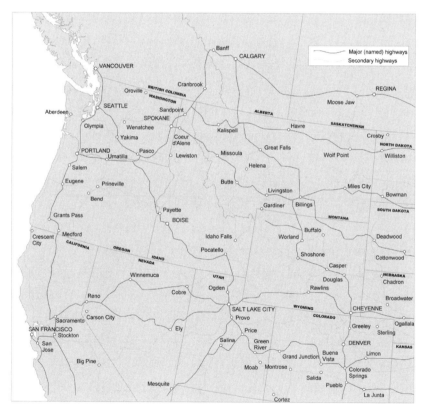

Map 13.3   Western highway network, 1926. The earliest federal highway networks in Canada and the United States clearly mirror the existing rail net. Note that the primary route across the Rockies between Calgary and Vancouver lies south of the border, a situation that would persist until the 1960s.

Source: Rand McNally, *Auto Road Atlas of the United States* (Chicago: Rand McNally, 1926).

policies in order to promote nation building and economic development. NAFTA has changed all of that for it is a policy that emphasizes economic interdependence. As a result of this policy shift, the continental transportation network that presently exists is obsolete, a reflection of past economic realities, and is not capable of handling the traffic NAFTA has produced.

Changing Transportation Patterns and Current Traffic Problems

By the mid-1990s it was clear that commercial trucks moved more than 80 percent of the $250 billion of annual trade that takes place between Canada and the US[16] – a situation that has not changed significantly since then. This translates into over 30,000 trucks crossing the Canada-US

Map 13.4 Western highway network, 1941. Major north-south highways in the United States – denoted here by heavier lines – built between 1920 and 1940 are assigned odd numbers from US 85 to US 99. These routes have not been significantly improved since their original construction, especially US 95 in Idaho.
Source: Rand McNally, *Auto Road Atlas of the United States* (Chicago: Rand McNally, 1941).

border each day.[17] The twenty busiest border ports along the Canada-US border are listed in Table 13.1. Note that the four busiest ports handle over 50 percent of all trade, and they are all located in Ontario near the traditional manufacturing belt. However, six of the twenty busiest border ports are located in the west. Currently, western border ports handle one-third of all truck traffic between Canada and the US.[18] In addition, while the amount of traffic handled by eastern border posts has increased relatively slowly, or in some cases has remained flat, truck traffic at western border ports is increasing at a much faster rate.[19]

Neither the existing transportation corridors nor the border ports were designed to handle the amount of traffic that they are now attempting

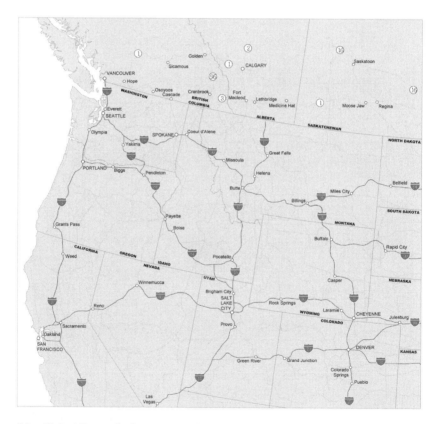

Map 13.5   Western highway network, 1999. The lack of north-south routes in the US Interstate Highway network is striking. Interstate 15, the only limited access corridor in the intermountain west, connects with Los Angeles rather than with the southern border, while Interstate 25 does not directly connect with the northern border.

Source: Rand McNally, *Auto Road Atlas of the United States* (Chicago: Rand McNally, 1999).

to serve. The free trade agreements have not only altered the economic relationship between Canada and the United States but they have also drastically altered the transportation patterns, particularly in the west. As previously noted, the historic transportation patterns have been predominately east-west; however, since the mid-1980s, that pattern has changed.

Today, ten times as much truck traffic crosses the US-Canada western border than moves between western and eastern Canada via the TCH, whereas the reverse was true the decade before.[20] The FTA and NAFTA have reoriented the flow of goods from an east-west direction to a north-south direction (Map 13.6).

This reorientation of transportation patterns to a north-south axis can be rationalized based on economics and geography.[21] In situations where countries share a long border, as in the case of Canada and the US, it is typically much cheaper to purchase and ship something across the international boundary than to ship it from another region across the country.[22]

Table 13.1

Daily truck traffic at the busiest Canada/US border ports, 1996

Port	Daily truck movements	Percentage of total	Cumulative percentage
Windsor, ON	7,554	25.4	25.4
Fort Erie, ON	3,292	11.1	36.5
Sarnia, ON	2,999	10.1	46.6
Queenston Bridge, ON	2,297	7.7	54.3
Pacific, BC	2,146	7.2	61.6
Lacolle, PQ	1,717	5.8	67.3
Lansdowne, ON	1,043	3.5	70.9
Emerson, MB	783	2.6	73.5
Phillipsburg, PQ	626	2.1	75.6
Rock Island, PQ	540	1.8	77.4
Coutts, AB	493	1.7	79.1
Huntingdon, BC	387	1.3	80.4
Sault Ste. Marie, ON	370	1.2	81.6
Woodstock, NB	361	1.2	82.8
Armstrong, PQ	351	1.2	84.0
North Portal, SK	324	1.1	85.1
Kingsgate, BC	254	0.9	86.0
Milltown, NB	240	0.8	86.8
Cornwall, ON	218	0.7	87.5
Aldergrove, BC	204	0.7	88.2
Others (96)	3,507	11.8	100.0
Total	29,706	100.0	

Source: Transport Canada, "Transportation and North American Trade," 1998, <http://www.tc.gc.ca/trucking/corridors/>.

Thus the FTA and NAFTA have permitted and encouraged the practice of buying goods from the nearest point of supply by reducing the economic and psychological barriers that were in place prior to this time. Although the relative importance of transportation costs has declined with improved transportation technology,[23] this does not indicate that distance, and thus transportation costs, are no longer significant economic factors. The fact that free trade blocs have developed among neighbouring nations demonstrates that geographic proximity and transportation costs are indeed of economic consequence.[24] The change in the transportation patterns simply reflects the fact that travel times between western Canada and most of the United States (that located west of the Ohio River) are less than the travel times from western Canada to Toronto or Montreal.[25] Thus, much of the emergence of a new north-south transportation pattern is simply the result of cost savings, especially among goods that have high transportation costs relative to the value of the goods.[26] This accurately characterizes the composition of goods exchanged along the rest of the western border.[27] As a result, the proximity of western Canada to the western United States and its markets, plus the similarities in economic and industrial activities across the border and the ease of cross-border trade, have created strong trade and transportation linkages across the border.

While the change in transportation patterns demonstrates the efforts made to capture economic advantages and reduce costs, the reality of the situation that has developed has resulted in limited economic benefits. Many of the border-crossing facilities and associated transportation links were built between 1950 and 1970, long before free trade was considered.

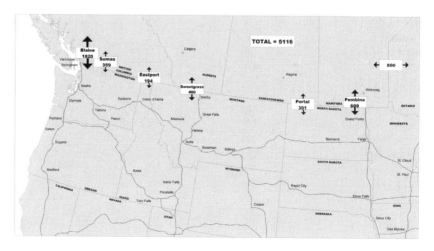

Map 13.6   Cross-border trucking movements, 1994. Expressed as trucks per day, notice the imbalance between north-south and east-west movements.
Source: University of Manitoba Transport Information Group, 1996.

Consequently, they were not designed to handle the amount and type of traffic currently being generated. The result is often long lines, congestion, and delays, which are estimated to cost private companies and the national economies millions of dollars every year.[28] Transportation infrastructure and costs are important to trading nations, especially among free trading nations, because the lower the transportation costs among member countries the greater the economic benefits of free trade.[29] The relationship between transportation and economic development is a long and well-established one, and improving transportation contributes to economic efficiency and growth.[30] Governments have long improved transportation infrastructure as a means to reduce costs and increase accessibility, open hinterlands, and enhance an area's competitive advantage.[31] This situation indicates that the full economic benefits associated with free trade and NAFTA cannot be realized because of inadequate transportation facilities.

Examining the six busiest western highway corridors and the border ports identifies the major weaknesses in the continental transportation system. Of the six major western border crossing ports, only three of them are linked to modern interstate highways.[32] The Douglas, BC-Blaine, WA border port is connected to Interstate 5 in the United States and Highway 99 in Canada; Pembina, ND-Emerson, MB is connected to Interstate 29/ Highway 29 in Canada, and Sweetgrass, MT-Coutts, AB is connected to Interstate 15 (Highway 4 in Canada). The other three border crossing stations are linked to national highways: Sumas, WA-Huntington, BC to US 9 (a two-lane state highway) and Highway 11 in Canada; Portal, ND-North Portal, SK to US 52 (Highway 39 in Canada); and Eastport, ID-Kingsgate, BC to US 95/Highway 95 (both two-lane national highways that are a product of 1920s engineering). But despite the fact that the individual national transportation systems of Canada and the United States are linked, they are not truly integrated.

The major weakness associated with creating a truly continental transportation system is the lack of connectivity with the infrastructure that already exists.[33] For example, the Pacific Highway crossing at Blaine, WA-Douglas, BC, which links Vancouver and the Lower Mainland of BC with the Interstate 5 corridor to Oregon, California, and Mexico, is the fifth busiest port on the northern border and handles the highest truck volume in the entire western borderland region. However, this crossing has no direct connection to the national highway system, except by local two-lane access roads. In fact, there is no direct connection for trucks between the national highway system and any US-Canada border crossing in all of BC, except for local access roads.[34] A similar situation exists along the southern border.

Another weakness associated with the existing transportation network is the lack of redundancy in the system. Redundancy is important in a transportation network because, if one segment of the system becomes inoperative – for instance, blocked because of a major accident, hazardous material spill, landslide, or avalanche – then alternative routes can be taken so that traffic and commerce do not come to a complete standstill. Most industrialized countries have built a certain amount of redundancy into their transportation system, but Canada has not.[35] As a result, any temporary blockage along the TCH can result in serious disruptions of both freight and passenger travel elsewhere in the network.

Problems with the continental transportation network are not limited to the borderlands region. Delays and congestion are found throughout the system, especially where major interstate highways pass directly through large metropolitan areas. For instance, Interstate 5 passes directly through six large urban core areas, each with populations of one million or more. Many of the highways and roads in the Lower Mainland of BC are currently operating at capacity or over-capacity.[36] The result is congestion that slows down freight traffic and increases operating costs for trucking firms. This is significant, given the fact that 15 percent of the cross-border truck traffic in this region consists of containers moving between the ports of Seattle and Vancouver.[37] Thus highway infrastructure and conditions also influence the competitive positions of the west coast ports as well. In addition, Interstate 35, which transects the centre of the United States connecting Winnipeg, MB, with Duluth, MN, and Laredo, TX, is estimated to carry the greatest amount of NAFTA trade of any highway corridor. However, it suffers from serious congestion problems in Dallas-Ft. Worth, Austin, San Antonio, Oklahoma City, Kansas City, and Minneapolis-St. Paul. It is estimated that it would cost $10 billion to relieve the congestion problems along this one route alone.[38] Based on these findings, two major policy questions come to mind: can an efficient continental transportation system be developed? And, if so, at what cost?

Perhaps the best way to respond to these questions would be to consider the costs and consequences associated with *not* building such a system. A recent survey of trucking companies in both Washington and BC estimated that "wait time" due to border congestion imposes private operating costs of $40 million per year on cross-border carriers.[39] However, more than costs need to be considered. In some cases the border facilities cannot be significantly improved because they lack the physical space to be able to expand operations. In addition, adequate numbers of personnel to staff the border is under strain, particularly in the US, as many immigration and customs officers have been moved to the more seriously stressed southern border.[40] Therefore, personnel limitations also contribute to border congestion and delays.

In order to create an efficient continental transportation system, more than just transportation must be considered. The transportation system must be integrated with the border to create a "seamless" system that can accommodate and respond to the increasing demands of free trade and global economic integration. This will require careful planning.

NAFTA Transportation Planning

If the full economic benefits of NAFTA are ever going to be realized, then it is going to take the coordinated effort of all three countries to make it happen. Substantial investments on roads and border facilities are needed in all three countries. While accords and memoranda have been signed, very little has actually been done. Under NAFTA over thirty working groups and committees were established to facilitate trade and investment and to ensure the effective implementation and administration of the agreement.[41] One of the committees established was the Land Transport Standards Subcommittee (LTSS). The objective of the LTSS is to facilitate increased travel and transportation between NAFTA nations by developing and implementing compatible and/or uniform standards for surface transportation, including the issues of drivers, roads, trucks, and railroads, and the transportation of hazardous materials. However, to date, this subcommittee has not accomplished its goal. The LTSS, like many other NAFTA committees, meets only once a year. The way the process works now is that the Mexican, Canadian, and American segment of each committee works independently of each other all year and then periodically unites to "discuss" or "share" issues of common interest. As a result, while there has been some agreement on common goals, nothing concrete has been accomplished. In other words, all have agreed to cooperate with each other, but so far this cooperation has not emerged "on the ground" through the actual implementation of study results.[42]

In 1995 Canada and the United States signed the Shared Border Accord. Its purpose was to facilitate trade between the two countries by harmonizing transportation regulation procedures and improving service to create what was to be "the most efficient border in the world." The two governments point to this accord as a demonstration of their commitment to working together to better manage the shared border. But once again, despite the numerous programs contained within the agreement, very little has actually been accomplished in the four years since the accord was signed.

The greatest hindrance to continental transportation planning has been the general lack of data. Although all three countries regularly collect data on trade flows, border traffic, number of visitors, and the like, none of what is collected is sufficient to accurately discern the current situation regarding transportation activity and impacts across and between the three countries. What are needed are data that identify the actual transportation corridors utilized as well as the origin, destination, and amount of goods traded. Section 5115 of the Transportation Equity Act for the 21st Century (TEA-21) requires the Bureau of Transportation Statistics (BTS) to conduct a study that will identify the needed improvements in data collection and to recommend changes in the law to ensure implementation of the identified changes in methods of data collection. As a result of these measures, the BTS is working in conjunction with Statistics Canada and the Mexican Transportation Statistical Agency to collect data. However, this information has only been available since June 2001.

Despite this lack of data, attempts to plan and create a continental transportation system continue. Private corporations like CN have struck out on their own, choosing not to wait for government action. In 1998 CN purchased the Illinois Central Railroad, with its legendary Chicago-New Orleans mainline, creating the first single-corporation network to connect the Atlantic, Pacific, and Gulf coasts. Through the integration of these railways goods can now be moved across Canada, through the Midwestern US, and on to Veracruz, Mexico. Although the attempt was ultimately abandoned, in December 1999 the Canadian National Railway Company and the Burlington Northern Santa Fe Corporation agreed to merge (pending government approval) – a move that would create the largest railroad in North America.[43] The new company was to be called North American Railways and was to consist of over 80,000 kilometres of track, connecting every major city across Canada and every state west of the Mississippi River. In July 2000, however, the Burlington Northern Santa Fe Corp. and Canadian National Railway "cancelled their proposed $5.1 billion merger ... becoming the first casualties of the 15-month moratorium on rail mergers imposed by federal regulators in March."[44] Nonetheless, in 2001 CN continued its continental agenda by acquiring Wisconsin Central (WC). CN observes that, "following the acquisition of WC by CN, the WC territory has become CN's sixth division – named the Wisconsin Central Division. Combining the two railroads strengthens CN's North American franchise."[45]

One of the greatest impacts of NAFTA on the continental transportation system will clearly include resurrecting the railroads as a major form of transportation. While truck traffic has increased approximately 10 percent per year since 1991, rail service has expanded at almost twice that rate.[46] Given the difficulties in planning and implementing NAFTA highway super-corridors, creating rail super-corridors may turn out to be cheaper, safer, and more environmentally friendly. The rail systems among the three countries are today much better integrated than the highways, and they are beginning to form a truly continental rail transportation system.[47] But there is another advantage: in contrast to publicly funded highway infrastructure, railroads provide their own infrastructure and are responsible for making capital investments to resolve any capacity constraint.[48] If a railway company fails to anticipate or forecast a capacity situation, then it will directly affect its ability to provide a competitive service to customers. Another advantage railways have over truck transport is the fact that they have been tracking shipments electronically since 1992.[49]

In any case, the United States is well ahead of Canada in terms of planning, designing, and creating an efficient national transportation system. The Intermodal Surface Transportation Efficiency Act (ISTEA) of 1991 contained provisions that specifically identified the necessity of creating an efficient north-south transportation system. ISTEA also provided further funding for studies on border congestion, including a federal highway administration assessment of border crossings and the transportation corridors that lead to them. As a result of ISTEA, twenty-one "trilateral corridors" were identified as being of the highest priority, and a number of studies have identified infrastructure and operational deficiencies near the US border with Canada.

Since ISTEA, other corridors have been added to the priority list. Eight corridors were added in the 1995 National Highway Designation Act, and another fourteen were added by the passage of the previously mentioned TEA-21 legislation in 1998. The purpose of TEA-21 is to develop and maintain the US transportation infrastructure. TEA-21 contains two programs specifically targeted towards transportation improvements to assist with the implementation of NAFTA: the National Corridor Planning and Development Program (NCPD) and the Coordinated Border Infrastructure Program (CBI). The purpose of the NCPD is to provide allocations to states and metropolitan planning organizations to help with the coordinated planning, design, and construction of corridors of national significance, economic growth, and international or interregional trade. The purpose of the CBI is to improve the safe movement of people and goods at or across the border between the United States and Canada, and the border between the United States and Mexico.

These border and corridor grants represent critical investments for the continued success of NAFTA. The combined authorized funding for these two programs is $140 million each year from 1999 to 2003, for a total amount of $700 million. In 1999, $124 million in grants were distributed. What is somewhat unusual about these two programs is that some of the funds can be used to support improvements in either Canada or Mexico. Allocations of money under the CBI program can be made for eligible uses anywhere in the border region. The border region is defined here as being 200 kilometres (124 miles) wide, corresponding to 100 kilometres (62 miles) on each side of the border. Most interestingly, under this definition the US government could provide funding for border and/or transportation improvements up to 100 kilometres *inside* Canada or Mexico.[50]

What is most worrisome now is that Canada currently has no national transportation policy in place. Although the prospect of a national highway program has been raised several times in cabinet meetings and among the provincial premiers, there remains an absence of consensus on how to pay for such a program. In 1988 an inventory found that 38 percent of Canada's national highway system was found to be deficient relative to minimum geometric design, serviceability, structural strength, and riding comfort.[51] Cabinet meetings that took place during the summer of 1999 were thought to have brought this issue to the forefront, but still a new national transportation policy has not materialized. In the meantime, studies have verified the poor condition of Canada's highway infrastructure.

Government Regulations and Policies

In addition to improving transportation infrastructure, attention must be paid to simplifying and streamlining paperwork and regulations if the full economic benefits of NAFTA are to be realized. Border-crossing formalities for commercial vehicles tend to be much more complicated than is typically assumed. At US entry points trucks must pass through three to four inspections, all conducted by different government agencies that have different authority, depending on the cargo. The minimum number of inspections each truck must pass is three: US Customs, US Immigration and Naturalization, and the US Department of Transportation. If the cargo involves food or agricultural products, then a fourth inspection is necessary (by the US Department of Agriculture). Despite measures to simplify and streamline the process, each agency currently requires separate paperwork and forms. This complexity is compounded as goods actually move across the border, where they are subject to additional inspections and the different paperwork requirements of Canada and its various government agencies (Canada Customs, Immigration Canada, Transport Canada, and Agriculture Canada). Congestion and delays at or near border-crossing points are thus largely the result of the dramatic increase in commercial trucking activity and the failure of these agencies to be able to respond to this trend.

Joint border facilities are another initiative that the United States and Canada are cooperating on in an effort to reduce costs and to increase the efficiency of border services. This initiative will involve the various national border inspection agencies sharing facilities and infrastructure at designated sites. Although four ports have been identified as test facilities, none has been completed, and controversy surrounds their operation and staffing. One major stumbling block concerns a law enforcement issue: US officers, both customs and immigration, wear firearms, while their Canadian counterparts do not. The Joint Facilities Working Group, a national committee consisting of representatives from agencies of both countries – the International Boundary Commission, the General Services Administration, the Immigration and Naturalization Service, the US Customs Service, the Department of Agriculture, the State Department, Revenue Canada, Public Works Canada, Immigration Canada, and Agriculture Canada – has been meeting twice a year for the past several years. Unfortunately, very little has been resolved regarding this issue. As has often been the case, agreements have been signed and plans have been developed, but very little action has taken place to implement these agreements.

A third program that the Shared Border Accord promoted was the North American Trade Automation Prototype (NATAP). Both governments are hopeful that improvements in technology will alleviate border congestion and improve efficiency. This program combines new technology, such as electronic transponders, to permit trucks to clear immigration and safety inspections electronically, along with harmonized customs procedures. Once again this program is in the testing phase, but it was scheduled for implementation in the summer of 1999. Difficulties associated with this program stem from the fact that several private companies have developed different transponder/tracking systems that are already on the market. Currently, the US government is trying to encourage the companies to coordinate their systems so that the computer hardware will work with both systems.

Despite the overall impression that the US government is committed to streamlining and improving the efficiency of the border, some recent actions have worked to undermine the underlying goodwill created by the Shared Border Accord. In 1996 the US Illegal Immigration Reform Immigrant Responsibility Act was passed into law. Concern, particularly by the Canadian government, focuses on Section 110 of this act, which would require the "physical documentation" (i.e., a computer entry) for *every* "alien person" as they enter or depart the US. Up to this point, Canadians have been exempt from having to acquire visas in order to visit the US. Canadians were ultimately exempted from this ruling in 2001.

Conclusions and Recommendations
Planning in the borderlands has failed to accomplish much beyond establishing goals and signing agreements. Most of the decision making concerning policy implementation has occurred at the national level in either Washington, Ottawa, or Mexico City, far removed from the border and based on little understanding and knowledge of the pressures, dynamics, and issues facing the borderland regions. One crucial element that seems to be lacking among the leadership of the three countries is a true commitment to, and appreciation of, a shared continental destiny. All three countries appear to recognize the need for coordination and cooperation, but they fail to commit with actions that attach money to targeted projects. Finally, and perhaps most important, is the lack of precedence for

many of the agencies and departments involved in this process. Interagency communication, let alone cooperation, among the players at the national level tends to be poorly developed, and all lack an understanding of each other's role and function. To fully implement NAFTA, each country must be willing to trade autonomy for interdependence not just in terms of trade and economic policies but also in terms of areas governing transportation, national security, and immigration policy. Compromises such as these are not easy to make, and are even harder to accomplish, because they involve significant cultural and ideological differences.

In comparison to the NAFTA situation, the European Union took advantage of the economic, political, and social compatibility of its members to forge a strong institutional structure that can address common problems and achieve shared goals.[52] In the mid-1980s the European transportation systems and, particularly, the cross-border transportation infrastructure was diagnosed as being insufficient to meet the increasing demands of growing trade.[53] As a result of these findings the EU developed a Common Transport Policy that identified goals to improve accessibility across the whole of Europe.[54] While each country continued to individually fund its own national transportation infrastructure, European funds could be used to assist parts of the EU that could not afford to undertake the necessary cross-border infrastructure improvements.[55] The result of these policies was the development of the Cohesion Fund to create Trans-European Transport Networks. While on the surface this appears to be similar to what happened with the working groups and committees established between Canada, the US, and Mexico, the institutional structure is remarkably different. What NAFTA, unlike the EU, failed to do was to provide the institutional structures necessary to implement its economic and related policies. For instance, in addition to funding transportation infrastructure, the EU countries have developed uniform border controls. In 1998 the EU introduced a single administrative document to be used universally among the member countries instead of the approximately 100 documents that were in use prior to that date.[56] Streamlining the inspection process at the border as well as simplifying and harmonizing the documentation has increased the efficiency of the transborder transportation network throughout all of Europe and has reduced costs by an estimated $10 billion annually.[57]

Within the EU four major institutions exist – the commission, the council, the Parliament, and the Court of Justice – all of which are responsible for formulating and implementing EU policies. The commission formulates and proposes legislation and provides for the implementation of EU policies. Members of the commission act not in the interest of individual nations but as representatives of the EU as a whole.[58] The council approves the legislation of the EU and is the main decision-making body. Although representatives of the Council represent individual nations, decisions are made based on a majority vote.[59] As a result, one country cannot dominate the decisions of the council; rather, decisions reflect the majority view. The 626-member Parliament works in a similar manner, based on the majority vote. Thus the institutional situation for the EU is more effective than is its counterpart in North America. There are several reasons that may account for this success. Europe has historically favoured a more centralized approach to planning. Also, the EU is much more a relationship among equals, whereas North American decision making tends to be dominated by the US. More important, members of the EU have a shared vision and a basic understanding that their economic futures are linked and that, in order for each to succeed, all must succeed. In addition, the economic agreement established institutions that operate and implement this shared vision. NAFTA, in comparison, lacks the institutional structure necessary to implement the agreement and the related transportation policies.[60]

As a result of this weakness, other measures are now being tried in North America – measures that focus on local-level binational planning efforts, such as what is being tried currently with the International Mobility and Trade Corridor Project (IMTC). The IMTC is one of several test projects funded under TEA-21's NCPD program. Although it remains unproven that local planning will be more successful than national efforts, there are several reasons to suggest that this approach is a good one. First, linkages and lines of communication already exist among the forty members of the IMTC steering committee. Interagency cooperation across the border has been taking place quite routinely among officials in both countries, even if it has been done somewhat informally.[61] Second, steering committee members live and work in the borderland region and are knowledgeable about the issues, problems, and constraints that they are facing locally. The steering committee consists of members from the private sector, public agencies, and various levels of government. Third, at the local level there is a greater appreciation of a shared destiny, of an awareness among the IMTC members that their economic futures are all inextricably linked. The borderlands have been subjected to dynamic and volatile changes during the last few years, and, because of the concomitant uncertainty, many organizations have been hesitant to make investments.[62] Most recognize that by cooperating in planning their futures they can achieve stability and be reasonably confident that investments will remain secure.

Local planning initiatives tend to be more creative and responsive to local needs than do "one-size-fits-all" national strategies. Certainly this strategy worked with the implementation of the PACE/CANPASS program, which expedited border clearance for regular, low-risk, non-commercial travellers. The US Immigration and Naturalization Service's PACE (Peace Arch Crossing Entry) Program and Revenue Canada's CANPASS program were first implemented at the Douglas, BC/Blaine, WA border port in 1992 as a temporary test program. By 1999, PACE/CANPASS cleared approximately 28 percent of all traffic through the port.[63] However, despite its success, this program was only expanded to one other US border port and, for nine years, remained a test program. In contrast, CANPASS received permanent approval from the Canadian government and was expanded to a number of land, sea, and airports.[64] Since the events of 11 September 2001, all of these programs were discontinued. At the present time a new, more security oriented program called NEXUS has been implemented along the Canada-US border. While attention and resources for planning transportation improvements were shifting toward local control, the events of 11 September reversed that trend. Border controls and policies are now firmly determined by the federal governments, illustrating just how quickly policy shifts can occur. What does the future hold for NAFTA and transportation planning? Only time will tell.

Acknowledgments

The authors gratefully acknowledge the support of the Government of Canada, the Canadian Consulate in Seattle, and Eastern Washington University for the research funding upon which this chapter is based. We also are indebted to Carrie Guiles of the Department of Geography at EWU for the cartographic content.

Notes

1 Dean Baker, Gerald Epstein, and Robert Pollin, *Globalization and Progressive Economic Policies* (Cambridge: Cambridge University Press, 1998).
2 Helen Milner, "Regional Economic Co-operation, Global Markets and Domestic Politics: A Comparison of NAFTA and the Maastricht Treaty," in *Regionalism and Global Economic Integration,* ed. William D. Coleman and Geoffrey R.D. Underhill (London: Routledge, 1998), 19-41; Thomas J. Biersteker, "Globalization and the North American Free Trade Agreement: Conceptual Changes within Major Institutional Actors and Their Potential Implications," in *NAFTA on Second Thoughts: A Plural Evaluation,* ed. David R. Davila-Villers (Lanham: University Press of America, 1998), 3-19.
3 Victor Konrad, "Borderlines and Borderlands in the Geography of Canada-United States Relations," in *NAFTA in Transition,* ed. Stephen J. Randall and Herman W. Konrad (Calgary: University of Calgary Press, 1995), 179-92.
4 Mel Hurtig, *The Betrayal of Canada* (Toronto: Stoddart, 1992); Mel Watkins, *Canada under Free Trade* (Toronto: James Lorimer, 1993); Sidney Weintraub, *NAFTA at Three: A Progress Report* (Washington, DC: Center for Strategic and International Studies, 1997).
5 Department of Foreign Affairs and International Trade, *NAFTA: A Partnership at Work,* 1997, <http://www.infoexport.gc.ca/nafta/partners-e.asp>; Transport Canada, *Transportation and North American Trade*; Thomas Hacker and Associates, *Western Washington/Lower British Columbia Border Comprehensive Plan* (Auburn, WA: General Services Administration, 1997).
6 Transport Canada, *Transportation and North American Trade.*
7 John Schofield, "Highway Lobbyists," *Maclean's,* 25 August 1997, 34; Gary Strauss, "NAFTA Jam," *USA Today,* 3 April 1998; Ken Ellingwood, "Boom at the Border," *Sun Sentinel* (Fort Lauderdale, FL), 9 January 2000, 3A.
8 Transportation Equity Act for the 21st Century (PL 105-178), 112 United States Statutes at Large (9 June 1998), 107-728.
9 Transport Canada, *Transportation and North American Trade.*

10 US Department of Transportation, *Western U.S.-Canada Crossborder Case Study,* 1995, <http://www.fhwa.dot.gov////////reports/tswstudy/tswrpt5.pdf>.

11 Bruce E. Moon, *Dilemmas of International Trade* (Boulder, CO: Westview Press, 1996).

12 D.W. Meinig, *The Shaping of America: Continental America, 1800-1867* (New Haven: Yale University Press, 1993); Meinig, *The Great Columbia Plain: A Historical Geography, 1805-1910* (Seattle: University of Washington Press, 1968).

13 Paul A. Bennett, Cornelius J. Jaenen, Nick Brune, and Alan Skeoch, *Canada: A North American Nation* (Toronto: McGraw-Hill Ryerson, 1989).

14 Daniel E. Turbeville III and Susan L. Bradbury, "From Fur Trade to Free Trade: Rethinking the Inland Empire," *American Review of Canadian Studies* 29, 3 (1999): 447-71.

15 Transport Canada, *Transportation and North American Trade.*

16 Department of Foreign Affairs and International Trade, 1997, *NAFTA: A Partnership at Work,* <http://www.infoexport.gc.ca/nafta/partners-e.asp>.

17 Transport Canada, *Transportation and North American Trade.*

18 US Department of Transportation, *Western U.S.-Canada Crossborder Case Study.*

19 Ibid.

20 Ibid.

21 Gerald Friesen, "From 54° 40' to Free Trade: Relations between the American Northwest and Western Canada," in *Terra Pacifica,* ed. Paul W. Hirt (Pullman: Washington State University Press, 1998), 93-108.

22 Mia Mikic, *International Trade* (New York: St. Martin's Press, 1998).

23 Reiner Martin, *The Regional Dimension in European Public Policy* (New York: St. Martin's Press, 1999).

24 William D. Coleman and Geoffrey R.D. Underhill, "Introduction: Domestic Politics, Regional Economic Co-operation, and Global Economic Integration," in *Regionalism and Global Economic Integration* (London: Routledge, 1998), 1-16.

25 US Department of Transportation, *Western U.S.-Canada Crossborder Case Study.*

26 Mikic, *International Trade.*

27 US Department of Transportation, *Western U.S.-Canada Crossborder Case Study.*

28 Arnold B. Maltz, James R. Giermanski, and David Molina, "The US-Mexico Cross-Border Freight Market: Prospects for Mexican Truckers," *Transportation Journal* 36, 1 (1996): 5-19; John Schofield, "Highway Lobbyists," *Maclean's,* 25 August 1997, 34.

29 Mikic, *International Trade.*

30 David Alan Aschauer, "Genuine Economic Returns to Infrastructure Investment," *Policy Studies Journal* 21, 2 (1989): 380-90; Aschauer, "Is Public Expenditure Productive?" *Journal of Monetary Economics* 23, 2 (1989): 177-200; Martin, *The Regional Dimension.*

31 Jeffery S. Luke, Curtis Ventriss, B.J. Reed, and Christine M. Reed, *Managing Economic Development: A Guide to State and Local Leadership Strategies* (San Francisco: Jossey-Bass, 1998).

32 US Department of Transportation, *Western U.S.-Canada Crossborder Case Study.*

33 Transport Canada, *Transportation and North American Trade.*

34 Transport Canada, *British Columbia Freight Transportation System Study* (Vancouver, BC: Transport Canada, 1996).

35 A.C. Lea and Nigel M. Waters, "The Role of Transportation in the Canadian Economy," in *Canada and the Global Economy,* ed. John N.H. Britton (Montreal: McGill-Queen's University Press, 1996).

36 Transport Canada, *Transportation and North American Trade.*

37 US Department of Transportation, *Western U.S.-Canada Crossborder Case Study.*

38 "Study Looks to Future of I-35 Trade Corridor," *Transport Topics,* 29 April 1999, <http://www.ttnews.com/members/topNews/0001487.html>.

39 Whatcom County Council of Governments, *Border System Study,* Phase 1 (Bellingham, WA: Whatcom County Council of Governments, 1998).

40 Colin Nickerson, "Canada Bristles at US Threats to Tighten Border," *Sun Sentinel* (Fort Lauderdale, FL), 28 January 2000, 20A.

41 Department of Foreign Affairs and International Trade, *Accord on Our Shared Border: Third Anniversary Report,* 1998, <http://www.dfait-maeci.gc.ca/geo/usa/accord-e.asp>.

42 Transportation Equity Act for the 21st Century.

43 "On Track to Creating a Rail Colossus," *Maclean's,* 10 January 2000, 38.

44 Burlington Northern Santa Fe Railway, "BNSF and CN Agree to Terminate Combination," <http://www.bnsf.com/media/html/news_2000_5.html>.
45 "Welcome to CN, North America's Railroad," <http://www.cn.ca/wc/>.
46 Transport Canada, *Transportation and North American Trade.*
47 Ibid.
48 Ibid.
49 Ibid.
50 Transportation Equity Act for the 21st Century.
51 Transport Canada, *British Columbia Freight Transportation System Study* (Vancouver, BC: 1996).
52 Bruce Moon, *Dilemmas of International Trade* (Boulder, CO: Westview Press, 1996).
53 Roundtable of European Industrialists, 1984.
54 Martin, *The Regional Dimension.*
55 Ibid.
56 Michael Calingaert, *The 1992 Challenge from Europe: Development of the European Community's Internal Market* (Washington, DC: National Planning Association, 1988).
57 Paolo Cecchini, *The European Challenge 1992* (Aldershot: Wildwood House, 1992).
58 Nicholas V. Gianaris, *The North American Free Trade Agreement and the European Union* (Westport: Praeger Publishers, 1998).
59 Ibid.
60 Moon, *Dilemmas of International Trade.*
61 Jay R. Brandt, Chief Inspector, US Customs Service, Blaine, Washington. Interview, 1 July 1999.
62 Daniel E. Turbeville III and Susan L. Bradbury, "From Fur Trade to Free Trade."
63 Whatcom County Council of Governments, *Border System Study,* Phase 2 (Bellingham, WA: Whatcom County Council of Governments, 1999).
64 Department of Foreign Affairs and International Trade, *Accord on Our Shared Border.*

Part 6
Borders as Metaphors

Part 6 focuses on a theme that is implicit throughout *Holding the Line:* borders are discursive processes rooted in spatialization of power arrangements and consociative dialogues. In this section we begin a process of theorizing borders (continued in Parts 7 and 8), interrogating the perceptual, ethnocentric, and hegemonic cultural and political practices that produce commonly understood metaphors concerning the nature and importance of boundaries within global, regional, and internal contexts. Borders are not just cartographic conventions, territorial markers, or shorthand symbols for functional divisions among the various parts of a global whole: they are also spatializations that delimit the nature and character of power, support political hegemonies, and determine geopolitical discourses. The consistent theme in Part 6 is that boundaries are metaphors – the way we construct our world is consistent with "the stories we tell about it." The chapters in this part build upon this theme, deriving insights from the work of Lefebvre and a tradition of scholarship in which borders are not just "unquestionable elements of physical space but, rather, diacritics of a socially produced and reproduced arena."

The discursive nature of borders, the symbolic rendering of borderlines as lines separating parallel universes, is an important theme. In Chapter 14 Mathew Coleman suggests that there is an unsettling dimension to the construction of borders because they construct separate worlds and, having done so, attach meaning to them. They encourage a misappreciation of the fluidity and fragility of social constructions, in which accounts of affluence, migration, and ecology "speak the familiar language of borders and sovereignty": this "candidly presented fear generated by a challenge to sovereign subjectivities, socialities, and securities ... demonstrates the currency and supposedly intuitive bordered character of both natural environments and sociopolitical community." Moreover, these imaginative border discourses and the convenient metaphors they represent are reified as spatial justifications for border arrangements, which then become misrepresented as "neutral assessments." Indeed, As Steven Jackson observes in Chapter 15, even "the borderless world metaphor presents itself as unobjectionable [and] makes sense to so many, in large part because it follows upon a set of technological assumptions deeply embedded in the popular (but also academic) imagination."

Applying this reassessment of spatialization to the construction of new rounds of development and boundary making within the Malaysian realm, Jackson sums up the relationship adroitly, extending Coleman's argument and linking the importance of metaphor, perception, and praxis. Arguing that "speaking of the production of space means taking seriously the interaction of the perceived, the conceived, and the lived, the outcome of which is never determined in advance," Jackson suggests that we need to take seriously "the potential for that politics to produce unanticipated results. The story of information technology and spatialization conveyed by the borderless world metaphor has the advantage of a clear and happy ending; the alternative view suggested here is unavoidably committed to an ambiguous future." In this case, the unintended consequences are that the borderless world metaphor justifies and legitimizes inequitable arrangements in the structuring of development "rewards," reinforcing the centrality of the elite at the expense of those at the margins.

The chapters in this part are extremely powerful and lead us to consider a number of ways of looking at globalized understandings of development. While in Chapters 7 and 8, Schofield and Nicol, respectively, suggest that there are functional benefits to developing countries undergoing the regional integration, reassessment, and reorganization of their borders – an assumption based upon normative political theories concerning functional spillover, resource sharing, and cooperation among nationstates – both Coleman and Jackson point both to the hegemonic practices encoded in such reorganizations of space and to the metaphors that sustain them.

14
Permeable Borders and Boundaries in a Globalizing World: Feeling at Home amidst Global Poverty
Mathew Coleman

> Space is never produced in the sense that a kilogram of sugar or a yard of cloth is produced ... Though a product to be used, to be consumed, [space] is also a means of production; networks of exchange and flows of raw materials and energy fashion space and are determined by it.
>
> – Henri Lefebvre

The cover illustration on the December 1994 issue of the *Atlantic Monthly* may be read as a map, replete with borders, fears of (in)security, and what has been understood as a "pervasive ... search for a lasting and stable order, for a resilient architecture that might withstand the assaults and erosions of temporal change, unexpected dangers and volatile fortunes."[1] The journal's provocative artwork depicts a white male sporting an apron embroidered with the phrase "Home Sweet Home," barbecuing hot dogs in a well-kept, uncluttered backyard. The man is glancing disconcertedly over his right shoulder, beyond the limits of his bordered real estate. Outside and pressed against the fenced-in backyard is an ambiguous and seemingly chaotic crowd of onlookers, contrasted en masse, as dark and disorganized, against the orderly white picket fence lining the borders of the affluent property.[2]

Any ambiguity presented in the *Atlantic Monthly* cover art is quickly clarified in the opening paragraphs of Matthew Connolly and Paul Kennedy's related piece, entitled *Must It Be the Rest against the West?* A quote from Jean Raspail's *The Camp of the Saints*, detailing a fictitious oceanic pilgrimage of thousands of Calcutta's most desperate and impoverished to Europe's shores, reproduces the cover's imagined theme and introduces the article:

> It was like trying to count all the trees in the forest, those arms raised high in the air, waving and shaking together, all outstretched toward the nearby shore. Scraggy branches, brown and black, quickened by a breath of hope. All bare, those fleshless Ghandi-arms ... thirty thousand creatures on a single ship.[3]

The cover art, in conjunction with this controversial excerpt, initiates an interesting account of politics under conditions of global environmental change. The homogenous and nameless crowd, both at the picket fence and on the decks of ships of Indian origin, are, to borrow from Ramachandra Guha and Madhav Gadgil, environmental refugees displaced by ecological degradation driven by the consumptive lifestyles of omnivores located largely in the North.[4] The complexity of Guha and Gadgil's formulation is, however, not the concern of this particular article; rather, the piece makes difficult an understanding of the flows present between the nomadic mob and the fenced-in homeowner. Indeed, in drawing from Raspail's novel and asking "must it be the Rest against the West?" Connolly and Kennedy, rather than detailing constitutive exchanges across the picket fence, frame politics in distinctly bordered terms: politics is captured as a spatialized fear of those "inside" and as an aspiration of those "outside."[5] The result is that a complex networked appreciation of late modern life in the so-called First World is supplanted by a conventional realist international map of community and threat, itemizing supposedly distinct peoples, environments, and politics.

The textual script/legend accompanying the artwork/map makes clear this sense of disconnectedness: "Whether it's racist fantasy or realist concern, it's a question that won't go away: As population and misery increase, *will the wretched of the earth overwhelm the Western paradise?*" Accordingly, the artwork/map presents migration as a sociopolitical problem and consumption as a sociopolitical norm, and it fails to highlight the links between Southern migration and Northern consumption, which clearly render suspect a claim that Western lifestyles are not the pressing political issue at stake when considering migration driven by ecological degradation. Of note is how this account of poverty, migration, and ecology speaks in the familiar language of borders and threats: the raw fear associated with a challenge to sovereign subjectivities, socialities, and securities by migrating "hoards" demonstrates the cultural currency of strictly bordered accounts of both natural environments and sociopolitical community.[6]

A similar geographical commitment underwrites recent reports concerning boats of migrating Chinese nationals reaching Canadian shores. A quick look at the 14 August 1999 edition of Canada's national newspaper, the *Globe and Mail,* demonstrates the currency of the white picket fence script. The front-page story announces that a boat overflowing with Chinese "criminals," en route from Lithuania, is expected shortly on Canada's east coast.[7] In this piece, Canadian immigration officials suggest that the "recent flood" of Chinese migrants (note the easy translation from criminals to migrants) should help bolster Canadian immigration procedures and bring Canadian refugee laws in line with the "expedited removal" laws currently practised south of the border. In the same edition, another piece suggests that Canada is the "soft underbelly" of the United States, alternatively referred to as a "mythical land of plenty ... known to millions of Chinese as Gold Mountain, the place where you get rich."[8] Finally, in the letters-to-the-editor section, tellingly entitled *Anger Over the Illegals,* three self-affirmed Canadians lament the recent arrival of the Chinese migrants/refugees/criminals. One letter suggests that Canada should be concerned with illegal immigration because resources for "deserving Canadians" are being unfairly redirected towards unexpected illegal migrants. Another letter suggests that the Canadian government "had better start redirecting a lot of money to immigration because the whole world will be getting into boats." The last letter berates then Immigration Minister Elinor Caplan's refusal to turn back the boatloads of Chinese nationals. The letter's author suggests that the current "abandonment of traditional immigration standards," identified as European, is leading Canada towards "insoluble social and economic problems and ultimately the disintegration of the country as we know it."[9]

The question asked by Connolly and Kennedy in the 1994 *Atlantic Monthly* article, "will the wretched of the earth overwhelm the Western paradise?" is clearly the issue at stake in these articles and letters. Much as dark brown faces are pitted against the soon-to-be-marred suburban ideal in Connolly and Kennedy's Raspailian essay, the *Globe and Mail's* recent coverage of Chinese migration, as well as popular responses to this coverage, turn on a crude notion of geopolitical encounter between the wretched and the paradisiacal. And, as with the *Atlantic Monthly's* interrogation of migration in an era of globalization, migration is presented as a sociopolitical problem and Canadian affluence as a sociopolitical norm, and little is said of the specifically consumptive transborder flows that confound the easy contrast drawn between so-called "criminal" Chinese and so-called "vulnerable" Canadians – an apparent attempt to read complex geographical realities in terms of reified entities and (threatened) stable spatial metaphors.[10]

"Geo-graphy," or scripting human lives, relations, and experiences in spatialized terms, is of central importance to the popular white picket fence script detailed above.[11] The question here, in fact, asks how it is that particular conceptions of spatiality (the bordered backyard, for example) organize thoughts and rationalize practices. Following this, a quite simple query takes shape: how might particular spatialities "act to encourage some thoughts and discourage others ... [telling] us *what and who belong where*"?[12] This path of inquiry encourages thought as to how spatial imaginings – such as the inside/outside logic described above – author, order, and authorize the *quotidien*.[13] It is in this sense that a Lefebvrian investigation of the production of space is compelling, for if white picket fences, for example, can be represented not as unquestionable elements of physical space but, rather, as the markers of a socially produced and reproduced arena, then the specific representations of ecological degradation empowered by the white picket fence script are rendered unsettled. In turn, a tradition of security writings, which, arguably, provide the basis for Connolly and Kennedy's understanding of ecological degradation in demographic terms, may be usefully problematized. In following a path borne by studies not normally juxtaposed with one another (studies of society and space and security-oriented scarcity-conflict literatures), it should be possible to, first, contest demographically concerned scarcity-conflict interpretations of ecological degradation and, second, explore a loosely defined Lefebvrian political economy approach to the study of matters of ecological origin.

Lefebvre and Borders

Lefebvre's inquiries in the opening pages of *The Production of Space* (1991) are critical of mathematical conceptualizations of space that disengage *res cogitans* from *res extensa:* for Lefebvre, this sovereign demarcation of spaces either mental or material, spaces governed by the inside/outside Cartesian logic of subject and object, refuse a treatment of space in corporeal terms. In other words, argues Lefebvre, Cartesian thought tends to fetishize space; it renders inaccessible the social, political, economic, cultural, gendered, and/or ecological processes that constitute space. This binarism, implying a possible categorization of problems in mechanistic, atomistic, and empiricist terms, precludes space that is both physical and social, thus making practical political action, premised on a recognition of "the outside world" as corporeal, difficult.[14]

Lefebvre's work, in contrast, treats "outside" space as a product of the human body: space is conceived, perceived, and practised – not simply given. For Lefebvre, this lesson is well taught by the Cartesian methodology itself, "for a binary physical-mental spatial logic, most obviously its vocabularies and embodied codes, is really only made possible by intervening in social space and ... taking on body,"[15] or, in other words, by dictating how bodies are to relate to physical space in the first place. Accordingly, Lefebvre's "anatomy of space generated by living bodies,"[16] unlike the Cartesian approach, serves notice that it is impossible to speak of space as an inanimate surface or environment beyond the living body. As such, space is not a bare architectural arena but rather, something that "*permits* fresh actions to occur, while *suggesting* others and *prohibiting* yet others."[17] This interrogation of space as social morphology recognizes that "any determinate and hence demarcated space necessarily *embraces some things and excludes others*,"[18] thereby opening for discussion the materiality of space and the notion that there are both users and producers of space.

Lefebvre's contemplation of space is, in part, facilitated by introducing representations of space (spaces of representations/lived spaces and spatial practices/perceived space comprise the remainder of Lefebvre's spatial triad). Representations of space are "conceived spaces, born of savoir and logic: maps, mathematics, the instrumental space of social engineers and urban planners,"[19] as well as of journalists, academics, activists, and intellectuals of statecraft, among others. At question in representations of space is authorship. Who is mapping the spaces in which people live? What does this mapping imply for people charted by such representations? The specifically corporeal element in representations of space – that such spaces exercise control over bodies – is highlighted:

> Representations of space have a *practical impact*, that they *intervene in and modify spatial textures* that are informed by effective knowledge and ideology ... Their intervention occurs by way of construction, in other words, by way of architecture, conceived not as the building of a particular structure, palace or monument, but rather as a project embedded in a spatial context and a texture which call for "representations" that will not vanish into the symbolic and imaginary realms.[20]

From this Lefebvre proposes a study of space as "architexture." The architextural inquiry refuses to treat spaces as mere architectures or unproblematic physical externalities; rather, space is addressed as a production with ordering capabilities. In this spirit, the architextural inquiry looks to borders not as simple and pre-existent physicalities but as social representations that enforce a spatial code of proxemics, or distances. Rather than an ontological condition of community and belonging, then, the border is a (normalized and naturalized) logic of property in space that articulates the idea that "places and things belonging to you do not belong to me."[21] One outcome of this bordered Cartesian logic of property in space is a refutation of people as producers and reproducers of space: borders are understood as sacrosanct and inviolable remnants of former times, and little thought is given to borders in terms of human innovation, renovation, and renewal. As such, space is decorporealized; ignored and refuted is the presence of the body in the constitution of space and the effects it has on space. Another outcome of this bordered logic is a refutation of flows between supposedly hermetic spaces. Accordingly, Lefebvre warns of the spatial trap that occasions sovereignty.[22]

Lefebvre's discussion encourages a general understanding that the social is spatial and that, conversely, spatial delineations are socially grounded. Thinking about space, in other words, is not simply thinking about abstract puzzles; rather, it is central to an examination of materiality, politics, and justice. Lefebvre's key point is, in fact, that spatiality is not a purely philosophical or mathematical enterprise: space is bodily; it both constrains and enables certain activities and imaginations, and is thus necessarily political.[23] This sociological and geographical mapping suggests that space (as those flows or relations between and including peoples, objects, and organizations) and place (as the product of such flows and relations), imbued with meaning and capable of imparting design on flows, "take on meaning through, and are permeated by, historically defined social relations (and vice versa)."[24] Consequently, representations of space, in designating flows between places (as well as the creation of these very places) and in bestowing definition to social relationships, provide the contours of place, perhaps a sense of familiarity and interconnectedness, or, as is witnessed by the white picket fence, a sense of isolation, containment, and difference. In turn, it is reasonable to suspect that these "senses of place" are capable of authoring and ordering (notably peopled) flows between places.

Rereading Connolly and Kennedy via Lefebvre

To return briefly to the Connolly and Kennedy piece, it is clear that the order imposed by the white picket fence is, in Lefebvrian terms, a representation of space with distinct corporeal implications. The backyard may be understood, for example, as an instatement of spatial fixity or as a spatial code of proxemics that details distances based on a logic of property in space. In this sense, the fence may be reread as a social arrangement and, thus, as a contestable bordered space. On the one hand, the backyard may be this man's "Western paradise," to be overwhelmed by the "wretched of the earth," but for those on the other side of the enclosure the fenced-off area enjoys only a tenuous claim to borderedness. Indeed, if one returns to Guha and Gadgil's discussion of environmental refugees, it is not only clear that the land is not the sovereign piece of property assumed by the suburban homeowner but that it (in that it is constitutive of and constituted by a largely unbound Western culture of consumption) is an active determinant in the fate of numerous (unrecognized) Others assumed to be geographically removed from "paradise." In other words, the backyard may be understood as a social morphology, a space of social and ecological exchanges, and not simply as a bordered real estate. It serves to note that this appreciation of the porosity of human existence contrasts markedly with Connolly and Kennedy's voiced concern over bodily transgressions of the sovereign yard, which is refused as anything except an ontological given. The central lesson to be drawn from Lefebvre in this context is that sovereign mappings of space, presented in terms of naturally occurring pre-cast sociopolitical containers, for instance, refute people as unbordered producers of space and disallow a recognition of the (social and ecological) expansiveness of human activity.

Demography, Scarcity, and Security

A central argument above is that mapping, as a set of practices by which citizens, non-citizens, academics, activists, journalists, intellectuals of state-craft, and others ascribe characteristics and meanings to various land-scapes, is an inherently political activity. This movement from the map as neutral to the map as an imposition of order[25] is particularly relevant in the context of the Raspailian artwork examined above. It is interesting to note, for example, that it is only when supposedly immutable sovereign borders are challenged that politics is explicitly invoked; otherwise, sover-eign space is understood as a physical given and not a site of political con-tention. In this sense, most telling is what is deemed contestable: it is the "mob" at the picket fence, and not the fence itself, that is the subject of political dispute. This focus renders the notion of bordered and sover-eign spaces incontestable and obscures the politics constituted by and constitutive of such demarcations of space.

Explaining ecological degradation *via* the metaphor of the distinct and disconnected backyard evinces a simplistic demographic politics that explains just how the "mob" is rendered as the principal object of political attention.[26] The white picket fence script brings to the surface what Betsy Hartmann calls a vision of an "overpopulated, environmentally degraded and violent Third World" in which both poor women, as racialized and othered agents, and the social movements representing poor women, are positioned as a security problem.[27] This demographic focus, where threats are referenced according to a Cold War identity trope of global disorder wrought by "surging" populations, poverty, and refugee flows, has fast become conventional political counsel in national security spheres.[28] Kap-lan's *The Coming Anarchy* (1994), which, as with Connolly and Kennedy's piece, suggests that the "political and social impact of surging popula-tions ... will be the core foreign-policy challenge" of the West in the post-Cold War environment[29] has, for example, been widely referenced in the United States by the White House and in Congress.[30] In a corroborative manner, top US State Department officials have blamed violent conflict in Chiapas, Rwanda, and Haiti on population-induced ecological degrada-tion and scarcity.[31] The more recent US war on terrorism also articulates the dangerous and unpredictable character of hyper-mobile and growing populations of so-called Islamic fundamentalists.

But it is important to point out that this image of environmental-demographic global disorder permeates bodies that are not readily associ-ated with the realist world of foreign policy prescription. The 1998 US Sierra Club debate concerning immigration is a case in point. A large portion of the club's voting membership (approximately 40 percent) supported Alter-native A, a "resolution that would have declared all immigration [to the US], legal and otherwise, to be an environmental ill."[32] Backed by 31,134 members, including: Dan Stein (head of the anti-immigrant Federation for American Immigration Reform), Gaylord Nelson (founder of Earth Day), Dave Foreman (founder of Earth First!), Paul Watson (founder of Greenpeace), Lester R. Brown (president of the Worldwatch Institute), and members of Californians for Population Stabilization,[33] the defeated proposal suggested that steps need to be taken to, first, stabilize the US population and, second, reduce net immigration to the United States.[34] Although the debate and subsequent vote produced Alternative B or a neutral stance on immigration, it nonetheless consolidated support in the Sierra Club for international birth control programs. Carl Pope, the Sierra Club's executive director, despite having championed Alternative B, digressed little in his post-vote speech from the spatialized fear-of-those-"inside"-and-the-aspiration-of-those-"outside" dilemma explored above: "The Sierra Club cannot protect our environment by building a wall around our borders. The common sense solution to reducing our population is birth control, not border patrols."[35] What is interesting here is Pope's specifically demographic segue to matters of ecology for, wall or no wall, the Raspailian imagery of masses of waving arms remains prevalent. Hence, despite his pre-vote talks about US energy *consumption* and global ecological damage,[36] Pope's attempt to rally the opposing groups in the club focused on controlling bodies rather than on exploring the different ways bodies are positioned, specifically as regards consumption, with respect to one other.

The importance of the fence imagery is evident. The normalized white picket fence script provides a crucial political and sociospatial backdrop for "foreign and security policy prescriptions [dependent] in large part on how the questions of appropriate policy prescriptions are practically understood within the larger geopolitical discourse and their interpretations of geopolitical order."[37] As Nalini Visvanathan suggests, by far the most important aspect of such scripts is how they articulate with a popular belief that population growth in the developing world is a major security and environmental issue.[38] In this sense, the *Atlantic Monthly*'s popularized adventures are of notable consequence because of their affirmation, through an ontologizing of borders, of homogenous selves and Others, exactly the segmented human geography requisite for foreign policy.[39] In drawing attention to issues of security, the white picket fence script allows concerns with consumption to be supplanted by a definition of corporeal well-being in terms of a spatial distinction between "here" and "there."[40] And the result, as Hartmann notes, is a masking of "the deeper political and economic forces generating poverty, environmental degradation, violence and migration."[41]

Indeed, the above accounts of ecological degradation and the migration of peoples cannot be sustained, particularly in the capitalist Western societies where the *Atlantic Monthly* audience is largely resident, without reference to a notion of localized scarcity or natural resource shortage that discounts a larger global political economy of commodity flows and consumption networks. Here, scarcity references the management of supposedly finite and sparse resources in other parts of the world, without addressing the complex linkages between those supposedly living and not living within the constraints of ecological scarcity. In other words, and most ironic given the contemporary fascination with things global, attention is rarely turned to the production of scarcity over great distances and, instead, focuses on methods of coping in specific contexts. This approach strengthens an ontologizing of borders (in as much as environments and peoples are considered disconnected and localized entities).

The rewriting of scarcity in localized terms betrays the Lockean existential foundations of the "white picket fence anxiety." Lockean governance assumes a population committed to a supposedly productive and fruitful sovereign demarcation, extraction, and consumption of natural resources.[42] Nomadic peoples, according to the Lockean criteria deemed suitable for order and prosperity, do not make proper use of land because land is neither possessed nor settled permanently. The nomadic orientation to territory is, thus, understood as a move away from the supposedly stable (and desirable) political, social, economic, and ecological order generated by permanent, fixed, regularized, and propertied Lockean environments.[43] In the Lockean mindset, then, an unsettled and itinerant refusal to occupy and undertake productive activity from a specified locale is scripted as a direct security threat to the maintenance of (Lockean) political communities committed to fixed populations and the bordered use of natural resources. It is specifically this reluctance to relate to natural resources in a "settled" fashion that pens nomads (Them) as a potential source of violation or trespass to "Lockeans" (Us) who, it is presupposed, relate to nature in a particularly arboreal fashion.

Two points follow. First, Lockean citizenship and social reproduction is (problematically) understood in terms of strictly local practices. The absence of a sovereign jurisdiction enabling and enforcing insides and outsides is thought to preclude citizenship and hence the formation of political identity, thus making social reproduction consonant with an exacting geography of boundaries. As a result, a more complex geography of global interdependencies and involvements is missed. Second, Lockean place is only made meaningful when residents are successfully distinguished from non-residents (nomads or residents of other places) or when a binary geography is established that differentiates "here" from "there," "modern" from "backwards," or "civilized" from "barbaric."[44] As such, the spatial code of proxemics established by Lockean governance informs a politics of security that details distances based on a logic of property in space. With this in mind, it is particularly telling that Connolly and

Kennedy speak of scarcity in terms of "rich versus poor," "race versus race," "developed versus developing countries," and "the Rest against the West," in categories of familiarity and foreignness. It is in exactly this spirit that a more encompassing discussion of global consumption is trumped by a simple security discourse concerned with fortifying white picket fences.

Significantly, the self/Other constitution of this inside/outside security discourse does not invite thinking "from the inside" about the constitution of security; rather, it is concerned with "external" peopled threats to established sovereign states/backyards. Indeed, to think "from the inside" is to confound the security cartography's linear internal/external dichotomy. Interrogating the "multiple interconnected causalities and feedback loops" of extractive, productive, and consumptive institutions and practices being rendered secure in the North (i.e., thinking "from the inside" about the constitution of security) demonstrates that security "does things."[45] Specifically, security renders secure not only boundaries but also key consumptive practices and polluting institutions housed in those boundaries. Indeed, if security is to be understood as the maintenance of such practices and institutions, then a "dilemma appears here because these ... are the very things that are causing many of the contemporary global environmental difficulties."[46] This problem is indicative of a need to rethink bordered ontologies and to challenge assumptions about what constitutes socioecological and political community.

Thinking Otherwise

Borrowing from Lefebvre, Smith suggests that the concept of scale is particularly salient when considering issues of ecological origin: the resolution of social and ecological issues, argues Smith, in terms of bordered places, often depends on an (unrecognized) translation of ecologically destructive practices and wastes to other sites at different geographical scales. In this sense, Smith wonders how a Western backyard can be described in terms of a bordered "environmental cleanliness" when this very condition is dependent on a capacity to move consumptive and extractive wastes across borders, specifically making other places sites of ecological degradation.[47]

From this, Smith offers an interesting (eco)political insight. Recounting Alix Kates Shulman's 1995 memoir *Drinking the Rain,* Smith suggests that much can be learned from Shulman's retreat from New York City life to an island in Maine. Faced with the daily difficulties on the island, and armed with a country cookbook, Shulman pragmatically "takes to eating whatever is scavengable in the environment."[48] Important for Smith is the fact that Shulman's engagement with nature is a "consumptive production of nature," an eating and transformation of nature "in an array of starkly pragmatic practices."[49] In this sense, Shulman, through consuming wild salads and fish, is consciously involved in a production of nature that eventually becomes a source of self-knowledge and understanding. Most important, Shulman becomes aware of the environments that sustain her lifestyle of "busyness." In traversing the scale back to her New York City life, Shulman "grasps her predicament more clearly" by understanding the ecological politics of foods and of a consumption pattern that she had not previously considered. In other words, Shulman's experiences "elsewhere" find a place in Shulman's urban life and prompt her to consider "elsewheres" in terms of the immediacies of her cosmopolitan lifestyle.

This unsettling potential politics of scale, which confounds categories of "here," "there," "Us," and "Them," and which encourages one to think of the many potential linkages and exchanges that make such terms difficult, accentuates the "intellectual necessity of distancing oneself from one's fondest fears to look again at one's identity in the light of its being rendered strange."[50] Such a politics challenges the popularized association of ecological degradation with the physical movement of people beyond the white picket fence and, instead, asks how the lifestyles maintained within might be understood or experienced from an alternate viewpoint.

Most relevant in this sense is Smith's inversion of the assumptions presented in the scarcity-conflict arguments forwarded by Kaplan, and Connolly and Kennedy. It will be recalled that these authors speak of the bodily transgression of spaces as a principal source of threat. For Smith, in contrast, the traversibility of spatial scale, an indisputable expression of nomadism, provides not for sociopolitical and ecological chaos but, rather, for the basis of a reconstructed political project. Specifically, Smith professes that the bodily transgression of demarcated sites, or a "politics of jumping scale," usefully challenges the notion of property claims over nature.[51] Thus, fundamental to the distinction between Smith and the scarcity-conflict position is the concept of ownership. The artwork/map presented in Connolly and Kennedy's *Atlantic Monthly* article, for instance, demonstrates the centrality of ownership to scarcity-conflict politics, and it is clearly informed by a sense of property-based sociopolitical order. For Smith, the translation present in this propertied reasoning between "reality and the [fenced] description of nature is fully erased; the discourse and the reality are rendered interchangeable."[52] Lost is a sense of "who is doing the production [of space] and under what circumstances."[53]

This "creative translation" becomes prominent when bodies traverse spatial scale. This is precisely the political project that Lefebvre understood to be the result of the dismissal of everyday experiences by representations of space – a political project defined by the confrontation of (migrating) spatial practices with (fixed) representations of space.[54] In this sense, Smith's (postsovereign) bodily politics of scale usefully entails challenging territorializations that encode space as a "field, an infinite, universal, and unchanging box within which material events occur ... as a set of philosophical lenses [through which] the symptoms of spatial restructuring appear as just so many separate processes at separate scales with very separate causes and explanations."[55] Thus the ontological, epistemological, and methodological reductionism of human sociality to sovereign parameters, which suspends complex ecologically based interactions and ignores the possibility that socioecological activity need not be confined to fenced-in backyards, is rendered usefully unstable.

To conclude, it might be noted that to engage the white picket fence imagery at this level is to study security studies that centre borderedness and is, most important, to become involved in a politics that asks about the horizons embedded in such approaches. The task at hand is informed by production: rather than focus on space as given, one focuses on space as something socially constituted, as something socially produced and reproduced. One also focuses on studies that employ specific designations of space and asks questions about how space, defined as such, is itself constitutive of both the everyday and social study – about how, in other words, spatiality produces and reproduces particular focal points in lived experiences and in social study. To pursue such a course is to engage in a study of the social constitution of spaces and places as well as in a study of the social constitution of study about spaces and places. As Kuehls suggests: "It is important to pay attention to the lines within ... text[s], to become intimate with these boundaries. *Where have they been drawn? How have they been used?*"[56] This suggests that a more comprehensive account of global ecological flows and politics might focus on the social constitution of space, on the ordering of peoples and locales – and exchanges between peoples and locales – in order to understand people and places as relational rather than as absolutely bordered and, in so doing, to demonstrate that spaces and people are dynamic.

Notes

1 R.J.B. Walker, *Inside/Outside: International Relations as Political Theory* (Cambridge: Cambridge University Press, 1993), 3.
2 S. Dalby, "The Environment as a Geopolitical Threat: Reading Robert Kaplan's 'Coming Anarchy,'" *Ecumene* 3, 4 (1996): 472-96.
3 Quoted in M. Connolly and P. Kennedy, "Must It Be the Rest against the West?" *Atlantic Monthly* 274, 6 (1994): 61-84; 61, emphasis added.
4 M. Gadgil and R. Guha, *Ecology and Equity: The Use and Abuse of Nature in Contemporary India* (London: Routledge, 1995); S. Dalby, "Ecological Metaphors of Security: World Politics on the Biosphere," *Alternatives* 23, 3 (1998): 291-319.
5 Dalby, "The Environment as a Geopolitical Threat," 487.
6 S. Dalby, "Contesting an Essential Concept: Reading the Dilemmas in Contemporary Security Discourse," in *Critical Security Studies: Concepts and Cases,* ed. K. Krause and M.C.

Williams (Minneapolis: University of Minnesota Press, 1997), 3-32; S. Dalby and F. MacKenzie, "Reconceptualizing Local Community: Environment, Identity and Threat," *Area* 29, 2 (1997): 99-108.

7   A. Mitrovica and J. Armstrong, "Shipload of 'Criminals' Heads for East Coast," *Globe and Mail*, 14 August 1999, A1, A3.

8   P. Cheney, "Smuggling Route to Gold Mountain Paved with Greed," *Globe and Mail*, 14 August 1999, A3.

9   For all quotations in this paragraph, see Cheney, "Smuggling Route to Gold Mountain."

10 Dalby, "The Environment as a Geopolitical Threat," 487.

11 Geo-graphy is "the writing of human spaces according to physical places," what Ó Tuathail refers to as "not a noun but a verb ... an [ambitious] earth-writing ... [organized] to fit [particular] cultural visions and material interests." See Gearóid Ó Tuathail, *Critical Geopolitics: The Politics of Writing Global Space* (Minneapolis: University of Minnesota Press, 1996), 2.

12 T. Cresswell, "Weeds, Plagues and Bodily Secretions: A Geographical Interpretation of Metaphors of Displacement," *Annals* 87, 2 (1997): 334.

13 D. Sibley, "Sensations and Spatial Science: Gratification and Anxiety in the Production of Ordered Landscapes," *Environment and Planning* 30 (1998): 235-46.

14 H. Lefebvre, *The Production of Space,* trans. Donald Nicholson Smith (Oxford: Blackwell Press, 1991).

15 R. Peet, *Modern Geographical Thought* (Oxford: Blackwell, 1998), 104.

16 L. Stewart, "Bodies, Visions, and Spatial Politics: A Review Essay on Henri Lefevre's *The Production of Space,*" *Environment and Planning D, Society and Space* 13 (1995): 612.

17 Lefebvre, *The Production of Space,* 73, emphasis added.

18 Ibid., 99, emphasis added.

19 Ibid., 610.

20 Ibid., 42, emphasis added.

21 Ibid., 57, emphasis added.

22 Ibid., 105-6.

23 Stewart, "Bodies, Visions, and Spatial Politics," 609.

24 A. Merrifield, "Social Justice and Communities of Difference: A Snapshot from Liverpool," in *The Urbanization of Injustice,* ed. A. Merrivale and E. Swyngedouw (New York: New York University Press, 1997), 525.

25 Ó Tuathail, *Critical Geopolitics;* M. Shapiro, *Violent Cartographies: Mapping the Cultures of War* (Minneapolis: University of Minnesota Press, 1997).

26 S.L. Arizpe, M.P. Stone, and D.C. Major, *Population and Environment: Rethinking the Debate* (Boulder, CO: Westview Press, 1994); G. Sen, "Development, Population and the Environment: A Search for Balance," in *Population Politics Reconsidered: Health, Empowerment and Rights,* ed. G. Sen, A. Germaine, and L.C. Chen (Boston, Harvard University Press, 1994), 63-73.

27 B. Hartmann, "Population, Environment and Security: A New Trinity," *Political Environments* 5 (1997): 14, 16.

28 Gearóid Ó Tuathail and T.W. Luke, "On Videocameralistics: The Geopolitics of Failed States, the CNN International and (UN)governmentality," *Review of International Political Economy,* 4, 4 (1997), 709-33.

29 R.D. Kaplan, "The Coming Anarchy: How Scarcity, Crime, Population, Tribalism and Disease Are Rapidly Destroying the Social Fabric of Our Planet," *Atlantic Monthly,* February 1994, 58.

30 For example, former US President Bill Clinton suggested: "I was so gripped by many things that were in that [Kaplan's] article and by the more academic treatment of the same subject by Professor Homer-Dixon ... You have to say, if you look at the numbers, you must reduce the rate of population growth." Quoted in B. Hartmann, "Population, Environment and Security: A New Trinity," *Political Environments* 5 (1997): 12.

31 See Hartmann, "Population, Environment and Security," 8; Deputy Secretary of State Strobe Talbott before the Environmental Issues in American Foreign Policy Seminar at the National Foreign Affairs Training Center, Arlington, Virginia, 10 September 1996, <http://www.state.gov/www/global/oes/960910.html>:

Struggles over land, water, and other natural resources affect our national interests overseas as well, since they can lead to instability in regions of critical importance to the United States ... closer to the US, where I've spent a lot of time, including in recent weeks, is Haiti.

When President Clinton went to Haiti in March of 1995, he looked out the window of Air Force One as it passed over the Dominican-Haitian border. What most struck him was that you could tell which country was which from high in the air. The Dominican side was canopied with forests, while on the Haitian side, there were mostly bare mountains. The President had been to Haiti in the '70s, with Mrs. Clinton, and he remembered it as a lush, green land. Haiti is an agricultural country that has lost 98 per cent of its forests, as much as 50 percent of its topsoil, much of it in the last thirty years. No wonder rural incomes are stuck at $50 per year. In the next 30 years, Haiti's population will nearly double, and 13 million Haitians will have to survive on an island with even less arable land than it has now. Democracy, like Haiti's crops of rice, corn and sugarcane, needs arable land in order to grow and survive.

32 G. Goldin, "The Greening of Hate," *The Nation*, 18 May 1998, 7; J. Cushman, "Sierra Club Defeats Move to Oppose Immigration," *New York Times*, 26 April 1998, A1.
33 Goldin, "The Greening of Hate," 7.
34 W. Branigin, "Sierra Club Votes for Neutrality on Immigration and Population Issue Intensely Debated," *Washington Post*, 26 April 1998, A16.
35 J. Cushman, "Sierra Club Defeats Move to Oppose Immigration," *New York Times*, 26 April 1998, A1.
36 Goldin, "The Greening of Hate," 7; J. Motavalli, "Birth Control or Border Control? The Sierra Club Votes Down an Immigration Initiative," *E: The Environmental Magazine* 9, 4 (1998): 18-23.
37 Dalby, "The Environment as a Geopolitical Threat," 474.
38 N. Visvanathan, "Population Control and National Security: A Critique of the Coming Anarchy," *Political Environments* 2 (1994): 18-19.
39 D. Campbell, "Violent Performances: Identity, Sovereignty, Responsibility," in *The Return of Culture and Identity in IR Theory*, ed. Y Lapid and F. Kratochwi (London: Lynne Rienner Publishers, 1996), 163-80.
40 Dalby, "The Environment as a Geopolitical Threat," 472-96.
41 See Hartmann, "Population, Environment and Security," 14.
42 T. Kuehls, *Beyond Sovereign Territory: The Space of Ecopolitics* (Minneapolis: University of Minnesota Press, 1996); Dalby, "Ecological Metaphors of Security"; Dalby, "Reading Rio, Writing the World: The New York Times and the Earth Summit," *Political Geography* 15, 6/7 (1996): 593-613; V. Shiva, "Conflicts of Global Ecology: Environmental Activism in a Period of Global Reach," *Alternatives* 19 (1994): 195-207.
43 Kuehls, *Beyond Sovereign Territory*.
44 J. Agnew, *Geopolitics: Revisioning World Politics* (London: Routledge, 1998), 20-21.
45 S. Dalby, "Security, Intelligence, the National Interest and the Global Environment," *Intelligence and National Security* 10, 4 (1995): 175-200; Dalby, "Ecological Metaphors of Security," 291-319; S. Dalby, "The Kiwi Disease: Geopolitical Discourse in Australia/New Zealand and the South Pacific," *Political Geography* 12, 5 (1993): 437-56.
46 Dalby, "Security, Intelligence, the National Interest," 176.
47 N. Smith, "Antinomies of Space and Nature in Henri Lefebvre's *The Production of Space*," in *Philosophy and Geography II: The Production of Public Space*, ed. A. Light and J.M. Swift (Boulder: Rowman and Littlefield Publishers, 1998), 66.
48 N. Smith, "Nature at the Millennium: Production and Re-enchantment," in *Remaking Reality: Nature at the Millennium*, ed. B. Braun and N. Castree (London: Routledge, 1998), 282.
49 Ibid., 283.
50 Dalby, "The Environment as a Geopolitical Threat," 309.

51 N. Smith, "Antinomies of Space and Nature," 66.
52 Ibid., 274.
53 Ibid., 273.
54 Lefebvre, *The Production of Space*, 52.
55 N. Smith, *Uneven Development* (Oxford: Blackwell Press, 1984), ix.
56 T. Kuehls, *Beyond Sovereign Territory: The Space of Ecopolitics* (Minneapolis: University of Minnesota Press, 1996), 30 (emphasis added).

15
Technopoles and Development in a "Borderless" World: Boundaries Erased, Boundaries Constructed

Steven Jackson

This chapter is about metaphors. It begins from the premise that how we talk about things matters, that the way in which we think and act upon the world is shaped by the stories we tell about it. I take up the case of a particularly powerful metaphor through which changes associated with recent information and communication technologies (ICTs) have been represented: the story of the movement towards a "borderless world." This metaphor has risen to particular prominence in recent years, permeating social and policy debates of many types and levels. The nature of globalization, the prospects for development, the proper scale and meaning of governance – in these and other debates the metaphor of the borderless world has profoundly influenced the way we talk, think, and act about new communication technologies as well as the broader sociopolitical processes of informational change.

The vehicle for this discussion is a technological development project of considerable scope and significance: the Multimedia Super Corridor (MSC) currently being promoted and developed by the Malaysian government in collaboration with a handful of domestic and multinational technology firms. At once technology park, free trade zone, and social experiment, the MSC has been described by its founder and chief promoter, Malaysian Prime Minister Dr. Mahathir Mohamad, as "a giant test-bed for experimenting with not only multimedia technology but also, and more important, the evolution of a new way of life in the unfolding age of information and knowledge."[1]

It forms the heart of an "information-led" development strategy celebrated as the springboard by which Malaysia may "leapfrog" into the ranks of the "information," or "knowledge," societies of the advanced capitalist world. It is also hailed as a visionary model of political economic cooperation, combining public and private, global and local interests, in productive and mutually beneficial partnerships. These, in turn, are shaped to reflect the realities of a new global economy, the borderless world, brought about by the spread of new information and communication technologies.

At the same time, the MSC reveals some of the deep ambiguities that characterize a wide range of similar information-led and borderless-world development strategies. To begin with, in contrast to its futuristic rhetoric, the MSC is a deeply historical phenomenon, profoundly influenced by past patterns of social and political economic conflict and the policy outcomes that these have produced. Furthermore, despite its connotations of liberty and claims to informational free-flow, the drive to create and promote the MSC has contributed significantly to a discursive closure that has undermined broader social discussion of the means and ends of technological development in Malaysia.[2] Finally, in contrast to its legitimating narrative of the borderless world, the MSC has functioned in part by systematically *putting boundaries up*.

The MSC is a particularly interesting reference point for the present discussion of informational change and the metaphors by which it is represented for at least two reasons. First, in its design, execution, and promotion (both domestic and international) the MSC has been explicitly shaped and driven by the idea of the borderless world. This is perhaps unsurprising, given that one of the chief architects of the project, as an influential advisor to the Malaysian government and member of the MSC's International Advisory Panel, is Kenichi Ohmae, who has been a leading international advocate of the borderless-world concept. Indeed, his 1990 book of the same title first popularized the term.[3] Beyond this, the MSC lies at the intersection of some of the key social and policy debates of our time. For instance: What is the appropriate role for the state in economic and technological development within a (selectively) liberalizing world economic order? How is the understanding of what was once called "Third World development" being recast in the "information age," and should this move be greeted with celebration or apprehension? What forces will shape the character of postcolonial technopoles,[4] like the MSC, both within the global political economy and within a wide variety of more immediate social, cultural, and political economic contexts? How might the social and cultural characteristics of postcolonial societies challenge present ethnocentric assumptions concerning the nature of "information societies"?

It is not my purpose to answer all of these questions, any one of which would extend well beyond the space available here. Nor do I profess to offer anything remotely resembling a final word on Malaysian information-led development strategies, which remain highly dynamic and subject to processes of daily experimentation and revision as well as the ongoing possibility of broader social negotiations leading to more fundamental reorientations.[5] Instead, what I wish to argue is precisely the need for a new way of talking and thinking about these processes, one that better captures the full range and tone of the social negotiations surrounding informational change. I also want to demonstrate the deeply *political* character of our ways of representing informational change, by showing how the borderless-world discourse that frames the MSC has enabled certain analyses while disabling others, brought certain social practices into sharp relief while obscuring others, and supported a particular politics of socio-technical change while removing others from the field of social possibility. In short, I argue (1) that the metaphor of the borderless world that has shaped the development of the MSC and other technopoles is deeply inadequate to the task of understanding current social and spatial reorganizations associated with the expansion of new ICTs and (2) that we need to find new ways to conceptualize these processes. I suggest that clear thinking about technopoles and the global(izing) effects of new information technologies might begin by replacing the simple notion of boundary erasure central to the borderless-world narrative with a more complex understanding of simultaneous boundary erasures *and constructions.*

The final section of the chapter considers two possible sources from which we might begin to rethink the complex and power-laden relationships connecting space, communication, and technological change. The first comes from British geographer Doreen Massey, who has written perceptively on what she terms the "power geometry of place" to argue the need for placing present discussions of an undifferentiated globalization within the context of a variable "politics of mobility" stratified along lines of class, race, and gender. I conclude by suggesting the usefulness of Henri Lefebvre's theory of the "production of space" as a starting point for reconceptualizing the relationship between contemporary informational development and spatial reorganization.

A Borderless World

Much contemporary usage of the "borderless-world" metaphor is owed to Japanese management consultant Kenichi Ohmae, whose influential 1990 book, *The Borderless World,* first popularized the term. For Ohmae, the rich countries of the world (especially the "triad" of the US, Europe, and Japan) increasingly constitute an Interlinked Economy (ILE), whose primary policy objective lies in "ensuring the free flow of information, money, goods and services as well as the free migration of people and corporations."[6] For the people/consumers of these nations, as well as those of the enlightened NICs who aspire to join the club, this would necessarily produce a substantial increase in well-being and personal liberty. The new centre of power is the individual consumer, now freed from both the repressive apparatus of government and unresponsive corporations who failed to realize that, in the new order, "multinational companies are truly the servants of demanding consumers around the world."[7] All that stood in the way of this happy outcome was the short-sighted and self-interested resistance of government bureaucrats who were slow to grasp the fact that their role had changed from protecting their people and their natural resource base from outside economic threats to ensuring that their people had the widest range of choice among the best and the cheapest goods and services from around the world.[8]

The nature of this borderless world, argues Ohmae, definitively settles the development debate. The only reasonable option for the governments and peoples of less-developed countries is to abandon all nationalist sentiments and protectionist programs and to seek the fullest possible integration into the interlinked economy. The unprecedented track records of interventionist governments in Japan, South Korea, and Taiwan in fostering economic development, while acknowledged, are claimed to belong to an earlier and definitively finished era, in which a different set of economic rules applied. In the present conjuncture, argues Ohmae, nationalist policies could reflect only two things: first, a profound misunderstanding of economic process (either an outmoded mercantilism or what he castigates as the "resource illusion"); second, the cynical manoeuvrings of political and bureaucratic elites willing to put their personal hold on power ahead of the welfare of their people. Indeed, in the present era the very idea of "nation" or "national interest" has become irrelevant. In his concluding "Declaration of Interdependence," Ohmae asserts:

> Inevitably, the emergence of the interlinked economy brings with it an erosion of national sovereignty as the power of information directly touches local communities; academic, professional, and social institutions; corporations; and individuals. It is this borderless world that will give participating economies the capacity for boundless prosperity.[9]

Underlying all of this is an assumption implicit throughout much of the argument but evident in the final quotation above; namely, that it is the fundamental nature of *information, and information technologies, to break down boundaries*. This is a prominent and long-standing theme in most accounts of communication technologies (old and new) that, if anything, has become even more prevalent now than at the time Ohmae was writing. Indeed, the borderless-world metaphor presents itself as unobjectionable, and makes sense to so many, in large part because it follows upon a set of technological assumptions deeply embedded in the popular (but also academic) imagination. Numerous scholars and popular commentators have pointed out the strong libertarian bent of discussions surrounding the new technologies, in which information and information technologies emerge – by argument but more commonly by assumption – as a powerful symbol of freedom. In this representation, the essence of information is the power to subvert, to undermine existing structures of restraint, to route around control. Thus liberal communication scholar Ithiel de Sola Pool can describe the new communication tools (and, indeed, entitle whole volumes) as *Technologies of Freedom* and *Technologies without Boundaries*.[10] Global software firms can build international advertising campaigns around the provocative question: Where do you want to go today?

This is closely aligned to a second prominent way of imagining the spatial effects of the new communication technologies: namely, their tendency to eliminate distance, or "annihilate space." It has become commonplace, even banal, to observe that new communication and transportation technologies have played an important part in "making the world a smaller place." Three decades of historical evidence to the contrary, McLuhanite visions of a benign "global village" display an enduring hold on the popular imagination. A prominent contemporary variant of this argument can be found in Frances Cairncross's *The Death of Distance*, which identifies the elimination of spatial barriers brought about by advances in communication technologies as "the single most important force shaping society in the first half of the next century."[11] The implications of this change are regarded as truly revolutionary, producing, among other things, "near-frictionless markets," "the proliferation of ideas," a "shift from government policing to self-policing," the "rebirth of cities," "increased mobility," a new "market for citizens" (with competition conducted on the basis of lower tax rates), the "rebalancing of political power" (away from governments, towards people), and even "global peace" (on the basis of economic interdependence).[12]

Certain costs associated with the transition are grudgingly acknowledged; Cairncross dwells in particular on the loss of privacy through surveillance (though this will also produce a sharp decline in crime) and the growth of income differences within countries (though this is more than compensated for by reduced income differentials *between* countries). Overall, however, the death of distance is hailed as an inevitable and overwhelmingly positive advance. Critics of the process are treated, rather patronizingly, as understandably confused by the accelerating whirl of historical progress. This, as well as the general spirit and principal argument of the book, is accurately captured in the following quote from Cairncross:

> For many people, this prospective new world is frightening. Change is always unsettling, and we are now seeing the fastest technological change the world has ever known. But at the heart of the communications revolution lies something that will, in the main, benefit humanity: global

diffusion of knowledge. Information once available only to the few will be available to the many, instantly and (in terms of distribution costs) inexpensively.[13]

As a result, new ideas will spread faster, leaping borders. Poor countries will have immediate access to information that was once restricted to the industrial world and travelled only slowly, if at all, beyond it. Entire electorates will learn things that once only a few bureaucrats knew. Small companies will offer services that previously only giants could provide. In all these ways, the communications revolution is profoundly democratic and liberating, levelling the imbalance between large and small, rich and poor. The death of distance, overall, should be welcomed and enjoyed.[14]

"In the main," "the many," "overall" – the prevalence of these terms and others like them identifies what is perhaps the chief failing of the "borderless-world" and "death-of-distance" narratives; namely, an almost complete lack of social differentiation. Complex social histories are in this way averaged out into general (and generally favourable) historical trajectories; the divergent, often conflictual, interests of specific groups and individuals are overwritten with a general human interest, sometimes elevated to the level of "humanity" or "mankind." This is closely tied to a second difficulty with such narratives: their failure to give an adequate account of the power relations that have shaped and continue to shape the very changes they are describing. Rather than beginning with the new communication technologies (which then inevitably emerge as the chief protagonists of the story, the heart of the critique of technological determinism), the proponents of such accounts would be well advised to take a step further back, to consider what forces and social relations might have contributed to the development of present technological and spatial forms in the first place. This denaturalizing critique would also form a necessary part of the effort to account for social differentiation in the relationship between information technologies and space that is absent in accounts of the borderless world.

It is considerations such as these that separate the borderless-world and death-of-distance arguments from a wide variety of critical accounts that nevertheless employ a similar imagery in portraying the relationship between technological and spatial change. A leading contemporary version of this sort of critical "annihilation theory" is offered by David Harvey, who draws on Marx's famous phrase, "the annihilation of space by time"[15] to develop his own theory of "time-space compression," a phenomenon shaped by "processes that so revolutionize the objective qualities of space and time that we are forced to alter, sometimes in quite radical ways, how we represent the world to ourselves."[16]

Continuing, Harvey writes:

> As space appears to shrink to a "global village" of telecommunications and a "spaceship earth" of economic and ecological interdependencies, to use just two familiar and everyday images, and as time horizons shorten to the point where the present is all there is (the world of the schizophrenic), so we have to learn how to cope with an overwhelming sense of compression of our spatial and temporal worlds.[17]

Rather than appearing as a disembodied and free-floating phenomenon, as it does in Ohmae and Cairncross, for Harvey the current experience of spatial and temporal shrinkage represents only the latest round in a historical series of time-space compressions, a series in turn rooted in periodic spatial and economic restructurings within capitalism. The immediate roots of the current round of time-space compression can be traced to the emergence of regimes of "flexible accumulation" in response to crisis conditions prevailing in the advanced industrialized economies in the early 1970s. Far from information technology *determining* the general course of social development, as Ohmae and Cairncross would have it, the character of the technologies themselves are in large part *determined by* processes of social reorganization contemporaneous with their development, and both are in turn rooted in the more general process of political economic restructuring.

This provides a starting point for the type of social differentiation lacking in more optimistic variants of the shrinking world hypothesis. Crucially, it allows us to begin to think about power in relation to the constitution and spatial effects of new communication technologies. For Harvey, the annihilation of space through time expresses the broader dynamic of intensifying capitalist competition on the basis of information control and geographic expansion; accordingly, the empowering aspects of the borderless world are skewed to privilege the interests of capital.

But this doesn't tell the whole story. As Scott Kirsch asks, "What happens to space after its collapse, how do these spatio-temporal transformations impact our everyday lives, and how does this notion of a shrinking world help us to understand the social relations which that world embodies?"[18] An exclusive focus on the annihilating tendencies of time-space compression, the point at which Harvey touches popular accounts of spatial change such as the borderless world, captures only part of the larger spatial process that he is describing. I want to suggest that some of the political and analytical points that this critique seeks to raise might be better made by bringing to the fore a second formulation present but sometimes neglected in Harvey's account, one that discards the notion of erasure (of space, of boundaries) and begins instead by considering the part played by technology in their active *production*. This brings us to a field of social theory most famously pioneered by Henri Lefebvre. Before that, however, I want to provide a concrete frame of reference for these rather abstract discussions. The next section takes up the case of the MSC.

The Multimedia Super Corridor

As noted above, choosing the MSC as an exemplar of the borderless-world metaphor in action is far from an arbitrary decision. Each stage of the project, from design to implementation to domestic and international promotion, owes a clear and explicit debt to the particular vision of a borderless world shaped by new information technologies found in Ohmae's writings. The MSC is also a project of deep social significance, central to the restructuring of Malaysian development strategies and priorities, and widely regarded as a potential model for other countries considering similar informational development paths. Each of these points is emphasized by Prime Minister Mahathir, who has declared that

> Malaysia is taking a single-minded approach to developing the country using the new tools offered by the Information Age. The MSC will be the R and D centre for the information-based industries, to develop new codes of ethics in a shrunken world where everyone is a neighbour to everyone else, where we have to live with each other without unnecessary tension and conflicts. Indeed, the MSC is a pilot project for harmonizing our entire country with the global forces shaping the Information Age.[19]

At the level of physical detail, the MSC consists of a fifteen-by-fifty-kilometre zone lying immediately south of the capital, Kuala Lumpur. It stretches from Kuala Lumpur's central business district, including the Kuala Lumpur City Centre and the world's tallest buildings, the Petronas Towers, to the new Kuala Lumpur International Airport, completed to the south of the capital in 1998. Falling within this zone are a number of residential zones, past commercial and industrial developments, the national sports complex, and the pre-existing National Technology Park, along with large stretches of plantation land, held by the Federal Land Development Agency, the Selangor State Government, and a variety of smallholders and private developers.

The true heart of the MSC, however, lies in two new "intelligent," or "garden," cities: Putrajaya, the new administrative capital, and Cyberjaya, its private-sector counterpart. Announced in 1994 at a projected cost of RM20 billion (at the time, US$7.1 billion) Putrajaya will eventually house the Prime Minister's Department, the Ministry of Finance, and fifteen other ministries, plus a range of other state and federal agencies. When complete, it is expected to be home to some 79,000 government and

59,000 private-sector workers, with a total population exceeding 240,000. It will be governed by Putrajaya Corporation, a quasi-private body with "the regulatory authority of City Hall and the development powers of a State Economic Development Corporation."[20] After a delay of several months, the Prime Minister's Department officially relocated operations to Putrajaya in June 1999.

Immediately to the west of Putrajaya and forty-five minutes from downtown Kuala Lumpur lies Cyberjaya, projected as the commercial heart of the MSC and home to a group of corporations and "knowledge workers" engaged in a range of advanced technological and commercial activities. Infrastructural provisions are scheduled to include a fibre-optic network capable of handling advanced telephony; data exchange and interactive multimedia services; high-speed road and rail links to Kuala Lumpur, Port Klang, and the airport; and customized office space suitable to corporate research and commercial activities. Also planned is a multimedia university, which will train workers and encourage joint academic-industry research. Cyberjaya is being promoted as an experiment in eco-friendly living, based on "symbiotic harmony between man, the environment and technology."[21] Initial planning documents describe a range of mid- to high-level accommodation options, including "hillside mansions, lakefront houses, and condominiums."[22] For the foreign and Malaysian knowledge workers envisioned as its future residents, Cyberjaya is touted as an idyllic "garden city," which will "ensure that a suitable environment is created for promoting spiritual, mental and physical health and the enjoyment of nature and cultural pursuits."[23]

Beyond these infrastructural and environmental factors, potential investors in Cyberjaya are wooed by a range of financial and institutional incentives, laid out in the government's "Bill of Guarantees" to MSC investors. Participating firms are offered the option of complete income tax forgiveness for up to ten years or (if their MSC operations represent a cost centre) a 100 percent investment tax allowance. Duties on imported multimedia equipment are being waived. Local firms may participate in the R and D Grant Scheme, covering up to 50 percent of allowable research costs. Foreign firms are granted complete freedom of ownership, capital sourcing, and remission of profits, including exemption from foreign exchange controls. MSC firms also enjoy unlimited freedom to import foreign knowledge workers. Furthermore, as part of the MSCs "soft infrastructure," a number of changes to the Malaysian legal system are being introduced. These include the Digital Signatures Act (designed to facilitate electronic commerce), the Copyright Amendment Act (which strengthens intellectual property protection), a Multimedia and Communication Act (which establishes a legal framework for media convergence), a Data Protection Act (which governs the gathering and exchange of personal information), and more specific measures designed to facilitate applications like telemedicine and electronic governance.[24]

The promotion and long-term management of Cyberjaya, as well as the MSC more generally, is governed by the Multimedia Development Corporation. It has received strong public support from the prime minister, who has led a number of promotional missions to corporations and potential investors in the United States, Europe, and Japan. The MDC is officially incorporated under the Companies Act, 1965, but is 100 percent publicly owned; in Mahathir's words, "It combines the efficiency and effectiveness of a private company having entrepreneurial flair, with the decision-making and authority of a high-powered government agency."[25]

Responsibility for the design and strategic direction of the MSC is shared among a number of bodies. First among these is the National Information Technology Council (NITC), a group representing Malaysian corporate interests, along with officials drawn from relevant government ministries and headed by the prime minister. The NITC is responsible for setting the general framework and strategies for incorporating information technologies into national development goals. A second influential group is the International Advisory Panel on the MSC, which is made up primarily of the heads of many of the world's largest IT companies (including Sun, Microsoft, IBM, Netscape, NTT, etc.). This group, also chaired by the prime minister, solicits the advice of leading international technology firms and other "expert" advisers. Telekom Malaysia, which took over the activities of the Telecoms Department in 1987, and the Malaysian Institute of Microelectronics (MIMOS), a public corporation housing the NITC secretariat, have also played important steering roles.

The research activities of the MSC, and its most immediate point of articulation with the broader social and economic life of the country, are organized around a series of seven "flagship applications." The "Smart Schools" flagship aims to develop tools and strategies for expanding the use of information technologies within the national public education system. The "Multi-Purpose Card" encourages the development of a single chip-based card capable of performing national ID, driver's licence, immigration, health, and electronic cash functions as well as data-processing and file management (later versions may also include credit card, pension fund, student card, bill payment, and voter registration features). "Telemedicine" is aimed at promoting general health information and education as well as at allowing remote diagnoses and consultations. "Electronic government" promises to "reinvent the concept of government through connectivity"[26] (e.g., by improving internal government efficiency and delivery of government services through Internet and public kiosk technologies). "Worldwide Manufacturing Web" promotes the MSC as a site for regional manufacturing support and coordination activities, while

"Borderless Marketing" encourages firms to centre their regional and global marketing activities in the MSC, including telemarketing, online information services, electronic commerce, and digital broadcasting. Finally, the "R&D Cluster" flagship is designed to promote collaborative research and information sharing among private- and public-sector researchers.[27]

These initial plans, ambitious as they are, constitute only the first step in what is envisioned as a dramatic and longer-term process of economic, social, and cultural restructuring, whose end goal the prime minister has identified as "the evolution of a new way of life in the unfolding age of information and knowledge."[28] In its third and final stage (scheduled to coincide with the achievement of the country's earlier "Vision 2020" development goals), the MSC is projected to catalyze the transformation of Malaysia as a whole into a "super corridor." In this it will join other "islands of excellence" throughout the world and become an integral element in the Global Information Infrastructure governing the open and "informational" world of the future.

The changes expected are clearly fundamental and far-reaching, going well beyond purely "technical" questions of economic development policy. The project is deeply indebted, in both its design and rhetoric, to the vision of a borderless world. The reshaping of national development policy around new information technologies is predicted to produce precisely those benefits connoted by the broader discourses of informationalism outlined above – the elimination of borders and distance – leading to a vast increase in personal freedom, mobility, and general well-being. These are the themes that have dominated domestic promotional efforts and much of the general social discourse surrounding informational change in Malaysia to date. The prime carriers of these messages have been public education initiatives (most famously, the national "Love IT" campaign, featuring billboards, nightly prime-time television ads, and an "IT song" instantly recognizable to all Kuala Lumpur residents), the advertising efforts of high-tech firms (e.g., in the rapidly growing computer, software, and mobile phone industries), and the domestic media, including newspapers, radio, and television.

The very saturation of these images, however, and the resulting dominance of the borderless-world imagery within public and popular discourse, has limited the range of debate over the nature and social meaning of informational change in Malaysia. I argue that this raises serious and disturbing questions about a sort of "informational authoritarianism" within the politics of technological change in Malaysia (though clear parallels, I believe, can be drawn here between Malaysia and other contexts, not all of them to be found in the "developing" world). All of this stands in stark and ironic contrast to the more upbeat visions of freedom and liberty that characterize the narrative of the borderless world. Given the depth of change that the MSC and the Malaysian information-led development strategy is intended to produce, such limits on the range of public discourse and imagination should be taken very seriously indeed.

Out of Bounds in the Borderless World

Interviews with a range of social actors, government officials, representatives of international and domestic IT firms, NGOs, citizen groups, and political opposition figures revealed a number of concerns generally neglected in the prevailing discourse on the MSC and informational change, at least that part of it represented in official announcements and mainstream media coverage.[29] Some of these came in the form of a "technical" critique, which accepted the terms in which the debate had been framed (i.e., upheld the notion of the borderless world and the general soundness of Malaysia's information-led development model) but questioned the feasibility of the MSC's ambitious development targets.[30] While far from common, such questions have periodically made it into the realm of "legitimate" public discussion.

Others, however, raised concerns whose marginalization was far more pronounced. This marginalization was the product of at least two factors. First and most obvious was the long-standing power relationship connecting the interests and policies of the state to most of the mainstream media outlets.[31] This ensured that news about the MSC and information-led development received prominent and sustained coverage within the domestic media, nearly all of which enthusiastically endorsed the government's efforts and indeed played a crucial role in the attempt to mobilize popular nationalist sentiment around the MSC. However, alternative critiques were just as seriously undermined by the largely successful effort to position the question of the MSC, and questions of technological development more generally, within the borderless-world narrative of technical and social change. Beginning from this starting point brought certain issues immediately to light while rendering others obscure, offered a ready vocabulary for describing some social processes while leaving others nameless. In short, the installation of this particular structure of representation had a real and limiting effect on the types of social questions that could be effectively communicated.

What were some of these concerns? One set of questions had to do with the changing distribution of power between public and private actors embedded in the long-term vision of the MSC and the information society it is projected to produce. It was questioned whether the "technological imperative" wasn't being mobilized to support a shift towards a corporatized mode of governance that was not (despite attempts to link the two) automatically embedded in the logic of informational development itself. This critique may seem counter-intuitive, given the crucial role of the state (and the dynamic leadership of the prime minister himself) in the early stages of the project; certainly the model of the MSC challenges any easy understandings of a simple state-market dichotomy. Nevertheless, concerns were raised over the vastly disproportionate weight accorded to corporate, as compared to civil society, representatives in the key design and steering decisions of the project. As noted above, the majority of seats on the NITC, the body responsible for setting the means and ends of national informational development, are held by the heads of domestic communication and high technology firms, while groups such as NGOs, citizens movements, unions, and so on are entirely unrepresented. At the most immediate level, this has raised serious conflict-of-interest questions, as many NITC members represented firms who stood to reap substantial benefits from MSC infrastructure and flagship projects.[32] Respondents also questioned the role of the International Advisory Panel in the strategic direction of the MSC. The fear was raised that this move would locate substantial decision-making power beyond the reach of local and national accountability.[33] This concern was particularly pronounced when it came to such sensitive areas of social provision as health and education.

The longer-term vision for the MSC and Malaysia's information society expressed by the prime minister clearly extends this model of social decision making. Responsibility for leadership in important social sectors is described as shifting increasingly from the state to the realm of corporate social responsibility. As Mahathir argues: "People, especially corporate managers, must lead business and society with a social responsibility that displays not only a balanced set of values and ethics, but one that will inculcate the spirit of corporate integrity."[34]

This move in the direction of private governance does not begin with the MSC or with the idea of information-led development in Malaysia; rather, it continues long-standing trends first evinced by the Mahathir government's aggressive privatization and liberalization campaigns from the mid-1980s onwards.[35]

A number of NGO representatives noted with apprehension the deep tensions running between a recent history of informational closure in Malaysia and the vision of openness and democratic potential sometimes ascribed the MSC. Although the government has promised freedom of the Internet within its "Bill of Guarantees" to investors, and proponents speak of IT's power to produce a democratized and empowered civil society, past experience should suggest some caution in this regard. As revealed by events surrounding the dismissal and prosecution of former deputy prime minister Anwar Ibrahim in 1998, including the ousting of perceived Anwar supporters from the editorial board of media outlets such as the *New Straits Times* and the dismissal of leading academic Chandra Muzaffar from his post at the University of Malaya, controls over the channels of public communication remain strong in Malaysia.[36] Older pieces of legislation that have been used in the past to control media freedom and political dissent, including the Printing Presses and Publications Act, Official Secrets Act, and the Internal Security Act, remain in place.[37]

Thus, while the new information technologies promoted by the MSC may indeed pose new challenges to regulators and offer new openings to domestic NGOs and social movements,[38] they have not escaped past patterns of information control. Evidence of this was provided in the so-called "Internet-rumour-mongering" case of August 1998, when reports of ethnic rioting in a downtown Kuala Lumpur market spread quickly via e-mail, sparking runs on stores throughout the capital region as people stocked up in preparation for a prolonged period of civil unrest. After several days of official silence (during which established media outlets made no reference to the story) the government came out strongly against the report, branding it a malicious fabrication, the work of "traitors" and "cowards." The country's chief Internet service provider was enlisted to gain access to private e-mail files in an attempt to determine the source of the rumour. Three people were eventually detained under the terms of the Internal Security Act for their part in the incident.[39] Partly in response to this, in December 1998 a bill was introduced requiring the country's numerous "cyber cafés" to identify and register all users and to make this information available to the police.

Finally, a large number of the MSC's domestic critics expressed concern over the polarizing effects that the current information-led development strategy could be expected to produce. It was feared that the promised benefits of information would merely become the latest field for the iteration of long-standing socioeconomic divisions. Thus, where once the categories of rich and poor were defined primarily according to access to material resources, the move to informationalism would shift the terms of the debate (e.g., to notions of the "information-rich" versus "information-poor") while doing little to address fundamental questions of social and material inequality.[40] To the extent that background and training prepared the elite and upper middle classes to be the most immediate beneficiaries of the MSC, and as Malaysia moved to restructure its economy around informational production, it was feared that information-led development would only widen the already large gaps in levels of prosperity throughout society as a whole.[41]

I wish to emphasize that these concerns about social distribution were at one and the same time questions of spatial organization. Several respondents pointed out that the MSC's central location, while perfectly logical given the need for advanced transport and communication infrastructure, as well as access to the business community and skilled labour market of Kuala Lumpur, was likely to only widen the already considerable gap separating the capital region from other, more remote, parts of the country. The vision of a futuristic zone of advanced technology and "informational" living (as suggested by the MSC's promotional literature) with stronger links to a global economic system than to its immediate local and national surroundings was seen as a potential challenge to social cohesion. Different respondents described the challenge in different ways. Some spoke of growing divisions along the lines of socioeconomic class, as described above. Others suggested a growing cultural split separating the MSC and its associated forms of development from other regions of the country. This reflected, in part, a concern over the "foreign" nature of the MSC both in the composition of its workforce and the cultural values attributed to it.[42] But it also revealed an interest, while avoiding the question of "Malaysian" versus "foreign," in the cultural forms that might be produced by the day-to-day experience of living and working in the MSC. In short, what sort of "cultural space" might the MSC come to represent? What factors would determine the character of this space? And what relationship might it have to other cultural spaces within the country?

These concerns were made particularly acute by the powerfully contradictory element of exclusion embedded in the design and promotion of the MSC. Consider once again, for example, the design of the "cyber cities" projected as the nucleus of the project. The stated goal of Cyberjaya planners, to create a city combining "a world-class urban development," "a human-friendly urban environment," and "an eco-friendly sustainable environment," is shaped by the desire to give MSC companies a first-of-its-kind working and living environment where the full potential of multimedia technologies can be explored without any physical limits.[43] Specific features of the new city will include

a wide choice of hillside mansions, lakefront houses, and condominiums to suit varying family needs, as well as a commercial precinct comprising [sic] of shopping facilities, first-class, resort-style hotels, convention centres, food outlets, and service apartments to accommodate business professionals and activities.[44]

These, along with numerous references to the "top management and knowledge workers" envisioned as the future residents of Cyberjaya, raise serious questions about who may be expected to gain access to the social space of the MSC and who may be held out "at the borders." This immediately suggests a different way of posing the question of information technology, space, and borders, one that brings to light an entire "micropolitics" of space organized around boundary practices more localized, often more subtle, but ultimately no less significant or compelling than borders prevailing at the level of the nation-state.

It should be noted that this exclusive nature is not incidental, an unintended by-product of the project's design. The need for a bounded zone with an explicitly "global" character is clearly central to the government's appeal to international investors and foreign (arguably also Malaysian) professionals. It is also key to the MSC's position as the new symbolic centre of national development aspirations. As several respondents (including many enthusiastic supporters of the project) argued, it was important that the MSC be something of a space apart, if indeed it was to provide an example to which the rest of the country could, in time, aspire. Paradoxically, its separate status in this way (and in the present discursive frame) contributed to its ability to act as the masthead of an increasingly technologically oriented nationalism. For all these reasons, the MSC (and many other technopole developments existing or under construction elsewhere in the world) depends upon and is constituted by practices of social and spatial exclusion. Or, to push the point somewhat: *exclusion may in fact be the sociospatial logic of information-led development,* at least as presently conceived and practised.

But here we are moving into a set of questions for which the borderless-world narrative offers little guidance. Indeed, the insistence upon erasure as the dominant motif within its particular vision of spatialization makes such practices of exclusion hard even to see. We clearly need a new way of talking about the relationship between contemporary processes of technical and spatial reorganization. The final section of this chapter suggests two sources from which such a rethinking might begin.

Information Technologies, the Politics of Mobility, and the Production of Space

We can now return to the more general discussions broached in the first section of this chapter. There I argued that one of the principal failures of the borderless-world narrative is its lack of social differentiation, its tendency to convey the impression that borders everywhere are disappearing or becoming porous, that communication and mobility (recall, "the free flow of information, money, goods and services, as well as the free migration of peoples and corporations")[45] are undergoing an unchecked and universal expansion.

Against this, drawing on the evidence of the MSC, I wish to set a formulation advanced by British geographer Doreen Massey. Massey argues that what such global analyses inevitably forget or obscure is the simple point that spatial transformations (the rise of the borderless world, the death of distance) are experienced in radically different ways by different people.

For different social groups and different individuals are placed in very distinct ways in relation to these flows and interconnections. This point concerns not merely the issue of who moves and who doesn't, although that is an important element of it; it is also about power in relation to the flows and the movement. Different social groups have distinct relationships to this anyway-differentiated mobility: some are more in charge of it than others; some initiate flows and movement, others don't; some are more on the receiving end of it than others; some are effectively imprisoned by it.[46]

We are reminded here that questions of communication and mobility (now as always) are deeply and inescapably *political;* that is, that the experience of these phenomena is accorded to different groups in different ways, with different effects.

To illustrate, consider two groups of workers central to the success of the MSC. The first are the "knowledge workers," the hi-tech and business professionals (both Malaysian and foreign) that MSC planners have been eager to attract. Some will have recently been transferred, by choice or assignment, from offices abroad in Japan, Australia, California, Boston, and Ottawa. Many will use the MSC as a base, spending much of their time travelling to clients and branch offices elsewhere in the region. Some will have recently returned from jobs or education in Australia, the US, Europe, and Japan. Many will leave the country on weekends, vacationing and shopping in Bali, Thailand, Singapore, and Hong Kong. Most will live in one of the new designer suburbs (and, eventually, Cyberjaya) with an easier commute to the new international airport than to downtown Kuala Lumpur. For the foreigners among them, immigration procedures will be quick and painless, with a guaranteed forty-eight-hour turnaround on all permit applications.

Compare this to the experience of a second group, the construction workers who are, quite literally, building the MSC. Many of these will also be foreigners, although they are far more likely to come from Indonesia or Bangladesh than the US, Australia, or Japan. Immigration procedures do not flow so smoothly for these workers; in recent months the price of a work permit has soared beyond reach, when permits are available at all. In better times these were "guest workers"; now, with the economy in crisis, they are more commonly simply "illegals," subject to periodic (and well-publicized) round-ups and deportation. It should be emphasized that these workers are also mobile, also part of the expanding global flows, though the circumstances surrounding their movement are vastly different.

Two groups of workers, both deeply implicated in the process of informational development, and two radically different experiences of boundaries. My point is simply this: that *both* of these experiences, not merely the first one, must be taken into account before we can begin to meaningfully discuss the processes of technological and spatial reordering currently under way. Assertions of the borderless world (or, for that matter, any of the other global narratives currently in vogue) must therefore be met with certain questions: *Whose* borderless world? And for what purpose?

A second way of reconsidering the relationship between space, boundaries, and informational change might begin from the theoretical frame supplied by French philosopher and social theorist Henri Lefebvre. For Lefebvre, far from being given, the empty Cartesian grid upon which sociality, as historical process, is written, space is actively and socially produced; put simply, "[Social] space is a [social] product."[47] Space is not only a neutral *medium* to be overcome or annihilated but also the *outcome* of social practice. It represents at once the "sedimentation" or "inscription" of history (i.e., the physical embodiment of historical social struggles, and the site and object of ongoing social negotiation and struggle).

Lefebvre has suggested a three-part schema, or "trialectic,"[48] by which the production of space may be understood to occur. The first component he identifies as "spatial practice," or *perceived* space. This consists of the material embodiments of place and location (e.g., buildings, road construction, park areas, urban zoning patterns, etc.) and the practices by which they are produced and reproduced. This corresponds to our everyday and commonsensical understandings of the social function and meaning of space; or, as Lefebvre biographer Rob Shields puts it, the myriad practices by which "space is dialectically produced as human space."[49] The second component consists of "representations of space," made up of the knowledges, signs, and codes by which the immediate experience of space is abstracted and restructured into systems of knowledge and logic. This is a *conceived* space precisely because of its power to overwrite the distinctly corporeal and material nature of space with a set of mental abstractions, philosophies, theories, and the science of planning, which portray space as uniformly divisible and quantifiable, capable of being mapped onto a consistent and universal grid. This is the space of scientists and planners, and the primary site a technocratic power intimately connected to prevailing relations of production.

The final element of Lefebvre's triad is made up of "spaces of representation," or *lived* space. For Lefebvre this represents the "clandestine," or "underground," side of social life (including art), in which may evolve symbolisms and practices rooted in the lived experience of community – symbolisms and practices that may differ from both the dominant "common-sense" understandings of perceived space and the technocratic impositions of conceived space. Spaces of representation are thus identified as potential sites of resistance and sources for new forms of spatial practice through acts of appropriation. Lefebvre gives as examples the activities of slum, favela, and barrio-dwellers, which put space to uses other than those mandated by the practice and conception of prevailing social orders.

It is precisely the relationship, frequently antagonistic, between perception, conception, and lived experience that accounts for the production of space; for Lefebvre, the radically different spatial outcomes evident today and historically have been determined by complex interactions among the three "poles" of this triad. The role of technology in this process is best understood not through its ability to erase space but, rather, through how it shifts the balance of influence among these three constitutive elements of spatial production. Technology's general tendency, for Lefebvre, is to privilege the *conceived* over the *lived*, the abstract spaces of technocratic planners and capital over the daily experience of living in community. In his urban writings this corresponds to the rise of the city as product (characterized by homogeneity, calculation, and the dominance of exchange value) over the city as work, or *"oeuvre"* (marked by creativity, difference, use value).[50]

While this particular reading of technology (which is not, it should be added, a prominent feature of Lefebvre's writings on space) has come under considerable criticism, the general framework established in the *Production of Space* can act as an important corrective to many of the failings of the borderless-world narrative outlined above. It will be apparent that beginning with an analytical frame built around active spatial production immediately renders such ideas as the erasure of space or the death of distance, strictly speaking, nonsensical. In doing so it forces us to engage with the multiple and complex relations prevailing (and persisting) in the concrete conditions of particular times and places. This grants technopole projects such as the MSC a specificity denied by borderless world arguments, which would cast the technopole in the simplest terms as a generic creature of policy whose social character merely reflects an emergent global economic logic.

Lefebvre's insistence upon the importance of lived experience in the production of spaces may also offer a useful entry point for the sorts of cultural questions identified in early responses to the MSC project. While the precise forms that this might take remain unknown at this early stage of the project, the evolving character of everyday life in the new cybercities of the MSC will clearly bear heavily on the broader and longer-term social outcomes likely to proceed from it. The uncertainty here stems from more than the new and unfinished character of the MSC, however; taking a Lefebvrian trialectic of spatiality seriously also means remaining sensitive to the potentially transformative character of everyday experience, introducing a necessary degree of openness and flexibility into the analysis of spatial phenomena.

Finally, starting with the framework laid out by Lefebvre might give us a way of approaching the sort of "micropolitics of space" neglected within discussions of the MSC to date. It would allow us to ask more interesting, if more complex, questions about *all* of the boundary practices by which the MSC and other technopoles are constituted. For example: Who/what has access to this space, and on what terms? Who/what is held out at the border? Within the technopole, who moves where, and under what conditions? Or, as Massey reminds us to ask, for whom is freedom and mobility enhanced, and for whom is it constrained?

These are questions for which no clear answers presently exist. The MSC, at the time of writing in early 2000 and certainly in mid-1998 (when the primary research for this study was conducted), remains a plan on the way to reality (though there is no guarantee that these two will bear a close resemblance). Quite apart from the longer-term considerations raised by respondents and conveyed here, the MSC faces some real and immediate challenges of a more strictly economic nature, including the need to attract higher levels of domestic and foreign investment, the availability of public and private funds to finance the costs of infrastructure development, and intensifying competition from other regional technopoles, old and new. But it should be emphasized that, in any serious engagement with the conceptual contributions of Massey and Lefebvre, it is necessary to acknowledge contingency. Speaking of the production of space means taking seriously the interaction of the perceived, the conceived, and the lived, the outcome of which is never determined in advance. Arguing for a politics of mobility means taking seriously the potential for that politics to produce unanticipated results. The story of information technology and spatialization conveyed by the borderless-world metaphor has the advantage of a clear and happy ending; the alternative view suggested here is unavoidably committed to an ambiguous future.

Acknowledgment
The author wishes to thank the Social Sciences and Humanities Research Council of Canada and the Asia Pacific Foundation of Canada for support during the research and writing of this project, and Professor Vincent Masco for guidance and co-authorship of an earlier version of this research. Versions of paragraphs 22-27 of the current chapter first appeared in an article by Steven Jackson and Vincent Masco, "The Political Economy of New Technological Spaces: Malaysia's Multimedia Super Corridor," *Journal of International Commuication* 6, 1 (1999): 23-40. They are reproduced here with the publisher's permission.

Notes
1 Mohamad Mahathir, *Excerpts from the Speeches of Mahathir Mohamad on the Multimedia Super Corridor* (Subang Jaya: Pelanduk Publications, 1998), 7.
2 A more detailed presentation of some of these arguments can be found in Zaharom Nain and Mustafa Anuar, "Malaysia: The Multimedia Super Corridor," a paper presented at the United Nations Research Institute for Social Development International Conference on Information Technologies and Social Development, Geneva, June 1998; and Steven

Jackson and Vincent Mosco, "The Political Economy of New Technological Spaces: Malaysia's Multimedia Super Corridor," *Journal of International Communication* 6, 1 (1999): 23-40.

3 Kenichi Ohmae, *The Borderless World: Power and Strategy in the Interlinked Economy* (Harper Business, 1990).

4 I adopt the terminology of Castells and Hall, who describe technopoles as various deliberate attempts to plan and promote, within one concentrated area, technologically innovative, industrial-related production: technology parks, science cities, technopoles, and the like. See Manuel Castells and Peter Hall, *Technopoles of the World: The Making of 21st Century Industrial Complexes* (New York: Routledge, 1994), 8.

5 Interested readers are referred once again to Nain and Anuar, "Malaysia"; Jackson and Mosco, "The Political Economy of New Technological Spaces"; and the official Web site of the Multimedia Development Corporation at <http://www.mdc.com.my>.

6 Ohmae, *The Borderless World*, xii-xiii.

7 Ibid., x.

8 Ibid.

9 Ibid., 216 (emphases added).

10 Ithiel de Sola Pool, *Technologies without Boundaries: On Telecommunications in a Global Age*, ed. Eli Noam (Cambridge, MA: Harvard University Press, 1990); Ithiel de Sola Pool, *Technologies of Freedom* (Cambridge, MA: Belknap Press, 1983).

11 Frances Cairncross, *The Death of Distance: How the Communications Revolution Will Change Our Lives* (Boston: Harvard Business School Press, 1997), 1.

12 Ibid., xi-xvi.

13 Ibid., 4.

14 Ibid.

15 Karl Marx, *Foundations of the Critique of Political Economy*, trans. Martin Nicolaus (New York: Random House, 1973).

16 David Harvey, *The Condition of Postmodernity* (Cambridge, MA: Blackwell, 1989), 240.

17 Ibid.

18 Scott Kirsch, "The Incredible Shrinking World? Technology and the Production of Space," *Environment and Planning D: Society and Space* 13 (1995): 529.

19 Ibid., 30.

20 Mahathir, *Excerpts from the Speeches*, 35.

21 Ibid.

22 Multimedia Development Corporation (MDC), *Cyberjaya: The Model Intelligent City in the Making* (Kuala Lumpur: Multimedia Development Corporation, 1998).

23 Mahathir, *Excerpts from the Speeches*, 32.

24 Multimedia Development Corporation (MDC), *Cyberjaya*.

25 Ibid.

26 Mahathir, *Excerpts from the Speeches*, 68.

27 Ibid.

28 Ibid., 7.

29 These interviews were conducted in July and August 1998. It should be noted that this was a time of considerable political and economic uncertainty. Politically, barely concealed tensions were mounting between the prime minister and his deputy, Anwar Ibrahim, within United Malays National Organization and the Barisan National (the leading party and ruling coalition, respectively). Economically, great uncertainty existed as to appropriate policy responses, as well as the probable length and severity, of the recession brought on by the Asian financial crisis of late 1997. A discussion of these political dynamics can be found in Meredith Weiss, "What Will Become of Reformists? Ethnicity and Changing Political Norms in Malaysia," *Contemporary Southeast Asia* 21, 3 (December 1999): 424-50. For more on the economic impact of the financial crisis in Malaysia, see K.S. Jomo, ed., *Tigers in Trouble: Financial Governance, Liberalisation and Crises in East Asia* (New York: Zed Books, 1998).

30 Concerns of this nature included the availability of suitable "knowledge workers," the scarcity of venture capital willing to support new technology start-ups, fierce regional investment competition (particularly from Singapore), short-term inadequacies in

communication and transportation infrastructures, and, above all, in the summer of 1998 the uncertain effects of the Asian financial crisis on long-term regional development and investor confidence. A fuller account of these concerns can be found in Jackson and Mosco, "The Political Economy of New Technological Spaces"; AMSC, "Confronting the Realities," *PC Magazine Malaysia*, July 1998; *Businessweek* (international edition), 22 March 1999.

31 See, for example, Nain Zaharom, "Rhetoric and Realities: Malaysian Television Policy in an Era of Globalization," *Asian Journal of Communication* 6, 1 (1996): 43-64; Nain Zaharom, "Commercialization and Control in a Caring Society: Malaysian Media towards 2020," *Sojourn* 9, 2 (1994): 178-99; F. Loh Kok Wah and Anuar Mustafa, "The Press in Malaysia in the Early 1990s: Corporatization, Technological Innovations and the Middle Class," in *Critical Perspectives: Essays in Honour of Syed Husin Ali*, ed. Muhammed Ikmal Said and Zahid Emby (Petaling Jaya: Malaysian Social Science Association, 1996).

32 This fear was heightened by a series of questionable corporate-political connections stemming from past rounds of privatization. For more on this, see K.S. Jomo and E.T. Gomez, *Malaysia's Political Economy: Politics, Patronage and Profits* (Cambridge: Cambridge University Press, 1997); K.S. Jomo, ed., *Privatizing Malaysia: Rents, Rhetoric, Realities* (Boulder, CO: Westview Press, 1995); and E.T. Gomez, *Money Politics in the Barisan Nasional* (Kuala Lumpur: Forum Publications, 1991).

33 The extent of this body's decision-making power remains unclear. On the one hand, as an advisory panel it would appear to have little formal authority; on the other hand, because it includes representation from several key present and prospective investors, its *informal* influence would seem to be, at least potentially, substantial. The question is clouded by a disjuncture between the MSC's international and domestic promotional efforts: the first of these asserts the important steering role of the International Advisory Panel, while the second tends to emphasize local project control.

34 Mahathir, *Excerpts from the Speeches*, 87.

35 For more discussion of these historical connections, see Jackson and Mosco, "The Political Economy of New Technological Spaces"; excellent accounts of the changing orientation of Malaysian economic policy can be found in Jomo, *Privatizing Malaysia*.

36 For a description of the continuing (and in some ways deepening) restrictions upon the Malaysian press and media system, see Nain Zaharom, "Rhetoric and Realities"; and Wah and Mustafa, "The Press in Malaysia in the Early 1990s."

37 Zaharom, "Rhetoric and Realities; Wah and Mustafa, "The Press in Malaysia in the Early 1990s."

38 E-mail and Internet strategies have indeed been adopted by many NGO activists to network and exchange information with domestic and international supporters. There are also, however, limits to the reach and effectiveness of such net-activism. For a discussion of these, see Anna Har and John Hutnyk, "Languid, Tropical, Monsoonal Time? Net-Activism and Hype in the Context of South East Asian Politics," *Saksi* 6 (1999) at <http://www.saksi.com/jul99>.

39 See *New Straits Times*, the *Star*, 8-13 August 1998.

40 For one version of this argument, see Lim Kit Siang, *IT For All* (Petaling Jaya: Democratic Action Party, 1997).

41 One respondent thus characterized the public monies spent on the MSC as a regressive net transfer of resources from poor to rich. These issues were viewed with special concern within the context of domestic economic turmoil, where money directed towards the advanced technology sectors was money not spent on a system of basic social services under severe stress.

42 In this, the MSC was inevitably caught up in the larger and highly sensitive debate (given the history and politics of Malaysian interethnic relations) over what might properly constitute a Malaysian culture or identity. One of the most immediate public expressions of this came in questions surrounding the range of allowable Internet communications, including the issue of Internet pornography. Efforts were also under way to define the relationship of Islam to informational development – a particular version of the cultural negotiation of technology that would appear to be a universal of informational change. One example of the politics of this process can be found in the prime minister's suggestion

that Malaysian religious groups should embrace information technologies in order to play a leading role in developing Islamic content for the World Wide Web.

43 Multimedia Development Corporation (MDC), *Cyberjaya*, 7.

44 Ibid.

45 Ohmae, *The Borderless World*, xii-xiii.

46 Doreen Massey, "Power-Geometry and a Progressive Sense of Place," in *Mapping the Futures: Local Cultures, Global Change*, ed. J. Bird, B. Curtis, T. Putnam, G. Robertson, and L. Tickner (New York: Routledge, 1993).

47 Henri Lefebvre, *The Production of Space*, trans. Donald Nicholson-Smith (Blackwell: Oxford, 1991), 26.

48 See also Edward Soja's *Thirdspace: Journeys to Los Angeles and Other Real-and-Imagined Places* (Cambridge, MA: Blackwell, 1996), for a treatment of these themes heavily influenced by Lefebvre.

49 Rob Shields, *Lefebvre, Love and Struggle: Spatial Dialectics* (New York: Routledge, 1999), 162.

50 Henri Lefebvre, *Writings on Cities*, trans. and ed. Eleonore Kofman and Elizabeth Lebas (Oxford: Blackwell, 1996).

Part 7
Rethinking Borders – Lines, Spaces, and Continua

The theme of Part 7 of *Holding the Line* is the continuing importance of the nation-state as an actor, the continuing relevance of borders not as linear phenomena carved in stone and set for time immemorial but, rather, as outcomes of geopolitical processes, diplomatic efforts, global institutions, changing international conditions, and evolving discourses on borders. We begin with a discussion of the continuing importance of the nation-state in the face of multinational and multi-institutional demands for the internationalization of relief efforts. We then go on to identify the diplomatic dialogues (and the geopolitical underpinnings) that have consistently authorized the understanding of borders and transnationalism as spatial processes, and we conclude that what is required of the twenty-first century is a new definition of borders as processes, or continua, that frame bounding activities.

There is no discrepancy between these three overall themes; indeed, they are all facets of a singular and larger theme – the changing meaning of borderland in the international arena. In Chapter 16, William Wood suggests that, contrary to what occurred in the past, the new recognition of the complex basis of multilateral, cross-border initiatives involve strategic alliances that challenge old technologies and old internationalist formulae, while in Chapter 17 Alan Henrikson discusses the deliberate development of strategic geopolitical discourses that discriminate between "front" and "back" orientations of diplomacy. Henrikson builds upon ideas about borders presented in Chapter 1 by Gerald Blake; these concern the importance of understanding borders as the outcome of processes that move not only beyond the map but also beyond recently revived realist interpretations in the international political arena that see borders as "limits" or "fighting spaces."

Particularly important in Part 7 is the idea that, over a century ago, when geopolitical discourse was in its formative stages, the notions of "choice," "discourse," and/or "constructed reality" had little currency. The chapters in this section suggest that this is no longer the case. Wood, for example, does not argue that the problems posed by the increasing application of technical expertise to pragmatic issues such as humanitarian relief are immune from the complexities of multiple contextual choices and multivocal texts. Indeed, he observes that, in terms of the context within which the problem – and possible solutions – exist, a pragmatic "crisis assessment" requires "not just an understanding of the immediate humanitarian needs of victims but also of the social, political, economic, and military factors that will influence the international community's ability to assist in their recovery."

The main idea developed in Part 7, therefore, is that borders are tightly linked to processes that are not merely economic, legalistic, and political but also discursive, diplomatic, and rooted in the experience of human tragedy and renaissance. Borders are a product of the mind – both in terms of idealizations and in terms of geopolitical dialogue. The chapters in the following section deliver the coup de grace to the notion that, somehow, borders are "stand-alone" phenomena that can be understood in and of themselves without reference to broader political, social, economic, cultural, and geopolitical realities. They substantiate claims made in earlier chapters that the spatial reorganization of borders in the twenty-first century provides evidence of the dynamic and multifaceted nature of borderland studies. Borders do not exist independently of states and geopolitical discourses, and their job is to meet rather than to collapse in the face of geospatial challenges. Henrikson concludes Chapter 17 with a statement that serves to encapsulate this idea. He observes that international political boundaries are neither, as the geopolitiker Karl Haushofer thought, "fighting places" nor simply "meeting places"; rather, "borders and border control systems are more complex phenomena: they both divide and unify. When synthesized across national lines they can be, in addition, 'joining places,' capable of connecting wholly different countries, consociatively, in certain kinds of organized cooperation."

16
Complex Emergency Response Planning and Coordination: Potential GIS Applications
William B. Wood

Complex emergency responses are invariably difficult, multifaceted, and highly charged undertakings, with international relations implications and urgent lifesaving requirements. Accurate, relevant, and timely data can play a critical role in humanitarian missions, yet a cohesive information plan has been largely absent from recent multilateral emergency responses. This chapter explores the potential use of geographic information system (GIS)-linked data collection, organization, and dissemination prior to and during multilateral humanitarian operations. The multiple functions of international boundaries in such operations are raised, as are the challenges of meeting crisis-response objectives. The use of GIS tools in Kosovo provides a model for projecting informational requirements onto future complex emergency responses that will involve both peacekeepers and civilian agencies.

Complex Emergency Operations
A growing body of literature on humanitarian relief and intervention describes the significant institutional, moral, and operational challenges such activities pose. While humanitarian relief operations are those that bring food, shelter, medicine, and other basic needs to vulnerable groups, a complex emergency operation entails something more. Traditional relief operations usually unfold with the consent of the government in which the crisis, usually a natural disaster, takes place. Such efforts include a number of organizations, urgent life-saving measures, and difficult working conditions, but the common purpose is taken for granted: to assist with the recovery process. Depending on the extent and intensity of the disaster – an earthquake, flood, hurricane, drought, or even a toxic chemical spill – survivors can expect that life-threatening conditions will eventually recede, allowing them to return to the mundane challenges of daily survival, at least until the next disaster strikes.[1] Reviews of "natural disasters" underscore underlying conditions of poverty, income inequity, and

poor resource management, which are often not adequately addressed by international relief efforts. While these studies also acknowledge that such natural disasters can spill across borders, international boundaries per se usually do not play a critical role other than as a logistical and bureaucratic hurdle to relief deliveries.[2]

Complex emergency operations, in contrast to a "traditional" humanitarian relief operation, almost always involve a multilateral military and civilian response to a life-threatening crisis that is deliberately imposed and manipulated rather than one stemming from a "natural" or accidental disaster. That key difference accounts for the much greater political, socioeconomic, security, and even logistical difficulties faced by the international community in dealing with the victims of civil war, human rights abuses, ethnic violence, and compelled impoverishment.[3] The international effort to help a war-ravaged community to recover can thus become highly contentious, requiring outside responders to understand the context in which the problem – and possible solutions – exist. A "crisis assessment" requires not just an understanding of the immediate humanitarian needs of victims but also the social, political, economic, and military factors that will influence the international community's ability to assist in their recovery.

Complex emergency responses are frequently implemented over the objections of the government that has internationally recognized sovereign power over the crisis zone. The spatial dimensions of a humanitarian crisis are influenced by, but not necessarily confined within, the delimited boundaries of the state, which attempts to legitimize its national authority by exerting control over its territory.[4] Under normal conditions, national territorial controls, such as those at border checkpoints, are taken for granted as part of the recognized rights of a government. They become problematic when the state in effect loses control over the conflict zone or is deemed by the United Nations Security Council (UNSC) to bear responsibility for the crisis. The UN secretary general has argued that sovereignty should not be used as an excuse to abuse human rights: "we [the United Nations] will not, and we cannot, accept a situation where people are brutalized behind national boundaries."[5] Complex emergencies, though, generally result from widespread and systematically brutal treatment of minority groups, which the national government may actively participate in or implicitly condone.

Multilateral Response
Multilateral operations are often undertaken amidst ongoing hostilities between armed belligerents who have all too often targeted civilians as part of their military campaigns. These multilateral responses can involve

peacekeeping forces, human rights monitors, refugee officers, civil affairs experts, negotiators, and special envoys of the UN secretary general. They can force the UN and its member states to make difficult choices between the safety of UN peacekeepers and civilian staff and the protection of civilian war victims, especially those unable to cross an international boundary to the relative safety of another country.[6] International responses to complex emergencies, particularly those in which a lack of public security weakens relief capabilities, invariably require involvement by a variety of civilian agencies and peacekeepers from several governments, international and regional organizations (such as the UN, Organization for Security and Co-operation in Europe [OSCE], and North Atlantic Treaty Organization [NATO]), and non-governmental organizations (NGOs).

Volatile and fluid military and political conditions that surround a complex emergency operation make the functions of international boundaries of critical importance. Initially, the UNSC must review the threats facing a vulnerable group and the implications for regional stability. If a mission is launched, then international organizations may establish multilateral operations that must often negotiate their way through government and militia forces that may attempt to deny access, obstruct their work, steal their supplies, and even kidnap or kill their personnel. Additionally, relief agencies and peacekeepers must deal with the other products of war: landmines, atrocity sites, ongoing clashes between ethnic groups, de facto divisions of communities along ceasefire lines, and even the creation of new subnational (Bosnia) and international (Ethiopia/Eritrea) boundaries.

Complex emergency responses involve two sets of actors – victims of various types and groups of responders – and a set of operational goals, or pillars.[7] Multilateral intervention in a complex emergency entails coordination among a variety of agencies collecting many different types of data coming from various agencies. Geospatial data are critical to the success of complex emergency responses because of the multitude and complexity of factors that can affect these missions. "Geospatial," in this sense, refers to any data, including maps and imagery, "georeferenced" to a point or area on the earth's surface. These data can relate to physical features of the affected area as well as infrastructure, population locations, and other factors relevant to both peacekeeping and civilian operations.

GIS software is uniquely capable of sorting through such "data layers" and displaying not-so-subtle relationships that underlie the context of the crisis and implications for multilateral response operations, from immediate relief through long-term development. This chapter looks at how GIS tools were used to assist international agencies responding to the humanitarian crisis in Kosovo, and it goes on to discuss how such tools might be applied to other complex cross-border emergencies.

Boundaries

Perhaps the most important geospatial data for multilateral operations are those only indirectly linked to physical geography. Current international land boundaries, for example, have often been imposed with little appreciation for local ecological conditions (watersheds), economic ties, land uses, or the distribution of ethnic groups. The variable functions of these boundaries can have profound influences on cross-border socioeconomic interactions.[8] They can also either facilitate or impinge upon cross-border relief operations, depending on the degree and consistency of their openness. Kosovo's border crossings into Macedonia and Albania, for example, were alternatively open or closed depending on the numbers of refugees attempting to cross, security conditions, and bilateral relations.

Both the belligerents responsible for a humanitarian crisis and those attempting to resolve it work across permeable borders, where porosity can vary greatly by place and time. The same border crossing can be open or closed to refugee flows or relief efforts depending on the policies of governments on both sides of the boundary line. Similarly, weapons can be smuggled quietly across one border while food shipments are hung up for days on another. Thus, border porosity is a critical, yet often ignored, function in multilateral response operations. Measures of cross-border relief flows, as well as operational impediments (such as multi-day delays at customs checkpoints), would be a useful addition to a GIS-linked set of data for emergency operations.

In addition to international boundaries, subnational administrative lines can also influence the spatial parameters of the conflict. They can divide a zone of safety from one of danger, determine the future of ethnic groups demanding self-determination, and even dictate the political and economic fate of specific communities located on one side or the other of the new line (or, in some unfortunate cases, straddling it). The responding agencies themselves can introduce new de facto boundaries, such as those that allocate peacekeeping operational responsibilities for specific "sectors" to particular countries. In Bosnia, the Dayton-created inter-entity boundary line (IEBL) between the Bosniak-Croat "Federation" and the "Serb Republic" has taken on many of the functions of an international boundary, with divergent political structures and migration impediments. In Kosovo, the ethnically and administratively divided city of Kosovska Mitrovica has been a continuing source of violence well after the arrival of NATO Kosovo Force (KFOR) peacekeepers.

Civil-Military Coordination

Complex contingency operations are invariably costly, complicated, and lengthy missions led by the UN and some member states.[9] Multilateral responses across international boundaries are often divided into those aspects managed by either military (peacekeeping) or civilian (relief) agencies. Military roles call for peacekeeping or observer forces under UN or regional organization (NATO) leadership. Military missions usually bring with them impressive logistical capabilities, a relatively disciplined workforce, and clear command and control structures. More often than not, however, they do not bring much expertise in handling large humanitarian crises, and often these forces believe they are much better suited to dealing with military security concerns than with relief delivery. Military operations are also expensive to launch and maintain.[10]

Civilian agencies vary greatly, but in comparison with military forces are generally much smaller and less well structured.[11] These agencies can range from widely experienced UN administrators to NGO entrepreneurs. Together they are supposed to help move an atrocity-ravaged society from chaos towards a durable peace. Such multilateral humanitarian efforts are optimistically mandated in UNSC resolutions but can be quickly bogged down in operational, political, and security dilemmas. While civilian agencies might agree in principle to a division of labour, in the "field" (the crisis area) tensions among relief personnel can arise over poor mission coordination, funding problems, staff shortages, miscommunication, and insufficient protection for staff members.

Mission success requires effective integration of various aspects of military activities with many civilian entities across a broad range of functions. While implementation problems will invariably recur with each new crisis, they could be lessened with appropriate information management tools that improve interagency communication. Such information management tools and shared data need to be part of a broader process of collaborative planning between civilian and peacekeeping programs. When such cooperation is lacking, the result is disjointed missions that, at a minimum, involve costly duplication of effort. Without corrective measures to improve information sharing, civilian and military operations can become disjointed and, thereby, negatively affect the well-being and safety of crisis victims.

GIS as a Planning and Coordination Tool

Both civilian agencies and peacekeepers are beginning to harness new information technologies that can assist their efforts to improve preparedness and responsiveness to natural disasters and complex emergencies.[12] While each responding agency usually brings specialized skills to a set of complementary mission goals, these are not enough: different agencies need to work together. New computer-based information management tools can help with the always-difficult tasks of planning, implementing, and successfully completing a multilateral mission. GIS-based applications offer one set of information management tools to assist contingency planning for complex emergencies. GIS software, for example, has been used to describe the ethnic cleansing of Kosovo as well as to assist with operational planning for the safe return of Kosovars and the reconstruction of their homes.[13]

GIS is a means to spatially organize a variety of data for any given place or area. The premise is simply that natural features (a mountain or stream) and events (an earthquake or flood), as well as human activities, tend to occur on the earth's surface and can thus be linked by their relative location. Observations of such activities – a birth, a death, a crop yield, a road, a town, or the GDP of a whole country – can thus be "georeferenced" to a defined place or area. Once they are thus organized, these disparate data can be "layered" to study patterns of human activities and their societal and environmental consequences.[14] These data layers can also be linked to earth observation images of the earth surface and precisely tied to specific points on that surface through the use of global positioning system (GPS) receivers. GIS software and GIS-linked data sets, if properly applied, can track a broad range of local, national, and international problems.[15]

In the Kosovo context, GIS was used to document a systematic pattern of forcible expulsions of ethnic Albanians from their communities. In that process tens of thousands of dwellings were destroyed and hundreds of thousands of Kosovars were forced into Albania, Macedonia, and beyond.[16] Since October 1998, with the advent of the Kosovo Verification Mission (KVM), the troubled province has served as a testing ground for new information management tools. A GIS-based innovation involves both a methodology for collecting, organizing, and using place-based crisis information as well as the software that allows such information to be shared among a diverse set of civilian and military agencies. This chapter reviews how GIS was used as a multilateral information-sharing and mission-coordination tool, beginning with the KVM and ending with the establishment of the UN Interim Administration Mission in Kosovo (UNMIK) in July 1999.

GIS for Kosovo

Since the early 1990s genocidal actions in the former Yugoslavia led to frustrating diplomatic impasses over how to respond to the latest threats by Serb nationalists against other ethnic groups.[17] By 1998, three years after the Dayton Peace Accords helped stabilize Bosnia, widespread violence erupted in the province of Kosovo. By the fall of 1998 GIS software was used to enable two of the lead international agencies involved in Kosovo – the OSCE-supported KVM and the UN High Commissioner for Refugees (UNHCR) – to work together. The KVM was responsible for monitoring human rights violations and maintaining public security, with an emphasis on limiting hostilities between Yugoslav military and policy units and ethnic Albanian guerrilla forces. The UNHCR had responsibility for coordinating the relief activities of over forty UN and NGO agencies, which collectively delivered food, built shelters, surveyed damage and water availability, and performed many tasks to meet the urgent needs of internally displaced persons (IDPs). A GIS package was developed as a means of data sharing between the KVM and the UNHCR. While this project got off to a good start, escalating violence in the spring of 1999 postponed the creation of GIS-enhanced databases related to security and relief activities.

The foundation for the use of GIS in Kosovo was an "electronic base map" of the province assembled by the US National Imagery and Mapping Agency (NIMA), which is the lead federal agency for collecting worldwide cartographic and imagery-based geospatial data. An initial product was a "humanitarian planning map" that was used in its paper copy form by many relief agencies. More important, though, was the underlying GIS product that contained several data "layers" (topography, roads, places, administrative units, etc.). A complementary NIMA project was a Kosovo gazetteer of over 1,500 place-names and geocoordinates. This NIMA map and gazetteer in effect created an objective spatial framework for collecting data about the unfolding ethnic cleansing tragedy. The KVM, for example, used the GIS-generated map to begin a database of reported landmines and booby traps that was later adopted by KFOR. The UNHCR used the same map to support its survey of dwelling damage; this effort was continued following renewed hostilities against ethnic Albanians.

Following the NATO air campaign, KFOR and UNMIK quickly deployed into Kosovo, facing the difficult task of ensuring stability in the province as well as providing assistance to over a million Kosovars who had been displaced and were now returning en masse. GIS tools were used to map refugee camps in Macedonia and Albania, where over half a million Kosovars had sought refuge under very difficult conditions. The need for GIS tools in late spring and summer 1999 was even greater than it was during the previous fall and winter. Returnees to Kosovo faced many obstacles: landmines and unexploded ordnance; destroyed infrastructure; tens of thousands of damaged dwellings; abandoned farms; lingering mistrust between returning ethnic Albanians and those ethnic Serbs who had decided to stay; and, finally, a devastated economy.

The US government-led Kosovo Repatriation Information Support (KRIS) project identified data of relevance to safe cross-border repatriation and included them within GIS-linked databases. The rapid pace of spontaneous returns precluded a well-ordered and prioritized repatriation from Albania and Macedonia but added even more urgency to the need for shareable data between KFOR and the UNHCR. A priority was data on landmines and unexploded ordnance that could be used by KFOR and

UNMIK-coordinated agencies to identify and disable these pervasive threats to returnees. Another valuable data set was a NIMA imagery-derived assessment of damage to dwellings. The KRIS team brought in laptops loaded with GIS software and NIMA-supplied foundation data, and worked with UNHCR GIS experts. A particularly important UNHCR field staff contribution was the creation of standardized "place codes" to facilitate data collection. As the lead humanitarian agency under the UNMIK aegis, the UNHCR launched a rapid village assessment survey that used these "place codes" to georeference field data. Another operational innovation was the use of an agreed-upon assessment form and template that could be directly linked to a relational database, which, in turn, could interact with and be displayed through a GIS. These standardized assessments were used to produce an initial report on destruction, population returns, and other critical variables.[18] In addition, GIS-linked datasets were used to support the work of the newly established Kosovo Humanitarian Community Information Centre, which provides relevant data to the UN and NGO relief agencies working in the province.

Planning for Future Multilateral Responses

Traditionally, the international community has responded to humanitarian emergencies with relief efforts directed primarily at refugees. More recently, however, relief agencies are attempting to reach victims who remain within a country racked by war.[19] The UN has had some success in providing urgent relief supplies to stave off starvation and epidemics but has been less able to cope with causal factors and protecting internally displaced persons.[20] A report by the International Council of Voluntary Agencies criticized the UNHCR-led multilateral effort to assist Kosovar refugees for weak coordination among UN agencies, donor governments, and NGOs.[21] The likelihood of more destabilizing spillovers suggests the need for improved contingency planning and coordination prior to future missions, but such efforts have been easier to propose than to implement.[22]

Multilateral responses are now called upon to confront deep-rooted hostilities, curtail arms flows, strengthen democratic institutions, and address educational biases. Such ambitious objectives are now considered essential for the creation of a "culture of prevention."[23] In areas of mass atrocities, though, NGOs argue that political and militia leaders hinder their access to victims because relief agencies are viewed as obstacles to the elimination of targeted communities.[24] Refugee advocacy groups also claim that they can assist victims only if the international community acts firmly to support cross-border relief, initiate human rights monitoring, and, most important, protect those forcibly displaced, whether they stay in their country or leave. A more vigorous UN and/or regional response capability requires a longer-term investment in conflict prevention measures and a consistent "firm but fair" challenge to those committing atrocities.[25] Preventive diplomacy measures, though, need a well structured information base about the geopolitical and situational context of each crisis.[26]

GIS for Coordinated Responses

GIS capabilities, especially when enhanced with high-resolution imagery, have been well tested under a variety of civilian and military applications, but their use by agencies responding together to a complex emergency is relatively new. Kosovo was a promising test case, despite the unpredictable and complicated problems that arose because of the rapid returns, extensive damage, lack of winterization supplies, and continuing political problems. Both peacekeepers and civilian agencies involved in Kosovo now have improving computer-based information management capabilities. But these took many months to develop. The international community's challenge is to incorporate these new decision-making tools into a multilateral contingency planning process before the next crisis erupts.

NIMA's "humanitarian-planning map" established a critical geospatial foundation for other disparate types of crisis- and relief-related data. Such a GIS-based map must be developed quickly and accurately prior to the intervention so that emergency response agencies can focus on integrating just those data layers that are relevant to their mission and help with overall mission coordination. Unfortunately, such maps are often taken for granted and/or assumed to already exist when, more often, they do not exist at the scale required for multilateral response operations in remote areas – especially border regions where crises often erupt. For base maps to be truly useful, they need to be clearly organized, standardized, and fully GIS-compatible. Dynamic base maps must form the core of an information package that interveners bring with them because once they cross into a war-ravaged country, they will have their hands full with the crisis.

Regardless of its computing power, a GIS is only as good as the data it displays. While GIS technology is affordable, powerful, and user-friendly, it is still heavily dependent upon the accuracy and currency of the databases that support it and the skills of the people who use it. In most war-devastated countries, basic socioeconomic and population data are poor to begin with and, since they are usually collected under prewar conditions, they are literally overtaken by events and are usually out of date for repatriation requirements. Similarly, remote sensing imagery and other data are becoming increasingly more accessible via the Internet, but the volume of data online is not a good measure of success for complex emergency responses; rather, any GIS program should be judged by how well it manipulates relevant data layers to help answer tough cross-border mission problems.

GIS for Basic Needs

GIS tools can help organize the logistical requirements for effective and timely relief deliveries. A humanitarian crisis is largely defined by the immediacy of the threat to the lives of those affected. The scale of basic needs response – the provision of food, water, medicine, clothes, and shelter – is dependent upon the spatial extension of the emergency.[27] For example, famines can be the result of both a lack of food supply (from crop failures) or, often more important, the inability of victims – usually the rural poor – to buy available food. Indicators of such a crisis can be seen in changing agrarian conditions – the rising price of grain and the declining price of livestock (as farmers sell off herds that they can no longer afford to maintain). A local famine can best be ameliorated with food imported from the regional and national levels; a national famine usually entails an international response. When the famine has been fuelled by warfare and/or corrupt regimes, efforts to import donated food across an international boundary can become a highly charged and internationalized political problem. GIS tools can help to demonstrate the spatial extent and severity of a drought and resulting crop failures, changes in the price of food staples, and the locations of acutely malnourished communities (e.g., this was accomplished in Africa by the Famine Early Warning System). Such combinations of war and natural disasters, which have occurred almost annually in the Horn of Africa, can hit both subnational and transnational areas and can shift from year to year, thus requiring an international response strategy.

In complex emergencies, many victims are left with next to nothing (other than their determination) to help them survive under dangerous conditions. Over a million forcibly displaced Kosovars demonstrated this resolve during the dangerous months prior to their return following the NATO air campaign. While those who escape across a border are often provided better care and protection by the international community than are those who remain within their country, both refugees and internally displaced persons (IDPs) require basic provisions for survival.[28] At the peak of such a crisis, delays of hours and, more likely, days can take a high toll in lost lives. Clean water is often the most urgent supply problem. Closely following clean water come other basic needs requiring deliveries to often isolated and distant sites: food, sanitation facilities, rudimentary shelters, and vaccinations. Data about supplies and demands are often lacking and fluctuating. A well-prepared GIS package can be used to assess campsites, populations in need, health threats, border checkpoint bottlenecks, delivery supply routes, water sources, food stockpiles, and other critical data for multilateral operations.

GIS for Public Security

Unlike a natural disaster, where the biggest public security threat may be pillaging, human-made emergencies are made more problematic and dangerous by well-armed belligerents who all too often place a higher priority on diverting or stopping relief deliveries than on helping the people they claim to represent. Food becomes a weapon of war and a means of controlling people.[29] Loosely controlled militias can and do hijack relief trucks, kidnap relief workers, and steal food directly from relief victims. In many conflict zones there are no civilian police capable of providing protection to IDPs and residents. Despite a sizable KFOR presence in Kosovo, violence between ethnic Albanians and Serbs continued into 2000. Another major public security threat in many civil wars is landmines and unexploded ordnance. While a GIS can itself do nothing to curb ongoing violence, it can be used by peacekeepers to plan safe routes, locate illegal militia checkpoints, determine ceasefire lines, and, perhaps most important, delineate suspected landmine fields along military lines of control and porous international borders.

GIS for Political Dialogue

Since political confrontations underlie all complex emergencies, international responders must also include a process for negotiating a stable outcome. The more violent and deep-rooted the internecine conflict, the more difficult the challenge of reconciliation and the more arduous the negotiations for an acceptable power-sharing regime among armed antagonists. The hatred and distrust that flourishes in civil wars does not end with a ceasefire. Even with Kosovo's ethnic Albanian community there are tensions among political groups attempting to dominate local institutions and exclude those with different political objectives. Elections are an important element in the introduction of democratic institutions that can help overcome such alienation, but they are only a means and, unless carefully nurtured, can reinforce nationalistic tensions. GIS can be used to assist organizations that aim to encourage democratic practices by helping to organize data related to voter registration, electoral districting, and election results at the local and national levels. A GIS-based approach can be used to clarify territorial aspects of the underlying conflict and can be an important aid in looking at political solutions based on the creation of new and/or reconfigured subnational and/or international political jurisdictions, such as the Dayton peace talks.[30] Relevant data layers for such territorial redistricting might include population distribution, ethnic composition, economic ties, and transportation linkages. The downside for partition schemes, such as in Bosnia, is that they can be used by nationalist groups to reinforce ethnic segregation and to discourage the return of IDPs and refugees to areas where they would be the minority group.

GIS for Human Rights/Justice

Systematic human rights abuses, crimes against humanity, and even genocide have been closely identified with recent civil wars.[31] The vast majority of deaths in such wars are no longer soldiers on the battlefields but civilians who are often deliberately targeted. Ethnic cleansing is the process of forcibly expelling an ethnic group from its community; it can involve torture, massacres, methodical destruction of homes and places of worship, and, of course, the generation of large numbers of IDPs and refugees. GIS tools were used to analyze ethnic cleansing patterns in Bosnia based on data collected by several agencies, including the UNHCR, the International Committee of the Red Cross, and the International Criminal Tribunal for the former Yugoslavia.[32]

In civil war-prone countries, the rule of law and human rights principles are frequently ignored, and criminal gangs, often associated with militias, can wield life and death power. In Kosovo as many as 10,000 people may have been killed since 1998, most of whom would have been noncombatants. A GIS-based project for Kosovo included showing patterns of ethnic cleansing, identifying the locations and conditions of massacre sites, and estimating levels of destruction in war-ravaged communities.[33] GIS can help war crime prosecutors, truth commissions, and human rights investigators determine the physical dimensions of atrocities against civilians and the impact of those crimes on the landscape. It can also be used to help plan for the safe deployment of peacekeepers and human rights monitors, under the United Nations Security Council's Chapters 6 and 7 provisions, to violence-prone areas within the sovereign space of UN members.

GIS for Sustained Economic Development

The ultimate goal for multilateral emergency operations is to transform the conflict zone into a politically and economically stable country, with decreasing ethnic tensions and improving living conditions. All are long-term prospects and are difficult to achieve under the best of conditions. Political and economic conditions are interrelated, with positive and negative trends feeding back to affect the likelihood of democracy on the one hand or economic growth on the other. Economic development is difficult to catalyze and sustain in postconflict societies; foreign investment can be skittish, and legitimate business can be scared away by the institutionalized corruption that war encourages. Once basic needs are established, a country struggling to recover from the devastation of war needs considerable investment in reconstruction of destroyed homes, damaged energy, transportation, telecommunication infrastructure, and public health.

Kosovo, despite a large international presence, will likely continue to face problems with power outages, lack of building supplies, and weak economic prospects. A current relief-to-development project for Kosovo is using GIS tools to assess reconstruction requirements and priorities, from estimating the extent of housing damage to road and utility repairs. GIS can also be used to look at agricultural and resource extraction prospects: what lands can be returned to productivity most quickly and which natural resources might be tapped to generate revenues? It can also be used to look beyond the crisis country to regional markets and trading networks, which are vital to long-term development goals.

GIS for Multilateral Synergy
GIS is most effective as an "enterprise-wide" tool to improve planning and coordination among the five mission areas outlined above. While the interrelations among these goals are obvious, the international community's crisis response is often based on institutions with stove-piped information flows. Each institution is given a mandate to address a particular goal – such as supplying building materials or organizing elections – but is constrained in how it interacts with other institutions. From the perspective of the war victim, though, they need all of the above in varying levels. Victims need effective management and leadership that will produce an integrated approach that minimizes duplication of effort and maximizes efficient services. GIS can be used to institute "mission-wide" strategic planning and complementary relief, security, human rights, and development services. The first step is to establish a GIS-enhanced data-sharing regime among all the key actors responding to the crisis. The second is for such an information strategy to be used by the senior-most members of the multilateral operation. In Kosovo, such responsibility lies with the UN secretary general's special representative, who administers UNMIK. The daily challenge of implementing a strategic information plan then takes up the many intervening steps of collecting, organizing, analyzing, and sharing data related to operational objectives. The last step is arguably the most important: leaving the GIS-structured information system to the local and host nation institutions that will take over from the responders once they leave.

Conclusions
Poor planning and insufficient data sharing often weaken international responses to complex emergencies, which can be regionally destabilizing. As diplomats, peacekeepers, human rights monitors, and relief agencies continue to wrestle with the challenge of implementing peace operations, relief deliveries, and even civil administrations in war-ravaged areas, they will need to rely more on new geographic information technologies and

methodologies.[34] For inevitable complex future emergencies, the issue will not be what GIS is capable of but, rather, how it can be best applied to support effective collaborations before, during, and after responders deploy into the crisis zone.

Acknowledgments
The views in this chapter are those of the author and do not necessarily reflect those of the US government. This chapter is dedicated to the memory of Bradford L. Thomas, master cartographer and boundary scholar. It was originally published in *Geopolitics* 5, 1 (2000): 19-36 (reproduced with permission from Frank Cass Publishers).

Notes
1 I. Burton, R. Kates, and G. White, *The Environment as Hazard* (New York: Guilford Press, 1993).
2 P. Blakie, T. Cannon, I. Davis, and B. Wisner, *At Risk: Natural Hazards, People's Vulnerability and Disasters* (London: Routledge, 1994).
3 F. Cuny, *Famine, Conflict and Response: A Basic Guide* (West Bloomfield, CT: Kumerian Press, 1999).
4 D. Knight, "People Together, Yet Apart: Rethinking Territory, Sovereignty, and Identities," in *Reordering the World: Geopolitical Perspectives on the 21st Century,* 2nd ed., ed. G. Demko and W. Wood (Boulder, CO: Westview Press, 1999), 209-26.
5 K. Annan, *Towards a Culture of Prevention: Statements by the Secretary General of the United Nations* (New York: Carnegie Commission on Deadly Conflict, 1999).
6 J. Moore, ed., *Hard Choices: Moral Dilemmas in Complex Emergency Operations* (Lanham, MD: Rowman and Littlefield, 1998).
7 W. Wood, "From Humanitarian Relief to Humanitarian Intervention: Victims, Interveners and Pillars," *Political Geography* 15, 8 (1996): 671-95.
8 Bradford Thomas, "Lines in the Sand (and Sea)," in Demko and Wood, *Reordering the World,* 69-93.
9 L. Sohn, "Broadening the Role of the United Nations in Preventing, Mitigating or Ending International or Internal Conflicts That Threaten International Peace and Security," International Rule of Law Center, Occasional Papers, 2nd series, no. 1, The George Washington University Law School, Washington, DC.
10 National Defense University, "Beyond Jointness: The Civil-Military Dimensions of Peace Operations and Humanitarian Assistance," Institute for National Strategic Studies Symposium, 23 June 1999.
11 D. Lute, *Improving National Capacity to Respond to Complex Emergencies: The US Experience* (New York: Carnegie Corporation, 1998) (a report to the Carnegie Commission on preventing deadly conflict).
12 Global Disaster Information Network, *Harnessing Information Technology for Disaster Management* (Washington, DC: 1997).
13 M. Dziedzic and W. Wood, "Kosovo Brief: Information Management Offers a New Technology for Cooperation between Civilian and Military Entities as a Catalyst for Civil-Military Unity of Effort," *Virtual Diplomacy Series,* no. 9, United States Institute of Peace, Washington, DC, August 2000.
14 D. Martin, *Geographic Information Systems: Socioeconomic Applications,* 2nd ed. (London: Routledge, 1996); W. Wood, "Geography: A Lesson for Diplomats," *The Fletcher Forum of World Affairs* 23, 2 (Fall 1996): 5-20.
15 R. Greene, *GIS in Public Policy* (Redlands, CA: ESRI Press, 2000).
16 US Department of State, *Erasing History, Ethnic Cleansing in Kosovo* (Washington, DC: US Department of State, 1999).
17 S. Woodward, *Balkan Tragedy: Chaos and Dissolution after the Cold War* (Washington, DC: The Brookings Institute, 1995); W. Zimmermann, *Origins of a Catastrophe* (New York: Time Books, 1996); R. Holbrooke, *To End a War* (New York: Random House, 1998).

18 See some of these data at <http://www.reliefweb.int>; J. Bouchard, "Winning the Peace in Kosovo," *GEOEurope* (July 2000): 36-41.

19 A. Dowty and G. Loescher, "Refugee Flows as Grounds for International Action," *International Security* 21, 1 (1996): 43-71.

20 Moore, *Hard Choices;* "The Independent Evaluation of UNHCR's Emergency Preparedness and Response to the Kosovo Refugee Crisis," *Talk Back* 2, 1 (February 2000).

21 International Council of Voluntary Agencies, 2000.

22 D. Lute, *Improving National Capacity to Respond to Complex Emergencies: The US Experience* (New York: Carnegie Corporation, 1998) (a report to the Carnegie Commission on preventing deadly conflict).

23 Annan, *Towards a Culture of Prevention.*

24 Médecins Sans Frontières, *World In Crisis* (London: Routledge, 1997).

25 International Peace Academy, *Peacemaking and Peacekeeping for the Next Century* (New York: International Peace Academy, 1995) (Report of the 25th Vienna Seminar).

26 B. Jentleson, "Preventative Diplomacy and Ethnic Conflict: Possible, Difficult, Necessary," policy paper no. 27, University of California Institute on Global Conflict, 1996.

27 M. Wolde-Mariam, *Rural Vulnerability to Famine* (New Delhi: Vrikas Press, 1981).

28 United States Committee for Refugees, *World Refugee Survey* (Washington, DC, Immigration and Refugee Services of America, 1997).

29 Cuny, *Famine, Conflict and Response.*

30 M. Corson and J. Minghi, "The Political Geography of the Dayton Accords," *Geopolitics and International Boundaries* 1, 1 (1996): 77-92.

31 J. Stremlau, *People in Peril: Human Rights, Humanitarian Action and Preventing Deadly Conflict* (New York: Carnegie Corporation, 1998) (a report to the Carnegie Commission on preventing deadly conflict).

32 W. Wood and D. Smith, "Mapping War Crimes: GIS Analyzes Ethnic Cleansing Practices in Bosnia," *GIS World,* September 1997, 56-58.

33 US Department of State, *Erasing History: Ethnic Cleansing in Kosovo – An Accounting* (Washington, DC: US Department of State, 1999).

34 W. Wood, "Geography: A Lesson for Diplomats," *Fletcher Forum of World Affairs* 23, 2 (1999): 5-20.

17
Good Neighbour Diplomacy Revisited
Alan K. Henrikson

The nature of border relationships qualifies the overall relationship between member states in the international system. Without mutually acceptable relations across borderlands, satisfactory relationships between adjoining nations, including diplomatic relationships, may be almost impossible to achieve. Transboundary stability and border-area comity may thus be necessary conditions of wider international stability and comity. Is peace along international borders, however, also a sufficient condition of world peace? Can the amelioration of conditions along borders produce – actually, by itself, generate – global reconciliation, cooperation, "good neighbourhood"? In what circumstances might diplomatic strategies that are aimed at, across, and about borders begin to have such a transformative effect?

A diplomacy of *bon voisinage,* which might significantly contribute to peace between nations and in the world, would depend on the fulfilment of a number of major conditions. In this chapter I seek to identify what these are and to explain their causal importance. Let me state them briefly at the outset. The first is that the nations in question must "face," or consciously confront and also formally address, one another – the crucial issue here being whether the countries and their leaders are sufficiently oriented towards, and therefore attentive to, one another. Whether they thus emphasize and highlight their mutual relations may depend on the historically conditioned geopolitical orientations of the countries involved; that is, where the general population of each of the adjoining countries conceives the "front" and the "back" of that country to be. A "front"-to-"front" relationship is more likely to have diplomatic significance than is a "back"-to-"back" one, or even a "front"-to-"back" or "back"-to-"front" one.

A second requirement is that the two facing countries must be internally organized, constitutionally ordered, and socially connected in such a way as to allow the effects of positive transborder relations to flow throughout their respective national "bodies." At issue is not just whether the border area is transparent and permeable but also whether the remainder of each of the national societies involved can efficiently process, and beneficially absorb, what is transmitted at the border – the goods and services that may pass through as well as the ideas and the images conveyed. The very "picture," or visual landscape, of a border zone – natural features as well as border installations – helps to give content to a nation's view of its transborder and other relationships with a neighbouring country. It is a "lens" through which the other is seen. The more positive (physically and socially attractive) the borderscape on both sides, the better. "Positive"-"positive" imagery here is obviously to be preferred to "negative"-"negative," or "positive"-"negative" or "negative"-"positive." The border-area picture, whatever its character, must be socially communicated in order to be politically effective.

A third condition of successful bordering diplomacy, particularly to be emphasized in this chapter, is that the "skins" of countries – reflecting the geographer Friedrich Ratzel's notion of the boundary as the "peripheral organ" of a state[1] – should somehow be bonded, legally and even institutionally, to the political epidermises or borders of the countries adjacent. The key issue here is whether the mutual chafing that can occur at borders from discrepancies that exist between countries can be avoided by joint management. The effectiveness of most bilateral transborder relationships around the world can usually be reinforced by systems, bilateral or multilateral, of transfrontier cooperation. Such "internationalization" of border-area cooperation can create large common-border systems, like those now developing within the geographic area of the expanding European Union (EU). In most parts of the globe, however, this degree of amalgamation, with supranational controls, is not possible. Therefore, international diplomacy as opposed to supranational administration of border arrangements must be emphasized. Even in Europe, especially in the east and south, continued diplomatic attention to borders is warranted.

In most countries or regional groupings of countries there is an interplay between capital communities and border areas: between "centres" and "peripheries."[2] As is the case in Europe, where there is wider international involvement – particularly big-power or supranational-organization interest – in the making of local boundary arrangements, there may be different levels of centre/periphery forces at play. For convenience, those forces operating at the national level, within nations or directly between nations, will be noted as national-"central" (with a small "c") and national-"peripheral" (with a small "p"), and those of a wider scope as international-"Central" (with a capital "C") and international-"Peripheral" (with a capital "P").

Increasingly today, in negotiations concerning borderlands and cross-border issues, there is a complex involvement of national-level centres and peripheries – in the immediately juxtaposed or neighbouring countries – and Centres and Peripheries – representing factors in the larger international community. An examination of *bon voisinage*, or "good neighbour," diplomacy must take account of these multilevel dynamics. Border-focused diplomacy, to be successful, must coordinate the interests of centres and peripheries within and across national lines, and it must also respond to Central and Peripheral concerns (where they exist). At present, it is still usually the national-level relationships that are the dominant ones. Both of the central governments and also both of the peripheral communities that are involved must be able, in harmonizing their relations, to define a border-related dispute between them in terms of a common interest.

Two pairs of centres and peripheries are implicated under these circumstances, and these can interact, directly and indirectly, regardless of national lines. There can be "inter-State" transactions between the neighbouring countries (i.e., between central-government officials situated in their respective national capitals or perhaps meeting one another elsewhere). There can be "core-periphery" transactions between the central areas and border regions within each of the two countries, and also "frontier zone," or immediate cross-border, transactions. Finally, there can be "core-periphery adjacent State" transactions, involving some (limited) contact between the centre of one country and the periphery of the other.[3]

Even if these four actors actually do engage in active exchanges, they may vary in their attitudes and their responses. In order for successful border-based diplomacy to occur, all four of the actors (c's and p's) must recognize that such interchange, possibly to result in an international agreement, is advantageous to them, individually as well as collectively. So, too, if the larger international community is involved, should the major powers or leading organizations therein (the C's), and also the weaker but nonetheless influential powers (P's), appreciate the advantage that a particular border agreement may bring. For an international border accord to be perceived as fair and just, and for it to be implemented effectively, all four parties must concur. This outcome can be achieved more readily if there is a guiding concept to inspire and direct the diplomacy of international border making.

The Concept of "Good Neighbourhood"/*Bon Voisinage*

"In the field of world policy," declared Franklin D. Roosevelt in his first inaugural address as US president in March 1933, "I would dedicate this nation to the policy of the good neighbour – the neighbour who resolutely respects himself and, because he does so, respects the rights of others – the neighbour who respects his obligations and respects the sanctity of his agreements in and with a world of neighbours."[4]

Roosevelt's statement is echoed in the *Preamble of the Charter of the United Nations*, signed at San Francisco on 26 June 1945: "We the Peoples of the United Nations" express determination "to practice tolerance and live together in peace with one another as good neighbours."[5] The French-language text, always a little different, replaces "good neighbour" with "esprit de bon voisinage" (spirit of good neighbourliness).[6] Article 74 of Chapter 11, concerning Non-Self-Governing Territories, commits members of the UN holding such territories to respect, on the colonial periphery no less than in metropolitan international areas, "the general principle of good-neighbourliness, due account being taken of the interests and well-being of the rest of the world, in social, economic, and commercial matters."[7] The French text, almost identical, affirms *"le principe général du bon voisinage dans le domaine social, économique et commercial, compte tenu des intérêts et de la prospérité du reste du monde."*[8]

It is obvious from these historically celebrated and important international expressions of the good neighbourhood idea that the "policy," or "principle," of good neighbourhood is not a strictly defined legal concept. Nonetheless, certain distinct elements of the neighbourly spirit-idea are clear, the most basic being the notion of mutuality or reciprocity and of the equivalency of station and interchange. Neighbours are to be accepted as being equal and thus deserving of respectful regard when an action that might adversely affect them is being contemplated, just as if the shoe were on the other foot. Moreover, there is an implied acceptance of a commitment to tolerance of difference. Force must not be used to change things. There is thus a specific implication of non-interference in the internal affairs of others. Noteworthy also is the possible generality of the concept, its being considered as an important element in the development of "world" policy.

These were the meanings associated with the idea from the time of the Roosevelt administration's "Good Neighbour Policy." In practice, this policy was applied mainly to US relations with Latin American and Caribbean countries (i.e., the western hemisphere). At the Seventh Pan-American Conference in Montevideo, Uruguay, in December 1933 the American republics approved a Convention on the Rights and Duties of States, prohibiting intervention by any state "in the internal or external affairs of another." This expressed an absolute commitment to non-intervention. This pledge also had it origins in the dialectic of US-Latin American relations during the preceding Republican administrations.[9] As far back as February 1848, with the signature of the Treaty of Guadalupe Hidalgo on "Peace, Friendship, Limits, and Settlement" that ended the war between the United States and Mexico, the "good neighbourhood" (and presumably *buen vecindad*) phrase was used. Suggested by the Mexican delegation,[10] this mention is considered the locus classicus of the modern concept.[11]

The preamble to the Treaty of Guadalupe Hidalgo states that the United States and Mexico, as between themselves, would "establish upon a solid basis relations of peace and friendship, which shall confer reciprocal benefits upon the citizens of both, and assure the concord, harmony and mutual confidence, wherein the two Peoples should live, as Good Neighbours." Article 21 of the treaty provides specifically for what should and should not be done if "disagreements" arose. It stated that there must be no resort by either country to reprisals, aggression, or hostility "until the Government of that which deems itself aggrieved, shall have maturely considered, in the spirit of peace and good neighbourship, whether it would not be better that such difference should be settled by arbitration of Commissioners appointed on each side, or by that of a friendly nation."[12] The possibility, even then, of third-party or international involvement in the maintenance of bilateral US-Mexican relations is worthy of particular note.

The broader meaning of Roosevelt's 1933 use of the Good Neighbour expression, in its conceptual character and in its span of geographical application (into the realm of "world" policy), "has been lost," as Sumner Welles later commented.[13] Moreover, events of the early twenty-first century suggest that good neighbour diplomacy may become increasingly important under conditions of heightened insecurity along and across borders around the world. The present re-examination of the concept of good neighbourhood is an effort to recover some of the lost content of the idea in an age of globalization.

In truth, *bon voisinage* is not a practice that has been unknown to other parts of the world. The antecedents are many, but they have rarely been seen to serve a larger political purpose. The historical geography of Europe, which happens to have more kilometres of political boundary per unit of land than any other continent, is replete with examples of boundary cooperation. Most of these have been very localized. John House, for example, describes Europe's designation of parallel frontier zones of varying widths on either side of a border within which local residents are granted special customs and other privileges. Such zones, promoting small-scale frontier exchanges, have usually been negotiated bilaterally and are in the limited interest of the border residents.[14]

An illustrative historical case is the boundary arrangement contained in a 1926 commercial treaty between Hungary and Yugoslavia.[15] Its purpose was "to afford reciprocal traffic between the frontier zones the facilities required for daily needs," and, to that end, the text defined two ten-to-fifteen-kilometre border zones on either side of the line. The agreement enumerated the foodstuffs (e.g., fresh vegetables and milk) and other necessary items (e.g., firewood and building materials) that could be transported across the border without payment of duties. For the benefit of local-area farmers, it provided that fields could be tilled and livestock pastured on the other side of the boundary line. "Frontier permits" would also be issued to other persons who needed to cross the border regularly. Specific crossing places and times were designated. In urgent situations, frontier passes could be given out summarily. During emergencies such as floods, forest fires, or other widespread calamities, frontier residents were authorized "to cross the frontier by all routes by day or by night."

The 1926 Hungarian-Yugoslav treaty provided as well for some bilateral cooperation of an institutional kind. With a view to "ensuring mutual assistance" and to "creating between the frontier authorities on both sides the atmosphere of good neighbourliness," the chief officers of the two nations' frontier authorities were to meet regularly. Those officers were to "endeavour to remove any difficulties arising from incidents of slight importance and redress any grievances of the inhabitants of the frontier zones." This suggests different levels at which border-related diplomacy can be conducted, although the full international potential of good neighbour diplomacy is not yet recognized.

Three Levels of Border Diplomacy

A diplomacy of *bon voisinage* can occur at any or all of three levels. The first, and highest, level is "summit" meetings between national political leaders. These may include discussion of border-related matters and, not uncommonly, take place at border locations. Such sites at or near the political boundaries between countries may be seen as symbolically located, even if they are not exactly situated geometrically, midway between the two nations' capitals, making it possible for their leaders "to meet each other halfway." These meetings remain essentially centre-to-centre encounters, though the border setting highlights the two countries' contiguity.

The "halfway" sites chosen may not actually be at formal boundary lines but, rather, at the common edges of their respective spheres of control – geopolitical equilibrium points. Sometimes they are at military fronts, where armies meet. An example of this is the historic 1897 meeting spot of Napoleon and Alexander the First on a raft in the Neman River near Tilsit (now Sovetsk, on Russia's Kaliningrad Oblast border with Lithuania), where, between them, they divided European power. When leaders' meetings take place at settled borders of already recognized state domains, they can gain resonance. The border location enhances (as does the very boundary line) the concept of "equal sovereignty."

An example of a regular series of border-situated leaders' meetings, occurring within the North American context, are the encounters that, traditionally, have taken place at the border between the United States and Mexico when a new US president is elected. The *encuentro* that occurred in January 1981 between the American president-elect, Ronald Reagan, and the president of Mexico at the time, José López Portillo, illustrates the pattern. For Americans, this border powerfully defines the US-Mexican relationship. "Our friends south of the border" was the way President Reagan referred to the leaders and officials of Mexico (and even of other, more distant, Latin American nations). It is also worth noting that Reagan's actual "first trip out of the country" following his inauguration was "a get-acquainted meeting," as he termed it, with the prime minister of Canada, Pierre Elliott Trudeau.[16] This took place in Ottawa, the capital of Canada – a political centre, but also a location close to the northern border of the United States and, thus, perhaps from a Washington-centric perspective, also a peripheral location.

President Reagan's first instinct, as the new American leader, was to keep the fences of the United States mended with the nation's "friends" to the south and to the north. There happened to be a larger, longer-term policy purpose in his diplomatic design as well: to lay a basis of neighbourly understanding at the leadership level for negotiation of what he had termed, in November 1979, a "North American accord" – the germ of what became the North American Free Trade Agreement (NAFTA). As Reagan later recalled, he had long believed that "the largest countries" of North America should "forge a closer alliance and become more of a power in the world." A grouping of the United States with Mexico and Canada would be "to our mutual economic benefit," and the example of the three North American countries working together "might be able to help the Latin American countries help themselves." Reagan's notion of tripartite North American cooperation was deeply rooted in the concept of neighbourhood. His very term, "accord," suggests direct, heart-to-heart contact between nations. Revealingly, when he initially proposed the North American accord idea in 1979, he said: "It is time we stopped thinking of our nearest neighbours as foreigners."[17]

The second, or middle, level of the diplomacy of good neighbourhood is that which occurs through ministerial or subministerial contacts. These, too, are often regularized and may even be institutionalized. Besides ministries of foreign affairs such as the US State Department, there are other departments or agencies of national governments that may be interested in border-related policy matters. Not only commerce and immigration authorities but also those dealing with the environment, public health, and crime may be involved. In 1976, in order to coordinate the handling of US-Mexican relations across a broad institutional front, President Jimmy Carter and President López Portillo established a consultative mechanism. The following year a border subgroup was set up to study, and cooperate in the management of, common economic and social problems under the general oversight of the consultative mechanism.[18]

At this subsummit or, more generally, the intermediate level, there should also be included the continuing transactions of such treaty-based, binational or international commissions as have been established for the management of problems that may develop on borders, including the possible adjustment of the borderline itself. In the context of US-Mexican border relations there is the International Boundary and Water Commission (IBWC), dating from the 1848 Treaty of Guadalupe Hidalgo, and also a boundary water treaty of 1889. In the US-Canadian context, there is the International Joint Commission (IJC), created by the 1909 Boundary Waters Treaty. This has a somewhat broader purview.

The third, and lowest, level is the subnational level. "Diplomacy" at this level may be thought of as including consultations that take place directly across national lines between state (or provincial) and also municipal authorities. Discussions that occur between non-governmental or private-sector groups desirous of good-neighbourly relations also might be included. Examples are the US Southwest Border Regional Commission and, on the Mexican side, the Co-ordinating Commission of the National Programme for the Borders and Free Zones, both of which were set up in 1977.[19] To the extent that such entities are established not just for the purpose of advancing interests of the resident communities in the border areas but also for the sake of a wider comity between neighbouring countries, they can be understood to have a "political" purpose. This broader national-level, and even international, purpose may justify the non-strict use of the term "diplomatic" to describe the politically relevant portion of such interlocal representation and discourse.[20] "Citizen diplomacy" can exist if it is structured and also if it is strategic.

Local and National "Mending Walls": Consociative Peacemaking

Ideally, a political boundary between communities should be a "Mending Wall," to use the title of Robert Frost's widely known poem about boundary-keeping in New England.[21] Frost posited that, in "walking the line" between fields, physical neighbours could become, by virtue of their common effort of jointly maintaining a boundary line, neighbours in a further sense – together making a neighbourhood. Boundaries are, as a chief cartographer of the US State Department, Bradford Thomas, has written, the "mortar" that holds together, as well as delineates, "the giant mosaic" that is the global map.[22] To a degree, they are the "mortar" that binds the political world itself.

Conventional thought suggests that there are two basic strategies for making peace between communities: those of an associative kind and those of a dissociative kind. The former are based on the premise that removing barriers between hostile or suspicious parties will help to reconcile

them. The latter hold to the opposite assumption, that keeping antagonistic parties apart will reduce their antagonism and, in time, even
placate them. Here a third strategy, the "consociative," is proposed.[23] More
than just a combination of the first two strategies, it is based on the idea
that the interaction, and even actual linking, of societies at and across
boundaries in space, with the semi-permeable boundary zone working to
form as well as to define a relationship, is a key to peacemaking.[24]

There are "schools" of belief concerning this subject. Those of an idealistic turn of mind have tended to favour the associative approach, prefer-
ring boundaries that are "meeting places." A few writers, such as the
British geographer Lionel William Lyde (in 1915), have argued that boundary lines should be drawn where they can have an "assimilative" effect. He
went so far as to propose, during the First World War, that boundaries
should be "anti-defensive." He meant not only that boundaries should not
be highly fortified but also that they should be "identified with geographical features which are associated naturally with the meeting of peoples
and persons in the ordinary routine of *peaceful* intercourse."[25]

The dominant perspective on political boundaries, however, has surely
been the realistically minded assertion that boundaries are, by definition,
dissociative – or "dissimilative," in Lyde's lexicon. As a former geographer
of the US Department of State, Samuel Whittemore Boggs, pointed out in
1940, "To at least some degree they restrict the movements of peoples and
the exchange of goods, of money, even of ideas."[26] Much the same basic
outlook on boundaries is adopted by Stephen B. Jones. Taking issue with
Lyde's assimilationist argument, Jones declared: "Almost inevitably an international boundary offers some impedance to the circulation of people and
goods. Therefore there may be some advantage – other things being equal
– in locating a boundary in a zone where circulation is relatively weak."[27]
Earlier, Lyde's "academic idealism" had been criticized by the British
boundary maker Colonel Sir Thomas H. Holdich, who asserted that "the
first and greatest object of a national frontier is to ensure peace and goodwill between contiguous peoples by putting a definite edge to the national
political horizon, so as to limit unauthorized expansion and trespass."[28]

The trouble with both of these contending "schools" is that they do
not clearly recognize the essential relation between the associative and dissociative aspects of boundaries. A consociative border strategy integrally
connects these. Its essence is structured cooperation – spatial and functional. Consociatively connected countries are confederated in contiguity, so to speak, through formal and informal transborder linkages. The
human use of these joint structures, in day-to-day local dealings and in
wider transactions as well, can stitch foreign and even alienated countries
together. This style of politically conscious border-based exchange and
communication between countries may be called "consociative diplomacy."

The Relevance of Boundary Making Today

Generally, boundaries have been thought of as problems. As Jean Gott-mann has observed, "The record of history demonstrates that political limits in geographic space have been and remain a major source of tension and conflict."[29] The emphasis of the present chapter is, instead, on the potential role of political boundaries, including administrative regimes to control them, as *solutions* – as ameliorative factors in situations that might, otherwise, erupt in local or general recrimination and violence. "Border incidents," in other words, can lead to peace as well as to war. What is required is a new way of looking at boundaries – a way that will enable us to better accommodate the actively pacific roles that boundary lines and boundary systems can play.

In advancing this argument, however, one must acknowledge that there is a growing belief in some regions of the world, especially in Western Europe, that the very idea of boundary divisions is losing significance. Economic interdependence, social mobility, technological exchange, and communications flows – in a single word, globalization – have made the very notion of achieving such aims as security, prosperity, or liberty through better territorial partitioning seem to some unrealistic and unreasonable. Nonetheless, there has not been a complete revolution. The shock of 11 September 2001 – the terrorist attacks on the World Trade Center in New York and the Pentagon in Washington – has heightened feelings of vulnerability, even within and among otherwise strong societies.

A British diplomat, Robert Cooper, has argued that three different mentalities simultaneously exist in today's world: the premodern, which is essentially a tribal outlook, focused on ethnic identity and survival; the modern, which is fixated on the notions of nation-state and sovereignty and emphasizes territorial integrity; and the postmodern, which transcends political-territorial foundations and walls, and allows, even requires, openness to the outside.[30] Two-way transparency is seen as advantageous. For certain purposes, such as human rights advancement, even external intervention in a country's internal affairs may be welcomed.

The European Union (EU) has carried the notion of postmodernity the furthest. Within the EU, national sovereignties have, to some extent, been pooled. Among the allies of the North Atlantic Treaty Organization (NATO) too, there has been a certain joining of vital national interests in a way that reduces the importance of boundaries. Article 5 of NATO Allies' Washington Treaty (1949) affirms, remarkably, that "an armed attack against one or more of them in Europe or North America shall be considered an attack against them all."[31] The countries in the European and Euro-Atlantic sphere, and to some degree their nearby neighbours as well, as *The Economist* observed in a comment on Cooper's conceptual scheme, now operate "in a system that encourages mutual interference in each other's domestic affairs and invites constraints and surveillance in military affairs," and increasingly in other areas of policy as well.[32]

Postmodernism does not mean, however, that boundaries are obliterated. They are, rather, becoming more differentiated. Their functions are now more various. Some borders themselves are becoming extended. Countries located along or amidst oceans now in most cases have wider national maritime boundaries than they did before.[33] The sea frontiers of the world are today much more inclusive and complex than they once were. For small island states, however, the vast spatial enlargement is an enormous complication, for it entails increased national administrative responsibility and diplomatic involvement with neighbours and others.

So numerous, layered, and diversified have boundary arrangements become that, as Bradford Thomas suggests, they cannot, as before, even be graphically delineated on the map: "'Full international boundaries,' those boundaries agreed by the two states being separated, came to have relatively uniform functions and be represented by a single symbol on the world political map." Departures from that symbol "represented not a change in function but such differences in legal status as disputed boundaries, cease-fire lines, and provisional administrative lines." Today, however, "changing concepts of territorial sovereignty and even of the state are bringing more variation in the functions of international boundaries and a tendency for decline in the number or level of functions a boundary may perform. A single 'international boundary' symbol no longer will suffice for the world political map."[34] Boundaries of "postmodern" economic and political communities (such as the EU is becoming), or even the common outer limits of merely "modern" bilateral or multilateral international free trade areas (such as Canada, the United States, and Mexico have together formed with their NAFTA) should perhaps be drawn on the political map. They are certainly now parts of most Europeans' and North Americans' "mental maps."[35] Particularly since the events of 9/11 there has been an increased consciousness among Europeans and North Americans of their continental "perimeters." The EU member states and the NAFTA countries thus could be represented as collectivities or groupings as well as individual nations.

Within some countries too, certain lines of division, including premodern ones, might need to be drawn in order better to indicate current and changing realities. The disintegration of the Socialist Federal Republic of Yugoslavia is an example of an ethno-national dialectic that has taken clearer and clearer linear form. To be sure, the Yugoslavian administrative borders that have emerged as interstate boundaries have not, except in the case of the Croatia-Slovenia interrepublican line, conformed well to the actual ethnographic map. As conveniences, however, they have been used as the basis of what have become in some cases international frontiers.[36]

There must be a better way to make as well as to represent boundaries between countries – a way that will help to resolve international tensions and engender peaceful and productive relations. As indicated earlier, there are three basic conditions that an effective peace-through-bordering, or good neighbour, diplomacy may need to fulfil. It is to these that we now turn.

Geographical Confrontation and Diplomatic Attention

The first premise of effective transborder[37] diplomacy, as suggested at the outset of this chapter, is that, in order for border relations to bring larger intercommunal or, if between sovereign parties, international peace, the political actors, seated in their respective territories, must think of themselves as "facing," or geopolitically confronting and also directly addressing, one another. Indeed, the very word "frontier," derives from the Latin word *frons*, which means "forehead." Thus an anthropomorphic factor is built into the very idea of international relations at and across frontiers.

The orientation of a country is a very complex matter, involving not only geography itself but also history and culture as well as, more specifically, a country's foreign policy traditions and habitual style of diplomacy. Nonetheless, certain fundamental things can be said. Any geographic space is altered by the conscious outlook of the human intelligence, individual and collective, residing in the corporeal entity, or "body," of the people occupying it. As Immanuel Kant wrote long ago, "our geographical knowledge, and even our commonest knowledge of the position of places, would be of no aid to us if we could not, by reference to the sides of our bodies, assign to regions the things so ordered and the whole system of mutually relative positions."[38] The geographer Yi-Fu Tuan epitomizes this Kantian psycho-geographical perception as follows: "The human being, by his mere presence, imposes a schema on space."[39] That is to say (generalizing from a single person to a part or the whole of a society), the way a community "faces" makes an area, whether a linear border zone or a broader territory ahead, a "front."

The basic point, in the present context, is a deceptively simple one: in order to negotiate effectively with another country, a country must *face* that country. It is only thus that a vista of opportunity can be opened up, which an entire society as well as its leadership can "see." And, of course, the diplomatic confrontation should be mutual: the neighbouring country must "see" these vistas, too. As suggested earlier, "front"-"front" negotiations, though not the only ones possible, are the most likely to result in breakthroughs for peace.

Some contiguous, or nearly contiguous, countries "face" each other, and others do not. Some peripheral zones in Europe, particularly those marginal territories between the great state-building cores, have been termed "interface peripheries."[40] The historical relationship between France and

Germany, fraught with fear as well as familiarity, is an example of a genuine face-to-face dialectic, and it may be used to illustrate the above-mentioned point. Following the Second World War, hundreds of communities within France and Germany joined in bilateral cooperative relationships, notably *jumelage,* or twinning, pacts. At the highest level of national leadership too, direct transborder politics were emphasized, for symbolic as well as for substantive reasons.

One can cite, at the personal leadership level, the roles of the French foreign minister, Robert Schuman, and the German chancellor, Dr. Konrad Adenauer, both Rhinelanders, in constructing the postwar French-German relationship, including the European Coal and Steel Community (ECSC), partly on the basis of their own commonly experienced neighbourhood. Indeed, their approach to reconciliation was more than neighbourly: it was consociative. It was aimed at joining their countries geo-functionally. When Schuman visited Bonn for the first time as foreign minister in January 1950, he said that "when one day the history of our time and its problems is written, it will be recognized that we attempted an important piece of work here on the Rhine, our Rhine, the German and French Rhine, this river that is one entity despite all national frontiers."[41]

Countries that are larger and geopolitically more detached, such as the United States on its transcontinental base in North America, have somewhat more freedom of orientation. The United States can "face" Europe, towards which it was originally and traditionally oriented.[42] Or, alternatively, it can swing towards the Asia-Pacific region, focusing on challenges there. In so doing, it "turns its back" on the Old Country. To be sure, it is probably still the northeastern seaboard of the United States, for most of its history the main gateway for imports and immigration, that is considered by most Americans to be the nation's "front."[43] Nonetheless, the geopolitical constraints on Uncle Sam are not so great as to prevent a shifting of the national "geobody" towards other horizons.

The smaller countries of North America, Mexico, and Canada are weaker and more vulnerable, and cannot so easily turn away from their immediate neighbourhood – and neighbour. In the words of President Porfirio Díaz, "Pobre México, tan lejos de Dios y tan cerca de los Estados Unidos" (Poor Mexico, so far from God and so close to the United States). For Mexicans, the Colossus of the North simply cannot be ignored. Thus, whether or not to "face" the US is not really an option. Mexico's northern frontier is the place where most of the exchanges with the US occur. It is thus not surprising that former Mexican foreign minister Rosario Green, in her initial ministerial address, accepted responsibility for coordinating "los diversos aspectos de la relación compleja e intensa con los Estados Unidos de América, vecino geográfico, socio comercial y con quien compartimos la mayor de nuestras fronteras" (the diverse aspects of the complex and intense relationship with the United States of America, geographic neighbour, commercial partner and with whom we share the largest of our frontiers).[44] Her counterpart, Canada's then foreign minister Lloyd Axworthy, also described the preservation of the "world's longest border" relationship with the US as a priority: "The Canada-US border is a potent symbol of the enduring partnership between our two countries," he wrote. "It is symbolic of the many ties that link our citizens and our destinies. Much more than a simple dividing line, our common border is a model of trust, mutual respect and cooperation between our two nations."[45]

It is unlikely that any US secretary of state at any time in American history would have so emphasized the management of relations with neighbouring Mexico or Canada. Geopsychologically, those two next-door countries lie somewhat to the "left" or "right" of the main course of American concerns, depending on which way the US happens to be facing – towards Europe or towards Asia. "In our experience as mobile animals," writes Yi-Fu Tuan, "front and back are primary, right and left are secondary."[46] To the extent that American society is similar to individual persons in its psychology of spatial orientation, it requires a "turn" for US authorities, at the national headquarters in Washington, to address relations with either Mexico or Canada head-on, "frontally," with full attention. Except on rare occasions, as during the Reagan administration (which was exceptional in its initial North American continental-policy interest) or the George W. Bush administration in its early days (when it was focused on Mexico), those countries tend to be dealt with "sideways," as a consequence of US officials' major foreign policy attention being directed across the Atlantic or the Pacific. Indeed, Canadian officials, especially, have often complained about being "sideswiped" by US policies that have, as their primary focus, some other part of the world.

The US's great counterpart, Russia, has scarcely been in direct contact with the US at all. Historically, the US and Russia have seemed to be on opposite sides of the globe. This changed somewhat during the Cold War, when the geostrategic attention of Soviet and US planners came to be focused on the Arctic zone. When Uncle Joe (Stalin) and Uncle Sam, as personifications of the two countries, faced each other at the top of the globe, as in a 1947 cartoon by the *Washington Post*'s Herbert Block, the geographical context ("One World") of their political confrontation was a vast territorial, maritime, and aerial expanse.[47] The High North strategic frontier, vitally important in defence, had very little transformative potential for the Russian and American nations in general, however, for it was "watched" mainly by the military, a specialized subculture. Only large-scale economic development, including the projection of shipping and air transport routes into the relatively inaccessible though resource-rich circumpolar zone – an "Arctic Mediterranean," as some fancied it – might have caused widespread Russian and American ties to form themselves into a transarctic international "neighbourhood."[48] As it was, the only immediate Russian-US boundary "interface" was between Big Diomede Island (Ostrov Ratmanova) and Little Diomede Island in the Bering Strait.

National Organization and Internal Transmission

Besides the requirement that countries must "face" each other in order for an improvement of transborder relations to have a pervasive effect throughout their societies, there is a second condition that, as has been suggested, needs to be met: that the physically juxtaposed societies be organized internally in such a way as to enable relevant information and imagery from the border areas to be communicated to the centre and around the rest of the country. The country must work cybernetically.[49] The national "body" must be well articulated. It must have a solid skeleton – that is to say, a strong constitutional-political framework as well as a sound transportation infrastructure grid. It must have an efficient digestive, or economic, system so that internal flows of goods and services occur without price discrimination or other distorting effects. It must have a responsive nervous system as well, so that impulses from the periphery are transmitted freely and throughout the whole society. The effectiveness of transfrontier diplomacy requires that border zones and their populations must be adequately represented at the centre, or at least have sufficient communication with it. The capital or, more broadly, the national government must have some presence in, or at least good correspondence with, the border areas. The importance of the internal "structure" of a country in shaping its external geographical relationships, as Jean Gottmann noted, has not been well recognized.[50]

An example of how things can go wrong, even in a democratic country where centre and periphery may be assumed to be mutually responsive, may be seen in the furor that resulted from an exchange of notes (conducted "in secrecy," or so it seemed to some critics of the action)[51] by the governments of the United States and the Soviet Union in 1977 with regard to the US-Soviet maritime boundary. Since the US purchase of Russian Alaska in 1867, this sea frontier had for the most part remained vaguely defined. In 1977, when establishing 200-nautical-mile fisheries conservation zones, both governments understood they would mutually have to respect, and be limited by, the 1867 Convention Line. There was considerable uncertainty regarding the exact location of the new fisheries limits, however, owing to a technical difference in the way the two governments depicted the 1867 Convention Line cartographically. The Soviet government showed it as a series of rhumb (compass) lines and the US government showed it as a series of great circle arcs. This produced a vast area of overlap in the Bering Sea of almost 21,000 square nautical miles.

Already there had been fisheries enforcement problems, and these became more difficult.

A formal US-Soviet Maritime Boundary Agreement resolving the dispute, essentially by splitting the difference between the competing claims, was signed on 1 June 1990 at a Washington summit meeting.[52] The treaty still has not gone into effect, however, because the Russian side, with the Duma refusing to give its consent, has not been able to ratify it. There is continued pressure for the cross-boundary exploitation of resources and also for their conservation, resulting from the belief of US-based fishers that Russian (and Russian-licensed) fishers take too many juvenile pollock, thus depleting the stock.

The controversy has helped to draw attention not merely to the 1990 treaty but also to an executive agreement that soon afterward accompanied it. The latter understanding was effected by an exchange of notes between US secretary of state James A. Baker and Soviet foreign minister Eduard Shevardnadze. It committed the two sides to abide by the terms of the 1990 treaty until it came into force. Although State Department and other federal officials dutifully conferred with the governor of Alaska and his colleagues in Juneau, it seemed to some Alaskans that the whole arrangement had been negotiated at a distance, without sufficient input from them. Partly in response to this local feeling, Representative Don Young (R., Alaska), as well as some other members of the US Congress, protested against the executive agreement "giveaway" of oil and gas resources as well as fish. They requested more information from the administration and insisted that any boundary-and-resources agreement with the Russians be validated in treaty form only.[53] Alaskans were not alone. Fishing and other interests in the Pacific Northwest state of Washington were also involved. The legislature of California, apparently fearing that, if the federal government could ignore one state in negotiating international maritime boundary agreements, then it could ignore California as well, passed a resolution in support of Alaska's right to be represented in US-Russian boundary talks.[54] Thus, in both countries, the importance of central-peripheral coordination in the making of diplomacy affecting the national domain has been demonstrated.

The US-Canada maritime frontier has also been the scene of controversy, most recently over salmon fishing. In both the United States and Canada, peripheral interests – including Aboriginal groups with "premodern" rights – have been at odds not just with each other, as fishing competitors, but also with their respective national centres, the federal governments in Washington and Ottawa. At issue has been the setting of quotas for the two countries under the 1985 Pacific Salmon Treaty. Pacific salmon hatch in rivers in the United States and Canada, then go to sea, and eventually return to their native rivers to reproduce, migrating down the coast from Alaska to Oregon. In 1997 a flotilla of Canadian fishers at Prince Rupert, BC, forcibly blockaded an Alaska ferry in protest against the intercepting of too many of "their" fish by Alaskan fishers. The Province of British Columbia's populist premier, Glen Clark, threatened to deny the US Navy continued use of a torpedo test range in Nanoose Bay off the BC coast over this issue. His provocative expressions prompted the Canadian federal government to assert national jurisdiction. Accordingly, the Canadian fisheries minister, David Anderson, negotiated with the US government for a new quota regime (even if not a perfect "salmon peace"). The US-Canadian salmon agreement, concluded in June 1999, set future quotas according to the scientific basis of abundance rather than according to equity. The US side, whose share of the total Pacific salmon harvest was expected to drop from 20.5 percent to 16.5 percent, promised to contribute funds for salmon population restoration. Secretary of State Madeleine Albright and Foreign Minister Lloyd Axworthy commented in a joint statement, implicitly acknowledging the centre-periphery and periphery-periphery tensions that existed, that the new arrangement "represents a victory for all those on both sides of the border interested in salmon conservation and the long-term viability of our salmon industries."[55]

With regard to the southwestern border of the United States, too, there have been serious disjunctions between federal authority and local action. At the centre in Washington there have often been considerations of policy, regarding relations with the government of Mexico within an international relations context, that do not have much bearing on the lives of those American and Mexican citizens who live at the border. The interplay of broader federal-level policy initiatives can be stressful for border communities. A recent example is the US government's post-September 11 global "War on Terror," which has given President Bush an excuse to suspend consideration of the proposal made by Mexico's president, Vicente Fox, for the free movement of labour between the two countries, leading perhaps to a North American common market. As John House, in his study of the problem of inadequate coordination between centre and periphery in managing border relations between the United States and Mexico, observed, "It will be entirely within the verdict of history if all decision-making continues to be centralized in Washington DC and México DF, whether or not this may be to the detriment of the dwellers on both banks of the Rio Grande."[56]

In the southeastern corner of the United States as well, tensions have arisen from the different perspectives of federal capital and local community interests. Florida is only 144 kilometres from Cuba, from which many present-day Floridians have fled. An example of centre-periphery misunderstanding in this setting is the strong opposition of many anti-Castro

"Miami Cubans" to former president Bill Clinton's decision, expressed in a joint communiqué with the government of Cuba on 9 September 1994, to revise the status of fleeing Cubans under the Cuban Adjustment Act, 1966. Accordingly, all Cubans subsequently coming into the United States were no longer presumptively to be treated as political refugees but were, rather, to considered to be ordinary immigrants, without assurance of automatic admission to the United States.

A general "key," if one such salient factor exists, to solving problems of internal coordination between centre and periphery in dealing with neighbouring countries, may be found in consociative diplomacy. Ways need to be found to somehow bridge the wide gap that usually exists between central government and peripheral areas on *both sides* of a dividing line. Local communities and even individual states, or provinces, usually lack the power, in themselves, to command attention as anything like "equal" partners in national decision-making regarding relationships with neighbours. At home, within their own country, they are often just one periphery among many. They may need to concert their efforts and combine their weights, *transnationally,* with the border community with which they have a direct interface and proximate interests. This can be done with interstate, interprovincial, and even somewhat broader interregional "alliances," including public-private partnerships, that extend across national lines.

International Agreements and Transfrontier Cooperation
The third condition for a successful "peace-through-neighbourhood" strategy, as indicated, is the international one. There can be agreements across borders, including not only bilateral pacts but also, where relevant, multilateral pacts affecting whole international regions, which advance and support transfrontier relationships. These agreements, because they join pairs or groups of countries formally, can enhance international stability and serve as a basis of confidence for transactions of economic and other kinds. They are legal commitments. They are to be taken seriously because they are binding. In particular, treaties that include good neighbourhood, or *bon voisinage,* provisions joining countries together via cooperative border arrangements are needed not only to symbolize but also to actually secure "close" relations between contiguous nations.

In the part of the world of the original good neighbour policy there have been many occasions for the practice of transfrontier diplomacy, sometimes resulting in formal accords. The New World, born in intercolonial rivalry with a plurality of premodern heritages, is notorious for its territorial and boundary disputes.[57] Some of the notable ones have been those between Bolivia and Paraguay, Peru and Colombia, Haiti and the Dominican

Republic, Guatemala and British Honduras, and Peru and Ecuador (a recurrent conflict that, in 1995, again broke out in open warfare). In every one of these cases, the peace machinery of the Inter-American System, a moral-legal framework, was used to help contain and resolve the controversy.

The Peru-Ecuador case is unusual in that a number of the hemisphere's great powers were directly involved as guarantors of a settlement – functioning as a kind of "Western Hemispheric Centre." The effective instrument was the Peruvian-Ecuadorian Protocol of Peace, Friendship, and Boundaries signed in Rio de Janeiro in 1942 both by the disputants and by Argentina, Brazil, Chile, and the United States. Brazil has been the leader of the guarantors group. The controversy was not completely settled in 1942, in part because of specific alignment disagreements (termed *impases*) concerning several sectors of the Rio Protocol boundary line.[58] After further fighting in 1981, in 1984, and in 1995, the matter was finally resolved in an agreement – the Brasilia Presidential Act – signed by Peru's and Ecuador's presidents under Brazilian auspices on 26 October 1998. This new treaty was "sealed" and put into effect not in Brazil but on the frontier itself on 13 May 1999, at the border town of Puesto Cahuide. Peru's president, Alberto K. Fujimori, and Ecuador's president, Jamil Mahuad, met there, shook hands, and ceremoniously dedicated an orange-painted boundary stone. This was the last of the settings marking the border, and it completed the boundary gestalt, so to speak, spatially and temporally. "Here is the final frontier [boundary] between two neighbouring peoples that managed to come together and reach agreement," declared President Fujimori. "We are putting an end to disputes," said President Mahuad, "closing wounds to start a new, healthy life."[59] Photographs and other recordings publicized the event throughout Peru and Ecuador, Latin America, and the world.

In its substance, the Peru-Ecuador border agreement might not have been possible but for the two countries' acceptance of an arbitration decision rendered by the Brazil-chaired guarantors – the Centre. The agreement was a "package deal." It collectively settled all of the issues assigned to binational commissions dealing with commerce and navigation, with border integration, with confidence-building measures, and with on-site border demarcation. A vital element of the package was Ecuador's final acceptance in principle of the 1942 Rio Protocol's line of division, which had precluded it from being an "Amazon" (and thus Atlantic) country as well as a Pacific coastal country. This favoured Peru, though Ecuador did actually gain a square kilometre of private – not formally sovereign – territory on the Peruvian side of the border. This symbolic piece of real estate, at Tiwinza on top of the Cordillera del Condor, was the site of Ecuador's last military holdout against Peru in the 1995 war. The place was to be consecrated by a monument to the country's war dead. The other key element was Ecuador's gaining navigation rights, again without sovereign access, to the Amazon River and its tributaries in Peru, along with two trading centres thereupon. The treaty further provided for establishment, by both countries, of a transborder ecological park across which transit would be guaranteed and within which no military forces (only police) would be allowed.[60] In separate understandings, the two countries also planned to link up their electrical grids; and Peru agreed that Ecuador, an oil producer, could have access to one of its underutilized pipelines.[61]

The "incentives" for this border accord were both national and international. Each country would save in terms of defence expenses and the cost of human lives. It was clearer than ever before to both Peru and Ecuador that mending fences between themselves was a de facto precondition of their being accepted, by other hemispheric countries, in a broader neighbourhood of international cooperation. This included involvement with the trading group, MERCOSUR, as well as some $1.5 billion in international loans for future development of the two countries' poorer regions (a loan that was on offer from the Centre).[62] The internal and external attractions of the agreement were such that it could be observed from afar that "South America may, for the foreseeable future, in 1995 have seen its last war over territorial claims."[63]

The eastern hemisphere, too, is progressing towards peace on and via boundaries. A major factor in this process is the Final Act of the Conference on Security and Cooperation in Europe (CSCE), signed in Helsinki on 1 August 1975. While neither a peace treaty between the Second World War adversaries nor a formal legitimization of the basic Cold War geographic division of Europe, the Helsinki Final Act, with thirty-five initial signers, was a fundamental commitment to the principle of the "territorial integrity" of states – a precondition, though not of itself the essence, of "good neighbourhood." Recognizing that frontiers can be modified in accordance with international law, by peaceful agreement, the act also solemnly declares: "The participating States regard as inviolable all one another's frontiers as well as the frontiers of all States in Europe and therefore they will refrain now and in the future from assaulting these frontiers." There was an affirmative, or constructive, aspect to their commitment as well. Under the rubric of "co-operation among States," the participants in Helsinki stated that they would "endeavour, in developing their cooperation as equals, to promote mutual understanding and confidence, friendly and good-neighbourly relations among themselves, international peace, security and justice."[64]

Subsequently there was concluded, originally with a focus on Western Europe, a European Outline Convention on Transfrontier Cooperation between Territorial Communities or Authorities. It was negotiated under the auspices of the Council of Europe at a meeting in Madrid on 21 May

1980.[65] This master framework text authorizes agreements for cooperation between neighbouring *non-central* authorities in such fields as urban and rural development, protection of the environment, improvement of public facilities and services, and mutual assistance in case of emergencies. It is aimed especially at improving conditions in the "frontier regions." Those of Eastern Europe – Europe's great regional "Periphery" – were now politically accessible as well. Thus the convention could contribute to "the spirit of fellowship which unites the peoples of Europe."

Even more recently in Europe, just following the collapse of the USSR and the reunification of Germany, there seemed a need to intervene to stabilize relations among, especially, the smaller European states in the East, which had been held together firmly, and even forcibly, by the Warsaw Treaty Organization. The government of France proposed a treaty that would be not an assistance pact but, rather, a kind of code of conduct for countries wishing to join the Western institutions, particularly the European Union. In April 1993 the French premier, Edouard Balladur, proposed an international conference, on the model of Europe's past great international conferences, to realize the French aim. The Balladur Initiative resulted in the Pact on Stability in Europe of March 1995. Taken up by the EU, the Stability Pact idea, though watered down somewhat in both its organizational and its funding implications, was important as an initial Joint Action of the EU's Common Foreign and Security Policy (CFSP). The Organization for Security and Cooperation in Europe (OSCE), successor to the CSCE, was to administer the pact.

A major emphasis of the Stability Pact, an international-Centrally (capital C) driven project, was a consolidation of frontiers. Balladur's original idea of suggesting possible minor frontier rectifications was dropped as likely to open a Pandora's box. It was, perhaps, considered too "modern" an approach to territorial problems. Nonetheless, international-Peripheral (capital P) states wishing benefits, including possible future organizational membership, were to reaffirm their commitment to the inviolability of frontiers and to make agreements between themselves pledging good neighbourliness. In addition, they were asked, in appropriate cases, explicitly to acknowledge the rights of national minorities in their midst, a controversial international recognition of the concept of collective rights.

A notable example may be found in the sizable Hungarian minority in Romania, along the border area with Hungary and in interior Transylvania. In consequence of the Balladur Initiative, there was negotiated a Treaty on Understanding, Co-operation and Good Neighbourly Relations between Romania and the Republic of Hungary. This included minority protections as well as a mutual recognition of the boundary. National minorities were recognized as "integral parts" of the societies in which they lived, and "territorial claims" were forever disavowed. Signed on 16

September 1996 in Romania (near the Hungarian border) at Timisoara, considered the cradle of the 1989 Romanian democratic revolution (in which many ethnic Hungarians participated), this was a politically complicated but psychologically greatly needed accord.[66] Hungary's prime minister, Gyula Horn, went to Timisoara to sign it. This was his first trip to Romania since he had taken office more than two years before. The Hungarian-Romanian treaty is one of the most important of the more than 100 such bilateral agreements facilitated by the Balladur Initiative and the ensuing Stability Pact in Europe.

In most of these cases, the existence of an international political-juridical framework worked together with the enticement of eventual membership in the EU and also in NATO to encourage countries in Eastern Europe to set aside their historical grievances against their neighbours. Formal bilateral agreements, promising good neighbourliness, by themselves would not have been sufficient to initiate processes of real reconciliation, if only because the countries of that region had historical recollections of the failure of such agreements during the interwar period and the later "fraternal" Soviet era.[67] In this context, the CSCE and EU initiatives, along with the more specifically frontier-oriented programs of the Council of Europe, have helped to give shape, if not all the requisite emotional content, to a new general movement of European fence mending.

Conclusion

How significant are these peace-via-borders international arrangements? Are they likely to prove to be effective in engendering further bilateral processes of reconciliation and, more generally, the spread of a spirit of regional good neighbourhood? Are they, in short, relevant today, given that they emphasize action at the level of the nation-state, or modernity, and may not take adequate account either of premodern ethnicity issues or of the future prospect of postmodern, postinternational integration on the global plane? Maybe the very idea is anachronistic.

The upshot of the matter seems to be that borders, though their technical functions and policy contours are changing, are as important as ever. In Europe the 1985 Schengen Agreement (named after a town on the Moselle in Luxembourg bordering France and Germany) has progressively lifted internal border controls within the common area of the participating countries while at the same time providing for tight coordination of controls at their external borders as well as for concerting visa policies and asylum procedures. A computerized Schengen Information System gives police and immigration officials a database to assist in regulating entry into "Schengenland." However, the signers of the Schengen Agreement, not wishing to be exclusive, have agreed on the harmonization of visa arrangements with some 160 countries around the world, and they are still extending the list.

In North America, the Schengen Agreement Area has been considered as a possible model for harmonization of Canadian and US border controls. Especially since the traumatic events of 9/11, which generated border grid-lock at a number of major crossing points, there has been increased interest in Schengen-type visa controls at the two countries' North American "perimeter" and also in smart-card technology, which would enable speedier passage of vehicles, cargo, and persons across the internal Canadian-US border. We have got to stop viewing the border as a "thing," said George Haynal, a former senior Canadian civil servant involved in coordinating North American policies, and start seeing it as a "shared asset."[68] The greatest difficulty will come in sharing this asset, directly and indirectly, with the world.

To be sure, the processes of "globalization" would seem to be indifferent, or even hostile, to borders. "But it is almost as though international politics obeyed some strange principle of the conservation of finitude," *The Economist* speculatively observes. "As some borders fall, so others rise."[69] In Europe, in particular, one has seen that, as internal restrictions on the flow of goods, capital, and persons within the EU itself are being removed, pressures increase for greater controls at the outer margins of the expanding EU. Some relatively new EU members, such as Austria, that, in the past, had quiet border towns on their frontiers, have found themselves on the administrative front lines for Europe generally. This has increased the need for the EU "to arrive at more coherent frontier region policies."[70]

The signing of the EU Treaty of Accession in Athens on 16 April 2003, by ten additional countries (which increased the membership of the EU to twenty-five in May 2004), has made these policies even more important. "Within our borders, which today stretch further, we have established peace," stated European Commission president Romano Prodi at the ceremony in Athens. "But we need to develop a ring of friends around us, a circle of friendly nations on our borders, stretching from Morocco, along the southern shores of the Mediterranean and up along the eastern confines of our Union to Russia. With this ring of neighbours and friendly countries we intend to share all the benefits of the Union that contribute to stability and prosperity. All except our institutions."[71]

In this context, formal diplomacy of the kind that produced the Hungarian-Romanian Treaty on Understanding, Co-operation, and Good Neighbourly Relations can assume a new importance not just as fulfilment of a *conditio sine qua non* for membership in the EU but also as a practical basis for closer community, based on reciprocity, in the region of cohabitation itself (regardless of whether or when EU membership comes). The Timisoara treaty and others like it must actually be used. Even though these treaty arrangements may be endowed, in institutional terms, with little more than joint intergovernmental committees and thus may lack

strong methods or means of implementation, they do constitute significant international assurances of stability. If national minorities across borders, such as the Magyars in Transylvania, do remain safely in place owing
in part to these basic treaties, then these groups will be in a position, especially as borders become more open, to realize "their most progressive
endeavour," which is to be "a bridge between two neighbouring nations"
rather than a cause of division and conflict.[72]

Transboundary diplomacy, whether based on treaties or not, may not
produce enormous "spillover" effects.[73] This is true even though some
boundary-focused international agreements, such as the 1996 Hungarian-
Romanian treaty, reach well into the interiors of the countries involved,
illustrating the "core-periphery adjacent State" type of transaction that
is described in House's model. Some of these contacts and exchanges
may seem legal and technical. Moreover, "functional integration" across
borders does not automatically lead to "political and social integration,"
as Michael Keating concludes from an extensive analysis of European
regional cooperation policies.[74] Nevertheless, international contacts across
borders, which may be facilitated by programs such as those sponsored by
the Council of Europe or by the European Commission's INTERREG program, do form networks that can have a definite cohesive force.[75]

Increasingly, there is developing (and not only in Europe) a phenomenon that Keating describes as "an interpenetration of territorial policy
spaces."[76] This interpenetration can blur the distinctions between places
and it can confuse identities in what might otherwise be a beneficial postmodern fashion. Premodern patterns – that is, the relationships of ethnic
or nationality groups to their homelands – may fade badly. Even modern,
or nation-state, ties of belonging – the psychological level at which diplomacy traditionally is conducted – may loosen, pulled apart by a welter of
competing jurisdictions, on different geographical scales, varying with
the different policy purposes being served. Ways of holding social entities
together are needed. "Traditional diplomacy," as Keating rightly recognizes but does not stress positively enough, "covers the whole range of
state interests and seeks to present a united front to the world."[77]

There is something to be said for keeping conventional political boundaries of nations at the fore. They are the sovereign interface between countries. The entities that they define remain, still, the locus of loyalty, of
patriotic feeling, for peoples in most parts of the world. The international
system is yet, basically, an interstate system. Diplomacy, the method by
which states address each other, retains a fundamental importance. This
may even be increasing. Diplomatic contact is the only way by which
countries can deal with each other as wholes. For diplomacy to work,
nations must continue to have "personalities." *Persona,* by definition, is
unitary.[78]

In this situation, the personification of international relations through meetings between nations' political leaders at borders can have a pivotal, even transformative, role for such encounters interconnect the "bodies politic" of countries in ways that other kinds of communication, even summit meetings held elsewhere, may not. The national body "gestures" made at border locations have a directness, spontaneity, and force that those emanating from capital cities rarely have. They actually touch another country; and its people, and those of the country doing the touching, can feel it.

Consider, as a final example of the diplomacy of *bon voisinage*, the trip, by bus, that India's prime minister Atal Behari Vajpayee made across "Line Zero" at Wagah on the Punjabi border between India and Pakistan on 20 February 1999 to meet his Pakistani counterpart at the time, Prime Minister Nawaz Sharif. These two countries, suffering "cartographic anxiety"[79] owing to their origin in partition, are acutely sensitive to one another. What occurred at that normally closed border post was felt throughout the subcontinent. Nominally a journey to inaugurate scheduled bus service between New Delhi and Lahore, Prime Minister Vajpayee's novel exercise in "bus diplomacy" was much more. "I bring the good will and hopes of my fellow Indians, who seek abiding peace and harmony with Pakistan," he said when he met, and embraced, Prime Minister Sharif at the border. "I am conscious that this is a defining moment in South Asian history, and I hope we will be able to rise to the challenge."[80]

This "challenge" included the difficult issues of sovereignty and military control over Kashmir and also lesser boundary matters, including the western sea border between India and Pakistan. The basic survival issue posed by the two countries' nuclear rivalry was of even more existential concern. The fact that the modest Vajpayee-Sharif summit occurred, and occurred at the very centre of the national fronts of both countries, provided an optimal geodiplomatic setting for beginning to resolve, or at least to restrict, these conflicts. It is a method that should be tried again.

Boundaries do make friends as well as foes. They function, at any level, to stabilize social relationships. As John Brinckerhoff Jackson, philosopher of landscape, has written, "They make residents out of the homeless, neighbours out of strangers, strangers of enemies."[81] They can be transformative, and so can a diplomacy that imaginatively takes account of them.

It has been the fundamental purpose of this chapter to challenge the notion that international political boundaries are chiefly, as the geopolitiker Karl Haushofer considered them, "fighting places." They are not, however, simply "meeting places," either. Borders and border control systems are more complex phenomena: they both divide and unify. When synthesized across national lines they can be, in addition, "joining places," capable of connecting wholly different countries, consociatively, in organized cooperation, in good neighbourhood.

Acknowledgments

An earlier and different version of this chapter, "Facing across Borders: The Diplomacy of Bon Voisinage," appeared in the *International Political Science Review/Revue international de science politique* 21, 2 (2000): 121-47. We thank the editors of this journal for their willingness to let us use and revise that article.

Notes

1   F. Ratzel, "The Laws of the Spatial Growth of States," in *The Structure of Political Geography*, ed. R.E. Kasperson and J.V. Minghi (Chicago: Aldine Publishing, 1969), 23.
2   J. Gottmann, ed., *Centre and Periphery: Spatial Variation in Politics* (Beverly Hills: Sage Publications, 1980).
3   J.W. House, "The Frontier Zone: A Conceptual Problem for Policy Makers," *International Political Science Review/Revue internationale de science politique* 1, 4 (1980): 466.
4   Quoted in E.A. Guerrant, *Roosevelt's Good Neighbor Policy* (Albuquerque: University of New Mexico Press, 1950), 1.
5   United Nations, *Charter of the United Nations and Statute of the International Court of Justice* (New York: Department of Public Information, United Nations, 1990), 1.
6   Nations Unies, *Charte des Nations Unies et Statut de la Cour internationale de Justice* (New York: Département de l'information des Nations Unies, 1997), 3.
7   United Nations, *Charter of the United Nations*, 39.
8   Nations Unies, *Charte des Nations Unies*, 48.
9   S. Welles, *The Time for Decision* (New York: Harper and Brothers, 1944), 185-241; B. Wood, *The Making of the Good Neighbor Policy* (New York: Columbia University Press, 1961).
10 Wood, *The Making of the Good Neighbor Policy*, 124.
11 *Dictionnaire de la terminologie du droit international* (Paris: Libraire du Recueil Sirey, 1960), 94.
12 C.I. Bevans, comp., *Treaties and Other International Agreements of the United States of America, 1776-1979* (Washington, DC: US Printing Office, 1972), 792, 803.
13 Welles, *The Time for Decision*, 192-93.
14 House, "The Frontier Zone," 459.
15 League of Nations, "Treaty of Commerce Between Hungary and Yugoslavia Concluded 24 July 1926," *Treaty Series* 97, 2222 (1929-30): 117-29; S.W. Boggs, *International Boundaries: A Study of Boundary Functions* (New York, Columbia University Press, 1940), 237-45.
16 R. Reagan, *An American Life* (New York: Simon and Schuster, 1990), 240.
17 Ibid.; A.K. Henrikson, "A North American Community: 'From the Yukon to the Yucatan,'" in *The Diplomatic Record, 1991-1992*, ed. H. Binnendijk and M. Locke (Boulder: Westview Press, 1993), 77.
18 J.W. House, *Frontier on the Rio Grande: A Political Geography of Development and Social Deprivation* (Oxford: Clarendon Press, 1982), 256.
19 Ibid.
20 The political scientist Ivo Duchacek has a more complex nomenclature for subnational transborder diplomacy. He distinguishes between "*global microdiplomacy* (or *paradiplomacy*)" and "*transborder regionalism.*" The former refers to "processes and networks through which subnational governments search for and establish cooperative contacts and compacts on a *global* scale, usually with foreign central governments and private enterprises." The latter refers to "the sum of the various informal and formal networks of communications and problem-solving mechanisms which bring *contiguous* subnational territorial communities into decisional dyads or triads – that is, bicommunal or tricommunal transfrontier regimes." See I.D. Duchacek, "International Competence of Subnational Governments: Borderlands and Beyond," in *Across Boundaries: Transborder Interaction in Comparative Perspective*, ed. O.J. Martínez (El Paso: Texas Western Press, 1986), 14, 17.
21 R. Frost, *The Poems of Robert Frost* (New York: The Modern Library, 1946), 35-36.
22 B.L. Thomas, "International Boundaries: Lines in the Sand (and the Sea)," in *Reordering the World: Geopolitical Perspectives on the 21st Century*, 2nd ed., ed. G.J. Demko and W.B. Wood (Boulder: Westview Press, 1999), 69.

23 There is, perhaps, no such thing as a completely novel word or even novel application of a word. Upon checking in *Webster's*, I find "consociation," a voluntary council or union of neighbouring Congregational churches (*Webster's Third New International Dictionary* (Springfield: G. and C. Merriam Company, 1961, 484). There is an inbuilt geographical component in this historical meaning. Geographical closeness is implicit, too, in the political scientist Arend Lijphart's notion of "consociational democracy," which deals with the structuring of relations between proximate or even intermingled ethnic or religious groups within the same, plural society. If secession or partition should occur, then "the model of international diplomacy," which is emphasized in this chapter, would apply. See A. Lijphart, *Democracy in Plural Societies: A Comparative Exploration* (New Haven: Yale University Press, 1977), 45.

24 Elements of all three theories – associative, dissociative, and consociative – may be found in Frost's poem, "Mending Wall." The associative view is implied by the line: "Something there is that doesn't love a wall." The forces of nature itself, during the upheavals of winter, have caused boundary stones to tumble down, thus seeming not to want the wall to exist. The dissociative view (surely not Frost's primary view) is expressed by the Yankee farmer who, moving along the stone barrier as in a dark age, keeps repeating his father's saying, "Good fences make good neighbours." The consociative view is captured in the poem's metaphorical description of the collaborative process – an anticipated and requisite event – of annually repairing the stone fence between farm plots by mutual action: "And on a day we meet to walk the line / And set the wall between us once again" (Frost, *Poems*, 35-36). The reciprocating process of boundary maintenance pulls the divided parties together – like a zipper. A boundary, cooperatively restored, binds as it bounds. In being jointly mended, the wall itself mends.

25 L.W. Lyde, *Some Frontiers of To-morrow: An Aspiration for Europe* (London: A. and C. Black, 1915), 2.

26 Boggs, *International Boundaries*, 11.

27 S.B. Jones, *Boundary-Making: A Handbook for Statesmen, Treaty Editors and Boundary Commissioners* (Washington, DC: Carnegie Endowment for International Peace, 1945), 8.

28 T.H. Holdich, *Political Frontiers and Boundary Making* (London: Macmillan, 1916), x.

29 J. Gottmann, "Spatial Partitioning and the Politician's Wisdom," *International Political Science Review/Revue internationale de science politique* 1, 4 (1980): 433.

30 R. Cooper, *The Postmodern State and the World Order* (London: Demos, 1996).

31 North Atlantic Treaty Organization, *NATO Handbook* (Brussels: NATO Office of Information and Press, 1995), 232.

32 "Foreign Policy: Not Quite a New World Order, More a Three-way Split," *The Economist*, 20 December 1997, 41-43.

33 This is a result of the 1982 United Nations Convention on the Law of the Sea and, particularly, the articulation therein of a "contiguous zone" of up to twelve nautical miles (beyond a twelve-mile-maximum "territorial sea"), within which infringements of customs, fiscal, immigration, or sanitary laws and regulations pertaining to the territorial sea can be prevented or punished, and also of a novel "exclusive economic zone" (EEZ) of up to 200 nautical miles. The EEZ concept gives to a state claiming such an economic zone the right to control resources both on or under the seabed and in the water column above it. This prerogative encompasses the management of all resources, protection of the marine environment, conduct of scientific research, and erection and use of artificial structures. Moreover, for some countries with the right geographies, a "continental shelf" of up to 350 nautical miles also can be claimed if the submarine physical topography so justifies this. Thomas, "International Boundaries," 82-87; L.B. Sohn and K. Gustafson, *The Law of the Sea in a Nutshell* (St. Paul: West Publishing, 1984), 94-95, 113-71.

34 In particular, as Thomas predicts, the "mounting pressure for marine resource development can be expected to lead to representation of offshore boundaries on political maps." Political maps might, for example, "extend the color applied to a state's land area into the seas over which it exercises economic jurisdiction in a screen of reduced values of the same color. Whatever the method of symbolization chosen, it seems clear that in order realistically to reflect human responses to political changes around the world, future political maps will need to display a number of different kinds of 'international' boundaries

– on land and in the sea." B.L. Thomas, "Changing Functions of International Boundaries," *Geographic and Global Issues Quarterly* 3, 1 (1993): 1-2.

35 A.K. Henrikson, "The Geographical 'Mental Maps' of American Foreign Policy Makers," *International Political Science Review/Revue internationale de science politique* 1, 4 (1980): 495-530; A.K. Henrikson, "Mental Maps," in *Explaining the History of American Foreign Relations*, ed. M.J. Hogan and T.G. Paterson (Cambridge: Cambridge University Press, 1991), 177-92; A.K. Henrikson, "A North American Community: 'From the Yukon to the Yucatan,'" in *The Diplomatic Record, 1991-1992*, ed. H. Binnendijk and M. Locke (Boulder: Westview Press, 1993), 69-95; A.K. Henrikson, "The US 'North American' Trade Concept: Continentalist, Hemispherist, or Globalist?" in *Toward a North American Community? Canada, the United States, and Mexico*, ed. D. Barry, with M.O. Dickerson and J.D. Gaisford (Boulder: Westview Press, 1995), 155-84.

36 On the legal aspects of this general problem, see S.R. Ratner, "Drawing a Better Line: *Uti Possidetis* and the Borders of New States," *American Journal of International Law* 90, 4 (1996): 590-624.

37 The term "trans*border* diplomacy" may be used more or less interchangeably with "trans*frontier* diplomacy," ignoring, for present purposes, subtle differences between these terms in different languages and geographical contexts. *Frontière*, in French, and *Grenze*, in German, are relatively inclusive, single terms. "Frontier" and "boundary," however, are contradistinguished by Ladis Kristof, who sees a frontier as outer-oriented, directed towards outlying areas that are both a source of danger and a prize, and a boundary as inner-oriented, created and maintained by the will of a central government. The former is a manifestation of centrifugal forces, and the latter is drawn by centripetal forces. A frontier, because it is a "zone of transition" from the sphere *(ecumene)* of one way of life to another, is an *integrating* factor; and a boundary, because it impedes transitional flows between such spheres, is a *separating* factor. Kristof accepts the assertion of the German geopolitician Karl Haushofer (1927) that boundaries are "zones of friction." L.K.D. Kristof, "The Nature of Frontiers and Boundaries," in Kasperson and Minghi, *The Structure of Political Geography*, 126-31.

38 I. Kant, "On the First Ground of the Distinction of Regions in Space" (1768), in *Kant's Inaugural Dissertation and Early Writings on Space*, trans. J. Handyside (Chicago: Open Court, 1929), 22-23, quoted in Y.F. Tuan, *Space and Place: The Perspective of Experience* (Minneapolis: University of Minnesota Press, 1977), 36.

39 Y.F. Tuan, *Space and Place*, 36.

40 S. Rokkan, "Territories, Centres, and Peripheries: Toward a Geoethnic-Geoeconomic-Geopolitical Model of Differentiation within Western Europe," in Gottman, *Centre and Periphery*, 175.

41 Quoted in K. Adenauer, *Memoirs, 1945-53* (Chicago: Henry Regnery Company, 1965), 235.

42 D.W. Meinig, *Atlantic America, 1492-1800*, vol. 1 of *The Shaping of America: A Geographical Perspective on 500 Years of History* (New Haven: Yale University Press, 1986).

43 Tuan, *Space and Place*, 42; J. Gottmann, *Megalopolis: The Urbanized Northeastern Seaboard of the United States* (Cambridge: MIT Press, 1961).

44 R. Green Macías, "Palabras de la Senadora Rosario Green Macías, durante la ceremonia en la que el Presidente Ernesto Zedillo la designó Secretaria de Relaciones Exteriores," *Los Pinos*, 7 January 1998.

45 L. Axworthy, *The 49th Parallel and Beyond: A Border for the 21st Century* (Ottawa: Department of Foreign Affairs and International Trade, 1999).

46 Tuan, *Space and Place*, 42.

47 T.A. Bailey, *America Faces Russia: Russian-American Relations from the Early Times to Our Day* (Ithaca: Cornell University Press, 1950), 321; A.K. Henrikson, "The Map as an 'Idea': The Role of Cartographic Imagery during the Second World War," *American Cartographer* 2, 1 (1975): 46.

48 A.K. Henrikson, "A World 'Arctic Mediterranean'? Open Skies and Transpolar Civil Aviation," in *Legal Problems in the Arctic Regions*, ed. T. Utriainen (Rovaniemi: The Institute for Nordic Law, University of Lapland, 1990), 24-64; O.R. Young, "Institutional Linkages in International Society: Polar Perspectives," *Global Governance: A Review of Multilateralism and International Organizations* 2, 1 (1996): 1-23.

49 K.W. Deutsch, *The Nerves of Government: Models of Political Communication and Control* (New York: Free Press, 1966).
50 J. Gottmann, *The Significance of Territory* (Charlottesville: University Press of Virginia, 1973), 143-54.
51 C.L. Olson, M.J. Seidenberg, and R.W. Selle, "US-Russian Maritime Boundary Giveaway," *Orbis: A Journal of World Affairs* 42, 1 (1998): 75.
52 J.I. Charney and L.M. Alexander, eds., *International Maritime Boundaries* (Dordrecht: Martinus Nijhoff, 1993), 447-60.
53 Olson, Seidenberg, and Selle, "US-Russian Maritime Giveaway," 84-85.
54 Ibid., 85, 86-87.
55 T. Kenworthy and S. Pearlstein, "US, Canada Reach Landmark Pact on Pacific Salmon Fishing," *Washington Post,* 4 June 1999.
56 House, *Frontier on the Rio Grande,* 256.
57 Victor Prescott distinguishes between *territorial* boundary disputes, arising from the broad attractiveness of a neighbouring territory to the initiator of a border conflict, and *positional* boundary disputes, concerning the actual location of a boundary and often, as well, the terms by which that line is to be defined. J.R.V. Prescott, *Political Frontiers and Boundaries* (London: Allen and Unwin, 1987), 98. In the Latin American context, the two types are often difficult to tell apart.
58 Thomas, "International Boundaries," 79, 80.
59 "Peru and Ecuador Leaders Seal Border Treaty," *New York Times,* 14 May 1999.
60 B.A. Simmons, *Territorial Disputes and Their Resolution: The Case of Ecuador and Peru* (Washington, DC: United States Institute of Peace), 15, 20.
61 "Peru and Ecuador Sign Treaty to End Longstanding Conflict," *New York Times,* 27 October 1998.
62 "Peru and Ecuador Leaders Seal Border Treaty."
63 "Peace in the Andes," *The Economist,* 31 October 1998, 35-36.
64 "Conference on Security and Cooperation in Europe: Final Act," signed at Helsinki, 1 August 1975, United States Department of State *Bulletin* 73 (1888), 1 September 1975, 324-26. Even before this Europe-wide commitment to general principles of coexistence, cooperation, and comity was made, the Federal Republic of Germany, following its policy of *Ostpolitik,* signed treaties with some of its eastern neighbors – the German Democratic Republic (1969), the Soviet Union (1970), and the People's Republic of Poland (1970) – that prepared the way for the later CSCE approach. For example, in its preamble the Draft Treaty on the Establishment of Equal Relations between the German Democratic Republic and the Federal Republic of Germany, dated 17 December 1969, acknowledged the two signatories' common "endeavour to make an effective contribution to *détente* and securing of peace in Europe, to remove tension between the two German states step-by-step, to bring about good neighbourly relations as equal sovereign states, and to advance the creation of a European security system." L.L. Whetten, *Germany's Ostpolitik: Relations Between the Federal Republic and the Warsaw Pact Countries* (London: Oxford University Press, 1971), 218.
65 Council of Europe, *Annuaire Européen/European Yearbook 27* (La Haye/The Hague: Martinus Nijhoff, 1982).
66 L. Székely, "Bilateralism vs. Euroatlanticism: Central and Eastern European Stability in the Early 1990s" (MA thesis, the Fletcher School of Law and Diplomacy, Tufts University, Medford, Massachusetts, 1999).
67 Ibid.
68 D. Fagan, "It's the Year 2025 ... There Is No US Border: Has Canada Become the 51st State?" *Globe and Mail,* 16 March 2002.
69 "Good Fences," *The Economist,* 19 December 1998, 19-22.
70 M. Anderson, *Frontiers: Territory and State Formation in the Modern World* (Cambridge, UK: Polity Press, 1996), 126.
71 R. Prodi, President of the European Commission, address at the Ceremony of the Signing of the Treaty of Accession, Athens, Greece, 16 April 2003.
72 Székely, "Bilateralism vs. Euroatlanticism."
73 J. McCormick, *The European Union: Politics and Policies* (Boulder: Westview Press, 1996), 15-20.

74 M. Keating, *The New Regionalism in Western Europe: Territorial Restructuring and Political Change* (Cheltenham: Edward Elgar, 1998), 182.

75 Anderson, *Frontiers*, 121; Keating, *The New Regionalism in Western Europe*, 180-81.

76 Keating, *The New Regionalism in Western Europe*, 183.

77 Ibid., 178.

78 P.F. Strawson, *Individuals: An Essay in Descriptive Metaphysics* (London: Methuen, 1959), 87-116.

79 S. Khrishna, "Cartographic Anxiety: Mapping the Body Politic in India," in *Political Geography: A Reader*, ed. J. Agnew (London: Arnold, 1997), 83.

80 B. Bearak, "India Leader Pays Visit to Pakistan," *New York Times*, 21 February 1999.

81 J.B. Jackson, *American Space: The Centennial Years, 1865-1876* (New York: Norton, 1972), 15.

Part 8
Conclusions

The two chapters in Part 9 stand alone, tying together the themes introduced throughout *Holding the Line*. They contain observations about the contemporary dilemmas facing border studies outlined in previous chapters. They develop what may well be a postmodern approach to border studies in that they acknowledge the need for critical, multivocal, and multitextual approaches to the theorization and definition of borders and border studies as well as the identification of the multiple borderlines that divide parallel universes of experience. While these universes may exit simultaneously, they require individual boundaries for divergent purposes. The problem then becomes one of incorporating the human experience, making the problem of life and living cornerstones in much of what social, policy, and natural sciences think and write about. To Stanley Brunn et. al., in Chapter 18, the problem of reinventing borders to accommodate twenty-first-century globalization is not an objective exercise; rather, it is intensely subjective.

A similar argument is made in Chapter 19 by David Newman, who acknowledges the difficulties of recasting borders not as lines that contain everywhere equal processes – that is, the territorial definition of nation-state – but as continua or multitextual and multipurposeful bounding activities. He observes that, given the changing nature of boundaries and their hierarchical and functional attributes, tools used to measure them require a built-in flexibility that takes account of their internal dynamism. Boundaries simply cannot be conceived of as static and unchanging phenomena. According to Newman, the lack of a conceptual and theoretical base for the study of international boundaries has led to the notion that the "bounding" phenomenon can be measured without becoming entrapped within a specific form of boundary language (be it the international, the municipal, or the aspatial-sociological). This is what Brunn et. al. define as "parallel universes."

In the final analysis, these chapters leave us to consider how the study of borders will accommodate the new realities and perceptions that have crept into the fields of political geography, geopolitics, international law, and political studies: this is not a bad place to finish our discussions, and the answer remains open-ended. Both Brunn et al. and Newman offer alternative, but not mutually exclusive, approaches to the problem of "where to from here," and they lay the groundwork for a retheorizing of borders. The significance of borders to "life and living" raises the ultimate question, also posed by Newman: what is the role of borders and boundaries, both real and perceived? According to Newman, this touches "upon the essential question concerning the relationship between territorial organization – at a number of scales – and the location of power within society."

18
Towards a Geopolitics of Life and Living: Where Boundaries Still Matter

Stanley D. Brunn, John F. Watkins, Timothy J. Fargo, Josh Lepawsky, and Jeffery A. Jones

While the world political map provides evidence of where boundaries are permeable or disappearing in importance, they remain significant and firm with regard to many issues related to life and living. States define citizenship and alien status, and determine the rights of those persons living within or moving across their borders. Quality of life and living, as influenced by boundaries, include state policies influencing family size; the rights to employment, movement, and human services; the rights of new minorities and women seeking abortions; the access to health care of terminally ill patients; and the rights of prisoners and prisoners of conscience. States also deal with "life" issues in the regulations they establish on the production, import, and sale of certain foods, including genetically produced and altered foods (and food additives), and the availability of medicines, blood, and organs to those in need. Environmental life issues of a transboundary nature include the protection of threatened fish and wildlife, the establishment of biosphere reserves, regional treaties on air and water pollution, and negotiations to halt weapons of mass destruction. We investigate space and quality of life questions, from local to global scales, that affect the privacy and protection of children, the elderly, the disabled, and the disenfranchised in areas of social conflict and war, and we also address the protection of biota. We conclude by looking at issues of freedom, privacy, protection, and citizen participation in cyberdemocracies and cybertyrannies, where boundaries are both real and imagined.

Several years ago the senior author attended an international political geography conference in Nicosia, Cyprus, and took a leisurely Sunday afternoon field trip with geography friends along the border separating Greek and Turkish portions of this divided city. As they walked along the walls and fence and around abandoned buildings on the Greek side, he noticed that there was little human life, which was in quite sharp contrast, so he understood, to an active café and street culture on the Turkish side. Just as remarkable was the life moving unimpeded across the border – a black and white cat climbing effortlessly across the wall and through vacant buildings and lots, birds flying overhead, and insects (especially bees) doing their business and disregarding the effect of this impenetrable border on human activity. In short, these fauna "owned" a territory in both countries. The author remarked to his friends that humans, it seems, were the only life forms who erected fixed borders. Non-human animals may ignore human boundaries, but other borders do exist for them, such as "natural" and "instinctual" borders that define areas in which they feel safe from predation. If animals cross into regions controlled by hostile animals, then a type of policing occurs and an attempt is made to remove the trespasser. Behaviours change when an animal enters a different territory.

Interestingly, borders also exist in three dimensions. For humans, consider US and British aircraft flying over Iraq or subsurface mineral (land or ocean-bed) rights. Birds experience three-dimensional spaces and may feel safer in the air than on land, or in a tree than on the ground. Animal territories may be either transitory or permanent, regional or linear. Human boundaries may be both physical (i.e., concrete barriers or obstructions) or non-physical (i.e., perceptual). The boundaries for non-human animals may also be both physical and ephemeral. For example, non-human animal territories may be marked by scents that dissipate over time.[1] And if they did cross into regions and territories controlled by other animals, policing still would occur. Boundary regulation and enforcement are distinctly human endeavours, and the example of Cyprus illustrates the focus of this chapter.

It is commonplace to hear and read, both in the popular media and in academic literature, about references to boundaries and their meaning on the world political map. Publications and presentations by political leaders, social scientists, and policy analysts include such phrases as "a world without boundaries," "opening up the East to the West," an "Internet world," and "the disappearance of boundaries" – especially when talking about "a Europe of regions" or "what NAFTA means to transboundary Canadian-US-Mexican relations." Forecasters, postmodernists, and extra-territorial specialists also describe "the demise or end of the state" and "the end of a bounded world."[2] Analysts attribute these transboundary changes to a variety of events, including the end of the Cold War, the expansion of regional economic unions and pacts (such as the European Union), the shrinking of time and space through information and communications technologies, globalization, and the activities of corporations, intergovernmental organizations (IGOs), and non-governmental organizations (NGOs).[3] Individually and collectively these events and processes are thought/said/assumed to contribute to the inexpensive, easy, and rapid flow of information (especially money and ideas) and goods across international boundaries. They also contribute to the easier and greater mobility of individuals who wish to cross international borders and enter new political spaces.[4]

Humans as Animals: Animals as Territorial

The central premise of our thinking is that life and living are important and that politics is integral to understanding both. We are not interested in simply measuring life and living in numerical terms (e.g., life expectancy or income level); rather, we emphasize the quality of life and living, the often subjective attributes of existence that are both highly dynamic and difficult to ascertain. We examine three themes. First, we discuss the meaning of boundaries for those who live in "state or containerized spaces" and who are both restricted in their movement across international boundaries and discover completely different rights and freedoms once they enter new states. These issues of life and living, or human well-being, hinge largely on definitions of rights and freedoms rather than on the easy flow of ideas and money (attributed to electronic commerce, which increasingly drives "successful development"). Second, we examine the impacts of fixed boundaries on non-human biotic populations (i.e., plants and animals, from microorganisms to the largest vertebrates) whose "rights," "protection," and "freedom" are affected by the human organization of political spaces. Many members of plant and animal communities cross international boundaries. They move naturally through dispersal of seeds by wind and water or as part of seasonal migrations for feeding and reproduction. Human forces also shape the movements of such biota through trade agreements/restrictions or state policies on the acceptability/unacceptability of certain species. These are important issues and are related to the patenting of life. Disruptions to the lives and habitats of biotic populations are political issues because how these habitats are protected, preserved, or eliminated are life issues defined by states. Third, we address impermeable boundaries; that is, boundaries that still "make a difference." In a world of impermeable boundaries – a world that is perhaps much less optimistic than is the world of those who envision the end of the state and the coming irrelevance of international borders – boundaries remain very important.

In our attempt to understand the interfaces of politics, life, and livelihood, we draw from a host of different literatures. We do this because we believe that it is important for political geographers and others looking at the organization of space and boundary questions to be exposed to theories and schema from diverse literatures. The fields from which we draw include animal behaviour, ecology, gerontology, demography, and epidemiology. This research encompasses the rights of women, children, the elderly, the disabled; ethnic minorities, refugees, immigrants, and new diaspora communities; electronic democracies and human rights in electronic space; intellectual property and indigenous rights; social inequities related to information technologies; and the local-global debates. First, we address the nature of boundaries. Then we discuss our notion of "life and living," which we extend beyond the common indicators used in state and international assessments to include the subjective nature of the human condition. We then discuss the integration of bounded space and life quality by looking at technological innovations and global economic decisions that affect the rights, freedoms, and geographies of individuals and groups. Politics is a common ground in all these issues. We offer specific examples of where state boundaries remain impenetrable barriers to human freedom, mobility, and opportunity. We then discuss boundary issues pertaining to non-human biota. Finally, we contend that boundaries still matter and, for some individuals and groups, will continue to be of increasing importance. Drawing together the main threads of our analyses, in our conclusion we ask several questions that merit the attention of those geographers, biologists, social, and political scientists concerned with permeable and impermeable boundaries.

A World of Parallel Universes: *Paradoxes Extraordinaires*
A critical reader of the contemporary world political map is likely to conclude that, in so far as international boundaries are concerned, we live in a world of "parallel universes." In other words, one "map" presents a world in which, during the past two decades, political boundaries have lost much of their meaning and influence with regard to commerce and human interaction. This map applies to the worlds of global financial transactions and other forms of e-commerce (electronic commerce), where many international boundaries cease to have meaning.[5] The other map presents a world in which the international boundaries are equally or more important than ever, especially with regard to the movement of humans and human products (ideas, regulations, technologies, etc.). The juxtaposition of these worlds is evident when considering the diffusion of some recent information and communication innovations; glaring gender, race, and ethnic disparities; and political/military conflicts in Europe, Africa, and Asia.

On the one hand, with greater regional economic dialogue and planning, the world's borders have become less important (e.g., among European states). An expanded EU and the Maastricht Treaty promote more and closer cooperation on the transfer of products and labourers across international boundaries. Transboundary economies, including a European currency and political regionalism, are by-products of discussions by political leaders who see the advantages of a unified continental market. The economic significance of the US-Canada boundary, and also the boundary between the United States and Mexico, diminished with the

North American Free Trade Agreement (NAFTA). The location of *maqui-ladoras* along the US-Mexico border illustrates that the boundary remains increasingly important economically not only for the location of plants but also for workers. The US-Mexico border is, however, far from open as it restricts the movement of workers and allows labour markets in both countries to play off one another and to reduce labour costs, thereby increasing the profits of companies locating along the border. The General Motors plants are cases in point. This international border also remains a major physical and psychological barrier for residents from Mexico wishing to enter the United States, either legally or illegally. Some Mexicans wishing to enter the United States will fly to Canada and enter via the Canadian-US border.

We can also identify other regions where international boundaries are fortified and where barriers to human traffic and commerce exist. These include Palestinian workers in Israel and those living in the West Bank and Gaza; South and Southeast Asian women who form part of the "maid trade" and seek employment in Canada, Germany, and the Persian Gulf states; married couples in the United States who adopt children from Romania and Russia; and refugees from wartorn West Africa seeking asylum in Central and Northern Europe. Along with these impermeable or difficult-to-cross borders are other international borders – borders that are seamless and transparent (especially if one uses the Internet and various telephone networks). Thus, depending on their socioeconomic context, boundaries have different meanings.

Values and Vagaries of Life and Quality of Life
We can approach human well-being and quality of life issues by examining those attributes that enhance life and living. These include what the United Nations and other organizations consider to be basic human needs; that is, the right to food, water, proper housing, and adequate health care. Such attributes are measurable and exhibit geographic variability. For example, how many people have access to sufficient potable water or have daily caloric levels below the world average? How many live in permanent structures and have a doctor or clinic nearby? Where are those malnourished and poorly housed populations? Where are the "doctorless" regions? All these are geographical questions. It is also worth noting that these needs may not necessarily be a priority in all countries. For example, Chinese leaders object to European and North American leaders calling attention to human rights violations in China and demanding that China implement programs to reduce environmental pollution levels before being admitted to the World Trade Organization.

Housing quality, running water, caloric intake, and physician availability are important with regard to measuring quality of life, but quality of life is more than what can be measured statistically. It also includes non-quantifiable measures and dimensions, including the difference between "house" and "home"; family and community support systems for the disabled, sick, and dying; civic responsibility; and caring and humane values. These qualitative quality of life indicators extend to how one cares for the natural world, including plants and animals, endangered species, sacred spaces, and the appreciation that comes from being able to experience a beautiful sunrise, seasonal vegetation changes, quietness in empty spaces, spiritual voices, and so on.

Decisions about life and living are decisions about places and spaces; in short, they are about how the state chooses to value those individuals and groups residing temporarily or permanently, legally or illegally, within its legal or administrative spaces.[6] Do citizens have certain rights, privileges, and services that are significantly different from those of non-citizens? Are there barriers to access to children's and adults' education, nutrition, and health care? Are quality of life measures and humane care provided to asylum seekers, the mentally ill, and the homeless as well as to victims of hate crimes, spousal and child abuse, ethnic cleansing, ecocatastrophes, and pandemics? In the United States a patchwork pattern of laws exists. All states except Nebraska, South Carolina, Wyoming, and the District of Columbia have passed hate crime legislation. Oregon passed legislation permitting physician-assisted suicide, while California, Washington, and Michigan have rejected such proposals. Nine states – Alaska, Arizona, California, Colorado, Hawaii, Maine, Nevada, Oregon, and Washington – have approved the use of medical marijuana. Those thirty-eight states that allow capital punishment see no conflict between a citizen's right to life and protection and the death penalty.

Also, groups in rural areas are affected by those who draw boundaries regardless of differential rights, freedoms, and opportunities. They are "gerrymandered" victims of de facto or de jure social, religious, ethnic, and age discrimination.[7] The criteria for delimiting regions for school attendance, political representation (voting), health care, financial loans and credit, and recreation opportunities may be drawn on the basis of census-derived racial data, ethnic inclusiveness, religious and linguistic mixes, and even bigotry. Several examples of gerrymandering, or the "social manipulation of space," come to mind. Two historical cases are the legacy of spatial and social segregation controls imposed by whites in rural and urban areas of the US South and urban North until the 1960s, and the apartheid policy in South Africa, under which the minority white South African government imposed rigid and harsh laws on Africans and "Coloureds." Another example of gerrymandering is the "Swiss cheese" political landscape of Israel/Palestine, where, when travelling about, one needs a large-scale detailed map to know whether one is in Israel, Israeli administrative territory, or Palestinian territory. And there are the efforts by the Baltic States to use gerrymandering and other political and legal manoeuvrings to restrict the political influences of large near-abroad Russian minorities.

Convoluted, jury-rigged, invisible, and blatant boundary manipulation may result in ghettoized or spatially constricted and restricted enclaves and exclaves. "Ghettoized landscapes" exist among the very poor and very rich in developed and developing market economies. Sometimes these groups exist side by side, sometimes they exist in separate zones. "Reservations" for Native Americans in the United States is one example of the latter: their rural locations are generally in isolated and poorly endowed resource environments. In some reservations the indigenous populations have their own governments and economies (e.g., casino gambling) that are outside federal and state jurisdiction. Other examples include retirement communities that dot the suburban landscapes of the Sunbelt, along with "military retirement ghettos" in Central America and the English-speaking Caribbean islands. Those living in protected "gated communities" often enjoy special tax benefits, luxuries, and state protection not guaranteed to ordinary citizens living in the same state.[8] Ethnic, age, income, religion, language, refugee, underworld, and gay ghettos are other examples of people voluntarily or involuntarily residing in segregated and separate communities. They may "live together separately," to use a book title by Israeli geographer Michael Roman, who applied this concept to Arabs and Israelis living in Jerusalem.

Other phenomena related to quality of life issues, and affected by state boundary machinations, include opportunities for refugees to participate in literacy programs and job training, rights to property for poor and landless populations, programs to feed and house a state's poor and refugee populations, medical programs for those with incurable diseases and those permanently disabled and disfigured, welfare programs for the uninsured and indigent, and blood and organ donor programs for the sick and dying. While many of these examples are well known, others are "hidden." The latter include the establishment of strict air, water, noise, and visual pollution laws; where these exist and are enforced, some human lives may be been enhanced. Where they do not exist or are weak, quality of life measures are likely to be lower, as in the case of Taiwan, China, Russia, and a number of Eastern European countries.[9] States that ban the sale and use of genetically altered foods, or foods with certain additives, or prohibit the use of pesticides seek to prolong the life of their residents. Recent examples include food stores on continental Europe concerned about the cross-species infections of farm animals. In late 2000, deaths and illnesses caused some European governments, including the Netherlands (which was the first), Spain, Austria, Greece, and Italy, to ban the sale and import of British and French beef because of the threat of Mad Cow (or Bovine Spongiform Encephalopathy [BSE]) disease.[10] More recently, the same problems have been encountered in North America.

Another food scare in Europe concerned Coca-Cola being tainted. In the United States there is concern about the dangers of tobacco and consuming high cholesterol, sugar, and fat products. There is also concern about flaws in a variety of consumer products, including auto airbags, child safety locks on pharmaceuticals, tires, toys, guns, microwave ovens, and cellular telephones. While to those in poor states these may seem frivolous consumer concerns, they illustrate the point that people in some states are more protected than are people in others. Similar variations in protection extend to victims of drug abuse, alcoholism, gambling, spousal and child abuse, and sexual and verbal harassment. These are very important public health and quality of life concerns in some societies but not in others. For those IGOs and NGOs working with AIDS victims and with those with mental and physical disabilities, where one lives makes all the difference in the quality of health care, prolonged longevity, and quality living. While governments in Northern and Central Europe provide barrier-free access to those with physical disabilities, much of Africa does not.

Human Rights and Freedoms

There is much discussion in the academic and public policy literature about globalization and what it means for global economies; new world orders or disorders; and the speed with which people, products, and information can be moved from place to place. These seamless webs of electronic commerce and rapid movement of information appear to erase national boundaries.[11] Open borders and boundaries, as noted above, are the norm today in much of Western Europe. Indeed, one can cross an international border without even knowing it. And openness and ease of movement is apparent in much of former Eastern Europe as well, certainly more so than a decade ago. Economies in Europe that were once defined largely by national boundaries now have to deal with transboundary issues and regional and continental economies. The expanded EU, which includes states in Eastern Europe, will further change the nature of regional boundaries with regard to commerce and human migration.

Individuals and groups who live in "timeless and spaceless/placeless worlds," such as much of Europe and North America, experience these "boundaryless" and digital worlds with daily Internet usage, e-commerce, and personal networking. While this scenario may describe the easy and inexpensive movement of money, datasets, information conveyed by radio and television, and visual displays of international information, it does not characterize the state and territorial variations that remain in many other regions of the world.

States still define the rights, freedoms, and opportunities for those within their spaces. In other words, "spatial rights" are the order of the day. States, even those states that are considered socially and politically progressive, may differ in how they define the rights of children, women, gays, the mentally and physically disabled, linguistic and religious minorities, and new diaspora members. States also decide who is welcome, and they do this by setting quotas and establishing "filters" for those entering under special circumstances (e.g., political refugees, unusual scientific and artistic merit, athletic skills). A state defines refugees, aliens, and immigrants through defining their rights to residence, movement, employment, property ownership, and political participation. In Afghanistan women once enjoyed some "spatial freedoms," but until very recently they were demeaned by the very strict laws enforced by the Taliban. The rights of women in Central Asia and North Africa differ in secular as opposed to fundamentalist Islamic states.[12] Roma (gypsies) sought entry into Finland and Switzerland only to be returned because they were unwelcome. A town in the Czech Republic erected a wall to separate the Czech and Roma populations – a wall that was eventually torn down because of a public outcry. Eriterians and Pakistanis in Norway are officially welcomed by the state (open borders) but not by villagers. Sports stars (especially soccer players) are given special permission to enter countries and granted citizenship so they can become members of competitive "national" teams.

And what about boundaries and rights of children in wartorn areas? Do these children merit special treatment; that is, protection from the ravages of war? During the past decade we have seen on television child soldiers in Congo, Liberia, and Sierra Leone committing brutalities as vicious as those perpetrated by their elders. Children and young women of minority populations have been enslaved by revolutionaries for sex and prostitution or as part of sex tourism. The United Nations Convention on the Rights of the Child contains articles about children that reflect their status in a European or North American world rather than in the developing world. Articles on the Web site of the UN High Commission for Human Rights include those that define the child as an individual under age eighteen, with a right to education, to protection from economic exploitation, and to non-participation in armed conflict. This same child has a right to freedom of expression, religion, peaceful assembly, access to information from national and international sources, and a standard of living "adequate for the child's physical, mental, spiritual, moral, and social development."[13] The geopolitics of children in a state's foreign policy and in discussions in the UN, as well as NGOs and IGOs, begs for attention on the part of scholars in various disciplines.

States also establish policies and regulations regarding another range of social issues that relate to life and living. These include making decisions about students in public schools who are taught sex education and parenting, programs for the homeless, those with chemical dependencies, unwed mothers, single fathers, disabled veterans, children with learning disabilities, and the elderly who require financial support. Some states also define the rights of the unborn, political prisoners, and prisoners of conscience. And states make decisions about those eligible for AIDS testing, genetic counselling, and inoculation for diseases as well as for those with permanent disabilities, those on life-support systems, those who wish to die with dignity (living wills and other advance directives), those diagnosed with serious mental problems, and those who are willing to be tested for new pharmaceutical products. In November 2000 the Netherlands became the first country to allow euthanasia and physician-assisted suicide.[14]

Other paradoxes of "boundary or transboundary life" involve the worlds that exist in virtual and real space. Space is both problematic and relational.[15] And these worlds we live in and experience, whether in cyberspace or mental or physical space, are different in size, shape, volume, and geometry.[16] Those who are mobile may desire "mobile rights," yet rights are "fixed" by two-dimensional boundaries. Cyberspace is as material as it is immaterial in that it requires material and energy throughputs. Cyberspace involves identifying, extracting, and using nature as a resource at scales and rates not previously possible. It also involves the application of state-specific technologies in remote sensing, geographic information system (GIS), and automated manufacturing.

Sometimes paradoxes and conflicts between the "real" and the "virtual" emerge when using the Internet.[17] For example, when using the Internet "we can be anyone, anywhere, anytime" and yet be in a "real" world where our freedoms of movement and expression are defined by state decisions.[18] In some ways the Internet transcends boundaries, yet where one lives largely determines how any information or communication gleaned from the Net can be used. In 2000 the French court stated that Yahoo! must block French users from gaining access to Nazi memorabilia; this set a precedent that could require Web companies to tailor their practices to the laws of individual countries.[19] Another example would be a homosexual gaining access to information on homosexuality and yet being unable to use such information openly (or even openly acknowledge their own sexuality), depending on where she/he lives.[20] In this sense, lived reality is not separate from cyberspace.

Technological and political decisions affect our lives, the spaces in which we live, and the communities we form.[21] For some, Internet boundaries and electronic communities are more elusive than are other communities to which we belong. These electronic spaces have invisible boundaries, and some users do not cross them, even in chat rooms or as contributors to "listservs" or on electronic communities like eBay. Community loyalty and even territorial boundaries exist, though they do so in ways that do not necessarily match our everyday sense of what constitutes space. The juxtaposition of these open and closed, visible and invisible, temporary and permanent spaces and boundaries can cause discomfort, unease, and conflict. These conflicts even exist for those residing in the same political spaces and for those governing in states that have new electronic technologies, such as GIS.[22] The boundaries where humans reside are "fixed" for some, permeable or porous for others, and fuzzy for still others. Rights may apply to a lifelong and permanent resident but not to a newcomer (whether welcomed or not); to those who are rich but not to the indigent; to men and not to women; to inherited and privileged elites, and not to the middle and lower classes; to the literate and not to the illiterate; to the able and not to the disabled.

Biological Boundary Issues
Our third area of interest addresses a topic too little considered by political geographers but one that we think is crucial to examining the importance of local, regional, and international boundaries. We are not discussing "panda diplomacy" between China and the United States or the biological/pest problems accompanying the rabbit in Australia, as fascinating as these are for political geography inquiry. Rather, we want to look at animal and plant populations and communities and consider them in light of their territories, movement, protection, and regulation – all environmental issues that were raised above when we examined human communities and boundaries.[23] As we determined, the state is the organizational unit that defines boundaries for its flora and fauna communities.

In this light, we consider three political geography/biology questions. First, do states address these issues? The answer is in the affirmative. Various examples illustrate the politics of plants and animals. These include defining exclusive economic zones for coastal, intercoastal, and high seas fishing; setting fish quotas; establishing fishing and hunting seasons; limiting catches and protecting unique plant and animal species by developing lists of threatened and endangered species; setting limits on timber harvests on state-owned properties; and establishing regulations (including fines and other penalties) for removal of endangered plants and animals from one state to another. Second, do plants and animals have rights? While this issue may appear to some to be frivolous and to others as of deep philosophical interest, animal and plant rights are high priorities in the minds of conservationists, preservationists, and ecologists who consider plant and animal species introductions, invasions, declines, and losses. For example, in October 1999 the New Zealand Parliament passed an Animal Welfare Act, which extended many rights to non-human hominids (five species also known as great ape species).[24] Many environmental and ecological NGOs operate and network across international boundaries and are concerned about individual state decisions that may affect the protection of a species on one side of a boundary but not on another as well as about human-constructed barriers that preclude seasonal movement of migratory species across transboundary spaces.[25] Reindeer move without passports across northern Norway, Sweden, and Finland, as do the Sami who hunt them. They also move unimpeded into Russia; however, Sami entrance into Russian space is prohibited. Large and small non-human mammals in a park along the China-Nepal border likewise can pass through political boundaries without problems. A similar condition also exists along the Waterton-Glacier International Peace Park between Montana and Alberta, which straddles the Canada-US border. Sharp agricultural land use differences along the US-Mexico border also display sharply different plant and animal communities. Along the Colorado River these differences are visible, in part because the United States virtually removes all water before it enters Mexico. Similarly, there are differences in agricultural land use along sections of the Canada-US border.

The "rights" of animals and plants are evident in national and international lists of endangered and threatened species included in international treaties and agreements (e.g., The World Conservation Union [IUCN]). Removing endangered plants illegally and transporting them across international boundaries violates international law, as does taking animals, or parts of animals, for souvenir, medical, or fashion purposes. In these cases, plants and animals have rights and merit protection.

The third question is: what role does the state play in what we term "the politics of biological destruction"? The crux of this question relates to the politics of economic development and what that means for biological communities as opposed to commercial developers. Biological communities include miniature plants and huge forests as well as individual fish and bird populations in inland and coastal locations, along with the routes and paths used by migrating species (especially their feeding and nesting areas). Many communities are being reduced or eliminated by the omnipresent bulldozers building suburban housing, office, and shopping centre developments, interstate highways and airports, military training sites and installations, and mega-engineering projects. In places of high population density – for example, Israel and the Netherlands – establishing, maintaining, and expanding nature preserves are sometimes in conflict with military training and testing grounds. These human-constructed landscapes, often sponsored directly by the state or with state authority and monetary support, will often destroy unique and common plant and animal species and, indeed, entire ecosystems by levelling hills, draining swamps, changing the course of rivers (Huang Ho and the Three Gorges project are an example), burning forests, and concreting a surface that once held places for fish to spawn, birds to feed and nest on long flyways, and large mammals to hunt, hibernate, and play. Conservation and preservation groups raise legitimate questions about "whose rights" are being violated by developments and who does and does not merit state protection.

The rights of plants and animals, the delimitation of biosphere reserves, and definitions of fragile land and water ecosystems are all for the state to decide. One may ask whether parks and preserves are becoming islands in the seas of landscape change. Are plants and animals and their communities (including their geometries) being protected, preserved, conserved for present and future generations? Sometimes threatened areas contain biodiversity levels that merit scientific research, often promising the discovery of new species (e.g., in late 1999 a new rabbit species was discovered along the Vietnam/Laotian border). Who "speaks" on behalf of the species that are threatened, endangered, and being destroyed? Debate in Colorado in late 2000 centred on the potential removal of prairie dogs, who were perceived as pests (by farmers and real estate developers), to "preservation pockets."[26] A "pock marked" ecological landscape is often the result of these political/biological decisions, unless there are international and interstate agreements protecting biological reserves and parks established so as to ensure that migrating fish, birds, and both large and small mammals can move unimpeded across international boundaries.[27]

Not only are the rights of animals raised but also their protection and welfare. Are animals (chickens, turkeys, hogs, beef cattle, etc.) raised in inhumane, unhealthy, and constrained spaces such as factory farms to be protected? Should they be allowed to enjoy sunlight, fresh air, and movement? Are zoos, which cater to the "gaze" of tourists, inhumane environments for animals? These are environmental, political, legal, and thus geographical questions.

Legal boundaries between humans and other species are also important with regard to in life and quality of life decisions. Legal boundaries usually privilege human well-being at the expense of the well-being of other species as most laws pertaining to society, nature, and animals are based upon anthropocentric principles. Anthropocentrism presumes that moral value is centred exclusively in human beings. Geographer William Lynn distinguishes the dominant value paradigm of anthropocentrism from non-anthropocentric value paradigms.[28] He emphasizes other relevant value paradigms that can be understood as non-anthropocentric, as not catering to a moral value centred exclusively on human beings. For example, supporters of biocentrism place moral value on individual beings, whether these beings are human or non-human. Those groups and organizations placing a high value on moral values support biocentrist values. Proponents of ecocentrism value ecological communities, including populations, species, and collectives. The traditional environmental movements and academics (e.g., conservation biologists) support ecocentrist values. Geocentrism, as outlined by Lynn, integrates anthropocentrism, biocentrism, and ecocentrism. All animals, including human beings, can be understood as ends in themselves (intrinsic value) as well as means to other ends (extrinsic value). Supporters of geocentrism value parts and wholes and see all animals as individuals, as members of certain species, and as parts of ecosystems.[29]

In this regard he proposes four principles of geoethics.[30] The first is the principle of geocentrism, which recommends the recognition of the moral value of all animals and nature. The second is the principle of equal consideration, which attempts to ensure that no creatures are inherently valued over any other creatures (although, according to Lynn, this should not justify outlandish comparisons and does not lead to sameness of treatment). The third is the principle of hard cases, which acknowledges the inevitable difficulties encountered within a contextual system and attempts to suggest a course of action that does not immediately privilege humans over non-humans. The fourth is the principle of moral carrying capacity, and it urges humans to consider the geographic communities in which they live (at many scales of organization) and to act in accordance with geographical morality.

Issues related to the maintenance of non-human biota, natural processes, and human influence illustrate the relevance of a geocentric perspective. Maintaining non-human biota is a complicated concern, and it raises issues of fixity and progress. Attempting to restore communities to their former condition does not allow for progress or change and does not recognize the inherent value of the dynamism of nature. Natural processes are cut out of the picture as it is assumed that nature has reached a pinnacle and that the environment should be maintained at that level while humanity continues to adapt and change. It also assumes that humanity is not a part of nature but, rather, belongs to a separate sphere of activity. This leaves us with an image of a Swiss cheese, with holes of progress and bordered off preserves of unchanging nature. It should not be forgotten that humans are a part of nature.

Delimiting preserves and reserves for plants and animals raise additional questions, especially in food-hungry parts of the world. Some African countries have chosen to preserve habitats for threatened wildlife, which may help promote tourist dollars in the "pleasure periphery,"[31] rather than to open up valuable rangeland for human settlement and increased cultivation.

It might be argued that maintaining non-human biota is the state's responsibility not only because of their inherent value but also because of their contributions to enhancing spiritual, artistic, educational, and humanistic dimensions. We need to remember that open and unrestricted boundaries present opportunities for unwelcome plants and animals to move across, whether these be airborne and water viruses, alien plants, species unknowingly brought in by tourists, or rabid animals (e.g., the case of foxes and raccoons along the Russia-Finnish border).

There is also the question of the "body" as a boundary.[32] These questions emerge, especially given the very rapid developments in genetic technology. Consider, for example, the cross-border consequences of selling genetically modified foods, in which the "borders" being crossed are both "state" boundaries and those of the body (via consumption). There is also the issue of the boundary of the plant/animal body being transgressed in order to be genetically manipulated. Another controversial issue is the use of genetically altered animals for human organ growth, which transgresses the imagined boundary between "human" and "animal." The US Patent and Trade Office has been granting "life patents" for twenty years. In 1980 a US Supreme Court decision ruled that microorganisms were patentable; in 1985 the US Patent and Trademark Office declared that plants and seeds were patentable; and in 1997 the patent commissioner stated that the licence to patent includes animals. The Institute for Agriculture and Trade Policy is an organization that seeks to ban the patenting of life.[33]

In January 1997 the US government decided to allow genetically modified food to be sold in stores; however, in late 2000, a number of controversies arose over the safety of many products with regard to human and livestock consumption. Some countries have more relaxed laws vis-à-vis pesticide use for agricultural products than do others. Discussions in the scientific, policy, and public arenas connect the local (the body) and global (international genetic scientific consortia). They look closely at the commercial and ethical ramifications of the Human Genome Project in diagnosing and treating mental and physical illnesses as well as the ethical issues of food and pharmaceutical research on the part of multinational agribusiness and chemical corporations (such as Monsanto and Ciba-Geigy). Another ticklish ethical issue relates to eugenics. While most European countries outlawed such policies last century, India, China, and Russia still support them.[34] In 1995 China passed a eugenics law that was specifically related to maternal and infantile health.[35] These and other issues bring into political geography relevant literature from such fields as medical ethics, health care law, cultural studies, anthropology, science and technology, and bioethics.

Summary: Where Do We Go from Here?

Our major purpose in addressing questions about the geopolitics of life and quality of life is to call attention to the fact that boundaries still matter to many humans and other living creatures on the planet. We believe it is important that international conferences address such topics as digitizing the earth, permeable boundaries, extraterritorial and extralegal politics, and the homogenization that accompanies globalization. Many individuals and groups on this planet remain "prisoners of space," to use a concept developed by our colleague Graham Rowles.[36] While he used this concept to refer to elderly persons, we know there are others in both rich and poor societies around the world who remain prisoners of spaces. Within state boundaries we see human worlds containing residents who are restricted and inhibited because of their refugee or alien status, their physical and/or mental disabilities, their lifestyle choices, and the boundary machinations that deny them equal access and opportunities. And we point to the need for political geographers to interface with biologists, in particular, biogeographers, ecologists, conservationists, preservationists, geneticists, and those working on maintaining biodiversity as well as addressing the issues of intellectual property, biopatenting, and biopiracy. Transboundary genetically modified organisms call for transboundary and global dialogue, regulation, and enforcement. Life and living should be the cornerstones of what concerns the social, policy, and natural sciences.

In writing this chapter we anticipate that it will stimulate further discussion on the geopolitics of life and living. We identify three topics and one project that we believe merit the attention of geographers, political scientists, sociologists, anthropologists, economists, and others interested in gender, class, race, religion, and law. The first topic is the "ethics of life and living," especially as these are related to state, interstate, and multistate issues. These would include concerns about who is eligible for donor organs (the rich countries?) and the legal and illegal trade in therapeutic "miracle" plants and body parts (of humans or other animals) or artificial organs. The second topic is the transboundary movements of individuals and groups. This would include political refugees and ecorefugees as well as those desiring or possessing multiple citizenships. It would also include women escaping serfdom, disabled populations seeking a healthier life, faith communities seeking religious freedom, and migrating plant and animal species and epiphenomenal communities. The third topic is plant and animal communities that cross international boundaries, particularly their habitat, nesting, and reproduction spaces and the threats to these from urban and suburban expansion as well as economic development schemes. We hope that these three topics will become foci for future international conferences.

Our project calls for the compilation, preparation, and publication of an

Atlas of Life and Living that will be similar to existing thematic atlases on women, environmental quality, and military spending. We can envision sections on children, women, the elderly, refugees, the mentally and physical disabled, immigrants, and prisoners of conscience. There would also be sections on regulations and trade in body parts and artificial organs, consumer product safety, boycotts, food scares, AIDS, pollution levels, humane and inhumane zoos, endangered species, habitat losses, and conservation/preservation areas. We envision a multilingual print and electronic atlas that would include topics important to both governments and NGOs. This undertaking might become the product of a multidisciplinary and international research team; potential funding might come through international governmental or non-governmental organizations.

In conclusion, we return to the Cyprus landscape discussed at the beginning of this chapter. It is important for scholars coming from different disciplinary and transdisciplinary perspectives and nationalities (and internationalities) to seize opportunities to study the geopolitics of life and living by welcoming the contributions of non-traditional political geographers. We need to encourage contributions both by political geographers and by social and natural scientists as well as those in the humanities who are willing to work on integrated scientific, medical, and humanitarian transdisciplinary research efforts. What is certain is that borders will continue to be important in life and living, and the extent to which we enjoy our lives will, in some measure, be affected by the boundaries "on the ground" and "in our minds."

Acknowledgments
We want to thank these individuals for helping us develop our thoughts and for the examples used in this paper: Harri Andersson, Kathleen Braden, Ruth Butler, Mary Ann Curulla, Susan Cutter, Mike Dorn, Margo Kleinfeld, Anssi Paasi, Barney Warf, and Douglas Young.

Notes
1 Diane Ackerman, *A Natural History of the Senses* (New York: Random House, 1990).
2 John W. Holmes, *The United States and Europe after the Cold War: A New Alliance?* (Columbia, SC: University of South Carolina Press, 1994); Kenichi Ohmae, *The Borderless World: Power and Strategy in the Interlinked Economy* (New York: Harper and Row, 1990).
3 Stanley D. Brunn and Thomas R. Leinbach, eds., *Collapsing Space and Time: Geographic Aspects of Information and Communication* (New York: HarperCollins, 1991); T.W. Luke and Gearóid Ó Tuathail, "Global Flowmations, Local Fundamentalisms, and Fast Geopolitics: 'America' in an Accelerating World Order," in *Unruly Worlds: Globalization, Governance, and Geography,* ed. A. Herod, Gearóid Ó Tuathail, and S.M. Roberts (New York and London: Routledge, 1998), 72-95; Stanley D. Brunn, Jeffrey A. Jones, and Shannon O'Lear, "Geopolitical Information and Communication in the Twenty-first Century," in *Reordering the World: Geopolitical Perspectives on the 21st Century,* 2nd ed., ed. George J. Demko and William B. Wood (Boulder, CO: Westview Press, 1999), 292-318.
4 Ibid.
5 Brunn and Leinbach, *Collapsing Space and Time;* James O. Wheeler, Yuko Aoyama, and

Barney Warf, *Cities in the Telecommunications Age: The Fracturing of Geographies* (New York and London: Routledge, 1991); M.I. Wilson and Kenneth E. Corey, eds., *Information Tectonics* (Chichester: Wiley, 2000).

6   Nicholas Blomley, *Law, Space, and the Geographies of Power* (New York: Guilford, 1994); Audrey Kobayashi, "Multiculturalism: Representing a Canadian Institution," in *Place/Culture Representation*, ed. James Duncan and David Ley (New York: Routledge, 1993), 205-31.

7   Donald J. Zeigler and Stanley D. Brunn, "Urban Ethnic Islands," in *Ethnicity in Contemporary America: A Geographical Appraisal*, ed. Jesse O. McKee (Lanham, MD: Rowman and Littlefield, 2000), 375-411.

8   Stanley D. Brunn, Harri Andersson, and Carl T. Dahlman, "Landscaping for Power and Defence," in *Landscapes of Defence*, ed. John Gold and George Revell (Essex: Pearson Education, 2000), 68-84.

9   Murray Feshbach, *Environmental and Health Atlas of Russia* (Moscow, Russia: Paims Publishing House, 1995).

10   See <http://Europe.cnn.com/2000/WORLD/Europe/UK/10/26/bse.science.index.html>.

11   T.R. Leinbach and S.D. Brunn, eds., *The Worlds of E-Commerce: Economic, Geographical and Social Dimensions* (London: Wiley International, 2001).

12   Joni Seager, *The Status of Women* (London: Penguin, 1997).

13   This language is in Article 27 of the United Nations Convention on the Rights of the Child. See <http://www.unhrc.ch/html/menu3/b/k2crc.htm>.

14   The Netherlands euthanasia legislation is found at <http://www.aph.gov.au/library/pubs/m/2000-01/01RN31.htm>.

15   Derek Gregory, *Geographical Imaginations* (Oxford, Blackwell, 1994); David Harvey, *Justice, Nature and the Geography of Difference* (Oxford: Blackwell, 1996); H. Lefebvre, *The Production of Space* (Oxford: Blackwell, 1991); Doreen Massey, *Space, Place, and Gender* (Minneapolis: University of Minnesota Press, 1994); Neil Smith, *Uneven Development* (London: Blackwell, 1990).

16   Martin Dodge and Rob Kitchen, *Mapping Cyberspace* (New York and London: Routledge, 2001).

17   D.J. Haraway, *Simians, Cyborgs and Women: The Reinvention of Nature* (New York: Routledge, 1991); D.J. Haraway, *Modest-Witness@Second-Millennium.FemaleMan-MeetsOncoMouse: Feminism and Technoscience* (New York: Routledge, 1997).

18   Francis Harvey and Stanley D. Brunn, "Here, There, and Everywhere: Geoliminality and the Burden of *Dasein*," *Limen: Journal for Theory and Practice of Liminal Phenomena*, 3, 1-2 (2002), <http://www.human.pefri.hr/cro/limen.htm>.

19   M. Mangalindan and K. Delaney, "Yahoo! Ordered to Bar the French from Nazi Items," *Wall Street Journal*, 21 November 2000, B1.

20   Rob Kitchen, *Cyberspace: The World in Wires* (Chichester: Wiley, 1998).

21   S.D. Brunn, "Human Rights in the Electronic State," in *Information Tectonics: Space, Place and Technology in an Electronic Age*, ed. M.I. Wilson and K.E. Corey (Chichester and New York: John Wiley, 2000), 41-64.

22   John Pickles, *Ground Truth: The Social Implications of Geographic Information Systems* (New York, Guilford Press, 1995).

23   Seager, *The Status of Women*.

24   New Zealand's Animal Welfare Act is presented at <http://www.maf.govt.nz/biosecurity/legislation/animal-welfare-act>.

25   D. Zbicz and M.J.B. Green, "Status of the World's Transfrontier Protected Areas," *Parks* 7, 3 (1997): 5-10.

26   National Public Radio, "Morning Edition," 1 December 2000.

27   S.D. Brunn and D.C. Munski, "The International Peace Garden: A Case Study in Locational Harmony," *IBRU Boundary and Security Bulletin* 7, 3 (1999): 67-74.

28   William Lynn, "Aniclas, Ethics and Geography," in *Animals Geographies*, ed. Jennifer Wolch and Jody Emel (London: Verso, 1998), 280-97.

29   Ibid., 288-90.

30   Ibid., 292-94.

31 David Zurick, *Errant Journeys: Adventure Travel in a Modern Age* (Austin: University of Texas Press, 1995), 18-21.
32 Barney Warf, "Compromising Positions: The Body in Cyberspace" in *Cities in the Telecommunications Age: The Fracturing of Geographies,* ed. J.O. Wheeler, Yuko Aoyama, and Barney Warf (New York and London: Routledge, 2000), 54-68.
33 See Institute for Agriculture and Trade Policy, <http://www.iatp.org>.
34 D. Dickson, "Survey: Some Countries Side with China on Genetic Issues," *Nature Medicine* 4 (1998): 1096.
35 Roger Pearson, "Whatever Happened to Eugenics?" *Mankind Quarterly* 37 (1996): 203-15.
36 Graham D. Rowles, *Prisoners of Space? Exploring the Geography Experiences of Older People* (Boulder: Westview Press, 1970).

19
From the International to the Local in the Study and Representation of Boundaries: Theoretical and Methodological Comments
David Newman

Introduction: Seeking a Conceptual Approach to the Study of Boundaries

Much of the boundary literature of recent years has commented on the lack of a conceptual or theoretical framework that can be used as a means of drawing the increasingly diverse strands of "boundary" studies into an integrated and analytical framework.[1] The study of international boundaries continues to be seen as a separate subset of the overall study of the boundary phenomenon, a phenomenon that can best be described as one that draws lines around social and spatial compartments and that serves to include some and exclude others, be they states, ethnic or social groups, religions, or even virtual associations. The study of international boundaries has traditionally been differentiated from any other form of boundary – internal, administrative, and municipal – because of the sovereignty and barrier dimensions of the lines enclosing the state territory, which do not apply to the other forms of boundary. But the impact of globalization has meant that international boundaries are now much more permeable than has been the case in the past, with greater movement of capital, information, people, and goods taking place at the state interface. Thus the focus for the study of boundaries is the bounding or bordering process; namely, the functional impact of the boundary rather than its descriptive and static locational characteristics. A deeper understanding of the boundary phenomenon places all types of boundaries on a single functional continuum. The precise location of any boundary along this continuum will be dependent on the extent to which the boundary is permeable to a greater or lesser degree, allowing movement of people, goods, information, or other sorts of transboundary interaction, from one side to the other.

Any attempt, therefore, to create a methodological and conceptual framework for the understanding of boundaries must be concerned with the process of "bordering," rather than simply with the means through which physical lines of separation are delimited and demarcated. The use of the term "boundary," or "border," has become an important part of the discourse in many disciplines during the past decade and has acquired a diversity of specific and particularistic meanings, ranging from the geographic to the economic and sociological and on to the anthropological.[2] In some cases, it represents the point (line) of separation between two entities (be they states, academic disciplines, or social groups), in others they represent the delimiters of the containers that include some and exclude others, while in yet others they denote the point of contact between two (or more) separate entities as well as (to use some of the classic political geography and international boundary jargon) the borderlands or frontier zones that mark a gradual and smooth transition from one entity to another.

This chapter attempts to suggest some pointers with regard to creating an all-embracing methodology to deal with the bordering process. Such a methodology needs to take account of different forms and definitions of boundaries, ranging from the territorial to the aspatial and from the social to the virtual and cyber lines of compartmentalization. The international boundary is but one – important – subset of the wider phenomenon. The discussion focuses on four dimensions of the boundary phenomenon:

1   Boundaries will be seen as hierarchical phenomena, including international, internal, and administrative lines of separation on a single functional continuum.
2   Boundaries will be understood as not only enclosing physical spaces and territories but also as social groups and affiliations, many of which may not have a fixed territorial focus.
3   Boundaries need to be understood as dynamic and constantly changing, rather than as static and unchanging, phenomena, given the longer sweep of human history throughout which territorial change, at all levels of spatial analysis, has been in perpetual flux.
4   In representing boundaries as part of a geographical text, particularly through the agency of mapping and cartography, it is necessary to link the political and the social understanding of boundaries and their impact on society with the technical methods that are currently available for depicting these boundaries, both in terms of their hierarchical structure (see 1 and 2 above) and as constructs whose location along the "closed-open" continuum (see 3 above) can be continually plotted.

Boundaries and the Contemporary World Political Map

Despite all the talk of a "borderless" world, international boundaries have not disappeared from the world political map, nor are they likely to do so in the near future. Despite the notions of a deterritorialized and a "borderless" world that have been posited so strongly in recent years, these phenomena have been seen as existing, at the most, within specific cultural milieus – North America and Western Europe – and as relevant to specific functions such as the transboundary movement of capital and/or the dissemination of information through electronic and cyber means.[3] But boundaries remain important features of the political and geographical landscape, especially in regions of ethno-territorial conflict, where those involved seek to demarcate their new lines of territorial separation.[4] Indeed, many cultures are only now beginning to come to terms with the notions of territorial fixation imposed upon them in the past by colonial powers – the same powers that, under different names, are today in the forefront of the borderless world theories. At the most, international boundaries are, like most social and political features, geographically differentiated – retaining a greater impact in some regions and places than in others.

Boundary characteristics have changed in that they have become increasingly permeable during the past decade, as technology has brought about the means of transboundary movement of capital and information. This freedom of movement has impacted strongly upon the nature of state sovereignty, such that the territorial reconfigurations of power that have been taking place during the past decade have also brought about a parallel globalization and localization (together, a localization) of political activity as territorial notions of power become diffused through different levels of spatial activity.[5]

The recent boundary literature has attempted to tie in different concepts and notions of boundaries in an attempt to create a holistic model of the impact of boundaries on both society and space.[6] In addition to the traditional function of boundaries as lines that separate state territories, boundaries play other roles. Boundaries are social constructs that determine the limits of group and national identity, including some and excluding others.[7] While national identity is tied up with the geographical location of the members of the group within a defined and compartmentalized territory (often, but not exclusively, the state), identity boundaries increasingly have a non-spatial dimension in that they include members of the group who live outside the territorial hearth or homeland of the group, while excluding non-members of the group who reside – temporarily or permanently – within that same territorial core. This is a major factor in explaining the "end of the nation-state" thesis, which has traditionally argued that the relationship between states and nations is determined by the spatial dispersion of members of the national group within the territory that is enclosed by the state boundaries. Given today's technological means of communication, diaspora, refugee, and migrant communities can continue to be part of the national group on an active and daily basis without necessarily residing within the territory of the nation-state (their boundaries are fixed elsewhere), while an increasing number of ethnic and migrant groups who are not part of the "nation" are part of the citizen population of the state, whose rights and obligations are determined by the territory within which they reside and are enclosed by the state boundaries.

Identities are multi-layered and hierarchical in that the individual is a member of many groups, ranging from the national to the family, the religious, the social, the neighbourhood (to name but a few), all of which have their own boundaries – some spatial, some social. While the territorial boundaries of the state continue to be the major reference point of group (national) belonging for most people, it is the other group affiliations and feelings of belonging that are coming to the fore in a world undergoing rapid reterritorialization. We use the term "reterritorialization" to describe not only the process through which new states are established, new boundaries demarcated, and the territorial shape of the state reconfigured, but also – and perhaps more important – the process through which the structural impact of globalization affects the relative importance of state – as contrasted with global, regional, and local – territories, and, by association, the functions and characteristics of the boundaries that enclose these state territories. As such the importance of boundaries may diminish and become partial rather than absolute, but they do not disappear altogether. In this sense, the notion that the world is undergoing a process of "deterritorialization" is rejected since there is no such phenomenon.[8] There is, and only can be, a process of "reterritorialization," one that has both a spatial and a structural impact. It is true that contemporary notions of power and control do not necessarily have to be defined in exclusively territorial or spatial terms; nevertheless, territory remains a central component of power, and the state continues to retain a major, albeit no longer hegemonous, place within the hierarchical power structure.

Permeability and Boundary Hierarchies

While state boundaries continue to demarcate the de jure sovereign territory of the state, it is the nature and function of sovereignty that are undergoing change as a result of the greater permeability of boundaries. As flows of capital and information pass, unimpeded, through state boundaries, so too do states lose control of the exclusive decision-making powers they previously held.[9] No longer are states able to maintain absolute control of economic, migration, and social policy that takes place within the state boundaries, notwithstanding the fact that the precise location and configuration of these boundaries has not necessarily changed.

But the "enclosure" function of boundaries continues to play an important role at a variety of social and spatial scales – both globally and locally. In particular, the relative impact of administrative and municipal boundaries is increasing in importance as the impact of the state boundary decreases. The localization of human activity that has resulted, paradoxically, from the globalization process has brought about the empowerment of local and regional groups, be they ethnic/national, or simply local/neighbour-hood with a common interest in preserving, and improving, their quality of life. The boundaries of their locales may be the formal administrative boundaries of the autonomous or planning regions inside the state, or the residents of a particular region or neighbourhood may simply perceive them. In many cases, the perceived functional boundaries of the locale may be stronger in explaining the spatial activity patterns of the residents than the formal planning and municipal lines that separate the diverse neighbourhoods. Perceived lines are not marked on maps, nor do they determine to which municipal authority we pay taxes, or in which state we are citizens, but they normally reflect, much more accurately, the real lines of group inclusion and exclusion, and the people with whom we feel, instinctively, most comfortable in our daily lives.[10]

Clearly, boundaries that are not state boundaries are perceived as being far more permeable and easy to cross. This is the case with respect to the lines that separate municipal, planning, and administrative areas from each other. We are not normally aware when we physically cross these invisible lines that separate our own neighbourhood or city from the neighbouring areas. There may be a sign on the roadside, but we are not stopped or asked for documentation that permits, or limits, our access to these neighbouring areas. At the same time, these lower-level hierarchical boundaries normally affect our daily life patterns to a much greater extent than do the boundaries of the state. They determine to whom we pay municipal taxes, to which schools we can send our children, and to which hospitals we can go for treatment. As such, they may be more permeable than state boundaries in one sense (the act of physical movement) but less permeable in terms of their functional impact upon our daily lives. For most of the world's population, it is the act of registering at a local health centre, or a local school, that is determined by the demarcation of admin-istrative boundaries and with which we are concerned on a daily basis, as contrasted with the rare occasions we have to cross the national boundary, a process that still requires most of us to have the correct passport, visa, and other documentation.

Similarly, the social boundaries that determine our various group affilia-tions display both "open" and "closed" characteristics. They are permeable in the sense that we cannot define their geographic or spatial location, and we are not normally aware when we cross the invisible boundary separat-ing one from the other. The exceptions to this rule are those cases where strong processes of ethnic residential segregation create a spatial homo-geneity of a particular ethnic, linguistic, or religious group, normally as part of an ethnic ghetto inside a city, or a mono-ethnic village in countries that are characterized by ethno-territorial conflict. At the same time, these social boundaries display almost "sealed" characteristics in terms of our ability to move from one social territory into another. This is particularly true with respect to our religious and/or family affiliations, to which membership is defined by very rigid boundaries that include some and exclude most others. It is not impossible to cross this type of boundary but it requires a great deal of effort, the visa to which normally requires conversion (to another religion), marriage (into another family), retraining (into another job), and/or learning to speak another language. Where the social and spatial boundaries coincide, the degree of impermeability, the inability to cross from one territory/group to the other, is the most difficult, and this takes on its most extreme from where claims to power and/or territory are contested, characterized by conflict – often violent – between the groups.

These hierarchical boundaries within which our lives are compartmentalized is not a new phenomenon. They have been with us for as long as human society has been ordered. But the relative importance of these boundaries is increasingly coming to the fore as state boundaries lose their predominant role in the ordering of human society and as global notions such as the rights of the individual and/or group empowerment take on an added dimension. The rights of the individual and/or the small group compete for allegiance with that of the state, normally defined through a combination of citizenship and geographical location of residence, and, whereas in the past it was the state that automatically determined the hegemonic boundary in this hierarchical relationship, this is no longer the case. Individual and group identities compete with state affiliation and membership, particularly in the Western postindustrial world, with the result that these can take increasing predominance over what was traditionally perceived as a primordial allegiance to the state. This is part of a postnationalism discourse that is becoming increasingly relevant to the changing realities of many parts of the world, not least Western Europe and, to a lesser extent, North America.

This changing relationship between the hierarchy of layered boundaries on the one hand, and the exclusion and inclusion functions of both social and spatial boundaries on the other, is a more structural definition of the process of reterritorialization that has been experienced during the past decade and that is continuing to redefine the relationship between society and space, people and territory. It touches upon the essential question concerning the relationship between territorial organization – at a number of scales – and the location of power within society. Thus, to limit the definition of contemporary territorial change to the spatial reconfiguration of state territories, as is the case with most studies of international boundaries, is missing the point and fails to adequately deal with the spatial and territorial impact of globalization. Such studies do continue to provide us with an important source of data relating to territorial change. They also show us the way in which new technologies can be used as a means of resolving demarcation and delimitation issues. But, standing alone, they do not adequately deal with the process through which society is bounded and rebounded in a hierarchy of wrappings and packages, only one of which – albeit a thicker wrapping – is that compartment known as the state.

Measuring Permeability: Some Methodological Issues

How, in this hierarchical world of boundaries, is boundary permeability to be measured? In contrast to the previous discussion, we will focus on the way in which the permeability of state boundaries can be measured, in the hope that this will contribute towards the creation of a model for the measurement of any type of boundary permeability, be it at a different spatial scale (internal and administrative), or be it a group/social, aspatial line of demarcation. While state boundaries have become more permeable to certain functions – such as the movement of capital or the diffusion of information through cyberspace and the Internet – they still retain their barrier characteristics for other functions, not least the restriction on the movement of people, and the practise of law and order within the state territory. It is not only an issue of awareness. The state is aware of the fact that certain functions cross the boundary, and it would prefer to re-establish its sovereignty by preventing the continued transboundary movement of these phenomena, but is simply unable to do anything. In this sense, technology is far stronger than the power of the state since the state is unable to restrict the free movement of those functions – capital and/or information – even where it expresses its desire to do so.

While boundaries have therefore become open to some phenomena, they remain closed to others. As such, boundaries cannot simply be defined on a single continuum of "open-closed" as has been the case in many past boundary typologies. This is made even more complex by the fact that no particular function – be it the movement of capital, information, or migrants – is uniform in the extent to which it does, or does not, move freely through a boundary. Some boundaries are permeable to certain features, other boundaries are less permeable to these same features but more permeable to others. Culture and location play an important role in determining the extent to which any boundary is more or less permeable to different functions of global movement. Thus, the measurement of boundary permeability must take account of geographical differentiation in the functional nature of boundaries. Rather than attempt to create a new boundary prototype, it is necessary to locate boundaries along a continuum, ranging from "closed and sealed" to "open and permeable." The boundaries of any particular country will move along this continuum (normally from a "closed" location to a more "permeable" location but not categorically so in every instance) as the impact of technology, capital, and cyberspace gradually take effect. The sum permeability of any particular boundary will take into account the location along the continuum with respect to each different function separately, rather than as a predetermined "whole." Thus one state boundary may be more permeable to capital markets and migrant labour, and less permeable to information flows (if only because many Third World countries simply do not yet have access to the technology), while another state boundary may be totally open to information and cyber flows but be more restrictive to the movement of labour and goods. Thus the sum total of such a permeability index may be similar in two or more cases but may be derived from different subcomponents that reflect on the contrasting nature of these boundaries in comparative perspective.

The Representation of Boundary Permeability

The way in which boundaries, as, indeed, other spatial features are represented on maps is an important part of the process through which their functions, not just their locations, are understood. Part of the process through which the boundary phenomenon can be understood concerns the way in which boundaries are represented – normally through the agency of mapping and cartography, which creates the social and spatial visual images through which we identify and recognize the spaces within which we live and interact. As such, the representation of boundaries is an important part of the political and territorial socialization processes through which our respective understandings of the world, global and local, are formed.

The texts through which physical and territorial boundaries can be understood, and deconstructed, are maps. The political map and its representation of state boundaries and territories is an important text for political geographers. The importance of maps as part of the process through which national and state identities are formed over long periods of time, and the way in which states and empires have put maps to work in their attempt to expand and consolidate control over territories, has become an important theme in human geography during the past decade.[11] Central to this work has been an analysis of just who drew up the maps, in the service of which governments and institutions, and using what symbols and semantics as a means of creating a visual impression of the political and territorial constructions of reality. In this way, the deconstruction of maps as political-geographic texts is no less important than is the deconstruction of written texts, be they political manifestos or pieces of literature. The ways in which specific maps, with their images, are used as part of the education system, in school textbooks, in media advertisements, and so on are, in turn, influential in creating the spatial images of regions, territories, and bounded spaces that are conceived as constituting the "correct" ordering of the world political map and that influence the political positions adopted by individuals and governments with relation to state territories and political power.

The study of the textual content of maps, of which political boundaries are but one component, has tended to focus exclusively on the role of state/international boundaries. But contested municipal and administrative boundaries are also the subject of cartographic representation on behalf of interested clients and pressure groups (local authorities, municipal councils, planning agencies) in the submission of claims to arbitration and decision-making authorities. The expertise required for an immediate understanding of a map is not always present and, as such, interest groups may often be visually deceived when presented with specific spatial images and texts. The fact that certain features appear while others are absent, or the scale dimensions of villages, borderlines, and physical resources, are not always immediately apparent to the untrained observer. This can, and often is, manipulated by the boundary "drawers" to advance their own cause, or the cause of the interests they represent, in creating a false spatial impression of reality and, as such, influencing decision makers to demarcate lines that serve specific interests.

The way in which the lines are represented – as thick or thin, red or black – the names given to the territories that they enclose, and the size of the territorial fonts all go a long way to creating the spatial impression necessary for reaching a demarcation decision in favour of one, or the other, claimants. Publication of such maps also goes a long way in constructing the public image of what "should" and "should not" be the "correct" means of boundary demarcation and territorial partition. Important in this respect is the language/semantics used (do we use Arabic or Hebrew in Israel/Palestine, Greek or Turkish in Cyprus, German or Polish in Western Poland, and so on) and the size of the lettering or symbols used to depict particular features of the landscape (for example, in my own research, Israeli maps sometimes depict West Bank settlements containing no more than a few thousand people in brighter colours and larger sizes than the neighbouring Palestinian townships that, in reality, contain tens of thousands of inhabitants). Historical maps may often be distorted or exaggerated to justify competing ethnic claims to territory, just as they may be used to justify competing municipal claims. The series of short articles by Denis Rushworth, which appeared in consecutive issues of the *Boundary and Security Bulletin,* provide ample evidence for the importance of mapping in support of frontier arbitration.[12] The time period and the nature of the claim may be different, but the process through which the visual images are constructed by interested parties in order to strengthen their own respective claims is a powerful process that, until recently, has been neglected but that requires a great deal of research.

It is possible to devise means of mapping through which the hierarchies and/or the relative permeability of boundaries is shown. At the simplest level, boundaries can be marked in different colours and/or graded as A, B, and C categories, depending on the nature of the boundary (external, internal, administrative, etc.) or on the extent to which it displays greater or lesser permeability. The importance of such a categorization is the recognition that the international boundary is part of a boundary continuum, of which state boundaries are but one type (in some senses this is similar to the argument in International Relations that has become so prominent in recent years; namely, that foreign policy and internal policy cannot be understood as two distinct, unrelated, categories but, rather, are part of a single continuum of decision making, each influencing the outcome of the other). Such a categorization would focus on the functions and impacts of boundaries, rather than simply acknowledging their existence as lifeless and static lines. The extent to which each of the boundary types performs a barrier or permeability function, and the nature of the permeability ("openness") of the boundary in different spheres of human activity, should be represented by the diverse ways in which the cartographer represents the boundary. This need not only relate to the more blatant dimensions of transboundary movement, such as the flow of capital, information, or illegal migrants: it can also take into account additional factors, such as crime[13] or the sex industry,[14] which, while less prominent in the literature on boundaries, are also important indicators of the extent to which boundaries are located along the permeability continuum.

In an age of computer cartography, this technical task should not be too difficult. But the determination of the values and weightings to be included is a sensitive issue and, however determined, they will, no doubt, be open to critical analysis and constant attempts at modification. A simple computer-GIS (geographic information system) program should have little difficulty in creating a hierarchical pattern of boundary permeability. Placing map layers, each of which depicts a different boundary function, on top of each other, could create an aggregate picture of boundary permeability. Equally, this form of cartography would enable the relative status of a boundary, be it state, regional, or municipal, to be constantly revised and updated as conditions on the ground – for any particular form of human activity that affects boundary permeability – change. Thus boundaries would not only be viewed from a hierarchical perspective enabling state and local boundaries to be taken as a single geopolitical category, but they would also be recognized for their essential functional dynamics (which undergo constant change) rather than as unchanging and static physical constructs whose location rarely changes, and even when it does is only depicted on maps at a much later stage.

Using Technology to Resolve Boundary Issues

In recent years, the application of GIS techniques to solving problems of international relations in general, and boundary issues in particular, has been proposed.[15] Geographic information technologies are an important tool for integrating remote sensing data gathered by satellites and aircrafts. Such data includes aspects of land use, environmental management, and socioeconomic parameters. The anticipated outcome of such a boundary demarcation project would be to determine whether an automated information and mapping system can assist in the resolution of territorial conflict. Similar techniques have been used for many planning and decision-making problems in the local and urban areas of analysis, but not for national political boundary demarcation. While the technology does not substitute for the emotive process of political decision making, it provides a level of sophistication and detail that does not exist today.

By using GIS to assess potential boundaries between contested claims (such as Israel and the Palestinian Authority) it would be possible to define, construct, and test a system that would automatically propose boundaries based on predetermined criteria.[16] By producing a score table that quantifies gains and losses, the system would optimize the costs and benefits of different "separation lines" for each of the parties to the negotiation process. Relevant criteria could include such factors as: land use patterns, strategic elevations, location of critical areas of the water aquifer and information regarding the availability of water, Israeli settlement on both sides of the "green line," Arab/Palestinian settlement on both sides of the "green line," transboundary transportation and other heavy infrastructure. The criteria can be given "value" weightings based on perceived importance or priority and/or economic values. For example, land can be assigned a price relatively easily based on its current market value. Water, of critical importance to this process, can also be assigned a value. If these were the only criteria, then the party for which the analysis is being conducted (the Israelis or Palestinians) would achieve control over the entire area in dispute.

Such an exercise would not, nor would it be intended to, propose an "optimum" boundary line, as it is assumed that there is no such thing. Optimal lines are difficult, in many cases impossible, to demarcate, since the optimal line for one side is often the worst line for the other side in the conflict. As such, mutual territorial concessions are a necessary element within any negotiated demarcation process. The determination of either side to focus on historical and/or ideological attachment to a territorial homeland may make this problem insoluble, especially where more than one side lays claim to the same territory. Mutual compromise based on pragmatic considerations as they relate to the spatial realities has to be a basic pre-condition for any such form of territorial negotiation. The relative advantages and disadvantages for each side have to be clearly outlined and visible, if contesting sides are to arrive at a balanced, and mutually acceptable, solution. The greater the knowledge of mutual costs and benefits of any particular boundary demarcation scenario, the greater the possibility that negotiations can, where necessary, bring about a more equitable partition of territory.

Rather than create the "optimum" line of separation, such an exercise would create a boundary database, including maps, showing the relative costs and benefits to each side emanating from a number of alternative lines. The maps would show the implications for each of the criteria for each of the participants. Different combinations of maps could be presented, so that the aggregated costs and benefits to each side could be clearly determined. An additional series of maps could depict the main areas of potential conflict between the two sides based on the individual and aggregated criteria, thus reducing the area of contention to those areas where real conflict of interest is to be found. It should be noticed, however, that the symbolic dimensions of ethnic and territorial conflict – the dimensions around which it is often impossible to arrive at conflict resolution and around which negotiations often collapse – cannot be adequately quantified or depicted as cartographic measures. Notwithstanding, the use of such techniques to represent the quantifiable and tangible dimensions of competing claims to territory and boundaries is a tool that has not yet been fully exploited by governments, diplomats, and negotiators.

An alternative, more sophisticated, method of dealing with such a boundary issue would be to have a program written that would determine the line of maximal separation (if this is the political objective of the boundary demarcation) for any given characteristic (security, settlements, land-uses, water aquifers, transportation routes, sites of historic and symbolic significance, etc.). Different lines would be achieved for each characteristic, the maps of which could then be layered on top of each other in an attempt to determine those areas where the desired separation is easily achievable, as contrasted with those areas where the lines conflict with each other and where political bargaining and trade-offs would have to be made in order for a political solution to be reached.

Decision makers will be able to compare the relative costs and benefits accruing from any preferred solution according to their own sets of priorities. Notwithstanding, given this level of cartographic and demarcation sophistication, the ultimate decision concerning boundary demarcation is a political, rather than a technical, one. However, decision makers often bemoan the lack of spatial information available to them (although they conveniently use such lack of information as a post-factum excuse for having reached a poor decision), and this would provide them with the necessary boundary database from which to derive a more informed solution, enabling them and negotiators to weigh up the pros and cons of different boundary lines.

Concluding Comments

This chapter has attempted to draw together some theoretical comments concerning the changing nature and understanding of boundaries and to provide some methodological suggestions concerning how boundaries can be adequately measured and represented as cartographic images. The underlying theme is that, given the changing nature of boundaries and their hierarchical and functional attributes, the tools used to measure these phenomena must have some sort of in-built flexibility that recognizes their internal dynamism rather than – as has been the case in much of the past literature – conceiving of boundaries as static and unchanging phenomena. The lack of a conceptual and theoretical base for the study of international boundaries has, paradoxically, enabled us to suggest some ideas for the measurement and representation of the "bounding" phenomenon, as contrasted with the boundary line, without becoming entrapped by a specific form of boundary language (be it the international, the municipal, or the aspatial-sociological). These comments and suggestions should serve as the start of a debate that can contribute to the creation of a framework for the understanding of boundaries and bounding in such a way that they can be constantly updated and brought into line with the reality of political change – be it global or local – and, as such, provide an important tool for decision making and the determination of policy.

Notes

1 D. Newman and A. Passi, "Fences and Neighbors in the Postmodern World: Boundary Narratives in Political Geography," *Progress in Human Geography* 22, 2 (1998): 186-207; D. Newman, "Boundaries," in *A Companion to Political Geography,* ed. J. Agnew, K. Mitchell, and G. Toal (Oxford, UK: Blackwell, 2002), 123-37.

2 H. Donnan, and T. Wilson, eds., *Border Approaches: Anthropological Perspectives on Frontiers* (New York and London: University Press of America, 1994); H. Eskelinen, I. Liikanen, and J. Oksa, eds., *Curtains of Iron and Gold: Reconstructing Borders and Scales of Interaction* (Aldershot: Ashgate Press, 1999); M. Pratt and J. Brown, eds., *Borderlands Under Stress* (London: Kluwer Academic Press, 2000).

3 D. Newman, "Geopolitics Renaissant: Territory, Sovereignty and the World Political Map," *Geopolitics* 3, 1 (1998): 1-16.

4 D. Newman, "Into the Millennium: The Study of International Boundaries in an Era of Global and Technological Change," *Boundary and Security Bulletin* 7, 4 (1999): 63-71; G.H. Blake, "State Borders in a Globalizing World: Observations on Form and Function," *Geopolitics* 5, 2 (2000): 1-18.

5 J. Agnew, *Place and Politics: The Geographical Mediation of State and Society* (London: Allen and Unwin, 1987).

6 Newman and Passi, "Fences and Neighbours in the Postmodern World"; J. O'Loughlin and V. Kolossov, "New Borders for New World Orders: Territorialities at the Fin-de-Siècle," *Geojournal* 44, 3 (1999): 259-73; D. Newman, "Boundaries, Borders and Barriers: On the Territorial Demarcation of Lines," in *Identity, Borders, Orders: New Directions in International Relations Theory*, ed. M. Albert, D. Jacobson, and Y. Lapid (Minnesota: University of Minnesota Press, 2001); D. Newman, "The Lines That Separate: Boundaries and Borders in Political Geography," in J. Agnew and G.Ó Tuathail, eds., *A Companion to Political Geography* (Oxford: Blackwell, 2001).

7 A. Paasi, *Territories, Boundaries and Consciousness: The Changing Geographies of the Finnish-Russian Border* (Chichester: John Wiley, 1996); M.J. Shapiro and H.R. Alker, eds., *Challenging Boundaries: Global Flows, Territorial Identities* (Minneapolis: University of Minneapolis Press, 1996); H. Donnan and T. Wilson, eds., *Border Approaches: Anthropological Perspectives on Frontiers* (New York and London: University Press of America, 1994).

8 D. Newman, "Boundaries, Territory and Postmodernity: Towards Shared or Separate Spaces?" in *Borderlands Under Stress*, ed. M. Pratt and J. Brown (London: Kluwer Academic Press, 2000).

9 Gearóid Ó Tuathail, "Borderless Worlds: Problematizing Discourses of Deterritorialization in Global Finance and Digital Culture," *Geopolitics* 4, 2 (1999): 139-54.

10 D. Sibley, *Geographies of Exclusion: Society and Difference in the West* (London: Routledge, 1996).

11 Jeremy Black, *Maps and Politics* (Chicago, University of Chicago Press, 1997); Jeremy Black, *Maps and History: Constructing Images of the Past* (New Haven: Yale University Press, 1997).

12 D. Rushworth, "Mapping in Support of Frontier Arbitration I," *Boundary and Security Bulletin* 4, 2 (1996): 60-62; D. Rushworth, "Mapping in Support of Frontier Arbitration II," *Boundary and Security Bulletin* 4, 3 (1997): 57-61; D. Rushworth, "Mapping in Support of Frontier Arbitration: Delimitation and Demarcation," *Boundary and Security Bulletin* 5, 1 (1998): 61-64; D. Rushworth, "Mapping in Support of Frontier Arbitration: Maps as Evidence," *Boundary and Security Bulletin* 5, 4 (1998): 51-55; D. Rushworth, "Mapping in Support of Frontier Arbitration: Boundary Definition, Boundary Disclaimer Notes, Toponymy," *Boundary and Security Bulletin* 7, 1 (1999).

13 P. Chalk, "Cross-Border Crime and the Gray Area Phenomena in Southeast Asia," *Boundary and Security Bulletin* 6, 3 (1998): 67-75.

14 C. Grundy-Warr, R. King, and G. Risser, "Cross-Border Migration, Trafficking and the Sex Industry: Thailand and Its Neighbours," *Boundary and Security Bulletin* 4, 1 (1996): 86-97.

15 H. Starr and W. Bain, "The Application of Geographic Information Systems to International Studies," *International Studies Notes* 20, 2 (1995): 1-8; H. Starr, "Using Geographic Systems to Revisit Enduring Rivalries: The Case of Israel," *Geopolitics* 5, 3 (2000); W. Wood, "Complex Emergency Response Planning and Coordination: Potential GIS Applications," *Geopolitics* 5, 2 (2000); D. Blumberg and D. Jacobson, "New Frontiers: Remote Sensing in Social Science Research," *American Sociologist* 28, 3 (1997): 61-68.

16 D. Newman, J. Isaac, and D. Blumberg, "Utilizing Geographic Information Technologies to Propose Alternative Scenarios for Resolving Border Conflicts: The Israel-Palestine Case," submitted to the Truman Institute for Peace Research, Hebrew University of Jerusalem, Israel, 1997.

Conclusion
Heather Nicol

The hotly debated topic of the 1990s was whether globalization had indeed encouraged the development of a borderless world: *Holding the Line* has not revisited this issue. Its starting point is that borders have continuing relevance and that "borderlessness" has not become the new basis of international organization in the late twentieth and early twenty-first centuries, nor have the geographies of globalization served to reinforce the state of deterritorialization. Blake (Chapter 1), who touches off the discussion of contemporary bordering processes, suggests that there is a need to recast the study of bordering processes and the geopolitical and geoterritorial dimensions represented by the physical and cognitive definition of "borders" in contemporary studies.

This is a reality that practitioners, strategists, and defence planners in the developed world have been forced to confront with respect to global politics. In the United States, for example, Ó Tuathail argues that "a postmodern geopolitical imagination attuned to globalization, informationalization and scientific-environmental challenges [has been] increasingly evident in the public thinking, alongside its traditional concerns with territorial enemies, security alliances and balance of power politics."[1] Certainly this issue is all the more relevant given the events of fall 2001, when the current Bush administration was forced to face the challenge of increasingly deterritorialized threats to national security (e.g., environmental degradation, the proliferation of weapons of mass destruction, transnational terrorism, and ethnic nationalism). The metaphor of the "fence" rather than the filter has become increasingly popular in describing the function of American borders. While perhaps helpful in addressing the immediate question of how to "keep the bad guys out," such thinking is of limited utility in a broader context. While to Americans the question becomes how to manage such issues as national security within an international political context that remains state-centred (i.e., where security is a strategic domestic issue), for much of the world the question remains ultimately transnational in character: are there alternatives to "state-centred" systems that still maintain national sovereignty and self-determination? Indeed, are there alternatives to transborder cooperation that fall outside of a "strategic" security paradigm?

We have seen throughout this volume that, while territory and power are embodied within borders, permeable borders do not negate sovereignty but may, in fact, be instrumental in extending and revitalizing national legitimacy beyond the context of geographical territory. Consequently, while much emphasis has recently been placed upon traditional security, and the institutions of postindustrial Western states have engaged in defence planning for the new millennium, more work needs to be done in cultivating the popular imagination with regard to reinvigorating the functional role of permeable borders, particularly in areas of economic and political cooperation. Although recent terrorist events have given the idea of open borders a bad name, and popular journalists and the media have tended to stress the negative aspects of globalization (the "threat" of NAFTA or the Multilateral Agreement on Investment [MAI] and transnational corporate culture), it is nonetheless true that the world is a stage upon which many successful transnational border stories are played out. No nation can impose any kind of an embargo on itself and not suffer significant damage.

The prospect of recasting border scholarship in the light of global processes is daunting but necessary. Political maps give a false sense of stability and territorial uniformity; they imply a consensus about the nature of territoriality and international relations that is problematic in today's world primarily because bordering processes and political territories are as much conceptual constructions of economic, national, and political discourses as they are of anything "material." We now recognize that the lines on the map were never intended to represent a world of immutable political design and, conversely, that the presence of transnationalism in the guise of TNCs does not signal the end of political territory as we know it today. In the final analysis political territories demarcated by borders of one type or another represent "the last man standing" in a world and world economy that has sought to forge interconnections and to construct commonalities out of differences. The reasons why borders hold, although undergoing tremendous transformation, is the real subject of *Holding the Line*, not what is now the rather unexceptional observation that borders have held their ground. So the question becomes: Why and how have borders been reinvented, and recast, so as to result in new rounds of economic, political, and cultural territorialization. How are processes that erode the traditional role of borders – as lines in the sand or linear walls built to differentiate one peoples from another – to be identified in the multiplicity of new responses that defend discrete political territories from obliteration?

At one level, as various chapters in this volume make clear, the global infrastructure needed in order to redefine the territory of informational technologies has its own set of borders, within which global and local are mutually constitutive. This results from the propensity of global transnational corporate culture to respond to borders as they would to market sectors: differentiating and reinforcing differences in national sensitivities precisely because of the requirement of transnationalism. Several chapters make this point, observing that information is the raw material of economies and that informational geopolitics require the ability to sell in as many differentiated places as possible. The battle lines are drawn, then, along the lines of TNC and nation-state or sovereign state, resulting in increasing competition and differentiation at the conceptual level. This is a process within which TNCs, nation-states, and individuals all have constitutive, but newly defined, roles.

While increased competition and the rising importance of informational geopolitics may result in new roles for multiple partners – a growing roster of actors vertically connected on the global stage – *Holding the Line* asks to what degree increasing competition is coordinated with new sensitivities regarding cooperation. We have seen that there are strong tensions in the area of international law, where multilateralism has assumed a growing importance precisely because of the overlap between global and local. Yet bilateralism and, more recently, unilateralism are also products of these same forces, and there is a growing trend to approach global issues with unilateral logic. This is evident in contemporary approaches to global problems such as terrorism, the environment, international trade, weapons of mass destruction, and regime change, where consensus has often become unachievable. Concomitant with globalization, therefore, is not so much a state of borderlessness or world consensus as divisions based upon individual responses to conflated global/domestic issues. Borders become the stuff of international law: themes and issues that may be conceptual in their general application fall out along borders precisely because the principal of sovereignty, enshrined in international law, creates insurmountable fault lines. So while there is a growing confluence between what constitutes domestic and international issues, processes of supranationalism, multilateralism, transnationalism, and the propensity for states to cross borders through a complex series of mutually enforced agreements concerning all manner of issues are matched and undercut by equal and opposite processes promoting new types of divisions and borders – regional, bilateral, and even unilateral distinctions and initiatives in international decision making, which take as their point of origin either the threat or potential of global interconnectivity.

Where does this leave successful transnational initiatives such as the EU or the Association of Caribbean States (ACS)? Both are regional institutions that have responded to economic globalization by redefining the nature of territory and territorial borders. It is clear that EU member states have not seen a loss of national sovereignty and/or the end of internal borders but, rather, a new type of border in which sovereignty has been reimagined at the community level. Many chapters in this volume point to the importance of regionalism and state policy in the bordering process and, in so doing, explain how we can recast the study of bordering processes so as to interrogate their geopolitical and geoterritorial representations. As it turns out, the EU and ACS are classic examples of reterritorialization, with diffuse, zonal, and non-hierarchical boundaries replacing traditional, crisp lines on the map.

But so, as it turns out, is Africa, and it is precisely this point that becomes clear when we take a closer look at the postcolonial territorial redefinition of African peoples. Borders erased within the context of postcolonial Africa are neither necessary nor desirable. Asiwaju believes that Afroregions, like Euroregions, hold the key to political, cultural, and economic stabilization among the African states in a process not unlike that unfolding in the EU. At the same time, questions are raised regarding the incomplete nature of transnationalism in North American contexts. Cascadia and NAFTA evoke powerful images of a North American continent with a north-south rather than an east-west grain. However, in reality, integration has not occurred, and the degree of cooperation along the western North American border, in the Cascadia region, remains exceptional. The process of transnationalism has been limited in this area of the globe, and, as the chapters in *Holding the Line* suggest, this is in no small measure the result of the limited strength of cross-border relationships as well as the configuration of geographical and political structures linking communities of interest. The notion that the Canada-US and US-Mexican borders are, de facto, frontiers of continental integration proves unsupportable. Regional initiatives are more political than cultural and, indeed, are impeded by international borders in unique ways.

These particular examples raise issues: given that the question is not "is it a borderless world" but, rather, "what are the alternative responses to traditional boundary-making?" several new questions are posited. Two of these are "What is the role of a collective imagination in this process?" and "What role does rhetoric play under such circumstances?" Collective imaginations, as many of the chapters in this volume demonstrate, are not sufficient conditions for transborder regionalism, yet they remain essential preconditions. Moreover, in what way are collective imaginations embedded in readings of space and place, and to what extent are these readings themselves constitutive of diplomatic discourses? Each of the chapters in this volume grounds the question of imagination within a bigger framework. Coleman, for example, asks how the collective imaginations that define borders are forged, what understandings of territory are embedded in people's consciousness and how they are understood collectively, and to what broader processes these uderstandings appeal. Even more important, he raises the question of who makes borders and for what purpose.

In this sense, the challenge is to understand borders not only as zones of confrontation between political groups but as competing schools of thought and competing ideologies. The bordering process is accompanied by discourses that privilege certain issues, certain spaces, certain narratives and dismiss others. While Jackson identifies the consequences of such discourses in terms of their economic and political disparities, Wood is concerned with a parallel process – the development of an international response to the kinds of complex humanitarian crises that unfold, for example, in the former Yugoslavia, as the renegotiation of borders, bounding discourses, and geopolitical territories takes place. In other chapters, there is more than a theoretical importance to this issue. Moreover, as more than one chapter in this volume suggests, the process of reterritorialization and the renegotiation of borders is inimical to the discourse of diplomacy itself: priorities are constructed within diplomatic universes, while discourse becomes embedded in the process of geopolitical and territorial bounding. Facing across or turning one's back on borders constitutes an act of meaning, one that reverberates through the political negotiations of border and territory. This is no small observation and, indeed, recalls the issue raised at the conclusion of this volume: the question of how to address borders is constitutive of what borders to address. What are the parallel universes that are represented? "The juxtaposition of these worlds is evident when considering the diffusion of some recent information and communication innovations; glaring gender, race, and ethnic disparities; and political/military conflicts in Europe, Africa, and Asia" (Brunn et al., Chapter 18). To this might be added the hard borderlines of South America's old colonially constructed realms (Bradshaw, Chapter 9). It is really a question of whose world and whose border, of the possibility of envisioning borders outside of the framework of the grade-school political map (to which we have all become accustomed) and to undertake multiple readings of the politics of geographical territory and the discourses that make them understandable.

It seems clear from the discussion thus far that scholars as well as decision makers, and even the general public at large, must be encouraged to engage in debate about new border arrangements in which alternative modes of "control" are considered, while the battle lines between corporate interests and the interests of the state need to be softened and new modes of functional cooperation discussed. Moreover, while political and economic sectors will always have different short-term goals, new bridges of cooperation and soft controls should be negotiated to ensure long-term success. Economic integration and cooperation can offer tremendous possibility for enhancing national sovereignty, provided that public policies are appropriate to national interests.

In the final analysis, then, what *Holding the Line* may contribute to the field of boundary studies is its attempt to respond to the call to search for a conceptual framework for boundary studies. Newman (Chapter 19) argues that the study of boundaries is integrated by the fact that boundaries are dynamic continua concerned with the process of bounding. Bounding is not necessarily the process of defining the line on the map or the ground, the process that gives shape to, and constantly reshapes, the relationships between a multitude of parallel universes, worlds, and geographical spaces. In this sense boundaries are both walls and points of contact. The chapters in this volume all contribute to the exercise of theorizing boundaries and lead us to the conclusion that these are not just lines, or special places, or even zones with meaning in and of themselves but, rather, special places that respond to, and exert influence upon, the ongoing process of contact between bounding – a process that has been sensitive to the changing nature and respective weight of political, economic, and cultural imperatives. Each chapter speaks from the point of a divergent perspective on border function and the nature of bounding activities. It is in this sense that this collection presents a discussion that pushes us closer to the goal of theorizing and understanding borders in the twenty-first century.

Notes
1 Gearóid Ó Tuathail, "De-Territorialized Threats and Global Dangers: Geopolitics and Risk Security," *Geopolitics* 3, 1 (1988): 18.

Acknowledgments

The chapters in this volume were presented at the Permeable Borders and Boundaries Conference, in Vancouver, BC, in August 1999. In the course of organizing the conference and its proceedings, several acknowledgments are necessary.

We are grateful to the Social Science and Humanities Research Council of Canada for provided funding for the Vancouver conference. SSHRCC made funding available for conference travel and keynote speakers.

Len Evenden, of Simon Fraser University, was instrumental in his efforts to assist in the organization of the conference. The production of this volume of proceedings would not have been possible without his efforts.

We would also like to acknowledge the contribution made by the John Holmes Research Fund, and the Centre for Canadian Foreign Policy Development, in providing funding for editorial assistance for the first draft of these proceedings.

We would like to thank Gerald Blake, Michelle Speak, Martin Pratt, and Clive Schofield, all on staff at the International Boundaries Research Unit, University of Durham, UK, for their assistance in organizing, promoting, and participating in the conference; and we would like to thank the University College of the Cariboo, which provided logistical and financial support for several conference events. Brooks Pearson, of the University of West Georgia, assisted in the technical modification of maps and charts prepared for the manuscript.

Finally, Canada's Maritime Command, Pacific Region, is most gratefully acknowledged for its assistance in providing a venue for the conference field trips, as is Microsoft Corporation, which was also a sponsor.

Heather Nicol and Ian Townsend-Gault
May 2003

Contributors

Robert Adamson is director of the Liu Institute for Global Issues Program on Global Justice. He has worked on international issues with law firms, governments, international organizations, NGOs, and academic institutions throughout the world, including projects on the International Criminal Court, international human rights, international and domestic environmental legal development, and regulatory and management models for governments and corporations.

Donald K. Alper is professor of political science and director of the Center for Canadian-American Studies at Western Washington University. His research interests focus on Canadian-American transboundary issues. He is co-editor of *Sustaining the Forests of the Pacific Coast* (UBC Press), and his research has appeared in many publications, including *Canadian Public Policy-Analyse de politiques,* the *American Review of Canadian Studies, Social Science Journal,* and *BC Studies.*

Alan F.J. Artibise is dean and Professor, College of Urban and Public Affairs, University of New Orleans. Dr. Artibise is author of numerous books and articles on Canadian issues, including those concerned with Cascadia and transnationalism in North America, and the role of Canada's urban places in economic and regional development.

Anthony I. Asiwaju is professor of history and director of the Centre for African Regional Integration and Border Studies at the University of Lagos, Lagos, Nigeria, and former commissioner (international boundaries), National Boundary Commission of Nigeria. He is author of many publications, mostly on African boundaries and borderlands as factors of regional integration.

Gerald Blake is professor emeritus at the University of Durham, UK. Until retirement in 2001, Dr. Blake was director of the International Boundaries Research Unit, professor of geography, and principal of Collingwood

College at the University of Durham. He is the author of numerous books and articles, and has been a major force in defining the field of political geography and border studies.

Eberhard Bort is the academic co-ordinator of the Institute of Governance and a lecturer in politics at the University of Edinburgh. From 1997 to 1999 he was associate director of the International Social Sciences Institute at Edinburgh University. Recent publications include *The Boundaries of Understanding* (ISSI, 1999); ed., with Neil Evans, *Networking Europe: Essays on Regionalism and Social Democracy* (Liverpool University Press, 2000); with Malcolm Anderson, *The Frontiers of the European Union* (Basingstoke and London: Palgrave, 2001).

Susan L. Bradbury is an associate professor of community and regional planning at Iowa State University. Her research interests include economic development, telecommunications planning, small town and rural planning, plan development and implementation as well as NAFTA issues and transportation policy. Professor Bradbury received her bachelor's degree in geography from McMaster University, her masters in regional planning and resource development from the University of Waterloo, and her PhD from the University of Florida.

Roy Bradshaw is a senior lecturer in the School of Geography, at the University of Nottingham, UK. After completing a PhD on regional development policies in Spain he worked in Spain, Portugal, and in Central and South America on various projects. He is the author of a monograph on the Venezuelan-Colombian border dispute and takes a deep interest in borderland questions. He currently lectures on GIS, quantitative methods, and environmental economics.

Stanley D. Brunn is professor, Department of Geography, University of Kentucky; his research interests include human interaction across boundaries (real, imaginary, and cyberspace), images and representations of places, identities and worldviews, innovative cartographies, and time warps.

Theodore H. Cohn is a professor of political science at Simon Fraser University in Burnaby, BC, Canada. He is the author and editor of a number of books and articles in the areas of international political economy, the politics of international trade, global cities, and Canada-US-Mexico relations. His recent publications include two authored books entitled *Governing Global Trade: International Institutions in Conflict and Convergence* (Ashgate, 2002) and *Global Political Economy: Theory and Practice,* 2nd ed. (Addison Wesley Longman, 2003).

Mathew Coleman is a PhD candidate in geography at the University of California, Los Angeles, and a graduate of the Institute of Political Economy at Carleton University in Ottawa, Canada. His current research explores post-9/11 US trade and security policy in the US-Mexico border region. He has published in *Political Geography* and *Geopolitics*.

Thomas M. Edwards has worked for Microsoft Corporation since 1992. Over the years, he has served as a geopolitical consultant on many Microsoft products and has also taught cartography part-time. In April 1998 he was given the opportunity to create a small internal research team called Geopolitical Strategy, which helps Microsoft avoid making geopolitical and cultural mistakes in its content. Edwards has BA and MA degrees in geography and is a PhD candidate at the University of Washington currently completing his PhD (on the subject of "information geopolitics") while working full-time at Microsoft.

Timothy J. Fargo (MA, geography, University of Kentucky) is in the doctoral program in geography at UCLA. He is interested in the philosophical and theoretical interfaces between geography, theology, science, and environmental thought.

Ian Townsend-Gault is a professor in the Centre for Asian Legal Studies, Faculty of Law, at the University of British Columbia, where he teaches and researches in international law, focusing especially on marine resource law, maritime boundaries, maritime cooperation, and the protection of the marine environment. Dr. Townsend-Gault has acted as a consultant to the United Nations; the Asian Development Bank; and the international development agencies of Canada, Norway, Sweden, and Finland; and he has advised governments in Southeast Asia and Eastern Europe on international legal issues.

Alan K. Henrikson is associate professor of diplomatic history at The Fletcher School of Law and Diplomacy, Tufts University, where he teaches US diplomatic history, American-European relations, and political geography. During the spring of 2003, he was Fulbright Diplomatic Academy Visiting Professor at the Diplomatische Akademie in Vienna. He has written widely on American foreign policy and on the role of geography of international relations. A recent study of his, connecting these two areas, is "Distance and Foreign Policy: A Political Geography Approach," *International Political Science Review* 23, 4 (2002).

Steven Jackson is a graduate of the Institute of Political Economy at Carleton University and is currently completing a PhD in the Department of

Communication and the Science Studies Program at the University of California, San Diego. His current research focuses on environmental and computer-mediated communication and governance in the US-Mexico border region.

Jeffery A. Jones (PhD, geography, University of Kentucky) is a senior public health researcher at the University of Kentucky's Center for Preventive Research. His social geography and public health interests include HIV/ AIDS, early childhood interventions, school health, pregnancy prevention, and historical community formations.

Josh Lepawsky is a PhD candidate in geography at the University of Kentucky. He has strong interests in the policies and geographies of the Internet, cyberspace, high-technology corridors, and technology transfer.

David Newman is professor of political geography in the Department of Politics and Government at Ben Gurion University in Israel. He is currently editor of the journal *Geopolitics*. He has published widely on issues relating to territory and boundaries, with a particular focus on territorial dimensions of the Israel-Palestine conflict. He has contributed to the counter-debate on deterritorialization and the borderless world.

Heather Nicol is assistant professor of geography at the University of West Georgia and Director of the UWG Center for Canadian Studies. Her research interests include North American transnationalism and Caribbean integration, critical geopolitics, and economic globalization. She is the author and editor of numerous books and articles on all of these topics, including *Canada, the United States and Cuba: An Evolving Relationship* (with Sahadeo Basdeo) and *(Re)Development at the Urban Edges* (with Greg Halseth).

Clive Schofield is a research fellow at the School of Surveying and Spatial Information at the University of New South Wales, Sydney, Australia. He has written numerous articles on maritime borders and has a research interest in the Southeast Asia region.

James Wesley Scott, BA (University of California, Berkeley), MA and PhD (Free University Berlin), is assistant professor of geography at the Free University of Berlin. He is also a research fellow at the Institute for Regional Development and Structural Planning in Erkner (Germany). His principal research topics include: urban and regional development, border regions, regional governance, metropolitan area problems, and European and North American Geography.

Daniel E. Turbeville III is professor of geography and geography program director at Eastern Washington University in Cheney/Spokane. He holds a PhD from Simon Fraser University (1985), an MA from Western Washington University (1976), and a BSc from the University of South Carolina (1968). His current research interests include Canada-US border issues, NAFTA, and North American transportation infrastructure.

John F. Watkins is an associate professor in the Departments of Geography and Gerontology at the University of Kentucky. His major research interests are in life course decision making, elderly migration in rural communities, and regional demographic modelling.

William B. Wood is deputy assistant secretary for analysis and information management, Bureau of Intelligence and Research, US Department of State. He oversees the work of analytical offices covering global issues and African affairs as well as those providing information management services for the bureau, geographic information systems (GIS), and remote sensing imagery support to the department. He also serves as the geographer for the Department of State.

Index